Amazing Grace

Amazing Grace

AN ANTHOLOGY OF POEMS
ABOUT SLAVERY, 1660–1810

edited by

JAMES G. BASKER

Yale University Press
New Haven & London

Published with assistance from the Annie Burr Lewis Fund and from the foundation established in memory of Amasa Stone Mather of the Class of 1907, Yale College.

Designed by Mary Valencia.
Set in Fournier type by Integrated Publishing Solutions, Grand Rapids, Michigan.
Printed in the United States of America by Vail-Ballou Press, Binghamton, New York.

Library of Congress Cataloging-in-Publication Data
Amazing grace : an anthology of poems about slavery, 1660–1810/ edited by James G. Basker.
    p. cm.
  Includes bibliographical references and index.
  ISBN 0-300-09172-9 (alk. paper)
    1. Slavery—Poetry. 2. English poetry—Early modern, 1500–1700. 3. English poetry—19th century. 4. English poetry—18th century. 5. Slave trade—Poetry. 6. Slaves—Poetry. 7. American poetry. I. Basker, James G.

  PR1195.S44 A45 2002
  821.008'0355—dc21   2002069171

A catalogue record for this book is available from the British Library.

∞The paper in this book meets the guidelines for permanence and durability of the Committee on Production Guidelines for Book Longevity of the Council on Library Resources.

10 9 8 7 6 5 4 3

To Angela, Anne, and Katherine
and
To the memory of my parents,
James W. and Anne G. Basker

Contents

CONTENTS

CONTENTS

CONTENTS

CONTENTS

CONTENTS

CONTENTS

CONTENTS

CONTENTS

CONTENTS

CONTENTS

CONTENTS

Acknowledgments

Without the assistance and support of many people, this anthology would not have been possible. I am grateful to the directors and staffs of the following institutions: Butler Library, especially the Rare Books Room, Columbia University; Wollman Library, Barnard College; Bobst Library, New York University; the Gilder Lehrman Collection, on deposit at the Morgan Library; the New York Public Library; the Schomberg Library; the Library of the New-York Historical Society; Yale University Libraries, particularly the Beinecke Library; Harvard University Libraries, particularly the Houghton Library; Sidney Sussex College Library and Muniments Room; the Cambridge University Library; the British Library; and the Bodleian Library, Oxford University. For particular advice and assistance I would like to thank Paul Romaine of the Gilder Lehrman Collection, Margaret Heilbrun of the New-York Historical Society, Virginia LaGoy of the Schenectady County Historical Society, Patrick Stevens of the Cornell University Library (Rare Books Division), and Janet Schwarz of the Virginia Historical Society.

I am very grateful to those who brought specific poems to my attention, including my colleague Quandra Prettyman of the Barnard College English Department and my former student Cinnamon Kennedy of the Columbia Graduate School, in addition to fellow scholars whose research provided other leads, especially Kwame Anthony Appiah, Vincent Carretta, Frank Felsenstein, Henry Louis Gates, Jr., Gretchen Gerzina, Alan Richardson, and Michael Sappol. William J. Burling and Odai Johnson generously allowed access to their excellent database, *The Colonial American Stage, 1655–1774,* for background information on specific poets. For help compiling the timeline I am grateful to historians Robert Forbes, Steven Mintz, Herb Sloan, and especially David Brion Davis. Stephen Marsh, classicist and longtime friend, has my deepest thanks for translating Coleridge's Greek ode on the slave trade and allowing its use in this book.

Thanks are due also for research grants and leaves provided by Barnard College, and I am grateful for the encouragement and support of President Judith Shapiro, Provost Elizabeth Boylan, Professors Christopher Baswell and Anne

Prescott, Department Administrator Connie Budelis, and all the members of the Barnard English Department. Other invaluable support was provided by the Gilder Lehrman Institute of American History, its founders Richard Gilder and Lewis Lehrman, Executive Director Lesley Herrmann, and all the staff.

I truly appreciate the advice and encouragement I received from friends and colleagues, especially the late Walter Jackson Bate, Tina Bennett, Paul-Gabriel Boucé, Christopher Brown, Vincent Carretta, Arthur Cash, David Brion Davis, James Engell, Frank Felsenstein, Rob Forbes, Annette Gordon-Reed, the late Alan Heimert, Roger Lonsdale, Linda Merians, Steve Mintz, Peter Sabor, Michael Seidel, Michael Shinagel, and Herb Sloan.

An array of researchers and other assistants helped in this project at various stages. Thanks are due to several research assistants who contributed in the early stages and have since gone on to their own scholarly and professional careers: Greg Brown, Tony Dangerfield, Steven Epley, Steven Farrelly-Jackson, David Liss, Lee Morrissey, Simon Pickard, and Jonathan Skinner. I am truly grateful to several other students who have done research work more recently, including Rachel Abramowitz, Catherine Dille, Janet Jun, Grace Lee, Sally Magdi, Malissa Marshall, Matt Matlack, Ottessa Moshfegh, and Elizabeth Stephens. Leslie Kendrick of Oxford University helped on frequent occasions with texts in the Bodleian Library. Amy Matthews and especially Anna Zintl are due enormous thanks for their help with logistics, computer technology, printouts, and morale.

Three graduate students in particular have contributed brilliantly over the past several years. Corey A. Olsen and Joan Obra worked long hours, chased down innumerable leads, and produced first-class research. Above all, Nicole Seary of the Columbia Graduate School has been for five years a mainstay of the project, invariably insightful, exacting, and indefatigable in her work. I shall be forever grateful. My family have always been unspeakably generous and supportive, including especially my siblings, Mary Anne, Toni, Judy, and Bob, and their families. My debts to my parents, James W. and Anne G. Basker, my wife, Angela Vallot, and my daughters, Anne and Katherine, are beyond words, though intimated in the dedication. I hope they might be pleased with this effort to readmit into history and literature the voices of those who—like the "strong and vigorous" black slaves of Blake's "America: A Prophecy"—"play[ed] on instruments/Stringed or fluted to ameliorate the sorrows of slavery."

Introduction

This anthology brings together for the first time hundreds of poems about slavery published in English during a crucial historic period, 1660 to 1810. The book is intended for scholars, students, and general readers, for all of whom the subject of slavery and its legacy seems to be growing in importance with every passing year. The editorial approach is both inclusive and radically historical. Many of the poems in this volume have not been reprinted for more than two hundred years. Taken together, they carry us back to a time before the antebellum crises and Civil War—which made slavery seem a particularly American problem—into a context that involved the whole of the anglophone world.

At the heart of the book lies a series of questions. To what degree was the British public aware of slavery in the seventeenth and eighteenth centuries? How did slavery figure in the collective imagination and the shared cultural life of the time? What relation did the literary treatment of slavery have to social attitudes, public policies, and economic realities? Above all, how can we explain the historic paradox that the very years of the European Enlightenment were also the period of greatest expansion in the slave trade and in slave-based economies? To address these and many other questions, I have gathered every poem or poetic fragment from the period that brings slavery into view, whether as its main subject, in a single passage or character, or, more glancingly, in bits of allusion or metaphor.

The result is something like a vast archeological dig. There are love poems, passages from dramatic pageants and verse plays, hymns, anthems, religious poems, ballads, songs from operas and musical comedies, epics, verse essays, children's poems, political poems, eclogues, elegies, dialogues, ditties and doggerel of many kinds, even "found poems" taken from newspapers, graffiti, and gravestone inscriptions. Inevitably the quality of the material varies wildly, from the sublime to the insufferable. But whatever the unevenness in aesthetic value, because poetry fills the interstices of our culture, from public spaces to private corners, in moments of high ceremony and in the spontaneous effusions of popular culture, this material maps the emergence of a collective awareness, the gradual appropriation of a subject charged with aesthetic and moral power, and the spread of that awareness through the collective imagination of the Enlightenment.

Why poetry only? The immediate answer is practical. For all the novels and other prose works that bear on the subject, the focus on poetry allows for greater range: it enables this anthology to include some 400 different titles by more than 250 different writers. Even that understates the reach and richness of the material, for many of the poems are short excerpts from much longer works, twenty lines or so from texts that often run to several hundred lines in the original. To enable readers to explore these longer texts in full, I have used the endnotes to provide full citations of original sources.

The focus on poetry has other benefits. This anthology includes some works that are primarily performative and ephemeral, demonstrating how poetry helps bridge oral culture and print, preserving poetic utterances that fall outside a book-reading culture's notions of "literature" and might otherwise have perished. The generic conventions and verbal allusiveness of poetry also make it easier, having assembled all these poems beside each other, to discern lines of influence and imitation. We can see Phillis Wheatley's or the missionary poet Joshua Marsden's debts to Alexander Pope, or those in turn of later white female poets such as Mary Deverell and Mary Scott to Phillis Wheatley, or of Samuel Taylor Coleridge to William Cowper and Robert Southey, and so forth, across an endlessly complex web of literary connection. And of course the variety of forms and voices and idioms available in poetry, and the celebrated tradition of imaginative freedom ("poetic license"), give poetry unsurpassed versatility in capturing extremes of emotion, experience, or fantasy. Poetry is all the more valuable because with a subject like slavery the violence and brutality, the suffering and destruction—most of the historic reality and psychological experience—can seem somehow ineffable, too terrible for words. Poetry, of all forms of language, best enables us to approximate or intimate the unspeakable.

Indeed, there is a transformative power that is in some way applicable to almost all the poetry in this anthology: the transformation of sin and sorrow into grace, of suffering into beauty, of alienation into empathy and connection, of the unspeakable into imaginative literature. That power is best dramatized in the story behind the hymn from which this volume takes its name, "Amazing Grace." Assumed by many people to be a "Negro spiritual" of the nineteenth century, it was originally composed in the 1770s by the English clergyman and abolitionist John Newton, whose preaching and writing inspired generations of abolitionists, including William Cowper, William Wilberforce, and Hannah More. The twist is that in his youth Newton had been a slave trader, sailing on several slaving voyages and eventually serving as captain of a slave ship. To the discomfort of some, the famous lyrics that are so widely heard as the slave's yearning for deliverance from the sufferings of this world—"Amazing grace!

(how sweet the sound)/That sav'd a wretch like me!"—were orginally the words of a penitent slave trader giving thanks for his deliverance from the sinfulness of slave trading. In a further twist, by the mid-1800s Newton's hymn had indeed been taken up by black Christians, enslaved and free alike, to such a degree that in Harriet Beecher Stowe's *Uncle Tom's Cabin* (1852), at his deepest moment of crisis (chap. 38), Tom achieves a kind of ecstatic transcendence by singing "Amazing Grace"—an act that, given the popularity of Stowe's novel, did effectively canonize the hymn as the paradigmatic expression of Negro piety and spirituality.

There is another aspect to this transformative power, one that emerges most clearly when the material in this volume is considered as a whole. By giving form to the previously unimagined, poetry helps shape reality, offering new models or blueprints for change, both personal and societal. As Percy Bysshe Shelley (himself a fierce critic of slavery) wrote in his great *Defence of Poetry*, "Poets are the unacknowledged legislators of the world." The 400 poems in this anthology trace 150 years of poetic expression about slavery leading up to the abolition of the slave trade in the first decade of the 1800s. A half-century later, when Abraham Lincoln made his famous comment to Mrs. Stowe about her book causing the American Civil War, he was, in more ways than he realized, echoing earlier generations of poets who believed in the power of literature to affect the course of history.

The Historical Context and the Rationale for 1660–1810

Any periodization is problematic, but there is a clear rationale for the period 1660 to 1810 as the natural framework for this anthology. It is rooted in historical circumstances. The English were relative latecomers to the African slave trade. Beginning in the 1430s and 1440s the Portuguese shipped African slaves back to the Iberian Peninsula, and they extended the traffic to the Azores and other Atlantic islands as they pushed their incursions south along the West African coast over the course of the fifteenth and sixteenth centuries. Columbus's voyages to the New World at the close of the fifteenth century opened the way for the transatlantic slave trade of the 1500s, which continued to be dominated by the Portuguese (later joined by the Dutch and French) and carried tens of thousands of slaves to Portuguese Brazil and to the Spanish possessions across South America and the Caribbean. Apart from isolated slaving voyages by Sir John Hawkins in the 1560s, the English showed little interest. This changed in the early seventeenth century—after the famous arrival of a load of slaves in Virginia in 1619 (carried by a Dutch ship) and the acquisition of Barbados (where sugar would be grown) in 1625—but only slowly.

It is the year 1660 around which major events and geopolitical changes in the Anglo-Atlantic world cluster, from London to New York to the Caribbean. The British takeover of Jamaica in the late 1650s was pivotal: the Spanish left behind plantations and the African slaves who worked them, and the vast size of the island (twenty-six times the size of Barbados) made huge expansion possible. During the Anglo-Dutch Wars of the 1660s the English also acquired new territories, including various African and Caribbean possessions and, most importantly, New Amsterdam/New York. The year 1660 also marked the restoration of the English monarchy, after two decades of civil war and fractious commonwealth, which not only brought stability at home but ushered in an era of burgeoning trade and colonial expansion overseas. In 1663 the Company of Royal Adventurers to Africa was formed, and then was succeeded by the Royal African Company in 1672. With these developments, English involvement in and awareness of African slavery began to grow dramatically. Significantly, Aphra Behn, whose *Oroonoko, or the Royal Slave* (1688) would do more to raise English awareness of New World slavery than any other literary work of the century, gathered her observations about slavery in the early 1660s when she traveled to Surinam with her father, a newly appointed colonial official.

By the end of the eighteenth century, the picture had changed beyond recognition. Between 1672 and 1713 the Royal African Company sent five hundred ships to Africa which, in addition to other trade, carried away 125,000 slaves for transatlantic sale.* By 1730, Britain (as it was called after the Union with Scotland in 1707) had become the world's leading slave-trading nation, and would occupy that position until the abolition of the slave trade in 1807. And it wasn't just as cargo that slaves were entering British consciousness. Beginning in the 1730s, articles about slave insurrections appeared regularly in London periodicals: a total of 52 articles about 43 different insurrections, for example, were published in the *Gentleman's Magazine* between the late 1730s and the eve of the American Revolution.† By the late eighteenth century slavery was practiced throughout the British colonies, including those that would become the United States; in the economies and agricultural systems that depended on slave labor there had been phenomenal growth in numbers. To take just one example: in 1700 Virginia had 16,000 black slaves; by 1780 there were 220,000. In the last years of the eighteenth century, British ships were carrying 45,000 slaves per year across the Atlantic. By 1810 British ships had carried more than three million slaves to the New World, of which more than 1,361,000 had been imported into the British West Indies, and a further 376,500 into British North America.

---

* This and most of the following statistical information is derived from Robin Blackburn, *The Making of New World Slavery: From the Baroque to the Modern, 1492–1800* (London: Verso, 1997), and James Walvin, *Slaves and Slavery: The British Colonial Experience* (Manchester: Manchester University Press, 1992). A comprehensive source for such information is the recently published CD-ROM, *The Trans-Atlantic Slave Trade: A Database*, ed. David Eltis, et al. (Cambridge: Cambridge University Press, 1999).

† Basker, "'The Next Insurrection': Johnson, Race, and Rebellion," *The Age of Johnson*, ed. Paul J. Korshin, vol. 11 (New York: AMS Press, 2000).

Thus it is all the more remarkable that at the same time, the anglophone Atlantic community also led the world in opposition to slavery. At first individuals took the lead, people like the Philadelphia Quaker Anthony Benezet, who ran a charity school for blacks and wrote a stream of pamphlets against slavery, and Granville Sharp in England, who filed legal actions against slaveholders and forced the landmark Somerset ruling of 1772, that no master could forcibly remove his slave from England. Gradually, more organized efforts emerged. While pious individuals of various denominations had spoken out against slavery at intervals since at least 1688, in the second half of the eighteenth century Quaker societies and other religious groups on both sides of the Atlantic began to denounce slaveholding as sinful with greater frequency, and in 1775 the first abolition society was formed in Pennsylvania. In the mid-1770s a group of activists (including Samuel Johnson) helped Joseph Knight secure his manumission in the Scottish courts, in a case I will return to below. In 1785 Cambridge University set the slave trade as the topic of an essay competition, and Thomas Clarkson's winning essay marked the beginning of his lifelong career as an abolitionist. In 1787 the British Abolition Society was founded in London and launched a national campaign. Largely through its efforts, thousands of petitions calling for the abolition of the slave trade flooded into Parliament from churches, town councils, corporate bodies, and citizen groups of all kinds. In May 1789 William Wilberforce led a group of antislavery MPs that began the struggle to pass an abolition bill, a struggle they would be forced to continue for almost twenty years, before a meaningful bill was passed in 1807. Meanwhile in America individual states in the North began to abolish slavery: first Vermont in 1777, followed, during the years 1780 to 1804, by Pennsylvania, Massachusetts, New Hampshire, Connecticut, Rhode Island, New York, and New Jersey. In 1807 the government of the United States, in parallel with Britain, outlawed the overseas slave trade, though of course the practice of slavery itself remained and a clandestine traffic in slave importation was to persist for another fifty years.

The year 1810 thus marks the appropriate closure for this volume, as major historic shifts occurred about that time. Both the British and American abolition of the slave trade took effect on January 1, 1808. Thereafter the British government dispatched ships of the Royal Navy to patrol the African coast and occasionally used the illegality of the slave trade as an added pretext to interfere with American shipping (they also were seeking to impress sailors alleged to have deserted from British ships). In 1812, as a result of this interference on the high seas and other grievances, America and Britain went to war, and during that war the British not only sacked and burned Washington, D.C., but also carried away hundreds of slaves they had enticed over to their side. From about 1810, America and Britain followed rapidly diverging trajectories on the slavery question. In Britain, popular opposition to slavery grew throughout the 1810s and 1820s, leading to further legislation and the peaceful abolition of slavery throughout the British colonies in 1833. Meanwhile America lurched through a series of moral and constitutional crises, beginning with the debates over admitting Missouri and other territories as free or slave states in the 1810s, and eventually descended into a bloody civil war. A dramatic reminder of these diverging trajectories is the fact that the American "Underground Railroad" for fugitive slaves eventually led to sanctuary in the British territory of Canada. After 1810, slavery in British and American cultural life became two different stories.

Slavery in English Literature

There were scattered treatments of slavery in English literature before 1660. Most impressive of them, perhaps, is the moment when Shakespeare allows Shylock to defend himself in terms that suggest chattel slavery and Christian humanism are ultimately incompatible:

> You have among you many a purchas'd slave,
> Which like your asses, and your dogs and mules,
> You use in abject and in slavish parts,
> Because you bought them. Shall I say to you,
> "Let them be free! Marry them to your heirs!
> Why sweat they under burthens? Let their beds
> Be made as soft as yours, and let their palates
> Be season'd with such viands"? You will answer,
> "The slaves are ours." So I do answer you:
> The pound of flesh which I demand of him
> Is dearly bought as mine, and I will have it.
>   (*The Merchant of Venice* [c. 1596], IV.i.89–100)

In *The Tempest*, shifting the scene to a vague representation of the New World, Shakespeare has Caliban complain about his treatment as Prospero's slave ("This island's mine . . . Which thou tak'st from me" and "[I] first was mine own king; and here you sty me / In this hard rock" [*The Tempest* (1611), I.ii.339–41, 342–3]. But despite the fact that he also touched on racial issues in his majestic portrayal of Othello (which in turn generated sharp comments on racism and racial inequality by at least one seventeenth-century critic),* neither

---

* See Charles Gildon's essay "Othello," printed in *Miscellaneous Letters and Essays on Several Subjects* (London, 1694), in which he writes "'Tis granted, a *Negro* here does seldom rise above a Trumpeter, nor often perhaps higher at *Venice*. But then that proceeds from the Vice of Mankind . . . 'Tis certain, there is no reason in the nature of things, why a *Negro* of equal Birth and Merit, should not be on an equal bottom, with a *German, Hollander, French-man*, &c. . . . [Shakespeare] has therefore well chosen a polite People [the Venetians], to cast off this customary Barbarity, of confining Nations, without regard to their Virtue, and Merits, to slavery, and contempt for the meer Accident of their Complexion" (pp. 97–98).

Shakespeare nor other early seventeenth-century English writers paid significant attention to transatlantic racial slavery per se.

As the contours of this anthology suggest, and scholars confirm, images of African slaves and the whole subject of New World slavery began to enter English literature in significant ways after 1660.* To map that process comprehensively would be a complex and perhaps impossible task. Indeed, my experience in compiling this anthology over several years convinces me that I have captured only a fraction of the relevant material; additional poems on slavery continue to turn up and doubtless will do so in perpetuity, as long as scholars and readers continue to search for them.† But if the contents of this volume can be taken as representative, some details about its overall shape and proportions may be enlightening. First, considered chronologically, the number of poems grows steadily over the whole course of the period: twenty-seven poems between 1660 and 1700 and another seventeen between 1700 and 1730, then a rough doubling to about thirty-three poems in the years 1730 to 1760. After 1760 the rate of increase shoots up again: seventy poems in the twenty-year period 1760 to 1780, then more than seventy in the single decade of the 1780s, rising immediately by another 50 percent to more than ninety in each of the last two decades, 1790–1800 and 1800–1810. Of course many factors influenced these trends beyond just the writers' attention to the subject: political and historic events; the availability of new publishing vehicles such as periodicals, anthologies, and children's books; and the spread of literacy, printed material, and print culture generally. But any quantitative measure would confirm that attention to slavery in English poetry had multiplied many times over between the late 1600s and 1800, with all the implications about intellectual, cultural, and political life that might entail.

In the early decades slavery tends to be incidental to the texts, a detail or a short passage in a work devoted primarily to something else. The excerpts from Dryden are typical: six or seven incidental references of a few lines each, scattered over twenty-five years. Only gradually, following Thomas Southerne's *Oroonoko* (1695), do writers begin to dedicate whole poems to the subject (John Saffin, Bernard Mandeville, and Frances Seymour are early examples). By con-

---

* See Winthrop D. Jordan, *White over Black: American Attitudes Toward the Negro, 1550–1812* (1968; repr. New York: W. W. Norton & Co., 1977), pp. 3–43, for a summary of the few glimpses of Africans in English literature before 1660.

† The most interesting, and tantalizing, example to arise so far is a poem that we know was published but of which no copy seems to have survived: *The Dictates of Indignation. A Poem on the African Slave Trade*, a twenty-eight-page work "By an Under Graduate [at] Oxford," which was reviewed in *The Monthly Review* in April 1791, but cannot be found in any archive today. Similarly, the original text of Elizabeth Bonhote's "Feeling" (1810) remains elusive, although at least one scholar has referred to it (see Moira Ferguson, *Subject to Others: British Women Writers and Colonial Slavery, 1670–1834* [New York: Routledge, 1992], p. 121.)

trast, at the end of the period the subject of the African diaspora has been elevated to heroic status: by 1810 writers as various as William Roscoe, James Stanfield, James Grahame, Thomas Branagan, and James Montgomery, among others, had composed full-scale epics on the subject, some running to thousands of lines, with titles such as "The Wrongs of Africa" and "Africa Delivered; or, the Slave Trade Abolished." Other poetic genres were seen as particularly suited to the subject and appeared more frequently over time. One can trace lyric forms such as the sonnet, ode, ballad, and elegy as they flourish in this collection, especially after 1750, the result of both the growing taste for sentimentalism and the deepening desire of poets to achieve subtler effects in voice and image. Beginning about mid-century, with William Dodd's "African Prince" (1749) and "Zara" (1749), a vogue began for poems—sometimes in the form of "African eclogues"—that gave voice and romantic personal histories to African captives, exemplified in the works of Thomas Chatterton, Thomas Day, Hugh Mulligan, Eliza Knipe, and Edward Rushton, among many others.

Similarly, important themes can be traced through this material: African homeland and culture, spouses and lovers, family, children, dreamlife, natural law, Christianity, ideas of beauty, race, interracial love, racial equality and, looming over all of them, the inevitable themes of violence, rape, suicide, insurrection, escape, physical and spiritual refuge. The list is endless, but the proliferation of such themes in this poetry reflects a general increase in efforts to humanize slaves and to deepen the pathos of their condition. In general, and in keeping with the larger literary trends of the century, there is a shift from the rhyming couplets and intellectual arguments of neoclassicists like Alexander Pope and Richard Savage, to the more subjective and sentimental modes of the later poets. Indeed, the whole transition from classicism to romanticism could be traced through this poetry. Reading antislavery excerpts from Pope's *Essay on Man* (1733) against Wordsworth's sonnet about an enigmatic black woman he saw on a ship ("September 1, 1802"), for example, highlights the difference between appeals to reason, principle, and moral codes, on the one hand, and emotion, empathy, and intuition on the other, as the basis for one's revulsion at slavery.

But analytical overviews, or "master narratives," must not overshadow the complexity of the material. Diverse and often sharply contrasting aesthetics were at work throughout the period. One could point, for example, to the contrast in the 1790s between Hannah More, with her rhyming couplets and arguments based on Christian doctrine and moral reason, and her contemporary William Blake, whose prophetic outpourings in verse defy conventional poetics, religion, and logic alike, while operating with equal force against the evil of slavery. But this was equally true sixty years earlier, when Richard Savage and James Thomson took up the subject. Savage's attack on slavery in "Of Public Spirit" (1737) is characteristically neoclassical: rhyming couplets and antithetical phrases, arguments based on universal truths and historic precedents, all informed by the ideals and values of classical civilization. Thomson, by contrast, uses the more daring form of blank verse in *The Seasons* (thus allying himself with "warblers wild" like Shakespeare and Milton, rather than Dryden and Pope) and works impressionistically through images of a catastrophic storm and a giant killer shark destroying a slave ship—the inarticulate forces of Nature avenging themselves on the moral deformity that was the slave trade. But these disparate poetic treatments turn out to be radically connected: private letters show that it was from Savage the classicist that the proto-Romantic Thomson got the idea to address the slave trade in the first place. In these and countless other instances, the material in this volume challenges our generalizations and our preconceptions.

Canonical Poets

One such challenge is to our memory of canonical authors. Among the 250 writers in this book are at least fifteen canonical writers whose attention to slavery has been largely forgotten, including Dryden, Defoe, Pope, Gay, Richardson, Johnson, Blake, Boswell, Chatterton, Burns, Cowper, Wordsworth, Coleridge, Mary and Charles Lamb, among others. The number of them raises questions about the history of canon formation and returns us to an old problem about historical research, that what we recognize and retrieve from the past is often limited to what we have set out to look for. Until about ten years ago, I had little idea what these canonical writers had to say about slavery (though I had read and taught most of them) because I had never really looked at them in this light. In some cases, this focus brings to the fore texts that had been shunted aside and opens a new perspective on a major author. Two examples must stand for many. The first is Coleridge's prize-winning Greek ode on the slave trade, written while he was a student and presented here in a new English translation, showing how central, and early, antislavery feeling was in his imaginative development. The second, as dramatic though far less attractive, is James Boswell's forgotten poem "No Abolition of Slavery," which has rarely been reprinted and yet, in its defense of slavery, has tremendous importance in documenting both his disagreement with Johnson (who was relentlessly antislavery) and Boswell's own place in eighteenth-century history.

The whole question of the disappearance of slavery as a subject from the poetic canon remains vexed. The most striking example of how completely the topic vanished from historic treatments of English poetry is an anthology published in 1908—precisely one hundred years after the abolition of the slave trade—called *The Book of Georgian Verse*, edited by a Boston man of letters, William Stanley Braithwaite. Of the 708 poems in this voluminous collection, only three overlap with the contents of the present volume (Blair's "The Grave," Blake's "The Little Black Boy," and Wordsworth's "Toussaint L'Ouverture"). The subject of slavery is so far excluded from Braithwaite's selections that even poets such as William Cowper and James Montgomery who were known in their own time precisely for their antislavery poetry are represented in his collection by poems that don't even hint at their interest in the cause. What makes Braithwaite's bleached-out rendering of the canon all the more dramatic and poignant (though it was scarcely his responsibility and was common to his era) is the fact that Braithwaite himself was African American.

Almost a century later the situation is not very different. Again, a single example speaks volumes. Among the more than three hundred poems representing the period 1660 to 1810 in the latest edition of *The Norton Anthology of Poetry* (4th ed.), only six coincide with those collected here in *Amazing Grace*.* As in Braithwaite, Cowper is presented without so much as a line from any of his antislavery poems. (This time Montgomery is omitted altogether.) Of course poems are chosen for many criteria—genre, author, aesthetic quality, as well as subject matter. But that Norton's three hundred-plus poems have scarcely any overlap with the four hundred poems in the present collection illustrates the degree to which slavery, by whatever process, has been relegated to the historical background. In more ways than one, *Amazing Grace* challenges canon formation over the past two hundred years and could be said to constitute a kind of shadow canon.

Black Poets

Also impressive is the number of black poets: at least twenty are represented here, and potentially more, their identities veiled for now behind the dozens of "Anonymous" poems scattered throughout the book. The eighteen include well-known figures such as Phillis Wheatley, Jupiter Hammon, Ignatius Sancho, Olaudah Equiano, and Benjamin Banneker, as well as others who have never before been anthologized. Two were university-educated: Francis Williams and Jacobus Elisa Johannes Capitein, at Cambridge and Leyden respectively. At least two others, much humbler, remain nameless, although their life stories are among the most interesting in the whole collection: the author of "The American in Algiers" (1797), who describes himself as a black veteran of the Revolutionary War who went to sea as a merchant sailor and was re-enslaved in Algiers, and the author of "The African Slave" (1802), who recounts his life, from capture in Africa and bondage in America, to his present condition as "a person confined in the [New Jersey] state-prison."

These writers also challenge our assumptions, not just about the numbers of black writers, but about the range of black voices, the degree and desirability

---

* *The Norton Anthology of Poetry*, ed. Margaret Ferguson, et al. (New York: W.W. Norton & Company, 1996). The coincident poems are Wheatley's "On Being Brought from Africa to America" and "To S. M., A Young African Painter," Blake's "The Little Black Boy," Freneau's "To Sir Toby" (in *Amazing Grace* as "The Island Field Hand"), and passages from Pope's "Rape of the Lock" and More's "The Slave Trade."

of acculturation, and the intertwining influences of black and white writers on each other. The academic cadences of Williams and Capitein contrast with the pious idioms and biblical inflections of Wheatley and Hammon, and both stand apart from either Sancho's London society banter or Lucy Terry's frontier folk ballad. Assimilation and acculturation figure for all of them, but with different outcomes. The free black Francis Williams, after his astonishing success at Cambridge University, nonetheless returned to Jamaica and stayed there for the rest of his career. The former slave turned sailor, entrepreneur, and writer Olaudah Equiano, on the other hand, having experienced life all around the Atlantic perimeter (Europe, Africa, the West Indies, and America) opted for England as his final residence. The interconnectedness of black and white writers surfaces in remarkable moments, as when Equiano in his autobiography quotes Thomas Day's "Dying Negro" (a poem written by a white in the voice of a black slave) to describe his own experience, or when a poor white woman such as Jane Dunlap attributes her poetic inspiration to reading the poems of Phillis Wheatley. Collectively, these black writers should weigh as heavily in our modern reconsideration of the period as they did in the work of the French writer Henri Grégoire, who in 1808 expounded at length on the achievements of Wheatley, Banneker, Capitein, Williams, Equiano, Sancho, and many others, as he sought to prove definitively, at the height of the European Enlightenment, that racism was philosophically and historically unjustified and that blacks were the full intellectual equals of whites.*

Women Poets

Remarkable also are the number of women poets represented: at least forty in all, including Aphra Behn, Hannah More, Helen Maria Williams, Joanna Baillie, Amelia Opie, Anna Letitia Barbauld, and Charlotte Smith, but many more whose names are completely unfamiliar. Most of them wrote after 1780, but as early as the 1720s there is a figure such as the extraordinary Frances Seymour (Countess of Hertford, later Duchess of Somerset), the first poet to put into verse the tale of "Inkle and Yarico," a story of interracial love and betrayal that would be retold in verse and prose (mostly by male writers) dozens of times before the end of the eighteenth century.† At the other end of the social spectrum are working-class women such as Jane Dunlap, the poor Bostonian born to an "obscure station of life," Susanna Pearson, a household servant in Sheffield,

---

* Henri Grégoire, *On the Cultural Achievements of Negroes* (Paris, 1808) was first published in English in Brooklyn, 1810, and has been republished with a modern translation and notes by Thomas Cassirer and Jean-François Brière (Amherst: University of Massachusetts Press, 1996).

† For a full account of the sixty or more versions of the "Inkle and Yarico" story produced during the eighteenth and nineteenth centuries, see Frank Felsenstein, *English Trader, Indian Maid: Representing Gender, Race, and Slavery in the New World* (Baltimore: Johns Hopkins University Press, 1999).

England, and Ann Yearsley, the spirited "milkmaid poet" of Bristol, England, in addition to the two who were themselves slaves, Lucy Terry and Phillis Wheatley.

The poems by women open fresh angles of vision on cultural and social history. The teenage "Cecilia" Stiles gives us a glimpse of the inner workings of a prominent and passionately antislavery New England family in the 1770s. In "The Slave" (1787) the genteel Elizabeth Tomlins explores, in potentially self-revealing ways, a story of the forbidden love a West Indian slave had for his master's sister—with lethal consequences. Poems by Mary Stockdale, Mary Lamb, and others take us into the minds of children, black and white, whose struggles to understand and articulate their experience of racism only deepen the disgrace of adult society. Overall, these poets throw into question our assumptions about the presence and force of women writers in this period, particularly in their engagement with a topic in the public realm such as slavery that might have been considered the appropriate, if not exclusive, concern of the governing male elite.

A Story Behind Every Poem

As with poems by women, so with the collection as a whole: behind every poem is a story, usually interesting in its own right and almost always full of implications for our understanding of history. Sometimes the interest is tonal or topical. Miscegenation, for example, is debated by anonymous poets (one defends it) in a South Carolina newspaper in the 1730s. The same topic, treated more coarsely, dominates a handful of political poems prompted by the Thomas Jefferson–Sally Hemings scandal in 1802 (one of the most scurrilous of them by young John Quincy Adams). A tiny poem about "the progeny of Ham" by John Wesley (orginally published in his *Thought upon Slavery*) rejects the racist ideology that "descendants-of-Ham" pseudo-biblical theorists propounded. Sympathetic comments about African slaves in Daniel Defoe's "Reformation of Manners" (1702) shed new light on *Robinson Crusoe*, arguably the most important novel in the English language. Expressions of admiration for the beauty of black women, as in Isaac Teale's "Sable Venus" (c. 1760–1763), and interracial love poems, beginning with Henry King's pair of courtship poems in 1660, occur with surprising frequency. Calls for insurrection and images of white bloodshed also appear in a startling numbers of works, from Savage's in the 1730s, to Captain Marjoribanks's in the 1780s, to Thomas Branagan's in the 1800s. On the other hand, one is also struck by the tone of those writers (admittedly a handful) who used poetry to defend or praise slavery, from John Saffin in 1701 to James Boswell ninety years later—proslavery attitudes and poetic sensibilities seeming as they do so completely antithetical.

More often the special interest is biographical. James Revel's poem of 1680 gains power as one realizes that his descriptions of being sold at auction alongside African slaves and worked nearly to death are drawn from his own harrowing experience of fourteen years as an indentured servant. A century later, Robert Southey's ballad about a penitent slave trader becomes even more haunting when his footnote reveals that it is based on an actual man, found crazed and raving in a Bristol cow barn in 1798. In addition to Newton, at least three others of the poets themselves were former slave traders, one of whom—Edward Rushton—went blind from a disease he contracted from the slaves he ministered to below decks. Another, James Grainger, served as physician on a Jamaican plantation. The young poets Philip Freneau, Timothy Dwight, Joel Barlow, and John Trumbull form another interesting group not because they were personally involved in slavery, but because accidents of history made them the first generation of self-defined "American" poets to have to address (or evade) the slavery question. The young Londoner Edward Kimber visited the American colonies in 1744 and sent back a poem called "Fidenia, or the Explanation," written to honor the beautiful young black woman who saved his life when he fell into the Chesapeake Bay—though what exactly he is "explaining" remains an open question. Perhaps most dangerous of all was the life of Joshua Marsden, a missionary who spent years trying to minister to slaves and free blacks in the West Indies and wrote many damning poems about what he observed, although he prudently waited to publish them until he was safely arrived in New York.

An Afrocentric Poetics of the Enlightenment

As compelling as the individual stories are, they also form a larger picture. The bringing together of this material makes possible an Afrocentric perspective on the English poetry of the Enlightenment—traditionally viewed as the period during which "Eurocentric" forces began to impress themselves indelibly on world history. Without seeking to displace the traditional canon, or to overturn or distort the history of the Enlightenment, one can nonetheless—by foregrounding the experience, the voices, and the perspectives of African slaves—see it through a new prism. The result might be called "an Afrocentric poetics" of the Enlightenment. Recent historical books such as Gretchen Gerzina's *Black London* (1995), W. Jeffrey Bolster's *Black Jacks: African American Seamen in the Age of Sail* (1997), Marcus Wood's *Blind Memory: Visual Representations of Slavery in England and America, 1780–1865* (2000), and Peter Linebaugh and Marcus Rediker's *The Many-Headed Hydra: Sailors, Slaves, Commoners, and the Hidden History of the Revolutionary Atlantic* (2000) have advanced similar perspectives, as indeed has the whole flowering of imperial history and related fields that include in their focus the slave trade and slave-holding societies.* Modern novel-

---

* For excellent examples of this new historiography, see Philip D. Morgan, "The Black Experience in the British Empire, 1680–1810," and David Richardson, "The British Empire and the Atlantic Slave Trade, 1660–1807," in P. J. Marshall and Alaine Low, eds., *The Eighteenth Century*, vol. 2 of *The Oxford History of the British Empire* (Oxford: Oxford University Press, 1998).

ists have also begun to reimagine the period from an Afrocentric perspective, as evidenced by such works as Barry Unsworth's *Sacred Hunger* (1992), S. I. Martin's *Incomparable World* (1996), and Caryl Phillips's *Cambridge* (1991) and *The Atlantic Sound* (2000).

Using a parallel approach in literary history enables us to see the degree to which Africans were a presence and a force in the European imagination, shaping sensibilities and cultural life. If one focuses for a moment on the power of Phillis Wheatley, who has only recently been raised to the level of canonical visibility, one has a suggestive example. Wheatley's impact spread in all directions. She achieved fame in New England as a teenager; her 1773 visit to London took the literary and social world by storm; thousands of readers admired her, critics praised her, and other writers, black and white, responded to her in print; her poem in honor of George Washington moved him to correspond with her and, some would argue, marked the beginning of his change in attitude toward blacks; Thomas Jefferson, even as he argued the inferiority of blacks, felt compelled to take account of her in his *Notes on the State of Virginia;* Henri Grégoire featured her achievement in his landmark book of 1808. (Indeed, her presence is the only one in this volume curtailed by deliberate editorial decision: I have included only ten of her more than fifty poems, chiefly because her work is so widely reprinted and anthologized today.)[*]

But perhaps we must allow that Wheatley was exceptional, a kind of starburst in the center of the literary culture. We could still gauge the validity of an Afrocentric perspective by tracing instead the impact of slavery on poets situated along the periphery, living farthest from the actual scenes of slave ships and plantations. The results are equally telling. Of the poets in this volume, at least seven were based in Ireland and another ten or more in Scotland, places where the populace rarely (if ever) saw black people and African slavery literally had to be imagined. They include such figures as the Irish lawyer Richard Alfred Millikin, who spent his whole career in his native Cork but wrote antislavery verse in the "Inkle and Yarico" tradition, and the Scottish academic James Beattie who, though based in remote Aberdeen, nonetheless laced his university lectures (according to his former students) with harangues against slavery from the 1760s well into the 1790s.

The most powerful example from the periphery, however, has to be the Scottish lawyer John Maclaurin. An amateur poet, Maclaurin had been writing verse against slavery and other imperial abuses since at least 1760, when, in the mid-1770s, he got the chance to become an activist. Joseph Knight, an African slave brought to Scotland by his master, petitioned for his freedom in the Scottish

---

[*] See especially Phillis Wheatley, *Complete Writings*, ed. Vincent Carretta (New York: Penguin Books, 2001).

courts: in 1774 Maclaurin took the case, waived his fees, and led a four-year court battle that, in January 1778, produced a Court of Session decision that officially abolished slavery in Scotland. (Tellingly, one of the other Scottish poets in this collection, Francis Garden, Lord Gardenstone, was a judge in the case.) In the colonies, in the capital, and at the periphery, whether as an immediate reality or an abstract idea, racial slavery challenged not only the poetic imagination, but law, religion, moral philosophy, economic theory, public policy, and international relations. By focusing on the visibility of slavery in literature, we can deepen our sense of how it played out in the culture, and influenced European, American, and Pan-African history.

New Questions and Challenges

The overwhelming majority of the 400 poems in this collection portray slavery as ugly and evil. Only a small subset of the poems, perhaps five to ten percent, condone or defend slavery. The question naturally follows, given the preponderance of writing against slavery, how then did it persist so long? Why was there such a gulf (or was it a lag?) between wider cultural attitudes and the economic and political reality? Were the poets merely an impotent body of social critics or did they have an effect on public attitudes and, eventually, public policy?

The poems at the very close of this book mark an almost uniform crescendo of jubilation. The slave trade had been abolished on both sides of the Atlantic and slavery itself seemed destined to end soon after. Poets raised their voices in praise and celebration, from Robert Southey's poetic tribute to Lord Grenville at a ceremony in Oxford, to the hymns of Robert Sidney, Peter Williams, Jr., William Hamilton, and so many others, sung by African American congregations at annual thanksgiving services in Boston, Philadelphia, and New York. What happened thereafter to dissipate the momentum and dispel the jubilation? How did what had seemed a broad historical trend fracture into so many shards: fugitive slave laws, repatriation and colonization schemes, delays and reversals, the divergent and uneven developments that defined the British and, more painfully, American paths toward emancipation? What role did literature and culture have in that history?

There is one last question, one that challenges us to think again about how we write cultural history. In the late twentieth century a view prevailed in some academic circles that English literature was "complicitous in Empire," that the majority of writers supported and condoned the goals and practices of the "imperial project," including its worst features such as the slave trade and plantation slavery. Recently scholars have challenged that view and in some cases begun to turn it on its head: one leading scholar of the early modern period has concluded that writers "may have hampered" rather than helped in building an "overseas empire for Britain."* The material in this anthology adds weight to such revisionist views. Indeed, this volume documents in massive detail the degree to which poets were the most outspoken and persistent critics of slavery, and fostered massive changes in public perception and attitude. Not that this revision is so novel: almost two hundred years ago, it was also the studied conclusion of both Thomas Clarkson and Henri Grégoire, in their seminal books, that writers played a centrally important role in bringing the slave trade to an end. Clarkson devoted long sections of his landmark *History of the Rise, Progress, and Accomplishment of the Abolition of the African Slave-Trade* (1808) to the influence of English writers from Milton, Behn, and Southerne in the seventeenth century down to those of his own time. At the same time, Grégoire actually dedicated his monumental book *On the Cultural Achievements of Negroes* (1808) to a long list of authors who had written against slavery, including more than thirty-five poets who are represented in this volume. The question for us is, how could theories that are so far at odds with the historical evidence have flourished in the first place? This was among the concerns that moved me to gather and publish these poems. This volume provides, I hope, the raw material for further historical explorations and analyses. Such primary sources are the essential and irreducible basis for our continuing efforts to understand the past and its implications for the world we live in.

* David Armitage, "Literature and Empire," *The Origins of Empire: British Overseas Enterprise to the Close of the Seventeenth Century,* ed. Nicholas Canny and Alaine Low (Oxford: Oxford University Press, 1998).

A Chronology of Major Events

1430s–1490s   Origins of modern slave trade: Portuguese explore West Africa and begin importing slaves into Iberia and the Canary Islands.

1492   Columbus's voyage to America opens the way to transatlantic slave trade; Columbus himself brings Indian slaves back to Spain and in 1498 recommends transporting to America African slaves such as were already present in cities like Seville and Valencia. Spanish and Portuguese traders begin carrying black slaves to the New World in the early 1500s.

1562   Sir John Hawkins makes first of three voyages carrying slaves from West Africa to Hispaniola, but Queen Elizabeth disapproves (she also tried to deport all blacks from England) and English involvement only continues after 1603, during reign of James I.

1571   French merchant's attempt to import African slaves into Bordeaux is disallowed; French slave trade doesn't develop until 1640s.

1602   Dutch East India Company is founded, begins carrying African slaves to present-day South Africa and Indonesia. Dutch West India Company officially commences transatlantic slave trade to Caribbean and South America in 1621.

1619   Dutch slave trader imports Africans into Jamestown, Virginia, although some blacks appear to have been there already.

1625   England settles Barbados and from the 1640s gradually begins sugar production using slave labor.

1636   Barbados becomes first English colony to sanction slavery by law.

1641   Massachusetts becomes first North American colony to give statutory recognition to slavery, followed by Connecticut, 1650; Virginia, 1661; Maryland, 1663; New York and New Jersey, 1664; South Carolina, 1682; Rhode Island and Pennsylvania, 1700; North Carolina, 1715; Georgia, 1750.

1655–1658   England takes Jamaica from Spain, extends slave-based sugar economy.

1660   Restoration of English monarchy, with Charles II.

1663   England charters the Company of Royal Adventurers (renamed Royal African Company in 1672) whose African trade includes slaves and other commodities.

1664   England acquires New Netherland and New Amsterdam from the Dutch, renames colony and city New York.

1688   First formal protest against slavery in English America is made by Quakers in Germantown, Pennsylvania; Quakers lead movement and produce antislavery writings for decades to come, although some Quakers own slaves as late as 1770s.

1698   Parliament ends Royal African Company's monopoly, allowing competitors to enter the slave trade.

1713   Britain wins the Asiento as part of the Treaty of Utrecht, gaining the exclusive right to supply slaves to the Spanish colonies and marking a rapid escalation of the British slave trade.

1738/9   After decades of insurrection and guerrilla warfare, British sign treaty with Jamaican maroons recognizing their independence in exchange for maroons' promise to return fugitive slaves.

1739   Stono slave revolt in South Carolina.

1758   Philadelphia Quakers pass measure condemning the ownership of slaves by their members.

1759   Pennsylvanian Anthony Benezet publishes his first pamphlet against slavery; his writings inspire generations of abolitionists on both sides of the Atlantic.

1760s   Wave of broad-based slave insurrections in Jamaica, followed by increasingly repressive legislation.

1769   Granville Sharp publishes his first attack on slavery and begins legal action on behalf of escaped slave that will lead to the Somerset decision.

1772   Lord Mansfield rules on the Somerset case: once in Britain slaves cannot be compelled to return to the colonies, thus granting them de facto emancipation.

1773   Phillis Wheatley travels to England, publishes her landmark *Poems on Various Subjects*.

1775   As American Revolution breaks out, Governor Dunmore in Virginia offers freedom to slaves of American rebels who come over and fight on British side. British generals repeat the tactic through much of the Revolutionary War (1775–1783).

————— Pennsylvania Society for the Abolition of Slavery is founded (then suspended until end of the war).

1777   Samuel Johnson contributes legal brief in aid of John Maclaurin's case on behalf of Joseph Knight, the former slave seeking manumission in Scottish courts.

————— Vermont becomes first future U.S. state to abolish slavery, followed by

Pennsylvania in 1780 and Massachusetts in 1783; gradual emancipation laws are passed between 1784 and 1804 in Rhode Island, Connecticut, New York, and New Jersey.

1778   Scottish Court of Session rules in favor of Joseph Knight, declares slavery does not exist in Scotland.

1780   William Wilberforce first elected to Parliament (same year as his friend William Pitt); under influence of John Newton and others leads abolitionist movement from late 1780s on.

1782   Publication of *Letters of the Late Ignatius Sancho, an African.*

1783   American independence established, British fleet departs with 3,000 former slaves, bound for resettlement in Nova Scotia, London, and eventually Sierra Leone.

1785   Thomas Clarkson submits prize-winning Cambridge essay on the slave trade, begins his career as abolitionist leader.

1787   British Abolition Society forms in London, under leadership of Wilberforce, Clarkson, and others.

——— Quobna Ottobah Cuguano publishes *Thoughts and Sentiments on the Evil of Slavery.*

——— U.S. Constitution drafted, allowing slavery in states that decide to continue it, counting black slaves as three-fifths of a person in calculating proportional representation, and postponing Congressional attention to slave trade until 1807.

1788   Jacques Pierre Brissot and others, inspired by the British Abolition Society, found the Société des Amis des Noirs.

——— Massive petition campaign in Britain against the slave trade.

1789   Wilberforce introduces bill in British Parliament to abolish the slave trade; debate and postponement continue for three years.

——— Publication of *Narrative of the Life of Olaudah Equiano, or Gustavus Vassa, the African* (whose origins are recently disputed).

1791   Slave insurrections in French colony of Saint Domingue begin the Haitian revolution, which would end after Toussaint L'Ouverture is captured and taken to France in 1802, followed by the defeat of Napoleon's army and Haitian independence in 1804.

1792   In a victory for slaveowners, the House of Lords defeats Wilberforce's bill approved by the Commons, that would have ended the British slave trade in 1796; this and war with revolutionary France effectively postpones abolition indefinitely.

——— African American scientist and writer Benjamin Banneker publishes first of his six almanacs.

1794   Wilberforce introduces another abolition bill, but it too is defeated.

——— African American Methodist Richard Allen founds the Bethel Church in Philadelphia.

———— French National Convention abolishes slavery throughout the French Empire.

1795   African American Peter Williams, Sr., founds African Methodist Episcopal Zion Church, the first black church in New York.

1801   Jefferson elected to first of two terms as U.S. President (disputed 1800 election settled by Congress); during second term (March 4, 1805) he signs bill abolishing the slave trade.

1802   Napoleon restores slavery and slave trade in French colonies.

———— Allegations surface of Thomas Jefferson's affair with his slave Sally Hemings.

1807   Britain and America abolish the slave trade, effective January 1, 1808.

1808   Clarkson publishes *History of the Abolition of the African Slave-Trade* and Abbé Henri Grégoire publishes *De la littérature des nègres* (*On the Cultural Achievements of Negroes*).

1812–1814   The War of 1812: British again employ tactic of inviting American slaves to flee to their side. American slavery begins period of explosive expansion, fueled by the Louisiana Purchase, the cotton gin, and cotton press.

1814   The Dutch officially end slave trade (but retain slavery until 1863).

1815   The Congress of Vienna issues a bland decree against slave trade, but France and especially Portugal revive African slave trade that thrives for many decades.

1820   Missouri Compromise, in clear victory for the South, establishes precedent of balancing admission of slave and free states to the United States. Thereafter fierce debates flare up over every proposed new state.

1833   British Parliament votes to end slavery in the British colonies, paying huge sum of twenty million pounds' compensation to slave owners; transitional "apprenticeship" period extends to 1838.

1845   Frederick Douglass publishes his *Narrative*, makes celebrated journey to Britain.

1848   France abolishes slavery throughout its colonies

1850   U.S. Congress passes Fugitive Slave Act, effectively preventing northern states from prohibiting slavery within their borders and forcing them to cooperate in delivering up runaway ("fugitive") slaves.

———— Under pressure from Britain, Brazil ends slave trade.

1857   Dred Scott decision, by which U.S. blacks, free and enslaved, are denied constitutional rights.

1859   John Brown leads armed abolitionist raid on Harpers Ferry arsenal.

1861–1865   American Civil War, the bloodiest in U.S. history.

1863   President Lincoln's Emancipation Proclamation frees slaves in rebellious Confederate states.

1865   Thirteenth Amendment to the U.S. Constitution abolishes slavery.

Selected Bibliography

Printed Sources

Anstey, Roger. *The Atlantic Slave Trade and British Abolition, 1760–1810*. London: Macmillan, 1975.

Appiah, Kwame Anthony, and Henry Louis Gates, Jr. *Africana: The Encyclopedia of the African and African American Experience*. New York: Basic *Civitas* Books, 1999.

Armitage, David. "Literature and Empire." In Nicholas Canny and Alaine Low, eds., *The Origins of Empire: British Overseas Enterprise to the Close of the Seventeenth Century*. Oxford: Oxford University Press, 1998.

Bennett, Lerone, Jr. *Before the Mayflower: A History of Black America*. Chicago: Johnson Publishing, 1962.

Berlin, Ira. *Many Thousands Gone: The First Two Centuries of Slavery in North America*. Cambridge: Harvard University Press, 1998.

Blackburn, Robin. *The Making of New World Slavery: From the Baroque to the Modern, 1492–1800*. London: Verso, 1997.

Carretta, Vincent. *Unchained Voices: An Anthology of Black Authors in the English-Speaking World of the 18th Century*. Lexington, Ky.: University Press of Kentucky, 1996.

Curtin, Philip D. *The Atlantic Slave Trade: A Census*. Madison: University of Wisconsin Press, 1969.

Davis, David Brion. *The Problem of Slavery in Western Culture*. Ithaca: Cornell University Press, 1966.

————. *The Problem of Slavery in the Age of Revolution, 1770–1823*. Ithaca: Cornell University Press, 1975.

Du Bois, W. E. B. *The Suppression of the African Slave Trade to the United States of America, 1638–1870*. First published 1896; reprinted Baton Rouge: Louisiana State University Press, 1969.

Felsenstein, Frank. *English Trader, Indian Maid: Representing Gender, Race, and*

Slavery in the New World: An Inkle and Yarico Reader. Baltimore: Johns Hopkins University Press, 1999.

Ferguson, Moira. *Subject to Others: British Women Writers and Colonial Slavery, 1670–1834.* New York: Routledge, 1992.

Gerzina, Gretchen. *Black London: Life Before Emancipation.* New Brunswick, N.J.: Rutgers University Press, 1995.

Grégoire, Henri. *On the Cultural Achievements of Negroes.* First published Paris, 1808. New edition and translation by Thomas Cassirer and Jean-François Brière. Amherst: University of Massachusetts Press, 1996.

Jordan, Winthrop D. *White over Black: American Attitudes Toward the Negro, 1550–1812.* New York: W.W. Norton & Company, 1977.

Kaplan, Sidney, and Emma Nogrady Kaplan. *The Black Presence in the Era of the American Revolution.* Amherst: University of Massachusetts Press, 1989.

Kitson, Peter J., and Debbie Lee, eds. *Slavery, Abolition, and Emancipation: Writings in the British Romantic Period.* 8 vols. London: Pickering & Chatto, 1999.

Linebaugh, Peter, and Marcus Rediker. *The Many-Headed Hydra: Sailors, Slaves, Commoners, and the Hidden History of the Revolutionary Atlantic.* Boston: Beacon Press, 2000.

Morgan, Philip D. "The Black Experience in the British Empire, 1680–1810." In P. J. Marshall and Alaine Low, eds. *The Eighteenth Century.* Vol. 2 of *The Oxford History of the British Empire.* Oxford: Oxford University Press, 1998.

Richardson, David. "The British Empire and the Atlantic Slave Trade, 1660–1807." In P. J. Marshall and Alaine Low, eds. *The Eighteenth Century.* Vol. 2 of *The Oxford History of the British Empire.* Oxford: Oxford University Press, 1998.

Shyllon, Folarin Olawale. *Black People in Britain, 1555–1833.* London: published for the Institute of Race Relations by Oxford University Press, 1977.

Sypher, Wylie. *Guinea's Captive Kings.* Chapel Hill: University of North Carolina Press, 1942.

Walvin, James. *Slaves and Slavery: The British Colonial Experience.* Manchester: Manchester University Press, 1992.

————. *Black Ivory: A History of British Slavery.* London: Fontana Press, 1993.

Wood, Betty. *The Origins of American Slavery: Freedom and Bondage in the English Colonies.* New York: Hill and Wang, 1997.

Wood, Marcus. *Blind Memory: Visual Representations of Slavery in England and America, 1780–1865.* New York: Routledge, 2000.

Electronic Sources

Davis, David Brion, Robert Forbes, et al. *The Gilder Lehrman Center for the Study of Slavery, Resistance, and Abolition.* Web site: www.yale.edu/glc.

SELECT BIBLIOGRAPHY

Eltis, David, Stephen D. Behrendt, David Richardson, and Herbert S. Klein. *The Trans-Atlantic Slave Trade: A Database on CD-ROM.* Cambridge: Cambridge University Press, 1999.

Mintz, Steven. "The Origins and Nature of New World Slavery." In *Gilder Lehrman History Online.* Web site: www.gilderlehrman.org.

Schwarz, Philip J. *The Roots of American Slavery: A Bibliographical Essay.* Web site: www.stratfordhall.org/schwarz.htm.

Textual Note

The text for each poem in this anthology is taken from the author's latest amended version, if known, and otherwise from the first edition. In a handful of instances where early editions were unobtainable, the best available modern edition was used. The texts have been reprinted as they originally appeared except for the silent correction of a few obvious typographical errors and the modest standardization of some elements in the punctuation and capitalization. Sources for texts are listed in the Notes.

Footnotes were deliberately kept to a minimum, except those from the author's original text that bear particularly on the subject of slavery or the historical context. In each case the author's notes are identified as such.

Given space constraints, the headnotes have been kept as brief as possible, although in each an effort is made to situate the poem biographically and historically, and to highlight salient features of the text.

HENRY KING (1592–1669)

Educated at Westminster and Christ Church, Oxford, King was a clergyman who eventually became Bishop of Chichester. He was also a literary man who counted Ben Jonson and John Donne among his friends, and who from early in life composed large numbers of occasional poems that began to appear in print about 1657, on the eve of the Restoration. King's pair of lyrics add an interracial charge to the conventions of courtship poetry and pose an early challenge to race-based assumptions about beauty. These two poems remained popular in the eighteenth century and were reprinted in anthologies as late as *The Poetical Farrago* (London, 1794).

A Blackamore Maid to a Fair Boy

Stay lovely boy! why fly'st thou me?
Who languish in these flames for thee!
I'm black 'tis true—why so is night,
Yet love does in its shades delight!
One moment close thy sparkling eye,
The world shall seem as black as I.
Or look—and see how black a shade
Is by thy own white body made!
That follows thee wher'er thou go,
(Ah who allow'd would not do so!)
Oh let me then that shadow be,
No maid shall then be blest like me!

The Boy's Answer

Black maid, complain not that I fly
When fate commands antipathy!
How monstrous would that union prove
Where night and day should mingled move?

1

And the conjunction of our lips,
Not kisses make, but an eclipse?
In which, the black shading the white,
Portends more terror than delight!
Yet if my shadow thou wilt be,
Enjoy my shadow's property;
Which tho' attendant on my eye,
Yet hastes away as I come nigh.
Else stay till death has struck me blind,
And then at will thou mayst be kind.

(wr. c. 1660/pub. 1742)[1]

EDMUND HICKERINGILL
(1631–1708)

A Cambridge graduate who came of age during the tumultuous Civil War era, Hickeringill served three years in Cromwell's forces in Scotland and then several years as a mercenary on the Continent. A convert to Baptism, he briefly became a Quaker and then lapsed into deism, before spending the balance of his life as an ordained but cantankerous Anglican. The volatility of his convictions was never more evident than when this former Cromwellian soldier dedicated the second edition of the poem below to King Charles II.

Jamaica Viewed (1661) is a versified report based on Hickeringill's expedition to the Caribbean. It is thought to have helped influence Charles II to retain and develop Jamaica in the 1660s, rather than return it to the Spanish (as he had promised). In the passage below, although he never precisely distinguishes the races and ethnicities of the slaves (whether native or African or mixed race), Hickeringill illustrates the bloody context in which the English saw New World slavery as they took possession of Jamaica. Here he describes the mores of the Caribs, including their ownership of slaves.

from Jamaica Viewed

When any dies, into his Urne is hurl'd
All that he hath; (to use, i'th' other world:)
His Axe, Bill, Knife, his Bow and Hammock too,
And this the best of service they can doe
For their dead Friend. If he a Captain be,
Then if he have a Slave, he then must die;
And the same Rouge burn both; thus is supply'd
Each one i'th' other world, as 'fore he dy'd.
But usually their Slaves, when captive ta'ne,
Are to the English sold; and some are slain,
And their Flesh forthwith Barbacu'd and eat
By them, their Wives and Children as choice meat.

Thence are they call'd Caribs, or Cannibals;
The very same that we Man-eaters call.
And yet herein lies not their chief content
To eat for food, but as a Sacrament;
To bind them and their Children to be fierce,
And into th' entrails of their foes to pierce.

(1661)[2]

JOHN DRYDEN (1631–1700)

Dryden, the Poet Laureate and dominant figure of Restoration literature, never composed a poem focused primarily on the slave trade, but images of blacks, the African trade, and slavery are scattered throughout his works. Thus in his 1662 "Satire on the Dutch" Dryden casually mentions the "Guinea trade"—which after 1660 included a rapidly growing slave trade—among the issues underlying the ongoing Anglo-Dutch wars. Dryden later incorporated the poem almost verbatim into the text of the prologue to his tragedy *Amboyna* (1672).

from "Satire on the Dutch"

> The dotage of some Englishmen is such,
> To fawn on those who ruin them,—the Dutch.
> They shall have all, rather than make a war
> With those who of the same religion are.
> The Straits, the Guinea trade, the herrings too;
> Nay, to keep friendship, they shall pickle you.
>
> (1662)[3]

Two years later, to conjure up an ironic image of desolation in his verse tragicomedy *The Rival Ladies*, Dryden invoked the bitter choice slaves faced between cruel captivity or starvation in the wild.

from The Rival Ladies

> *Julia:* Your Favour from constraint has set me free,
> But that secures not my Felicity;
> Slaves, who, before, did cruel Masters serve,
> May fly to Desarts, and in Freedome starve.
> The noblest part of Liberty they loose,
> Who can but shun, and want the Pow'r to choose.
>
> (1664)[4]

In 1689, when Dryden wrote the prologue to Aphra Behn's *The Widow
Ranter,* he was introducing one of the first plays to present New World African
slaves on a London stage, yet chose to treat transatlantic trade and life in the
"dear plantation[s]" primarily as food for wit and beau monde satire.

from "Prologue" to The Widow Ranter or The History of Bacon in Virginia, A Tragicomedy

> Plays you will have; and to supply your store,
> Our poets trade to every foreign shore:
> This is the product of Virginian ground,
> And to the port of Covent-Garden bound.
> Our cargo is, or should at least, be wit . . .
> You sparks, we hope, will wish us happy trading;
> For you have ventures in our vessel's lading;
> And though you touch at this or t'other nation;
> Yet sure Virginia is your dear plantation.
> Expect no polished scenes of love should rise
> From the rude growth of Indian colonies.
>
> (1689)[5]

By 1690 the presence of black servants in fashionable London households
had become familiar enough that Dryden could allude, in the "Prologue" to *The
Prophetess,* to the copper collars these enslaved status symbols customarily wore.

from "Prologue" to The Prophetess

> Go Conquerors of your Male and Female Foes;
> Men without Hearts, and Women without Hose.
> Each bring his Love, a Bogland Captive home,
> Such proper Pages, will long Trayns become:
> With Copper-Collars, and with brawny Backs,
> Quite to put down the Fashion of our Blacks.
>
> (wr. 1690/pub. 1708)[6]

In the "Prologue" to *Cleomenes* the value of black and white bondsmen as
slave labor in the colonies becomes fodder for comic banter in a London play-
house.

from "Prologue" to Cleomenes

> I think or hope, at least, the Coast is clear,
> That none but Men of Wit and Sence are here:

JOHN DRYDEN

That our Bear-Garden Friends are all away,
Who bounce with Hands and Feet, and cry Play, Play. . . .
Let 'em go People Ireland, where there's need
Of such new Planters to repair the Breed;
Or to Virginia or Jamaica Steer,
But have a care of some French Privateer;
For if they should become the Prize of Battle,
They'll take 'em Black and White for Irish Cattle.

(1692)[7]

In light of the growing awareness of black slavery in his era, even Dryden's 1693 treatment of the Ethiopian episode in Juvenal's *Sixth Satire* (composed 1,500 years earlier) takes on new interest and resonance.

from The Sixth Satire of Juvenal

But thou, whatever slops she will have bought,
Be thankful, and supply the deadly draught;
Help her to make manslaughter; let her bleed,
And never want for savin at her need.
For, if she holds till her nine months be run,
Thou may'st be father to an Ethiop's son;*
A boy, who, ready gotten to thy hands,
By law is to inherit all thy lands;
One of that hue, that, should he cross the way,
His omen would discolour all the day.
I pass the foundling by, a race unknown,
At doors exposed, whom matrons make their own;
And into noble families advance
A nameless issue, the blind work of chance.
Indulgent fortune does her care employ,
And, smiling, broods upon the naked boy:
Her garment spreads, and laps him in the fold,
And covers with her wings from nightly cold:
Gives him her blessing, puts him in a way,
Sets up the farce, and laughs at her own play.
Him she promotes; she favours him alone,
And makes provision for him as her own.

(1693)[8]

* [Dryden's footnote:] Juvenal's meaning is, help her to any kind of slops which may cause her to miscarry, for fear she may be brought to bed of a black Moor, which thou, being her husband, art bound to father; and that bastard may, by law, inherit thy estate.

SAMUEL BUTLER (1613–1680)

Little is known about this anti-Puritan satirist except that he refrained from publishing anything until after the death of Cromwell in 1658, when Butler was almost fifty, and that his mock-epic *Hudibras* (Part I 1663, Part II 1664) was an enormous critical and popular success in the pro-Royalist atmosphere of the Restoration. In this passage from his fierce and raucous satire, Butler imagistically stigmatizes the "Negro" as a demonic other, in league with the Devil. This kind of minor, casual, but nonetheless racist reference became more common over time, as awareness of Africa and the transatlantic slave trade grew.

from Hudibras

Quoth Hudibras, These sad effects
Spring from your Heathenish neglects
Of Love's great pow'r, which he returns
Upon your selves with equal scorns;
And those who worthy Love[rs] slight,
Plague's with prepost'rous appetite;
This made the beautious Queen of Crete
To take a Town-Bull for her Sweet;
And from her greatness stoop so low,
To be the Rival of a Cow.
Others to prostitute their great Hearts,
To be Baboons, and Monkeys Sweet-hearts.
Some with the Dev'l himself in League grow
By's Representative a Negro,
'Twas this made Vestal-Maids love-sick,
And venture to be bury'd Quick.

(1664)[9]

ANONYMOUS

The unknown author of this stanza includes it, without explanation, in a prose tract about West Africa ("Guinney") that combines travelogue, geography, and commercial advice. Celebrating Britain's growing economic power, the writer situates the nation's burgeoning African trade in a vision of Britain's potential dominance of world commerce: "Commanding the commerce of all Nations; our *Negotiation* being not limited in a narrower compass than the whole Earth, and our dealing knowing no bounds but those of the world." The growing European interest in racial difference and cross-cultural perspectives is evident in the poem.

Untitled [from The Golden Coast]

The Land of *Negroes* is not far from thence,
    Neerer extended to th'*Atlantick* Main,
Wherein the Black Prince keeps his Residence,
    Attended with his Jeaty-coloured train.
      Who in their native beauty most delight,
      And in contempt do paint the Devil white.
               (1665)[10]

MICHAEL WIGGLESWORTH
(1631–1705)

A conscientious Puritan who had lived in New England since the age of seven, Wigglesworth was a Harvard-educated minister, physician, and author. His "Meditation X," for all its advice to blacks that they be pious and submissive, also shows remarkable compassion for their suffering and attempts to elevate their ordeal as a paradigm of Christian grace. Perhaps the first to suggest that black slaves may be God's chosen people ("they to him are dear"), Wigglesworth also anticipated by a century the symbolic interplay of black and white as both physical and metaphysical qualities—skin color and spiritual condition—that Blake would explore in "The Little Black Boy" (1789).

"Meditation X" from Meat out of the Eater

Although Affliction tanne the Skin,
Such Saints are Beautiful within.

1
How amiable is
The face of suffering Saints,
Where God thus quieteth their hearts
And stilleth their complaints!
Where 'tis their daily care,
And earnest hearts desire,
To love, and bless, and honour God
In middest of the fire.

2
Where nothing grieves them more
Then what their God doth grieve:
Where nothing pleaseth them like that
Which make them sin to leave.
Where though they have a will
And wishes of their own:

Yet at the foot of Jesus Christ
    They meekly lay them down.

3

    These are the happy men,
      Judge of them what thou please
Vain world, amongst thy Darlings all
    Thou hast not one like these.
    As God is dear to them,
      So they to him are dear,
And he to all the world ere long
    Will make it to appear.

4

    The Daughter of the King,
      All glorious is within,
How Black soever and Sun-Burnt,
    May seem her outward Skin.
    Because I Blackish am,
      Upon me—look not ye,
Because that with his Beams the Sun
    Hath looked down on me.

5

    A patient suffering Saint
      Is a right comely one:
Though black as *Kedar's* Tents, and as
    Curtains of *Solomon*.
    Thus beautifie my soul
      Dear Saviour; thus adorn it.
As for the Trappings of the world,
    And Bravery, I can scorn it.

6

    Some deck the outside fair;
      But are like Graves within:
Some sweep and wash their houses clean;
    Whose hearts most nasty been.
    Some bodies fat and fair
      Have Souls both foul and lean:
But howsoe're my Body fare,
    Lord make my soul more clean.

               (1667)[11]

THOMAS JORDAN (?1612–1685)

A native Londoner who pursued a career as actor, playwright, versifier, and occasional writer, Jordan struggled to survive the mid-century closure of the theaters (1643–59) but came into his own after the Restoration, especially with his appointment as "Poet of the Corporation of London" in 1671. In this post his chief duty was to compose elaborate pageants for the annual Lord Mayor's show, an event that celebrated the glories of British trade and commerce. The pageants combined elements of lavish parades, street theater, and musical performance, and Jordan wrote and directed these with great success for fourteen years.

Many of these pageants, unconsciously reflecting the emerging racial dimension of overseas trade, include large numbers of black characters. In one of his first pageants, *London Triumphant* (1672), Jordan confuses and conflates Native Americans with Africans under a variety of ambiguous terms. His elaborate stage directions present a cast consisting of several "Negro" characters and "Black-Moors," some of them in the roles of "Princes of West-India" and "Princes of Peru and Mexico," all of them with physical features described in terms of "black Faces" and "short curl'd black wool-like Hair." One of them, "the Indian Emperour," delivers an opening tribute to the Grocers' Company that rejoices in the growth of British commerce in the most idyllic terms, rosily painting over the historic reality experienced by people of color in the Americas.

from London Triumphant

> *The first speech, spoken by the* Indian *Emperour:*
> To fill your Triumphs, and compleat this Show,
> The Princes of *Peru* and *Mexico*
> With our Imperial Train appear in State,
> Your Royal Revellings to Celebrate:
> Especially to be receiv'd a Guest
> By those that bear this *Camel* in their Crest;

THOMAS JORDAN

Because it is reported (as Fame saith,)
That *England's* great Defender of the Faith,
Head of four Thrones, doth not disdain to be
A Member of the *Grocers* Companie.
If their indulgent Soveraign be so good
As to consociate in Brotherhood,
And be concorporated, well may I
(That furnish them with Fruits and Spicery)
Give them a visit, and congratulate
Their Noble-natur'd, new-made Magistrate;
For I have heard He is a person free
And liberal in Hospitalitie . . .

    Justice supports the World, for without that
No man hath title to his own Estate;
Which mix'd with *Mercy,* gives mankind new birth,
And may be fitly styl'd *Heaven* upon *Earth,*
Which there's no question, but you will dispense
To punish Guilt, and cherish Innocence;
And with your Eagles eyes to search out those
That are your God's, your King's, and Country's foes;
Such as ly lurking, only to grow higher
By Civil Wars, or Cities set on fire,
Which they'll pretend to quench: But (in a word,)
You bear this Sword of Government (my Lord)
In such a peevish Age, that (I may say)
Many are studious how to Disobey,
And yet Speak well, but if they Act not so,
We are better Moralists in *Mexico.*

    But I am well assur'd, my Lord, you'll do
What Love and Equity shall prompt you to,
And future Ages shall your praises sing
With a choice Pen pluckt from an Eagles wing.

In this second excerpt, another idealized depiction of the blessings of the English on these peoples—sharply contrasted with the evil ways of the Spanish and Dutch—is followed by one of the earliest renderings of "the happy slave" motif in English literature. The monologue is delivered by "America," described in the text as "A proper Masculine Woman, with a tawny Face, Raven-black long Hair, curling up at the ends, on her Head a Crown Imperial; her Breast naked and tawny." The jolly refrain that follows is sung by the many black field hands—"tawny Moors"—who form the large chorus of the pageant.

The Third Speech, spoken by AMERICA

That I the better may Attention draw,
Be pleas'd to know I am *America*,
The Western Quarter of the World, whose Climes
Were not discover'd till these later Times:
When first *Columbus* found me out, where I
Lay hid a long time in obscurity,
(Unknown to *Christendom*) I liv'd at ease,
Enrich'd with Gold, Tranquility and Peace;
But when, by fierce Invasions, they did know
The Treasures of *Peru* and *Mexico*,
(My two great Empires) I became a Prey
To divers Nations, who did rob and slay
My naked Natives, such as knew no Art
In War-like Weapons, but the Bow and Dart.
Then came the winged ship, with thundring Gun,
Which dimm'd the Eyes of our great God, the Sun,
The only Deity we worship'd, and
Ransack'd my riches, over'ran my Land,
Ruin'd my Princes, (my sad Fate was such)
The haughty *Spaniard* and the cruel *Dutch*
(Than which the Devil is not worse) did Build
Fortifications, rout me in the Field,
Brought over Priests, and Monks with Holy Hoods,
To teach Religion, whilst they stole my Goods:
Only the *English* Nation I did find
Amongst the rest more peaceable and kind,
Full of Humanity, who did perswade
Me to a generous and fair way of Trade;
Faithful in Word and Deed, which makes me come
To this Celestial Part of *Christendome*,
And bear my share in the Triumphant Glory
Of *London's* Magistrate, whose Fame and Story
Throughout the Western World I'll boldly sing,
A Faithful Subject to a Gracious King:
And may they both ever preserved be
From publick Force or private Treachery,
That so the GROCER's Traffick may prevail
So long as ships on the curl'd Ocean Sail. . . .
      This Speech being ended the Planters, the Gatherers, and Reapers,
      Sing this ensuing Song, with a Chorus at the end of every Verse.

THOMAS JORDAN

A Song

This Wilderness is
A place full of Bliss,
   For caring and sparing
We know not what 'tis:
By the sweat of our brows
   We do purchase our meat:
What we pluck from the boughs
   We do lye down and eat.

   Chorus [of "tawny Moors," the plantation laborers]:
We labour all day, but we frollick at Night,
With smoaking and joking, and tricks of Delight.

      II.
The Merchant that Plows
On the Seas rugged brows,
   Submits all his hits
To what Fortune allows:
   If she do but frown
   The Trader is down;
   Till he comes to Port he has nothing his own.

   Chorus:
We labour all day, but we frollick at Night,
With smoaking and joking, and tricks of Delight.

      III.
Of Fruits that are ripe
   We all freely can take;
With Tongues and Bag-Pipe
   Jolly Musick we make:
In our Pericraniums no mischief doth lurk;
We are happier then they that do set us a work.
   We never are losers
      What ever wind drive;
   Then God bless the *Grocers,*
      And send them to thrive.

   Chorus:
We labour all Day, yet we frollick at Night,
With smoaking and joking, and tricks of Delight.

                                        (1672)[12]

The 1678 pageant mounted similar scenes, once again blurring the distinctions between the Indies, East and West, and their respective peoples. Again stage directions call for a "Negro boy," "two Active Negroes" mounted on golden gryphons, three "Black *Indian* Princes," and a chorus of similar folk presented as Plantation "Labourers, Planters, and Drolls." The lyrics of the song reveal a rather telling concern about the plantation workers' loyalty, submission, and distaste for "Rebellion" or "Sedition." A decade later, with Aphra Behn's *Oroonoko* (1688), British society was presented with a radically different vision, based on treachery and violence, of master-slave relations in the plantations.

"A Song" from The Triumphs of London

I

With Mattock, Spade, Pruning-Hook, Shovel & Sieve,
What a Life of Delight do we Labourers live?
The bonny brisk Planter (for delving design'd)
Hath Health in his Body, and Peace in his Mind.
Though this as a Curse in the Scripture we read,
In the Sweat of thy brows thou shalt purchase thy Bread.
Chorus. Yet by Patience and Labour, in Digging and Dressing,
    Th' old Curse is converted into a new Blessing.

II

With Cinamon, Cloves, Murr, and all other spice,
We Planters have planted a New Paradise.
We feel no Effects of the Fault that was Adam's,
Here's Pepper for Gallants, and Nutmegs for Madams.
We work, and we sweat, yet are never the worse;
At the most we have but a Spice of the Curse.
Chorus. But by Patience and Labour our Treasure encreasing
    Hath made a Conversion on't into a Blessing.

III

For *London's* great *Grocers* we Labour and Work,
No Plots against Princes in our Heads do lurk:
We Plant, Set, and Sow, likewise for the Physician,
But Plant no Rebellion, and Sow no Sedition.
The *Grocers* and Merchants are Men of Renown,
They are just in their Trading, and true to the Crown.
Chorus. And we faithful Planters; since all this is so Sirs,
    Let's Pray for King Charles, and his Brethren, the *Grocers*.

(1678)[13]

THOMAS FLATMAN (1637–1688)

An Oxford-educated poet and miniature painter, Flatman pursued the clever similes and elaborate conceits of the metaphysical poets. Indeed, he was said to have carefully imitated Cowley, for whom the term was invented. In this passage, Flatman is one of the first to bring into view the actual buying and selling of slaves as a poetic image. Significantly, the image is of a child. Thus he distantly foreshadows the poignant images of children and families on the auction block that would become so widespread in the sentimental poetry of the later eighteenth and nineteenth centuries.

from "Pastoral"

Unlucky stars poor Shepheards have,
Whose love is fickle *Fortune*'s Slave:
Those golden days are out of date,
When every Turtle chose his Mate:
Cupid that mighty Prince then uncontroul'd
Now like a little *Negro*'s bought and sold.

(1674)[14]

APHRA BEHN (c. 1640–1689)

Celebrated by Virginia Woolf in *A Room of One's Own* as the first professional woman writer, Behn seems (despite a shortage of hard biographical facts) to have led an extraordinarily adventurous life. Born in England, she spent a year of her youth in Surinam, where she apparently witnessed a major slave insurrection. As a young woman she married a Dutch merchant and moved in London social and literary circles that included Dryden, Rochester, and others. Soon widowed, she served as a spy in Holland during the Anglo-Dutch War, afterward returning to London where, driven by penury, she pursued a twenty-year career as playwright, poet, and novelist. No writer before 1700 did more to make New World slavery visible in English literature, both directly, through her novella *Oroonoko, or the Royal Slave* (1688), and indirectly, through the several dramatic adaptations based on it by Thomas Southerne and others.

Like Dryden and many other Restoration playwrights, Behn fashioned a verse tragedy out of the history and lore of the fifteenth-century clash between Moors and Christians. In the excerpt below, the Moorish prince Abdelazer not only bridles with resentment at his enslavement in the Spanish court, but exhibits a proud self-consciousness about the racism with which his captors view him. Later, in *Oroonoko*, about an African prince who becomes a slave and leads an insurrection in Surinam, Behn would carry over into prose fiction the heroic and sentimental treatment of slavery that characterized plays like *Abdelazer*.

from Act I, Scene i of Abdelazer, or the Moor's Revenge. A Tragedy

> Abdelazer: The Queen with me! with me! a Moor! a Devil!
> A Slave of *Barbary!* for so
> Your gay young Courtiers christen me:—but Don,
> Although my skin be black, within my veins
> Runs bloud as red, and Royal as the best.—
> My Father, Great *Abdela*, with his Life

Lost too his Crown: both most unjustly ravisht
By Tyrant *Philip;* your old King I mean. . . .
I was but young, yet old enough to grieve,
Though not revenge, or to defie my Fetters;
For then began my Slavery: and e'er since
Have seen that Diadem by this Tyrant worn,
Which Crown'd the Sacred Temples of my Father,
And shou'd adorn mine now;—shou'd! nay and must.

(wr. 1676/pub. 1677)[15]

In the passage below, from an ode addressed to a newly appointed governor of Jamaica, "the sun-scorch'd natives" would seem to include all the inhabitants, black and white. If so, it is remarkable that nothing else is said in this poem about the slave system or population, by a writer so well known for her treatment of the subject in prose fiction. The poem is made all the more difficult by Behn's subtly ironic tone, in praising a young aristocrat who was notorious for his self-indulgence and dissipation.

from To the Most Illustrious Prince Christopher Duke of Albemarle, on His Voyage to His Government of Jamaica. A Pindarick

Prepare, ye Sun-scorch'd Natives of the Shore,
Prepare another Rising Sun t'adore,
Such as has never blest your Horizon before.
And you the Brave Inhabitants of the Place,
Who have by Conquest made it all your own,
Whose Generous and Industrious Race
Has paid such Useful Tribute to the Crown;
See what your Grateful King for you has done!
Behold a Prince high in His Favor plac'd,
By Fortune Blest, and lavish Honour Grac'd,
Lov'd by the Great, and Worshipp'd by the Crowd,
Of whom the Nation has so long been proud,
The Souldiers Honour and the Brave Mans Friend.

(1687)[16]

ANONYMOUS ["EPHELIA"]
(fl. 1670s and 1680s)

This poem, which appeared in a volume titled *Female Poems on Several Occasions. Written by Ephelia,* reveals a striking irony in the unknown Ephelia's life. She who had laced many of her love poems elsewhere in the volume with the metaphor of slavery (e.g., "when your Eyes first made my Heart your Slave" and "Being your Slave, I'm not so vain . . .") here discloses that her lover "Strephon," a merchant in the African trade (and by one account a slave trader),* has jilted her for an "Afric Nymph." Tantalizingly short on detail, the poem opens wide the field for speculation on interracial relationships and European perspectives on Africans during the Restoration.

from "My Fate"

    Midst our Joys, [Destiny] snatch'd my Shepherd hence
To Africa: yet tho' I was neglected,
I bore it better than could be expected:
Without Regret, I let him cross the Sea,
When I was told it for his Good wou'd be;
But when I heard the Nuptial Knot he'd ty'd,
And made an Afric Nymph his happy Bride:
My Temper then I could no longer hold,
I curs'd my Fate, I curs'd the Pow'r of Gold;
I curs'd the Easiness believ'd at first,
And (Heaven forgive me) Him I almost curs'd.
Hearing my Loss, to him was mighty Gain;
I check'd my Rage, and soon grew Calm again:
Malicious Fate, seeing this wou'd not do,
Made Strephon wretched, to make me so too.

* Moira Ferguson, *Subject to Others,* p. 23 and n. 65.

ANONYMOUS

Of all her Plagues, this was the weightiest Stroke,
This Blow, my resolv'd Heart hath almost broke:
Yet, spight of Fate, this Comfort I've in store,
She's no room left for any Ill thing more.

(1679)[17]

JAMES REVEL (fl. c. 1659–1680s)

An indentured servant turned poet, Revel was born in London, serving there from age thirteen as apprentice to a tin-man, before falling into a life of crime. Three of his fellow criminals were hanged, but he was sentenced to fourteen years of bonded service in the colony of Virginia. In those early years, as his poem indicates, white indentured servants were bought and sold, and lived and worked, alongside African slaves, with the all-important distinction that the latter's servitude never ended and descended upon their offspring. Revel disappears from the historical record after finishing his sentence, but his gritty poem reveals in extraordinary detail the miserable life of slave laborers in seventeenth-century America.

from "The Poor Unhappy Transported Felon's Sorrowful Account of His Fourteen Years Transportation, at Virginia, in America"

> To refresh us, we were wash'd and cleaned
> That to our buyers we might the better seem;
> Our things were gave to each they did belong,
> And they that had clean linnen put it on.
> Our faces shav'd, comb'd out our wigs and hair,
> That we in decent order might appear,
> Against the planters did come down to view,
> How well they lik'd this fresh transported crew.
> The Women s[e]parated from us stand,
> As well as we, by them for to be view'd;
> And in short time some men up to us came,
> Some ask'd our trades, and others ask'd our names.
> Some view'd our limbs; and others turn'd us round
> Examening like Horses, if we're sound . . . .
>
> At last to my new master's house I came,
> At the town of Wicocc[o]moco call'd by name,

Where my Europian clothes were took from me,
Which never after I again could see.

    A canvas shirt and trowsers then they gave,
With a hop-sack frock in which I was to slave:
No shoes nor stockings had I for to wear,
Nor hat, nor cap, both head and feet were bare.

    Thus dress'd into the Field I nex[t] must go,
Amongst tobacco plants all day to hoe,
At day break in the morn our work began,
And so held to the setting of the Sun.

    My fellow slaves were just five Transports more,
With eighteen Negroes, which is twenty four:
Besides four transport women in the house,
To wait upon his daughter and his Spouse,

    We and the Negroes both alike did fare,
Of work and food we had an equal share;
But in a piece of ground we call our own,
The food we eat first by ourselves were sown,

    No other time to us they would allow,
But on a Sunday we the same must do:
Six days we slave for our master's good,
The seventh day is to produce our food.

    Sometimes when that a hard days work we've done,
Away unto the mill we must be gone;
Till twelve or one o'clock a grinding corn,
And must be up by daylight in the morn.

    And if you run in debt with any one,
It must be paid before from thence you come;
For in publick places they'll put up your name,
That every one their just demands may claim,

    And if we offer for to run away,
For every hour we must serve a day;
For every day a Week, They're so severe,
For every week a month, for every month a year
But if they murder, rob or steal when there,
Then straightway hang'd, the Laws are so severe;
For by the Rigour of that very law
They're much kept under and to stand in awe.

    Part IV
At length, it pleased God I sick did fall
But I no favour could receive at all,

23

For I was Forced to work while I could stand,
Or hold the hoe within my feeble hands.
  Much hardships then in deed I did endure,
No dog was ever nursed so I'm sure,
More pity the poor Negroe slaves bestowed
Than my inhuman brutal master showed.
  Oft on my knees the Lord I did implore,
To let me see my native land once more;
For through God's grace my life I would amend
And be a comfort to my dearest friends. . . .

Thus twelve long tedious years did pass away,
And but two more by law I had to stay:
When Death did for my cruel Master call,
But that was no relief to us at all.
  The Widow would not the Plantation hold,
So we and that were both for to be sold,
A lawyer rich who at James-Town did dwell,
Came down to view it and lik'd it very well.
  He bought the Negroes who for life were slaves,
But no transported Fellons would he have,
So we were put like Sheep into a fold,
There unto the best bidder to be sold,

(c. 1680)[18]

THOMAS TRYON ["PHILOTHEOS PHYSIOLOGUS"] (1634–1703)

A radical experimentalist in religion and personal mores, Tryon was a hatmaker who at different times belonged to the Anabaptists and Boehmenists, and practiced vegetarianism, temperance, and pacifism. Having spent several years in Barbados in the 1660s, Tryon criticized slavery from firsthand knowledge. This little poem, apparently adapted from an unidentified source, is embedded in his antislavery treatise *Friendly Advice*. There, amidst a prose dialogue between a "Negro-Slave, and a Christian That Was His Master," the slave recites this stanza to mock the hypocrisy of his master's social class.

Untitled [from Friendly Advice to the Gentlemen-Planters of the East and West Indies*]*

If my foul Deeds of Darkness may
Be wrapt in Clouds as black as they;
If being ugly I can Paint,
And act the *Devil*, yet seem a *Saint*,
Cheat and Oppress, Forswear and Lye,
Yet scape the *Law* and *Infamy*,
I mind no further Honesty.

(1684)[19]

ANONYMOUS

Nothing is known of this author except what can be gathered from his poem and the book in which it appeared, *Poetical Recreations* by Jane Barker (fl. 1688–1726). A Royalist poet and novelist, Barker included this poem with others attributed to "Several Gentlemen of the Universities." Obviously a supporter of the newly appointed governor of Jamaica, the Royalist Duke of Albemarle, the poet (unlike Behn in a similar poem printed above) shows a sympathetic awareness of the slaves in Jamaica even as he idealizes the likely impact of the new governor's arrival.

from "To Their Graces, the Duke and Dutchess of Albemarle, Upon Their Voyage for Jamaica"

Go then, lov'd Prince, Success your Actions crown,
Guarded with vertuous Honours there unknown . . .
How shall the slaves to Labour born, and Toil,
When Your kind Person shall refresh the Isle,
Wonder with joy to see each other smile?
The Spirits which, to them, You shall dispence,
So much their once-vex't Souls will influence,
That they shall banish all sad sorrows thence.
What ease shall Natives, what delight possess,
Who from blest You derive their Happiness?

(1688)[20]

ELKANAH SETTLE (1648–1724)

A rival of Dryden's and a prolific playwright, Settle had left Oxford without a degree to pursue a literary career in London. After writing a long series of conventional but popular plays from 1666 to 1690, Settle was named "City Laureate" in 1691 and charged with producing the annual pageant in celebration of British commerce and power. Like Jordan in the 1670s and 1680s, Settle presented a range of black characters to his London audience.

In the first passage, Arachne (the mythical seamstress and patroness of the Drapers' Guild) is presented in a chariot drawn by two lions mounted by "two *Negroes* in their Native Habit." She opens her poetic address by directing the attention of her black charioteers to the awesome power of the Lord Mayor and goes on to stress the themes of subservience, industry, and wealth creation.

from The Triumphs of London

Hold, hold my sooty sun burnt Charioteers,
Behold the awfull Lord of Pow'r appears:
Bid my Triumphant Driving Chariot stay,
Till to bright HONOUR I my Homage pay.
That Pow'rful Hand must stop my rolling Wheels,
Whilst to such WORTH even my proud Lyon Kneels.
My Lyons! Yes; at that commanding Word,
They know their Duty and must own their Lord.
If such their Homage, Sir, what must be mine,
I who but only from Your Favour shine?
Though proud Arachne does her self profess,
Of Arts the Mistress, and the Patroness.
Fair Industry and Arts your Hand-Maids stand;
Th'improving Age and the Enriching Land,
All spin their Thred from Your Encouraging hand.
My Wheel then and my Loom are all Your own,

And 'tis Your Smiles that mount me to my Throne.
Then from that Throne, my Lord, I bend thus low;
And to Acknowledge the vast Debt I owe,
My Founders Fame in my own Loom enroll'd,
For that Rich Web I'll spin a Thread of Gold.

(1691)[21]

THOMAS SOUTHERNE
(1659–1746)

The Anglo-Irish writer Thomas Southerne was educated at Trinity College, Dublin but came to London in the late 1670s to become a playwright. With Dryden's help, Southerne enjoyed a moderately prosperous career, producing plays from 1682 until 1726. *Oroonoko* was by far his greatest success. Adapted from Aphra Behn's novella *Oroonoko, or the Royal Slave* (1688) and influenced by Shakespeare's *Othello* (both in its blank verse and its interracial romantic theme), Southerne's *Oroonoko* was an immediate hit when produced in 1695 and went on to be performed 315 times during the eighteenth century—an average of three performances a year. The play was also adapted by others, including John Hawkesworth (1759), Francis Gentleman (1760), and John Ferriar (1788). If eighteenth-century London theatergoers formed any idea of slavery from the stage, it would most likely have been from *Oroonoko*.

In the first excerpt, Oroonoko, who has been tricked into slavery by a treacherous sea captain, defiantly proclaims his dignity as he is marched ashore to be sold as a field slave in Surinam.

from Oroonoko

Act I, Scene II.
    Oroonoko. Let the guilty blush . . . Honest Black
Disdains to change its Colour. I am ready:
Where must I go? Dispose me as you please.
I am not well acquainted with my Fortune,
But must learn to know it better: So I know, you say:
Degrees make all things easy. . . .
Tear off this Pomp, and let me know my self:
The slavish Habit best becomes me now.
Hard Fare, and Whips, and Chains may overpow'r
The frailer flesh, and bow my Body down.

But there's another, Nobler Part of Me,
Out of your reach, which you can never tame.

In the following scene, Oroonoko resists pressure from his loyal lieutenant
Aboan to lead a rebellion of the slaves, although later he will change his mind
and fight for freedom when he learns that his beloved Imoinda is pregnant with
their child.

Act III, Scene II.
Oroonoko. Though I languish for my liberty,
I wou'd not buy it at the Christian Price
Of black Ingratitude: they shannot say,
That we deserv'd our Fortune by our Crimes.
Murder the Innocent!
    Aboan.   The Innocent!
Oroonoko. These men are so, whom you wou'd rise against:
If we are Slaves, they did not make us Slaves;
But bought us in an honest way of trade:
As we have done before 'em, bought and sold
Many a wretch, and never thought it wrong.
They paid our Price for us, and we are now
Their Property, a part of their Estate,
To manage as they please. Mistake me not,
I do not tamely say, that we should bear
All they could lay upon us: but we find
The load so light, so little to be felt,
(Considering they have us in their power,
And may inflict what grievances they please)
We ought not to complain.
    Aboan.   My Royal Lord!
You do not know the heavy Grievances,
The Toyls, the Labours, weary Drudgeries,
Which they impose; Burdens, more fit for Beasts,
For senseless Beasts to bear, than thinking Men.
Then if you saw the bloody Cruelties,
They execute on every slight offence;
Nay sometimes in their proud insulting sport:
How worse than Dogs, they lash their fellow Creatures:
Your heart wou'd bleed for 'em. O cou'd you know
How many Wretches lift their Hands and Eyes
To you, for their Relief.
    Oroonoko.   I pity 'em,
And wish I cou'd with honesty do more.

Aboan. You must do more, and may, with honesty.
O Royal Sir, remember who you are,
A Prince, born for the good of other Men . . .

Here Oroonoko exhorts his fellow slaves to overcome their fears and join in an insurrection. His plan is for the slaves to escape into the bush and subsist in the wild until they can capture a ship to carry them back to Africa.

Act III, Scene IV.
Oroonoko. Impossible! nothing's impossible:
We know our strength only by being try'd.
If you object the Mountains, Rivers, Woods
Unpassable, that lie before our March:
Woods we can set on fire: we swim by nature:
What can oppose us then, but we may tame? . . .
Slave. Great Sir . . .
Were we only Men, [we] wou'd follow such,
So great a Leader, thro' the untry'd World.
But, oh! consider we have other Names,
Husbands and Fathers, and have other things more dear
To us, than Life, our Children, and our Wives,
Unfit for such an expedition:
What must become of them?
Oroonoko.   We wonnot wrong
The virtue of our Women, to believe
There is a Wife among 'em, wou'd refuse
To share her Husband's fortune. What is hard,
We must make easie to 'em in our Love:
While we live,
And have our Limbs, we can take care for them;
Therefore I still propose to lead our march
Down to the Sea, and plant a Colony:
Where, in our native innocence, we shall live
Free, and be able to defend our selves;
Till stress of weather, or some accident
Provide a ship for us.

For all its depiction of the ugliness of slavery and the heroism of African slaves, the play has never neatly fit into the category of "antislavery text." Here Oroonoko, embittered at the failure of their insurrection, reviles his fellow slaves for their lack of courage and resolution.

Act IV, Scene II.

    Oroonoko. I own the Folly of my Enterprise,
The Rashness of this Action, and must blush
Quite thro' this Vail of Night, a whitely Shame,
To think I cou'd design to make those free,
Who were by Nature Slaves; Wretches design'd
To be their Masters Dogs, and lick their Feet.
Whip, whip 'em to the Knowledge of your Gods,
Your Christian Gods, who suffer you to be
Unjust, dishonest, cowardly, and base,
And give 'em your Excuse for being so.
I wou'd not live on the same Earth with Creatures,
That only have the Faces of their Kind:
Why shou'd they look like Men, who are not so?

Oroonoko's tenderness for his own unborn child leads to his downfall. In this scene he is moved to surrender, in hopes Imoinda and the child may eventually be spared. (His hope proves futile and the further treachery of the whites in the final scenes pushes the tragic couple to a dismal double suicide reminiscent of both *Romeo and Juliet* and *Othello*.)

Act IV, Scene II.

    Oroonoko.   I feel
A Father's Fondness, and a Husband's Love.
They seize upon my Hart, strain all its strings,
To pull me to 'em, from my stern resolve. . . .
Methinks I see the Babe, with Infant Hands,
Pleading for Life, and begging to be born:
Shall I forbid his Birth? Deny him Light?
The Heavenly Comforts of all-cheering Light?
And make the Womb the Dungeon of his Death?
His Bleeding Mother his sad Monument?
These are the Calls of Nature, that call loud,
They will be heard, and Conquer in their Cause:
He must not be a Man, who can resist 'em.
No, my *Imoinda!* I will venture all
To save thee, and that little Innocent:
The World may be a better Friend to him,
Than I have found it. Now I yield my self: [*Gives up his Sword.*]
The Conflict's past, and we are in your Hands.

                                  (1695)[22]

ANONYMOUS

Undoubtedly provided by a theatrical friend of Southerne's, the prologue to *Oroonoko* (first performed November 1695 at Drury Lane) avoids raising racial or imperial issues, focusing instead on the competition between theatres for audience share. Although the prologue was delivered by the actor who played Aboan, the most rebellious of the black slaves, not a mention is made of slavery or insurrection: even the phrase "man-destroying trade" here refers, ironically, to the metaphorical war between Drury Lane and Covent Garden. Only in the allusion to the play as a "means to mend [the viewer's] thinking" does the writer suggest a moral reading of *Oroonoko*.

from "Prologue to Oroonoko. Sent by an Unknown Hand. And Spoken by Mr. Powell."

As when in Hostile Times two Neighbouring States
Strive by themselves, and their Confederates;
The War at first is made with awkward Skill,
And Soldiers clumsily each other kill:
Till time at length their untaught Fury tames,
And into Rules their heedless Rage reclaims:
Then every Science by degrees is made
Subservient to the Man-destroying Trade:
Wit, Wisdom, Reading, Observation, Art;
A well-turn'd Head to guide a Generous Heart.
So it may prove with our Contending Stages,
If you will kindly but supply their Wages:
Which you with ease may furnish, by retrenching
Your Superfluities of Wine and Wenching.
Who'd grudge to spare from Riot and hard Drinking,
To lay it out on means to mend his thinking? . . .

(1695)[23]

WILLIAM CONGREVE
(1670–1729)

It is a measure of Southerne's prominence that he enlisted the brilliant young William Congreve, the hottest new playwright of the 1690s, to write the epilogue to *Oroonoko*. Significantly, the epilogue was written for the actress who played Charlotte Welldon, a wisecracking husband-hunter whose antics in Surinam are meant to offset Oroonoko's tragic story. Her epilogue extends the ribald tone of the comic subplot, an element that grates on modern ears and already by the 1750s had offended such writers as Johnson and Hawkesworth. (Hawkesworth's revised version of 1759 appears elsewhere in this book.)

For all her unconscious racism ("save us from a Spouse of Oroonoko's Nations!"), Charlotte makes an ironic concession to the moral superiority of non-Europeans ("they make a Conscience of their Vows!"). Note also the plasticity of racial categories and terms at this time: Imoinda, an African-born white enslaved in Surinam, is referred to as an "Indian"—as in "*West* Indian."

from "Epilogue, Written by Mr. Congreve, and Spoken by Mrs. Verbruggen"

To follow Fame, Knights-Errant make profession:
We Damsels fly to save our Reputation:
So they their Valour shew, we our Discretion.
To Lands of Monsters, and fierce Beasts they go:
We, to those Islands, where rich Husbands grow:
Tho' they're no Monsters, we may make 'em so.
If they're of English growth, they'll bear't with Patience:
But save us from a Spouse of Oroonoko's Nations!
Then bless your Stars, you happy London Wives,
Who love at large each Day, yet keep your Lives:
Nor envy poor Imoinda's doating Blindness,
Who thought her Husband kill'd her out of Kindness.
Death with a Husband ne'er had shewn such Charms,

Had she once dy'd within a Lover's Arms.
Her Error was from Ignorance proceeding:
Poor Soul! She wanted some of our Town Breeding.
Forgive this Indian's Fondness of her Spouse;
Their Law no Christian Liberty allows:
Alas! they make a Conscience of their Vows!
If Virtue in a Heathen be a Fault;
Then damn the Heathen School, where she was taught.
She might have learn'd to Cuckold, Jilt, and Sham,
Had Covent-Garden been in Surinam.

(1695)[24]

Like Dryden, Behn, and other Restoration playwrights before him, Congreve wrote a verse tragedy based on the epic struggle between Moors and Christians in Spain in the 1400s. Though not about New World slavery, the play's treatment of the enslavement of Africans and their ordeal informs many of the heroic tropes and sentimental conventions that it would share with the emerging literature about transatlantic slavery. The theme of African royalty reduced to bondage was treated similarly in Southerne's *Oroonoko* and in later works such as William Dodd's "The African Prince" and "Zara"—in both of which Dodd borrowed the African heroine's name directly from Congreve's play.

from Act II, Scene ii of The Mourning Bride, A Tragedy

ZARA: I urg'd my Husband
On to this Invasion; where he was lost,
Where all is lost, and I am made a Slave.
Look on me now, from Empire fall'n to Slavery;
Think on my Suff'ring first, then, look on me;
Think on the cause of all, then, view thy self:
Reflect on *Osmyn,* and then look on *Zara,*
The fall'n, the lost, the Captive *Zara.*

(1697)[25]

ANONYMOUS

The unknown poet applauds the founding of a Scottish trading company modeled on English ones such as the Guinea Company (1618) and particularly the more successful Royal Africa Company (1672). The poet celebrates free trade and the civil liberty it makes possible, while paradoxically basing his economic vision on a slave labor force. Very tellingly, in this excerpt black slaves are depicted collectively as industrious and productive—"like bussie Bees"—but without any individual identity, or indeed any characteristic that would mark them as human beings at all.

from "A Poem upon the Undertaking of the Royal Company of Scotland Trading to Africa and the Indies"

On some such Shoar from all Preluctancy,
This Company designs a Colony.
To which all Mankind freely may resort,
And find quick Justice in an open Port.
To that the weary Labourer may go,
And gain an easie Wealth in doing so.
Small Use of tiresome Labour will be there,
That Clyme richly rewards a little Care,
There every Man may choose a pleasant Seat,
Which poor Men will make Rich, & Rich Men Great.
Black Slaves like bussie Bees will plant them Canes
Have Juice more sweet than honey in their Veins
Which boil'd to Sugar, brings in constant gains,
They'l[l] raise them Cotton, Ginger, Indigo,
Luscious Potatoes, and the rich Coco[a].
Ships thence encrease to fetch these Goods away,
For which the Stock will ready Money pay.
By Manufacturers here the Poor will live,
So they that go and they that stay will thrive.

(1697)[26]

JOHN SAFFIN (1632–1710)

Saffin wrote the first poem in English that defends slavery. A prominent Boston Puritan who owned slaves, Saffin got into a legal and literary conflict on the subject with a fellow Bostonian, Samuel Sewall (included elsewhere). In his tract *The Selling of Joseph* (1700), Sewall had attacked slavery, urged citizens to manumit their slaves, and proposed to outlaw the slave trade in Massachusetts. Saffin immediately responded with the pamphlet in which this poem appeared. In these rough couplets, Saffin departs from the more humane views on slavery expressed by Sewall and other leading Puritans such as Richard Baxter and Cotton Mather, and he becomes one of the first colonial apologists to posit innate racial inferiority as a justification for slavery.

The Negroes Character

Cowardly and cruel are those *Blacks* Innate,
Prone to Revenge, Imp of inveterate hate.
He that exasperates them, soon espies
Mischief and Murder in their very eyes.
Libidinous, Deceitful, False and Rude,
The spume issue of Ingratitude.
The premises consider'd, all may tell,
How near good *Joseph* they are parallel.

(1701)[27]

DANIEL DEFOE (1660–1731)

The famous writer presented scenes of slavery and the slave trade in several of his imaginative works, including an educational book, *The Family Instructor* (1715), and his first two novels, the classic *Robinson Crusoe* (1719) and the less familiar *Captain Singleton* (1720). In this early poem, a long critique of contemporary British society (as the generic subtitle suggests), Defoe sympathizes with Africans and Native Americans who are so ruthlessly exploited and enslaved by Europeans. Particularly noteworthy is Defoe's criticism of the hypocrisy of Christians owning slaves, a theme that would recur ubiquitously in the antislavery literature of the next 160 years. Ultimately, however, Defoe resists easy generalizations, as elsewhere in his writings he intersperses moments of compassion for slaves among other episodes that suggest a merchant's indifference to the human costs of a profitable trade.

from Reformation of Manners: A Satyr

Some fit out Ships, and double Fraights ensure,
And burn the Ships to make the Voyage secure;
Promiscuous Plunders thro' the World commit,
And *with the Money* buy their safe Retreat.
Others seek out to *Africk*'s Torrid Zone,
And search the burning Shores of *Serralone;*
There in insufferable Heats *they fry,*
And run vast Risques to see the Gold, *and die:*
The harmless Natives basely they trepan,
And barter Baubles for the *Souls of Men:*
The Wretches they to Christian Climes bring o'er,
To serve worse Heathens than they did before.
The Cruelties they suffer there are such,
Amboyna's nothing, they've out-done the *Dutch.*
    Cortez, Pizarro, Guzman, Penaloe,

Who drank the Blood and Gold of *Mexico*,
Who Thirteen Millions of Souls destroy'd,
And left one third of God's Creation void,
By Birth for Nature's Butchery design'd,
Compar'd to these are merciful and kind;
Death cou'd *their* cruellest Designs fulfil,
Blood quenched *their* Thirst, and it suffic'd to kill:
But these the tender *Coup de Grace* deny,
And make Men beg in vain for leave to die;
To more than *Spanish* Cruelty inclin'd,
Torment the Body, and debauch the Mind:
The ling'ring Life of Slavery preserve,
And vilely teach them both to sin and serve.
In vain they talk to them of Shades below,
They fear no Hell *but where such Christians go;*
Of *Jesus Christ* they very often hear,
Often as his Blaspheming Servants Swear;
They hear and wonder what strange Gods they be,
Can bear with Patience such Indignity:
They look for Famines, Plagues, Disease and Death,
Blasts from above, and Earthquakes from beneath:
But when they see regardless Heaven looks on,
They curse our Gods, or think that we have none.
Thus Thousands to Religion are brought o'er,
And made worse Devils than they were before.

(1702)[28]

SAMUEL SEWALL (1652–1730)

A Harvard-educated Puritan merchant and leader, Sewall emerges as one of America's original moral heroes. First, in 1697 he publicly repented his involvement as a judge in the Salem witch trials. Then in 1700 he published the first antislavery work in the history of New England, *The Selling of Joseph*. The latter sprang from Sewall's advocacy on behalf of a slave named Adam, who was seeking freedom from his owner John Saffin (included elsewhere). Sewall's antislavery feelings were deeply conscientious and long held. On June 19, 1700, he recorded in his private diary that, "Having been long and much dissatisfied with the Trade of fetching Negroes from Guinea . . . I began to be uneasy that I had so long neglected doing anything." Three years later, when despite his efforts the Court still had the black man Adam in slavery, Sewall inserted this righteously angry poem in his diary.

Untitled [from The Selling of Joseph, A Memorial*]*

Superanuated Squier, wigg'd
   and powder'd with pretence,
Much beguiles the just Assembly
   by his lying Impudence.
None being by, his bold
   Attorneys push it on with
   might and main
By which means poor simple
   Adam sinks to slavery again.
            (1703)[29]

ANONYMOUS

These stanzas about Southerne's *Oroonoko* appeared in a poetic survey of twenty-four leading poets of the day, each evaluated by the unnamed author (who probably saw himself as a competitor). His only serious criticism is that Southerne transformed Imoinda (who in Behn's version is black) into a white character.

from The Tryal of Skill: or, A New Session of the Poets. Calculated for the Meridian of Parnassus, in the Year, MDCCIV

Not but *Oroonoko* some Merit might plead,
    And take off from the weight of 's Offence,
Were but every Character Just which we read,
    And Consistent with Reason and Sence.

Were his Heroine but like his Heroe, not Fair,
    Since their Breath in one Country they drew,
And She that was Born in an *Indian* Air,
    Set forth in an *Indian* Hue.

Yet for all that Mistake, it would be worth his while,
    And his Interest might not be lost,
For if this Contradiction he could reconcile,
    He might stand assur'd of the Post.

                   (1704)[30]

?BERNARD MANDEVILLE
(c. 1670–1733)

This long poem, akin to a versified tract on slavery, has repeatedly been attributed to Bernard Mandeville, although modern scholars are still uncertain of his authorship. The ideas and ironic manner accord with those of the learned Dutchman, who came to London sometime after 1689—perhaps to seek his fortune under the newly enthroned William and Mary—and who eventually pursued a literary career. Particularly noteworthy are his insistence on the humanity of Africans, his assertion of racial equality in God's eyes, and his apparent attack (beneath a densely ironic tone that is hard to decode) on the hypocrisy of "Christians" who justify slavery by quoting scripture, yet deny baptism to their slaves.

The Planter's Charity

I Have often pitied the Miserable Condition of those Heathen Wretches, *that being captivated in* Africa, *are hurried up and down the World, and sold to cultivate the* American *and other Plantations. Their being used both in their Labour and Diet, like so many Heads of Cattle, must move, not only a Generous Man, but every Human Creature, that esteems his Kind. But their being surrounded with the Light of the Gospel, and yet kept in the Dark of Ignorance, and shut up from our Holy Faith by the very Professors of it, shocks (I need not say the pious) but the Meanest Christian. The vast Benefit which* Europe, *but more especially* England, *receives from those Islands, and the impossibility of maintaining 'em without the Hands of those* Unhappy Savages, *made me always think their Case was desperate, and their Conversion impracticable; because with the Vulgar I believed, that the way to* Christianity *led also to* Liberty; *that after* Baptism, *the Owner lost his Right, and the Slave changed his Condition into that of an Hired Servant. But some time ago I was happily drawn from my Errour by an Ingenious Discourse on this Subject, the Author of which demonstrates, That Slaves are allowed of from the* Old *and* New Testaments, *the Customs of* Christendom, *and the Statutes of* England; *and from the very Epistle of St.* Paul *to* Philemon, *he*

proves, That Slaves after Baptism *cease not to be so, by an undeniable In-*
stance of Onesimas *that ran away from* Philemon, *and was made a* Christ-
ian . . . *This Sermon, to which I refer the Reader, is full of Eloquence and*
Learning, and call'd, After Baptizatus, *or the* Negro Baptized. *And as the*
Author by Preaching and Printing of it, could have no other Aim, than the
Eternal Welfare of these Captive Souls, so his Labour ought to be valued as a
Pious Deed, and the meer Effect of Christian Charity. . . *If ever [the fol-*
lowing lines] may contribute to the Spiritual Good of a Heathen, or but rouse
the Conscience of any one Planter, *I shall reckon, that no Work of mine ever*
could turn to a better Account, than this Days Amusement.

You that Oppress the Captive *African,*
Abuse the Black, and Barbarously treat Man
Like Beast, in spight of his great Attribute,
Which only can distinguish him from Brute,
Reason, the lawful Claim to Human-kind;
As if you thought God's Image was confin'd,
To *European White!* Why should your Slave,
Feel your Unrighteousness beyond the Grave?
Lay on the Burden, till you break his Back,
And let him labour till his Sinews crack,
Draw out the Marrow from the aking Bone,
Feed on his Flesh, but let his Soul alone.
Tho' upon Earth you cause his Misery,
Strive not to stretch it to Eternity;
For whilst your Principles won't let you doubt
But all are sav'd thro' Christ, and none without
And you confess the Sacred Font to be
The Gate that lets in Christianity:
If you barr Men from that, how do you know,
But that you damn 'em to Eternal Woe?
Did ever *Turk* deny a *Christian,*
That had a mind to turn *Mahometan?*
Lewis himself, the Gallick Tyrant, grants
More Mercy to Dissenting *Protestants;*
He makes 'em Slaves, but then recals the Doom,
On their Submission to the Church of *Rome;*
You need not preach to Princes, nor reveal
Religious Truths with Apostolick Zeal
To Persecutors, or at Bloods expence,
Draw Savage Nations from their Ignorance.
The Task is easier, than to propagate

43

The Holy Gospel at so dear a rate;
Spread but the Name of Christ, where without pains
Or hazard you may act like Sovereigns;
But far from acting for it, you controul
The Zeal to Faith, when God has touch'd the Soul;
You won't be Passive, and let them receive
The Sacred Mysteries, in which you believe.
Sure it's unnatural not to wish Success
To those Opinions, we ourselves profess.
If on the Cruel Deed you ruminate,
Consult your conscience, and a future State,
Must you not fear, the Baptism you suppress,
Will one Day make your own avail you less?
Since you prey on the Flock of Christ, pray, why
Think you, he won't resent the Robbery?
For Human-kind he died, none so despis'd,
But he invites 'em all to be Baptiz'd:
Yet you may boast, you're able to retain
The Nations, which your Saviour calls in vain;
Should we look on the Character that's due
To Antichrist, what must we think of you?

But Negroes have no Souls! O Ignorance!
Behold, your Slave smile at the vile Pretence;
The stupid Notion makes your Cause the worse,
It shews you strugling with a just Remorse,
And striving to extenuate your Fault;
Yes, Negroes have a Soul, blush on the Thought:
A Soul, which, if you might, you would not save;
A Soul, that shall not enter in the Grave;
A Rational, an Everlasting one,
Part of the bright Æther'al Substance, blown
Into the Nostrils by the immediate care
Of the Omnipotent, whose Image they're:
A Human Soul, that whilst y'allow 'em none,
Is not so black and sordid as your own.

But says the hardned Planter, the Black Knave
Knows that a *Christian* cannot be a Slave;
He wants his Freedom; Must I be undone,
And lose that *Labour* which I live upon?
They are my Portion by my Father's Will,
I found 'em Slaves, and so I'll keep 'em still:

God can be serv'd, sure, at a cheaper rate,
Than with the loss of Right and of Estate.
  The Estate is the Concern, tho' you would hide
Your Thoughts, and deck your Avarice and Pride
With *Right* and *Lawfulness,* the poor Pretext
That may serve in this World, not in the next.
How dares a *Christian* make the Impious Plea,
For robbing Christ to feed his Luxury?
Suppose you'd lose: What would y'infer from thence,
But that you'd rather, at your Soul's Expence,
Spread *Satan's* dark Dominions, than inlarge
God's Holy Kingdom at your Temporal Charge?
  But then the Notion's false, tho' vulgarly
Receiv'd, That slaves when once Baptiz'd are free,
You'll have no loss, by *Baptism* they may be
Made free from Sin, but not from Slavery.
Slaves, tho' made *Christians,* shall remain so still;
Consult for solid Proof, the Learned HILL:
There you'll be taught, that whilst you strive to save
A Human Soul, you shall not lose your Slave.
That *Christianity* won't rob you from
A Victor's Right, nor injure *Christendom.*
Then turn to Christ, be call'd no more (for shame)
Anti-Apostles to his Sacred Name;
And think, when'er you pray, *Thy Kingdom come,*
What Kingdom 'twas you kept the *Heathens* from.
  Baptize your Slave, th'*Almighty God* shall bless
The Labour of his Hands with more success;
Lead him the way to Truth, instruct his Mind
With Holy Duties, and you'll quickly find
The difference that's between the Stubborness,
The Craft and Fraud of *Heathen* Principles;
Their inborn Malice, and th'Obedience,
Meekness and Honesty of *Christians.*
The Heavenly Shepherd shall increase your Stock,
When every Slave shall help to augment his Flock;
Angels shall guard your souls, and you receive
Content and Peace of Conscience, whilst you live;
Till God at the end of Time shall have prepar'd
The infinite unspeakable Reward.

                                        (1704)[31]

EDMUND ARWAKER (1655–1730)

Chaplain to the Duchess of Ormond, Arwaker also had an Anglican parish in Ireland. He wrote volumes of religious poetry and, like his contemporary Jonathan Swift, tracts on behalf of the Irish addressed to the British government. In this poem, from a collection of didactic fables in verse, Arwaker unexpectedly brings in African slaves as the subject of a rather crude conceit. Arwaker's morbid and naive fascination with racial difference, specifically black skin pigmentation, is less surprising if we remember that in this era scientists were beginning to study whether skin color was acquired or innate.

Fable XII— "The Negro: or, Labour in Vain"

A shallow 'Squire, who had a Negro bought,
His sooty Face too long neglected thought;
And, in great hope to make him White and Fair,
Had him well Scour'd with wond'rous Pains and Care:
But spent his Labour, Soap, and Time, in vain;
The Native Black, did still a Black remain.

The MORAL.
The Characters that Nature has impress'd,
Keep their primaeval Stamp on ev'ry Breast;
And he that wou'd, what's printed there, erase,
As well might hope to blanch a Negro's Face.
No Pow'r an Innate Quality can sway,
That to its Native Bent will force its Way:
And still, the more it is diverted thence,
Recurrs with more impetuous Violence.

(1708)[32]

THOMAS WALDUCK
(fl. 1696–1710)

A sea captain who settled in Rupert's Fort, Barbados in 1696, Walduck left few traces of his life except some letters to a friend in London, James Petiver. In one of them he included the following acrostic (a cross between a poem and a puzzle) that, despite its playful form, expresses a bleak view of a slave-holding society held by someone living in its midst. Although the poem circulated in manuscript, its publishing history is uncertain until its modern rediscovery in 1947.

An Acrosti upon the Island of Barbados & the Inhabitants Thereof

B   Barbadoes Isle inhabited by Slaves
A   And For one Honest man ten thousand Knaves
R   Religion to thee's a Romantick Storey
B   Barbarity and ill gott wealth thy glory
A   All sodoms Sins are Centred in thy Heart
D   Death is thy look and Dearth in every part
O   Oh Glorious Isle in Vilany Excell
S   Sin to the Height thy fate is Hell.

(wr. 1710/pub. 1947)[33]

ALEXANDER POPE (1688–1744)

Pope is a good example of how even a famous writer's attention to slavery can be largely forgotten. The dominant poet of the first half of the eighteenth century, Pope is famous for his satiric wit, his virtuosity with rhyming couplets, and his mastery of the mock heroic. Less well remembered are the moments in his major poems when an awareness of New World slavery surfaces as an image or a theme.

In *Windsor-Forest*, Pope's sustained poetic reflection on the royal wood at Windsor, the idea of trees being made into ships leads to a reverie on expanding overseas trade and relations with non-European peoples. Typical of his era, Pope uses the word "Indians" to refer without distinction to Africans, Asians, and Amerindians—the term derives of course from "Indies," both West and East. Pope's disapproval of conquest and enslavement is evident, as is his hope that global trade might foster ethnic and racial harmony.

from Windsor-Forest

Thy Trees, fair *Windsor!* now shall leave their Woods,
And half thy Forests rush into my Floods,
Bear *Britain's* Thunder, and her Cross display,
To the bright Regions of the rising Day;
Tempt Icy Seas, where scarce the Waters roll,
Where clearer Flames glow round the frozen Pole;
Or under Southern Skies exalt their Sails,
Led by new Stars, and born by spicy Gales!
For me the Balm shall bleed, and Amber flow,
The Coral redden, and the Ruby glow,
The Pearly Shell its lucid Globe infold,
And *Phoebus* warm the ripening Ore to Gold.
The Time shall come, when free as Seas or Wind

Unbounded *Thames* shall flow for all Mankind,
Whole Nations enter with each swelling Tyde,
And Seas but join the Regions they divide;
Earth's distant Ends our Glory shall behold,
And the new World launch forth to seek the Old.
Then Ships of uncouth Form shall stem the Tyde,
And Feather'd People crowd my wealthy Side,
And naked Youths and painted Chiefs admire
Our Speech, our Colour, and our strange Attire!
Oh stretch thy Reign, fair *Peace!* from Shore to Shore,
Till Conquest cease, and Slav'ry be no more:
Till the freed *Indians* in their native Groves
Reap their own Fruits, and woo their Sable Loves,
Peru once more a Race of Kings behold,
And other *Mexico's* be roof'd with Gold.
Exil'd by Thee from Earth to deepest Hell,
In Brazen Bonds shall barb'rous *Discord* dwell:
Gigantick *Pride*, pale *Terror*, gloomy *Care*,
And mad *Ambition* shall attend her there.
There purple *Vengeance* bath'd in Gore retires,
Her Weapons blunted, and extinct her Fires:
There hateful *Envy* her own Snakes shall feel,
And *Persecution* mourn her broken Wheel:
There *Faction* roar, *Rebellion* bite her Chain,
And gasping Furies thirst for Blood in vain.

(1713)[34]

In the card table episode in *Rape of the Lock,* Pope incorporates, rather startlingly, images of "colored" troops on the battlefield. Beyond the obvious reference to Asian and African nations at war, Pope's simile draws on a general awareness of black troops fighting with and against British forces, from Francis Drake's adventures among Central American maroons in the 1570s, to the intermittent guerilla war against Jamaican maroons from 1655 to 1738.

from Canto III of The Rape of the Lock

Clubs, Diamonds, Hearts, in wild Disorder seen,
With Throngs promiscuous strow the level Green.
Thus when dispers'd a routed Army runs,
Of *Asia's* Troops, and *Africk's* Sable Sons,
With like Confusion different Nations fly,

Of various Habit and of various Dye,
The pierc'd Battalions dis-united fall,
In Heaps on Heaps; one Fate o'erwhelms them all.

(1714)[35]

In this key passage from his philosophical poem *An Essay on Man*, Pope evokes the admirable simplicity of a "poor Indian's" vision of heaven. By describing his paradise in terms of some "happier island" where "slaves" have returned to their "native land," Pope clearly seems to have in mind—despite the ambiguity of "Indian"—the enslaved peoples of the Caribbean and their hopes for the afterlife.

from An Essay on Man: Epistle I

Hope humbly then; with trembling pinions soar;
Wait the great teacher Death, and God adore!
What future bliss, he gives not thee to know,
But gives that Hope to be thy blessing now.
Hope springs eternal in the human breast:
Man never Is, but always To be blest:
The soul, uneasy and confin'd from home,
Rests and expatiates in a life to come.
Lo! the poor Indian, whose untutor'd mind
Sees God in clouds, or hears him in the wind;
His soul proud Science never taught to stray
Far as the solar walk, or milky way;
Yet simple Nature to his hope has giv'n,
Behind the cloud-topt hill, an humbler heav'n;
Some safer world in depth of woods embrac'd,
Some happier island in the watry waste,
Where slaves once more their native land behold,
No fiends torment, no Christians thirst for Gold!
To Be, contents his natural desire,
He asks no Angel's wing, no Seraph's fire;
But thinks, admitted to that equal sky,
His faithful dog shall bear him company.

(wr. 1730–32/pub. 1733)[36]

ANONYMOUS

Even in Ireland black figures turn up in the literature of the early eighteenth century. These lines are an excerpt from an anonymous verse celebration of an annual procession, or "Cavalcade," around Dublin, organized by the trade guilds. Here the poet records a black servant appearing in the pageant of the Saddlers' Guild, a figure probably seen by the crowds as rarer and more exotic than the thoroughbred horse he is leading. Very likely he was one of the individual black servants brought back from the New World by successful Irish adventurers.

from "The Cavalcade: A Poem on the Riding the Franchises"

Next march the Saddlers, glorious to behold,
On Sprightly Beasts, their Saddles shine with Gold:
A Warlike Steed most proudly walks before,
Richly attir'd, led by a Black-a-moor.
Proud of his Furniture he paws the Ground,
And champs the Bit and throws the Foam around.

(c. 1716)[37]

FRANCES SEYMOUR [née THYNNE], COUNTESS OF HERTFORD, LATER DUCHESS OF SOMERSET (1699–1754)

A well-connected noblewoman who served as "Lady of the Bedchamber" to the Princess of Wales, later Queen Caroline, Seymour was the friend of many literary figures, including the Countess of Winchilsea, Elizabeth Rowe, James Thomson, Isaac Watts, Richard Savage, and William Shenstone. She published only a few of her own poetic efforts, but helped other writers who were in trouble. She ended her life in rural seclusion, mourning the deaths of her son and husband.

Although the tragic story of Inkle and Yarico had been known in England since Richard Ligon's *True and Exact History of the Island of Barbados* (1657), it only became popular when retold in Richard Steele's *Spectator*, no. 11 (March 13, 1711). Seymour is the first to render it in verse and her version emphasizes the romantic aspects of a terrible tale. The Englishman Inkle, shipwrecked somewhere in the New World and rescued by the beautiful "Indian" (here also called a "Negro virgin") Yarico, promises to take his pregnant lover back to England as his wife. But when they dock in Barbados en route, Inkle, tempted by the offers of slave traders and deaf to her pleas, sells Yarico into slavery. Innumerable retellings of the story were composed over the course of the eighteenth and nineteenth centuries, including eight others included elsewhere in this anthology.

The Story of Inkle and Yarico. A Most Moving Tale from The Spectator [no. 11]

A YOUTH there was possessed of every charm,
Which might the coldest heart with passion warm;
His blooming cheeks with ruddy beauty glowed,
His hair in waving ringlets graceful flowed;
Through all his person an attractive mien,
Just symmetry, and elegance were seen:
But niggard Fortune had her aid withheld,

And poverty th'unhappy boy compelled
To distant climes to sail in search of gain,
Which might in ease his latter days maintain.
By chance, or rather the decree of Heaven,
The vessel on a barbarous coast was driven;
He, with a few unhappy striplings more,
Ventured too far upon the fatal shore:
The cruel natives thirsted for their blood,
And issued furious from a neighbouring wood.
His friends all fell by brutal rage o'erpowered,
Their flesh the horrid cannibals devoured;
Whilst he alone escaped by speedy flight,
And in a thicket lay concealed from sight!

    Now he reflects on his companions' fate,
His threatening danger, and abandoned state.
Whilst thus in fruitless grief he spent the day,
A negro virgin chanced to pass that way;
He viewed her naked beauties with surprise,
Her well-proportioned limbs and sprightly eyes!
With his complexion and gay dress amazed,
The artless nymph upon the stranger gazed;
Charmed with his features and alluring grace,
His flowing locks and his enlivened face.
His safety now became her tend'rest care,
A vaulted rock she knew and hid him there;
The choicest fruits the isle produced she sought,
And kindly to allay his hunger brought;
And when his thirst required, in search of drink,
She led him to a chrystal fountain's brink.

    Mutually charmed, by various arts they strove
To inform each other of their mutual love;
A language soon they formed, which might express
Their pleasing care and growing tenderness.
With tigers' speckled skins she decked his bed,
O'er which the gayest plumes of birds were spread;
And every morning, with the nicest care,
Adorned her well-turned neck and shining hair,
With all the glittering shells and painted flowers
That serve to deck the Indian virgins' bowers.
And when the sun descended in the sky,
And lengthening shades foretold the evening nigh,
Beneath some spreading palm's delightful shade,

Together sat the youth and lovely maid;
Or where some bubbling river gently crept,
She in her arms secured him while he slept.
When the bright moon in midnight pomp was seen,
And starlight glittered o'er the dewy green,
In some close arbour, or some fragrant grove,
He whispered vows of everlasting love.
Then, as upon the verdant turf he lay,
He oft would to th'attentive virgin say:
'Oh, could I but, my Yarico, with thee
Once more my dear, my native country see!
In softest silks thy limbs should be arrayed,
Like that of which the clothes I wear are made;
What different ways my grateful soul would find
To indulge thy person and divert thy mind!';
While she on the enticing accents hung
That smoothly fell from his persuasive tongue.
    One evening, from a rock's impending side,
An European vessel she descried,
And made them signs to touch upon the shore,
Then to her lover the glad tidings bore;
Who with his mistress to the ship descends,
And found the crew were countrymen and friends.
Reflecting now upon the time he passed,
Deep melancholy all his thoughts o'ercast:
'Was it for this,' said he, 'I crossed the main,
Only a doting virgin's heart to gain?
I needed not for such a prize to roam,
There are a thousand doting maids at home.'
While thus his disappointed mind was tossed,
The ship arrived on the Barbadian coast;
Immediately the planters from the town,
Who trade for goods and negro slaves, came down;
And now his mind, by sordid interest swayed,
Resolved to sell his faithful Indian maid.
Soon at his feet for mercy she implored,
And thus in moving strains her fate deplored:
    'O whither can I turn to seek redress,
When thou'rt the cruel cause of my distress?
If the remembrance of our former love,
And all thy plighted vows, want force to move;
Yet, for the helpless infant's sake I bear,

FRANCES SEYMOUR

Listen with pity to my just despair.
Oh let me not in slavery remain,
Doomed all my life to drag a servile chain!
It cannot surely be! thy generous breast
An act so vile, so sordid must detest:
But, if thou hate me, rather let me meet
A gentler fate, and stab me at thy feet;
Then will I bless thee with my dying breath,
And sink contented in the shades of death.'

    Not all she said could his compassion move,
Forgetful of his vows and promised love;
The weeping damsel from his knees he spurned,
And with her price pleased to the ship returned.
                (c. 1726/rev. 1738)[38]

WILLIAM PATTISON (1706—1727)

A rebellious young student who quit Sidney Sussex College, Cambridge, just as he was about to be expelled, Pattison went to London to seek his fortune as a writer. Sadly, he died a year later, scarcely aged twenty-one. Obviously drawn to the pathos of the "Inkle and Yarico" tale, he left behind this fragment of a version he did not live to complete.

Yarico to Inkle: An Epistle [a fragment]

Dear, faithless Man! if e'er that cruel Breast
Love's pleasing Toys, and soft Delights, confest;
Distress like mine, may sure thy Pity move,
For tender Pity is the Child of Love!
But can Compassion from thy Bosom flow?
Source of my Wrongs, and Fountain of my Woe!
Wilt thou, repentant, soften at my Grief,
Melt at my Tears, and lend a late Relief!
What have I done? ah! how deserv'd thy Hate?
Or was this Vengeance treasur'd up by Fate?
Then will I mourn my Fate's severe Decree,
Nor charge a Guilt so black, so base on Thee;
For O! I know, ah no! I knew, thy Mind
Soft as the Dove, and as the Turtle kind;
How have I seen thy gentle Bosom move,
And heave, contagious, to some Tale of Love!
How have I heard thee paint the faithfull'st Pair,
Describe their Bliss, and e'en their Raptures share!
Then have thy Lips, with sweet Transition swore
Thy Love more lasting, and thy Passion more!

And what, is Truth, if Signs like these deceive?
Signs! that might win the wariest to believe.

(c. 1727)[39]

JOHN GAY (1685–1732)

A popular poet, playwright, and satirist, Gay earned his place in literary history with the spectacularly successful *Beggar's Opera,* which has remained influential for more than two hundred fifty years. Embedded within his innovative comic opera is this duet suggesting how far images of slave trading had entered contemporary culture. The heroine, Polly, straining to dramatize her passion for Macheath, compares herself to a slave sold on the auction block and put to work in the fields.

Air XVI: "Over the hills and far away"
from *The Beggar's Opera*

Macheath:	Were I laid on Greenland's coast,
	And in my arms embraced my lass;
	Warm amidst eternal frost,
	Too soon the half year's night would pass.
Polly:	Were I sold on Indian soil,
	Soon as the burning day was closed,
	I could mock the sultry toil,
	When on my charmer's breast reposed.
Macheath:	And I would love you all the day,
Polly:	Every night would kiss and play,
Macheath:	If with me you'd fondly stray
Polly:	Over the hills and far away.

(1728)[40]

Tellingly, *Polly,* the sequel that Gay immediately wrote to the *Beggar's Opera,* is set on a slave-holding Caribbean island, suggesting that Gay (like Defoe, Johnson, and others) saw such a setting as the natural extension of the London criminal underworld—a realm of vice, illegality, and depravity. Gay does not foreground slavery as a subject, but in a play rife with racial passing,

interracial warfare, mixed-race pirate bands, threatened insurrections, and un-
free laborers of all races, an awareness of plantation slavery inflects all the ac-
tion. Whether for these anarchic elements or for its antigovernmental satire,
Polly was promptly banned and, though published, was not staged for decades.

In the following poem, Polly, newly arrived on the island and threatened
with rape or enslavement by the rich plantation owner Ducat, invokes slavery
metaphorically in a song of distress. Later, to protect herself and continue her
search for Macheath, she disguises herself as a man.

Air XVI: "A Swain long tortur'd with Disdain"
from Polly: An Opera. Being the Second Part of the Beggar's Opera

> Polly: Can I or toil or hunger fear?
> For love's a pain that's more severe.
> The slave, with vertue in his breast,
> Can wake in peace, and sweetly rest.

Here Morano, the "black" leader of the invading pirate band, sings a love
duet with Jenny, his white mistress, herself an escaped indentured servant. A
few lines later Morano reveals to the audience that he is really Macheath, having
disguised himself as an escaped slave to ingratiate himself with the pirates and
to protect himself "from women who laid claim to me where-ever I went."
Later in the play a pirate lieutenant reports a further influx of "slaves that have
deserted to us from the plantations [and] are all brave determin'd fellows" (act
II, sc. 8).

Air XXX: "Sawny was tall, and of noble race"
from Polly

> Morano: Shall I not be bold when honour calls?
> You've a heart that would upbraid me then.
> Jenny: But, ah, I fear, if my hero falls,
> Thy *Jenny* shall ne'er know pleasure again.
> Morano: To deck their wives fond tradesmen cheat;
> I conquer but to make thee great:
> Jenny: But if my hero falls,—ah then
> Thy *Jenny* shall ne'er know pleasure again!

Here Macheath, still disguised as Morano, the black leader of the pirates, has
been sentenced to death by the chief of the victorious Indians. The irony within
Morano's song converges with many ironies in this scene, as a virtuous Indian

condemns to death a "black" pirate for practicing and defending European mores of acquisitiveness and dishonesty. Morano exits protesting.

Air LXI: "Mad Moll"
from Polly

Morano: All crimes are judg'd like fornication;
        While rich we are honest no doubt.
    Fine ladies can keep reputation,
        Poor lasses alone are found out.
    If justice had piercing eyes,
    Like ourselves to look within,
    She'd find power and wealth a disguise
  That shelter the worst of our kin.

(wr. 1728/pub. 1729)[41]

ANONYMOUS

A glimpse of African American life in Philadelphia in the 1720s emerges from this rambling poem printed in Andrew Bradford's magazine, *The American Weekly Mercury*. Although Pennsylvania was to become a center of Quaker-led abolitionism, slavery remained legal there until 1780 when the state adopted a gradual emanicipation law. Here the speaker juxtaposes a scene from slave life (perhaps a folk dance) with a respectful, even sympathetic, visit to the Negro burial ground.

[Untitled]

Passing those fields where negroe slaves are found
At Rustick Gestures to a dismal sound
I into a place arrived in which is laid
Poor Negroe's ashes when his debts are paid.

(1729)[42]

STEPHEN DUCK (1705–1756)

The earliest and best known of the "working-class poets" who emerged in the eighteenth century, Duck was something of a celebrity. Born and raised a farm laborer, the self-taught youth achieved fame in 1730 when he published "The Thresher's Labour," a long poem about rural working-class life. Taken up by high society and patronized by Queen Caroline, Duck enjoyed several years of fame in the London literary world before committing suicide in 1756.

In the following excerpt from "The Thresher's Labour," Duck compares dust-covered farm workers to African slaves. His metaphor conveys a sense of the degrading and alienating effects of mechanized labor and at another level, despite its racist implications, suggests an ambivalent kinship between exploited laborers on both sides of the Atlantic. Poetically, there is a nod to that pathetic moment in the *Iliad* when Hector's war helmet frightens his infant son.

from "The Thresher's Labour"

When sooty pease we thresh, you scarce can know
Our native colour, as from work we go:
The sweat, and dust, and suffocating smoke
Make us so much like Ethiopians look,
We scare our wives, when evening brings us home,
And frighted infants think the bugbear come.

(1730)[43]

Duck's sympathy for enslaved peoples developed with time. Within a short while, he was drawn to the tragic story of Inkle and Yarico. Symbolically renaming the characters Avaro (for avarice) and Amanda (for love), Duck amplifies the familiar story into a 4,000-line saga of betrayal and enslavement. In these excerpts, Duck displays a lush sentimentalism while also embellishing the traditional story by having Avaro eaten by a wolf after he sells Amanda into slavery.

from Avaro and Amanda

An Indian princess [was] . . .
Smit with the beauty of the god-like man.
His dress and fair complexion charm'd her sight;
Each glowing feature gave her new delight:
While love and pity both arose within,
And kindled in her soul a flame unseen.
With equal joy Avaro now survey'd
The native graces of the Negro maid:
He view'd her arms, with various ribbands bound;
Her downy head, with painted feathers crown'd;
With bredes, and lucid shells, in circles strung,
Which shone refulgent, as they round her hung.

    As when, in splendid robes, a courtly maid
Begins the dance at ball or masquerade;
The pearls and diamonds shine with mingled light,
And glitt'ring pendants blaze against the sight.

    So shone the beauteous shells around her waist.
And sparkling gems, that deck'd her jetty breast;
All which Avaro's gazing eyes pursue,
Charm'd with her lovely shape, disclos'd to view:
Each limb appears in just proportion made,
With elegance thro' ev'ry part display'd:
And now his cares dissolve, new passions move;
And Nature intimates the change is Love. . . .

    Yet, still to give her lover more delight,
(Lest what he daily saw, should pall the sight)
When Sol with purple cloath'd the western sky,
And shades extended shew'd the ev'ning nigh,
She to some verdant grove the youth convey'd,
Where nightingales harmonious musick made:
Soft flow'rets were their couch; and, all around,
Diffusive sweets perfum'd the fragrant ground.
There oft she would his snowy bosom bare,
Oft round her fingers wind his silver hair;
Charm'd with the contrast, which their colours made,
More pleasing than the tulip's light and shade.
Nor was the youth insensible; but soon
Repaid her love by shewing of his own.
Oft would his bosom heave with speaking sighs;
Oft would he gaze, and languish with his eyes:

Now on her panting breast his head repose;
To meet his head her panting breast arose;
While in her soul extatic raptures glow'd,
And her fond arms believ'd they clasp'd a God. . . .

A scene of woes remains to be display'd,
Indulgent love with slavery repaid.
Ingratitude, and broken vows, and lyes,
The mighty ills that spring from avarice,
Provoke my lays: your aid, ye muses, bring;
Assist my tragick numbers, while I sing;
Say, what ensu'd, when, on the briny deep,
The watchful dame beheld a floating ship?
She call'd, and beckon'd to it from the shore,
Then to the youth the grateful tidings bore . . .

    The British bark was to Barbadoes bound;
Th' expected shore the sailors quickly found:
Where, safe from danger, now the perjur'd youth,
False to his former vows of sacred truth,
Reflecting, counts the int'rest he had lost,
While fate detain'd him on the Indian coast;
The frugal thoughts suppress his am'rous flame,
And prompt him to betray the faithful dame.
Yet scarce he can the cursed fact pursue;
But hesitates at what he fain would do:
For, tho' his av'rice moves him to the ill,
His gratitude within him struggles still;
And, 'twixt two passions, neither guides his will. . . .
    So stood the doubtful youth awhile; nor wou'd
Forsake the evil, nor pursue the good:
Till, as the sailors in the haven stay,
To purchase slaves, the planters croud the key.
One asks, for what the Negro may be sold;
Then bids a price, and shews the tempting gold:
Which, when Avaro views with greedy eyes,
He soon resolves to gain th' alluring prize;
Nor oaths, nor gratitude, can longer bind,
Her fate he thus determines in his mind.
    "Suppose I should conduct this Indian o'er,
And thus, instead of gold, import a Moor;
Would not my sire, with stern contracted brows,
Condemn my choice, and curse my nuptial vows?

Was it for this I learn'd the merchant's art?
Only to gain a doating Negro's heart!
Was it for this the raging seas I cross'd?
No! gold induc'd me to the Indian coast;
And gold is offer'd for this simple dame:
Shall I refuse it, or renounce my flame?
Let am'rous fools their tiresome joys renew,
And doat on love, while interest I pursue."
He added not; for now, intent on gold,
And dead to all remorse, the dame he sold. . . .

"O base! ungrateful youth!" she loudly cries;
"O base! ungrateful youth!" the shore replies:
"And can'st thou, cruel, perjur'd villain! leave
Thy tender infant, too, an abject slave;
To toil, and groan, and bleed beneath the rod?
Fool, that I was, to think thou wert a God!
Sure from some savage tiger art thou sprung—
No! tigers feed, and fawn upon their young:
But thou despisest all paternal cares;
The fate of infants, and their mothers pray'rs."
    In vain she does her wretched state deplore;
Pleas'd with the gold, he gladly quits the shore. . . .

The giddy ship on circling eddies rides,
Toss'd, and re-toss'd, the sport of winds and tides;
Redoubled peals of roaring thunder roll,
And flames, conflicting, flash from pole to pole,
While guilty thoughts distract Avaro's soul.
Of life despairing, though afraid to die,
One fatal effort yet he means to try:
While all the busy crew, with panting breath,
Were lab'ring to repel the liquid death;
Avaro from the stern the boat divides,
And yields up to the fury of the tides.
Toss'd on the boist'rous wave, the vessel flies;
Now sinking low, now mounting to the skies:
Till soon the storm decreas'd; and, by degrees,
Hush'd were the winds, and calm the ruffled seas;
The sailors safely steer their course again,
And leave Avaro floating on the main;
Who landed quickly on a lonely isle,
Where human feet ne'er print the baleful soil.

STEPHEN DUCK

A dreary wilderness was all appear'd,
And howling wolves the only sound he heard;
A thousand deaths he views before his eyes,
A thousand guilt-created fiends arise:
A conscious hell within his bosom burns,
And racks his tortur'd soul, while thus he mourns.
    "Curs'd be the precepts of my selfish sire,
Who bade me after fatal gold aspire!
Curs'd be myself, and doubly curs'd, who sold
A faithful friend, to gain that fatal gold!—
O! could these gloomy woods my sin conceal,
Or in my bosom quench this fiery hell!
Here would I pine my wretched life away,
Or to the hungry savage fall a prey.
But can the gloomy woods conceal my sin?
Or cooling shadows quench the hell within?
No; like some spirit banish'd heav'n, I find
Terrors in ev'ry place to rack my mind;
Tormenting conscious plagues increase my care,
And guilty thoughts indulge my just despair.
O! where shall I that piercing eye evade,
That scans the depths of hell's tremendous shade!"
    So saying, straight he gave a hideous glare,
With rolling eyes, that witness'd strong despair:
Then drew his pointed weapon from the sheath,
Confus'dly wild, and all his thoughts on death;
To pierce his trembling heart he thrice essay'd,
And thrice his coward arm deny'd it's aid.
Meanwhile, a howling wolf, with hunger press'd,
Leap'd on the wretch, and seiz'd him by the breast:
Tore out his heart, and lick'd the purple flood;
For earth refus'd to drink the villain's blood.

(1734)[44]

ANONYMOUS

Miscegenation is the subject of this short verse sent in to the *South Carolina Gazette* by an anonymous South Carolinian in 1732. Given the topic, and the fact that the paper was one of the most widely read journals in the South, the author's disapproval of race-mixing was bound to stir a response. The next week's issue carried two replies: a letter from someone who shared the poet's indignation at this "Evil . . . spreading itself among us" and a poem from another citizen who disagreed (see Anonymous, "Cameleon's Defense," in the following section). It is remarkable that seventy years before the Sally Hemings–Thomas Jefferson controversy (see Joseph Dennie and John Quincy Adams, included elsewhere), the sensitive subject of miscegenation was being aired by these southern writers.

The Cameleon Lover

If what the *Curious* have observ'd be true,
That the *Cameleon* will assume the *Hue*
Of all the Objects that approach its *Touch;*
No Wonder then, that the *Amours* of *such*
Whose *Taste* betrays them to a close Embrace
With the *dark* Beauties of the *Sable* Race
(Stain'd with the Tincture of the *Sooty* Sin,)
Imbibe the *Blackness* of their *Charmer's* Skin.

(1732)[45]

ANONYMOUS ("SABLE")

His pseudonym obviously playing on the race issues raised in "The Cameleon Lover," this anonymous South Carolinian voiced a more libertine view of interracial sexual relations in his poem published a week later (March 18, 1732). Although not expressly advocating white-black liaisons, "Sable" tries to lighten the stigma of such relationships. His cavalier tone ignores the underlying pattern of sexual exploitation suffered by enslaved African women throughout slaveholding society.

Cameleon's Defense

All Men have Follies, which they blindly trace
Thro' the dark Turnings of a dubious Maze:
But happy those, who, by a prudent Care,
Retreat betimes, from the fallacious Snare.
The eldest Sons of Wisdom were not free,
From the same Failure you condemn in me.
If as the Wisest of the Wise have err'd,
I go astray and am condemn'd unheard,
My Faults you too severely reprehend,
More like a rigid Censor than a Friend.
Love is the Monarch Passion of the Mind,
Knows no Superior, by no Laws confin'd:
But triumphs still, impatient of Controul,
O'er all the proud Endowments of the Soul.

(1732)[46]

JOHN WHALEY (1710–1745)

Little is known of Whaley except that he was educated at Eton (where he later served as an assistant master) and King's College, Cambridge (where he became a fellow), and that he published several works of poetry, including *Blenheim* (1728) and *Original Poems and Translations* (1745). This poem, apparently inspired by the experience of a friend ("Lucretia"), testifies to the continuing power of Southerne's *Oroonoko* to move audiences decades after its premiere in 1695. Consciously or not, viewers who wept for Oroonoko and Imoinda were imaginatively enlisted in a doomed but heroic slave rebellion.

On a Young Lady's Weeping at Oroonooko

At Fate's approach whilst Oroonooko Groans,
Imoinda's Fate, undaunted at his own;
Dropping a gen'rous Tear *Lucretia* Sighs,
And views the Heroe with *Imoinda*'s Eyes.
When the Prince strikes who envy's not the Deed?
To be so Wept, who wou'd not wish to Bleed?

(1732)[47]

The next poem, addressed to an unnamed friend and written in imitation of Horace, opens an unusual window on eighteenth-century social life and race relations. Whaley writes to support a friend who seems to feel embarrassed about having fallen in love with a black woman. Whaley says he himself likes the "paler Northern Beauties," but he justifies his friend's preference for darker "Æthiopian Beauty" by invoking ancient examples such as Cleopatra with her "jetty Charms." The treatment of interracial romance here seems far from what it was to become by the nineteenth century.

To a Gentleman in Love with a Negro Woman. In Imitation of Horace, Lib. 2 Od. 4.

Don't Blush, dear Sir, your Flame to own,
Your sable Mistress to Approve;
Thy Passion other Breasts have known,
And Heroes justify your Love.
By Æthiopian Beauty mov'd,
Perseus was clad in Martial Arms;
And the World's Lord too feeble prov'd
For Cleopatra's jetty Charms.
What tho' no sickly White and Red,
With short liv'd Pride adorn the Maid?
The deeper Yew, its Leaves ne'er Shed,
While Roses and while Lillies Fade.
What tho' no conscious blush Appear;
The Tincture of a guilty skin?
Her's is a Colour that will wear,
And honest Black ne'er harbours Sin.
Think'st thou such Blood, in Slaves can roll,
Think'st thou such Lightnings can arise,
Such Pow'r was lodg'd to pierce the Soul,
In vulgar and Plebeian Eyes?
No, Sir, by Air, and Form, and Dress,
Thy Fusca, of uncommon Race,
No doubt an Indian Princess is;
And swarthy King's her Lineage Grace.
Such decent Modesty and Ease!—
But, least my Rapture be suspected,
Cease, prying jealous Lover, cease,
Nor judge the Muse too much Affected.
Me paler Northern Beauties move,
My Bosom other Darts receives,
Think not I'll Toast an Indian Love,
While Fielding or a Shirley Lives.

(1732)[48]

ANONYMOUS

In the 1730s the Inkle and Yarico story became something of a set piece for aspiring poets. This anonymous and amateur woman poet ("an artless dame"), probably moved by Seymour's and Duck's versions, contributed to a London magazine the longest and most melodramatic version yet to appear. In a florid pastoral style, the poet embellishes the story of this "negro virgin" and her faithless English lover with a number of new thematic elements. She makes Yarico's homeland a generic non-European setting, inhabited by a barbarous people who combine edenic innocence with cannibalism. The poet also espouses a kind of ethnodeterminism (northern peoples have "frozen souls"), and evinces a fierce dislike of commerce and its inhumane influence.

The Story of Inkle and Yarico

Ye virgin train, an artless dame inspire,
Unlearnt in schools, unblest with natal fire,
To save this story from devouring fate,
And the dire arts of faithless man relate. . . .
    Insatiate love of gold, and hope of gain,
Encourag'd him to cut the yielding main;
By winds, or waves, or the decrees of heaven,
His bark upon a barbarous coast was driven;
Possest by men who thirst for human blood,
Who live in caves, or thickets of the wood:
Untaught to plant (yet corn and fruits abound,
And fragrant flowers enamel all the ground).
Distrest, he landed on this fatal shore,
With some companions, which were soon no more;
The savage race their trembling flesh devour,
Off 'ring oblations to th' infernal power.
Dreadfully suppliant, human limbs they tore,

(Accursed rites) and quaft their streaming gore.
Immortal Jove stoop'd from his azure sky,
Grieving a form so like his own shou'd dye;
On the fair youth mercurial speed bestow'd,
Swifter than thought he reach'd the shady wood.

    Beneath a nightly shade he panting lies . . .
When lo! a negro virgin chanc'd to rove
Thro' the thick mazes of the nodding grove,
Whose glitt'ring shells and elegant undress,
With various plumes, a noble birth confess.
With reverential fear, the well-shap'd maid
Thought him a god, and low obedience paid.
His face like polish'd marble did appear;
His silken robe, and long-curl'd flaxen hair
Amaz'd the nymph; nor less her sparkling eyes,
And naked beauty, did the youth surprize.
Low at her feet, in suppliant posture laid,
With speaking eyes, he thus addrest the maid.

    O let soft pity touch that lovely breast!
Succour a man, by various ills opprest:
Such finish'd grace does thro' your person shine,
Sure 'tis enliven'd by a soul divine.

    The tender negro look'd a kind reply
Thro' pearls of pity, dropping from her eye;
With hands uplifted, did the gods implore,
That her relentless countrymen no more
Might stain their native land with native gore.
He seiz'd her hand, with tender passion prest,
While copious tears both love and fear confest.
The pitying maid view'd him with yielding eyes,
And from each bosom mutual sighs arise.

    His safety, now, became her only care,
A secret cave she knew, and hid him there . . .

    In soft repose the beauteous lover lies,
While *Yarico* with care unseals her eyes;
With anxious fear the matchless maid attends,
Careful to save him from her barb'rous friends. . . .

    Oft would say; my *Yarico*, with thee
(My only bliss!) cou'd I my country see,
If ever I forget my vows of love,
Unblest, abandon'd, may I friendless rove.
To thee, alone, I owe the vital air;

My love and gratitude for ever share.
I'll gems provide, and silks of curious art,
With gifts expressive of my grateful heart:
Thou in a house by horses drawn shalt ride,
With me, thy faithful lover, by thy side . . .
    Pleas'd with his words, desiring more to please,
She from a craggy cliff survey'd the seas;
A bark she spy'd, and did by signs implore,
That they would touch upon the sandy shore.
With joy she ran—My love make haste away,
A vessel waits us, on the foaming seas.
Soon he the vessel's lofty side ascends,
And finds them to be countrymen, and friends.
With lovely *Yarico,* puts off to sea;
With equal joy they plough the watery way.
    When the fair youth, despairing, calls to mind
All hopes eluded of his wealth design'd;
Riches the seat of his affection seize,
And faithful *Yarico* no more can please. . . .
This youth was born too near the northern pole,
Which chilled each virtue in his frozen soul:
But near the sun, the nymph her birth confest,
Where ev'ry virtue glow'd within her breast . . .
    Propitious *Zephyrs* fill their swelling sails;
They make *Barbadoes,* blest with prosp'rous gales.
The planters thick'ning on the key appear,
To purchase negroe slaves, if any there;
When the false youth, by cursed avarice sway'd,
Horrid to mention! sells his faithful maid. . . .
    She grasps his knees, in vain attempts to speak,
At length her words in moving accents break:
O much lov'd youth, in tender pity spare
A helpless maid, my long-try'd faith revere.
From you this worst of human ills to prove,
Must break a heart that overflows with love.
Break not my heart, nor drive me to despair,
Lest you deface your lovely image there.
Ah! do not with consummate woe undo
A soul, that father, mother, country, left for you. . . .
But if the swelling sorrows in my breast
Your heart of adamant can still resist,

Yet let the infant in my womb I hear,
The blessing taste of your paternal care.
    He thrust her from him with remorseless hand,
For her condition rais'd his first demand.
Pleas'd with success he cheerfully returns,
While hapless *Yarico* in bondage mourns.
The merchants all the prudent youth admire,
That could, so young, a trading soul acquire.
(1734)[49]

ANONYMOUS

Remarkable as a very early protest against the slave trade, this poem has a very local focus, attacking only Bristol slave traders rather than including those from Liverpool, London, and elsewhere. The speaker's treatment of cannibalism is wildly inaccurate, but seems to have been used primarily for rhetorical effect—to emphasize the barbarity of the Bristol traders—rather than to claim anthropological accuracy.

from "An Essay on Humanity. Inscrib'd to the Bristol Captains"

You Bristol Captains, who no Mercy shew,
Do you do what you wou'd have done to you?
When you submit yourselves to Passion's sway,
Your Minds are ruffled like the boist'rous Sea;
Alike you treat the Coward and the Brave,
And, as proud haughty Tyrants, kill or save;
By Piece-meal kill, a ling'ring Death procure,
Inflict such Pains no Mortal can endure,
Vaunt in your Cruelty, and strut with Pride,
And dying Groans, and dying Men deride.
Kind are the Cannibals, compar'd with you,
For we must give to every one his Due;
They are by Hunger prompted to destroy,
You murder with a Countenance of Joy;
They kill for the sake of Food, and nothing more,
You feed your Cruelty with Christian Gore:
Then talk no more of Savages for Shame,
All Men agree that you are most to blame,
And as a Punishment so justly due,
Which you deserve, henceforward each of you,
As a Reproach, shall be nick-nam'd by all
An unrelenting Bristol-Cannibal.

(1735)[50]

ANONYMOUS

The opening lines of this "Yarico to Inkle" make it the first version to frame the story as a pointed indictment of slavery, rather than just a tragic tale. Nothing is known of the anonymous author, except a clue in the dedication, "To Miss Arabella Saintloe"—apparently a wealthy young lady who, in 1737, married a London silk merchant named Cranke.* Other distinguishing elements of this version include greater emphasis on the lovers' sexual relationship and, at the poem's close, a special attention to the inhumanity of abandoning one's biological child to a life of slavery.

The poem was reprinted well into the 1800s, in more than ten editions in England, Ireland, and America. Its popularity confirms that the story of Yarico and Inkle "belonged," as Frank Felsenstein argues, "more to the public domain than to a single authorial consciousness."

from Yarico to Inkle. An Epistle.

From the sad place where sorrow ever reigns,
And hopeless wretches groan beneath their chains;
Where stern oppression lifts her iron hand,
And restless cruelty usurps command:
To sooth her soul and ease her aching heart,
Permit a wretch her sufferings to impart.—
To Inkle she complains—to him who taught
Her hand in language to express her thought.
Yet ere your sails before the winds are spread,
A woman's sorrow with compassion read;
Her dying farewell from her pen receive,
And to her wrongs, a tear in pity give. . . .

---

* For details, see Frank Felsenstein, *English Trader, Indian Maid: Representing Gender, Race, and Slavery in the New World* (Baltimore: Johns Hopkins University Press, 1999), 111.

Your eyes on all my naked beauty stray'd,
While mine your dress and fairer face survey'd.
If you my well proportion'd shape admir'd—
Your flowing locks my heaving bosom fir'd;
The fondest things in words unknown you spoke;
But the soft meaning from your eyes I took;
No other language we could use, or need,
For eyes beyond all eloquence persuade.
Inflam'd with love—with wanton joy you kiss'd
My trembling lips; and panting to be bless'd,
You press'd, and look'd, and strove, nor vainly strove,
For every power was soften'd into love:
Unskill'd in art—unable to deny,
Blushing I yielded to the silent joy.

  O! happy hours of love! where all my care,
Was but to please, and to preserve my dear:
Solicitous, for nothing else I knew—
No thought, no wish, for any thing but you.
Clasp'd in each other's arms, conceal'd we lay,
And in soft pleasures wasted all the day . . . .

And now I stand upon the long'd for shore,
And fondly hop'd my hour of sorrow o'er:
You smil'd, and as you kindly press'd my hand—
"Welcome!" you cry'd, "my Yarico to land—
"Thou kindest—dearest—tenderest—loveliest maid
Now shall my promis'd gratitude be paid."
Oh! how inhuman is the flattering lie,
That cheers but to inhance our misery;
For that which aggravates our sorrow most,
Is to know happiness, and know it lost.
Such soothing words conceal'd the vile deceit,
And lull'd me unsuspecting of my fate.
But now no longer need the mask be on,
The means was over for the end was come:
No more th'endearing look your falshood wears,
But all the monster in full light appears:
"Take her," you cry'd "my right I here resign;
Her life and labour are by purchase thine."
You ended; and the wretch to whom you spoke,
(Pride and ill-nature settl'd in his look)
Approach'd and sternly siez'd me by the hand,
And rudely haul'd me under his command.

ANONYMOUS

Such cruelty, what savage ever knew,
Or hearing, would believe you meant it true?
Too true I found it, when with barbarous scoff
And hate unknown before, you shook me off;
Plung'd me o'erwhelm'd in ev'ry human ill—
Not to be spoke, and what I only feel. . . .

I feel the infant struggling in my womb,
As conscious of its misery to come.
Oh! spare the guiltless babe; let nature move
Your heart to pity tho' 'tis deaf to love.
I could no more—your cruel looks, congeal'd
My flowing blood, and ev'ry vital chill'd;
No more my bosom heav'd—-my dying eyes
Were clos'd, and sense forsook me with my cries.
Oh! had it been for ever gone indeed,
From what a world of woes had I been free'd;
But fate conspiring to protract my grief,
Unseal'd my eyes and gave me back to life.
I found me, when my senses were restor'd,
In the curst house of him I call my lord. . . .
I told my fatal story o'er with pain,
And su[e]d for pity, but I su[e]d in vain!
Condemn'd to feel unutterable woes,
And all the wrongs that slav'ry can impose.

   Tho' deaf to justice, and love's softer claim,
O yet redeem me, in regard to fame!
For still the living Story of my woe
Shall follow, and exclaim where'er you go;
Mankind will shun you, and the blasting tongue
Shall hoot the monster, as you pass along.
                                    (1736)[51]

RICHARD SAVAGE (?1697–1742)

Brilliant, erratic, and often penniless, Savage is the embodiment of the eccentric grubstreet character. Writer of a stream of uneven work, including plays, satires, and poems of all kinds, Savage moved among the literati, walked the midnight streets of London with young Samuel Johnson, and vacillated between flashes of success and stretches in debtors' prison. He spent much of his adult life suing, unsuccessfully, to be acknowledged as the illegitimate son of Lady Macclesfield, to her chagrin and the amusement of society.

In this excerpt from a moralistic survey of contemporary Britain, Savage speaks in the voice of "Public Spirit" to attack British imperialism, particularly the abuse of Native Americans and enslaved Africans. The force of this passage seems to have moved Savage's friend and rival, James Thomson, to add his own protest against the slave trade to a later edition of his *Seasons* in 1744 (included elsewhere).

from Of Public Spirit in Regard to Public Works

    "Learn future Natives of this promis'd Land
What your Forefathers ow'd my saving Hand!
Learn what *Despair* such sudden Bliss shall see,
Such Bliss must shine from OGLETHORPE or ME!
Do you the neighb'ring blameless *Indian* aid,
Culture what he neglects, not His invade;
Dare not, oh dare not, with ambitious View,
Force or demand Subjection, never due.
Let by *My* specious Name no *Tyrants* rise,
And cry, while they enslave, they civilize!
Know LIBERTY and *I* are still the *same*,
Congenial!—ever mingling Flame with Flame!
Why must I *Afric's* sable Children see
Vended for Slaves, though form'd by Nature free,

RICHARD SAVAGE

The nameless Tortures cruel Minds invent,
Those to subject, whom Nature equal meant?
If these you dare, albeit unjust Success
Empow'rs you now unpunish'd to oppress,
Revolving Empire you and yours may doom,
(*Rome* all subdued, yet *Vandals* vanquish'd *Rome*)
Yes, Empire may revolve, give Them the Day,
And Yoke may Yoke, and Blood may Blood repay."
                          (wr. 1736/pub. 1737)[52]

ANONYMOUS

A blend of travelogue, pastoral, and Caribbean boosterism, this poem was published in the *Gentleman's Magazine* over two issues, March and April 1738. Clearly eager to shape perceptions of Jamaica in the British reading public, the anonymous colonial poet sings the virtues of the island's climate, society, and prosperity. In this excerpt, the poet's depiction of slave society (a very small part of the text) rises beyond idealization to sheer fantasy. Alert readers would have noticed that in 1737 the same magazine carried articles on a slave rebellion in Antigua, and in 1739 would begin reporting on a massive slave insurrection in Jamaica itself.

from "The Pleasures of Jamaica. In an Epistle from a Gentleman to His Friend in London."

Each rural object gratifies the sight,
And yields the mind an innocent delight;
Greens of all shades the diff'rent plots adorn,
Here the young cane, and there the growing corn;
In verdant pastures interspers'd between,
The lowing herds, and bleating flocks are seen:
With joy his lord the faithful Negro sees,
And in his way endeavours how to please;
Greets his return with his best country song,
The lively dance, and tuneful merry-wang.

When nature by the cane has done her part,
Which ripen'd now demands the help of art,
How pleasant are the labours of the mill,
While the rich streams the boiling coppers fill;
With gladden'd hearts we see the precious juice
From tend'rest plants the useful sweet produce;
Oh! may the seasons never fail again,

ANONYMOUS

Nor heav'n deny the kind refreshing rain,
To bless the soil, and fill the growing cane;
So shall our wealth with wonder still be told,
And sugar works be preferr'd to mines of gold.

(1738)[53]

?SAMUEL RICHARDSON
(1689–1761)

The authorship of the following poem is uncertain, although it is either by Richardson himself or adapted by him from an unidentified source. Like the duet from *The Beggar's Opera* (1728) anthologized above, the lines are a prime example of how poems about slavery can surface, upon reexamination, even within well-known canonical texts. Whatever its source, this poem is inevitably informed by an awareness of contemporary African slavery, given that later in the novel an English colonial in Jamaica is said to have sent a ten-year-old black slave back home as a "present" to Mr. B's illegitimate child. (The black boy died of smallpox one month after arriving in England.)

Untitled [from Pamela]

Wise Providence
Does various parts for various minds dispense;
The *meanest slaves*, or those who *hedge* and *ditch*,
Are useful, by their toil, to feed the *rich*.
The *rich*, in due return, impart their store;
To comfort and reward the lab'ring poor.
Nor let the *rich* the *lowest slave* disdain;
He's *equally* a *link* of nature's *chain;*
Labours to the *same end*, joins in *one view;*
And *both alike* the *Will Divine* pursue:
And, at the last, are levelled, *king* and *slave*,
Without distinction, in the silent grave.

(1740)[54]

ANONYMOUS

Enslaved Africans appeared in many poetic contexts, some quite unexpected. In this excerpt from an anonymous broadside published in May or June 1741 to celebrate Admiral Vernon's success at Cartagena, the presence of black troops is reported to have startled the besieged Spanish, much as their appearance in the poem may have surprised contemporary readers. In fact, both free and enslaved blacks fought at Cartagena, on both sides. The poem proved premature and wrong (although the Bostonian Mather Byles anthologized it in his *Collection of Poems, By Several Hands* in 1744). The British ultimately lost at Cartagena, in the worst military setback they were to suffer until the American Revolution.

from *"Some Excellent Verses on Admiral Vernon's Taking the Forts and Castles of Carthagena, in the Month of March Last"*

While these brave Things were done at Sea,
    Our Soldiers work'd for Blood,
Built on the Land a Battery,
    Behind a hideous Wood.

Wentworth commands, down go the Trees,
    With horrible Report;
Agast, the trembling *Spaniard* sees
    The Negroes and the Fort.

Our Picture shows all this with Art,
    (Was ever Work so pretty!)
And soon you'll see the second Part,
    When we have took the City.

             (1741)[55]

JACOBUS ELISA JOHANNES CAPITEIN [or CAPTAIN] (1717–1747)

One could hardly imagine a more unlikely fate for a former slave than Capitein's. Born in Africa, orphaned and enslaved at about age seven, and kept by a succession of masters in various African port towns, Capitein was brought to Holland at the age of eleven. Good fortune and prodigious intelligence led to an excellent formal education, culminating in degrees from the University of Leyden. He returned to Elmina in present-day Ghana as a Protestant missionary in 1742 where, after limited success and the ordeal of living between two cultures, he died at age thirty.

At Leyden, he wrote his dissertation in Latin on the question "Is Slavery Contrary to Christian Liberty?" in which the verses below first appeared. His writings later circulated in the anglophone world, in an American translation of Henri Grégoire's *Enquiry Concerning the Intellectual and Moral Faculties, and Literature of Negroes* (Brooklyn, 1810) and an antebellum edition of Capitein's work published in Kentucky in 1860. What adds to the mystery of Capitein is that, despite his own experience, his dissertation is not unequivocally opposed to slavery.

[Untitled autobiographical poetic fragments]

This land received me from dark Afric's shore,
Batavia, first, to Tempe was the door. . . .
This truly is the place where my dark youth
Was dedicated to ingenuous arts,
Hither Batavian Fathers come; and here,
In solemn conclave, keep the bonds of peace;
And here, through thousand paths and fair retreats,
All care thrown off, each spends his loved repose.

(1742)[56]

Capitein composed this elegy in Latin to mourn the death of his beloved teacher and mentor John Philip Manger. His anonymous translator's use of rhyming couplets captures the mid-eighteenth-century aura of neoclassical formality.

Elegy from Is Slavery Contrary to Christian Liberty?

Death envious hurls through all the earth his darts,
Frantic with zeal his stern commands imparts,
Fearless he enters the abode of kings:
"Resign your sceptres," the command he brings.
"No more your triumphs long enjoyed behold,
Your trophies leave adorned with shining gold."
The rich man's wealth, alike the beggar's cot,
He ruthless takes to make another's lot;
The old, the young, with no distinction made,
Like standing crops before his scythe are laid.
Hence the audacious tyrant, veiled in black,
On Manger's house directs his dire attack,
When at his door the mournful cypress stood,
Illustrious Hague sent forth her tears, a flood;
Him the dear wife with copious tears bedews,
And on her breast the frequent blow renews.
So thy Naomi when deprived of thee,
Elimelech, poured forth her tears as free.
Oft she invokes the manes of her spouse,
The trembling lips thus vent her heavy woes:
"As hides the sun behind the darksome cloud,
Folding Earth's tracts in one funereal shroud,
So, my Immortal Honor, sole delight,
Thou flee'st, irreparable loss, my sight.
I grudge not, Consort, that some swifter wings
Have borne thee upward to more joyful things;
But oft as evening's shade upon me falls,
Or day returns, fond memory thee recalls.
Nay more, sad sight, the pledges of our bed
Pour forth their tears, like rivers from their head.
As flocks by wolves disjected o'er the plain,
The faithful shepherd miserably slain,
So moanings fill our hall with plaintive signs,
While on its couch thy lifeless corpse reclines."
To her responsive, see the pious choir,
In wonted custom tune the funeral lyre.
Grand Honor of the sacerdotal corps!

Thy welcome face we hence behold no more.
My radiant glory too departed then,
Delight of God and love of pious men.
Closed the bland lips in sacred font immersed,
That font in which e'en I may quench my thirst.
How soon, alas! that eloquence has fled,
Which once distilled like nectar on my head!
Go, boast your Nestor, Bards of ancient song,
Nestor himself had not our Manger's tongue.
The Stygian Demon, at his potent word,
Flies from his house, his Leader, Christ the Lord.
From Hell's dark door the perishing he becks,
And bids them yield to Christ their willing necks.
With lucid order, how his words were fraught!
The better way how worthily he taught!
My prayers he bore before the holy throne;
His fervent prayer did God as quickly own.
Those eyes that beamed with heavenly lustre bright,
On thine, now fixed, perpetual slumbers light.
With them—a Watchman on the sacred wall—
The dart of Hell malignant harmless fall.
A bloodless pallor holds his modest face,
Where once was seated dignity with grace.
So leaves grow pale and wan and sere,
Touched by the rigors of the winter drear.
The rest, who shall relate! deep griefs arrest
My hand, attempting his last words expressed,
Although thy body, Sire, to earth is given,
Thy nobler part has scaled the gate of Heaven.
Arrayed in white, amid the heavenly guests,
Victorious thou, now taste the ambrosial feasts;
Exultant, drink, as from a chrystal flood,
The living water from the throne of God;
No day shall hence thy sure repose invade,
Death, vanquished foe, beneath thy feet is laid,
This, which thy weeping friends around thee sought,
O Father, thy last words most surely taught.

(1742)[57]

ROBERT BLAIR (1700–1746)

A Scottish clergyman of independent means, Blair wrote meditative verse that fed the eighteenth-century vogue for a "graveyard school" of poetry that also included Gray's "Elegy Written in a Country Churchyard" and Young's "Night Thoughts." In this excerpt from his 700-line poem, the speaker reflects on how death levels all distinctions between master and slave. Blair's diction seems deliberately vague so as to encompass both the medieval feudalism that was still dying out and the New World chattel slavery that had been growing since the early 1500s.

from The Grave

Here! all the mighty Troublers of the Earth,
Who swam to Sov'reign Rule thro' Seas of Blood;
Th'oppressive, sturdy, Man-destroying Villains!
Who ravag'd Kingdoms, and laid Empires Waste;
And, in a cruel Wantonness of Pow'r,
Thinn'd States of half their People, and gave up
To Want the rest: Now like a Storm that's spent,
Lye hush'd, and meanly sneak behind thy Covert.
Vain Thought! to hide them from the gen'ral Scorn,
That haunts and dogs them like an injur'd Ghost
Implacable. Here too the petty Tyrant
Of scant Domains Geographer ne'er notic'd,
And well for neighbouring Grounds, of Arm as short;
Who fix'd his Iron Talons on the Poor,
And gripp'd them like some Lordly Beast of Prey;
Deaf to the forceful Cries of gnawing Hunger,
And piteous plaintive Voice of Misery:
(As if a Slave was not a Shred of Nature,
Of the same common Nature with his Lord:)

Now! tame and humble, like a Child that's whipp'd,
Shakes Hands with Dust, and calls the Worm his Kinsman;
Nor pleads his Rank and Birthright. Under Ground
Precedency's a Jest; Vassal and Lord
Grossly familiar, Side by Side consume. . . .

Here the o'er-loaded Slave flings down his Burthen
From his gall'd Shoulders; and when the cruel Tyrant
With all his Guards and Tools of Pow'r about him,
Is meditating new unheard-of Hardships,
Mocks his short Arm, and quick as Thought escapes
Where Tyrants vex not, and the Weary rest.

$(1743)^{58}$

EDWARD KIMBER (1719–1769)

Poetry about interracial romance was not always tragic. Here Kimber, a twenty-five-year-old Londoner visiting the American colonies, sings the praises of a beautiful young black slave who saved his life and, apparently, captured his heart. Professing loyalty to his lover back in England, Kimber nonetheless devotes most of the poem to an idealization of the African Fidenia's virtues: beauty, modesty, innocence, inherent nobility, and exceptional intelligence. One can only imagine the response of English readers when the poem was published in the popular *London Magazine,* courtesy of his father (the editor) in March 1744. Kimber's first footnote makes clear, however, that colonial society did not entirely approve of his admiration for the black girl.

Fidenia* or, the Explanation

1.

Ye fair, whose worth I so esteem,
   Who sport on *Britain's* vivid plains,
Still may your smiles upon me gleam,
   For still your lover wears your chains.
Think not, tho' longer I endure
   This tedious absence from your eyes,
That time, or distance, e'er can cure
   Those passions that from you take rise.

2.

Tho' sweet *Fidenia,* born of kings,
   From *Afric's* shores, attracts my sight;

---

* [Kimber's note:] A very beautiful Negro Girl, aged 16, from James River in Guinea, who, by every superior Accomplishment, seems far beyond any of her Kind. She learnt the English Tongue in three Months Time, and in four, read the Spectators and Tatlers with inimitable Grace. She has endear'd herself to a grateful Master by her Fidelity and Affection, tho' he has been much censur'd for his Regard to her.

What tho' her praise, your *Strephon* sings,
    And eager grasps the new delight?
What tho' her soft and jetty hue
    Gives yet unfelt, untasted joy?
Remembrance speaks such charms in you,
    As all her blandishments destroy.

    3.

Tho' *Amblerena* spread her snare,
    And caught me in the am'rous vein;
Her vicious soul, her gloating air,
    The thrilling ecstacies restrain.
Unhappy females, loosely bold,
    Where southern climates raise desire,
Your faint attractions ne'er will hold,
    Where reason sprinkles but the fire.

    4.

Rather let me, where *Gambia* flows,
    With black *Fidenia* spend my days,
Than tempt those arms, where lust all glows,
    And mingle with the curs'd embrace.
See! With what majesty she walks!
    What modesty adorns her mien!
How simply innocent she talks,
    Inchanting slave! My *Indian* queen!

    5.

E'er my exalted, matchless friend
    Had sav'd me from the enraged deep,*
With what sad cries, thou wail'dst my end,
    And how my faithful slave did weep!
How shouts broke forth, with joy replete,
    When sav'd, they cast me on the shore!
With rapture, how you hugg'd my feet,
    And all thy gods, how didst implore!

    6.

For this, I'll grateful, thee convey,
    Where ev'ry precept shall combine,
To chace the savage quite away,
    And all thy motions to refine.

---

* [Kimber's note:] He was in Danger of drowning in the great Bay of C[hesapeake]; and 'tis impossible to express the tender Concern she show'd, in her Way, on that Occasion.

And ev'ry maid, and ev'ry swain,
   Shall melt at thy uncommon tale,
With admiration, tell thy name,
   And me, thy happy master, hail!
   7.
Nor you, ye fair ones, will condemn
   A grateful mind, for acts like these;
Nor such a tenderness arraign,
   Where sense, and wit, and prudence please,
Thou, my *Maria,* shalt embrace
   Fidenia, with a glad surprise;
Hortensia too, her beauties trace,
   And own the lustre of her eyes.

                    (1744)[59]

WILLIAM SHENSTONE
(1714–1763)

Oxford-educated and independently wealthy, Shenstone devoted his life to beautifying his country estate at Leasowes and to writing poetry expressive of his melancholy temperament. Shy and physically unattractive, Shenstone never married. His friends included Johnson, Percy, and other literati. Interestingly, he was the dedicatee of Book II of James Grainger's *The Sugar-Cane,* a poem that also treated the topic of slavery (included elsewhere).

Here, using an imagistic scheme that Boswell would take up in the 1790s (see his *No Abolition of Slavery*), Shenstone compares his sense of thralldom to his beloved "Delia" to the bondage of an African slave. But in a way that Boswell's poem never comprehends, Shenstone's elegy quickly acknowledges the absurdity of this premise and develops into a sympathetic account of the misery of slaves caught up in the African diaspora. Particularly noteworthy, in the last ten stanzas, is his effort to render the African experience in an imaginary captive's voice.

from "Elegy XX"

He Compares His Humble Fortune with the Distress of Others; And His Subjection to *Delia,* with the Miserable Servitude of an African Slave.

Why droops this heart, with fancy'd woes forlorn?
    Why sinks my soul beneath each wint'ry sky?
What pensive crowds, by ceaseless labours worn,
    What myriads, wish to be as blest as I! . . .

Slave tho' I be, to DELIA's eyes a slave,
    My DELIA's eyes endear the bands I wear;
The sigh she causes well becomes the brave,
    The pang she causes, 'tis ev'n bliss to bear.

See the poor native quit the Lybian shores,
    Ah! not in love's delightful fetters bound!

WILLIAM SHENSTONE

No radiant smile his dying peace restores,
    Nor love, nor fame, nor friendship heals his wound.

Let vacant bards display their boastive woes,
    Shall I the mockery of grief display?
No, let the muse his piercing pangs disclose,
    Who bleeds and weeps his sum of life away!

On the wild beach in mournful guise he stood,
    Ere the shrill boatswain gave the hated sign;
He dropt a tear unseen into the flood;
    He stole one secret moment, to repine.

Yet the muse listen'd to the plaints he made;
    Such moving plaints as nature could inspire;
To me the muse his tender plea convey'd,
    But smooth'd, and suited to the sounding lyre.

"Why am I ravish'd from my native strand?
    What savage race protects this impious gain?
Shall foreign plagues infest this teeming land,
    And more than sea-born monsters plough the main?

Here the dire locusts horrid swarms prevail;
    Here the blue asps with livid poison swell;
Here the dry dipsa writhes his sinuous mail;
    Can we not here, secure from envy, dwell?

When the grim lion urg'd his cruel chace,
    When the stern panther sought his midnight prey,
What fate reserv'd me for this* Christian race?
    A race more polish'd, more severe than they!

Ye prouling wolves pursue my latest cries!
    Thou hungry tyger, leave thy reeking den!
Ye sandy wastes in rapid eddies rise!
    O tear me from the whips and scorns of men!

Yet in their face superior beauty glows;
    Are smiles the mien of rapine and of wrong?
Yet from their lip the voice of mercy flows,
    And ev'n religion dwells upon their tongue.

Of blissful haunts they tell, and brighter climes,
    Where gentle minds convey'd by death repair,
But stain'd with blood, and crimson'd o'er with crimes,
    Say, shall they merit what they paint so fair?

* [Shenstone's note:] Spoke by a savage.

No, careless, hopeless of those fertile plains,
   Rich by our toils, and by our sorrows gay,
They ply our labours, and enhance our pains,
   And feign these distant regions to repay.

For them our tusky elephant expires;
   For them we drain the mine's embowel'd gold;
Where rove the brutal nations wild desires?—
   Our limbs are purchas'd, and our life is sold!

Yet shores there are, blest shores for us remain,
   And favour'd isles with golden fruitage crown'd
Where tufted flow'rets paint the verdant plain,
   Where ev'ry breeze shall med'cine ev'ry wound.

There the stern tyrant that embitters life
   Shall, vainly suppliant, spread his asking hand;
There shall we view the billow's raging strife,
   Aid the kind breast, and waft his boat to land."

                                        (1744)[60]

JAMES THOMSON (1700–1748)

A Scotsman who pursued a literary career in London, Thomson was, after Pope, the most eminent British poet of the first half of the eighteenth century. Writing in an era of neoclassical rhyming couplets, Thomson instead developed his powerful blank verse and romantic sensibilities, which would influence Cowper, Wordsworth, and Tennyson and remain popular for more than a century. Thomson was highly esteemed in literary circles, and counted among his friends Pope, Savage, and Frances Seymour, whose poems on slavery appear elsewhere in this anthology. Apparently moved by his friend Savage's recent lines on slavery, Thomson added the passage below to the "Summer" section of *The Seasons* when he revised it between 1738 and 1744. His vision of the forces of nature avenging themselves on the perpetrators of the slave trade proved so powerful that it is thought to have inspired J. M. W. Turner's great painting *The Slave Ship* (1840).

from "Summer" in The Seasons

With such mad seas the daring Gama fought
For many a day and many a dreadful night
Incessant, labouring round the stormy Cape,
By bold ambition led and bolder thirst
Of gold. . . .
    Increasing still the terrors of these storms,
His jaws horrific armed with threefold fate,
Here dwells the direful shark. Lured by the scent
Of steaming crowds, of rank disease, and death,
Behold he rushing cuts the briny flood
Swift as the gale can bear the ship along,
And from the partners of that cruel trade
Which spoils unhappy Guinea of her sons
Demands his share of prey, demands themselves.

The stormy fates descend: one death involves
Tyrants and slaves; when straight, their mangled limbs
Crashing at once, he dyes the purple seas
With gore, and riots in the vengeful meal.

(1744)[61]

THOMAS BACON (? 1700–1768)

Born on the Isle of Man, Bacon was an Anglican clergyman who was sent to Maryland in 1745. Although a slave owner, he took a deep interest in the education and spiritual well-being of the enslaved Africans. He published at least six sermons in 1749–50 addressed specifically to slaves and their masters, and he habitually referred in his sermons to "My well-beloved Black Brethren and Sisters." Bacon was instrumental in founding a charity school that educated the needy of all races. After his wife and only son died in 1755, rumors surfaced of an intrigue with a mulatto woman named Rachel Beck, leading to a "morals charge" and a countersuit for slander. Sympathetic to the suffering of slaves but never an abolitionist, Bacon in this poem urges resignation to the sufferings of this world, in hopes of deliverance in the next.

from "The Comforts of Religion"

O blest religion, heav'nly fair!
   Thy kind, thy healing pow'r;
Can sweeten pain, and soften care,
   And gild each gloomy hour.

'Tis thou canst make the heathen bless'd,
   And make their darkness light;
Cheer'd by thy blessings see them rise,
   To hope, to life, and light.

'Tis Thou canst sooth their troubled soul,
   In slavery, woe, and pain;
And Afric's sobs with grateful joy,
   Thy sacred peace shall gain!

When dismal thoughts, and boding fears,
   The trembling heart invade;
And all the face of nature wears,
   A universal shade;

Thy sacred dictates can assuage,
   The tempest of the soul;
And ev'ry fear shall lose its rage,
   At thy divine control. . . .

O let my heart confess thy pow'r,
   And find thy sweet relief:
To brighten ev'ry gloomy hour;
   And soften ev'ry grief.

         (c. 1745)[62]

LUCY TERRY (1730–1821)

Considered by many the first African American poet, Terry was abducted from Africa and sold into slavery as a small child, living most of her life in Deerfield, Massachusetts, where she was the property of Ebenezer Wells. Having produced her verse entirely in an oral context, Terry presents a glimpse of the slave poet as local bard. This poem is the only one of her works known to survive, having been passed down orally until it was transcribed in 1855 and published in Josiah Gilbert Holland's *History of Western Massachusetts*. The poem was occasioned by an Indian attack on Deerfield on August 25, 1746, and pointedly shows Terry's sense of herself not as a kindred spirit with the native Americans, but as a chronicler and eulogist for the English colonial population.

Untitled

"August 'twas the twenty-fifth,
Seventeen hundred forty-six;
The Indians did in ambush lay,
Some very valient men to slay,
The names of whom I'll not leave out.
Samuel Allen like a hero fout.
And though he was so brave and bold,
His face no more shall we behold.
Eleazer Hawks was killed outright,
Before he had time to fight,—
Before he did the Indians see,
Was shot and killed immediately.
Oliver Amsden he was slain,
Which caused his friends much grief and pain.
Simeon Amsden they found dead,
Not many rods distant from his head.
Adonijah Gillett we do hear

Did lose his life which was so dear.
John Sadler fled across the water,
And thus escaped the dreadful slaughter.
Eunice Allen see the Indians coming,
And hopes to save herself by running,
And had not her petticoats stopped her,
The awful creatures had not catched her,
Nor tommy hawked her on her head,
And left her on the ground for dead.
Young Samuel Allen, Oh lack-a-day!
Was taken and carried to Canada.

                    (1746)[63]

WILLIAM DODD (1729–1777)

A clergyman, writer, and bon vivant, Dodd achieved fame for his preaching and good works, but he came to a tragic end. Success having led to an extravagant lifestyle and huge debts, he forged a bond over Lord Chesterfield's signature, was caught, convicted, and, despite the appeals of supporters high and low, hanged in June 1777. The following poems, written in happier times while Dodd was a student at Cambridge, were inspired by real events. In 1749 the London press was full of the story of a young African prince from Anamaboe in West Africa who, having been entrusted by his father to a British sea captain for education in Britain, was instead betrayed and sold into slavery, from which he only narrowly escaped and came to England after all.

In these lines, Dodd imagines the newly freed African in London corresponding with his beloved "Zara" back home in Anamaboe. The sympathetic rendering of an African captive's experience proved popular, appearing first in the *Gentleman's Magazine* in 1749 and thereafter in such anthologies as *The Lady's Poetical Magazine, or Beauties of British Poetry* (1782).

from "The African Prince"

The African prince, now in England, to Zara at his father's court:
How vainly proud, the arrogantly great
Presume to boast a monarch's godlike state!
Subject alike, the peasant and the king,
To life's dark ills, and care's corroding sting.
From guilt and fraud, that strikes in silence sure,
No shield can guard us, and no arms secure.
By these, my fair, subdu'd, thy prince was lost,
A naked captive on a barb'rous coast.
Nurtur'd in ease, a thousand servants round,
My wants prevented, and my wishes crown'd,
No painful labours stretch'd the tedious day,

101

On downy feet my moments danc'd away.
Where'er I look'd, officious courtiers bow'd,
Where'er I pass'd, a shouting people crowd;
No fears intruded on the joys I knew,
Each man my friend, my lovely mistress you.
What dreadful change! abandon'd and alone,
The shouted prince is now a slave unknown;
To watch his eye, no bending courtiers wait,
No hailing crowds proclaim his regal state;
A slave, condemn'd, with unrewarded toil,
To turn, from morn to eve, a burning soil.
Fainting beneath the sun's meridian heat,
Rouz'd by the scourge, the taunting jest I meet:
Thanks to thy friends, they cry, whose care recalls
A prince to life, in whom a nation falls!
Unwholesome scraps my strength but half sustain'd,
From corners glean'd, and ev'n by dogs disdain'd;
At night I mingled with a wretched crew,
Who by long use with woe familiar grew;
Of manners brutish, merciless and rude,
They mock'd my suff'rings, and my pangs renew'd;
In groans, not sleep, I pass'd the weary night,
And rose to labour with the morning light. . . .
    The wretch, sordid hypocrite, that sold
His charge, an unsuspecting prince, for gold,
That justice mark'd, whose eyes can never sleep,
And death, commission'd, smote him on the deep.
The gen'rous crew their port in safety gain,
And tell my mournful tale, nor tell in vain;
The king, with horror of th' atrocious deed,
In haste commanded, and the slave was free'd. . . .
O! I have tales to tell, of love divine—
Such blissful tidings! they shall soon be thine.
I long to tell thee, what, amaz'd, I see,
What habits, buildings, trades, and polity!
How art and nature vye to entertain,
In public shows, and mix delight with pain.
O! Zara, here, a story like my own,
With mimic skill, in borrow'd names, was shown;
An Indian chief, like me, by fraud betray'd,
And partner in his woes, an Indian maid.

I can't recall the scenes, 'tis pain too great,
And, if recall'd, should shudder to relate.
To write the wonders here, I strive in vain,
Each word wou'd ask a thousand to explain.
The time shall come, O! speed the ling'ring hour!
When Zara's charms shall lend description power;
When plac'd beside thee, in the cool alcove,
Or through't the green Savannahs as we rove,
The frequent kiss shall interrupt the tale,
And looks shall speak my sense, tho' language fail.

(1749)[64]

The corresponding poem from the prince's lover, Zara, printed below, appeals primarily to the reader with a taste for sentimental romance. For all the clichés Dodd puts in her mouth, Zara is unequivocal about the slave trade, characterizing it as the work of "barbarians" in pursuit of empire.

from "Zara"

At the court of Anamaboe, to the African Prince when in England.

O! art thou safe on Britain's happy shore,
From winds that bellow, and from seas that roar?
And has my prince—(oh, more than mortal pain!)
Betray'd by ruffians, felt the captive's chain?
Bound were those limbs, ordain'd alone to prove
The toils of empire, and the sweets of love?
Hold, hold! barbarians of the fiercest kind!
Fear Heav'n's red lightning—'tis a prince ye bind!
A prince whom no indignities could hide,
They knew, presumptuous! and the gods defy'd.
Where'er he moves, let love-join'd reverence rise,
And all mankind behold with Zara's eyes!
    Thy breast alone, when bounding o'er the waves
To Freedom's climes, from slavery and slaves;
Thy breast alone the pleasing thought could frame
Of what I felt, when thy dear letters came:
A thousand times I held them to my breast,
A thousand times my lips the paper press'd:
My full heart panted with a joy too strong,
And 'Oh, my prince!' dy'd fault'ring on my tongue . . .

Alas, my prince!—yet hold, my struggling breast;
Sure we shall meet again, again be bless'd.
"Hope all," thou say'st, "I live, and still am free;"
O then prevent those hopes, and haste to me!
Ease all the doubts thy Zara's bosom knows,
And kindly stop the torrent of her woes.

(1749)[65]

SAMUEL JOHNSON (1709–1784)

Poet, journalist, biographer, lexicographer, and critic, Johnson was so much the dominant literary figure of his time that the period 1740 to 1800 is often called the "Age of Johnson." Most of his lifelong criticism of slavery was expressed in prose works, including *The Life of Francis Drake* (1740–41), the introduction to *The World Displayed* (1759), *Taxation No Tyranny* (1775), and the legal brief he wrote on behalf of the African slave Joseph Knight in 1777. He stunned an Oxford common room by proposing a toast "to the next insurrection of the Negroes in the West Indies." On two occasions, however, Johnson's antislavery feelings surfaced fleetingly in poetic works. The first is a metaphor about slave resistance in the manuscript draft of *The Vanity of Human Wishes,* a passage he replaced with more lighthearted lines when he published the poem.

from "The Vanity of Human Wishes"

What care, what rules your heedless charms shall save,
Each nymph your rival, and each youth your slave?
An envious breast with certain mischief glows
And slaves, the maxim tells, are always foes.

(1749)[66]

In his translation of Boethius, Johnson uses the following ironic lines to undercut the arrogance of northern European peoples filled with a sense of superiority over the races they dominate and enslave.

Book III, Metre 5 from Translations from Boethius

The man who pants for ample sway
Must bid his passions all obey;
Must bid each wild desire be still,
Nor yoke his reason with his will:
For tho' beneath thy haughty brow

105

Warm India's supple sons should bow,
Tho' northern climes confess thy sway,
Which erst in frost and freedom lay,
If sorrow pine or av'rice crave,
Bow down and own thyself a slave.

                 (wr. c. 1765/pub. 1788)[67]

JOHN WINSTANLEY
(c. 1678–1750)

An obscure Irish poet and self-described fellow of Trinity College, Dublin, Winstanley published his poetry in two volumes near the end of his life. That he chose to retell the story of Yarico's enslavement confirms how far the vogue had spread in the mid-century, even into Irish academic circles. Framing the poem in Yarico's voice, Winstanley offers a less melodramatic, more meditative version than those of predecessors like Frances Seymour and Stephen Duck. Despite Winstanley's largely conventional poetic language, there are moments—such as his proto-Yeatsian image of the swan—that can be arresting.

from "Yarico's Epistle to Inkle"

Here let a *Captive* fetch a panting Groan,
Dissolv'd in flowing Tears till now unknown;
And Swan-like enter with a mournful Strain,
A *Sea* of Toil, a *World* of boundless Pain.
Still is there left me Freedom to deplore,
To kiss and grasp my now abandon'd Shore,
Nor hope to taste it's short-liv'd Pleasures more;
Still have I Freedom to expose thy Shame,
Perfidious Man, and curse the hated Name.
    Ye conscious Breezes that around me play,
Bear the soft Breathings of my Soul away;
My Sighs in Whispers to his Breast impart,
And bend to Pity his relentless Heart.

(c. 1750)[68]

CORNELIUS ARNOLD
(1711–1757)

A businessman with poetic aspirations, Arnold eventually became beadle to the Distillers' Company in London. During the 1750s he published several works, including *Commerce,* the long poem that follows in the tradition of verse celebrations of British trade, from the City of London pageants of the 1670s down through Pope's *Windsor-Forest* (1713) and John Dyer's *The Fleece* (1757). In the following excerpt the poet momentarily sympathizes with the plight of enslaved Africans, but also seems to accept the widespread (though specious) notion that slaves were acquired by traders merely as a by-product of internecine African wars.

from Commerce: A Poem

See! the gay Fleet to various Ports consign'd,
Various their Freight—rich Industry at Helm
Smiles on the jovial Crew, joyous they hold
The swelling Canvas to th'impelling Wind . . .
Some the Atlantic plough, serener far,
Tho' oft the loud tongu'd Waves contentious brawl,
In Uproar wild—Onward they steer their Course,
To Afric's parched Clime, whose sooty Sons,
Thro' Rage of civil Broils—hard Destiny!
Forc'd from their native Home to Western Ind,
In Slavery drag the galling Chain of Life:
Or past the Streights, they coast the Tuscan Shore
To sea-born Venice, or the proud Levant:
Delicious Range! There variegated Scenes
Strike the enchanted Mind with new Delight.

(1751)[69]

ANONYMOUS

Incidental poetry about contemporary events often preserves serendipitous images of slaves in the general population. George Whitefield (1714–1770) was an evangelical Methodist whose open-air preaching and itinerant ministry were powerful forces in the Great Awakening. As these broadside stanzas by an anonymous New Englander indicate, his ministry was addressed to black and white alike. It is all the more ironic, therefore, that Whitefield purchased a South Carolina plantation (complete with slaves) in order to fund the charity school he had founded.

from "A Poem, on the Joyful News of the Rev. Mr. Whitefield's Visit to Boston"

Ye Widows all pray now attend,
    And little Maidens too,
Ye pretty Boys and little Girls,
    For *Whitefield* calls to you.

The *Negroes* too he'll not forget,
    But tells them all to come;
Invites the *Black* as well as *White*,
    And says for them there's Room.
                (1754)[70]

SAMUEL BOWDEN, M.D.
(fl. 1732–1761)

A physician based in Somerset, Bowden sent in occasional pieces to the *Gentle-man's Magazine* in London and published two books of poems, in 1733–35 and in 1754. A friend of Elizabeth Rowe who was also apparently influenced by the deistic views of Pope in his *Essay on Man,* Bowden expresses in these elegiac verses an enlightened view of racial equality. The poem honors the memory of a black servant who had died recently in the neighborhood. The unnamed African was typical of the many brought back to Britain as servants when their masters returned from the colonies.

An Epitaph, on a Negro Servant, Who Died at Governor Phipps's, at Haywood, near Westbury

European vain—mock not my hue,
    Nor ridicule a slave;
Death soon, like me, will blacken you,
    In darkness, and the grave.

Tho' nature o'er my swarthy skin
    Diffus'd a sable blot;
Yet was my mind unstain'd within,
    And free from vicious spot.

It boots not here, or black, or white,
    All colours suit the tomb;
Black guests, and *Æthiopian* night,
    Sit round this funeral room.

Releas'd from servitude, and woe,
    Here all my toils are o'er,
To some green island I shall go,
    And see my native shore.

SAMUEL BOWDEN

Tho' with reluctant mind I part,
    From my kind master here;
Yet my old country has my heart,
    And liberty is dear.

There in some shady, *Indian* grove,
    I shall forever stray;
Or o'er the pathless mountain rove,
    And hunt for savage prey.

It matters not, or rich, or poor,
    But 'tis the honest man;
Whether he lives on *India*'s shore
    In *Europe*, or *Japan*.

Live well—nor tremble at the grave,
    The good shall live again;
The wicked man's the truest slave,
    And death a tyrant then.

(1754)[71]

JOHN DYER (? 1700–1758)

A man of many talents, Dyer was by turns an office clerk, itinerant artist, clergyman, and successful writer. Esteemed in his time, he influenced Wordsworth and others who valued his taste for scenic description. In this excerpt from his long poem on the wool trade, Dyer, like Pope, Thomson, and Arnold before him, presents a poetic vision of British commerce sailing across the globe, creating new wealth, new knowledge, and new relations (beneficial and exploitative) among nations and peoples. For all his optimism, he was troubled by the slave trade. His closing warning is darkly reminiscent of his friend Savage's prophesy, that "blood may blood repay" (see Savage's *Of Public Spirit*).

from Book IV of The Fleece

> The whole globe
> Is now of commerce made the scene immense,
> Which daring ships frequent, associated,
> Like doves, or swallows, in the ethereal flood,
> Or, like the eagle, solitary seen.
>   Some, with more open course, to Indus steer;
> Some coast from port to port, with various men
> And manners conversant; of the angry surge,
> That thunders loud, and spreads the cliffs with foam,
> Regardless, or the monsters of the deep,
> Porpoise, or grampus, or the ravenous shark,
> That chase their keels; or threatening rock o'erhead
> Of Atlas old; beneath the threatening rocks,
> Reckless, they furl their sails, and bartering take
> Soft flakes of wool; for in soft flakes of wool,
> Like the Silurian, Atlas' dales abound. . . .
>   On Guinea's sultry strand, the drapery light
> Of Manchester or Norwich is bestowed

For clear transparent gums and ductile wax
And snow-white ivory; yet the valued trade,
Along this barbarous coast, in telling wounds
The generous heart, the sale of wretched slaves;
Slaves by their tribes condemned, exchanging death
For life-long servitude; severe exchange!
These till our fertile colonies, which yield
The sugar-cane, and the Tobago-leaf,
And various new productions, that invite
Increasing navies to their crowded wharfs.
  But let the man, whose rough tempestuous hours
In this adventurous traffic are involved,
With just humanity of heart pursue
The gainful commerce: wickedness is blind:
Their sable chieftains may in future times
Burst their frail bonds, and vengeance execute
On cruel unrelenting pride of heart
And avarice. There are ills to come of crimes.

$(1757)^{72}$

ANONYMOUS ("AGRICOLA")

This anonymous South Carolina poet chose an ingenious pseudonym: "Agricola" refers both to the Roman governor who ruled and "Romanized" Britain from 78 to 84 A.D. (implying a parallel with the "civilizing" impact of the British on the New World) and to the Latin word for farmer, which no doubt the poet himself was. This excerpt is from a specimen of a longer poem that was never published in full. Agricola follows in the tradition of georgics, or poems about farm life, that dates back to Virgil and was continued by poets such as John Dyer and James Grainger in the eighteenth century. He blithely imagines the cultivation of a profitable new crop (indigo) without a hint of sensitivity to the labor of African slaves on which it is all based.

from "Indico"

If Time permits, the shady Forest clear,
And turn the Fallow for the foll'wing Year;
Beneath the noxious Pine the Soil is sour,
And spreading Oaks prevent the genial Pow'r
Of mellowing Suns, but yet, Experience shows,
In these hot Climes that rich Herbage grows,
The foll'wing Summer, where in Winter past,
The hungry Swine had found a Winter Mast.
    Begin when first bleak Winter strips the Trees,
When Herds first shudder at the Northern Breeze,
'Tis time the Walnut and the Cypress tall
And tow'ring Pride of verdant Pines to fall.
Arm'd with destructive Steel thy Negroes bring,
With Blows repeated let the Woodlands ring;
With winged Speed, the tim'rous Deer from far
Shall fly the Tumult of the Sylvan War. . . .

ANONYMOUS

Most skilful Planters in the Judgment rest,
That rotten Soil for Indico's the best:
But let not that thy Hopes of Crops impair,
Some stiffer Soils great Droughts may better bear.

(1757)[73]

FRANCIS WILLIAMS
(c. 1700–c. 1770)

Born of free blacks in Jamaica, and destined to graduate from Cambridge University, Francis Williams may be the greatest example of black achievement in the eighteenth century. His excellence as a young pupil moved well-intentioned whites to sponsor his education in England, in an effort to demonstrate that blacks were as capable as whites. Although racialists such as Edward Long (who translated Williams's "Ode" from Latin) remained skeptical, Henri Grégoire and other enlightened thinkers held Williams up as irrefutable proof of black equality. After the early blaze of his Cambridge career, Williams returned to Jamaica where he ran a school for black children. He continued to endure prejudice and it is a sad irony that, as lines in his poem suggest, he eventually seemed to internalize a sense of racial inferiority that his life had otherwise proved so unfounded. His poem of tribute to the new governor conveys the ambivalence and awkwardness of an educated black man in his situation, living in a slave-holding society.

To that Most Upright and Valiant Man, George Haldane, Esq. Governor of the Island of Jamaica: Upon Whom All Military and Moral Endowments Are Accumulated. An Ode*

> At length revolving fates th' expected year
> Advance, and joy the live long day shall cheer,
> Beneath the fost'ring law's auspicious dawn
> New harvests rise to glad the enliven'd lawn.
> With the bright prospect blest, the swains repair
> In social bands, and give a loose to care.
> Rash councils now, with each malignant plan,
> Each faction, that in evil hour began,

---

* The text here is Long's translation of Williams's Latin ode. For Williams's original Latin text, see (Edward Long), *The History of Jamaica* (London, 1774), vol. 2, 478–81.

At your approach are in confusion fled,
Nor while you rule, shall raise their dastard head.
Alike the master and the slave shall see
Their neck reliev'd, the yoke unbound by thee
Till now, our guiltless isle, her wretched fate
Had wept, and groan'd beneath the oppressive weight
Of cruel woes; save thy victorious hand,
Long form'd in war, from Gallia's hostile land,
And wreaths of fresh renown, with generous zeal,
Had freely turn'd, to prop our sinking weal.
Form'd as thou art, to serve Brittania's crown;
While Scotia claims thee for her darling son.
Oh! best of heroes, ablest to sustain
A falling people, and relax their chain.
Long as this isle shall grace the Western deep
From age to age, thy fame shall never sleep.
Thee, her dread victor, Guadaloupe shall own,
Crush'd by thy arm, her slaughter'd chiefs bemoan,
View their proud tents all levell'd in the dust,
And while she grieves, confess the cause was just.
The golden iris the sad scene will share,
And mourn her banners scatter'd in the air,
Lament her vanquish'd troops with many a sigh,
Nor less to see her towns in ruins lie.
Favorite of Mars! believe, the attempt were vain,
It is not mine to try the arduous strain.
What! shall an Aethiop touch the martial string
Of battles, leaders, great achievements sing?
Ah no! Minerva, with the indignant nine,
Restrain him, and forbid the bold design.
To a Buchanan does the theme belong,
A theme, that well deserves Buchanan's song.
'Tis he should swell the din of war's alarms,
Record thee great in council, as in arms:
Recite each conquest by thy valour won,
And equal thee to great Peleides son.
That bard, his country's ornament and pride,
Who with Mars might e'en the bays divide:
Far worthier he, thy glories to rehearse,
And paint thy deeds in his immortal verse.
We live, alas! where the bright God of day,
Full from the zenith whirls his torrid ray:

Beneath the rage of his consuming fires,
All fancy melts, all eloquence expires.
Yet may you deign to accept this humble song,
Tho' wrapt in gloom, and from a falt'ring tongue
Tho' dark the stream on which the tribute flows,
Not from the skin, but from the heart it rose.
To all of human kind, benignant heaven
(Since nought forbids) one common soul has giv'n,
This rule was 'stablish'd by the eternal mind;
Nor virtue's self, nor prudence are confin'd
To color, none imbues the honest heart;
To science none belongs, and none to art:
Oh! muse of blackest tint, why shrinks thy breast,
Why fears to approach the Caesar of the West!
Dispel thy doubts, with confidence ascend
The regal dome, and hail him for thy friend:
Nor blush, altho' in garb funereal drest
Thy body's white, tho' clad in sable vest.
Manners unsullied, and the radiant glow
Of genius, burning with desire to know;
And learned speech, with modest accent worn
Shall best the sooty African adorn.
A heart with wisdom fraught, a patriot flame,
A love of virtue, these shall lift his name
Conspicuous, far beyond his kindred race,
Distinguish'd from them by the foremost place.
In this prolific isle I drew my breath
And Britain nurs'd, illustrious thro' the earth.
This my lov'd isle, which never more shall grieve
Whilst you, our common friend, our father live.
Then this my prayer, "May earth and heaven survey
A people ever blest beneath thy sway."

(wr. 1758–59/pub. 1770)[74]

JOHN HAWKESWORTH
(? 1715–1773)

An English poet, playwright, journalist, and editor based in Kent, Hawkesworth was an early and close friend of Samuel Johnson's. He wrote for the *Gentleman's Magazine* and produced a variety of successful literary works between 1752 and 1773, including *The Adventurer* (1752–54), *Almoran and Hamet: An Oriental Tale* (1761), *An Account of the Voyages Undertaken in the Southern Hemisphere* (1773), and at least five dramatic pieces.

In the play excerpted below, Hawkesworth rewrote Southerne's *Oroonoko* with two purposes. First, he aimed to eliminate the comic elements that Southerne had intermingled with the main plot. Second, he drew out and amplified the antislavery implications of the play, adding new speeches that articulated the slaves' suffering and hunger for freedom. His version proved successful and was republished several times in the later eighteenth century, with new editions in 1775, 1776, 1777, 1778, 1785, and 1791. Significantly, the passages reprinted here are precisely the same three that Johnson selected for his favorable review of the play in the *Critical Review* (December 1759), thus highlighting the antislavery feeling that the two friends shared.

Hawkesworth uses the "Prologue" both to praise and to distance himself from Southerne, whose inclusion of bawdy comedy detracted, in Hawkesworth's view, from the moral seriousness of the subject.

from the *"Prologue"* to Oroonoko, A Tragedy, as it is Now Acted at the Theatre Royal in Drury-Lane

This night your tributary tears we claim,
For scenes that Southern drew; a fav'rite name!
He touch'd your fathers' hearts with gen'rous woe,
And taught your mothers' youthful eyes to flow;
For this he claims hereditary praise,
From wits and beauties of our modern days;
Yes, slave to custom in a laughing age,

119

With ribbald mirth he stain'd the sacred page;
While virtue's shrine he rear'd, taught vice to mock,
And join'd, in sport, the buskin and the sock;
O! haste to part them!—burst th'opprobrious band!
Thus *art* and *nature,* with one voice demand:
O! haste to part them, blushing *virtue* cries;—
Thus urg'd, our bard this night to part them tries.

The following soliloquy by Oroonoko's chief lieutenant Aboan shows him wrestling inwardly, on the eve of an insurrection, with his fears and hopes. Resisting the slide into passivity that seems to have overcome others, he expresses a loathing for and absolute rejection of the docility that might "steal upon" slaves who become habituated to their captivity.

from Act I, scene iii

 Aboan alone. At length I am alone—but why alone?
My thoughts are worse society to me
Than the poor slaves with whom I'm doom'd to labour—
I cannot bear it—if I turn my view
Backward or forward, round me, or within,
'Tis all regret, oppression, and despair.—
Yet why despair!—something may yet be done;—
May yet be done—hold—let me most distrust
The flatterer Hope—if the one moment lures me
To patient suff'rance, from that fatal moment
Insidious slumbers steal upon my virtue—
I shall—distraction! *must* grow tame by habit—
I must—what else has quench'd in those around me
That indignation which now choaks my utt'rance?
All hell is in the thought—my struggle must be now,
This instant Now—precipitation's wisdom—
  Slaves at a distance.
 Slav. Hoa! hoa, Aboan, Aboan—
 Abo. Hark! here they come—It must, it shall be so—
Hackney'd they are in mis'ries new to me,
Like secret fire that smokeless embers hide.
Yet still the love of liberty must live.

The following song sequence subverts the myth of the "happy slave." The false contentment voiced in the first air is countered by the more compelling truth expressed in the second, that neither love nor any human emotion can flourish in bondage. Significantly, in the closing duet the man has been converted to the woman's view, and both lament the sadness of their plight, as lovers degraded by "the sounding scourge and galling chain."

> *Air by a man.*
> Come let us be gay, to repine is in vain,
> When our loss we forget, what we lose we regain;
> Our toils with the day are all ended at last,
> Let us drown in the present all thoughts of the past,
> All the future commit to the powers above,
> Come, give me a smile as an earnest of love.
>
> > *[To a woman taking her hand, she rises and comes*
> > *slowly forward.]*
>
> *Air by the woman.*
> Ah no—it will not, cannot be,
> Love, love and joy must still be free;
> The toils of day indeed are past,
> And gentle evening comes at last
> But gentle evening comes in vain
> To sooth the slave from sense of pain;
> In vain the song and dance invite,
> To lose reflection in delight;
> Thy voice, thy anxious heart belies,
> I read thy bondage in thy eyes;
> Does not thy heart with mine agree?
> *Man*—Yes, love and joy must both be free.
> *Wom.*—Must both be free, for both disdain
>   The sounding scourge, and galling chain.
> *Man*—'Tis true, alas! they both disdain
>   The sounding scourge, and galling chain.
> *Both together.* Love, love and joy must both be free,
>   They live not but with liberty.
>
> > (1759)[75]

ANONYMOUS

This version of *Oroonoko,* by an unidentified author, appeared a few months after Hawkesworth's and, despite the hopeful phrasing of its title, was apparently never produced. Like Hawkesworth, this author deletes the comic scenes and recasts the play as pure tragedy, while adding characters and speeches that deepen the play's antislavery theme.

In this excerpt from the opening scene, Imoinda protests the practice of slavery and the attendant racism as immoral, uncivilized, and un-British.

from Oroonoko, A Tragedy, Altered from the Original Play of That Name by the Late Thomas Southern . . . Intended for one of the theatres

from Act I, Scene i

> *Imoi.* I have heard, *Maria,* the Isle which gave thee Birth,
> Is mark'd for hospitable Deeds, humane
> Benevolence, extended Charities—
> With ev'ry social Virtue—Is't possible?
> A Nation thus distinguish'd, by the Ties,
> Of soft Humanity, shou'd give its Sanction,
> To its *dependant* States, to exercise,
> This more than savage Right, of thus disposing,
> Like th' marketable Brute, their Fellow-Creatures Blood?
> Whose equal Rectitude of fair Proportion—
> Their Strong Intelligence—their Aptitude,
> In Reason's Rules, loudly, nay, terribly pronounce,
> They stand the equal Work of Reason's God.

In this exchange between Blandford and Maria (an antislavery character added by this author), a common apology for the slave trade—that slaves were better off in captivity than dead on an African battlefield—is refuted in three lines, as untrue to human nature and useless in the face of slave rebellions.

from Act IV, Scene i

> *Blan.* There are, who say, this Practice carries Mercy,
> Rather than Marks of an unfeeling Stamp—
> Since in th' Wars, they wage, each with the other—
> Were not this Channel of commercial Intercourse
> Kept open, th' Pris'ners taken, would exchange
> This Slavery, for cruel, and tormenting Deaths.
>   *Mar.* Reasoning will not weigh with those, who feel
> Th' Oppression—nor *stop* their warm Impatience
> To purchase Freedom, with their Master's Blood.
>
> (1760)[76]

JAMES BEATTIE (1735–1803)

A Scottish poet, essayist, moral philosopher, and academic, Beattie defended Christianity against Hume and other Enlightenment skeptics. Beattie is recorded by contemporaries as having railed against slavery in his lectures at Aberdeen from 1762 to 1793. He wrote many books, including volumes of poetry and a work called *Elements of Moral Science* (1790–93) that contained a strong attack on the slave trade. Beattie composed "The Triumph of Melancholy" at the age of twenty-five, and with it helped establish the new sensibility of the "Graveyard School" of poetry led by Gray, Blair, and Young. Here his depiction of slavery is deliberately abstract, so as to evoke (as Blair had in *The Grave*) a universal image of human disenfranchisement, rather than focus only on African bondage.

from "The Triumph of Melancholy"

Haste, happy Days, and make All Nature glad—
But will All Nature joy at your return?
Say, can ye chear pale Sickness' gloomy bed,
Or dry the tears that bathe th'untimely urn?
Will ye one transient ray of gladness dart
Cross the dark cell where hopeless Slavery lies?
To ease tir'd Disappointment's bleeding heart
Will all your stores of softening balm suffice?
When fell Oppression in his harpy-fangs
From Want's weak grasp the last sad morsel bears,
Can ye allay the heart-wrung parent's pangs,
Whose famish'd child craves help with fruitless tears?
For ah! thy reign, Oppression, is not past.
Who from the shivering limbs the vestment rends?
Who lays the once-rejoicing village waste,
Bursting the tyes of lovers and of friends?

(1760)[77]

JOHN MACLAURIN, LATER LORD DREGHORN (1734–1796)

A Scottish lawyer and man of letters, a friend of Boswell and Johnson, Maclaurin later served with distinction as a Lord Justice on the Court of Session (Scotland's supreme court). Always an opponent of slavery, Maclaurin volunteered in 1774 to represent, gratis, the African slave Joseph Knight who was suing for his freedom in the Scottish courts. Aided by Samuel Johnson and others, Maclaurin eventually won the case, which abolished slavery in Scotland by judicial decision on January 15, 1778.

In the first piece, an excerpt from a meditative poem in the mode of Rousseau, the young Maclaurin voices the kind of idealism that would continue to inform his outlook as he became a leading figure of the Scottish Enlightenment.

from "The Walk"

What woes
The slave-trade, e'vn, ev'n by generous Britons driv'n!
Ambition, avarice, and various ills
Allow'd to rage and ravage on the earth!
The whole creation groans!* as well exclaim'd
The man of Tarsus, and from that remark
Consolatory consequences flow;
That all the living creatures, which compose
The wond'rous links of being's endless chain,
Now struggle through existence, in a state
Imperfect and progressive, that awaits
The final consummation; when, on them,
Felicity eternal and complete,
Shall be bestow'd by Him whose goodness call'd
Them forth into existence. This my creed,
Tho' stigmatiz'd as heretic by priests.

(1760)[78]

---

* [Maclaurin's note]: Epist. to the Romans, chap. viii. ver. 9.

These lines are from a long poem in which Maclaurin systematically criticizes Europe's conquest and exploitation of Africa, Asia, and the New World. Maclaurin's views parallel those of his admired friend Samuel Johnson, who, in his fiercely anti-imperialist introduction to *The World Displayed* (1759), declared: "The Europeans have scarcely visited any coast, but to gratify avarice, and extend corruption; to arrogate dominion without right, and practice cruelty without incentive."

Thoughts Occasioned by Reading L'Histoire General des Voyages

'Mongst all inventions none you'll trace
So hurtful to the human race.
Had *Gama*, less expert at sea,
To India miss'd the watry way:
Had great *Columbus* sought in vain
Another world beyond the main;
Their disappointment, you will find,
Had been a mercy to mankind.

Hot *Afric's* sons, in grief and pain,
Who toil to rear the sugar-cane;
Th' unwarlike natives of *Bengal*,
Whom London citizens inthrall;
Th' *Americans* of ev'ry tribe,
To this position all subscribe.

The first discov'rers were humane,
And gave no reason to complain;
But what an execrable rout
Pursu'd that path they pointed out:
Rapacity, the shining ore,
Soon tempted to the foreign shore;
Him *Murder* follow'd, at whose back
Came *Torture* with his wheel and rack,
And *Slav'ry* with his whip and chain,
And *Bigotry* was of the train,
Whose hands a crucifix uprear,
His shoulders fire and faggot bear.

The hardest heart must heave a sigh,
And moisten ev'n the stoic's eye,
At the recital of the woes
From such invasion that arose.

> Ev'n Europe cause has to repent,
> Her sons on such adventures went.

In the second excerpt, Maclaurin refers to the recent findings of the naturalist Joseph Banks (1743–1820), who voyaged with Captain Cook. Maclaurin points out that the scientific discoveries of the Enlightenment continue to come at considerable cost to the peoples thus "discovered."

> But from this hidden country *Banks,*
> I fear, had merited no thanks;
> Soon numbers must have been devour'd
> By *Europe's* cruel conquering sword,
> Or, ravish'd from their native soil,
> Condemn'd as slaves to endless toil.
> His crew the ladies of those places
> Had smitten with our worst diseases,
> Receiving others in exchange,
> That wou'd exact a great revenge.
>
> (1772)[79]

In this bitter denunciation of world developments in the early 1790s, Maclaurin begins with the bloody events taking place in France and then indicts Britain for its failure, despite the efforts of Wilberforce and his allies, to abolish the slave trade in 1791. The "improvements" of the title are illusory.

from "Verses on the Improvements of the Present Age"

> Think next, what eloquence display'd,
> What persevering efforts made,
> The Slave-trade to suppress:
> Nay more, that statutes we enact
> The beast of burden to protect,
> And make his labour less.
>
> We dine, we dance, at midnight hours,
> Many a fortune play devours,
> And wives are oft untrue:
> But th' imperfections of our day,
> 'Tis evident we much outweigh,
> By virtues that are new.
>
> (1791)[80]

In this rambling antiwar poem, inspired by the convulsions in Europe in the 1790s, Maclaurin condemns all regimes, past and present, that espouse the ideal of freedom yet practice slavery. He notes this recurrent contradiction in ancient Greece, Brutus's Rome, and, most recently, in George Washington's America.

from "Address to the Powers at War"

Greece how enabl'd to resist
Th'invasive millions of the East,
   To conquer nations Rome;
The Transatlantic planters how
The parent state to disavow,
   And Freedom's flag assume:

Yet as o'er slaves they tyranniz'd,
Their species' rights they sacrific'd,
   The many to the few;
And were Republics but in name,
Exhibited by partial Fame,
   As models to the view.

With them the citizens were kings,
The slaves not *persons* deem'd, but *things*
   Below the law's regard;
Hence every insult, grief, and pain,
That pow'r and passion could ordain,
   Th' abandon'd wretches shar'd.

Brutus ought to have hugg'd the chain,
Still less could Washington complain
   Of Britain's stamping tax;
To Freedom's genuine feelings lost
As each of slaves possess'd a host,—
   One whites, the other blacks.

In the final section of "Address to the Powers at War," Maclaurin turns from continental Europe to address "his native land" and outline "what [Britain] in future ought to do." Tellingly, his vision of progress takes as its starting point the problem of slavery.

Begin with Afric's sable race;—
But 'twere superfluous to trace
   The slave's progressive woes;
For not Apollo's self, in verse,

JOHN MACLAURIN

So well the story could rehearse
  As *Pitt* has done in prose.

Despotic power, arch sorceress!
More drastic poisons you possess
  Than Circe's magic bowl;
She metamorphos'd but the shape,
You, that permitting to escape,
  Unhumanize the soul.*

Th' impracticable task assign,
Instruct Injustice to combine
  Barbarity with art;
Not men alone forbid to feel,
But harden with no common steel
  The female planter's heart.†

Not the coincidence of sex,
That oft deserv'd chastisement checks,
  Her lawless lash arrests;
Nay, urg'd by her imperious cries,
The shock'd unwilling flogger plies
  The thong against the breasts.

She stands, the fury! in delight,
Her eyes regaling with a fight
  That Beelzebub would shun:
Great God! that ever woman could
See whip-extracted milk and blood
  In hideous contrast run.

But th' unsuspecting negro-maid,
Whom force compell'd, or fraud betray'd,
  To the kidnapping knave;
Tho' bitterly she wept, when sold,
Some consolation took when told
  She was a lady's slave.

Can Britons, who, with shudd'ring ear,
The horrible recital hear,
  A speedy change dissuade;
Or balance to forego the juice,

* [Maclaurin's note:] See the *Odyssey,* Book X.
† [Maclaurin's note:] See Steadman's *Voyages,* lately published, particularly Vol. II. P. 293.

Whose costly and too common use
   Maintains the monst'rous trade?

"How came (they'll cry) the candied cane,
From Nature's pencil to obtain
   The whiteness of the snow?
Fit but the black, or crimson dye,
Of carnage this the livery,
   The habit that of woe.

From our disgusted sight begone,
Ye fragments of the luscious cone,
   That sweeten bitter tea;
The blendid tastes no more allure,
Unless Humanity procure,
   The sugar that is free."

                         (1796)[81]

BRYAN EDWARDS (1743–1800)

Edwards's poems consistently express sympathy and admiration for the African slaves in Jamaica. By his later years, however, he had become an apologist for slavery who preferred amelioration to emancipation. Born and educated in England, Edwards came to Jamaica at age seventeen, where he eventually became quite prosperous. Meanwhile he wrote several books, including *History of the British Colonies in the West Indies* (1793) and *An Historical Survey of St. Domingo* (1797), both of which recount the history of slavery and slave rebellions in detail. He moved back and forth between Britain and the West Indies, standing several times (in 1796, successfully) for Parliament. He published pieces intermittently in the British press, and eventually collected his verse in *Poems Written Chiefly in the West Indies* (Kingston, 1792). His work shows how complex and contradictory the feelings of the plantation master class could be.

The first poem below, "The Death of Alico," displays the sympathies of the eighteen-year-old Edwards, newly arrived in Jamaica. Remarkably, coming just after the bloodiest slave insurrection of the century, Edwards's poem seems to glorify the failed rebels' cause. His speaker, a condemned slave, faces death with pathos and dignity, defiant to the end.

Stanzas, Occasioned by the Death of Alico, An African Slave, Condemned for Rebellion, in Jamaica, 1760

(He is supposed to address himself to his wife at the place of execution.)

'Tis past:—Ah! calm thy cares to rest!
  Firm and unmov'd am I:—
In Freedom's cause, I bar'd my breast,—
  In freedom's cause I die.

Ah stop! thou dost me fatal wrong:—
  Nature will yet rebel;
For I have lov'd thee very long,
  And lov'd thee very well.

To native skies and peaceful bow'rs,
    I soon shall wing my way;
Where joy shall lead the circling hours,
    Unless too long they stay.

O speed, fair sun! thy course divine;
    My ABALA remove;—
There thy bright beams shall ever shine,
    And I forever love!

On those blest shores—a slave no more!
    In peaceful ease I'll stray;
Or rouse to chace the mountain boar,
    As unconfin'd as day!

No christian tyrant there is known
    To mark his steps with blood,
No sable mis'ry's piercing moan
    Resounds thro ev'ry wood!

Yet have I heard the melting tongue,
    Have seen the falling tear,
Known the good heart by pity wrung,
    Ah! that such hearts are rare!

Now, Christian, glut thy ravish'd eyes,
    —I reach the joyful hour;
Now bid the scorching flames arise,
    And these poor limbs devour.

But know, pale tyrant, 'tis not thine
    Eternal war to wage;
The death thou giv'st shall but combine
    To mock thy baffled rage.

O death how welcome to th'opprest!
    Thy kind embrace I crave!
Thou bring'st to mis'ry's bosom rest,
    And *freedom to the slave!*

               (c. 1760)[82]

    These excerpts from Edwards's long unfinished georgic project a poetic fantasy onto the Jamaican landscape: limpid waters, languid (black) nymphs, sunshine and luxuriant nature everywhere. Eventually the terrible disjunction between idyll and reality struck even the poet himself. Edwards later said his "maturer judgment" led him to drop the idea and abandon the poem.

BRYAN EDWARDS

from Book I of "Jamaica, a Descriptive and Didactic Poem"

Ever gently roll, sweet stream, as now
Soft murm'ring; in thy chrystal waters still
May languor solace, and affliction's sons
Drink sweet oblivion. Bathe your wearied limbs,
Ye Lybian maidens, unreprov'd, unaw'd:
(Nor sportive smiles, nor hov'ring loves, disdain
Your harmless revels.) While the yielding wave
Some clasp with circling arm, and buoyant float
The profluent eddy; others, bolder still,
Plunge in the blue profound, and pleas'd far off
Emerge exulting. In the jocund toil
They waste th'unconscious hours; forgot awhile—
Could slavery but forget—past cruel wrongs,
And dread of future woes. But soon (too soon!)
The sportive smiles, and hov'ring loves, are fled—
For now, the bank obtain'd (th'invidious term
Of sweet indulgence pass'd) afflictive thought,
And aching memory, and anxious dread,
Cloud each dejected brow. Soft Ebo* nymphs
Awake the plaintive lay; their own sad fate,
Torn from their native fields and sable loves,
Lamenting loud. The hard impending rocks
Their sighs re-echo, and Agualta flows
In deeper murmurs. On the willow'd bank,
By Babylon's proud stream, thus Israel's sons
Bewail'd their captive doom, and Zion lost!

(c. 1763)[83]

In this elegy for a fellow white Jamaican, first published in the *Gentleman's Magazine* of 1764, Edwards emphasizes his friend Teale's compassion for the slaves. Edwards later included one of Teale's poems, a lyric tribute to an unnamed black woman, "The Sable Venus," in his own collection of 1792.

from "Elegy on the Death of a Friend [Isaac Teale]"

Nor folly's voice, nor envy's rage obscene,
    Thy gentle ghost, lamented friend, shall wound:

* [Edwards's note:] The Ebo Negroes are the gentlest and mildest of all the nations of Africa. They never rise into rebellion; but often sink under a sense of their condition, and destroy themselves.

Pure as thyself, shall kindred forms unseen
  Protect from aught profane the hallow'd ground.

Constant as eve, shall the poor Lybian slave
  Drag to Eugenio's turf his galling chain;
Then press, with accents wild, th'unconscious grave,
  And lift to heav'n th'imploring eye in vain.

For *he* still sympathiz'd in mis'ry's moan,
  And sooth'd the heart-drawn anguish of despair:
What *he* then paid to sorrows not his own,
  O pay to him——the tribute of a tear!

(c. 1764)[84]

In this elegiac ode, Edwards takes a slave's funeral as an occasion to reflect on the injustice of slavery. In this vision, death delivers the slave to an idyllic afterlife in his beloved Africa. Meanwhile a brutal vengeance is prophesied, in graphic terms, for the heartless Christians who had enslaved him.

"Ode, on Seeing a Negro Funeral"

Omalco dies! O'er yonder plain
His bier is borne; the sable train
  By youthful virgins led:
Daughters of injur'd Africk, say
Why raise ye thus th'heroic lay,
  Why triumph o'er the dead?

No tear bedews their fixed eye!——
'Tis now the hero lives, they cry,
  Releas'd from slav'ry's chain:
Far o'er the billowy surge he flies,
And joyful views his native skies,
  And long-lost bow'rs again.

On Koromantin's palmy soil,
Heroic deeds and martial toil
  Shall fill each glorious day:
Love, fond and faithful, crown thy nights,
And artless joys, unbought delights,
  Past cruel wrongs repay.

Nor lordly pride's stern av'rice there,
Alone, shall nature's bounties share;
  To all her children free:

For thee, the dulcet reed shall spring,
Her milky bowl the coco bring,
    Th'anana bloom for thee.

The thunder, hark!—'Tis Africk's god!
He wakes; he lifts th'avenging rod,
    And speeds th'impatient hours:
From Niger's golden stream he calls;
Fair freedom comes; oppression falls,
    And vengeance yet is ours!

Soon, Christian, thou, in wild dismay,
Of Africk's ruthless rage the prey,
    Shalt roam th'affrighted wood:
Transform'd to tygers, fierce and fell,
Thy race shall prowl with savage yell,
    And glut their rage for blood!

But soft—beneath yon tam'rind shade,
Now let the hero's limbs be laid;
    Sweet slumbers bless the brave:
There shall the breezes shed perfume,
Nor livid light'nings blast the bloom
        That decks Omalco's grave!
                    (c. 1773)[85]

Apparently a "found poem," this graveyard inscription shows that the influence of Gray's "Elegy Written in a Country Churchyard" (1751) extended to the outer reaches of the British colonial world. The epitaph romanticizes the anonymous African dead buried in their humble graveyard, in language that echoes Gray's tribute to the forgotten peasantry of rural England. Whether Edwards composed it himself or merely copied it down where he found it remains uncertain.

Inscription, over the Wicket of an Inclosed Burial-Ground for Negroes, in Trelawny Parish, Jamaica

Stranger or friend, with silent rev'rence tread,
Lo these, the lonely mansions of the dead!
His life of labour o'er, the wearied slave
Here finds at length soft quiet in the grave.
View not with proud disdain th'unsculptur'd heap,

Where injur'd innocence forgets to weep;
Nor idly deem, altho' not here are found
The solemn aisle and consecrated ground,
The spot less sacred: O'er the turf-built shrine,
Where virtue sleeps, presides the Pow'r Divine!

(c. 1776)[86]

JUPITER HAMMON (1711–?1800)

The first published African American poet, Jupiter Hammon was a slave who belonged to the Lloyd Family of Queens Village, Long Island (now in Queens, New York City). His poetry celebrates his deep Christian faith, which, given his status as a slave owned by Christians, is perplexing to many modern readers. The issue of slavery rarely surfaces in his verse, except as background. In 1786, however, he treated the topic in his *Address to the Negroes of the State of New York*, in which he shows a willingness to bear slavery meekly (for now) but expresses his disapproval and calls for eventual emancipation.

The following poem is the first ever printed by an African slave in America. In it, Hammon takes Christmas as the occasion for a religious meditation on salvation, a word that appears no fewer than twenty-three times in eighty-eight lines. The hymn-like metrics suggest the poem was probably meant to be sung.

An Evening Thought. Salvation By Christ, with Penetential Cries: Composed by Jupiter Hammon, a Negro belonging to Mr Lloyd, of Queen's-Village, on Long-Island, the 25th of December, 1760

SALVATION comes by Jesus Christ alone,
    The only son of God;
Redemption now to every one,
    That love his holy Word.
Dear Jesus we would fly to Thee,
    And leave off every Sin,
Thy tender Mercy well agree;
    Salvation from our King.
Salvation comes now from the Lord,
    Our victorious King;
His holy Name be well ador'd,
    Salvation surely bring.

Dear Jesus give thy Spirit now,
    Thy grace to every Nation,
That han't the Lord to whom we bow,
    The Author of Salvation.
Dear Jesus unto Thee we cry,
    Give us thy Preparation;
Turn not away thy tender Eye;
    We seek thy true Salvation.
Salvation comes from God we know,
    The true and only One;
It's well agreed and certain true,
    He gave his only Son.
Lord hear our penetential Cry:
    Salvation from above;
It is the Lord that doth supply,
    With his Redeeming Love.
Dear Jesus by thy precious Blood,
    The World Redemption have:
Salvation comes now from the Lord,
    He being thy captive Slave.
Dear Jesus let the Nations cry,
    And all the People say,
Salvation comes from Christ on high,
    Haste on Tribunal Day.
We cry as Sinners to the Lord,
    Salvation to obtain;
It is firmly fixt his holy Word,
    Ye shall not cry in vain.
Dear Jesus unto Thee we cry,
    And make our Lamentation:
O let our Prayers ascend on high;
    We felt thy Salvation.
Lord turn our dark benighted Souls;
    Give us a true Motion,
And let the Hearts of all the World,
    Make Christ their Salvation.
Ten Thousand Angels cry to Thee,
    Yea louder than the Ocean.
Thou art the Lord, we plainly see;
    Thou art the true Salvation.
Now is the Day, excepted Time;
    The Day of Salvation;

Increase your Faith, do not repine:
    Awake ye every Nation.
Lord unto whom now shall we go,
    Or seek a safe Abode;
Thou hast the Word Salvation too
    The only Son of God.
Ho! every one that hunger hath,
    Or pineth after me,
Salvation be thy leading staff,
    To set the sinner free.
Dear Jesus unto Thee we fly;
    Depart, depart from Sin,
Salvation doth at length supply,
    The Glory of our King.
Come ye Blessed of the Lord,
    Salvation gently given;
O turn your Hearts, accept the Word,
    Your Souls are fit for Heaven.
Dear Jesus we now turn to Thee,
    Salvation to obtain;
Our Hearts and Souls do meet again,
    To magnify thy Name.
Come holy Spirit, Heavenly Dove,
    The Object of our Care;
Salvation doth increase our Love;
    Our Hearts hath felt thy fear.
Now Glory be to God on High,
    Salvation high and low;
And thus the soul on Christ rely,
    To Heaven surely go.
Come Blessed Jesus, Heavenly Dove,
    Accept Repentance here;
Salvation give, with tender Love;
    Let us with Angels share.
        (wr. 1760/pub. 1761)[87]

Hammon's poem to Phillis Wheatley marks a major moment in American literary history: the self-conscious identification of one African American writer with another, his poem in dialogue with hers, on the issues of slavery, freedom, and salvation. In particular, stanzas two, four, and five take up the theme of her most famous poem, "On Being Brought from Africa to America" ("'Twas mercy brought me from my native land"). The marginal citations from the Bible, much like those found in sermons and other religious texts, serve as a gloss on the poem and provide a parallel body of readings that deepen and extend his message.

AN ADDRESS to Miss PHILLIS WHEATLY, Ethiopian Poetess, in Boston, who came from Africa at eight years of age, and soon became acquainted with the Gospel of Jesus Christ

Miss WHEATLY; pray give leave to express as follows:

1.

O Come you pious youth! adore
    The wisdom of thy God,   Eccles[iastes]. xii.
In bringing thee from distant shore,
    To learn his holy word.

2.

Thou mightst been left behind,
    Amidst a dark abode;   Psal[ms]. cxxxv,2,3.
God's tender mercy still combin'd,
    Thou hast the holy word.

3.

Fair wisdom's ways are paths of peace,
    And they that walk therein,   Psalm. i.1,2.
Shall reap the joys that never cease,   Prov[erbs]. iii,7.
    And Christ shall be their king.

4.

God's tender mercy brought thee here,
    Tost o'er the raging main;   Psalm. ciii,1,3,4.
In Christian faith thou hast a share,
    Worth all the gold of Spain.

5.

While thousands tossed by the sea,
    And others settled down,   Death.
God's tender mercy set thee free
    From dangers still unknown.

6.

That thou a pattern still might be,
    To youth of Boston town,   2 Cor[inthians].
The blessed Jesus set thee free,   v,10.
    From every sinful wound.

7.

The blessed Jesus, who came down,
    Unvail'd his sacred face,   Rom[ans]. v,21.
To cleanse the soul of every wound,
    And give repenting grace.

8.

That we poor sinners may obtain
    The pardon of our sin;   Psalm. xxxiv,6,7,8.
Dear blessed Jesus now constrain,
    And bring us flocking in.

9.

Come you, Phillis, now aspire,
    And seek the living God,   Matth[ew]. vii,7,8.
So step by step thou mayst go higher,
    Till perfect in the word.

10.

While thousands mov'd to distant shore,
    And others left behind,   Psalm. lxxxix,1.
The blessed Jesus still adore,
    Implant this in thy mind.

11.

Thou hast left the heathen shore,
    Thro' mercy of the Lord,   Psalm. xxxiv,1,2,3.
Among the heathen live no more,
    Come magnify thy God.

12.

I pray the living God may be,
    The shepherd of thy soul;   Psalm. lxxx,1,2,3.
His tender mercies still are free,
    His mysteries to unfold.

13.

Thou, Phillis, when thou hunger hast,
    Or pantest for thy God;   Psalm. xiii,1,2,3.
Jesus Christ is thy relief,
    Thou hast the holy word.

14.

The bounteous mercies of the Lord,
    Are hid beyond the sky,   Psalm. xvi,10,11.
And holy souls that love his word,
    Shall taste them when they die.

15.
These bounteous mercies are from God,
    The merits of his Son;   Psalm. xxxiv,15.
The humble soul that loves his word,
    He chooses for his own.

16.
Come, dear Phillis, be advis'd,
    To drink Samaria's flood: John iv,13,14.
There nothing is that shall suffice,
    But Christ's redeeming blood.

17.
While thousands muse with earthly toys,
    And range about the street,   Matth. vi,33.
Dear Phillis, seek for heaven's joys,
    Where we do hope to meet.

18.
When God shall send his summons down,
    And number saints together,   Psalm. cxvi, 15.
Best angels chant, (triumphant sound)
    Come live with me for ever.

19.
The humble soul shall fly to God,
    And leave the things of time,   Matth. v,3,8.
Start forth as 'twere at the first word,
    To taste things more divine.

20.
Behold! the soul shall waft away,
    Whene'er we come to die,   1 Cor. xv,51,52,53.
And leave its cottage made of clay,
    In twinkling of an eye.

21.
Now glory be to the Most High,
    United praises given,   Psalm. cl,6.
By all on earth incessantly,
    And all the host of heav'n.

(1778)[88]

In the following excerpts from a poetic dialogue that runs to thirty stanzas, Hammon raises a dangerous topic: the power relations between master and servant/slave. While carefully affirming the servant's obedience, the poem subtly undermines the unconditional authority the master asserts in the opening lines ("follow me / According to thy place"). The servant finds several ways to say that he will obey the master so long as the master himself serves the God they both worship. For all its reverence, the poem remains essentially a quiet act of resistance and a lesson in humility for the master.

from "A Dialogue; Entitled, the Kind Master and [the] Dutiful Servant"

1. *Master.*
Come my servant, follow me,
According to thy place;
And surely God will be with thee,
And send the heav'nly grace.

2. *Servant.*
Dear Master, I will follow thee,
According to thy word,
And pray that God may be with me,
And save thee in the Lord.

3. *Master.*
My Servant, lovely is the Lord,
And blest those servants be,
That truly love his holy word,
And thus will follow me.

4. *Servant.*
Dear Master, that's my whole delight,
Thy pleasure for to do;
As far as grace and truth's in sight,
Thus far I'll surely go.

5. *Master.*
My Servant, grace proceeds from God,
And truth should be with thee;
Whence e'er you find it in his word,
Thus far come follow me.

6. *Servant.*
Dear Master, now without controul,
I quickly follow thee;
And pray that God would bless thy soul,
His heav'nly place to see.

7. *Master.*

My Servant, Heaven is high above,
Yea, higher than the sky:
I pray that God would grant his love,
Come follow me thereby.

8. *Servant.*

Dear Master, now I'll follow thee,
And trust upon the Lord;
The only safety that I see,
Is Jesus's holy word.

9. *Master.*

My Servant, follow Jesus now,
Our great victorious King;
Who governs all both high and low,
And searches things within.

10. *Servant.*

Dear Master I will follow thee,
When praying to our King;
It is the Lamb I plainly see,
Invites the sinner in.

11. *Master.*

My Servant, we are sinners all,
But follow after grace;
I pray that God would bless thy soul,
And fill thy heart with grace.

12. *Servant.*

Dear Master I shall follow then,
The voice of my great King;
As standing on some distant land,
Inviting sinners in. . . .

19. *Master.*

We pray that God would give us grace,
And make us humble too;
Let ev'ry nation seek for peace,
And virtue make a show.

20. *Servant.*

Then we shall see the happy day,
That virtue is in power;
Each holy act shall have its sway,
Extend from shore to shore.

21. *Master.*
This is the work of God's own hand,
We see by precepts given;
To relieve distress and save the land,
Must be the pow'r of heav'n.

22. *Servant.*
Now glory be unto our God,
Let ev'ry nation sing;
Strive to obey his holy word,
That Christ may take them in.

23. *Master.*
Where endless joys shall never cease,
Blest Angels constant sing;
The glory of their God increase,
Hallelujahs to their King.

24. *Servant.*
Thus the Dialogue shall end,
Strive to obey the word;
When ev'ry nation act like friends,
Shall be the sons of God.

25.
Believe me now my Christian friends,
Believe your friend call'd HAMMON:
You cannot to your God attend,
And serve the God of Mammon. . . .

(1782)[89]

ISAAC TEALE (d. 1764)

Little is known of Isaac Teale except that he was a Church of England clergyman, a friend and mentor to Bryan Edwards in his early years in Jamaica, and, if the poem is to be believed, an ardent admirer of black beauty. In its stylized language, rife with Shakespearean echoes, the poem compares black women favorably with white beauties and explores the complex nature of black-white romantic relationships in a slave society. The poem seems to allude to real people, but how far it is rooted in Teale's own life remains a mystery.

from The Sable Venus: An Ode

Erato smil'd to see me come;
Ask'd why I staid so much at home;—
   I own'd my conduct wrong;
But now, the sable queen of love,
Resolv'd my gratitude to prove,
   Had sent me for a song.

The ladies look'd extremely shy,
Apollo's smile was arch and sly,
   But not one word they said.—
I gaz'd, sure silence is consent,
I made my bow, away I went;
   Was not my duty paid?

Come to my bosom genial fire,
Soft sounds, and lively thoughts inspire,
   Unusual is my theme.
Not such dissolving *Ovid* sung,
Nor melting *Sappho's* glowing tongue,—
   More dainty mine I deem.

Sweet is the beam of morning bright,
Yet sweet the sober shade of night.

ISAAC TEALE

On rich *Angola's* shores
While beauty clad in sable dye,
Enchanting fires the wond'ring eye,
    Farewel! ye *Paphian* bow'rs.

O sable queen! thy mild domain
I seek, and court thy gentle reign,
    So soothing soft and sweet:
Where meeting love, sincere delight,
Fond pleasure, ready joys invite,
    And all true raptures meet.

The prating *Frank,* the *Spaniard* proud,
The double *Scot, Hibernian* loud,
    And sullen *English* own
The pleasing softness of thy sway,
And here, transferr'd allegiance pay,
    For gracious is thy throne.

From east to west, o'er either Ind
Thy scepter sways, thy pow'r we find
    By both the tropics felt:
The blazing sun, that gilds the zone
Waits but the triumphs of thy throne,
    Quite round the burning belt.

When thou, this large domain to view,
Jamaica's isle, thy conquest new,
    First left thy native shore,
Gay was the morn, and soft the breeze,
With wanton joy the curling seas
    The beauteous burthen bore.

Of iv'ry was the car, inlaid
With ev'ry shell of lively shade,
    The throne was burnish'd gold:
The footstool, gay with coral beam'd,
The wheels with brightest amber gleam'd,
    And, glist'ring round they rowl'd. . . .

Her skin excell'd the raven's plume,
Her breath the fragrant orange bloom,
    Her eye the tropic beam:
Soft was her lip as silken down,
And mild her look as ev'ning sun
    That gilds the *Cobre* stream.

The loveliest limbs her form compose,
Such as her sister *Venus* chose,
   In *Florence,* where she's seen:
Both just alike, except the white,
No difference, no,—none at night,
   The beauteous dames between.

With native ease, serene she sat,
In elegance of charms compleat,
   And ev'ry heart she won:
False dress deformity may shade,
True beauty courts no foreign aid;
   Can tapers light the sun?—

The pow'r that rules old ocean wide,
'Twas he, they say, had calm'd the tide,
   Beheld the chariot rowl:
Assum'd the figure of a tar,
The Captain of a man of war,
   And told her all his soul.

She smil'd, with kind consenting eyes,
Beauty was ever valour's prize;
   He rais'd a murky cloud:
The tritons sound, the sirens sing,
The dolphins dance, the billows ring,
   And joy fills all the croud.

Blest offspring of the warm embrace!
Gay ruler of the saffron race!
   Tho' strong thy bow, dear boy,
Thy mingled shafts of black and white,
Are wing'd with feathers of delight,
   Their points are tipt with joy.

But when her step had touch'd the strand,
Wild rapture seiz'd the ravish'd land,
   From ev'ry part they came:
Each mountain, valley, plain, and grove
Haste eagerly to shew their love,
   Right welcome was the dame.

Port-Royal shouts were heard aloud,
Gay *St. Jago* sent a croud,
   Grave *Kingston* not a few:
No rabble rout, I heard it said,

Some great ones joined the cavalcade—
   I can't indeed say who.

Gay Goddess of the sable smile!
Propitious still, this grateful isle
   With thy protection bless!
Here fix, secure, thy constant throne;
Where all, adoring thee, do one,
   One Deity confess. . . .

Then, playful goddess! cease to change,
Nor in new beauties vainly range;
   Tho' whatsoe'er thy view,
Try ev'ry form thou canst put on,
I'll follow thee thro' ev'ry one,
   So staunch am I, so true.

Do thou in gentle *Phibba* smile,
In artful *Benneba* beguile,
   In wanton *Mimba* pout;
In sprightly *Cuba's* eyes look gay,
Or grave in sober *Quasheba*,
   I still shall find thee out.

Just now, in *Auba's* easy mien;
I think I saw my roving queen,
   I will be sure tonight:
Send *Quaco*, gentle girl, from home,
I would not have him see me come;
   Why should we mad him quite?

Thus have I sung, perhaps too gay
Such subject for such time of day,
   And fitter far for youth:
Should then the song too wanton seem,
You know who chose th'unlucky theme,
   Dear Bryan tell the truth.
         (c. 1760–63)[90]

CHARLES CHURCHILL
(1731–1764)

A prolific, erratic, and volatile satirist, Churchill was an impoverished clergyman who also, from age twenty-nine, pursued a London writing career. Notorious for his political wrangling, dissipated ways, and drunken outbursts, Churchill produced some of the most potent verse satire of the mid-century before suddenly dying of a fever in 1764. *Gotham*, a sustained attack on European imperialism, was one of six full-length verse satires he published in the year of his death.

The opening of Book I frames the whole vision of "Gotham" as an imaginary utopian alternative to the devastation caused by European expansionism. Churchill lacerates the hypocrisy of European (particularly British) imperialist rhetoric, that justifies the conquest and enslavement of "savage" peoples in the name of spreading Christian faith.

from Book I of Gotham

Far off (no matter whether east or west,
A real country, or one made in jest) . . .
There lies an island, neither great nor small,
Which, for distinction sake, I Gotham call.
 The man who finds an unknown country out,
By giving it a name, acquires, no doubt,
A Gospel title, though the people there
The pious Christian thinks not worth his care;
Bar this pretence, and into air is hurl'd
The claim of Europe to the Western world.
 Cast by a tempest on the savage coast,
Some roving buccaneer set up a post;
A beam, in proper form transversely laid,
Of his Redeemer's cross the figure made,
Of that Redeemer, with whose laws of life,

From first to last, had been one scene of strife;
His royal master's name thereon engraved,
Without more process, the whole race enslaved,
Cut off that charter they from Nature drew,
And made them slaves to men they never knew.

    Search ancient histories, consult records,
Under this title the most Christian lords
Hold (thanks to conscience) more than half the ball;
O'erthrow this title, they have none at all;
For never yet might any monarch dare,
Who lived to truth, and breathed a Christian air,
Pretend that Christ, (who came, we all agree,
To bless his people, and to set them free)
To make a convert ever one law gave
By which converters made him first a slave. . . .

    Never shall one, truly honest man,
Who, bless'd with Liberty, reveres her plan,
Allow one moment, that a savage sire
Could from his wretched race, for childish hire,
By a wild grant, their all, their freedom pass,
And sell his country for a bit of glass.

    Or grant this barbarous right, let Spain and France,
In slavery bred, as purchasers advance;
Let them, whilst conscience is at distance hurl'd,
With some gay bauble buy a golden world:
An Englishman, in charter'd freedom born,
Shall spurn the slavish merchandize, shall scorn
To take from others, through base private views,
What he himself would rather die, than lose.

    Happy the savage of those early times,
Ere Europe's sons were known, and Europe's crimes!
Gold, cursed gold! slept in the womb of earth,
Unfelt its mischiefs, as unknown its worth . . .

    Happy, thrice happy, now the savage race,
Since Europe took their gold, and gave them grace!
Pastors she sends to help them in their need,
Some who can't write, with others who can't read;
And on sure grounds the Gospel pile to rear,
Sends missionary felons every year;
Our vices, with more zeal than holy prayers,
She teaches them, and in return takes theirs:
Her rank oppressions give them cause to rise;

Her want of prudence, means and arms supplies,
Whilst her brave rage, not satisfied with life,
Rising in blood, adopts the scalping-knife:
Knowledge she gives, enough to make them know
How abject is their state, how deep their woe;
The worth of freedom strongly she explains,
Whilst she bows down and loads their necks with chains:
Faith, too, she plants, for her own ends imprest,
To make them bear the worst and hope the best;
And whilst she teaches, on vile interest's plan,
As laws of God, the wild decrees of man,
Like Pharisees, of whom the Scriptures tell,
She makes them ten times more the sons of Hell.
    But whither do these grave reflections tend?
Are they design'd for any, or no end?
Briefly but this—to prove, that by no act
Which Nature made, that by no equal pact
'Twixt man and man, which might, if Justice heard,
Stand good; that by no benefits conferr'd,
Or purchase made, Europe in chains can hold
The sons of India, and her mines of gold.
Chance led her there in an accursed hour;
She saw, and made the country hers by power . . .
    Europe discover'd India first; I found
My right to Gotham on the self-same ground . . .
With Europe's rights my kindred rights I twine;
Hers be the Western world, be Gotham mine.

(1764)[91]

JAMES GRAINGER (1721?–1766)

Physician and writer, Grainger worked as a military surgeon, an overseer on a West Indian slave plantation, and a London poet. A friend of Samuel Johnson's and a member of his circle, Grainger was one of the few writers who had lived in a slave-holding colony. Following in the tradition of Virgil, James Thomson, and John Dyer, Grainger intended his long agricultural poem *The Sugar-Cane* to convey to a British readership an edifying vision of the land, economy, and society of an island plantation. Although Grainger acknowledges how dangerously dependent colonials are on slave labor, and he repeatedly urges reforms, his poem overall envisions slaveholding as essential to a viable, even ideal, Caribbean society.

This excerpt is the first of several instances in which Grainger advocates the "humane" treatment of slaves. The passage echoes a line in Gray's "Elegy" ("And shut the gates of mercy on mankind,") that is, curiously, the same line Boswell invokes in *The Life of Johnson* (1791) when trying to rebut Johnson's antislavery views. Like Boswell, Grainger did not call for an end to slavery, but instead advocated ameliorative measures.

from Book I of The Sugar-Cane

The gemmy summits of the Cane await
Thy Negroe-train, (in linen lightly wrapt,)
Who now that painted Iris girds the sky,
(Aerial arch, which Fancy loves to stride!)
Disperse, all-jocund, o'er the long-hoed land.

    The bundles some untie; the withered leaves,
Others strip artful off, and careful lay,
Twice one junk, distant in the amplest bed:
O'er these, with hasty hoe, some lightly spread
The mounded interval; and smooth the trench:

Well-pleas'd, the master-swain reviews their toil;
And rolls, in fancy, many a full-fraught cask. . . .

[slave addresses his son:] "Whate'er their creed, God is the Sire of man,
His image they; then dare not thou, my son,
To bar the gates of mercy on mankind.
Your foes forgive, for merit must make foes;
And in each virtue far surpass your fire.
Your means are ample, Heaven a heart bestow!
So health and peace shall be your portion here;
And yon bright sky, to which my soul aspires,
Shall bless you with eternity of joy."

In this excerpt, Grainger tries to establish his poem in the georgic tradition of poets like Dyer who idealize agricultural life. Inevitably, though, the brutality of slavery (here compounded by the cruelty of a black slave driver) disrupts the bucolic vision. Even the Muse "averts her . . . ear."

from Book III of The Sugar-Cane

What of the Cane
Remains, and much the largest part remains,
Cut into junks a yard in length, and tied
In small light bundles; load the broad-wheel'd wane,
The mules crook-harnest, and the sturdier crew,
With sweet abundance. As on Lincoln-plains,
(Ye plains of Lincoln sound your Dyer's praise!)
When the lav'd snow-white flocks are numerous penn'd;
The senior swains, with sharpen'd shears, cut off
The fleecy vestment; others stir the tar;
And some impress, upon their captives sides,
Their master's cypher. . . .
  Nor need the driver, Æthiop authoriz'd,
Thence more inhuman, crack his horrid whip;
From such dire sounds the indignant muse averts
Her virgin-ear, where musick loves to dwell:
'Tis malice now, 'tis wantonness of power
To lash the laughing, labouring, singing throng.

When it was published in 1764, Grainger's Book IV was the longest sustained treatment of African slavery to have appeared in English poetry. It presents in great detail every aspect of slave life, from capture in Africa, to sale at auction, to working conditions, diseases, social customs, and religious rituals. For all of Grainger's self-professed humanity, readers have long been struck by his blindness to the indefensible evil of slavery. Grainger's admired friend Samuel Johnson, for example, publicly criticized him for discussing the slave trade "without the least appearance of detestation."

from Book IV of The Sugar-Cane

Planter, chuse the slave,
Who sails from barren climes; where art alone,
Offspring of rude necessity, compells
The sturdy native, or to plant the soil,
Or stem vast rivers for his daily food.
    Such are the children of the Golden Coast;
Such the Papaws, of negroes far the best:
And such the numerous tribes, that skirt the shore,
From rapid Volta to the distant Rey.
    But, planter, from what coast soe'er they sail,
Buy not the old: they ever sullen prove;
With heart-felt anguish, they lament their home;
They will not, cannot work; they never learn
Thy native language; they are prone to ails;
And oft by suicide their being end.—
    Must thou from Africk reinforce thy gang?—
Let health and youth their every sinew firm;
Clear roll their ample eye; their tongue be red;
Broad swell their chest; their shoulders wide expand;
Not prominent their belly; clean and strong
Their thighs and legs, in just proportion rise.
Such soon will brave the fervours of the clime;
And free from ails, that kill thy negroe-train,
A useful servitude will long support.
    Yet, if thine own, thy childrens life, be dear;
Buy not a Cormantee, tho' healthy, young.
Of breed too generous for the servile field;
They, born to freedom in their native land,
Chuse death before dishonourable bonds:
Or, fir'd with vengeance, at the midnight hour,
Sudden they seize thine unsuspecting watch,
And thine own poinard bury in thy breast. . . .
    The slaves from Minnah are of stubborn breed:

But, when the bill, or hammer, they affect;
They soon perfection reach. But fly, with care,
The Moco-nation; they themselves destroy.
    Worms lurk in all: yet, pronest they to worms,
Who from Mundingo sail. When therefore such
Thou buy'st, for sturdy and laborious they,
Straight let some learned leach strong medicines give,
Till food and climate both familiar grow. . . .

Nor, Negroe, at thy destiny repine,
Tho' doom'd to toil from dawn to setting sun.
How far more pleasant is thy rural task,
Than theirs who sweat, sequester'd from the day,
In dark tartarean caves, sunk far beneath
The earth's dark surface; where sulphureous flames,
Oft from their vapoury prisons bursting wild,
To dire explosion give the cavern'd deep,
And in dread ruin all its inmates whelm?—
Nor fateful only is the bursting flame;
The exhalations of the deep-dug mine,
Tho' slow, shake from their wings as sure a death.
With what intense severity of pain
Hath the afflicted muse, in Scotia, seen
The miners rack'd, who toil for fatal lead?
What cramps, what palsies shake their feeble limbs,
Who, on the margin of the rocky Drave,*
Trace silver's fluent ore? Yet white men these! . . .

Yet, planter, let humanity prevail.—
Perhaps thy Negroe, in his native land,
Possest large fertile plains, and slaves, and herds:
Perhaps, whene'er he deign'd to walk abroad,
The richest silks, from where the Indus rolls,
His limbs invested in their gorgeous pleats:
Perhaps he wails his wife, his children, left
To struggle with adversity: Perhaps
Fortune, in battle for his country fought,
Gave him a captive to his deadliest foe:
Perhaps, incautious, in his native fields,
(On pleasurable scenes his mind intent)
All as he wandered; from the neighbouring grove,

---

* [Grainger's note:] A river in Hungary, on whose banks are found mines of quicksilver.

Fell ambush dragg'd him to the hated main.—
Were they even sold for crimes; ye polish'd, say!
Ye, to whom Learning opes her amplest page!
Ye, whom the knowledge of a living God
Should lead to virtue! Are ye free from crimes?
Ah pity, then, these uninstructed swains;
And still let mercy soften the decrees
Of rigid justice, with her lenient hand.

    Oh, did the tender muse possess the power,
Which monarchs have, and monarchs oft abuse:
'Twould be the fond ambition of her soul,
To quell tyrannic sway; knock off the chains
Of heart-debasing slavery; give to man,
Of every colour and of every clime,
Freedom, which stamps him image of his God.
Then laws, Oppression's scourge, fair Virtue's prop,
Offspring of Wisdom! should impartial reign,
To knit the whole in well-accorded strife:
Servants, not slaves; of choice, and not compell'd;
The Blacks should cultivate the Cane-land isles. . . .

In magic spells, in Obia, all the sons
Of sable Africk trust . . . .

    Fern root cut small, and tied with many a knot;
Old teeth extracted from a white man's skull;
A lizard's skeleton; a serpent's head:
These mix'd with salt, and water from the spring,
Are in a phial pour'd; o'er these the leach
Mutters strange jargon, and wild circles forms.

    Of this possest, each negroe deems himself
Secure from poison; for to poison they
Are infamously prone: and arm'd with this,
Their sable country daemons they defy,
Who fearful haunt them at the midnight hour,
To work them mischief. This, diseases fly;
Diseases follow: such its wonderous power!
This o'er the threshold of their cottage hung,
No thieves break in; or, if they dare to steal,
Their feet in blotches, which admit no cure,
Burst loathsome out: but should its owner filch,
As slaves were ever of the pilfering kind,
This from detection screens;—so conjurers swear. . . .

Howe'er insensate some may deem their slaves,
Nor 'bove the bestial rank; far other thoughts
The muse, soft daughter of humanity!
Will ever entertain.—The Ethiop knows,
The Ethiop feels, when treated like a man;
Nor grudges, should necessity compell,
By day, by night, to labour for his lord.

    Not less inhuman, than unthrifty those;
Who, half the year's rotation round the sun,
Deny subsistence to their labouring slaves.
But would'st thou see thy negroe-train encrease,
Free from disorders; and thine acres clad
With groves of sugar: every week dispense
Or English beans, or Carolinian rice;
Iërne's beef, or Pensilvanian flour;
Newfoundland cod, or herrings from the main
That howls tempestuous round the Scotian isles! . . .

On festal days; or when their work is done;
Permit thy slaves to lead the choral dance,
To the wild banshaw's* melancholy sound.
Responsive to the sound, head feet and frame
Move aukwardly harmonious; hand in hand
Now lock'd, the gay troop circularly wheels,
And frisks and capers with intemperate joy.
Halts the vast circle, all clap hands and sing;
While those distinguish'd for their heels and air,
Bound in the center, and fantastic twine.
Meanwhile some stripling, from the choral ring,
Trips forth; and, not ungallantly, bestows
On her who nimblest hath the greensward beat,
And whose flush'd beauties have inthrall'd his soul,
A silver token of his fond applause.
Anon they form in ranks; nor inexpert
A thousand tuneful intricacies weave,
Shaking their sable limbs; and oft a kiss
Steal from their partners; who, with neck reclin'd,
And semblant scorn, resent the ravish'd bliss.

                                    (1764)[92]

* [Grainger's note:] This is a sort of rude guitar, invented by the Negroes. It produces a wild
pleasing melancholy sound.

MICHAEL WODHULL
(1740–1816)

Wodhull was a wealthy, Oxford-educated man of leisure who pursued book collecting and writing among his avocations. He was also, as the title of his youthful poem *The Equality of Mankind* suggests, a liberal republican influenced by the writings of Rousseau. Eventually he would also support the French Revolution. Amid Wodhull's conventional observations on slavery is his criticism, noteworthy at the time, of missionaries as enemies rather than friends to enslaved peoples.

from The Equality of Mankind

> View first the Slave, whom his unhappy fate
> In galling fetters to some foreign state
> Tears from his dearest home; there basely sold
> By those, who truck humanity for gold,
> Abus'd, neglected, sinking with distress,
> When all is dark, and Hope alone can bless;
> Ev'n then thro' Life's dim curtain he descries
> Some happier regions, and serener skies,
> Where Commerce never rears her impious head,
> No Fiends approach, no Missionaries tread.
>
> (1765)[93]

EDWARD JERNINGHAM
(1727–1812)

Well born and well educated, Jerningham came from an Anglo-Catholic family, moved in aristocratic circles, and produced a steady stream of plays and poetry—more than thirty-two separate titles—over a fifty-year career. Although his writings and his slightly foppish manner were later satirized, he caught the vogue for sentimentalism and his works enjoyed some popularity. Inevitably, given his sensibilities, Jerningham was drawn to the subject of slavery in several of his works.

The first is a short lyric he wrote in the 1760s that was frequently reprinted in later collections, including *The African Repository,* an abolitionist periodical of the 1820s. Using the pathetic voice of a boy whose mother has been abducted by slave traders, the poem dramatizes the human damage and emotional pain inflicted on Africans by slavery.

The African Boy

Ah! tell me, little mournful Moor,
Why still you linger on the shore?
Haste to your playmates, haste away,
Nor loiter here with fond delay.
When morn unveiled her radiant eye,
You hailed me as you wandered by;
Returning at the approaching eve,
Your meek salute I still receive.

Benign enquirer, thou shalt know,
Why here my lonesome moments flow:
'Tis said, my countrymen (no more
Like ravening sharks that haunt the shore,)
Return to bless, to raise, to cheer,
And pay compassion's long arrear.

'Tis said, the numerous captive train,
Late bound by the degrading chain,
Triumphant come, with swelling sails,
New smiling skies, and western gales;
They come with festive heart and glee,
Their hands unshackled—minds as free;—
They come, at mercy's great command,
To re-possess their native land.
The gales that o'er the ocean stray,
And chase the waves in gentle play,
Methinks they whisper, as they fly,
Juellen soon will meet thine eye.
'Tis this that soothes her little son,
Blends all his wishes into one.
Ah! were I clasped in her embrace,
I would forgive her past disgrace;
Forgive the memorable hour
She fell a prey to tyrant power;
Forgive her lost, distracted air,
Her sorrowing voice, her kneeling prayer;
The suppliant tears that galled her cheek,
And last, her agonizing shriek;—
Locked in her hair, a ruthless hand
Trailed her along the flinty sand;
A ruffian train, with clamours rude,
Th'impious spectacle pursued;
Still as she moved, in accents wild,
She cried aloud, my child! my child!
The lofty bark, she now ascends,
With screams of woe, the air she rends,
The vessel less'ning from the shore,
Her piteous wails I heard no more.
Now, as I stretched my last survey,
Her distant form dissolved away.
That day is past, I cease to mourn,
Succeeding joy shall have its turn.
Beside the hoarse resounding deep,
A pleasing anxious watch I keep.
For when the morning clouds shall break,
And darts of day the darkness streak,
Perchance along the glittering main,

(Oh, may this hope not throb in vain)
To meet these long-desiring eyes,
Juellen, and the sun may rise.
                    (1766)[94]

Like others before him, Jerningham found the story of "Inkle and Yarico"
deeply moving. In the mid-1760s he became the first to recast it in the voice of
the victimized Yarico, who is here unambiguously presented as an African
("Nubian") rather than Native American slave. In the first excerpt, Yarico re-
calls the barriers her interracial affair with Inkle had broken, at the same time
hinting (in line 4) at the internalized self-loathing that slavery fostered in people
of color.

from *"Yarico to Inkle, An Epistle"*

"Yet utter not to me the lover's vow,
All, all is thine that Friendship can bestow:
Our laws, my station, check the guilty flame—
Why was I born, ye powers, a Nubian dame?
Yet see around, at Love's enchanting call,
Stern laws submit, and vain distinctions fall:
And mortals then enjoy life's transient day,
When smit with passion they indulge the sway."

In her lamentation over Inkle's treachery, Yarico makes clear the debilitating
psychological effects of slavery on those subjected to it. Here Jerningham antic-
ipates modern insights into the subtle and persistent psychological damage of
racism.

And (do I live to breathe the barb'rous tale?)
His faithful YARICO expos'd to sale!
Yes, basely urg'd (regardless of my pray'rs,
Ev'n while I bath'd his venal hand with tears)
The tend'rest circumstance—I can no more—
My future child—to swell his impious store:—
All, all mankind for this will rise thy foe,
But I, alas! alone can endure the woe:
Endure what healing balms can ne'er controul,
The heart-lodged stings and agony of soul.—
Was it for this I left my native plain,
And dar'd the tempest brooding on the main?
For this unlock'd (seduc'd by Christian art)

The chaste affections of my virgin heart?
Within this bosom fan'd the constant flame,
And fondly languish'd for a Mother's name?
Lo! ev'ry hope is poison'd in its bloom,
And horrors watch around this guilty womb.

With blood illustrious circling thro' these veins,
Which ne'er was chequer'd with plebeian stains,
Thro' ancestry's long line ennobled springs,
From fame-crown'd warriors and exalted kings,
Must I the shafts of Infamy sustain?
To Slav'ry's purposes my infant train?
To catch the glances of his haughty lord?
Attend obedient at the festive board?
From hands unscepter'd take the scornful blow?
Uproot the thoughts of glory as they grow?

Here, in language reminiscent of Savage's *Of Public Spirit* (1737), Jerningham imagines a supernatural figure—the "Genius" of Africa—who threatens vengeance against the European nations that have so devastated non-European peoples.

Methought—nor was it childish Fancy's flight:
My country's Genius stood confess'd to sight:
"Let Europe's sons (he said) enrich their shore,
With stones of lustre, and barbaric ore:
Adorn their country with their splendid stealth,
Unnative foppery, and gorgeous wealth;
Embellish still her form with foreign spoils,
Till like a gaudy prostitute she smiles:
The day, th' avenging day at length shall rise,
And tears shall trickle from that harlot's eyes:
Her own Gods shall prepare the fatal doom
Lodg'd in Time's pregnant and destructive womb:
The mischief-bearing womb, these hands shall rend,
And straight shall issue forth Confusion's fiend:
Then shall my children urge the destin'd way,
Invade the Christian coast, and dare the day:
Sue, as they rush upon them as a flood,
Dishonour for dishonour, blood for blood."

In its closing lines, the poem becomes melodramatic, as Yarico prepares to kill herself and her child.

163

This poinard, by my daring hand imprest,
Shall drink the ruddy drops that warm my breast:
Nor I alone, by this immortal deed
From Slav'ry's laws my infant shall be freed.
And thou, whose ear is deaf to Pity's call,
Behold at length thy destin'd victim fall;
Behold thy once lov'd Nubian stain'd with gore,
Unwept, extended on the crimson floor:
These temples clouded with the shades of death,
These lips unconscious of the ling'ring breath:
These eyes uprais'd (ere clos'd by Fate's decree)
To catch expiring one faint glimpse of thee.
Ah! then thy YARICO forbear to dread,
My fault'ring voice no longer will upbraid,
Demand due vengeance of the pow'rs above,
Or, more offensive still, implore thy love.

(1766)[95]

In this political poem of the 1790s, Jerningham urges Pitt, Fox, William Windham, Richard Sheridan, and other pro-reform leaders to push ahead with their efforts—temporarily set back by the reaction to events in France—to abolish the slave trade.

from "Peace, Ignominy and Destruction"

Cou'd I, like Dryden, wield the bolts of war,
And fling amazement from the rushing car!
Did I possess that energetic strain
Which pours the sorrows of the negro train,
Brings the heart-rending tale to Britain's ear,
And bids compassion pay her long arrear;
The arguments that flow from Wyndham's sense,
Well guarded round by reason's strongest fence;
The sacred boon by Chatham's Son possest,
The muse of eloquence that fires his breast:
The quiver richly stored with attic darts,
Which genius to his Sheridan imparts:
Th' exalting winnow'd purity of soul
With which Fitzwilliam soars beyond controul;
Who, greatly daring, with a zeal severe
Stemm'd the wild deluge of opprobrious fear;
And, on the day eternally renown'd,

Like Abdiel, was the only faithful found:—
Had I these pow'rs concenter'd in one form,
I'd pour on England the resistless storm,
To wake her soul, to rouse her mental part,
And chace her sombrous lethargy of heart.

(1796)[96]

JOHN SINGLETON
(fl. 1752–1777)

Singleton was a strolling player of whom few traces survive. An Englishman, he came to America in the early 1750s as an actor in Hallam's Company, which, from 1752 until at least 1759, was the first British theater troupe to tour Williamsburg, New York, Philadelphia, Charleston, and the Caribbean. He wrote occasional prologues for the company, and in 1767, encouraged by Grainger's success with *The Sugar-Cane* (1764), Singleton published this long poem about the West Indies. Acclaimed in the colonies for his Shakespearean and comic roles, Singleton courted the favor of Charles Pinfold, former governor of Barbados, to whom he dedicated the second edition of his *West Indies*.

In the first excerpt, the poet vividly depicts the island custom of the *barbecue*, which, as a word and a social event, exemplifies how indigenous practices could circulate back into and influence the mores of the imperial culture. Little could Singleton have forseen that the exotic cookout he observed in the eighteenth-century Caribbean would by the twentieth century become a middle-class norm throughout the English-speaking world.

from Book I of A Description of the West-Indies
"The Barbecue"

> The sable cooks, with utensils prepar'd,
> Their several stations take, and crackling flames
> Enkindle, not with bellows, but with lungs
> Expert at blowing culinary blasts.
> Whilst Cuffé, Lovelace, Quasheba and Sal,
> With viands stor'd, the loaded baskets bring:
> This a variety of herbage holds,
> And that the solid sav'ry meat contains,
> The well cramm'd turkey, and the rosy ham:
> Nor is the mellow cheese forgot, of taste
> High relishing, when silver-tipp'd black jack,

Or tankard bright, fam'd Calvert's porter holds,
With flow'ry head high tow'ring o'er the brim.
The destin'd shoat on Ethiop's shoulders swags,
Grunting, as to the rural shrine he's brought:
Here one beneath a load of liquors bends,
Cooling sherbets, and choice of dainty wines;
Another the capacious bowl conveys,
With saccharissian loaf; the spirit fine,
From choicest cane distill'd, mellow'd by age,
Within its glossy bounds alluring smiles.

In this passage, Singleton describes the hiding place of a runaway slave and ruminates on the tragedy of his fate.

from Book II of A Description of the West-Indies

A dreary pit there is, of deep descent,
Where Nature, in mysterious mood, her stores
In secret hides; where sulph'rous atoms fume;
First found, through chance, by some delinquent slave,
Flying the lash of his revengeful lord,
Or overseer more cruel. Once he dwelt
A native of rich Ebo's sunny coast,
Or Gambia's golden shore; a prince perhaps;
By treach'rous scheme of some sea brute entrap'd,
When the steel-hearted sordid mariner
Shap'd out his wat'ry course for traffic vile,
Commuting wares for baneful dust of gold;
Or, what is worse, made spoil of human flesh.
Accursed method of procuring wealth!
By loading free-born limbs with servile chains,
And bart'ring for the image of his god.
Deal Christians thus, yet keep that sacred name?
Or does the diff'rence of complexion give
To man a property in man?—O! no:
Soft nature shrinks at the detested thought,
A thought which savages alone can form.

In this final excerpt, Singleton pauses from his idealized depiction of the Caribbean to focus briefly, but with an anthropologist's acuity, on a slave burial. The poet's vignettes of slave life form a striking counterpoint to the poem's overall tone of admiration for colonial society.

from Book III of A Description of the West Indies

But see! what strange procession hither winds,
With long continued stream, thro' yonder wood?
Like gentle waves, hundreds of sable heads
Float onwards; still they move, and still they seem
With unexhausted flow to keep their course.
    In calm succession thus th' unruffl'd main
Rolls on its peaceful waters to the shore,
With easy swell, wave gliding over wave,
Till the spectator can no longer count
Their breaks incessant, but the numbers past
Are in succeeding numbers quickly lost.
Behold the white-rob'd train in form advance
To yonder new-made grave: six ugly hags,
Their visage seam'd with honorary scars,
In wild contortive postures lead the van;
High o'er their palsied heads, rattling, they wave
Their noisy instruments; whilst to the sound
In dance progressive their shrunk shanks keep time.
With more composure the succeeding ranks,
Chanting their fun'ral song in chorus full,
Precede the mournful bier, by friendly hands
Supported: sudden stops the flowing line;
The puzzled bearers of the restive corpse
Stand for a-while, fast rooted to the ground,
Depriv'd of motion, or perhaps, impell'd
This way, or that, unable to proceed
In course direct, until the troubled dead
Has to some friend imparted his request;
That gratify'd, again the fun'ral moves:
When at the grave arriv'd, the solemn rites
Begin; the slave's cold reliques gently laid
Within their earthy bed, some veteran,
Among the sable archimages,* pours
His mercenary panegyric forth,
In all the jargon of mysterious speech;
And, to compose the spirit of the dead,
Sprinkles his fav'rite liquor on the grave.
This done, the mourners form a spacious ring,
When sudden shrill discordant notes, surprize

* [Singleton's note:] Obeah Magicians.

JOHN SINGLETON

The deafen'd ear; nor Corybantian brass,
Nor rattling sistrum, ever rung a peal
So frantic, when th'Idaean dactyli
At their intoxicated feasts ran wild,
Dizzily weaving the fantastic dance,
And with extended throats proclaiming high
Their goddess Rhea, thro' the giddy crowd.
Thus do these sooty children of the sun,
"Unused to the melting mood," perform
Their fun'ral obsequies, and joyous chant
In concert full, the requiem of the dead;
Wheeling in many a mazy round, they fill
The jocund dance, and take a last farewel
Of their departed friend, without a tear.

(1767)[97]

PHILLIS WHEATLEY
(?1753–1784)

In the context of slavery in English literature, Wheatley is the most important figure of the eighteenth century. Having risen to canonical status only in the late twentieth century, her works now widely republished, Wheatley had humble origins. Born in Africa, she was captured and sold into slavery as a child, and then purchased by John Wheatley of Boston. Her genius impressed her owners, who arranged for her to be educated by private tutors in several subjects, including Latin and Greek. So brilliant that she began to publish serious poems as a young teenager, Wheatley became a sensation among Boston intellectuals. Her fame spread to England when she traveled to London to publish her *Poems on Various Subjects* in 1773. She took the literary and social scene by storm, enjoying tributes from royalty, literati, and the press. Her later life declined into sadness. Manumitted by the Wheatleys, she endured an unhappy marriage, the deaths of two of her three children, poverty, and long illness before dying in 1784, scarcely aged thirty. Her poetic oeuvre is the cornerstone of the African American literary tradition, as well as a major force in the broader history of America.

Of the ten poems here included, the first shows the boldness, verging on audacity, of a fourteen-year-old female slave speaking with an authority usually reserved for ordained white males: that is, preaching on religious doctrine, in this case refuting the skepticism of deists. Her modest opening line slyly points up this irony, as she goes on to defend the divinity of Jesus and the existence of the holy trinity.

An Address to the Deist

Must Ethiopians be employ'd for you?
Much I rejoice if any good I do.
I ask O unbeliever, Satan's child
Hath not thy Saviour been too much revil'd
Th' auspicious rays that round his temples shine

Do still declare him to be Christ divine
Doth not the great *Eternal* call him Son
Is he not pleas'd with his beloved One—?
How canst thou thus divide the Trinity
The blest the Holy the eternal three
Tis Satan's snares are fluttering in the wind
Whereby he doth ensnare thy foolish mind
God, the Eternal Orders this to be
Sees thy vain arg'ments to divide the three
Canst thou not see the Consequence in store?
Begin th' Almighty monarch to adore.
Attend to Reason whispering in thine ear
Seek the Eternal while he is so near.
Full in thy view I point each path I know
Lest to the vale of black dispair I go
At the last day where wilt thou hide thy face
That day approaching is no time for Grace
Too late perceive thyself undone and lost
To late own Father, Son, and Holy Ghost.
Who trod the wine-press of Jehovah's wrath?
Who taught us prayer, and promis'd grace and faith?
Who but the Son, who reigns supremely blest
Ever, and ever, in Immortal rest?
The vilest prodigal who comes to God
Is not cast out but bro't by Jesus's blood
When to the faithless Jews he oft did cry
Some own'd their teacher some made him a lye
He came to you in mean apparel clad
He came to save us from your sins, and had
Compassion more than language can express.
Pains his companions, and his friends distress
Immanuel on the cross these pains did bear
Will the eternal our petitions hear?
Ah! wond'rous Destiny his life he laid
"Father forgive them," thus the Saviour pray'd
Nail'd was king Jesus on the cross for us
For our transgressions he sustain'd the Curse.

(1767)[98]

Wheatley began to emerge as a prodigy in the New England press, here via
the *Newport Mercury,* in 1767. The following poem, occasioned by a shipwreck
whose survivors were sheltered in the Wheatley household, offers the prospect

of an eternal afterlife as deliverance from any earthly terror. It remains unknown whether the two men found her words true to their experience.

On Messrs. Hussey and Coffin

To the PRINTER: Please to insert the following Lines, composed by a Negro Girl (belonging to one Mr. Wheatley of Boston) on the following Occasion, viz. Messrs Hussey and Coffin, as undermentioned, belonging to Nantucket, being bound from thence to Boston, narrowly escaped being cast away on Cape-Cod, in one of the late Storms; upon their Arrival, being at Mr. Wheatley's, and, while at Dinner, told of their narrow Escape, this Negro Girl at the same Time 'tending Table, heard the Relation, from which she composed the following Verses.

Did Fear and Danger so perplex your Mind,
As made you fearful of the whistling Wind?
Was it not Boreas knit his angry Brow
Against you? or did Consideration bow?
To lend you Aid, did not his Winds combine?
To stop your Passage with a churlish Line,
Did haughty Eolus with Contempt look down
With Aspect windy, and a study'd Frown?
Regard them not;—the Great Supreme, the Wise,
Intends for something hidden from our Eyes.
Suppose the groundless Gulph had snatch'd away
Hussey and Coffin to the raging Sea;
Where wou'd they go? where wou'd be their Abode?
With the supreme and independent God,
Or made their beds down in the Shades below,
Where neither Pleasure nor Content can slow.
To Heaven their Souls with eager Raptures soar,
Enjoy the Bliss of him they wou'd adore.
Had the soft gliding Streams of Grace been near,
Some favourite Hope their fainting Hearts to cheer,
Doubtless the Fear of Danger far had fled:
No more repeated Victory crown their Heads.
    Had I the Tongue of a Seraphim, how would I exalt thy
Praise; thy Name as Incense to the Heavens should fly, and the
Remembrance of thy Goodness to the shoreless Ocean of Beatitude!
——Then should the Earth glow with seraphick Ardour.
Blest Soul, which sees the Day while Light doth shine,
To guide his Steps to trace the Mark divine.

                                          (1767)[99]

Self-consciously turning to allegory (or "simile") to express a vision of America, Wheatley in the next poem shows an awareness of the growing tensions between the New England colonists and the British government while still hoping, obviously, for a reconciliation. Once again, her choice of topic and tone of voice seem remarkable for someone of her status, as does her strong affiliation with the white colonial citizenry.

America

New England first a wilderness was found
Till for a continent 'twas destin'd round
From field to field the savage monsters run
E'r yet Brittania had her work begun
Thy Power, O Liberty, makes strong the weak
And (wond'rous instinct) Ethiopians speak
Sometimes by Simile, a victory's won
A certain lady had an only son
He grew up daily virtuous as he grew
Fearing his Strength which she undoubted knew
She laid some taxes on her darling son
And would have laid another act there on
Amend your manners I'll the task remove
Was said with seeming Sympathy and Love
By many Scourges she his goodness try'd
Untill at length the Best of Infants cry'd
He wept, Brittania turn'd a senseless ear
At last awaken'd by maternal fear
Why weeps americus why weeps my Child
Thus spake Brittania, thus benign and mild
My dear mama said he, shall I repeat—
Then Prostrate fell, at her maternal feet
What ails the rebel, great Brittania Cry'd
Indeed said he, you have no cause to Chide
You see each day my fluent tears my food.
Without regard, what no more English blood?
Has length of time drove from our English veins
The kindred he to Great Brittania deigns?
Tis thus with thee O Brittain keeping down
New English force, thou fear'st his Tyranny and thou didst frown
He weeps afresh to feel this Iron chain
Turn, O Brittania, claim thy child again
Riecho Love drive by thy powerful charms

Indolence Slumbering in forgetful arms
See Agenoria diligent imploys
Her sons, and thus with rapture she replys
Arise my sons with one consent arise
Lest distant continents with vult'ring eyes
Should charge America with Negligence
They praise Industry but no pride commence
To raise their own Profusion, O Brittain See
By this New England will increase like thee.
(1768)[100]

Many regard the following as a pivotal poem in Wheatley's career. George Whitefield, evangelical preacher, co-founder (with the Wesleys) of Methodism, and celebrated leader of the Great Awakening, died in 1769 during his seventh tour of America. Wheatley's elegy reveals the depth of her own evangelical fervor and her attachment to Whitefield. Her diction and cadences invite the reader to see Whitefield's attentions to America (and to "Africans") as significant for their political, as well as religious, implications. Because of Whitefield's fame on both sides of the Atlantic, Wheatley's poem was widely reprinted throughout England and America, and brought her to prominence.

An Elegiac Poem, on the Death of that Celebrated Divine, and Eminent Servant of Jesus Christ, the Reverend and Learned *George Whitefield,* Chaplain to the Right Honourable the Countess of Huntingdon, &c. &c.

HAIL happy Saint on thy immortal throne!
To thee complaints of grievance are unknown;
We hear no more the music of thy tongue,
Thy wonted auditories cease to throng.
Thy lessons in unequal'd accents flow'd!
While emulation in each bosom glow'd;
Thou didst, in strains of eloquence refin'd,
Inflame the soul, and captivate the mind.
Unhappy we, the setting Sun deplore!
Which once was splendid, but it shines no more;
He leaves this earth for Heaven's unmeasur'd height:
And worlds unknown, receive him from our sight;
There WHITEFIELD wings, with rapid course his way,
And sails to Zion, through vast seas of day.

When his AMERICANS were burden'd fore,
When streets were crimson'd with their guiltless gore!
Unrival'd friendship in his breast now strove:
The fruit thereof was charity and love
Towards *America*—couldst thou do more
Than leave thy native home, the *British* shore,
To cross the great Atlantic's wat'ry road,
To see *America*'s distress'd abode?
Thy prayers, great Saint, and thy incessant cries,
Have pierc'd the bosom of thy native skies!
Thou moon hast seen, and ye bright stars of light
Have witness been of his requests by night!
He pray'd that grace in every heart might dwell:
He long'd to see *America* excell;
He charg'd his youth to let the grace divine
Arise, and in their future actions shine;
He offer'd THAT he did himself receive,
A greater gift not GOD himself can give:
He urg'd the need of HIM to every one;
It was no less than GOD's co-equal SON!
Take HIM ye wretched for your only good,
Take HIM ye starving souls to be your food.
Ye thirsty, come to this life giving stream:
Ye Preachers, take him for your joyful theme:
Take HIM, "my dear AMERICANS," he said,
Be your complaints in his kind bosom laid:
Take HIM ye *Africans,* he longs for you;
Impartial SAVIOUR, is his title due;
If you will chuse to walk in grace's road,
You shall be sons, and kings, and priests to GOD.

Great COUNTESS! we *Americans* revere
Thy name, and thus condole thy grief sincere:
We mourn with thee, that TOMB obscurely plac'd,
In which thy Chaplain undisturb'd doth rest.
New-England sure, doth feel the ORPHAN's smart;
Reveals the true sensations of his heart:
Since this fair Sun, withdraws his golden rays,
No more to brighten these distressful days!
His lonely *Tabernacle,* sees no more
A WHITEFIELD landing on the *British* shore:
Then let us view him in yon azure skies:

Let every mind with this lov'd object rise.
No more can he exert his lab'ring breath,
Seiz'd by the cruel messenger of death.
What can his dear AMERICA return?
But drop a tear upon his happy urn,
Thou tomb, shalt safe retain thy sacred trust,
Till life divine re-animate his dust.

(1770)[101]

Again remarkable for her courage in addressing major public issues, here the appointment of a new minister for America (William Legge, Second Earl of Dartmouth), Wheatley breaks through neoclassical formalities to reveal some of her personal experience of abduction and enslavement. In her extraordinary use of slavery as a metaphor for America's treatment at the hands of Britain, Wheatley seems to suggest that she has come to terms with her fate and her present condition. Or perhaps, at a deeper level, she is subtly encouraging American patriots to empathize with the misery African slaves endure.

To The Right Honourable William, Earl Of Dartmouth, His Majesty's Principal Secretary of State for North America, &c.

Hail, happy day, when smiling like the morn,
Fair *Freedom* rose *New-England* to adorn:
The northern clime beneath her genial ray,
Dartmouth, congratulates thy blissful sway:
Elate with hope her race no longer mourns,
Each soul expands, each grateful bosom burns,
While in thine hand with pleasure we behold
The silken reins, and *Freedom's* charms unfold.
Long lost to realms beneath the northern skies
She shines supreme, while hated *faction* dies:
Soon as appear'd the *Goddess* long desir'd,
Sick at the view, she languish'd and expir'd;
Thus from the splendors of the morning light
The owl in sadness seeks the caves of night.

No more, *America*, in mournful strain
Of wrongs, and grievance unredress'd complain,
No longer shalt thou dread the iron chain,
Which wanton *Tyranny* with lawless hand
Had made, and with it meant t'enslave the land.

Should you, my lord, while you peruse my song,
Wonder from whence my love of *Freedom* sprung,
Whence flow these wishes for the common good,
By feeling hearts alone best understood,
I, young in life, by seeming cruel fate
Was snatch'd from *Afric's* fancy'd happy seat:
What pangs excruciating must molest,
What sorrows labour in my parent's breast?
Steel'd was that soul and by no misery mov'd
That from a father seiz'd his babe belov'd:
Such, such my case. And can I then but pray
Others may never feel tyrannic sway?

For favours past, great Sir, our thanks are due,
And thee we ask thy favours to renew,
Since in thy pow'r, as in thy will before,
To sooth the griefs, which thou dids't once deplore.
May heavn'ly grace the sacred sanction give
To all thy works, and thou for ever live
Not only on the wings of fleeting *Fame*,
Though praise immortal crowns the patriot's name,
But to conduct to heav'ns refulgent fane,
May fiery coursers sweep th' ethereal plain,
And bear thee upwards to that blest abode,
Where, like the prophet, thou shalt find thy God.
                              (wr. 1772/pub. 1773)[102]

Wheatley's most famous poem is also, to modern readers, her most perplexing. Her apparent celebration of having been enslaved and carried to America makes sense only if one imagines her first line as a response to well-intentioned but misguided or condescending remarks from a sympathizer. That is, read with a stress on the word *mercy*, Wheatley's poem expresses her view that it was God's larger plan for her salvation, rather than the wickedness of slave traders, that determined the events of her life. Still, she also undermines white complacency, reminding Christians (with an apt pun on sugar cane processing) that blacks and whites are equal in the divine plan.

On Being Brought from Africa to America

'Twas mercy brought me from my *Pagan* land,
Taught my benighted soul to understand
That there's a God, that there's a *Saviour* too:
Once I redemption neither sought nor knew.

Some view our sable race with scornful eye,
"Their colour is a diabolic die."
Remember, *Christians*, *Negros*, black as *Cain*,
May be refin'd, and join th' angelic train.

(1773)[103]

Though infant mortality was a harsh commonplace of life, the death of a baby was nonetheless traumatic and gave rise to a genre of consolatory verse practiced by both men and women. The poem below demonstrates Wheatley's mastery of the form and her compassion for a friend's loss.

On the Death of J.C. an Infant

No more the flow'ry scenes of pleasure rise,
Nor charming prospects greet the mental eyes,
No more with joy we view that lovely face
Smiling, disportive, flush'd with ev'ry grace.

The tear of sorrow flows from ev'ry eye,
Groans answer groans, and sighs to sighs reply;
What sudden pangs shot thro' each aching heart,
When, *Death*, thy messenger dispatch'd his dart?
Thy dread attendants, all-destroying *Pow'r*,
Hurried the infant to his mortal hour.
Could'st thou unpitying close those radiant eyes?
Or fail'd his artless beauties to surprize?
Could not his innocence thy stroke controul,
Thy purpose shake, and soften all thy soul?

The blooming babe, with shades of *Death* o'erspread,
No more shall smile, no more shall raise its head,
But, like a branch that from the tree is torn,
Falls prostrate, wither'd, languid, and forlorn.
"Where flies my *James?*" 'tis thus I seem to hear
The parent ask, "Some angel tell me where
He wings his passage thro' the yielding air?"
Methinks a cherub bending from the skies
Observes the question, and serene replies,
"In heav'ns high palaces your babe appears:
Prepare to meet him, and dismiss your tears."
Shall not th'intelligence your grief restrain,
And turn the mournful to the chearful strain?
Cease your complaints, suspend each rising sigh,
Cease to accuse the Ruler of the sky.

Parents, no more indulge the falling tear:
Let *Faith* to heav'n's refulgent domes repair,
There see your infant, like a seraph glow:
What charms celestial in his numbers flow
Melodious, while the soul-enchanting strain
Dwells on his tongue and fills th'ethereal plain?
Enough—for ever cease your murm'ring breath;
Not as a foe, but friend converse with *Death*,
Since to the port of happiness unknown
He brought that treasure which you call your own.
The gift of heav'n intrusted to your hand
Chearful resign at the divine command:
Not at your bar must sov'reign *Wisdom* stand.

(1773)[104]

In the next poem, Wheatley displays a sense of pride in her race, in her ad-
miration for a talented young African American painter called Scipio Moorhead
("S. M."). Moorhead also lived in Boston, as a household slave of the Reverend
John Moorhead. He was apparently friends with Wheatley and is thought to
have drawn the portrait of Wheatley on which the frontispiece to her book was
based. The opening lines convey her appreciation for pictorial art, while the poem
as a whole offers clues about the connections among artists in the eighteenth-
century African American community.

To S. M., a Young African Painter on Seeing His Works

To show the lab'ring bosom's deep intent,
And thought in living characters to paint,
When first thy pencil did those beauties give,
And breathing figures learnt from thee to live,
How did those prospects give my soul delight,
A new creation rushing on my sight?
Still, wond'rous youth! each noble path pursue,
On deathless glories fix thine ardent view:
Still may the painter's and the poet's fire
To aid thy pencil, and thy verse conspire!
And may the charms of each seraphic theme
Conduct thy footsteps to immortal fame!
High to the blissful wonders of the skies
Elate thy soul, and raise thy wishful eyes.
Thrice happy, when exalted to survey
That splendid city, crown'd with endless day,

Whose twice six gates on radiant hinges ring:
Celestial *Salem* blooms in endless spring.

    Calm and serene thy moments glide along,
And may the muse inspire each future song!
Still, with the sweets of contemplation bless'd,
May peace with balmy wings your soul invest!
But when these shades of time are chas'd away,
And darkness ends in everlasting day,
On what seraphic pinions shall we move,
And view the landscapes in the realms above?
There shall thy tongue in heav'nly murmurs flow,
And there my muse with heav'nly transport glow:
No more to tell of *Damon's* tender sighs,
Or rising radiance of *Aurora's* eyes,
For nobler themes demand a nobler strain,
And purer language on th' ethereal plain.
Cease gentle muse! the solemn gloom of night
Now seals the fair creation from my sight.

                       (1773)[105]

The next poem combines elements of high classicism and personal memory. Although the lyric form and mythological allusions are typical of eighteenth-century neoclassical verse, the poem was said to be inspired by Wheatley's childhood recollection of her mother pouring out water every morning before the rising sun.

An Hymn to the Morning

Attend my lays, ye ever honour'd nine,
Assist my labours, and my strains refine;
In smoothest numbers pour the notes along,
For bright *Aurora* now demands my song.

    Aurora hail, and all the thousand dies,
Which deck thy progress through the vaulted skies:
The morn awakes, and wide extends her rays,
On ev'ry leaf the gentle zephyr plays;
Harmonious lays the feather'd race resume.
Dart the bright eye, and shake the painted plume.

    Ye shady groves, your verdant gloom display
To shield your poet from the burning day:
Calliope awake the sacred lyre,
While thy fair sisters fan the pleasing fire:

The bow'rs, the gales, the variegated skies
In all their pleasures in my bosom rise.

See in the east th' illustrious king of day!
His rising radiance drives the shades away—
But Oh! I feel his fervid beams too strong,
And scarce begun, concludes th' abortive song.

$(1773)^{106}$

The story of Wheatley's poetic tribute to Washington marks an important moment in American history. Wheatley, who supported the American cause, had fled to Providence with the Wheatley family when the British occupied Boston in 1775. Inspired by Washington's victory over the British in Boston that fall, Wheatley sent the General the following poem of tribute. Flattered and grateful, Washington responded with a warm and complimentary letter to "Miss Phillis." But this was private correspondence: the real significance lies in how the poem came to be published. Long thought to have first appeared in the abolition-friendly *Pennsylvania Magazine* (April 1776), the poem actually was first printed in the March 30, 1776, issue of the *Virginia Gazette*. By the indirect agency of friends, Washington apparently meant to show his fellow Virginians a slave who was not only literate, but loyal to the American cause—an astute tactic at a time when Virginia was wracked with fear of a major slave insurrection, incited by Governor Dunmore's call for slaves to come fight on the British side.

To His Excellency General Washington

The following LETTER *and* VERSES *were written by the famous* Phillis Wheatley, the *African Poetess, and presented to his Excellency Gen.* Washington.

SIR,

I Have taken the freedom to address your Excellency in the enclosed poem, and entreat your acceptance, though I am not insensible of its inaccuracies. Your being appointed by the Grand Continental Congress to be Generalissimo of the armies of North America, together with the fame of your virtues, excite sensations not easy to suppress. Your generosity, therefore, I presume, will pardon the attempt. Wishing your Excellency all possible success in the great cause you are so generously engaged in, I am,

Your Excellency's most obedient humble

servant,

PHILLIS WHEATLEY.

Providence, Oct. 26, 1775.
His Excellency Gen. Washington.

Celestial choir! enthron'd in realms of light,
Columbia's scenes of glorious toils I write.

While freedom's cause her anxious breast alarms,
She flashes dreadful in refulgent arms.
See mother earth her offspring's fate bemoan,
And nations gaze at scenes before unknown!
See the bright beams of heaven's revolving light
Involved in sorrows and veil of night!

   The goddess comes, she moves divinely fair,
Olive and laurel binds her golden hair:
Wherever shines this native of the skies,
Unnumber'd charms and recent graces rise.

   Muse! bow propitious while my pen relates
How pour her armies through a thousand gates:
As when Eolus heaven's fair face deforms,
Enwrapp'd in tempest and a night of storms;
Astonish'd ocean feels the wild uproar,
The refluent surges beat the sounding shore;
Or thick as leaves in Autumn's golden reign,
Such, and so many, moves the warrior's train.
In bright array they seek the work of war,
Where high unfurl'd the ensign waves in air.
Shall I to Washington their praise recite?
Enough thou know'st them in the fields of fight.
Thee, first in place and honours,—we demand
The grace and glory of thy martial band.
Fam'd for thy valour, for thy virtues more,
Hear every tongue thy guardian aid implore!

   One century scarce perform'd its destin'd round,
When Gallic powers Columbia's fury found;
And so may you, whoever dares disgrace
The land of freedom's heaven-defended race!
Fix'd are the eyes of nations on the scales,
For in their hopes Columbia's arm prevails.
Anon Brittania droops the pensive head,
While round increase the rising hills of dead.
Ah! cruel blindness to Columbia's state!
Lament thy thirst of boundless power too late.

   Proceed, great chief, with virtue on thy side,
Thy ev'ry action let the goddess guide.
A crown, a mansion, and a throne that shine,
With gold unfading, WASHINGTON! be thine.

                  (1775)[107]

ISAAC BICKERSTAFFE
(c. 1735–c. 1812)

A prolific Anglo-Irish playwright who lived a shadowy life, Bickerstaffe en-
joyed considerable success in London before being exiled to France in 1772,
amidst scandalous but still mysterious circumstances. *The Padlock* (1768) was an
enormously popular comedy that was staged throughout the English-speaking
world and beyond well into the mid-nineteenth century. In the Americas the
play was performed even in slave-holding communities such as Charleston, Bal-
timore, and Montego Bay. George Washington is recorded as having seen it at
least twice, in Williamsburg (1771) and Annapolis (1772).

In Mungo, the play presents the first African slave character to speak in
"black" dialect. Mungo's role anticipates the figure of the black minstrel in the
nineteenth century. Although modern scholars debate whether the character of
Mungo represents compassion or disdain for African slaves, contemporary au-
diences responded very sympathetically. During the play's early run, an anony-
mous antislavery epilogue (anthologized below) was added and recited by
Mungo, and it concluded the play in most performances thereafter.

Mungo's Song from Act I of The Padlock

Dear heart, what a terrible life am I led,
A dog has a better that's shelter'd and fed:
    Night and day 'tis de same,
    My pain is dere game;
Me wish to de Lord me was dead.

    What e'er's to be done,
    Poor black must run;
    Mungo here, Mungo dere,
    Mungo every where;
    Above and below,
    Sirrah come, Sirrah go;

Do so, and do so.
Oh! oh!
Me wish to de Lord me was dead.

Mungo's Song from Act II of The Padlock

Let me, when my heart a sinking;
Hear de sweet guittar a clinking;
When a string speak,
Such moosic he make,
Me soon am cur'd of tinking.
Wid de toot, toot, toot,
Of a merry flute,
And cymbalo,
And tymbalo,
To boot.
We dance and we sing,
Till we make a house ring,
And, tied in his garters, old Massa may swing.

(1768)[108]

ANONYMOUS ["A CLERGYMAN," d. 1786]

Little is known about the origins of this poem. An editorial note reports that it was composed "soon after the first representation" of Bickerstaffe's *The Padlock* (Drury Lane, October 3, 1768), by "a very worthy clergyman" who "died in the summer of 1786." More important is its performance history. Recited by "Mungo" as the epilogue to a play that was staged frequently from 1768 well into the 1850s, throughout the English-speaking world and beyond, the speech was heard by thousands of theatergoers. The poem suggests that as early as the 1760s, twenty years before the founding of the British Abolition Society, there was a significant vein of antislavery sentiment in the general public, or at least a receptiveness to strong antislavery rhetoric.

Untitled Epilogue to The Padlock

MUNGO speaks.

   Thank you, my Massas! have you laugh your fill?
Then let me speak, nor take that freedom ill.
E'en from *my* tongue some heart-felt truths may fall,
And outrag'd nature claims the care of all.
My tale, in *any* place, would force a tear,
But calls for stronger, deeper feelings here:
For whilst I tread the free-born British land;
Whilst now before me crouded Britons stand;
Vain, vain that glorious privilege to me,
I am a *slave*, where all things else are *free*.

   Yet was I born, as you are, no man's slave,
An heir to all that lib'ral Nature gave;
My thoughts can reason, and my limbs can move
The same as yours; like yours my heart can love;
Alike my body food and sleep sustain;
And e'en like yours—feels pleasure, want, and pain.

One sun rolls o'er us, common skies surround;
One globe supports us, and one grave must bound.

    Why then am I devoid of all to live
That manly comforts to a man can give?
To live—untaught Religion's soothing balm,
Or life's choice arts; to live—unknown the calm
Of soft domestic ease; those sweets of life,
The duteous offspring, and th' endearing wife.
To live—to property and rights unknown,
Not e'en the common benefits my own;
No arm to guard me from oppression's rod,
My will subservient to a tyrant's nod.
No gentle hand, when life is in decay,
To sooth my pains, and charm my cares away;
But, helpless, left to quit the horrid stage;
Harrass'd in youth, and desolate in age.

    But I was born on Afric's tawny strand,
And you in fair Brittania's fairer land.
Comes Freedom then from colour? Blush with shame!
And let strong Nature's crimson mark your blame.
I speak to Britons—Britons, then, behold
A man by Britons *snar'd,* and *seiʒ'd,* and *sold.*
And yet no British statute damns the deed,
Nor do the more than murd'rous villains bleed.

    O sons of Freedom! equalise your laws,
Be all consistent—plead the Negroe's cause;
That all the nations in your code may see
The British Negroe, like the Briton, free.
But, should he supplicate your laws in vain,
To break for ever this disgraceful chain,
At least, let gentle usage so abate
The galling terrors of its passing state,
That he may share kind Heav'n's all-social plan;
For tho' no Briton, Mungo is—a MAN!

                            (1768)[109]

THOMAS CHATTERTON
(1752–1770)

A literary prodigy who inspired Coleridge, Keats, Shelley, and all the Romantics (Wordsworth called him "the marvelous boy"), Chatterton began publishing poems as an eleven-year-old in his native Bristol. By his mid-teens his poems were appearing in several London magazines, as he fabricated a set of authentic-seeming medieval romances in verse. In 1770, just as he moved to London to try his fortunes, Chatterton briefly turned his attention to African themes. He produced a series of "African Eclogues" in which he invented a heroic and stylized poetic vision that, though set in Africa, is indistinguishable from the ethos of his Eurocentric medieval poems. Nonetheless, in the excerpts below, the ugliness of slavery surfaces. Two months after these were published, he committed suicide in a London garret, aged seventeen. Despite a myth (fed by his own writings) that he was neglected and spurned by the literary establishment, Chatterton received widespread encouragement and had many poems forthcoming when he died.

Perhaps influenced by what he saw and heard growing up in one of Britain's leading slave ports, Chatterton held a sympathetic view of Africans. In the first excerpt, the African hero Gaira recounts to his friend Heccar his painful memories of a wife ("Cawna") and children taken from him by slave traders. For all the lofty poetic language, Gaira's agony stirs in him a very realistic desire for vengeance against the whites.

from "Heccar and Gaira. An African Eclogue"

Gaira [to Heccar]:
Rouze not Remembrance from her shadowy Cell
Nor of those bloody Sons of Mischief tell
Cawna, O Cawna: deck'd in sable Charms
What distant region holds thee from my arms
Cawna the Pride of Afric's sultry Vales
Soft, as the cooling Murmur of the Gales

Majestic as the many color'd Snake
Trailing his Glorys thro' the blossom'd brake
Black as the glossy Rocks where Eascal roars
Foaming thro' sandy Wastes to Jagirs Shores
Swift as the Arrow hasting to the breast
Was Cawna the companion of my rest . . .
Upon my Cawna's Bosom I reclin'd
Catching the breathing Whispers of the Wind
Swift from the Wood a prowling Tiger came
Dreadful his Voice his Eyes a glowing flame
I bent the Bow, the never erring dart
Pierc'd his rough Armour, but escap'd his heart
He fled tho' wounded to a distant Waste
I urg'd the furious flight with fatal haste
He fell he dy'd, spent in the fiery toil
I stripp'd his Carcase of the furry Spoil
And as the varied Spangles met my Eye
On this I cry'd shall my lov'd Cawna lie . . .
Impelled by Love I wing'd the airy way
In the deep Valley and the mossy Plain
I sought my Cawna but I sought in vain
The palid shadows of the Azure Waves
Had made my Cawna and my Children slaves
Reflection maddens to recall the hour
The Gods had giv'n me to the Daemons Power
The Dusk slow vanish'd from the hated Lawn
I gain'd a Mountain glaring with the Dawn
There the full Sails expanded to the Wind
Struck Horror and Distraction in my Mind
There Cawna mingled with a worthless train
In common slav'ry drags the hated Chain
Now judge my Heccar have I cause for Rage?
Should aught the thunder of my Arm asswage?
In ever reeking blood this Javlin dy'd
With Vengeance shall be never satisfied
I'll strew the Beaches with the mighty dead
And tinge the Lilly of their Features red.

(1770)[110]

In these lines from a romantic duet, an African warrior sings of his beloved. Beneath the florid and hyperbolic diction, Chatterton strives to humanize Africans and to affirm, through the lover's voice, the beauty of black people.

THOMAS CHATTERTON
from *"An African Song"*

Far where the clouds of Bonny spread,
I sought the beauties of Mored,
    But ah! I sought in vain!
And thro' the ling'ring darkness trac'd
The wild inhabitable waste,
    To Chelmar's burning plain.
But now! propitious to my love,
The guardian Deities above,
    Have led me to thy arms:
But now! I'll shun the coming heat,
And in yon darkened, close retreat,
    Enjoy these godlike charms.

Black is that skin as winter's skies;
Sparkling and bright those rolling eyes,
    As is the venom'd snake.
O let me haste! O let me fly!
Upon that lovely bosom die,
    And all myself forsake.

(1770)[111]

THOMAS BOULTON
(fl. 1760s and 1770s)

Other than his English nationality, his medical background, and a period of residence in New England, little is known of Boulton. According to his note, he sailed as a surgeon (apparently from Liverpool) on an ill-fated slave-trading voyage in the 1760s. Boulton alludes to bloody battles with a mysterious "Captain Fisher" and with "the Negroes" (perhaps in a shipboard insurrection), from which he and two others were the only survivors. These lines from his long poem show Boulton to be another of those who worked in the slave trade and came to despise it.

from Part I of The Voyage, a Poem in Seven Parts
"A Farewell"

> To scorching AFRIC fortune bids me roam
> In quest of riches—hardly gain'd at home.
> Oh thirst of gold! How pow'rful is thy sway?
> What crouds, by thee, are daily borne away
> From placid rivers to a boist'rous sea?
> From scenes of bliss, if ought could bless mankind,
> When av'rice, or ambition fires the mind. . . .
> Earth, ocean, air, what boundless space contains,
> From thine immense omnipotence emanes.
> Teach me to trace thine hand thro' all thy ways,
> Or in the earth or thro' the boist'rous seas.
> While toss'd on billows; cast on foreign shores,
> Or in the power of more than savage MOORS,
> Tho' this sad traffic scarce will bear appeal,*
> Yet, LORD, thy servant only goes to heal.

* [from Boulton's note:] The AUTHOR of this piece was lately engaged in a voyage to AFRICA, in the capacity of *Surgeon;* upon which voyage all on board was killed, excepting himself and two others, who were in a most miraculous manner preserved, after having been exposed to the shot of not only the NEGROES, but also to the shot of Capt. FISHER, for several hours.

THOMAS BOULTON

from Part III of The Voyage
"A Moderate Breeze"

Such men there are, nor will they cease to be,
Whilst men o TITTLE copy after thee;*
To blush with shame, is foreign to thy race,
No crimson e'er was in an Ethiop's face,
And none so stupid, or so dimly blind,
But from thy looks may trace a vicious mind.

　　But here I'd not be thought to censure all,
Or let the lash upon the guiltless fall;
Many there are, who do such crimes detest,
And these my muse would sever from the rest.

　　I know the wretch whom this my cap doth fit,
Will damn my genius, and condemn my wit.

　　I value not his censure, or his praise,
I'd shun alike, his colour and his ways.

　　Of such I'd speak, to warn succeeding times,
To shun the mischiefs of his hateful crimes;
To warn them from a DIZIA's rule to fly,†
DIZIA who did my peace of mind destroy.
　　　　　　　　　　　　　(1770)[112]

---

* [Boulton's note:] A mulatto captain who sails out of Liverpool. "No friend to God, a foe to
all mankind" [ERASMUS].
† [Boulton's note:] DIZIA an *African* lady,
　　Whose sooty charms he was so wrapt in,
　　He strait ordain'd her second captain;
　　So strict was she in ev'ry matter,
　　She even lock'd the jar of water:
　　And whil'st in that high station plac'd,
　　No thirsty soul a drop must taste.

JANE DUNLAP (fl. 1765–1771)

Little is known about this pious Bostonian, except her self-description as a "poor person in [an] obscure station of life" who avidly followed the evangelist George Whitefield on his "Great Awakening" missions to New England. The excerpts below are from a 1771 volume of poems inspired by Whitefield's sermons and dedicated to his memory. Like Whitefield, Dunlap includes blacks in her vision of salvation. Remarkably, in one poem Dunlap acknowledges that she is moved to write by the example of the African American poet Phillis Wheatley (see Wheatley's poem on Whitefield, included elsewhere).

from [Untitled]

Shall his due praises be so loudly sung
By a young Afric damsel[']s virgin tongue?
And I be silent! and no mention make
Of his blest name, who did so often speak.

To us, the words of life,
Fetch'd from the fountain pure,
Of God's most holy sacred truths;
Which ever shall endure.

(1771)[113]

The Ethiopians Shall Stretch out Their Hands to God, or a Call to the Ethiopians

Poor Negroes flee, you'll welcome be,
Your colour's no exception;
But fly to Christ, he's paid the price,
Meet for your Souls redemption.

And though your souls made black with sin,
The Lord can make them white;
And cloath'd in his pure righteousness,
They'll shine transparent bright.

(1771)[114]

?THOMAS THISTLETHWAITE ["S.E."] (fl. 1770s)

An amateur poet about whom little is known, Thistlethwaite was inspired by Chatterton's series of "African Eclogues" to compose his own. Like Chatterton, Thistlethwaite lived in Bristol, a major slave-trading port, and may have been moved by seafarers' tales or black faces in the street to idealize African people in verse. Thistlethwaite sent this poem in to a London periodical (*Every Man's Magazine*)—a mode of publication that fostered a vogue for poetry about Africa and raised awareness of non-European peoples, however fictionalized.

from "Bambo and Giffar; an African Eclogue"

BAMBO. My charming *Squabee* was the loveliest maid
That e'er with kindness love like mine repaid;
Black as the glossy jet on yonder hill
Where *Eacal* forms the ever-murmuring rill;
Mild as the gentle breezes of the spring,
Whose fragrant gales the sweets of *Borno* bring;
Gay as the plumage of yon proud macaw;
Whose lengthened tail such various feathers draw;
Swift as an arrow from the well-string'd bow,
Sweeter than maize which in the vallies grow;
Majestic as the cocoa's graceful tree,
Her form display'd the justest symmetry.
The gold crown'd sun began to gild the plain,
And with fresh lustre spread its wide domain;
Reclin'd upon her breast I lay at ease,
Tasting the fragrance of the southern breeze;
When o'er our heads black rushing clouds did fly,
And sudden tempests mantled o'er the sky;
The lucid lightning danc'd upon the ground,
Whilst dreadful thunder hurl'd destruction round;

193

Wild boist'rous winds with fury shook the wood,
Loud as the noise of *Niger*'s roaring flood;
Impetuous torrents overflow'd the lake,
And desolation smote the flow'ry brake:
Let us be gone my love, alarm'd I cry'd,
Ere horrors hem us round on ev'ry side.—
When lo, I saw,—distraction seize my brain!
Squabee stretch'd lifeless on the drenched plain;
A fiery bolt had laid her on the green,
Her sable charms no more were to be seen;
Torn from my arms she never will return,
Whilst I in endless grief her absence mourn.

(1771)[115]

WILLIAM ROSCOE (1753–1831)

Truly a renaissance man, Roscoe rose from humble Liverpool origins to become a successful lawyer and banker, while also pursuing a career as a writer, civic leader, and social reformer. His achievements include the production of several literary works, a major role in the introduction of Italian literature into England, the founding of various cultural institutions, and a short but significant career in Parliament as an antislavery activist. This last cost him his seat in Parliament, and nearly his life, when, having voted to abolish the slave trade in the spring of 1807, he returned to Liverpool (a leading slave trade port) to face an angry mob.

The following excerpt, from a descriptive poem written when Roscoe was nineteen, follows in the style of Pope's *Windsor-Forest* and John Dyer's *The Fleece*. The poem is remarkable as an early and explicit denunciation of slavery on economic, political, and moral grounds.

from "Mount Pleasant"

There AFRIC's swarthy sons their toils repent,
Beneath the fervors of the noon-tide heat;
Torn from each joy that crowned their native soil,
No sweet reflections mitigate their toil;
From morn, to eve, by rigorous hands opprest,
Dull fly their hours, of every hope unblest.
Till, broke with labour, helpless, and forlorn,
From their weak grasp the lingering morsel torn;
The reed-built hovel's friendly shade denied;
The jest of folly, and the scorn of pride;
Drooping beneath meridian suns they lie,
Lift the faint head, and bend the imploring eye;
Till Death, in kindness, from the tortured breast
Calls the free spirit to the realms of rest.

Shame to mankind! But shame to BRITONS most,
Who all the sweets of Liberty can boast;
Yet, deaf to every human claim, deny
That bliss to others, which themselves enjoy:
Life's bitter draught with harsher bitter fill;
Blast every joy, and add to every ill;
The trembling limbs with galling iron bind,
Nor loose the heavier bondage of the mind.

Yet whence these horrors? this inhuman rage,
That brands with blackest infamy the age?
Is it, our varied interests disagree,
And BRITAIN sinks if AFRIC's sons be free?
—No—Hence a few superfluous stores we claim,
That tempt our avarice, but increase our shame . . .
—Blest were the days ere Foreign Climes were known,
Our wants contracted, and our wealth our own;
When Health could crown, and Innocence endear.
The temperate meal, that cost no eye a tear:
Our drink, the beverage of the crystal flood.
—Not madly purchased by a brother's blood—
Ere the wide spreading ills of Trade began,
Or Luxury trampled on the rights of Man.

(wr. 1772/pub. 1777)[116]

Writing in the year that the British Abolition Society was founded, Roscoe began a long political poem in two parts that editorialized against the slave trade in unambiguous terms. Amid the moral indignation, what stands out in the following excerpt is Roscoe's fantasy that the slave trade might have been extinguished at the start if the first European trader to try it had been slain by a defiant African.

from Part I of "The Wrongs of Africa"

But say, whence first the unnatural trade arose,
And what the strong inducement, that could tempt
Such dread perversion? Could not Afric's wealth,
Her ivory, and her granulated gold,
To her superfluous, well repay the stores
(Superfluous too) from distant Europe sent;
But liberty and life must be the price,
And man become the merchandise and spoil?
—O, when with slow and hesitating voice

The wily European first proposed
His hateful barter,—that some patriot hand,
Urged with prophetic rage, had stopt the source
Of future ill, and deep within his breast
The deadly weapon buried!—whilst aloof
Stood his pale brethren, paler then with fear,
And shuddering at the awful deed, had learnt
To venerate the eternal rights of man.

(1787)[117]

In this excerpt, Roscoe imagines the departure of a slave ship from the African coast, the panic of the slaves below decks, the eerie silence that descends after the first day, and the bloody shipboard insurrection that erupts from the stillness. Writing with the visual acuteness of a painter, Roscoe captures the shipboard scene as vividly as any writer of the century.

from Part II of "The Wrongs of Africa"

Deep freighted now with human merchandise,
The vessel quits the shore; prepared to meet
The storms and dangers of the Atlantic main;
Her motion scarce observed, save when the flood
In frequent murmurs beats against her prow,
And the tall cocoas slowly seem to change
Their former station. Lessening on the sight,
The distant mountains bowed their cloud-capped heads;
And all the bright and variegated scene,
Of hills, and groves, and lawns, and reed-built sheds,
That oft had caught the prisoners' ardent eye,
Not hopeless of escape, now gradual sunk
To one dim hue. Amongst the sable tribes
Soon spread the alarm; when sudden from the depths
Of crowded holds, and loathsome caverns, rose
One universal yell of dread despair,
And anguish inexpressible; for now
Hope's slender thread was broke; extinguished now
The spark of expectation, that had lurked
Beneath the ashes of their former joys,
And o'er despondency's surrounding gloom
Had shed its languid lustre. Bold, and fierce,
Of high indignant spirit, some their chains
Shook menacing, and from their lowering eyes,

Flashed earnest of the flame that burned within:
Whilst groans, and loud laments, and scalding tears
Marked the keen pangs of others.——Female shrieks,
At intervals in dreadful concert heard,
To wild distraction manly sorrow turned;
And ineffectual, o'er their heedless limbs
Was waved the wiry whip, that dropped with blood.

    Now sunk the mournful day; but mournful still
The night that followed: and the rising morn,
That spread before the hopeless captives' view
Nought but the wide expanse of air and sea,
Heard all their cries with double rage renewed.
Nor did the storm of headstrong passions rest,
Till the third evening closed; nor by degrees
Was hushed; but sudden, as the autumnal blast,
Its rage exhausted, sinks at once to rest,
Whilst the wide wood, that bowed beneath its course,
Declines its wearied branches, thus the strife
Ceased——not a groan, and not a voice was heard;
But, as one soul had influenced every breast,
A sudden stillness reigned. Resigned and mild,
As if forgot their former sense of wrong,
They took the scanty fare they lately spurned;
And if a tear should mingle with their food,
No prying eye perceived it: day by day
Saw the same scene renewed; whilst prosperous gales
Full towards her destined port the vessel bore;
And gently breathing o'er the seaman's mind
Came the remembrance of his native land;
The thoughts of former pleasures, former friends,
Of rest and independence; heedless, he,
That on the miseries of others rose
The fabric of his joys; and gratified
His selfish views, whilst multitudes bewailed
The eternal loss of nature's dearest gifts;——
To them, irreparable wrong; to him,
A slight accession to his stores of bliss.

    'Twas night; and now the ship, with steady course,
Pursued her midway voyage: subsided now
The tyrant's dread, a more indulgent lot
The slaves experienced; and their chains relaxed

Their biting cincture. Fearless trod the deck
The unsuspicious guard; whilst, from below,
Amidst the crowd of captives, not a sound
Of louder note ascended. Yet, even then,
Each eye was wake, and every heaving breast
Was panting for revenge. For now approached
The awful hour, long hoped for, long forefixed,
Sacred to vengeance, to the thirst of blood,
And bitter retribution. Slowly rolled
The moments, whilst, with anxious minds, the slaves
Waited the voice that loosed them from restraint,
And turned them on their tyrants . . .
A hollow murmur rises, that upbraids
The long delay—nor yet the voice is heard!
Whilst in each agitated breast, by turns,
Dismay, and doubt, and desperation reign;
And fancy, now triumphant, now depressed,
Luxuriant wantons through the scene of blood,
Or feels the fiery torture. "Rise, revenge—
Revenge your wrongs," the expected voice exclaims,
And meets a ready answer, from the tongues
Of countless numbers, from each gloomy cell,
In dreadful cries returned. But who shall tell
The wild commotion; who the frantic rage
Of savage fury, when with joint accord
They burst the opposing gratings, and poured forth
Impetuous as the flood that breaks its mound?
—What though unarmed!—upon the unsparing steel
They rushed regardless; and the expected wound
Deep, but not always deadly, roused their minds
To fiercer desperation: thronging close,
Fearless and firm, they joined the unequal war;
And when the fatal weapon pierced their side,
They struggled to retain it, and in death
Disarmed the hand that conquered.—Thick they fell,
But oft not unrevenged, for fastening close
Upon the foe, some gained the vessel's side,
And rushed together to a watery death;
Whilst from the hold, emerging throngs
Replaced the vanquished, and, with hideous cries,
Struck terror through the tyrants' chilling veins,
And bade oppression tremble. Nerveless stood

The hardened seamen: but recovering soon,
They gained the barrier, that across the deck
Its firm defence projected; then began
The scene of blood; then poured amongst the slaves,
Frantic and fierce, and maddening with their wrongs,
The volleyed vengeance . . .
                    —Terror and surprise,
Like deadly bloodhounds, seized the vanquished slaves,
That stood defenceless and exposed, that mark
Of uncontrolled revenge; and as they fell,
Without reluctance saw the purple stream
Slow welling from the fount of life, and, joined
In kindred currents, pour along the deck,
Tinging with guiltless blood the western wave.
                    (wr. 1787/pub. 1788)[118]

In this melodramatic ballad, co-authored with his friend Dr. Currie and published anonymously in 1788, Roscoe creates the voice of Maraton, an enslaved African, who pines for his lost love ("Adila"), hears her calling him from beyond the grave, and vows to commit suicide to be reunited with her. For all its sentimental stylization, the poem builds on the sad truth that suicide was common among slaves. Popular for decades after, the ballad became a staple of such anthologies as Mavor and Pratt's *Classical English Poetry, for the Use of Schools* (1801), which went through innumerable editions in the nineteenth century.

The African

Wide over the tremulous sea
    The moon spread her mantle of light;
And the gale, gently dying away,
    Breathed soft on the bosom of night.

On the forecastle Maraton stood,
    And poured forth his sorrowful tale;
His tears fell unseen in the flood,
    His sighs passed unheard on the gale.

Ah, wretch! in wild anguish he cried,
    From country and liberty torn,—
Ah, Maraton! would thou hadst died
    Ere o'er the salt waves thou wert borne!

Through the groves of Angola I strayed,
    Love and hope made my bosom their home;

WILLIAM ROSCOE

There I talked with my favorite maid,
  Nor dreamt of the sorrow to come.

From the thicket the man-hunter sprung,
  My cries echoed loud through the air;
There was fury and wrath on his tongue,
  He was deaf to the shrieks of despair!

Accursed be the merciless band,
  That his love could from Maraton tear;
And blasted this impotent hand,
  That was severed from all I held dear.

Flow, ye tears—down my cheeks ever flow—
  Still let sleep from my eyelids depart;
And still may the arrow of woe
  Drink deep of the stream of my heart.

But, hark! On the silence of night
  My Adila's accents I hear;
And, mournful beneath the wan light,
  I see her loved image appear.

Slow o'er the smooth ocean she glides,
  As the mist that hangs light on the wave;
And fondly her lover she chides,
  That lingers so long from his grave!

"O! Maraton, haste thee," she cries;
  "Here the reign of oppression is o'er;
The tyrant is robbed of his prize,
  And Adila sorrows no more."

Now sinking amidst the dim ray,
  Her form seems to fade on my view;
O stay thee, my Adila, stay!—
  She beckons, and I must pursue.

To-morrow, the white man in vain
  Shall proudly account me his slave;
My shackles I plunge in the main,
  And rush to the realms of the brave.

                    (1788)[119]

DANIEL BLISS (fl. 1773–1781)

The unrhymed but lyrical lines of this inscription for a slave in Concord, Massachusetts, open questions both about American history and about the proper form of epitaph poetry itself. Composed by the lawyer and Tory sympathizer Daniel Bliss, the epitaph commemorates the African John Jack in unsentimental terms and exposes the hypocrisy of Americans clamoring for liberty while holding slaves. The lines achieved the status of literary text in 1775 when a British soldier copied them down and sent them to be reprinted in a London newspaper. Years later the gravestone itself became the focus of a local abolitionist group, who decorated it and held ceremonies at the site.

[Untitled Epitaph for John Jack, a Native of Africa]

God wills us free; man wills us slaves.
I will as God wills; God's will be done
　　—Here lies the body of—
　　　　—JOHN JACK—
A native of Africa who died
March 1773, aged about 60 years.
Tho' born in a land of slavery
He was born free.
Tho' he lived in a land of liberty,
He lived a slave.
Till by his honest, tho' stolen labors,
He acquired the source of slavery,
Which gave him his freedom;
Tho' not long before
Death, the grand tyrant,
Gave him his final emancipation,
And set him on a footing with kings.
Tho' a slave to vice,
He practiced those virtues
Without which kings are but slaves.
　　　　　　　　(1773)[120]

THOMAS DAY (1748–1789)

An Oxford-educated idealist heavily influenced by Rousseau, Day was a self-conscious social reformer who practiced asceticism, tried Pygmalion-like educational experiments, and grew increasingly eccentric as he aged. Friends with Richard Edgeworth (father of Maria, the novelist) and Erasmus Darwin, Day published a variety of didactic and philosophical works before dying in a bizarre accident. True to his theory that kindness would tame any animal, he insisted on riding an unbroken horse on a journey; the horse threw him and Day died within the hour.

The Dying Negro, his first publication (possibly aided by the barrister John Bicknell, an old Oxford friend), made a huge impact. Enthusiastically reviewed and popular with the general public, the poem went through several editions. Purportedly based on a true story then in the news, the poem imagines the final soliloquy of the African: a tragic tale of enslavement, interracial love, heartbreaking separation, and dramatic suicide. For all its sentimental conventions and stylistic traces of Shakespeare, Milton, and Gray, the poem closes (like so many before it) with the prospect of African vengeance against Europe, in a vision of apocalyptic racial violence. The poem influenced a whole generation, including innumerable antislavery activists such as Clarkson and Grégoire, and even some African writers such as Olaudah Equiano.

The Dying Negro, a Poetical Epistle, Supposed to be Written by a Black, (Who lately shot himself on board a vessel in the river Thames;) to his intended Wife

> Blest with thy last sad gift—the power to dye,
> At length, thy shafts, stern fortune, I defy;
> Welcome, kind pass-port to an unknown shore!—
> The world and I are enemies no more.
> This weapon ev'n in chains the brave can wield,
> And vanquish'd, quit triumphantly the field.

    Yet ere this execrated being close,
Ere one determin'd stroke end all my woes.
O thou whom late I call'd too fondly mine,
Dearer than life, whom I with life resign!
How shall I soothe thy grief, my destin'd bride!
One sad farewell, one last embrace denied?
For oh! thy tender breast my pangs will share,
Bleed for my wounds, and feel my deep despair.
Thy tears alone will grace a wretch's grave,
A wretch, whom only thou would'st wish to save.
Take these last sighs—to thee my soul I breathe—
Fond love in dying groans, is all I can bequeathe.

    Why did I, slave, beyond my lot aspire?
Why didst thou fan, fair maid, the growing fire?
Full dear, for each deluding smile of thine
I pay, nor at thy fatal charms repine.
For thee I bade my drooping soul revive;
For thee alone I could have borne to live;
And love, I said, shall make me large amends,
For persecuting foes, and faithless friends;
Fool that I was! enur'd so long to pain,
To trust to hope, or dream of joy again.
Joy, stranger guest, too soon my faith betray'd,
And love but points to death's eternal shade,
There while I rest from mis'ry's galling load,
Be thou the care of every pitying God!
Nor may that Daemon's unpropitious power,
Who shed his influence on my natal hour,
Pursue thee too with unrelenting hate,
And blend with mine the colour of thy fate.
For thee may those soft hours return again,
When pleasure led thee o'er the smiling plain,
Ere, like some hell-born spectre of dismay,
I cross'd thy path, and darken'd all the way.
Ye waving groves, that from this cell I view!
Ye meads, now glitt'ring with the morning dew!
Ye flowers that blush on yonder purple shore,
That at my baneful step shall fade no more,
A long farewell!—I ask no vernal bloom—
No pageant wreaths to deck an outcast's tomb.
—Let serpents hiss and night-shade blacken there,
To mark the friendless victim of despair!

THOMAS DAY

And better in th' untimely grave to rot,
The world and all it's cruelties forgot,
Than dragg'd once more beyond the Western main,
To groan beneath some dastard planter's chain,
Where my poor countrymen in bondage wait,
The long enfranchisement of ling'ring fate.
Oh! my heart sinks, my dying eyes o'erflow,
When mem'ry paints the picture of their woe!
For I have seen them, ere the dawn of day,
Rouz'd by the lash, go forth their chearless way,
And while their souls with shame and anguish burn,
Salute with groans unwelcome morn's return,
And, chiding every hour the slow-pac'd sun
Pursue their toils, till all his race was run,
Without one hope—to mitigate their pain—
One distant hope, their freedom to regain;
Then like the dull unpitied brutes repair
To stalls more wretched, and to coarser fare,
Thank Heav'n, one day of misery was o'er,
And sink to sleep, and wish to wake no more.
Sleep on! dear, lost companions in despair,
Whose suff'rings still my latest tears shall share!
Sleep, and enjoy the only boon of Heav'n
To you in common with your tyrants giv'n.
O while soft slumber from their couches flies,
Still may its balmy blessings seal your eyes;
Awhile in sweet oblivion lull your woes,
And brightest visions gladden your repose!
Let fancy now, unconscious of the change,
Thro' your own climes, and native forests range,
Still waft ye to each well-known stream and grove,
And visit every long-lost scene ye love!
—I sleep no more—nor in the midnight shade,
Invoke ideal phantoms to my aid,
Nor wake again, abandon'd and forlorn,
To find each dear delusion fled at morn;
A slow-consuming death I will not wait,
But snatch at least one sullen boon from fate;
Yon ruddy streaks the rising sun proclaim,
That never more shalt beam upon my shame;
Bright orb! for others let thy glory shine—
The gloomy privilege to die, be mine.

Beneath such wrongs let pallid Christians live,
Such they can perpetrate, and may forgive.

    And thou, whose impious avarice and pride
Thy God's blest symbol to my brows denied,
Forbade me or the rights of man to claim,
Or share with thee a Christian's hallow'd name,
Thou too farewell!—for not beyond the grave,
Thy power extends, nor is my dust thy slave.
Go bribe thy kindred ruffians with thy gold,
But dream not nature's rights are bought and sold.
In vain Heav'n spread so wide the swelling sea;
Vast watry barrier, 'twixt thy world and me;
Swift round the globe, by earth nor heav'n controul'd,
Fly proud oppression and dire lust of gold.
Where'er the thirsty hell-hounds take their way,
Still nature bleeds, and man becomes their prey.
In the wild wastes of Afric's sandy plain,
Where roars the lion through his drear domain,
To curb the savage monarch in the chace,
There too Heav'n planted man's majestic race;
Bade reason's sons with nobler titles rise,
Lift high their brow sublime, and scan the skies.*
What tho' the sun in his meridian blaze
On their scorch'd bodies dart his fiercest rays?
What tho' no rosy tints adorn their face,
No silken ringlets shine with flowing grace?
Yet of etherial temper are their souls,
And in their veins the tide of honour rolls;
And valour kindles there the hero's flame,
Contempt of death, and thirst of martial fame.
And pity melts the sympathizing breast,
Ah! fatal virtue!—for the brave distrest.

    My tortur'd breast, O sad remembrance spare!
Why dost thou plant thy keenest daggers there,
And shew me what I was, and aggravate despair?
Ye streams of Gambia, and thou sacred shade!

* [Day's note:] "It is amazing, that such a rude and illiterate people should reason so perti-
nently in regard to the Heavenly Bodies; there is no doubt but that with proper instruments,
and a good will, they would become excellent Astronomers." M[ichel] Adanson's Voyage to
Senegal, &c.

THOMAS DAY

Where, in my youth's first dawn I joyful stray'd,
Oft have I rouz'd amid your caverns dim,
The howling tiger, and the lion grim,
In vain they gloried in their headlong force,
My javelin pierc'd them in their raging course.
But little did my boding mind bewray,
The victor and his hopes were doom'd a prey
To human beasts more fell, more cruel far than they.
Ah! what avails it that in every plain,
I purchas'd glory with my blood in vain?
Ah! what avails the conqu'ror's laurel meed,
The generous purpose or the dauntless deed?
Fall'n are my trophies, blasted is my fame,
Myself become a thing without a name,
The sport of haughty Lords and ev'n of slaves the shame.

    Curst be the winds, and curst the tides that bore
These European robbers to our shore!
O be that hour involv'd in endless night,
When first their streamers met my wond'ring sight,
I call'd the warriors from the mountain's steep,
To meet these unknown terrors of the deep;
Rouz'd by my voice, their generous bosoms glow,
They rush indignant, and demand the foe,
And poize the darts of death and twang the bended bow.
When lo! advancing o'er the sea-beat plain,
I mark'd the leader of a warlike train.
Unlike his features to our swarthy race.
And golden hair play'd round his ruddy face.
While with insidious smile and lifted hand,
He thus accosts our unsuspecting band.
"Ye valiant chiefs, whom love of glory leads
To martial combats, and heroic deeds;
No fierce invader your retreat explores,
No hostile banner waves along your shores.
From the dread tempests of the deep we fly,
Then lay, ye chiefs, these pointed terrors by.
And O, your hospitable cares extend,
So may ye never need the aid ye lend!
So may ye still repeat to every grove
The songs of freedom, and the strains of love!"
Soft as the accents of the traitor flow,

We melt with pity, and unbend the bow;
With lib'ral hand our choicest gifts we bring,
And point the wand'rers to the freshest spring.
Nine days we feasted on the Gambian strand,
And songs of friendship echo'd o'er the land.*
When the tenth morn her rising lustre gave,
The chief approach'd me by the sounding wave.
"O, youth," he said, "what gifts can we bestow,
Or how requite the mighty debt we owe?
For lo! propitious to our vows, the gale
With milder omens fills the swelling sail.
To-morrow's sun shall see our ships explore
These deeps, and quit your hospitable shore.
Yet while we linger, let us still employ
The number'd hours in friendship and in joy;
Ascend our ships, their treasures are your own,
And taste the produce of a world unknown."

He spoke; with fatal eagerness we burn,
Ah! wretches, destin'd never to return!
The smiling traitors with insidious care,
The goblet proffer, and the feast prepare,
'Till dark oblivion shades our closing eyes,
And all disarm'd each fainting warrior lies,
O wretches! to your future evils blind!
O morn for ever present to my mind!
When bursting from the treach'rous bands of sleep,
Rouz'd by the murmers of the dashing deep,
I woke to bondage, and ignoble pains,
And all the horrors of a life in chains.†

---

* [Day's note:] "Which way soever I turned my eyes on this pleasant spot, I beheld a perfect image of pure nature, an agreeable solitude bounded on every side by charming landscapes; the rural situation of cottages in the midst of trees; the ease and indolence of the Negroes, re-clined under the shade of their spreading foliage; the simplicity of their dress and manners; the whole revived in my mind the idea of our first parents, and I seemed to contemplate the world in its primitive state. They are, generally speaking, very good-natured, sociable, and obliging. I was not a little pleased with this, my first reception; it convinced me that there ought to be considerable abatement made in the accounts I had read and heard of the savage characters of the Africans." *M. Adanson's* Voyage to Senegal, &c.

† [Day's note:] "As we past along the coast, we very often lay before a town, and fired a gun for the natives to come off, but no soul came near us; at length we learnt by some ships that were trading down the coast, that the natives came seldom on board an English ship, for fear of being detained or carried off; yet at last some ventured on board; but if these chanced to

Where were your thunders in that dreadful hour,
Ye Gods of Afric! where your heavenly power?
Did not my prayers, my groans, my tears invoke
Your slumb'ring justice to direct the stroke?
No power descended to assist the brave,
No lightnings flash'd, and I became a slave.
From Lord to Lord my wretched carcase sold,
In Christian traffic, for their sordid gold:
Fate's blackest clouds still gather'd o'er my head;
And now they burst, and mix me with the dead.

Yet when my fortune cast my lot with thine,
And bade beneath one roof our labours join,
Surpriz'd I felt the tumults of my breast
Lull'd by thy beauties, and subside to rest.
Delusive hopes my changing soul enflame,
And gentler transports agitate my frame.
What tho' obscure thy birth, superior grace
Beam'd in the glowing features of thy face;
Ne'er had my youth such winning softness seen,
Where Afric's sable beauties danc'd the green,
When some bright maid receiv'd her lover's vow,
And bound the offer'd chaplet to her brow;
While on thy languid eyes I fondly gaze,
And tremble while I meet their azure rays,
O mildest virgin, thou did'st not despise
The humble homage of a captive's sighs.
By heav'n abandon'd and by man betray'd,
Each hope resign'd of comfort or of aid,
Thy gen'rous love could every sorrow end,
In thee I found a mistress and a friend;
Still as I told the story of my woes,
With heaving sighs thy lovely bosom rose;
The trick'ling drops of liquid chrystal stole
Down thy fair cheek, and mark'd thy pitying soul;

---

spy any arms, they would all immediately take to their canoes, and make the best of their way home." *Smith's* Voyage to Guinea.

"It is well known that many of the European nations, have, very unjustly and inhumanly, without any provocation, stolen away, from time to time, abundance of the people, not only on this coast, but almost every where in Guinea, who have come on board their ships, in a harmless and confiding manner; these they have in great numbers carried away, and sold in the plantations." *J. Barbot's* Description of Guinea.

Dear drops! upon my bleeding heart, like balm
They fell, and soon my wounded soul grew calm,
Then my lov'd country, parents, friends forgot;
Heaven I absolv'd, nor murmur'd at my lot,
Thy sacred smiles could every pang remove,
And liberty became less dear than love.

    —Ah! where is now that voice which lull'd my woes?
That Angel-face, which sooth'd me to repose?
By Nature tempted, and with passion blind,
Are these the joys Hope whisper'd to my mind?
Is this the end of constancy like thine?
Are these the transports of a flame like mine?
My hopes, my joys, are vanish'd into air,
And now of all that once engag'd my care,
These chains alone remain, this weapon and despair!

    —So may thy life's gay prospects all be curst,
And all thy flatt'ring hopes like bubbles burst,
Thus end thy golden visions, son of pride!
Whose ruthless ruffians tore me from my bride;
That beauteous prize Heav'n had reserv'd at last,
Sweet recompence for all my sorrows past.
O may thy harden'd bosom never prove
The tender joys of friendship or of love!
Yet may'st thou, doom'd to hopeless flames a prey,
In disappointed passion pine away!
And see thy fair-one, to a rival's arms,
Obdurate to thy vows, resign her charms.

    Why does my ling'ring soul her flight delay?
Come, lovely maid, and gild the dreary way!
Come, wildly rushing with disorder'd charms,
And clasp thy bleeding lover to thy arms,
Close his sad eyes, receive his parting breath,
And sooth him sinking in the shades of death!
O come—thy presence can my pangs beguile,
And bid th' inexorable tyrant smile;
Transported will I languish on thy breast,
And sink in raptures to eternal rest:
The hate of men, the wrongs of fate forgive,
Forget my woes, and almost wish to live.
—Ah! rather fly, lest ought of doubt controul
The dreadful purpose lab'ring in my soul,

THOMAS DAY

Tears must not bend me, nor thy beauties move,
This hour I triumph over fate and love.

    —Again with tenfold rage my bosom burns,
And all the tempest of my soul returns,
Now fiery transports rend my madding brain,
And death extends his shelt'ring arms in vain;
For unreveng'd I fall, unpitied die;
And with my blood glut Pride's insatiate eye!

    Thou Christian God, to whom so late I bow'd,
To whom my soul its fond allegiance vow'd,
When crimes like these thy injur'd pow'r prophane,
O God of Nature! art thou call'd in vain?
Did'st thou for this sustain a mortal wound,
While Heav'n, and Earth, and Hell, hung trembling round?
That these vile fetters might my body bind,
And agony like this distract my mind?
On thee I call'd with reverential awe,
Ador'd thy wisdom, and embrac'd thy law;
Yet mark thy destin'd convert as he lies,
His groans of anguish, and his livid eyes,
These galling chains, polluted with his blood,
Then bid his tongue proclaim thee just and good!
But if too weak thy boasted power to spare,
Or suff'rings move thee not, O hear despair!
Thy hopes, and blessings I alike resign,
But let revenge, let swift revenge be mine!
Be this proud bark, which now triumphant rides,
Toss'd by the winds, and shatter'd by the tides!
And may these fiends, who now exulting view
The horrors of my fortune, feel them too!
Be their's the torment of a ling'ring fate,
Slow as thy justice, dreadful as my hate,
Condemn'd to grasp the riven plank in vain,
And chac'd by all the monsters of the main,
And while they spread their sinking arms to thee,
Then let their fainting souls remember me!

                                    (1773)[121]

PERCIVAL STOCKDALE
(1736–1811)

A minor poet with an inflated sense of his own importance, peripherally con-
nected with Samuel Johnson's circle, Stockdale nonetheless supported various
enlightened causes, including the abolition of slavery. His poetic tribute to
Day's influential poem suggests how readily some contemporary readers em-
braced even the most violent and revolutionary elements of Day's antislavery
vision. Stockdale returned to the subject in the 1790s, in his pamphlet *A Letter to
Granville Sharp, suggested by the present Insurrection of the Negroes in the Island of
St. Domingo* (1791).

from "To the Author of a Poem Just Published, Entitled 'The Dying Negro'"

Accept, pathetic bard, these generous lays;
A poet will not spurn a poet's praise. . . .
May all the curses which thy youth implores
With speedy ruin reach West Indian shores!
Oh! may the Negroes, with an iron rod,
Avenge the cause of Nature, and of God!
May they in happy combination rise,
Torture their doom, or liberty their prize;
Rush with resistless fury on their foes,
By one great effort expiate Afric's woes;
Eager each mark of slavery to efface,
Of their pale tyrants murder all the race! . . .

Then will my mind be open to believe
That Christ, or Israel's awful king of kings,
Minutely regulates terrestrial things.

And as the poet's warm expansive soul
Spreads its benevolence from pole to pole,
Loves man, his brother, in Siberian snow,

Or where the spicy gales of Afric blow;
Then I'll enjoy the Negro's happy lot,
His purling rivulet, his peaceful cot;
Behold him, stretched beneath a fragrant shade,
Breathe fervid accents to a sable maid;
Or pass, in mirth, and festal song, the day,
Streams, groves, and hills responsive to his lay:
No northern ruffian near, importing woes,
No ruthless Christian to disturb repose!

(c. 1773)[122]

In these lines from a later poem about his retirement from London, Stockdale reaffirms his commitment to the antislavery cause. The passage is noteworthy for its empathy, as the poet imagines a radical reversal of fates in which whites like himself are kidnapped from Britain and forced into bondage.

from "On My Going to Live at Windsor"

But let the poor; the friendless; the distressed;
Scorned by the rich; avoided by the rest;
Plead with decisive pathos, in my breast.
When lords of millions not a mite bestow,
Even I may mitigate a brother's woe.
May I, when languid in the negro's cause,
On English ground, in vain imploring laws!
Be torne by ruffians from my native shore,
Like him; and destined ne'er to view it more:
Possess, while eager to resign my breath,
But a mere coffin's room, before my death!

(c. 1791/pub. 1810)[123]

ANONYMOUS ["BOB JINGLE, ESQ."]

In the era of the American Revolution, political propaganda often took poetic form. In this excerpt from an unknown American's pamphlet, defiance of British trade policies is coupled with a call to abolish the slave trade. In an appendix to his poem, the writer quotes with approval the Continental Congress's resolution to "neither import, nor purchase any slave imported, after the first day of December next; after which time, we will wholly discontinue the slave-trade." Many forget that the first draft of the *Declaration of Independence* also contained such a provision (deleted before final publication). Some critics of America, such as Samuel Johnson and David Hartley, pointed out that the institution of slavery itself, not just the trade, was the real immorality. In the end, however, all such attempts to link antislavery projects to the American Revolution failed.

from The Association, &c. of the Delegates of the Colonies, at the Grand Congress, Held at Philadelphia, Sept. 1, 1774

    First, that from and after December the first,
May *we,* meaning *you* all, forever be curst,
If we into *America—British,* import
Any Goods, Wares, or Merchandize, of any Sort,
From *England's* Kennels, or Boroughs, or Dens;
From *Scotland's* high Hills, or from *Ireland's* Fens;
Or East-India Tea, from *Guinea* or *Rome,*
Or Parts known or unknown, Abroad or at Home . . .
    Then, *secondly,* we do protest, vow and swear,
That we from the Slave-Trade, will wholly forbear;
Tobacco and Indigo, Rice, we may have,
Without the Assistance of one Negro-Slave;
The *Britons* will gladly come over and work,

ANONYMOUS

Tho' we use them as hard as a Jew or a Turk;
But if not, never fear, we can do well enough,
Our *poor Folks* can labour, when stript to the Buff;
And sure in the Cause of *American Freedom*,
They will not refuse to be *Slaves*, if we need 'em;
But if a Reflection so noble and fine fails,
They'll soon be brought to't, by a good Cat-o'nine Tails:
But yet, after all, if a Scheme that's so clever,
Should fail, it will *frighten Great-Britain*, however.
To conclude upon this Head, we've only to say,
We'll not eat, drink, or smoke, with a Man that says nay.

(1774)[124]

EDWARD LONG (1734–1813)

Whether his own composition or adapted from elsewhere, these lines confirm the tenacity of racial prejudice in the mind of this Jamaican judge and man of letters. Long inserted this disparaging poem into his commentary on Francis Williams (anthologized above), the Caribbean free black author and Cambridge graduate whose extraordinary accomplishments Long only grudgingly acknowledged.

Untitled from The History of Jamaica

What woeful stuff this madrigal would be
In some starv'd, hackney sonneteer, or me!
But let a *Negroe* own the happy lines,
How the wit brightens! how the style refines!
Before his sacred name flies ev'ry fault,
And each exalted stanza teems with thought!

(1774)[125]

WILLIAM HAYWARD ROBERTS
(c. 1736–1791)

A graduate of King's College, Cambridge, Roberts was a cleric, poet, and biblical scholar who spent much of his life on the faculty at Eton, including his final ten years as Provost. A mentor of the young William Hayley (whose antislavery poem is included elsewhere), Roberts contrived, amid this long theological poem, to pause and condemn the evils of slavery.

from Part I, A Poetical Essay on the Existence of God

Near the banks
Of Zaara, whence the merchant, dreadful trade!
Comes fraught with slavery to Caribbean isles,
The tawny African o'er Ocean's stream
Spreads forth his arms; on bended knee implores
The howling winds; and begs the storm to drive
The cruel Christian far from Congo's coast.

(1774)[126]

MARY SCOTT (fl. 1774–1788)

Only fragments survive about this early feminist author: she lived in Milbourne Port, Somerset, held fervent low-church Protestant beliefs, was friends with Anna Seward, admired the antislavery poetry of Helen Maria Williams, married the dissenting minister John Taylor in 1786, and published a poetic *Messiah* (Bath, 1788). Writing in the year after Wheatley's celebrated visit to London, Scott here includes Wheatley in her version of a pantheon of British women writers and links her to the earlier nature poet William Shenstone (included elsewhere).

from The Female Advocate; A Poem. Occasioned By Reading Mr. Duncombe's Feminead.

> Daughter of SHENSTONE* hail! hail charming maid,
> Well hath thy pen fair nature's charms display'd!
> The hill, the grove, the flow'r-enamell'd lawn,
> Shine in thy lays in brightest colours drawn:
> Nor be thy praise confin'd to rural themes,
> Or idly-musing Fancy's pleasing dreams;
> But still may contemplation† (guest divine!)
> Expand thy breast, and prompt the flowing line.
>
> (1774)[127]

---

* [Scott's note:] See original Poems by Miss *Wheatley*.
† [Scott's note:] This couplet alludes to a fine Poem of that Lady's, intituled, "The Pleasures of Contemplation."

JOHN WESLEY (1703–1791)

The famous religious reformer and founder of Methodism was also a prominent opponent of slavery. The following lines, which Wesley either composed himself or adapted from another source, appear in a substantive antislavery essay in which he denounces the sinfulness of slaveholding and asserts that "the African is in no respect inferior to the European." The essay closes with an emotional appeal to Jesus on behalf of the slaves ("Thou Saviour of all, make them free, that they may be free indeed!"), followed by this hymn-like coda.

Untitled from Thoughts Upon Slavery

The servile progeny of Ham
    Seize as the purchase of thy blood!
Let all the Heathen know thy name:
    From idols to the living GOD
The dark Americans convert,
And shine in every pagan heart!
(1774)[128]

ANONYMOUS

The following excerpts are from a serialized poem published anonymously in the May and June 1775 issues of the *London Magazine*. That an antislavery poem of such length and sentimental fervor could appear without controversy, in one of the most widely read magazines of the time, suggests the degree to which the literate public either shared or at least acquiesced in such views. More interesting for its ideas than its lyricism, the poem closes with a prophesy (so prescient) that the day would come when the devastated societies of Africa would have to be rebuilt.

from *"Remarks on the Slavery of the Negroes"*

Full in my view a num'rous train appears
Of wretched exiles, bath'd in briny tears,
Forc'd from their country by some ruthless hand,
And sold for captives in a foreign land:
Far from the comforts of domestick life,
Father from son, and husband torn from wife;
Compell'd to drag oppression's galling chain,
And till the land, whilst others reap the gain;
Expos'd half naked to the scorching rays
Of darting Phoebus in his noon-tide blaze:
Scarce time allow'd to eat their scanty meal,
And each small fault the dreadful scourge must feel:
Full oft the lash with purple gore is dy'd,
Whilst down their backs descends the crimson tide.
Woes follow woes, and griefs on griefs arise,
In vain the tears hang trembling on their eyes;
In vain their sighs, in vain their tears are spent,
Their cruel tyrants know not to relent. . . .
An easier labour to recount the grains

Of driving sand on parch'd Arabia's plains,
Than to declare the num'rous ills decreed
By cruel man, to Afric's sable seed.
Obdurate hearts! encas'd with harden'd steel
Who this can view, and not compassion feel!
O ye who lost to every sense of woe
Inflict the tortures that they undergo;
Who can your hands in human gore imbrue,
And the vile trade for viler gain pursue!
Sure no kind mother clasp'd you to her breast,
Sure by no father have you been caress'd
But torn from rocks amidst the wat'ry main
Suck'd some fierce tigress on Numidia's plain.
But oh! methinks, the dreadful day draws nigh;
When God himself will ev'ry action try,
At whose tribunal bribes will naught avail;
Where hood-wink'd justice lifts the impartial scale.
Methinks on high the vengeful sword I see
Edg'd with destruction, ready to obey,
Unless repentance for your cruel deeds,
Unless repentance to each crime succeeds.
When on your heads the writhen bolts shall fly,
And dreadful thunders roll along the sky,
Then will you tremble, tho' in soft repose
Now lull'd secure, ye disregard these woes.
But oh! I wish (might I that wish obtain) . . .
That Christian hearts no more might thirst for gold,
Nor th' human race for wretched slaves be sold;
That on the confines of Numidea's shore,
The brazen throat of dreadful war no more
Might kindle rage, nor mortal thunder roar:
Then in the covert of embow'ring groves,
Glad Afric's sons might woo their sable loves
Secure and undisturb'd, no danger near,
No hostile foe to mix their joys with fear.
Altho' at present they are sore distrest,
Some rays of hope illuminate my breast;
My spirits cheer, my withering joys renew,
And future ages open to my view.
Methinks I see the long expected day,
When gentle peace exerts her genial sway;
Her olive branch aloft in air she rears,

And dire ambition from his empire tears . . .
On Gambia's banks I see new towns arise
Whose curling smoke invades the azure skies;
And Whydah's cities from their ashes spring,
Laid low in ruins by their cruel king. . . .
O glorious day! O day of peace arise!
And with thy splendors glad my longing eyes.
(1775)[129]

ANONYMOUS ["T."]

Both the interracial contact and the initiative taken by the female are significant in this poem, which appeared immediately in the wake of other poems about slavery in the *London Magazine* of 1775 (included elsewhere). That the "beautiful young lady" (tacitly assumed to be white) controls the scene and plants the kiss suggests the boy is one of the black children so fashionable as servants in affluent English households of the time.

On Seeing a Beautiful Young Lady Kiss a Black Boy

Whoever saw a contrast half so true?
The spotless ivory with the ebon view!
Was such Adonis when the Queen of Love
Prais'd all his charms—and did his form approve?
Thrice happy boy, to riot in such bliss,
And take from beauty's lips a virgin kiss!
To have the sweet distinction, I would be
As Æthiop black;—O to be kiss'd by thee
Is such a rapture, that by Jove I'd part
With every worth—since I have pledg'd my heart.
Thus *Cato*'s daughter, in the day of Rome,
On black *Numidia*'s prince bestow'd her bloom;
Juba with rapture took the patriot maid,
And bless'd his *Marcia* in the rural shade.
More black than *Juba* is thy Æthiop boy,
And thou more fair than *Marcia* crown'st his joy.
Thrice happy boy—with such a mistress kind,
With spotless manners, and the purest mind.

(1775)[130]

ANONYMOUS

The routine use of racist language surfaces at unexpected moments. In these lines from a satiric ditty about the rag-tag American Revolutionary army, the speaker mocks the diversity of humble figures who came to enlist in Washington's forces—among them many blacks. Initially, there was controversy over whether to accept blacks in the American army but very soon, prompted in part by the British General Dunmore's enlistment of runaway slaves in Virginia, Washington felt able to admit black troops without alienating his fellow southerners. Eventually thousands of blacks served on both sides in the Revolutionary War.

from "Adam's Fall: The Trip to Cambridge. 1775"

When Congress sent great Washington
    All clothed in power and breeches,
To meet old Britain's warlike sons
    And make some rebel speeches . . . .

Full many a child went into camp,
    All dressed in homespun kersey,
To see the greatest rebel scamp
    That ever cross'd o'er Jersey.

The rebel clowns, oh! What a sight!
    Too awkward was their figure.
'Twas yonder stood a pious wight,
    And here and there a nigger.

               (1775)[131]

ANONYMOUS

The following anonymous poem, which appeared in colonial newspapers from Rhode Island to Virginia, suggests how widely antislavery sentiments were circulating on the eve of the American Revolution. The outbreak of the war prevented the emergence of any coherent abolitionist movement, and events during the war such as British calls for slaves to rise and fight against their masters made the issue more divisive than ever. After the war, when abolitionists appealed to the nascent American government, they faced a deeper, better defined, and more inflexible opposition. The poem is noteworthy for its reliance less on Christian doctrine than on sentimental identification with the captive Africans.

from "To the Dealers of Slaves"

See the poor native quit the Lybian Shores,
Ah? not in love's delightful fetter's bound?
No radiant smile his dying peace restores,
Nor love, nor fame, nor friendship heals his wound.
On the wild beach in mournful guise he stood,
E'er the shrill boatswain gave the hated sign;
He dropped a tear, unseen in the flood;
He stole one secret moment to repine—
"Why am I ravish'd from my native strand?
What savage race protects this impious gain? . . .
Where rove the brutal nation's wild desires;
Our limbs are purchas'd, and our life is sold!
Yet, shores there are, blest shores for us remain,
And favour'd isles with golden fruitage crown'd,
Where tufted flow'rets paint the verdant plain,
Where ev'ry breeze shall med'cine ev'ry wound.

There the stern tyrant that embitters life,
Shall, vainly, suppliant, spread his asking hand;
There, shall we view the billows raging strife,
Aid the kind breast, and waft his boat to land."

(1775)[132]

"CECILIA" [UNIDENTIFIED DAUGHTER OF EZRA STILES] (fl. c. 1775)

This delicate sonnet, left by one of Ezra Stiles's six daughters, was published anonymously in a volume of Stiles family verse edited by a son-in-law, Abiel Holmes. Stiles himself was a scholar, clergyman, president of Yale, and anti-slavery activist. In the 1770s he was teaching and ministering to African Americans in Rhode Island and in 1790 he became the founding president of the Connecticut Society for the Abolition of Slavery.

Here "Cecilia" writes about her sister "Eliza's" transfer of devotion from their mother, who died in 1775, to "Yarrow," the elderly black servant whom the dying mother had beseeched her to look after. Perhaps the most significant aspect is the sentimental reversal of roles, not yet as cliched as it would become in the nineteenth century: the now-grown child caring for the loyal old servant who had rocked her cradle.

"A Fragment"

ELIZA's blooming years are gone;
    Autumnal season marks the fair:
Now Yarrow, Afric's captive son,
    Shall be her future pleasing care.

For by her cradle oft he's mourn'd,
    And rock'd and sooth'd her infant cry;
His sable cheek he kindly turn'd
    To wipe the tear that fill'd her eye.

When twice eight years had grac'd the fair,
    Heaven call'd her parent to the sky:
Yarrow—she said—hence be thy care,
    And all his future wants supply.

Fix'd in her heart the soft injunction lay,
Nor can she ever trifle Yarrow's wants away.
            (wr. c. 1775/pub. 1796)[133]

MYLES COOPER (1737–1785)

Oxford-educated clergyman, Loyalist, and second president of King's College (now Columbia University), Cooper was so notoriously anti-independence that his contemporaries tended to attribute every pro-British pamphlet to him. In May 1775 he left America forever, returning to Britain, where he took up academic posts at Queens' College, Oxford, and then Edinburgh. In this excerpt from a rambling tirade against the American independence movement, Cooper attacks the rights-of-man optimism of the age as false and pernicious. He appeals crankily to history and common sense to teach foolish idealists that so-called natural societies, rather than being blissful, tend instead to foster slavery and inhumanity.

from The Patriots of North-America: A Sketch

Teach them, to view th' historick Page,
To trace the Scenes, of every Age;
    To look o'er Asia's, Africk's Coast,
And see Mankind, in Slavery lost.
Born, to fair Nature's equal Law,
Doom'd to hew Wood, and Water draw;
The Weak, the Strong, the Young, the Old,
Like Cattle bought, like Cattle sold;
Their Wives, their Daughters, bed, and board,
At will, of some imperious Lord.
Fawning like Spaniels, train'd, and link't,
And every free born Thought extinct;
The Book of Knowledge, fair conceal'd,
And Heaven's most sacred Laws, repeal'd.

(1775)[134]

LEMUEL HAYNES (1753–1833)

Abandoned as an infant by his African father and white New England mother, Haynes was raised as a servant in the house of Deacon David Rose in Granville, Massachusetts. Educated in the local school and at home by the minister and his wife, Haynes grew up to be a bookish and devout man. A patriotic American, he joined the local militia when he turned twenty-one in 1774, and went on to see action in various battles, including the siege of Boston and Ethan Allen's assault on Ticonderoga. Afterward he pursued a long career as a preacher in Vermont, publishing an account of his ministry and two of his sermons in 1820.

The poem below was written and probably circulated in the weeks after the Battle of Lexington, but, for reasons one can only surmise, was not published until 1985 when the manuscript resurfaced. Haynes's patriotic ardor is comparable to Phillis Wheatley's and, like her, he wrote a work of tribute to George Washington. Both writers are remarkable for their commitment to the American cause even as they and other blacks were denied the liberty and equality it promised. Notably, Haynes does not allude to the subject of African slavery in this ballad, but by the war's end had come to feel strongly enough to draft a treatise "On the Illegality of Slave-keeping" (it too remained unpublished until the 1980s).

from "The Battle of Lexington"

3

The Nineteenth Day of April last
We ever shall retain
As monumental of the past
most bloody shocking Scene

4

Then Tyrants fill'd with horrid Rage
A fatal Journey went

& Unmolested to engage
And slay the innocent . . .

6

At *Lexington* they did appear
Array'd in hostile Form
And tho our Friends were peacefull there
Yet on them fell the Storm

7

Eight most unhappy Victims fell
Into the Arms of Death
Unpitied by those Tribes of Hell
Who curs'd them with their Breath

8

The Savage Band still march along
For *Concord* they were bound
While Oaths & Curses from their Tongue
Accent with hellish Sound

9

To prosecute their fell Desire
At *Concord* they unite
Two Sons of Freedom there expire
By their tyrannic Spite

10

Thus did our Friends endure their Rage
Without a murm'ring Word
Till die they must or else engage
And join with one Accord

11

Such Pity did their Breath inspire
That long they bore the Rod
And with Reluctance they conspire
To shed the human Blood

12

But Pity could no longer sway
Tho' 't is a pow'rfull Band
For Liberty now bleeding lay
And calld them to withstand

13

The Awfull Conflict now begun
To rage with furious Pride

And Blood in great Effusion run
From many a wounded Side

    14

For Liberty, each Freeman Strives
As its a Gift of God
And for it willing yield their Lives
And Seal it with their Blood

    15

Thrice happy they who thus resign
Into the peacefull Grave
Much better there, in Death Confin'd
Than a Surviving Slave

    16

This Motto may adorn their Tombs,
(Let tyrants come and view)
"We rather seek these silent Rooms
Than live as Slaves to You"

                  (wr. 1775/pub. 1985)[135]

IGNATIUS SANCHO (1729–1780)

An African manservant turned London writer, Sancho was born aboard a slave ship en route from Guinea to the Spanish West Indies. Following the deaths of his mother (of disease) and father (a suicide), the two-year-old orphan was brought to England and raised as a household servant. His precocious intelligence attracted the patronage of the Duke of Montagu, who helped with his education and advancement. Along with various small business ventures, Sancho pursued his avocation as a writer and eventually became acquainted with Sterne, Johnson, Garrick, and others in their circles. The following pieces, which he incorporated into two of his letters of 1775, show Sancho imitating the witty and worldly tone of the fashionable social set with whom he was a favorite.

[Untitled]

For conscience like a fiery horse,
Will stumble if you check his course;
But ride him with an easy rein,
And rub him down with worldly gain,
He'll carry you through thick and thin,
Safe, although dirty, to your Inn.
(wr. 1775/pub. 1782)[136]

In this poem, Sancho jests about the subject of Samuel Foote's latest play, a scandal involving the Duchess of Kingston. Approving the playwright's mockery of moral lapses by the upper classes, Sancho introduces his lines (punningly and self-deprecatingly) as "black poetry."

"Some Black Poetry upon the Occasion [of Foote's dramatic satire on the Duchess of Kingston]"

With Satire, Wit, and Humour arm'd,
Foote opens his exhibitions;

IGNATIUS SANCHO

High-titled Guilt, justly alarm'd,
The Chamberlain petitions.

My Lord, quoth Guilt, this daring fiend
Won't let us sin in private;
To his presumption there's no end,
Both high and low he'll drive at.

Last year he smoak'd the cleric gown;
A D[uche]ss now he'd sweat.
The insolent, for half a crown,
Would libel all the Great.

What can I do, his Lordship cries,
Command you freely may,
Don't license him, the Dame replies,
Nor let him print his play.

(wr. 1775/pub. 1782)[137]

JOHN TRUMBULL (1750–1831)

An American prodigy who passed the entrance exam for Yale at age seven but wasn't allowed to matriculate until thirteen, Trumbull became a prominent educator, lawyer, and writer. He supported the American Revolution and emerged afterward as a leading member of the "Hartford Wits," a group of Connecticut writers that included Joel Barlow and Timothy Dwight.

In these excerpts from his patriotic mock epic (composed 1775–82), Trumbull satirizes American Tories—represented by M'Fingal, who speaks first—for blindly accepting British policies. Among the most appalling of these, to Trumbull, were British plans to free American slaves. Right-thinking Americans, in the voice of "Honorius," rejected these as mere military and political machinations—especially tactics such as Dunmore's November 1775 offer of freedom to slaves who came over and fought on the British side. For both sides, as Trumbull unwittingly reveals, slavery had an inescapable importance in the Revolutionary War.

from Canto I of M'Fingal

"And has she not assay'd her notes,
To rouze your slaves to cut your throats,
Sent o'er ambassadors with guineas,
To bribe your blacks in Carolinas?
And has not Gage, her missionary,
Turn'd many an Afric slave t'a Tory,
And made th'Amer'can bishop's see grow,
By many a new-converted Negro?
As friends to gov'rnment did not he
Their slaves at Boston late set free;
Enlist them all in black parade,
Set off with regimental red?
And were they not accounted then

Among his very bravest men? . . .
Till all this formidable league rose
Of Indians, British troops and Negroes.
And can you break these triple bands
By all your workmanship of hands? . . .

　　While Whigs subdued in slavish awe,
Our wood shall hew, our water draw,
And bless that mildness, when past hope,
Which sav'd their necks from noose of rope.
For as to gain assistance we
Design their Negroes to set free;
For Whigs, when we enough shall bang 'em,
Perhaps 'tis better not to hang 'em;
Except their chiefs; the vulgar knaves
Will do more good preserv'd for slaves."

　　"'Tis well," Honorius cried, "your scheme
Has painted out a pretty dream.
We can't confute your second-sight;
We shall be slaves and you a knight:
These things must come; but I divine
They'll come not in your day, or mine."

(1775)[138]

from Canto IV of M'Fingal

See plund'ring Dunmore's negro band
Fly headlong from Virginia's strand;
And far on southern hills our cousins,
The Scotch M'Donalds fall by dozens . . .

What females caught in evil hour,
By force submit to British power,
Or plunder'd Negroes in disaster
Confess king George their lord and master! . . .
Not Howe's humanity more deserving,
In gifts of hanging and of starving;
Not Arnold plunders more tobacco,
Or steals more Negroes for Jamaica.*

(1782)[139]

* [from Trumbull's note:] Arnold, in the year 1781, having been converted to the cause of
Great Britain, commanded a detachment of their army in Virginia; where he plundered many
cargoes of negroes and of tobacco, and sent them to Jamaica for his own account.

ANONYMOUS

When Lord Dunmore issued his proclamation in November 1775, offering freedom to slaves of Americans who would flee their masters and fight on the British side, the impact was felt throughout the colonies. One black woman in New York was reported to have named her new baby in honor of Dunmore, prompting an anonymous apologist for slavery to mock her quite understandable gesture in the following poetic squib.

[Untitled]

Hail! doughty Ethiopian Chief!
Thou ignominious Negro Thief!
This Black shall prop thy sinking name,
And damn thee to perpetual fame.

(1776)[140]

JAMES BOSWELL (1740–1795)

Born into the Scottish aristocracy (eventually to succeed his father as Laird of Auchinleck), Boswell became a lawyer and man of letters who achieved lasting fame for his biography of Johnson. Ironically, slavery was one of the issues on which Boswell differed from his idol most markedly. Whereas Johnson had criticized slavery relentlessly throughout his career, even writing a legal brief on behalf of Joseph Knight (a slave seeking manumission) in 1777, Boswell defended the institution both in the text of his *Life of Johnson* (1791) and in other writings that are less well remembered.

As early as 1776, in a poetic prologue he wrote for William Whitehead's play *Variety*, Boswell notes the presence of black characters among the exotic figures appearing in the theater of the day.

from "Prologue" to Variety: A Tale for Married People

Here all the sattin of Circassia shines,
Or homepsun stuff with Scottish plaid combines.
There checquer'd Harlequins fair Virtue calls
To Negro nymphs, in linsey-wolsey shawls;
Chictaws and Tictaws all the town entice—
True eastern splendour!—'nothing but full price.'
(wr. 1776/pub. 1777)[141]

In 1791, in the very weeks he was finishing the *Life of Johnson*, Boswell entered the public debate over Wilberforce's abolition bill. With a parliamentary vote expected that spring, Boswell defended slavery and attacked abolitionists in a long and, to modern ears, embarrassing poem. His framing metaphor (visible particularly at the close) compares black bondage to the thraldom of a lover to his lady. In these excerpts, Boswell mocks a series of antislavery leaders (including Wilberforce, Burke, and Pitt) and complains that the antislavery movement is part of the larger, and lamentable, democratic tendency of the age.

237

from No Abolition of Slavery; Or the Universal Empire of Love*

Noodles,† who rave for abolition
Of *th'Africans improv'd condition‡*,
At your own cost fine projects try;
Don't *rob*—from *pure humanity.*

Go, W[ilberforce], with narrow scull,
Go home, and preach away at Hull,
No longer to the Senate cackle,
In strains which suit the Tabernacle;
I hate your little wittling sneer,
Your pert and self-sufficient leer,
Mischief to Trade sits on thy lip,
Insects will gnaw the noblest ship;
Go, W[ilberforce], be gone, for shame,
Thou dwarf, with a big-sounding name.

What frenzies will a rabble seize
In lax luxurious days, like these;
THE PEOPLE'S MAJESTY, forsooth,
Must fix our rights, define our truth;
Weavers become our Lords of Trade,
And every clown throw by his spade,
T'*instruct* our minsters of state,
And *foreign commerce* regulate . . .

See in a stall three feet by four,
Where door is window, window door,
Saloop a hump-back'd cobler drink;
"With *him* the muse shall sit and think;"
He shall in *sentimental* strain,
That *negroes* are *oppress'd,* complain.

---

* [Boswell's dedication:] To the Respectable Body of West-India Planters and Merchants.

† [Boswell's note:] If the abettors of the Slave trade Bill should think they are too harshly treated in this Poem, let them consider how they should feel if *their* estates were threatened by an agrarian law [no unplausible measure]; and let them make allowances for the irritation which themselves have occasioned.

‡ [from Boswell's note:] That the Africans are in a state of savage wretchedness, appears from the most authentic accounts. Such being the fact, an abolition of the slave trade would in truth be precluding them from the first step towards progressive civilization, and consequently of happiness, which it is proved by the most respectable evidence they enjoy in a great degree in our West-India islands, though under well-regulated restraint.

JAMES BOSWELL

What mutters the decrepit creature?
THE DIGNITY OF HUMAN NATURE!

WINDHAM, I won't suppress a gibe
Whilst THOU art with the whining tribe . . .
Shalt THOU, a Roman free and rough,
Descend to weak *blue stocking* stuff,
And cherish feelings soft and kind,
Till you emasculate your mind.

Let COURTENAY sneer, and gibe, and hack,
We know Ham's sons are always black;
On sceptick themes he wildly raves,
Yet Africk's sons were always slaves;
I'd have the rogue beware of libel,
And spare a jest—when on the Bible.*

BURKE, art Thou here too? thou, whose pen,
Can blast the fancied *rights of men:*
Pray, by what logick are those rights
Allow'd to *Blacks*—deny'd to *Whites?*

But Thou! bold Faction's chief *Antistes,*
Thou, more than Samson Agonistes!
Who, Rumour tells us, would pull down
Our charter'd rights, our church, our crown;
Of talents vast, but with a mind
Unaw'd, ungovern'd, unconfin'd;
Best humour'd man, worst politician,
Most dangerous, desp'rate state physician;
Thy manly character why stain
By canting, when 'tis all in vain?
For thy tumultuous reign is o'er;
THE PEOPLE'S MAN thou art no more.

And Thou, in whom the mighty name
Of WILLIAM PITT still gathers fame,
Who could at once exalted stand,
Spurning subordinate command . . .
Why stoop to nonsense? why cajole
Blockheads who vent their *rigmarole?* . . .

* [from Boswell's manuscript note in MS. Yale [C842]:] The above [six] lines in [John] Courte-
nay's handwriting were of his own composition, and given by him to me to introduce into
my Poem "No Abolition of Slavery" . . . I inserted them with [the] alteration of one line.

He who to thwart God's system* tries,
Bids mountains sink, and valleys rise;
Slavery, subjection, what you will,
Has ever been, and will be still:
Trust me, that in this world of woe
Mankind must different burthens know;
Each bear his own, th'Apostle spoke;
And chiefly they who bear the yoke. . . .

Lo then, in yonder fragrant isle
Where Nature ever seems to smile,
The cheerful *gang!*†—the negroes see
Perform the task of industry:
Ev'n at their labour hear them sing,
While time flies quick on downy wing;
Finish'd the bus'ness of the day,
No human beings are more gay:
Of food, clothes, cleanly lodging sure,
Each has his property secure;
Their wives and children are protected,
In sickness they are not neglected;
And when old age brings a release,
Their grateful days they end in peace.

But should our Wrongheads have their will,
Should Parliament approve their bill,
Pernicious as th'effect would be,
T'abolish negro slavery,
Such partial freedom would be vain,
Since Love's strong empire must remain. . . .

O ————! Trust thy lover true,
I must and will be slave to you. . . .
By your keen roving glances caught,
And to a beauteous tyrant brought;
My head with giddiness turn'd round,
With strongest fetters I was bound;
I fancy from my frame and face,
You thought me of th'Angola race:‡

* [Boswell's note:] The state of slavery is acknowledged both in the Old Testament and the New.

† [Boswell's note:] Sir William Young has a series of pictures, in which the negroes in our plantations are justly and pleasingly exhibited in various scenes.

‡ [from Boswell's note:] The Angola blacks are the most ferocious.

JAMES BOSWELL

You kept me long indeed, my dear,
Between the decks of hope and fear;
But this and all the *seasoning* o'er,
My blessings I enjoy the more. . . .

My charming friend! it is full time
To close this argument in rhime;
The rhapsody must now be ended,
My proposition I've defended;
For, slavery there must ever be,
While we have Mistresses like thee!

(1791)[142]

PHILIP FRENEAU (1752−1832)

Long regarded as the most important American poet of his generation, Freneau was born to a prosperous New York family. Educated privately by tutors and then at Princeton, he saw himself as a poet from the beginning, although he worked variously as a farmer, seaman, and newspaper editor, in America and the West Indies. He ardently supported the American Revolution and, although he never took up arms, he was captured and tried by the British for his writings, and condemned to a prison ship. His later publications radiated Jeffersonian ideals and those of the French Revolution. In his poetry, slavery surfaces frequently, sometimes as background, often as main subject.

The first excerpt, ten stanzas from a poem of more than four hundred lines, was written during his time in the Caribbean island of Santa Cruz (today St. Croix). Amidst a pastoral idealization of life on the island, Freneau allows slavery into view and pauses to examine its horrors.

from "The Beauties of Santa Cruz"

70

On yonder steepy hill, fresh harvests rise,
Where the dark tribe from Afric's sun-burnt plain
Oft o'er the ocean turn their wishful eyes
To isles remote high looming o'er the main,

71

And view soft seats of ease and fancied rest,
Their native groves new painted on the eye,
Where no proud misers their gay hours molest,
No lordly despots pass unsocial by.

72

See yonder slave that slowly bends this way,
With years, and pain, and ceaseless toil opprest,

Though no complaining words his woes betray,
The eye dejected proves the heart distrest.

73

Perhaps in chains he left his native shore,
Perhaps he left a helpless offspring there,
Perhaps a wife, that he must see no more,
Perhaps a father, who his love did share.

74

Curs'd be the ship that brought him o'er the main,
And curs'd the hands who from his country tore.
May she be stranded ne'er to float again,
May they be shipwreck'd on some hostile shore . . .

76

O gold accurst! for thee we madly run
With murderous hearts across the briny flood,
Seek foreign climes beneath a foreign sun,
And there exult to shed a brother's blood.

77

But thou, who own'st this sugar-bearing soil,
To whom no good the great First Cause denies,
Let freeborn hands attend thy sultry toil,
And fairer harvests to thy view shall rise.

78

The teeming earth shall mightier stores disclose
Than ever struck thy longing eyes before,
And late content shall shed a soft repose,
Repose, so long a stranger at thy door.

79

Give me some clime, the favourite of the sky,
Where cruel slavery never sought to reign . . .
(wr. 1776/pub. 1779)[143]

After the British defeat at Yorktown in 1782, American independence was as-
sured. Freneau chose this moment to mock the much-hated Lord Dunmore, for-
mer governor of Virginia, who had been forced to withdraw to England. Here,
Freneau uses a satiric voice to attack Dunmore's 1775 call for slaves to join the
British side, which Americans remembered and resented as a murderous instiga-
tion of slave revolt.

from "Lord Dunmore's Petition to the Legislature of Virginia"

Though a brute and a dunce, like the rest of the clan,
I can govern as well as most Englishmen can;
And if I'm a drunkard, I still am a man:

I missed it some how in comparing my notes,
Or six years ago I had joined with your votes;
Not aided the negroes in cutting your throats.

Although with so many hard names I was branded,
I hope you'll believe, (as you will if you're candid)
That I only performed what my master commanded.
(1782)[144]

Freneau supported Washington as the natural leader of the new country. In this tribute to the future president, Freneau expresses confidence that slavery will soon be abolished.

from "Occasioned by General Washington's Arrival in Philadelphia, on His Way to His Residence in Virginia."

Not less in wisdom than in war
Freedom shall still employ your mind,
Slavery shall vanish, wide and far,
'Till not a trace is left behind . . .
(1783)[145]

In this melancholy poem indebted to the vogue for elegiac works like Goldsmith's "Deserted Village" (1770), Freneau laments the sad condition of Jamaica and seems to regret that he ever came there. Foremost among those things that depress him is the ubiquitous, soul-draining presence of slavery.

from "Lines, Written at Port-Royal in the Island of Jamaica"

No sprightly lads or gay bewitching maids
Walk on these wastes or wander in these shades . . .
A negro tribe but ill their place supply,
With bending back, short hair, and downcast eye;
That gloomy race lead up the evening dance,
Skip on the sands, or dart the alluring glance:
Sincere are they?—no—on your gold they doat—

And in one hour—for that would cut your throat.
All is deceit—half hell is in their song
And from the silent thought?—"You have done us wrong!"
A feeble rampart guards the unlucky town,
Where banish'd Tories come to seek renown,
Where worn-out slaves their bowls of beer retail,
And sun-burnt strumpets watch the approaching sail. . . .
    Why sail'd I here to swell my future page!
To these dull scenes with eager haste I came
To trace the reliques of their ancient fame,
Not worth the search!—what domes are left to fall,
Guns, gales, and earthquakes shall destroy them all—
All shall be lost!—tho' hosts their aid implore,
The Twelve Apostles* shall protect no more . . .
No priest shall mutter, and no saint remain,
Nor this palmetto yield her evening shade,
Where the dark negro his dull music play'd,
Or casts his view beyond the adjacent strand
And points, still grieving, to his native land,
Turns and returns from yonder murmuring shore,
And pants for countries he must see no more—
Where shall I go, what Lethe shall I find
To drive these dark ideas from my mind!
                    (wr. 1784/pub. 1788/rev. 1809)[146]

    This poem, retitled "To Sir Toby: A Sugar Planter in the Interior Parts of Jamaica" in later editions, is Freneau's angriest, most unflinching attack on slavery. In graphic imagery, he describes the hell on earth of Jamaican slavery—the brutal labor, the whippings and torture, the hunger and fear, the flight and recapture of runaways.

from "The Island Field Hand"

    "The motions of his spirit are black as night,
    And his affections dark as Erebus."—Shakespeare

    If there exists a hell—the case is clear—
Sir Toby's slaves enjoy that portion here:
Here are no blazing brimstone lakes—'tis true;
But kindled Rum too often burns as blue;

---

* [Freneau's note:] A Battery so called, on the side of the harbour opposite to Port-Royal.

In which some fiend, whom nature must detest,
Steeps Toby's brand, and marks poor Cudjoe's breast.*

　　Here whips on whips excite perpetual fears,
And mingled howlings vibrate on my ears:
Here nature's plagues abound, to fret and tease,
Snakes, scorpions, despots, lizards, centipedes—
No art, no care escapes the busy lash;
All have their dues—and all are paid in cash—
The eternal driver keeps a steady eye
On a black herd, who would his vengeance fly,
But chained, imprisoned, on a burning soil,
For the mean avarice of a tyrant, toil!
The lengthy cart-whip guards this monster's reign—
And cracks, like pistols, from the fields of cane.

　　Ye powers! who formed these wretched tribes, relate,
What had they done, to merit such a fate!
Why were they brought from Eboe's† sultry waste,
To see that plenty which they must not taste—
Food, which they cannot buy, and dare not steal;
Yams and potatoes—many a scanty meal!—

　　One, with a gibbet wakes his negro's fears,
One to the windmill nails him by the ears;
One keeps his slave in darkened dens, unfed,
One puts the wretch in pickle ere he's dead:
This, from a tree suspends him by the thumbs,
That, from his table grudges even the crumbs!

　　O'er yond' rough hills a tribe of females go,
Each with her gourd, her infant, and her hoe;
Scorched by a sun that has no mercy here,
Driven by a devil, whom men call overseer—
In chains, twelve wretches to their labors haste;
Twice twelve I saw, with iron collars graced!—

　　Are such the fruits that spring from vast domains?
Is wealth, thus got, Sir Toby, worth your pains!—
Who would your wealth on terms, like these, possess,
Where all we see is pregnant with distress—

* [Freneau's note:] This passage has a reference to the West Indian custom (sanctioned by law) of branding a newly imported slave on the breast, with a red hot iron, as evidence of the purchaser's property.
† [Freneau's note:] A small Negro Kingdom near the river Senegal.

Angola's natives scourged by ruffian hands,
And toil's hard product shipp'd to foreign lands. . . .
    Here Stygian paintings light and shade renew,
Pictures of hell, that Virgil's* pencil drew:
Here, surly Charons make their annual trip,
And ghosts arrive in every Guinea ship . . .
    Here, they, of stuff determined to be free,
Must climb the rude cliffs . . .
Beyond the clouds, in sculking haste repair,
And hardly safe from brother traitors† there.—
                (wr. 1784/pub. 1792)[147]

In a different mood, Freneau wrote these more romantic lines about Jamaica. But once again, the misery of the slaves presses on his consciousness and on the shape of his poem.

from "Stanzas Written in a Blank Leaf of Burke's History of the West India Islands"

Jamaica's sweet romantic vales
Invain with golden harvests teem,
Her endless spring, her balmy gales
Did more to me than magic seem:
    Yet what the god profusely gave
    Is here denied the toiling slave.

Fantastic joy and fond belief
Through life support the galling chain,
Hope's airy scenes dishearten grief
And bring his native climes again:
    His native groves his heaven display
    The *funeral* is the *happy* day.

For man reduc'd to such disgrace
Invain from Jove fair virtue fell:
Distress compells him to be base,
He has no motive to excel:
    In death alone his prospects end,
    The world's worst foe is his best friend.

---

* [Freneau's note:] See *Aeneid,* Book 6th.—and Fenelon's *Telemachus,* Book 18.

† [Freneau's note:] Alluding to the *Independent* negroes in the blue mountains who, for a stipu-
lated reward, deliver up every fugitive that falls into their hands, to the English Government.

How great their praise, let truth declare,
Who, smit with honour's sacred flame,
Bade freedom to these coasts repair,
Assum'd the slaves' neglected claim,
    And scorning interest's sordid plan
    Prov'd to mankind the rights of man.

Ascending here, may this warm sun,
With freedom's beams divinely clear,
Throughout the world his circuit run
Till these dark scenes shall disappear,
    And a new race, not bought or sold
    Springs from the ashes of the old.
               (wr. 1786/pub. 1787)[148]

Turning his focus back to America, Freneau discerns the underlying contradiction of a country peopled by those seeking freedom from Old World tyranny that still allows slavery in its midst. Freneau accurately predicts this tension deepening as the nation expands westward.

from "On the Migration to America, and Peopling the Western Country"

Forsaking kings and regal state,
    With all their pomp and fancied bliss,
The trav'ller owns—convinc'd—tho' late,
    No realm so free, so blest as this;
The east is half to slaves consign'd,
And half to slavery more refin'd.

O come the time, and haste the day,
    When man shall man no longer crush!
When Reason shall enforce her sway,
    Nor those fair regions raise our blush,
Where still the African complains;
And mourns his, yet unbroken, chains.

Far brighter scenes, a future age,
    The muse predicts, these states shall hail,
Whose genius shall the world engage,
    Whose deeds shall over Death prevail!
And happier systems bring to view,
Than ever eastern sages knew.
               (c. 1794)[149]

In this poem, Freneau sees the once noble state of Virginia as degenerate, corrupted by luxury and the slave labor system. The distinctions he draws between the "more vigorous" northern states and those of the slave-holding south (whose citizens are "averse to toil") mark a faultline that was to resurface insistently over the next sixty-five years.

from *"Virginia: A Fragment"*

Vast in extent, VIRGINIA meets my view,
With streams immense, dark groves, and mountains blue;
First in provincial rank she long was seen,
Built the first town, and first subdued the plain:
This was her praise—but what can years avail
When times succeeding see her efforts fail!
On northern fields more vigorous arts display,
Where pleasure holds no universal sway;
No herds of slaves parade their sooty band
From the rough plough to save the fopling's hand . . .
Averse to toil, the natives still rely
On the sad negro for the year's supply;
He, patient, early quits his poor abode,
Toils at the hoe, or totes some ponderous load,
Sweats at the axe, or, pensive and forlorn,
Sighs for the eve, to parch his stinted corn! . . .
At night returns, his evening toils to share,
Lament his rags, or sleep away his care,
Bind up the recent wound, with many a groan;
Or thank his gods that Sunday is his own.

(1795)[150]

ANONYMOUS

Though unnamed, this young Jamaican identifies himself in the preface to his poem as an eighteen-year-old white colonial and an aspiring poet. In his long (thirty pages) and passionate poem, the author records Jamaican life in lavish and stylized detail, focusing with particular sympathy on the plight of the slaves. Still, despite his criticisms of inhumane practices, the poet ultimately inclines more to ameliorative reforms than to outright abolition. In the first excerpt, the poet is struck by the exotic atmosphere of Jamaica, particularly the erotic beauty of black women. Perhaps revealing as much about the inner life of the poet as about the mores of the people he observes, the passage fosters the emerging racist stereotype of Africans as libidinous and sexually licentious.

from Part II of Jamaica

    Then first, O Muse! Attempt the motly fair,
From lank and long, to short and woolly hair;
From white to black, thro' ev'ry mixture run,
And sing the smiling daughters of the sun!

  'Tis true, few nymphs with British bloom we boast,
No rosy red adorns the tropic toast;
But here the lilly sheds her purest white,
And well-turn'd limbs the panting youth invite!
While sportive Cupids circle round the waist,
Laugh on the cheek, or wanton in the breast!
Our sultry sun (tho' fierce in vertic rage)
Ripes the young blood, and nourishes old age;
O'er ev'ry limb spreads more than mortal grace,
And gives the body what he robs the face.

    Next comes a warmer race, from sable sprung,
To love each thought, to lust each nerve is strung;

The Samboe dark, and the Mullattoe brown,
The Mestize fair, the well-limb'd Quaderoon,
And jetty Afric, from no spurious sire,
Warm as her soil, and as her sun—on fire.
These sooty dames, well vers'd in Venus' school,
Make love an art, and boast they kiss by rule.
'Midst murm'ring brooks they stem the liquid wave,
And jetty limbs in coral currents lave.
In field or houshold pass the toilsome day,
But spend the night in mirth-enlivening play:
With pipe and tabor woo their sable loves,
In sad remembrance of their native groves;
Or, deck'd in white, attend the vocal halls,
And Afric postures teach in Indian halls.
Not always thus the males carouse and play,
But toil and sweat the long laborious day;
With earliest dawn the ardent task begun,
Their labour ends not with the setting sun:
For when the moon displays her borrow'd beams,
They pick the canes, and tend the loaded teams,
Or in alternate watch, with ceaseless toil,
The rums distil, or smoaky sugars boil.
Ev'n while they ply this sad and sickly trade,
Which numbers thousands with the countless dead,
Refus'd the very liquors which they make,
They quench their burning temples in the lake . . .

    Lo! the Afric genius clanks his chains,
And damns the race that robs his native plains!

In Part III of this thirty-page poem, the speaker explores the injustice and cruelty of the slave trade in detail. In the closing stanzas, he addresses the Jamaican planters directly ("O Planter! be it yours to nurse the slave . . ."), apparently in hopes of generating more humane attitudes and practices among West Indian whites. But history reveals, with inexorable force, how radically incompatible were this poet's sentimental ideals and the reality of the slave system.

from Part III of Jamaica

    Thus far the Muse, when mad'ning at the scene
Of christian guile, and man-enslaving man:
Around my head aërial phantoms rise,
And soothing slumbers seal my tear-stain'd eyes. . . .

When lo! Out-issuing from surrounding night,
The goddess *Liberty* arrests my sight:
A cypress garland round each temple twines,
And at her feet the British lion pines.
The sugar-isles with furious frown she eyes,
And I attend while thus the goddess cries:
"Lo! Afric from your furthest shores complains,
Bares her soul wounds, and clanks your cruel chains;
Polluted Gambia mourns his country spoil'd,
And wild Zaara's fields become more wild . . .
Your cruelties reach beyond th'Atlantic main,
A people sigh, but all their sighs are vain!
These eyes have seen what this tongue can't reveal,
These ears have heard what I would blush to tell;
Whate'er the Briton, or the man could stain,
Or give the Christian, or the Heathen pain!
Thus Rome of old the barb'rous nations brav'd,
Ev'n Indus saw his tawny sons enslav'd,
Far to the North she spread her proud domain,
And bound ev'n Britain in a gilded chain.
But she who aw'd the world by arms and fame,
Now smoaks by slaves, now stands an empty name!
Fear then, like her, to meet an awful doom,
And let your sea-girt shores still think on Rome;
For your green isles, surcharg'd with bosom'd foes,
May yield to slaves,—you feel the captive's woes."
This said,—the goddess sheds ambrosial tears,
Spreads her fleet wings, and instant disappears!

O Planter! Be it yours to nurse the slave,
From Afric's coasts waft o'er th'Atlantic wave:
With tender accents smooth the brow of care,
And from his bosom banish dark despair:
So may rich sugars fill your roomy stores,
And rums in plenty reach your native shores:
So may no dire disease your stock invade,
But feed contented in the cooling shade!

Oft have I blush'd to see a Christian give
To some black wretch, worn out, and just alive,
A *manumission full,* and leave him free,
To brave pale want, disease, and misery!

ANONYMOUS

A poor reward for all his watchful cares,
Industrious days, and toil-revolving years!

　　And can the Muse reflect her tear-stain'd eye,
When blood attests ev'n slaves for freedom die?
On cruel gibbets high disclos'd they rest,
And scarce one groan escapes one bloated breast.
Here sable Caesars feel the christian rod;
There Afric Platos, tortur'd, hope a God:
While jetty Brutus for his country sighs,
And sooty Cato with his freedom dies!

　　Britons, forbear! Be Mercy still your aim,
And as your faith, unspotted be your fame;
Tremendous pains tremendous deeds inspire,
And, hydra-like, new martyrs rise from fire.

　　Inhuman ye! Who ply the human trade,
And to the West a captive people lead;
Who brother, sister, father, mother, friend,
In one unnat'ral hapless ruin blend.
Barbarians! Steel'd to ev'ry sense of woe,
Shame of the happy source from whence ye flow:
The time may come, when, scorning savage sway,
Afric may triumph, and ev'n you obey! . . .

　　If my lays can chace one captive sigh,
Care from his breast, a tear wipe from his eye;
Dispel one gloomy woe-dejected brow,
Make one full heart with kind compassion flow;
Torture award from one desponding slave,
Or one poor wretch from fire or gibbet save:
This is my utmost wish—the envy'd prize;
Above wealth, fame, and honour, this my choice!
　　　　　　　　(wr. 1776/pub. 1777)[151]

253

ANONYMOUS [SIGNED "KINGSTON, JAMAICA, TWENTIETH MAY 1776"]

The author of this poem was no doubt a friend of the poet above, since this "Poetical Epistle" was printed as an appendix to the latter's *Jamaica* (London, 1777) and, like it, is presented as having been composed in Jamaica in 1776. In these excerpts, the speaker loathes the barbaric ethos of plantation life and reveals he was so revolted by his own brief stint as a planter that he abandoned that work and withdrew into a kind of mental exile from his fellow colonials. Perhaps alluding to the frequent slave insurrections in Jamaica, he prophesies (like so many poets from Savage on) a future bloodbath: "Some Afric chief will rise . . . [and] repay us in some vengeful war, / And give us blood for blood, and scar for scar." Guilt and fear permeate the poem.

from "A Poetical Epistle, from the Island of Jamaica, to a Gentleman of the Middle-Temple"

From Coke and Lyttleton, from Law—attend,
And hear a Muse, by more than blood thy friend;
While midst th'Atlantic isle I fondly stray,
And in my mind the future bliss pourtray,
When fortune smiles, from these warm climes to roam,
And greet my friends, my country, and my home. . . .

   Ambition was my aim,
To raise a fortune, or erect a name:
Midst tropic heats, and sickly climes, to scan
The works of Nature, and the ways of man.

  The Muse, when first she view'd the destin'd isle,*
(Where slav'ry frown'd, and fortune ceas'd to smile,)
Was forc'd by fate to pass her joyless days,

---

* [Author's note:] Alluding to the author's stay for a few months in the country, as a Planter, after his arrival.

ANONYMOUS

'Mong men unknown to sympathetic lays.
To see the captive drag the cruel chain,
Repaid with tortures, and solac'd with pain;
To give the Afric's fate the pitying tear,
And spurn the slavery that she could not bear.
But soon she scorn'd on human woe to rise,
Nor with a tort'ring hand would stain the bays. . . .

But happy ye, who dwell midst Britain's isle,
Thrice happy men! if fortune deigns to smile.
No sighing slave there makes his heedless moan,
No injur'd Afric echoes forth his groan;
No tort'ring lord ransacks his fruitful mind,
Some unthought woe, some unknown rack to find.

At each new crime this labours in my breast,
And this each night denies a quiet rest:
Some Afric chief will rise, who, scorning chains,
Racks, tortures, flames—excruciating pains,
Will lead his injur'd friends to bloody fight,
And in the flooded carnage take delight;
Then dear repay us in some vengeful war,
And give us blood for blood, and scar for scar.

(wr. 1776/pub. 1777)[152]

WILLIAM JULIUS MICKLE
(1734–1788)

The Scottish heir to a brewery, Mickle used his inheritance to pursue a literary career in England. His magnum opus, five years in the making, was a free translation into English verse of the great Portuguese epic, Luiz Vaz de Camoëns's *Lusiad* (1572). The poem is an heroic commemoration of the Portuguese conquest of Africa and the East Indies in the fifteenth century. Mickle's choice of text suggests his admiration for the transoceanic commercial empires created by European powers.

The excerpt below presents an instance of the confusion and violence that ensued when the Portuguese explorers made contact with African peoples. From the mid-1400s, the Portuguese began to build forts along the west coast of Africa (as mentioned in Mickle's own note). These forts formed the basis of the Portuguese slave trade that was, over the next four hundred years, to send millions of African captives overseas into slavery. The violence in this episode foreshadows the dynamics of slave-taking and resistance for centuries to come.

from Book V of Camoëns's Lusiad

> Still to the south our pointed keels we guide,
> And through the Austral gulph still onward ride:
> Her palmy forests mingling with the skies,
> Leona's rugged steep behind us flies;
> The cape of palms that jutting land we name,
> Already conscious of our nation's fame.*. . .

---

* [Mickle's note:] During the reign of John II, the Portuguese erected several forts, and acquired great power in the extensive regions of Guinea. Azambuja, a Portuguese captain, having obtained leave from Caramansa, a Negro Prince, to erect a fort on his territories, an unlucky accident had almost proved fatal to the discoverers. A huge rock lay very commodious for a quarry; the workmen began on it; but this rock, as the Devil would have it, happened to be a Negro God. The Portuguese were driven away by the enraged worshippers, who were afterwards with difficulty pacified by a profusion of such presents as they most esteemed.

WILLIAM JULIUS MICKLE

Our sails wide swelling to the constant blast,
Now by the isle from Thomas named we past;
And Congo's spacious realm before us rose . . .

While thus attentive on the beach we stood,
My soldiers, hastening from the upland wood,
Right to the shore a trembling Negro brought,
Whom on the forest-height by force they caught,
As distant wander'd from the call of home,
He suck'd the honey from the porous comb.
Horror glared in his look, and fear extreme
In mien more wild than brutal Polypheme:
No word of rich Arabia's tongue he knew,
Nor sign could answer, nor our gems would view:
From garments striped with shining gold he turn'd,
The starry diamond and the silver spurn'd.
Strait at my nod are worthless trinkets brought;
Round beads of chrystal as a bracelet wrought,
A cap of red, and dangling on a string
Some little bells of brass before him ring:
A wide-mouth'd laugh confest his barbarous joy,
And both his hands he raised to grasp the toy.
Pleased with these gifts we set the savage free,
Homeward he springs away, and bounds with glee.

   Soon as the gleamy streaks of purple morn
The lofty forest's topmost boughs adorn,
Down the steep mountain's side, yet hoar with dew,
A naked crowd, and black as night their hue,
Come tripping to the shore: Their wishful eyes
Declare what tawdry trifles most they prize:
These to their hopes were given, and, void of fear,
Mild seem'd their manners, and their looks sincere.
A bold rash youth, ambitious of the fame
Of brave adventurer, Velose his name,
Through pathless brakes their homeward steps attends,
And on his single arm for help depends.
Long was his stay: my earnest eyes explore,
When rushing down the mountain to the shore
I mark'd him; terror urged his rapid strides,
And soon Coëllo's skiff the wave divides.
Yet ere his friends advanced, the treacherous foe
Trod on his latest steps, and aim'd the blow.

257

Moved by the danger of a youth so brave,
Myself now snatch'd an oar, and sprung to save:
When sudden, blackening down the mountain's height,
Another crowd pursued his panting flight;
And soon an arrowy and a flinty shower
Thick o'er our heads the fierce barbarians pour.
Nor pour'd in vain; a feather'd arrow stood
Fix'd in my leg, and drank the gushing blood.
Vengeance as sudden every wound repays,
Full on their fronts our flashing lightnings blaze;
Their shrieks of horror instant pierce the sky,
And wing'd with fear at fullest speed they fly.

(1776)[153]

ANONYMOUS

This poem emerges from the badinage of two (presumably male) satirists in the *Public Advertiser*, a London daily newspaper. The author of this palinode had earlier written an attack on Hannah More. His irreverent counterpart responded in the "voice" of Phillis Wheatley, pretending to defend More in a piece that was really an excuse to publish an obscene *jeu d'esprit*. Here, by return, the first satirist offers a tongue-in-cheek apology to Wheatley. Despite the racist views suggested by his heavy irony, the poem itself shows that four years after her London tour of 1773 Wheatley remained a literary celebrity.

Palinode to Phillis Wheatley

> *'Tis not a Set of Features or* COMPLECTION,
> *The* TINCTURE *of a Skin that* I *admire*—
> ADDISON.

Poetic Queen of parch'd WHIDAW!
With *sable* Beauties, void of Flaw,
   Obscurely, like the Night,
Steal softly to my throbbing Breast,
Where *Cupid* dwells, the little Guest,
   Who hates the garish Light.

Like *Phoebe* in Eclipse, you move
A *dark* Portent of fatal Love
   To those who sigh in vain!
Unbend on me, with gentle Smile,
Your *dusky* Features for awhile;
   Deceive or heal my Pain.

Let others sigh for *brighter* Charms,
For *rosy* Necks and round *white* Arms,
   And call all Beauty *fair;*

My Soul is fix'd on Nymphs, who lave
Their woolly Locks in *Niger's* Wave,
    And *Black* is all my Care.

Why do these Eyes in Passion roll?
Thou *Ebon* Tyrant of my Soul!
    Expel this causeless Spite;
I never meant to Phillis Harm,
Nor wing'd one Shaft at *sooty* Charm;
    My Rage was aim'd at *White*.

Should ev'n my *dusky* Beauty chuse
To shield *each* Daughter of the Muse
    Who deals in Classic Lore;
For her *their* Nonsense I'll forgive,
In *Christian* Patience with them live,—
    Nay, I'll do something—MORE!

(1777)[154]

MARY ROBINSON (1758–1800)

An actress and famous beauty, Robinson (nicknamed "Perdita" for one of her characters) parlayed a career on the stage into a series of relationships with prominent men, culminating in a run as mistress to the Prince of Wales. During a glamorous life that swung between affluence and debtor's prison, she produced volumes of poetry, plays, and other writings. She died prematurely, exhausted and paralyzed from illness, in her early forties.

Although she focused on slavery in many poems over her career, in this early work the eighteen-year-old Robinson allocates only a few lines to the subject in a long text concerning prisoners and other unfree people.

from "Captivity, A Poem"

Sweet Liberty, delights the free-born mind,
Which laws and fetters have not power to bind;
The wretched slave, inur'd to every pain,
By her inspir'd, disdains the Captive's chain;
Oppress'd with labour, murmuring they go,
And curse the source whence all their miseries flow;
Fainting and sad, they bend their toilsome way
Thro' all the burning heats of sultry day;
From every comfort, every pleasure driven,
Robb'd of the common gifts of bounteous Heaven;
Taught by experienc'd Cruelty to find,
That savage baseness taints the human mind,
Their mingled griefs in plaintive murmurs flow,
With all the energy of heart-felt woe;
Still one kind thought the ruling Pow'rs ordain,
With lenient art to sooth each anxious pain,
Whatever punishment the Fates decree
For erring mortals,—still the mind is free!

(1777)[155]

In 1791 Robinson paused to include Africans and other women of color in her enlightened refutation of racist assumptions about the superior beauty of English women.

from "Lines on Hearing It Declared that No Women Were So Handsome as the English"

Beauty, the attribute of Heaven!
In various forms to mortals given . . .
We trace her steps where'er we go;
The British Maid with timid grace;
The tawny Indian's varnish'd face;
The jetty African; the fair
Nurs'd by Europa's softer air;
With various charms delight the mind,
For Fancy governs *all* Mankind.

                                        (1791)[156]

In this passage from an enthusiastically Whiggish vision of liberal progress, Robinson uses an apocalyptic allegory to dramatize the overthrow of tyranny in all its forms. Just before her death in 1800, Robinson completed an expanded "Progress of Liberty" that incorporated revised versions of this poem and several others (including "The African," below). This early version is remarkable for the motifs of chaos and violence, most strikingly the prophesied vengeance of the enslaved Africans ("Their countless wounds wide yawning for revenge").

from "The Progress of Liberty"

The scene disclos'd, where on his iron throne
Terrifically frown'd DESPOTIC POW'R,
A giant strong! His vassals, bound in chains
(Artfully twin'd with wreaths of opiate flow'rs,
Thro' which the clanking links sad music made),
Stood trembling at his gaze. Beneath his feet
Pale captives groan'd; while shad'wy spectres dire,
Of persecuted Innocence and Worth;
Of GENIUS, bent to an untimely grave;—
Of ETHIOPS, burnt beneath their native sun,
Their countless wounds wide yawning for revenge,
Rose in a mighty host,—and yell'd despair!—

The flinty fabric shook! The thund'ring spheres
Frown'd, dark as Erebus! Upon its base

The Pandemonium rock'd! While with'ring bolts
From Heav'n's red citadel fell fast around.
The vex'd sea, swoln above its tow'ring walls,
Foam'd madly furious. The gigantic fiend
Wav'd high his adamantine wand in vain;
They potent grasp palsy'd the monster's arm,
And hurl'd him fathoms down his native Hell!
All Earth, convulsive yawn'd; while Nature's hand
Crush'd the infernal throne, and in its stead,
A thousand temples rose, each dedicate
To Valour, Reason, Liberty, and Fame!

(1798)[157]

Though weighed down by its heavy sentimentalism and hackneyed diction,
this lyric poem is nonetheless noteworthy for its attention to the violation of Af-
rican slave women by white masters and its call for not only the abolition of
slavery but the recognition of racial equality. It is remarkable here that Robin-
son, who in her own life survived by bartering her sexual favors, should, in her
imaginative writing, dwell on the sexual predations of white men against inno-
cent black women.

The African

Shall the poor African, the passive Slave,
Born in the bland effulgence of broad day,
Cherish'd by torrid splendours, while around
The plains prolific teem with honey'd stores,
Sink prematurely to a grave obscure,
No tear to grace his ashes? Or suspire
To wear Submission's long and goading chain,
To drink the tear that down his swarthy cheek
Flows fast, to moisten his toil-fever'd lip
Parch'd by the noon-tide blaze? Shall he endure
The frequent lash, the agonizing scourge,
The day of labour, and the night of pain;
Expose his naked limbs to burning gales;
Faint in the sun, and wither in the storm;
Traverse hot sands, imbibe the morbid breeze,
Wing'd with contagion; while his blister'd feet,
Scorch'd by the vertical and raging beam,
Pour the swift life-stream? Still his frenzied eyes,
Oh! worst of mortal mis'ries! behold

The darling of his heart, his sable love,
Selected from the trembling timid throng,
By the wan Tyrant, whose licentious touch
Seals the dark fiat of the Slave's despair!

　　　Oh Liberty! From thee the suppliant claims
The meed of retribution! Thy pure flame
Wou'd light the sense opake, and warm the spring
Of boundless ecstacy: while Nature's laws,
So violated, plead immortal tongu'd,
For her dark-fated children! Lead them forth
From bondage infamous! Bid Reason own
The dignities of Man, whate'er his clime,
Estate, or colour. And, O sacred Truth!
Tell the proud Lords of traffic, that the breast
Thrice ebon-tinted, owns a crimson tide
As pure,—as clear, as Europe's Sons can boast.
　　　　　　　　　　　　　　(1798)[158]

These lines are from a long romantic poem, told from a woman's perspective, about two lovers separated by the slave trade. For the African setting, the heroine's name "Zelma," and other details, Robinson may be indebted to William Dodd, Thomas Chatterton, and others who set such tales amidst the tumult of slave raids.

from "The Negro Girl"

"Yon vessel oft has plough'd the main
With human traffic fraught;
Its cargo—our dark Sons of pain—
For worldly treasure bought!
What had they done? O Nature tell me why
Is taunting scorn the lot of thy dark progeny? . . .
Is it the dim and glossy hue
That marks him for despair?
While men with blood their hands embrue,
And mock the wretch's pray'r,
Shall guiltless Slaves the scourge of tyrants feel,
And, e'en before their God! unheard, unpitied kneel.
Could the proud rulers of the land
Our Sable race behold;
Some bow'd by Torture's giant hand,
And other's basely sold!

Then would they pity Slaves, and cry, with shame,
Whate'er their tints may be, their souls are still the same!
Why seek to mock the Ethiop's face?
Why goad our hapless kind?
Can features alienate the race—
Is there no kindred mind?
Does not the cheek which vaunts the roseate hue
Oft blush for crimes that Ethiops never knew?
Behold! the angry waves conspire
To check the barb'rous toil!
While wounded Nature's vengeful ire
Roars round this trembling Isle!
And hark! her voice re-echoes in the wind—
Man was not form'd by Heav'n to trample on his kind!
Torn from my mother's aching breast,
My Tyrant sought my love—
But in the grave shall Zelma rest,
Ere she will faithless prove;
No, Draco!—Thy companion I will be
To that celestial realm where Negros shall be free!

(1800)[159]

JOHN CODRINGTON
BAMPFYLDE (1754–1796)

The second son of Sir Richard Warwick Bampfylde of Devonshire, John Bampfylde came to London to pursue a career as a poet. Gradually, his dissipation and melancholy grew into madness. Having published only one book of poems by the age of twenty-four and failed in his bizarre courtship of Joshua Reynolds's niece, Bampfylde spent much of his later life in a private madhouse. The sonnet below, admired by Southey and other Romantics, balances the sentimentalist's abhorrence of slavery with the liberal optimist's belief that trade and commerce were ushering in an era of enlightened progress.

Sonnet VIII

*On the Abbé REYNALL's History of the Establishments in the East
and West Indies*

Friend to the wretch, great Patron of Mankind,
Born to enlighten and reform the age;
Whose energetic and immortal page,
From Nature's laws, hath every art combin'd
Of mildest policy; whose soul refin'd,
Melts at the Slave's big tear, with generous rage
Dares to assert his rights, his griefs assuage,
And mould to industry the savage mind.
Tutor'd by thee, the nations blest shall see
Unbounded Commerce, Wealth and Peace arise,
And Truth, and spotless Faith, and Liberty:
Nor shall thy latest moment want the meed
Of praise and joy serene, which virtuous deed
Procures from Heaven for the Good and Wise.

(1778)[160]

JOEL BARLOW (1754–1812)

A Connecticut farm boy who went to Yale and later served in the American Revolution, Barlow pursued a varied career in law, business, and diplomacy (including seventeen years in England, France, and Algiers), through all of which his first desire was to be a major American poet. He died in Poland during the Franco-Russian War, on a failed mission to settle a treaty with Napoleon.

The first excerpt is from a poem he wrote at Yale and delivered at the commencement exercises in July 1778. Predicting American victory soon (the Revolutionary War was then in its fourth year), Barlow calls for an end to slavery as an essential element of the new nation that Washington and his troops were fighting to establish.

from The Prospect of Peace

No grasping lord shall grind the neighbouring poor,
Starve numerous vassals to increase his store;
No cringing slave shall at his presence bend,
Shrink at his frown, and at his nod attend;
Afric's unhappy children, now no more
Shall feel the cruel chains they felt before,
But every State in this just mean agree,
To bless mankind, and let th'oppressed free.
Then, rapt in transport, each exulting slave
Shall taste that Boon which God and nature gave,
And, fir'd with virtue, join the common cause,
Protect our freedom and enjoy our laws.

(1778)[161]

In this, the magnum opus of his career, composed, published in succeeding versions, and revised from 1779 to 1807, Barlow set himself up as the Homeric bard and prophet of America. Amidst more than seven thousand lines of rhyming couplets, Barlow saw the contradictions of a professedly free nation practicing slavery. Here in Book VIII, using the voice of "Atlas" (the mythological guardian of Africa), Barlow attacks American hypocrisy and points to the capture and enslavement of Americans by Algerians (then happening in the Mediterranean) as just retribution. The final twenty lines of this excerpt shift back to the voice of the poem's main speaker, who warns Americans not to fall back into European feudalism or burden their posterity with the poisonous inheritance of slavery.

from Book VIII of The Columbiad

    Thy proud sons, a strange ungenerous race,
Enslave my tribes, and each fair world disgrace,
Provoke wide vengeance on their lawless land,
The bolt ill placed in thy forbearing hand.—
Enslave my tribes! then boast their cantons free,
Preach faith and justice, bend the sainted knee,
Invite all men their liberty to share,
Seek public peace, defy the assaults of war,
Plant, reap, consume, enjoy their fearless toil,
Tame their wild floods to fatten still their soil,
Enrich all nations with their nurturing store
And rake with venturous fluke each wondering shore.—
Enslave my tribes! what, half mankind imban,
Then read, expound, enforce the rights of man!
Prove plain and clear how nature's hand of old
Cast all men equal in her human mold!
Their fibres, feelings, reasoning powers the same,
Like wants await them, like desires inflame.
Thro former times with learned book they tread,
Revise past ages and rejudge the dead,
Write, speak, avenge, for ancient sufferings feel,
Impale each tyrant on their pens of steel,
Declare how freemen can a world create,
And slaves and masters ruin every state.—
Enslave my tribes! and think, with dumb disdain,
To scape this arm and prove my vengeance vain!
But look! methinks beneath my foot I ken
A few chain'd things that seem no longer men;
Thy sons perchance! whom Barbary's coast can tell
The sweets of that loved scourge they wield so well.
Link'd in a line, beneath the driver's goad,

See how they stagger with their lifted load;
The shoulder'd rock, just wrencht from off my hill
And wet with drops their straining orbs distil,
Galls, grinds them sore, along the rampart led,
And the chain clanking counts the steps they tread.
By night close bolted in the bagnio's gloom,
Think how they ponder on their dreadful doom,
Recal the tender sire, the weeping bride,
The home, far sunder'd by a waste of tide,
Brood all the ties that once endear'd them there,
But now, strung stronger, edge their keen despair.
Till here a fouler fiend arrests their pace:
Plague, with his burning breath and bloated face,
With saffron eyes that thro the dungeon shine,
And the black tumors bursting from the groin,
Stalks o'er the slave . . .

    Nor shall these pangs atone the nation's crime;
Far heavier vengeance, in the march of time,
Attends them still; if still they dare debase
And hold inthrall'd the millions of my race;
A vengeance that shall shake the world's deep frame,
That heaven abhors and hell might shrink to name.
Nature, long outraged, delves the crusted sphere
And molds the mining mischief dark and drear;
Europa too the penal shock shall find,
The rude soul-selling monsters of mankind. . . .

    Ah, would you not be slaves, with lords and kings,
Then be not masters; there the danger springs. . . .

    Mark modern Europe with her feudal codes,
Serfs, villains, vassals, nobles, kings and gods,
All slaves of different grades, corrupt and curst
With high and low, for senseless rank athirst,
Wage endless wars; not fighting to be free,
But *cujum pecus*, whose base herd they'll be.

    Too much of Europe, here transplanted o'er,
Nursed feudal feelings on your tented shore,
Brought sable serfs from Afric, call'd it gain,
And urged your sires to forge the fatal chain.
But now, the tents o'erturn'd, the war dogs fled,
Now fearless Freedom rears at last her head
Matcht with celestial Peace,—my friends, beware
To shade the splendors of so bright a pair;

Complete their triumph, fix their firm abode,
Purge all privations from your liberal code,
Restore their souls to men, give earth repose
And save your sons from slavery, wars and woes.

(wr. 1779–1804/pub. 1807)[162]

JAMES DELACOURT
[OR DE-LA-COUR] (1709–1781)

A native of Cork, Delacourt was an Anglo-Irishman who, after attending Trinity College, Dublin, pursued a career as an Anglican clergyman and amateur poet. A mildly eccentric figure, Delacourt was influenced by James Thomson (included elsewhere), whose sensibility he admired and to whom he addressed some early poems. In the rhyming couplets of the ode printed below, Delacourt criticizes European artificiality, especially women's fashion and cosmetics, contrasting it with the unaffected natural beauty of an African woman. Whether he had a specific black woman in mind or instead drew on an idealized image, his poem radically challenges the racist aesthetics so prevalent at the time.

In Praise of a Negress

What shape I have, that form is all my own
To art a stranger, and to modes unknown;
To paint or patches, perfum'd fraud, no friend,
Nor know what stays and honey-water mend;
No spotted moons deform my jetty face,
I would be blacker than that speckled race!
My simple lotion is the purer rain,
And e'en that wash is labour took in vain.
But my pearl teeth, without tobacco's aid,
O'er snow or Indian iv'ry cast a shade!
My eyes eclipse the stars in all their flame,
Such as may not e'en Albion's daughters shame!
My softer skin with the mole's velvet vies,
Ah! who will on these altars sacrifice?
But if I please less in the sultry day,
My colour with the candles dies away;
Since to our hue the light is deem'd a foe,
Night will a THAIS in my charms bestow.

(1778)[163]

ANONYMOUS ["A NATIVE OF THE WEST INDIES"]

The author of the following poems remains unknown and only a few details about him can be inferred from his published volume of poetry, *Poems on Subjects Arising in England, and the West Indies* (London, 1783). Born in the West Indies, apparently in Antigua, the poet obviously spent considerable time both in the Caribbean and in England. He evinces equal confidence writing about life in the islands, and about politics and culture in London. While the poems set in England are conventional in genre and voice, the poems about the West Indies are truly extraordinary and succeed in their purpose, to distinguish the collection with exotic and original material.

The first excerpt, from a poem about the catastrophic famine in Antigua in the late 1770s, presents a firsthand account of slave burials. Both in the careful detail of his description and the tone of his voice, the poet displays remarkable sympathy for the miserable Africans who can find relief only in death.

from "The Antigua Planter; or War and Famine"*

No golden years, nor plenteous crops, I sing;
No harvests waving to the zephyr's wing:
Far other scenes, ye muses, join your train,
The dying negroe, and the drooping cane.
The sullen thunder rolling from afar;

---

* [Author's note:] This poem was written in the year 1779, when the French fleets were so much superior to us in the West Indies, and when the island of Antigua suffered from dry weather, and the scarcity of provisions. Not only the negroes, but several of the white inhabitants, felt the effects of hunger, in the most extreme degree. The slaves on several estates were swept away by sickness, and those who were intrepid enough to venture on the neighbouring cane pieces to steal and pillage, were either killed by the watchmen or chopped and mangled in so severe a manner, that they were laid up in the sick houses for a length of time. Amidst this scene of desolation, it was impossible for any heart, endued with humanity, not to be affected.

The seeds of famine, and the sword of war;
The ruffl'd roses of the British crown;
The world's disdain, and heav'n's imperial frown! . . .

Alas! poor slaves, your tedious toil is o'er;
A master's will shall vex your life no more.
No more you rise, at morning's early bell,
Nor leave your slumbers at the jarring shell.
No more we lead you to the farrow'd way,
Or curse you to the labours of the day.
    Let freemens' tears, the freeman's grave bedew,
Far other rites, ye slaves, attend on you;
For hark! what peals of horrid mirth resound,*
As yonder slaves enclose the neighb'ring ground.
High are their hands, and high their voices rais'd,
Like dancing furies madden'd and amaz'd!
See how they mock us, with indecent joy,
And hail the moment destin'd to destroy!
For them, oh! more than heav'n itself must bloom,
When horrid custom riots o'er the tomb.
Yet sure no words, no antick shapes are strange,
When death has giv'n the slave the pow'r to range.
No ear, in soft condolance, caught their woes;
No hand had rock'd their age to calm repose.
For them no freeman's pity dropt a tear,
Nor flow'rs of wildest nature grace their bier.
                    (wr. 1779/pub. 1783)[164]

The following poem is reprinted in full because it presents one of the best eyewitness accounts of slave life in all of eighteenth-century literature. Despite some conventional elements, the poem offers a wealth of anthropological detail (much of it in the author's notes), even recording African contributions to English such as *canoe* and *tamboreen*.

The Field Negroe; or the Effect of Civilization

SAY, lovely muse, what thoughts compel
    Thy poet's partial fire

---

* [Author's note:] Some negroes believe, that when they die, they return back to their native country; for which reason they often hang themselves at first coming to us.
                                    SMITH's Hist. of Nevis, &c.
This accounts for their dancing, festivity and joy on these occasions.

To sound, uncouth, th' Indian shell,
  Or strike the savage lyre?

From your own lov'd Parnassus smile,
  Ye muses, on my strain;
'Tis you that point a distant isle
  Beyond th' Atlantic main.

And though no laurels there succeed,
  To grace a poet's bier,
My hands, perhaps, shall cull a meed
  From off the prickly pear.

High on my brows this shrub shall stand,
  My humble muse to suit,
And keep, at once, the critic's hand
  From poetry and fruit.

O thither let my footsteps rove,
  Their own peculiar way;
Or lull me in an orange grove,
  Beneath a golden ray.

O, fancy, let me view the toil,
  When drooping, faint with pain,
The panting negroe digs the soil
  Of sugar's sweet domain.

And now I see thy *canes** arise,
  Like blades of springing corn;
And now thy *cocoas* meet my eyes,
  High waving as in scorn.

Here stand the slaves in even rows,
  And, though the season warms,
They throw, at once, their equal hoes,
  Like soldiers under arms.

On skins of goats their children lie,
  Or here and there they run;

---

* [Author's Note:] Sugar-canes; one Mr. Powers, a Cantabrigian, who was a predecessor of mine in the rectory of St. John's, at Nevis, wrote a poem called the *Sugar Cane,* which was looked upon there as a curious work, and as such, after his death, sent home hither to his relations. But, I believe, it was never printed; for, at my return to England, I made particular enquiry after it of Mr. Rivington, in St. Paul's Churchyard, and of many other London booksellers, but in vain. However, the subject was a field noble enough for the finest of poets to expatiate upon.

SMITH'S Voyage to the Caribbee Islands.

ANONYMOUS

And grow, beneath a torrid sky,
  Still blacker in the sun.

Hence, then, the polish'd skin, so meek,
  Of shining glossy black;—
The sable plumes are not so sleek
  Upon a raven's back.

O let me steal upon that soil,
  So long unbless'd by rain,
Which oft, with never-ceasing toil,
  The negroe digs in vain.*

'Twas here, as once I stroll'd along,
  With musing steps and flow,
I spied, the other slaves among,
  One leaning on his hoe.

Just by his famish'd side, I think,
  A *yabbah*† struck my view;
And, empty quite of meat and drink,
  A *calabash*‡ or two.

Poor Arthur was the wretch's name,
  And Guinea gave him breath;
While he to sad Antigua came,
  To meet, he fear'd, his death.

That negroe near the burning line
  That mov'd the swift canoe,
That stem'd the foamy ocean brine
  With paddle light and true.

Poor Arthur now, aloud cry'd I,
  You are not, sure, dismay'd!
Poor Arthur answer'd with a sigh,
  And scratch'd his woolly head.

I begg'd some water of a maid,
  To give the wretch relief;
He held it, trembling, to his head,
  Within a plantain leaf.

---

* [Author's note:] The allusion is here to the island of Antigua, once a flourishing and wealthy colony, but now desolated by a perpetual sun-shine.
† [Author's note:] An earthen pot or vessel to hold meat, provisions, and the like.
‡ [Author's note:] Spoons, bowls, and other utensils for slaves to eat out of are made of them [calabash fruit].

The sweat ran down his sun-burnt face,
    In troubl'd torrents fast;
While not a breeze, with tepid grace,
    Dispell'd it as it past.

I now my silk umbrella spread,
    To screen him from the sun;
And patient held it o'er his head,
    'Till all his work was done.

The slave then stoop'd and kiss'd my feet,*
    Low prostrate on the ground,
And made his arms in wonder meet
    My fainting knees around!

The bell of noon now open'd wide,
    The shell a signal sent;
Poor Arthur rubb'd each awkward side,†
    And home his footsteps bent.

But Arthur now has made a hut,‡
    And little garden wild,
Which keeps, contiguous to a gut,
    Himself, his wife, and child.

'Tis there the Jessamine demure,
    And fav'rite flow'ry fence,
Shall ev'ry holiday allure
    The negroe's simple sense.

'Tis here, oft as the gentle airs
    At morn and eve renew;
So oft a thrilling music bears,
    To tune the *diddledoe.*§

There Melancholy lifts her head,
    With soft dejected mien,

---

* [Author's note:] Their usual manner of expressing their gratitude for any great and unlooked for act of kindness.

† [Author's note:] Descriptive of a new negroe, or one who has not been long in the island, after leaving his native country.

‡ [Author's note:] Negroes live in huts, on the western side of our dwelling houses; so that every plantation resembles a small town; and the reason why they are seated on the western side, is, that we may breathe the pure eastern air, without being offended with the least nauseous smell. Our kitchens and boiling houses are on the same side, and for the same reason.

§ [Author's note:] The pod in which the seed of the aquafee grows, and which, when blown upon by the mouth or the air, produces a tone.

And rises from her mountain bed,
    To grace the palmy scene.

On Sunday, oft he joins the throng
    Of India's swarthy dames;
On Sunday, oft he sings the song
    Expressive of his flames.

Now Arthur and the youths advance
    With pleasure-smiling mien,
He leads, at once, the antick dance,
    And beats the *tamboreen.*

At cudgels* now, against all blows
    He nicely guards his head;
And boldly meets a thousand foes,
    Beneath the plantain shade.

And now the rank *baba* he throws†
    From off his polish'd limbs,
And every day he nicer grows,
    Improving in his whims.

A shirt of check that loss supplies,
    And other garbs below;
And rings of horn, of homely guise,
    Compleats the savage beau.

Now, faithful to his master's side,‡
    He takes his nimble course:
He braids his hair, with decent pride,
    And runs beside his horse.

And now we daily hear him sing,
    The merriest and the best:
He seems, he moves another thing,
    And portly rears his crest.

             (1783)[165]

---

* [Author's note:] An amusement common among negroes.
† [Author's note:] A blanket or loose kind of covering used by the meaner kind of slaves.
‡ [Author's note:] It is usual in the West Indies for the slave, who more immediately waits upon his master, to attend him on his journies, and airings on horseback, which he generally does on foot, with an activity and strength, which has, at first, very much surprized the Europeans who have gone to that part of the world. It is considered by them as a mark of distinction, and preferred to the more slavish office of digging the cane holes.

In the next piece, the poet tells a pathetic story about a Caribbean slave who rushes to aid the sole survivor of a sinking slave ship, only to discover she is his long-lost daughter ("Dina"). The irony of the poem's subtitle emerges belatedly.

from "The Guinea Ship;* or Liberty Restored"

From sable Guinea's horrid shore
    The lab'ring vessel came,
And on her deck some wretches bore
    To infamy and shame.

But welcome storms and tempests rose,
    The welkin lighten'd round;
The angry billows quickly close,
    And all the crew was drown'd.

One only board the seas above
    A trembling maiden bore;

* [Author's note:] As early as the year one thousand five hundred and three, a few negroe slaves had been sent into the new world. In the year one thousand five hundred and eleven, [King] Ferdinand permitted the importation of them in greater numbers.

They were found to be a more robust and hardy race than the natives of America; they were more capable of bearing fatigue; more patient under servitude: and the labour of one negroe was computed to be equal to that of four Indians. Cardinal Ximenes, however, when solicited to encourage this commerce, preemptorily rejected the proposition, because he perceived the iniquity of reducing one race of men to slavery, while he was consulting about the means of restoring liberty to another. But Las Casas, from the inconsistency natural to men, who hurry, with head-long impetuosity, towards a favourite point, was incapable of making this distinction.

While he contended earnestly for the liberty of the people born in one quarter of the globe, he laboured to enslave the inhabitants of another region; and in the warmth of his zeal to save the Americans from the yoke, pronounced it to be lawful and expedient to impose one still greater upon the Africans. Unfortunately, for the latter, Las Casas's plan was adopted. Charles [Holy Roman Emperor] granted a patent to one of his Flemish favourites, containing an exclusive right of importing four thousand negroes into America. He sold his patent to some Genoese merchants for twenty-five thousand ducats, and they were the first, who brought into a regular form, that commerce for slaves between Africa and America, which has since been carried on to such amazing extent.

ROBERTSON's Hist. of America, Vol. I.

Now and then these poor creatures are, by private traders, stole away out of their own countries, to the eternal scandal of us Christians. But the usual method of coming by them is, to purchase them, when taken in their wars with each other; and if some great persons concerned in the trade to Africa are not strangely belied, they frequently set those black princes together by the ears, purely that they may buy the prisoners for slaves.

SMITH's Hist. of Nevis, &c.

And in a pleasing hurry drove
    Against a coral shore.

Half breathless on the strand she lay,
    Serene in sable charms;
Till one poor negroe pass'd that way,
    And warm'd her in his arms.

Long o'er her corpse the negroe stands,
    With wild and savage gaze;
And now uncouthly wrings his hands
    In various savage ways.

What wonder struck the negroe's heart,
    As wildly on he gaz'd,
While trying ev'ry soothing part,
    'Twas Dina's form he rais'd.

That Dina, comfort of his life,
    Who travell'd at his side,
And whom his youthful tender wife,
    Had fondly felt her pride. . . .

O, tell it to the lofty air,
    To sporting billows wild;
To clouds that move in mad despair,
    The father found his child!

And now the angry winds are laid,
    The brooding halcyon's charm;
Fair Liberty uplifts her head,
    And all the sea is calm.

(1783)[166]

In this excerpt from a haunting nocturnal reverie, the poet presents another melodramatic tale. Two African lovers, Francis and Myrtilla, die in a futile attempt to escape slavery and find happiness together. By contrast with the unwitting whites who are asleep, the speaker is conscious of the slaves' "oppressive woe" and, at poem's end, involves the reader in a pilgrimage to the site of their demise.

from *"Scene in the West Indies"*

"The watchman sleeps, his dog has ceas'd to bark,
The happy white so lull'd in sleep profound,
That not an eye, thro' all the mazy dark,
Can trace a wand'ring footstep on the ground.

O come, my love, 'tis nature's fav'rite time,
For now no ear our am'rous plaints can tell;
And now, arising in their native clime,
Our country's chieftains raise a merry yell.

O fly, Myrtilla, from this cruel shore,
And fly the sunshine of the bitter day,
Where toiling servitude so sad and sore,
Has strew'd with prickles all our weary way.

Thy Francis calls, by love's endearing name,
That name that made you once so glad and gay!
O, bring not then his tender love to shame,
But hasten quick and steal with him away". . . .

"How," cry'd the female captive, in a fright,
"Dare I the cruel white-man's trust betray!
I am that cruel white-man's slave by right,
And dare I wander in your arms away?

What if the morning shews us on the sea,
He'll doom us then to ev'ry kind of ill;
Or worse, perhaps, he'll hide my face from thee,
And cruel whips Myrtilla's blood shall spill."

"The seas are vext, the angry surges rage,
Our fate admits," he cries, "no long delay;
Now nine times nine those seas, those sands engage,
Come, launch the crazy bark, and hence away."

Long on a wave of craggy height they rode,
Then headlong plung'd oblivious to their woe,
While ev'ry heart-felt grief that inward flow'd,
Found a calm harbour in the depths below.

Oft to the shore, with musing steps, I go,
To view the little creek and neighb'ring bay,
Where, heaving sad with life's oppressive woe,
Poor Francis and Myrtilla stole away.

(1783)[167]

JOHN NEWTON (1725–1807)

The author of "Amazing Grace" had an extraordinary early life for an antislavery activist. A seafarer from age eleven, Newton became a captain in the slave trade and carried several human cargoes to the Americas before his conversion to evangelical Christianity in the 1750s. Ordained in 1764, he led a popular ministry, first in the village of Olney (until 1780) and then at St. Mary Woolnoth in London, until his death. Among the many influenced by his antislavery views were William Wilberforce, Hannah More, and William Cowper (the latter two included in this anthology).

"Amazing Grace" was first published in 1779, in a collection of 348 hymns (68 by his friend Cowper) known as *The Olney Hymns*. Although Newton wrote the hymn to celebrate his delivery from the sinfulness of the slave trade, it was to become popular in the nineteenth century (set to new music) as an expression of the joy slaves felt at the prospect of Christian deliverance from the miseries of this world. Since the time of Harriet Beecher Stowe, who put the song on Tom's lips in the climactic chapter of *Uncle Tom's Cabin* (1852), the song has been viewed as the paradigmatic Negro spiritual.

Hymn XLI

Amazing grace! (how sweet the sound)
    That sav'd a wretch like me!
I once was lost, but now am found,
    Was blind, but now I see.

'Twas grace that taught my heart to fear,
    And grace my fears reliev'd;
How precious did that grace appear,
    The hour I first believ'd!

Thro' many dangers, toils and snares,
    I have already come;

'Tis grace has brought me safe thus far,
    And grace will lead me home.

The LORD has promis'd good to me,
    His word my hope secures;
He will my shield and portion be,
    As long as life endures.

Yes, when this flesh and heart shall fail,
    And mortal life shall cease;
I shall possess, within the vail,
    A life of joy and peace.

The earth shall soon dissolve like snow,
    The sun forbear to shine;
But GOD, who call'd me here below,
    Will be for ever mine.

                           (1779)[168]

EDWARD THOMPSON
(? 1739–1786)

A career British Naval officer, Thompson entered as a teenaged midshipman in the early 1750s, saw action in the Seven Years' and American Revolutionary Wars, rose to the rank of Commodore, commanded ships in the African coastal patrol and in the Caribbean fleet (where he was also involved in organizing colonial government in Guyana) in the 1770s and 1780s, and died at sea, unmarried, in 1786. Remarkably, this hardened sailor had a parallel career as a writer, publishing at least fifteen books of his own poetry and prose, and several edited volumes, between 1761 and 1784. Dubbed by fellow sailors "Poet Thompson," he was also known for producing erotic, uninhibited verse.

Here, in a lyric typically composed aboard ship (the *Hyaena*), Thompson unconsciously reveals his sympathy for Guinea slaves. Although his duty involved protecting British commerce on the African Coast, Thompson loathed the slave trade, as is evident in other poems below.

from "To Emma, Extempore. Hyaena, off Gambia, June 4, 1779"

What kind impulse touched on Cupid's breast
Last night, I cannot tell—but when at rest,
And rolling, tumbling, on this scorching wave,
A mere sea-drudge, a very Guinea slave——
Methought I met you, tidy, gay, and neat,
White with pink ribbons, in St. James's-street:
You smiled, you looked most fair, and smartly said,
"Come home to tea, and bless thy Emma, Ned."
Whether this pleasing assignation proved
Too great a transport to the mind that loved—
I waked—with horror cursed my cruel state,
That you was fled, and Africa my fate.

But be this coast my curse—make love my theme,
And beauteous Emma ev'ry night my dream!
(wr. 1779/pub. 1783)[169]

While much of Thompson's poetry expresses sexual longing, the following poem is remarkable because the object of his passion is a black woman in St. Kitt's. Parodying a popular song of the time, Thompson celebrates her physical charms while almost comically disclosing his own lust.

from "The Negro Naiad: A Parody on Fanny Blooming Fair. Composed Extempore on the Occasion in St. Kitt's. February 13, 1781"

Not *Fanny* blooming fair,
    Now caught my ravish'd sight,
But *Fanny,* plump and bare,
    And black as twelve at night!

Whilst eagerly I hung
    On beauties new and swart,
Into the stream the *Naiad* sprung,
    And bore away my heart! . . .

What strength my nerves invade,
    When I behold the breast
Of this bright charcoal maid,
    Rise—pouting to be press'd!

Venus, round Fanny's waist,
    Has not her cestus bound
With silks; nor is she lac'd
    To dance the circle round.

But when the *banjer** plays,
    Fann dances without shoes,
Or stockings—zone—or stays—
    The graces all unloose!
(wr. 1781/pub. 1783)[170]

In the voice of the mixed-race "Jacoba" ("My Indian sire, my *Negro* Dam"), Thompson imagines the anxieties of a young Caribbean woman who, in leaving

* [Thompson's note:] It is a discordant instrument the *Negroes* bring from *Africa,* made with three wires, like the *guittar;* which they strum to words of a lascivious sort, to inspire the dancers with zeal and activity.

her home to follow her white lover, feels torn between two cultures. Ironically, her ruminations lead her to idealize the life she is leaving behind, full of simple, sensual pleasures routinely enjoyed even by slave girls—such as Jacoba herself probably was.

from "The Maid of Marra-Carra's Soliloquy, [Composed] Between Barbados and Demararie, June 13, 1781"

Why did I leave my peaceful home,
And o'er the lifting billows roam
With *Europeans?*—Why so rash,
To quit my carved *Calabash.*
My *Troolie-house,* my *cocoa-dish,*
My roasted *plantain,* broiled fish,
My *pepper-pot* of *crab* and *yam,*
My Indian Sire, my *Negro* Dam?
Ah! tell me, why did I leave these,
With *Buckra* man to cross the seas? . . .
When I *Marra-Carra* name,
I feel a strange, uneasy flame;
A glow, a trilling, thro' my blood—
Then wish I ne'er had cross'd the flood:
Repine the loss of *cocoa* milk,
Now smile on *banffs, chintz, gauze,* or *silk.*
Thrice happy wench! undress'd and bare,
Who scorns the sun, and tanning air;
Who buxom pads the ground along,
And hears the *Indian's* savage song . . .
Who to the *banja* or the fiddle,
Dances, with *quaio** round her middle:
Nothing to hide her shape and mien—
Her bum and bosom equal seen!
When hot, she plunges in the wave—
Here's luxury, Christians, for a slave!
When cool, she tries the dance again,
And courts in *lap*† some active swain;

* [Thompson's note:] A sort of primeval fig-leaf, made of beads, and used by *Indian* belles, to hide their nakedness.
† [Thompson's note:] A covering round the middle of the men . . . fringed and ornamented; but it is a mere apology for hiding the filth of the privacies.

Who with her in a hammock swings,
Happier than *European* Kings;
Who make their loves their pleasing theme—
Draw health and pleasure from the stream.
These must *Jacoba* now resign.

           (wr. 1781/pub. 1783)[171]

Intimations of the Inkle and Yarico story that hover over the preceding poem become explicit in Thompson's note to the following. Here, in a tragic poem about a love triangle among African slaves that he presents as a true story, Thompson shows, especially in the early stanzas of the poem and his scathing footnote, the intensity of his moral outrage and his belief that the tale's significance extends beyond the lives of three people to the whole institution of slavery.

from "The True But Unfortunate Histories of Corrobana, Hobaboo, and Cyonie. An African Tale. Written at Sea, December 16, 1781"

For *Liverpool** and gallant ship,
    With tackle trim and gay,
Sail'd with a very wicked freight,
    For Slaves of *Africa*.

---

* [from Thompson's note:] Though the unnatural and ungenerous tale of *Yarico* and *Inkle* has moved the feelings of all that could be moved by the distresses of a fellow-creature; yet the *Liverpool* people employed in the *African* Trade, can look on the pregnancy of a *Yarico*, and sell her without any remorse, and take advantage of her pregnant situation. But although these circumstances, inhuman as they are, frequently pass and happen in the *African* Trade, yet none would believe a General Officer in the *British* Service, could be guilty of the enormity of such an action . . . A Commander in Chief, celebrated for his *vinegar* disposition, bought a Mullatto Girl in *Barbadoes*, on his arrival to be his bed-fellow. This was about the year 1780. On his departure for *England*, in the year 1782, (not honoured, regretted, or lamented . . .), he ordered his Secretary to sell her! in spite of her tears and distress, in spite of her plea of fidelity and affection!—The Secretary also interceded in her behalf, and argued the disgrace of the action—He was deaf to every remonstrance of honour and humanity—AND, ordered HER to be *sold!*—The Secretary, still hoping to succeed in the plea of Charity, told him with every feeling emotion of a generous mind, that the Wench was with child; and solicited him to reflect, that the child was his—The General paused, and seemed to be struck with the weight of her condition; then breaking from a seeming pensive mind, he said—'Tis well; 'tis all the better—demand *ten pounds more for her!*—and the hapless, wretched girl *was sold!*—and yet this blot to Humanity holds a place in Christian Society; but I trust he does not escape a gnawing and perturbed conscience.

EDWARD THOMPSON

Nor does the spread-out world produce
    Merchants so hard of heart,
As the rich Town of *Liverpool*,
    Which drives a human *mart*.

Nor are the Merchants' callous souls,
    Less piteous than the knave's
Which they employ on *Guinea* Coast,
    To buy, or steal the slaves.

They stink a proverb to the world,
    Rear'd in the basest school:
To epigrammatise a wretch,
    Call him of *Liverpool*. . . .

Soon did she let her anchor run,
    In *Gambia's* muddy waves;
And soon the diabolick trade
    Began, for wretched slaves! . . .

Among the many Slaves decoy'd
    Were three of fashion rare:
Hobaboo, and *Cyonie* tall,
    And *Corrobana* fair.* . . .

For Ladies fair, with linen cheeks,
    I do not ween more pure
Than lovely *Corrobana* liv'd;
    And nought was blacker sure! . . .

The friendship which *Hobaboo* shew'd,
    Cyonie did return;
Nor did the flame *Cyonie* nurs'd,
    With weaker passion burn.

But both did *Corrobana* love,
    And both did woe her heart;
And both she lov'd—nor could she spare
    To one the other's part.

One morn . . . she smil'd on both—when both,
    With mutual impulse start!
Each in the instant drew his knife,
    And stab'd her in the heart!

* [Thompson's note:] Will the Wits allow a Negro Maid, by nature black, to be called fair?
Philosophers will, if they refuse the epithet.

She sigh'd, and to her bleeding arms
    The wretched Lovers drew:
Kiss'd the assassins of her love,
    And bade the World adieu!

Stung with remorse, like light they flew,
    Then on each other prest,
And the same knives the Maiden slew
    Plung'd in each other's breast!

Thus fell *three* hapless *Lovers* rare,
    Of *Africk's* savage race;
With every sentiment of Truth,
    That chaster *Christians* grace.
                (wr. 1781/pub. 1783)[172]

CHARLES DIBDIN (1745–1814)

Musically accomplished from childhood, Dibdin pursued a prolific if volatile career as singer, actor, composer, and playwright in London. He is said to have composed more than nine hundred songs of his own and set to music countless others (usually for operas and musicals). He composed the music for Bickerstaffe's *The Padlock* (1768), in which he also starred in the role of Mungo, the African slave. The tremendous success of the play (it sold 28,000 copies) established Dibdin at the center of the London theater world. He acknowledged both Bickerstaffe and his breakthrough part by naming his illegitimate son (born 1768) "Charles Isaac Mungo Dibdin."

Dibdin never forgot the success of his role as Mungo, spoken in a slave dialect. His own writings further established a stereotypical image of African slaves, complete with dialect speech patterns that served, in various contexts, both comic and sentimental ends. The first two songs below are spoken by black characters in a popular comic opera of the 1780s.

"Air" [Sung by Orra], from The Islanders

When Yanko dear, fight far away,
   Some token kind me send;
One branch of olive—for dat say,
   Me wish de battle end,
Me wish de battle end.
   De poplar tremble, while him go,
Say of dy life take care,
   Me send no laurel, for me know,
Of dat he find him share.
   Me send no laurel, for me know,
Of dat he find him share.
   Of dat he find him share!

De ivy say, my heart be true,
  Me droop, say willow tree,
De torn, he say, me sick for you,
  De sun flower—tink of me.
'Till last me go weep wid de pine,
  For fear poor Yanko dead;
He come, and I de myrtle twine,
  In chaplet for him head.
                    (1780)[173]

"Air" [Sung by Yanko], from The Islanders

Poor Orra, tink of Yanko dear,
  Do he be gone for ever,
For he no dead, he still live here,
  And he from here go never.

Like on a sand, me mark him face,
  The wave, come roll him over,
De mark he go—but still de place,
  'Tis easy to discover.

I see fore now, de tree, de flower,
  He droop like Orra, surely,
And den, by'm bye, dere come a shower,
  He hold him head up purely.

And so some time, me tink me die,
  My heart so sick, he grieve me;
But in a lillee time, me cry
  Good deal, and dat relieve me.
                    (1780)[174]

Beneath the comic dialect and alley-cat atmosphere of sexual license, the following song (from a musical of the 1790s) hints at the complex social position of blacks in terms that foreshadow the "invisible man" of the twentieth century. The wry singer observes all, tells nothing, and pursues his own fun unnoticed.

"Rondeau" from The Wags

One Negro, wi my banjer,
  Me from Jenny come,
    Wid cunning yiei
    Me savez spy
  De buckra world one hum,

As troo a street a stranger
   Me my banjer strum.

My missy for one black dog about the house me kick,
Him say my nassy tawny face enough to make him sick;
But when my massa he go out, she then no longer rail,
For first me let the captain in, and then me tell no tale:

   So aunt Quashy say,
Do tabby, brown, or black, or white,
You see um in one night,
   Every sort of cat be gray.
     One Negro, &c.

To fetch a lilly money back, you go to law they call,
The court and all the tie-wig soon strip you shirt and all,
The courtier call him friend him foe,
   And fifty story tell,
To-day say yes, to-morrow no,
   And lie like any hell:
And so though Negro black for true,
He black in buckra country too.
     One Negro, &c.

$$(1790)^{175}$$

[?LEVI MAXCY] (fl. 1770–1780)

Engraved burial markers were rare enough for black people, but rarer still were those composed in rhyme. The lines below pay tribute to Caesar, a domestic slave who died at age seventy-seven, having worked faithfully for the Maxcy family through three generations. Probably composed by Caesar's owner, Levi Maxcy, the poetic inscription has stood in the cemetery of North Attleboro, Massachusetts, for more than two hundred years.

[Untitled gravestone epitaph]

In memory of
CAESAR
Here lies the best of slaves
Now turning into dust;
Caesar the Ethiopian craves
A place among the just.
His faithful soul has fled
To realms of heavenly light,
And by the blood that Jesus shed
is changed from Black to White.
Jan 15 he quitted the stage
in the 77th year of his age.
1780

(c. 1780)[176]

MARY DEVERELL
["PHILANTHEA"]
(c. 1737 – post-1792)

A self-educated Gloucestershire merchant's daughter, Deverell first came to notice in 1774 when—most unusually for a woman of her time—she published a volume of *Sermons*. In later years her writings included an epic poem, a verse tragedy, and her *Miscellanies in Prose and Verse*. The poem below first appeared in that volume, which attracted hundreds of subscribers, among them Samuel Johnson and Granville Sharp. They and other antislavery readers would have been gratified to read Deverell's warm tribute to Phillis Wheatley and its denunciation of racism.

On Reading the Poems of Phillis Wheatley

To shame the formal circle of the school,
That chain their pupils down by pedant rules,
Curbing the insolence of learned lore,
There lately came from India's swarthy shore,
In nature's sable charms, a lowly maid,
By fortune doom'd to languish in the shade;
Till Britain call'd the seeds of genius forth,
Maturing, like the sun, her native worth.
Though no high birth nor titles grace her line,
Yet humble PHILLIS boasts a race divine;
Like marble that in quarries lies conceal'd,
Till all its veins, by *polish*, stand reveal'd;
From whence such groups of images arise,
We praise the artist, and the sculpture prize.
Go on, sweet maid, of Providence once more
Divinely sing, and charm another shore;
No fetters thus thy genius shall controul,
Nor iron laws restrain thy towering soul.
$(1781)^{177}$

WILLIAM COWPER (1731 – 1800)

Although a standard work such as the *Dictionary of National Biography* omits any reference to Cowper's antislavery writings, he was one of the most prolific and influential antislavery poets of the eighteenth century. Plagued by mental illness and unable to pursue his intended legal career, Cowper lived off family inheritance, in rural retirement. A confidant and fellow evangelical of John Newton's, Cowper contributed more than sixty pieces to Newton's *Olney Hymns* (1779). During the 1780s Cowper introduced powerful antislavery passages into his long meditative poems and published shorter abolitionist lyrics in newspapers and magazines. After a life wracked with mental breakdowns and suicide attempts, Cowper died peacefully in 1800.

In the first poem, Cowper's advocacy of antislavery charity is undermined by an unconscious tone of condescension at the close. In the opening section the slave is humanized through his suffering, but later the "generous" master is shown rejoicing in the gratitude and pious loyalty of the slaves he has freed.

from "Charity"

But ah! what wish can prosper, or what pray'r,
For merchants rich in cargoes of despair,
Who drive a loathsome traffic, gage and span,
And buy the muscles and the bones of man?
The tender ties of father, husband, friend,
All bonds of nature in that moment end,
And each endures while yet he draws his breath,
A stroke as fatal as the scythe of death.
The sable warrior, frantic with regret
Of her he loves, and never can forget,
Loses in tears the far receding shore,
But not the thought that they must meet no more;
Depriv'd of her and freedom at a blow,

What has he left that he can yet forego?
Yes, to deep sadness sullenly resign'd,
He feels his body's bondage in his mind,
Puts off his gen'rous nature, and to suit
His manners with his fate, puts on the brute.
    Oh most degrading of all ills that wait
On man, a mourner in his best estate!
All other sorrows virtue may endure,
And find submission more than half a cure . . .
But slav'ry!—virtue dreads it as her grave,
Patience itself is meanness in a slave:
Or if the will and sovereignty of God
Bid suffer it awhile, and kiss the rod,
Wait for the dawning of a brighter day,
And snap the chain the moment when you may. . . .
    Canst thou, and honour'd with a Christian name,
Buy what is woman-born, and feel no shame?
Trade in the blood of innocence, and plead
Expedience as a warrant for the deed? . . .
    A Briton knows, or if he knows it not,
The Scripture plac'd within his reach, he ought,
That souls have no discriminating hue,
Alike important in their Maker's view.
. . . Slaves, by truth enlarg'd, are doubly freed:
Then would he say, submissive at thy feet,
While gratitude and love made service sweet,
My dear deliv'rer out of hopeless night,
Whose bounty bought me but to give me light,
I was a bondman on my native plain,
Sin forg'd, and ignorance made fast, the chain;
Thy lips have shed instruction as the dew,
Taught me what path to shun, and what pursue;
Farewell my former joys! I sigh no more
For Africa's once lov'd, benighted shore,
Serving a benefactor I am free,
At my best home if not exiled from thee.

                          (1782)[178]

These lines, from a long poem assigned to Cowper by a lady friend as a mental health exercise (hence its title *The Task*), give voice to the poet's hatred of slavery and racism. His famous expression of sympathy ("I had much rather be

myself the slave") was frequently repeated by abolitionists, especially after the
founding of the British Abolition Society in 1787.

from "The Time-Piece," Book II of The Task

        My ear is pain'd,
My soul is sick with ev'ry day's report
Of wrong and outrage with which earth is fill'd.
There is no flesh in man's obdurate heart,
It does not feel for man. The nat'ral bond
Of brotherhood is sever'd as the flax
That falls asunder at the touch of fire.
He finds his fellow guilty of a skin
Not colour'd like his own, and having pow'r
T' inforce the wrong, for such a worthy cause
Dooms and devotes him as his lawful prey. . . .
And worse than all, and most to be deplored
As human nature's broadest, foulest blot,
Chains him, and tasks him, and exacts his sweat
With stripes, that mercy with a bleeding heart
Weeps when she sees inflicted on a beast.
Then what is man? And what man seeing this,
And having human feelings, does not blush
And hang his head, to think himself a man?
I would not have a slave to till my ground,
To carry me, to fan me while I sleep,
And tremble when I wake, for all the wealth
That sinews bought and sold have ever earn'd.
No: dear as freedom is, and in my heart's
Just estimation priz'd above all price,
I had much rather be myself the slave
And wear the bonds, than fasten them on him.
We have no slaves at home.—Then why abroad?
And they themselves once ferried o'er the wave
That parts us, are emancipate and loos'd.
Slaves cannot breathe in England; if their lungs
Receive our air, that moment they are free,
They touch our country and their shackles fall.
That's noble, and bespeaks a nation proud
And jealous of the blessing. Spread it then,
And let it circulate through ev'ry vein

Of all your empire. That where Britain's power
Is felt, mankind may feel her mercy too.

(1785)[179]

Dryly ironic, the following stanzas use an equivocating citizen's voice to raise political consciousness about the slavery question that Wilberforce and the abolitionists thrust before the public in the years 1787–89. One by one, Cowper exposes the hollowness of the rationalizations for allowing slavery to continue.

from "Pity for the Poor Africans"

I own I am shock'd at this Traffic of Slaves,
And fear those who buy them, and sell them, are Knaves.
What I hear of their Hardships, their Tortures & Groans,
Is almost enough to draw Pity from Stones.

I pity them greatly, but I must be mum;
For how could we do without Sugar and Rum?
Especially Sugar so needful we see;
What, give up our Desserts, our Coffee, and Tea?

Besides, if we do, the French, Dutch and Danes
Will heartily thank us, no Doubt, for our Pains:
If WE do not buy the poor Creatures THEY will,
And Tortures and Groans will be multiply'd still.

If Foreigners *likewise* would give up the Trade,
Much more in Behalf of your Wish might be said;
But whilst *they* get Riches by purchasing Blacks,
Pray tell me, why we may not also go Snacks?

(1788)[180]

The following allegory offered the public a much more uplifting vision of the abolition movement, as part of the divine plan for British civilization. Although long thought to have first appeared in the *Gentleman's Magazine*, the poem was first published in Thomas Bellamy's *General Magazine and Impartial Review*, where a steady stream of antislavery writings by Cowper and others were printed between 1787 and 1792.

from "The Morning Dream"

I dreamt that, on Ocean afloat,
    Far West from fair Albion I sail'd,
While the billows high lifted the boat,
    And the fresh-blowing breeze never fail'd.

In the steerage a woman I saw,
    (Such, at least, was the form that she bore,)
Whose beauty impress'd me with awe,
    Ne'er taught me by woman before.

She sat, and a shield at her side
    Shed light, like a sun, on the waves;
And, smiling divinely, she cried,
    I go to make *freemen* of *slaves!*

Then raising her voice to a strain,
    The sweetest that ear ever heard,
She sung of the slave-broken chain,
    Wherever her glory appear'd. . . .

Thus swiftly dividing the flood,
    To a slave-cultur'd island we came,
Where a demon her enemy stood,
    Oppression his terrible name.

In his hand, as a sign of his sway,
    A scourge hung with lashes he bore;
And stood looking out for his prey
    From Africa's sorrowful shore.

But soon as approaching the land
    This Goddess-like woman he view'd,
The scourge he let fall from his hand,
    With blood of his subjects embrued.

I saw him both sicken and die,
    And, the moment the monster expir'd,
Heard shouts, that ascended the sky,
    From thousands with rapture inspir'd.

—Awaking, how could I but muse
    At what such a dream might betide?
But soon my ear caught the glad news,
    Which serv'd my weak thoughts for a guide;

That Britannia, renown'd o'er the waves,
    From the hatred she ever has shewn
To the black-sceptr'd Ruler of Slaves,
    Resolves to have *none of her own.*

(1788)[181]

One of the most perplexing of Cowper's poems, this song uses the voice of a
slaveship captain to bid mock-farewell to a trade that the author wrongly be-

lieved—with many others—was on the verge of extinction in 1788. Perhaps this explains why the poem was not published until thirty-five years after Cowper's death.

from "Sweet Meat Has Sour Sauce: or, The Slave-Trader in the Dumps"

A Trader I am to the African shore,
But since that my trading is like to be o'er,
I'll sing you a song that you ne'er heard before,
    Which nobody can deny, deny,
    Which nobody can deny.

When I first heard the news it gave me a shock,
Much like what they call an electrical knock,
And now I am going to sell off my stock,
    Which nobody, &c.

'Tis a curious assortment of dainty regales,
To tickle the Negroes with when the ship sails,
Fine chains for the neck, and a cat with nine tails,
    Which nobody, &c. . . .

Here's padlocks and bolts, and screws for the thumbs,
That squeeze them so lovingly till the blood comes,
They sweeten the temper like comfits or plums,
    Which nobody, &c.

When a Negro his head from his victuals withdraws,
And clenches his teeth and thrusts out his paws,
Here's a notable engine to open his jaws,
    Which nobody, &c.

Thus going to market, we kindly prepare
A pretty black cargo of African ware,
For what they must meet with when they get there,
    Which nobody, &c.

'Twould do your heart good to see 'em below
Lie flat on their backs all the way as we go,
Like sprats on a gridiron, scores in a row,
    Which nobody, &c.

But ah! if in vain I have studied an art
So gainful to me, all boasting apart,
I think it will break my compassionate heart,
    Which nobody, &c.

So this is my song, as I told you before;
Come buy off my stock, for I must no more
Carry Caesars and Pompeys to Sugar-cane shore,
    Which nobody can deny, deny,
    Which nobody can deny.
             (wr. 1788/pub. 1836)[182]

A moral recrimination addressed to the British public, ostensibly by an Afri-
can captive, the following poem was written by Cowper at the specific request
of the Abolition Society. First published in a 1788 antislavery pamphlet, it was
reprinted in many collections thereafter. The central themes, that racial differ-
ence was no justification for slavery and that slaveholding was un-Christian,
were no longer original by this date, but remained powerful nonetheless.

The Negro's Complaint

Forc'd from home, and all its pleasures,
    Afric's coast I left forlorn;
To increase a stranger's treasures,
    O'er the raging billows borne.
Men from England bought and sold me,
    Paid my price in paltry gold;
But, though theirs they have enroll'd me,
    Minds are never to be sold.

Still in thought as free as ever,
    What are England's rights, I ask,
Me from my delights to sever,
    Me to torture, me to task?
Fleecy locks, and black complexion
    Cannot forfeit nature's claim;
Skins may differ, but affection
    Dwells in white and black the same.

Why did all-creating Nature
    Make the plant for which we toil?
Sighs must fan it, tears must water,
    Sweat of ours must dress the soil.
Think, ye masters, iron-hearted,
    Lolling at your jovial boards;
Think how many blacks have smarted
    For the sweets your cane affords.

Is there, as ye sometimes tell us,
    Is there one who reigns on high?

Has he bid you buy and sell us,
   Speaking from his throne the sky?
Ask him, if your knotted scourges,
   Fetters, blood-extorting screws,
Are the means which duty urges
   Agents of his will to use.

Hark! he answers—Wild tornadoes,
   Strewing yonder sea with wrecks;
Wasting towns, plantations, meadows,
   Are the voice with which he speaks.
He, foreseeing what vexations
   Afric's sons should undergo,
Fix'd their tyrant's habitations
   Where his whirlwinds answer—No.

By our blood in Afric wasted,
   Ere our necks receiv'd the chain;
By the mis'ries we have tasted,
   Crossing in your barks the main;
By our suff'rings since ye brought us
   To the man-degrading mart;
All sustain'd by patience, taught us
   Only by a broken heart:

Deem our nation brutes no longer
   Till some reason ye shall find
Worthier of regard and stronger
   Than the colour of our kind.
Slaves of gold, whose sordid dealings
   Tarnish all your boasted pow'rs,
Prove that you have human feelings,
   Ere you proudly question ours!

                 (1788)[183]

Cowper was one of many to laud Wilberforce for his moral heroism in leading the antislavery campaign. Here Cowper tries to put a brave face on a legislative disappointment (the evisceration of the 1792 abolition bill) as he encourages Wilberforce to continue the struggle. Wilberforce did, for decades to come.

Sonnet, Addressed to William Wilberforce, Esq.

I praise thee, WILBERFORCE! and with disdain
Hear thee by cruel men and impious call'd

Fanatic, for thy zeal to loose th' enthrall'd
From exile, public sale, and slav'ry's chain.
Friend of the poor, the scourg'd, the fetter-gall'd,
Fear not lest labour such as thine be vain.
Thou hast atchiev'd a part; hast won the ear
Of Britain's Senate to thy glorious cause;
Hope smiles, joy springs, and though cold caution draws
Delay between, the better hour is near
That shall remunerate thy pains severe
By peace to Afric, fenced with British laws.
Then let them scoff—two prizes thou hast won—
Freedom for Captives, and thy God's—"Well done."

(1792)[184]

In this final piece, a strange blend of folklore, blood symbolism, and political protest, Cowper's poetical brew suggests the diabolic evil of slavery.

An Epigram

To purify their wine some people bleed
A *Lamb* into the barrel, and succeed,
No nostrum, planters say, is half so good
To make fine sugar, as a *Negro's* blood.
Now *Lambs* and *Negroes* both are harmless things,
And thence, perhaps, this wond'rous virtue springs;
'Tis in the blood of innocence alone—
Good cause why *planters* never try *their own.*

(1792)[185]

[GEORGE] GREGORY (1754–1808)

After a youth spent working as clerk to a Liverpool merchant, Gregory went on to become a clergyman and man of letters. He moved to London in 1782 and thereafter held various ministries, served as evening preacher at the Foundling Hospital, and received a doctorate in divinity in 1792. Meanwhile he had a career as a writer, publishing sermons, literary criticism, moral essays, and biography, including, importantly, a life of the antislavery poet Thomas Chatterton. Gregory gave voice to his own antislavery views in two major poems, published early in his career as a pair of "American Eclogues."

Although the first of these poems has sometimes been attributed to Hugh Mulligan (who is included elsewhere in this volume), it is clear from the details of their publication in the *Gentleman's Magazine* that Gregory wrote them both. The first is a monologue set vaguely in America: a lament by the slave Adala for his lost African homeland, and the wife and children he left behind. In describing the more fortunate life of his friend and fellow slave Arcona, whose master is the kindly Quaker Narbal, Adala acknowledges the enlightened convictions and practices of the Quakers. But overall Gregory's poem is a plaintive indictment of slavery in America in the Revolutionary era.

from "American Eclogues, Eclogue I: Morning; or the Complaint"

"Oh curs'd destroyers of our hapless race,
Of human kind the terror and disgrace!
Lo! hosts of dusky captives, to my view,
Demand a deep revenge! demand their due! . . .

Lift high the scourge, my soul the rack disdains;
I pant for freedom and my native plains!

With limbs benumb'd my poor companions lie;
Oppress'd by pain and want the aged sigh;
Through reedy huts the driving tempest pours,

Their festering wounds receive the sickly show'rs;
In mad'ning draughts our lords their senses steep,
And doom their slaves to stripes and death in sleep:
Now, while the bitter blast surrounds my head,
To times long past my restless soul is led,
Far, far beyond the azure hills, to groves
Of ruddy fruit, where beauty fearless roves—
O blissful seats! O self-approving joys!
Nature's plain dictates! ignorance of vice!
O guiltless hours! Our cares and wants were few,
No arts of luxury or deceit we knew.
Our labor, sport—to tend our cottage care,
Or from the palm the luscious juice prepare;
To sit indulging love's delusive dream,
And snare the silver tenants of the stream . . .

    Can I forget, ah me! the fatal day,
When half the vale of peace was swept away!
Th'affrighted maids in vain the gods implore,
And weeping view from far the happy shore;
The frantic dames impatient ruffians seize,
And infants shriek, and clasp their mother's knees;
With galling fetters soon their limbs are bound,
And groans throughout the noisome bark resound.
Why was I bound! why did not the Whydah see
Adala gain, or Death or Victory!
No storms arise, no waves revengeful roar,
To dash the monsters on our injur'd shore.
Long o'er the foaming deep to worlds unknown,
By envious winds the bulky vessel's blown,
While by disease and chains the weak expire,
Or parch'd endure the slow consuming fire.
Who'd in this land of many sorrows live,
Where death's the only comfort tyrants give?
Tyrants unblest! Each proud of strict command,
Nor age nor sickness holds the iron hand;
Whose hearts, in adamant involv'd, despise
The drooping female's tears, the infant cries,
From whose stern brows no grateful look e'er beams,
Whose blushless front no rape nor murder shames.
    Nor all I blame; for Narbal,* friend to peace,

* "Nastal" in later editions.

Thro' his wide pastures bids oppression cease;*
No drivers goad, no galling fetters bind,
Nor stern compulsion damps th'exalted mind.
There strong Arcona's fated to enjoy
Domestic sweets, and rear his progeny;
To till his glebe employs Arcona's care,
To Narbal's God he nightly makes his pray'r;
His mind at ease, of Christian truths he'll boast—
He has no wife, no lovely offspring lost.
Gay his Savannah blooms, while mine appears
Scorch'd up with heat, or moist with blood and tears.
Cheerful his hearth in chilling winter burns,
While to the storm the sad Adala mourns.
    Lift high the scourge, my soul the rack disdains;
    I pant for freedom and my native plains.

    Shall I his holy prophet's aid implore,
And wait for justice on another shore?
Or, rushing down yon mountain's craggy steep,
End all my sorrows in the sullen deep?
A cliff there hangs in yon grey morning cloud,
The dashing wave beneath roars hard and loud—
But doubts and fears involve my anxious mind,
The gulf of death once pass'd, what shore we find.
Dubious, if sent beyond th'expanded main,
This soul shall seek its native realms again:
Or if in gloomy mists condemn'd to lie,
Beyond the limits of yon arching sky.
A better prospect oft my spirit cheers,
And in my dreams the vale of peace appears,
And fleeting visions of my former life:
My hoary sire I clasp, my long-lost wife,
And oft I kiss my gentle babes in sleep,
Till with the sounding whip I'm wak'd to weep.
    Lift high the scourge, my soul the rack disdains;
    I pant for freedom and my native plains! . . .

    Thou God, who gild'st with light the rising day!
Who life dispensest by thy genial ray!
Will thy slow vengeance never, never fall,
But undistinguish'd favor shine on all?

* [Gregory's note:] The Quakers in America have set free all their Negroes, and allow them
wages as other servants.

O hear a suppliant wretch's last, sad pray'r!
Dart fiercest rage! infect the ambient air!
This pallid race, whose hearts are bound in steel,
By dint of suffering teach them how to feel.
    Or, to some despot's lawless will betray'd,
Give them to know what wretches they have made!
Beneath the lash let them resign their breath,
Or court, in chains, the clay-cold hand of death.
Or, worst of ills! within each callous breast,
Cherish uncurb'd the dark internal pest;
Bid Av'rice swell with undiminish'd rage,
While no new worlds th'accurst thirst assuage;
Then bid the monsters on each other turn,
The fury passions in disorder burn;
Bid Discord flourish, civil crimes increase,
Nor one fond wish arise that pleads for peace—
Till, with their crimes in wild confusion hurl'd,
They wake t'eternal anguish in a future world."*
                (wr. c. 1782/pub. 1783)[186]

In the second eclogue, Gregory presents an emotional conversation between two African slaves, one of them a desperate runaway pursued by a murderous master, who meet by chance in the bush. Holding his motherless infant in his arms, the runaway Zamboia tells his long-lost friend Mombaze the harrowing tale: his repulse of the white overseer who tried to rape his wife, Melinda, the punishments and beatings that followed, Melinda's death in childbirth, and his frantic flight with their newborn. Though hope flares briefly when gentle Mombaze offers him refuge, the poem reverts to reality when Zamboia is recaptured and led away to his death.

from "American Eclogues, Eclogue II: Evening; or, the Fugitive"

MOMBAZE.
    Sure rememb'rance mocks me, or I trace
In thine the semblance of Zamboia's face?
Yet scarce thyself; for in thy alter'd eye
I read the records of hard destiny.
From thy rack'd bosom sighs that ceaseless flow,
A man bespeak thee exercis'd in woe

---

* [Gregory's note:] This Eclogue was written during the American war.

GEORGE GREGORY

Say, then, what chance has burst thy rigid chains,
Has led thee, frantic, o'er these distant plains?
What potent sorrows can thy peace infest?
What crimes conceal'd prey on thy anxious breast?

ZAMBOIA.

No crimes this heart infest, this hand defile,
Or frantic drive me o'er a foreign soil.
A murder'd wife and wrongs unmatch'd I mourn,
And buried joys that never shall return!
If then thou'rt tempted by the traitor's meed,
Take this poor life, and prosper by the deed!

MOMBAZE.

Not the rich produce of Angola's shore,
Not all the miser's heap'd and glittering store,
Not all that pride would grasp, or pomp display,
Should tempt this hand the wretched to betray. . . .
Canst thou forget? One common lot we drew,
With thee enchain'd, a captive's fate I knew.
Distrust me not, but unreserv'd disclose
The anxious tale that in my bosom glows.

ZAMBOIA.

Dear to my sight that form, and doubly dear
Thy well-known accents meet Zamboia's ear.
O! had I died, and left the name of slave
Deep, deep entomb'd within an early grave! . . .
Tedious to tell what treach'rous arts were tried,
To sooth the smart of still revolting pride.
I liv'd, and lov'd—then kiss'd the fatal chain!
No joy but one to cheer a life of pain.
Yet witness bear, thou dear departed ghost,
That lonely rov'st thy Gambia's sacred coast!
How sweet the toil that met the morning's ray,
How light the labor that o'er-lasted day!
The reed-built hovel, and the scanty fare,
Imperial bliss could give, Melinda there!
Soft was my pillow, on thy gentle breast,
When o'er-prest Nature droop'd in want of rest! . . .

A wretch, who banish'd from his native clime,
Defil'd with many a black and monstrous crime,
Presided o'er us, and with iron hand
Held savage sway o'er all the servile band.

In him each hellish passion rudely glow'd,
And cruelty in him most cruel shew'd.
Him lust infernal, one sad ev'ning, led
T'invade the chasteness of my marriage bed:
I chanc'd to approach—the caitiff I surpris'd—
My wife preserv'd, and had his guilt chastis'd
While full with vengeance boil'd my wounded heart:
But chance reserv'd him for a baser part. . . .

    The baffled villain, now a foe profess'd,
Rolls scenes of blood within his rankling breast;
With coward arts he forg'd a crafty tale;
And hands unrighteous poise the partial scale.
Imputed crimes to crush the weak suffice,
Hearsay is guilt, and damning fact surmise.
Where uncurb'd will usurps the place of laws,
No friendly pleader takes the wretch's cause.
Our tyrant's fears each want of proof supplied,
We stand condemn'd, unquestion'd, and untried.

    O! had the grief and shame been all my own,
And the black vengeance lit on me alone!
But harsher fates a harder curse decreed;
These eyes were doom'd to see Melinda bleed.
I saw her by relentless ruffians bound,
The brandish'd scourge inflict the mortal wound;
Her tender frame abus'd, and mangled o'er,
I saw her welt'ring in a flood of gore.
The murd'rous scene had soon a dreadful close—
And do I live! and can I speak my woes!
Her pregnant womb no longer could sustain
The public shame, and agony of pain;
A birth abortive robb'd her of her breath,
And pangs convulsive seal'd her eyes in death.
One only pledge my weary soul retains,
This hapless infant, all that now remains;
The mournful image of my once-lov'd wife,
And ties me down awhile to hated life.
Else this bold hand should liberty restore,
And my rapt spirit seek a happier shore. . . .

MOMBAZE.

    Hapless Zamboia! had it been thy fate
With me to share my more propitious state;

Thy soul had breath'd no impious wish to die,
Nor the big tear had trembled in thine eye.
Disjoin'd from thee, I too to slavery went;
But Heaven a father, not a master, lent.
He seems as Virtue's self, in moral guise;
Tho' wealthy, simple; and tho' modest, wise. . . .
But, come! thy faint and weary limbs repose,
Forgetful of thy fears, thy griefs compose;
By morning's dawn with earnest foo[t] I speed,
Nor sleep these eyes till I behold thee freed.
Some wealth I have; and, did I prize it more,
Well spar'd for this I deem the sacred store.
    So talked these friends, and to the cottage haste;
While sad Zamboia his pursuers trac'd.
The ruffian band arrest the hapless swain,
And pray'rs, and tears, and promises are vain:
Their vengeful fervor, no—not gifts abate;
But bound in chains, they drag him to his fate.*

(c. 1783)[187]

---

* [Gregory's note:] A higher reward is generally offered for the *head* of a fugitive negro than for bringing him alive.

GEORGE CRABBE (1754–1832)

A former medical apprentice turned clergyman and writer, Crabbe struggled early but eventually succeeded and attracted the support of Burke, Johnson, Walter Scott, and many others over his long career. In the poem below, intended as an unsentimental response to Goldsmith's elegiac "Deserted Village," Crabbe blurs the distinction between New World slavery and the worst excesses of rural labor exploitation in Britain. Although he seems never to have commented extensively on African slavery, personal experience brought home its reality quite painfully: Crabbe's younger brother John, master of a slave ship, died after being set adrift by slaves who had risen and captured his ship.

from Book I of The Village

> In other scenes more fair in view,
> Where Plenty smiles—alas! she smiles for few,
> And those who taste not, yet behold her store,
> Are as the slaves that dig the golden ore,
> The wealth around them makes them doubly poor.
> Or will you deem them amply paid in health,
> Labour's fair child, that languishes with Wealth?
> Go then! and see them rising with the sun,
> Through a long course of daily toil to run;
> Like him to make the plenteous harvest grow,
> And yet not share the plenty they bestow;
> See them beneath the dog-star's raging heat,
> When the knees tremble and the temples beat;
> Behold them leaning on their scythes, look o'er
> The labour past, and toils to come explore;
> See them alternate suns and showers engage,
> And hoard up aches and anguish for their age;

Thro' fens and marshy moors their steps pursue,
When their warm pores imbibe the evening dew;
Then own that labour may as fatal be
To these thy slaves, as luxury to thee.

(1783)[188]

HENRY JAMES PYE (1745–1813)

An Oxford-educated man of property and Member of Parliament, Pye was appointed Poet Laureate by Pitt in 1790. He would serve twenty-three years, and was widely viewed as the worst poet ever to fill that post. This excerpt from one of his many mediocre poetic productions reveals Pye's assumptions about the inferiority of Africans within his larger theory of the environmental influences on human culture.

from The Progress of Refinement

What else exists beneath the cope of heaven
Is to the savage tribe of wanderers given,
Who unrestrain'd by precept or by law,
From climate, and from soil, their difference draw.
The sable African no culture boasts,
Fierce as his sun, and ruthless as his coasts;
And where the immeasurable forests spread
Beyond the extent of Ocean's western bed,
Unsocial, uninform'd, the tawney race
Range the drear wild, and urge the incessant chace.
Amid the wild expanse of southern seas
Where the blest isles inhale the genial breeze,
The happier native in the fragrant grove
Woos the soft powers of Indolence and Love:
But where more keen the ray, more rude the gale,
Manners less mild and harsher cares prevail;
Till in the sad extremes of polar frost,
The sacred beam of human reason lost,
Man scarcely rises from the shaggy brood
That prowl insatiate o'er the icy flood.

(1783)[189]

HUGH MULLIGAN
(fl. 1780s and 1790s, d. 1798)

Modern scholarship seems to have settled on Mulligan as the author of this poem, first published over the initials "H.M." in the *Gentleman's Magazine*. Little is known of Mulligan except that he was originally Irish, lived in Liverpool, wrote against slavery, and was friends with the circle of Liverpool antislavery writers that included William Roscoe, Edward Rushton, and William Sheperd (all represented elsewhere in this volume).

His eclogue is a romantic dialogue between two African captives, Zelma and her lover, Bura, who escape a British slave ship on the African coast (near the Volta River) and swim back to shore. They recount their harrowing experiences, including beatings, torture, and attempted rape. The end is cataclysmic: through the stormy night, the lovers can dimly discern a shipboard slave rebellion in progress, the ships adrift and ablaze, and then a huge explosion blasting all aboard to certain death.

from "The Lovers, An African Eclogue"

In Volta's flood the British bark was moor'd;
Th'unfeeling traders thought their prey secur'd;
What time the watch proclaim'd the midnight sound,
The sickly crew in flatt'ring slumbers bound:
When o'er the poop two sable lovers glide,
And pant for freedom on the swelling tide.
    The beach now gain'd, they joyful, hand in hand,
With glowing souls salute their native strand;
In mutual raptures on each other gaze;
Till Bura thus began with words of praise. . . .

     BURA.
    Now, Zelma, rise, and, ere this light's withdrawn,
We'll o'er the uplands pass the verdant lawn,
Far from the haunts of ruffian beach-men stray,
Or where the Whites with blood have mark'd their way. . . .

ZELMA.

Much Bura saw; yet, heaven! thou more didst see,
Of what I dar'd for liberty and thee.
Support me, love! support my feeble frame,
Nor let a woman's weakness meet thy blame.
Think how against the tyrant's wiles I strove,
Us'd every art t'evade his lawless love.——
Now all is hush'd, our weary'd limbs we'll rest,
My soul I'll pour into thy constant breast.
Yon verdant bank near that palmetto's shade
Invites our stay.

BURA.

——Come, then, thou lovely maid:
And now the wand'ring moon glides thro' the trees,
And sultry plains enjoy this cooling breeze,
We'll all our sufferings, all our woes, relate,
The captive's thraldom and our country's fate.
Once happy land! where all were free and blest,
And love and friendship sooth'd each care to rest:
Where age rejoic'd to see his offspring take
The quaint meander through the limpid lake;
Where nightly sports regal'd the sprightly throng,
And Plenty smil'd at cheerful Labour's song.
To ruthless strangers now an easy prey,
And native ruffians far more fierce than they.

ZELMA.

Once happy land! blest were thy blooming bowers,
Where youthful virgins pass'd their pleasing hours;
Where thou, impatient, sought'st the cooling grove,
And brought'st each eve the tokens of thy love.
Now in that grove the uncouth stranger's seen,
Frightful his arms, ghastly his threatening mien.

BURA.

Deceitful men! when first our flocks they view'd,
With plaintive tales they sued for needful food;
Their artful guides, from ANTE's faithless strand,
With proffer'd friendship hail'd our happy land;
But in the silent hour of peaceful night,
Consuming fires th'unwary hamlets fright,
When, like a lion eager for his prey,
Amongst the bloody throng I forc'd my way:

My strength full well their haughty leader knew,
When from my single arm the dastards flew.
Why need I say what swarms from ambush rose?
How dragg'd in chains by these unfeeling foes
O'er trackless sands, till on the Volta's tide
Thou blest my sight, my life, my better guide.

ZELMA.

    . . . Struck dumb with fear, I saw their strange attire,
When high in air they wav'd the dreadful fire. . . .
With tottering steps, by dire distraction led,
Thro' tangling woods and dreary dells we fled;
Nor aught avail'd—beset by fresh alarms,
They tore me fainting from a father's arms.
Nor need I now my sorrows here disclose,
Since blest with thee I half forget my woes.

BURA.

    Speak ever thus, and ever thus appear;
No traders' taunts nor shipmen's threats we fear;
Such rugged souls no sweet sensations prove,
Who spoils his country ne'er can taste of love.
Alas! what horrors fill'd my sinking soul,
To see such monsters rais'd above controul!
Unheard-of crimes and tortures met mine eyes,
That call'd for vengeance from th'impartial skies,
O, think what troubles tore my throbbing breast,
When thou, my Zelma, pin'd and sat distrest.

ZELMA.

    My frantic thoughts oft sunk me in despair;
Blown by the winds thro' seas we knew not where;
And, worse than all, to be their passion's slave;
T'avoid such lust I brav'd the dashing wave.
But know, ere morn, a warlike chief's prepar'd
With engines meet—he'll seize the drowsy guard,
And plunge him headlong in the gloomy deep,
Then free our friends, while yet the ruffians sleep.
My love-fraught bosom, ever prone to fear,
Still kept the precious secret from thine ear.

BURA.

    Too timid maid,—when could I better die,
Than thus for friendship, love, and liberty?
In all his aims still may that chief succeed!

315

Methinks I see the cruel tyrants bleed.
What! tho' unus'd to war, inspir'd I feel
My strength revive. O! for the pointed steel,
To hurl swift vengeance on the pallid foe!

    ZELMA.

    Hark, Bura! heard'st thou not the scream of woe,
Where sinks the moon beneath yon dusky hill?
Behold the bark!—what fears my bosom fill!
What moving fires around the decks now gleam,
And gain reflected horror from the stream!
This way they float; mark! how the flames ascend:
Just heaven, the old and innocent defend!

    BURA.

    The Gods are rous'd—hark! now their thunders roll,
And now shall shrink each trembling tyrant's soul.
O friends! O countrymen! be greatly bold,
For justice strike, nor thus be tamely sold;
You fight for heaven, the CAUSE that gave you breath;
Brave every fear, and challenge manly death.
Would I were there!—to clasp me thus forbear.—

    ZELMA.

    Why shook the earth? behold the darken'd air!

    BURA.

    Thus, rapt in clouds, the lofty mountain shakes
When from the skies the vivid lightning breaks. . . .
The Whites no more at suffering wretches smile,
Nor more majestic floats their lofty pile.

    ZELMA.

    Now all their fears, and tears, and sufferings cease;
The Gods are good, and take their souls to peace.
Guilty and guiltless now are seen no more;
Alas! my love, we'll fly this deathful shore.

    BURA.

    . . . Haste, to distant wilds we'll bend;
Content and Peace shall on our steps attend.
See ruddy clouds o'ertop the mountain's height,
The sun, now glorious, bursts the cave of night.

                         (1784)[190]

WILLIAM HAYLEY (1745–1820)

Educated at Eton and Cambridge (Trinity Hall), Hayley was a successful poet and translator who was deeply immersed in Spanish history and culture. In these lines, from his adaptation of Alonzo de Ercilla's Spanish epic about the conquest of South America, *La Araucana* (1569–90), Hayley dramatizes the defiance of an Amerindian queen whose husband and followers have been defeated. Though Hayley was not as critical of European imperialism as his admired fellow poets Cowper and Blake, he shows here the irony of a black member of the Spanish force (perhaps a slave himself) running to recapture the escaped Amerindian and restore her to bondage with her captive husband.

from Canto XXXIII of "The Araucana"

Setting: an island on the way to South America . . .

From a tent, that, plac'd on safer ground,
The neighbouring hill's uncultur'd summit crown'd,
A woman rush'd, who, in her hasty flight,
Ran through the roughest paths along the rocky height.
A Negro of our train, who mark'd her way,
Soon made the hapless fugitive his prey;
For thwarting crags her doubtful steps impede,
And the fair form was ill prepar'd for speed;
For at her breast she bore her huddled son;
To fifteen months the infant's life had run:
From our brave captive sprung the blooming boy,
Of both his parents the chief pride and joy.
The Negro carelessly his victim brought,
Nor knew th'important prize his haste had caught.
    Our soldiers now, to catch the cooling tide,
Had sallied to the murmuring river's side:
When the unhappy Wife beheld her Lord,

His strong arms bound with a disgraceful cord,
Stript of each ensign of his past command,
And led the pris'ner of our shouting band;
Her anguish burst not into vain complaint,
No female terrors her firm soul attaint;
But, breathing fierce disdain, and anger wild,
Thus she exclaim'd, advancing with her child: . . .

    "Where are the vaunted fruits of thy command,
The laurels gather'd by this fetter'd hand?
All sunk! all turn'd to this abhorr'd disgrace,
To live the slave of this ignoble race!"

(1785)[191]

CAPTAIN J. MARJORIBANKS
(fl. 1784–1793)

Little is known of this Scottish soldier poet beyond what can be gathered from
the poem itself: that he had extensive firsthand experience of plantation slavery
but was also familiar with genteel British society, that he was well versed in (and
appalled by) the rationales offered by slaveholders and their apologists, and that
he was resident in the Caribbean (probably Jamaica) when he composed this
poem. (During his career he produced three books of poetry, all published in
Scotland.)

Here his moral indignation is fierce. Even by the standards of the day, the
poem is remarkable for the shock value of its imagery: a fetus sold prenatally
into slavery, limbs casually lopped off, a pretty slave girl slowly poisoned to
death. Marjoribanks was obviously aware that he was engaged in a battle of
competing discourses for control of public opinion and government policy.

from "Slavery: An Essay in Verse"

What horrid fears must haunt th'untutor'd mind
(Too *just*, alas!) of torments yet behind!
On shocking feasts must savage fancy brood,
Where pale Europeans prey on human food!
His bloody limbs, yet quiv'ring on the board,
Glut the keen stomach of his ruthless lord!
Or on the shrine of vengeful gods he lies;
And, in atonement for a christian, dies!
Yes! Every slave must yield a master food,
Who slowly fattens on his vital blood
Blest, if at once his cruel tortures ceas'd,
And gave white cannibals a short liv'd feast!
Yes! Afric's sons must stain the bloody shrine!
But all those victims, Avarice, are *thine!*
On Mercy's God, those tyrants dare to call;

But Av'rice only is their lord of all!
To him their rites incessantly they pay;
And waste for him the Negro's life away!
　　"But hear!" say you. . . .
"On their own shore those wretches *slaves* we found,
And only mov'd them to a fairer ground.
Captives in war they met this wayward fate;
Or birth had doom'd them to a servile state.
Oft they are convicts, sentenc'd for their crimes
To endless exile from their native climes.
With plants they knew not on those sterile lands,
Here are they nourish'd by our friendly hands;
Of our own properties we give them share,
And food or raiment never costs them care.
On them no debts, no difficulties prey,
Not Britain's peasants half so blest as they!"
Hold, impious men! The odious theme forbear!
Nor with such treason wound a Briton's ear!
The British peasant! healthy, bold, and *free!*
Nor wealth, nor grandeur, half so blest as he!
The state of life, for *happiness the first,*
Dare you compare with this the *most accurs'd.*
You found them slaves . . . but who that title gave!
The God of Nature never form'd a slave!
Though Fraud, or Force acquire a master's name,
Nature and Justice must remain the same!
He who from thieves their booty, conscious, buys,
May use an argument as sound and wise:
That he conceives no guilt attends his trade,
Because the booty is already made.
　　For your own honour, name not Afric's wars!
Ye, whose curs'd commerce rais'd those civil jars!
Each petty chief, whose tribes were drain'd for you,
For *your vile traffic* roams in quest of new;
For you in guiltless blood imbrues his hands,
And carries havoc o'er his neighbour's lands!
They whom the feebler rage of war may spare,
A harder fate from you and slavery share!
For you . . . *sole instigators to the wrong,*
The brutal victor hurries them along.
From Afric's far interior regions driven,
To you . . . and anguish are those wretches given! . . .

But I, alas! May spare my idle strains,
Which ne'er can wrest them from European chains!
For int'rest speaks in language far too strong,
Either to heed a sermon, or a song!
Yet happy I, and not in vain I write,
If I could render but their chains more light;
Could I but wipe one tear from SLAVERY's eye,
Or save his heart one agonizing sigh! . . .

Soon as the trembling crew are landed *here,*
Their quiv'ring flesh the burning pincers sear;
Proudly imprinting your degrading brand
On men, created by your Maker's hand!
A dreadful specimen, we may suppose,
This *warm* reception gives of future woes!
Ere the poor savage yet can understand
The haughty language of a foreign land;
Ere he conceives your meaning, or your view,
The whip directs him what he is to do.
No sex, no age, you ever learn'd to spare,
But female limbs indecently lay bare;
See the poor mother lay her babe aside,
And stoop to punishment she must abide!
Nor midst her pangs, her tears, her horrid cries,
Dare the sad husband turn his pitying eyes.
Amongst your numbers, do we never meet
Villains so most atrociously complete,
Who, with accurs'd accuracy, count the days,
The hours of labour pregnancy delays;
Who nature's wond'rous work attempt to spoil
By stripes, by terrors, and excess of toil. . . .

Chains, hooks, and horns, of every size and shape,
Mark those who've once attempted an escape.
A sister isle once us'd, but *this* improves,
That curs'd invention call[ed] Barbadoes Gloves.
For your own sakes, your malice, and your whim
But *rarely* sacrifice a Negro's limb.
Unless a slave of sedentary trade,
(A luckless tailor well may be afraid);
Where there's no great occasion for a pair,
You may lop off the leg he has to spare. . . .
If int'rest teaches you their limbs to spare,

Immediate murders must be still more *rare*.
Though 'tis this selfish sentiment alone
That oft deters you to destroy *your own*.
But should your passions hurry you away
Another person's property to slay,
The guilty's consider'd in a venial light,
The proof is difficult; the sentence slight.
Nay, malice, safe, may find a thousand times
When no *white evidence* can prove his crimes.
Since, 'tis establish'd by your partial laws,
No slave bears witness in a *white* man's cause. . . .
A jealous mistress finds a ready sham
To give a handsome maid the sugar dram;
With her fair hands prepares the nauseous draught,
And pours the scalding mixture down her throat;
Closely confin'd for mad'ning nights and days,
Her burning thirst no liquid drop allays. . . .

    In mild Britannia many of you dwell,
Where tortur'd slavery ne'er is heard to yell.
You fly wherever luxury invites,
And dissipation crowns your days and nights;
The dire reflection never meets your view,
What pangs, what bloodshed, buy those joys for you!
Your injur'd slaves, perhaps, you *never saw;*
And doubt the picture I so *truly* draw. . . .
But, if from freedom's land you never stray'd;
By false descriptions you may be betray'd.
Self-interested men have met your ear;
I, *without int'rest,* will be more sincere!
Wretches by want expell'd from foreign climes;
Escap'd from debts, or justice due their crimes;
The base, the ignorant, the ruffian steer,
And find a desperate asylum *here*. . . .
By such caprice, are negroes doom'd to bleed,
The Slaves of Slavery . . . They are low indeed!
    He who has made an independence *here*,
At home in splendour hurries to appear;
London, or Bath, with lying fame resounds,
"A fresh Creole! . . . worth Fifty Thousand Pounds!"
Though ten he knows the limit of his store,
He must keep up the figure first he wore.
Thoughtless, he riots in the gay career;

And finds himself half ruin'd in the year. . . .
. . . Seiz'd by marshalls, and to market brought
By various masters families are bought.
Amidst their unregarded sighs and tears,
The wife and husband fall to different shares;
Their clinging offspring from their arms are tore,
And hurried from them, ne'er to meet them more!
    I knew a foetus, in mere wanton play,
Sold from the mother in whose womb it lay.
Unhappy mother! doom'd for months to bear
The luckless burden thou art not to rear! . . .

You, brutal ravishers! pretend in vain
That Afric's children feel no jealous pain.
Untaught Europeans, with illiberal pride,
Look with contempt on all the world beside;
And vainly think no virtue ever grew,
No passion glow'd beneath a sable hue.
Beings you deem them of inferior kind;
Denied a human, or a thinking mind.
Happy for Negroes were this doctrine true!
Were *feelings lost to them . . . or giv'n to you!*
                      (1786)[192]

JOHN WOLCOT (1738–1819)

Notorious as the slashing satirist "Peter Pindar," Wolcot was a prolific writer and critic who at different times attacked George III, Johnson, Boswell, Pitt, Burke, and nearly every other famous person of his time. From his early posting to Jamaica as a protégé of Governor Trelawney, Wolcot had gained firsthand experience of slave society, but in his writings his attitude toward slavery seems to vacillate.

In *Bozzy and Piozzi*, published two years after Samuel Johnson's death, Wolcot mocks the whole Johnsonian circle. In this episode about Johnson's kindness to his aged cat, sneeringly adapted from Hester Piozzi's *Anecdotes of Johnson* (1786), Wolcot twists the story to make Frank (the former slave, now household servant) sound arrogant, and even manages to insult the cat.

from Bozzy and Piozzi, or the British Biographers, a Town Eclogue

Madame Piozzi:
    The Doctor had a cat, and christ'ned Hodge,
That at his house in Fleet Street us'd to lodge . . .
To please poor Hodge, the Doctor, all so kind,
Went out, and bought him *oysters to his mind;*
This ev'ry day he did—nor ask'd black Frank,
Who deem'd himself of much too high a rank,
With *vulgar fish-fags,* to be forc'd to chat,
And purchase oysters, for a *mangy* cat.

In this squib, also based on Mrs. Piozzi's *Anecdotes,* Wolcot badly distorts what Johnson—who was a lifelong opponent of slavery and asserted the full humanity of blacks—actually believed.

Madame Piozzi:

    Th'affair of Blacks when Johnson would discuss,
He always thought they had not *souls* like *us;*
And yet, whene'er his family would fight,
He always said that* Frank was in the *right.*

Later in the poem, Wolcot has "Bozzy" (James Boswell) criticize Piozzi for including the Hodge story, as if a black servant and a pet cat were not worthy of mention in Johnson's biography. (In his *Life of Johnson,* published five years later, Boswell includes the story but effaces Frank by referring only to Johnson's unnamed "servants.")

Bozzy:

Who would have told a tale, so *very* flat,
Of Frank, the Black; and Hodge, the mangy cat?

Here Wolcot lampoons the competition among Johnson's would-be biographers. He has Sir John Hawkins (who would publish a *Life of Johnson* in 1787) attacking Boswell, while also exploiting Johnson's beloved Francis Barber for private information about the dead man.

Sir John:

    "For *thee,* James Boswell, may the hand of Fate
Arrest thy goose-quill, and confine thy prate:
Thy egotisms, the world, *disgusted* hears—
Then load with vanities, no more our ears
Like some lone Puppy yelping all night long;
That tires the *very echoes* with his tongue. . . ."
    Thus spoke the Judge, then leaping from the chair;
He left, in consternation, lost, the pair:
Black Frank, he sought, on anecdote to cram,
And vomit *first,* a Life of surly Sam.

(1786)[193]

In this verse attack on Roman Catholicism, Wolcot mockingly compares that faith to the practice of "Obiah" among the African slaves in Jamaica. Drawing on personal memories of a failed slave insurrection, Wolcot speaks with the flippancy characteristic of the slave-holding class when in psychological (and political) denial of the real dangers such rebellions posed.

---

* "Black Frank" in some later editions.

from "A Poetical, Serious, and Possibly Impertinent, Epistle to the Pope"

Thus in Jamaica, once upon a time,
(Ah! well remember'd by the man of rhime!)
Quako, high priest of all the Negro nation,
And full of Negro faith in conjuration,
Loaded his jackass deep with wonder-bags
Of monkeys teeth, glass, horse-hair, and red rags;*
When forth they march'd—a goodly, solemn pace,
To pour destruction on the Christian race;
To send the husbands to th'infernal shades,
Hug their dear wives, and ravish the fair maids;
To bring God Mumbo Jumbo into vogue,
And sanctify the names of wh[ore] and rogue!
By Fortune's foot behold the scheme disjointed;
And, lo, the Black Apostle, disappointed!
But mark! this diff'rence, to the world's surprise,
Between your Holiness and Quako lies:—
O'er France (no more an unbelieving foe,
Who bought thy reliques, and ador'd thy toe)
Divine dominion shalt thou stretch, O Pope,
While luckless Quako only stretch'd—a *rope*.

(1793)[194]

The satirist had a soft side too. Here he crafts a sentimental lyric, in Yarico's voice, distilled from the well-known story of Inkle's betrayal.

Yarico to Incle

When night spreads her shadows around,
    I will watch with delight on thy rest;
I will soften thy bed on the ground,
    And thy cheek shall be lodg'd on my breast.

Love heeds not the storm nor the rain;
    On *me* let their fury descend,
This bosom shall never complain
    While it shelters the life of a friend.

O tell me what tears thee away?
    To a *fair one*, ah! wouldst thou depart?

* [Wolcot's note:] These little bags are called by the Negroes, *Obia,* and are supposed to be possessed of great witchcraft virtues.

Alas! to thy Yarico say
    What maiden will love like this heart?

Though resolv'd not my sorrows to hear;
    Though resolv'd from a mourner to fly;
The ocean shall bear thee a tear,
    And the winds shall convey thee a sigh!

                (1793)[195]

In this not-unsympathetic lyric about a slave's longing for his beloved, Wolcot plays on what was widely thought to be an African belief, that after death one's soul returned to one's native country. Though his attempt at slave dialect grates on modern sensibilities, it may represent an effort to convey Azid's suffering in a more authentic voice.

Azid, or The Song of the Captive Negro

Poor Mora eye be wet wid tear,
    And heart like lead sink down wid woe;
She seem her mournful friends to hear,
    And see der eye like fountain flow.

No more she give me song so gay,
But sigh, "Adieu, dear Domahay."

No more for deck her head and hair,
    Me look in stream, bright gold to find;
Nor seek de field for flow'r so fair,
    Wid garland Mora hair to bind.

"Far off de stream!" I weeping say,
"Far off de fields of Domahay."

But why do Azid live a slave,
    And see a slave his Mora dear?
Come, let we seek at once de grave—
    No chain, no tyrant den we fear.

Ah, me! I hear a spirit say,
"Come, Azid, come to Domahay."

Den gold I find for thee once more,
    For thee to fields for flow'r depart;
To please de idol I adore,
    And give wid gold and flow'r my heart.

Den let we die and haste away,
And live in groves of Domahay.

                (1794)[196]

In this double-edged satire, the cruelty of a black slave to his mule is used to expose the deeper brutality of white "Christians" holding slaves.

from "Tempora Mutantur. An Ode"

How like the Negro on his Mule,
Tormenting him beyond all rule,
Beating him o'er the head and ears;
His spurs into the creature sticking,
Abusing, damning, cursing, kicking!
For Blacky like a *Christian* swears.

His *quondam* Master, passing by,
Beheld the Beast with pitying eye:
"You scoundrel, hold; is *murder* your design?"—
Quako turn'd round, with a broad grin,
Not valuing the rebuke one pin:
"Massa, *me* was *your* Nega; *dissy mine.*"

(1802)[197]

GEORGE COLMAN (1762–1836)

Born to a famous theatrical family, Colman pursued his own productive career as a theater manager and playwright. He wrote more than thirty-five works, among which *Inkle and Yarico* was an early and much acclaimed success. In a preface Elizabeth Inchbald later wrote for it, she reported that Colman took particular pride in this play because "it was popular before the subject of the abolition of the slave-trade was popular" and helped focus attention on "that great question." It was performed more than 160 times between 1787 and 1800.

Colman transformed the famous story (about a white trader betraying his black lover and selling her as a slave) into a madcap musical comedy. Here Inkle and Yarico sing a duet that establishes the play's dominant theme of interracial romance.

from "Duett" [by Inkle and Yarico], Act I, Inkle And Yarico, An Opera *

Inkle.	O say, simple maid, have you form'd any notion
	Of all the rude dangers in crossing the ocean?
	When winds whistle shrilly, ah! won't they remind you,
	To sigh with regret for the grot left behind you?
Yarico.	Ah! no, I cou'd follow, and sail the world over,
	Nor think of my grot, when I look at my lover!
	The winds which blow round us, your arms for my pillow,
	Will lull us to sleep, whilst we're rock'd by each billow. . . .

---

* [from Elizabeth Inchbald's 1806 preface:] This is a drama, which might remove from Mr. Wilberforce his aversion to theatrical exhibitions, and convince him, that the teaching of moral duty is not confined to particular spots of ground; for, in those places, of all others, the doctrine is most effectually inculcated, where exhortation is the most required— the resorts of the gay, the idle, and the dissipated. . . . This opera has been performed in every London theatre, and in every theatre of the kingdom, with the same degree of splendid success.

Both.   O say then, my true love, we never will sunder,
Nor shrink from the tempest, nor dread the big thunder;
Whilst constant, we'll laugh at all changes of weather,
And journey all over the world both together.

The parallel subplot is also interracial: Trudge, a lower-class white adventurer stranded with Inkle, falls for Wowski, Yarico's dark-skinned maidservant. Given a crude dialect for comic effect, Wowski expresses in her song the vulnerability felt by women of color in this drama.

"Song" [by Wowski], Act I

White man, never go away;
    Tell me why need you?
Stay, with your Wowski, stay;
    Wowski will feed you.
Cold moons are now coming in;
    Ah don't go grieve me!
I'll wrap you in leopard's skin;
    White man, don't leave me.

In this aria Yarico idealizes her life with Inkle before he sold her into slavery in Barbados.

from "Song" [by Yarico], Act II

Our grotto was the sweetest place!
    The bending boughs, with fragrance blowing,
Would check the brook's impetuous pace,
    Which murmur'd to be stopp'd from flowing.
Twas there we met, and gazed our fill:
Ah, think on this, and love me still. . . .

For him, by day, with care conceal'd,
    To search for food, I climb'd the mountain;
And when the night no form reveal'd,
    Jocund we sought the bubbling fountain.
Then, then would joy my bosom fill;
Ah, think on this, and love me still.

In his raucous way, Trudge here celebrates the beauty of his "quite Black" Wowski as superior to that of "English belles" and posits their romance as a comic inversion of Othello and Desdemona's.

from "Song" [by Trudge], Act III

Hey! for America I sail,
    Yankee doodle deedle;
The sailor boys cry'd, "Smoak his tail!"
    Jemmy linkum feedle.
On English belles I turn'd my back,
    Diddle, daddle, deedle;
And got a foreign Fair, quite Black,
    Oh twaddle, twaddle tweedle! . . .

Rings I'll buy to deck her toes,
    Jemmy linkum feedle;
A feather fine shall grace her nose,
    Waving sidle seedle.
With jealousy I ne'er shall burst,
    Who'd steal my bone of bone-a?
A white Othello, I can trust
    A dingy Desdemona.

By contrast with other writers' versions of *Inkle and Yarico* (eight of them elsewhere in this volume), in Colman's play Inkle ultimately repents, defies the racist norms of Caribbean society, and marries Yarico. Here in the polyphonic finale, everyone rejoices in the parallel interracial marriages of Inkle and Yarico, Trudge and Wowski. Even Patty, the skeptical white servant, grudgingly comes around and calls on the audience to approve the mixed-race unions.

from "Finale," Act III

Chorus.   Come then dance and sing,
        While all Barbadoes' bells shall ring, &c.
Trudge.   'Sbob's now I'm fix'd for life,
        My fortune's fair, tho' black's my wife,
        Who fears domestic strife—
           Who cares now a souse!
        Merry cheer my dingy dear
        Shall find with her Factotum here;
        Night and day, I'll frisk and play
           About the house, with Wows.   *Chorus.*
Patty.   Let Patty but say a word,
        A chambermaid may sure be heard—
        Sure men are grown absurd,

Thus taking black for white!
To hug and kiss a dingy miss,
Will hardly suit an age like this—
Unless here, some friends appear,
Who like this wedding night.   *Chorus.*

(1787)[198]

ELIZA KNIPE (fl. 1780s)

Little is known of Knipe except that she was an artist based in Liverpool who specialized in miniature paintings of flowers. Her work appeared in public exhibitions in Liverpool at least twice, in 1784 and 1787, and she taught drawing professionally. Active in the cultural circles of Liverpool that included so many antislavery writers, Knipe gives hints of her early feminist courage, not only in the public exhibition of her art but in her defiance of conventional modesty by placing her name on the title page of the book *Six Narrative Poems* she published in London in 1787. Here she describes the cruel capture and sale of two African lovers who, once they escape the hold of the slave ship, plunge to their deaths rather than endure slavery.

from *"Atomboka and Omaza; An African Story"*

Round their wounded limbs
A pond'rous chain they twin'd, and on a car
Of interwoven canes, beset with thorns,
In pomp barbaric, dragg'd them o'er the plain.
They heav'd no sigh; with patient scorn they brav'd
Insult and pain: the instruments of death
Pleas'd their glad sight; and on the tort'ring fire
They smil'd serene, and hail'd its rising blaze.

From a tall rock, a warrior-youth descry'd
A gallant ship that, bounding o'er the waves,
Spread her white wings, and hasted to the shore.
He gave the well-known sign.——On ev'ry side
Calm silence spread; exulting clamour ceas'd;
Av'rice prevail'd: down to the sandy beach
They led their patient captives: soon the ship
Arriv'd, and paid their price.——Two changing moons,
O'er the wide earth, had spread their silver light,

333

E'er, from surrounding hills, the wretched train
To slav'ry doom'd were brought.—In silent woe
Full many an hour proud ATOMBOKA spent;
While sad OMAZA, with heart-rending groans,
Indulg'd the keener transports of despair. . . .

ATOMBOKA.   Methinks the gentle waves
Invite us to repose, and, murm'ring soft,
Say, "Rest, O mortals, from the toils of life!"

OMAZA.   'Tis greatly thought! borne on the rolling main,
We soon shall reach that blissful island where
Our fathers' spirits rest, and with them raise
The song of triumph.—Our insulting foes
Shall lose their promis'd vengeance.—

ATOMBOKA.   Hark! I hear
A ghost's shrill voice! It chides our dull delay,
And waits to guide us to the happy shore.

Sudden they plung'd, clasp'd in a fond embrace,
And, o'er their heads, the closing waters roll'd.

                                        (1787)[199]

HANNAH MORE (1745–1833)

An evangelical Christian and social reformer with a conservative bent (educating the poor while defending the class system), More is thus quite remarkable as a fervent antislavery activist. Precocious and well educated, she grew up in genteel Bristol society and pursued a career as educator, playwright, poet, novelist, and civic reformer, this last most grandly through her famous Cheap Repository Tracts that ultimately appeared in more than 2,000,000 copies. An intimate member of Johnson's and Garrick's circles in the 1770s and early 1780s, from the late 1780s she began to admire and associate with Wilberforce, Newton, and others who were organizing the abolition campaign. Among the many antislavery writers she befriended, two stand out: the milkmaid poet Anne Yearsley, author of *On the Inhumanity of the Slave-Trade*, who later spurned More's patronage, and the young Eaglesfield Smith whose "Sorrows of Yamba" she reworked and distributed to a wide audience in 1795 as one of the Cheap Repository Tracts (both included elsewhere in this anthology).

More's verse attack on the slave trade is crucially important. Written by a woman, a conservative, and a reformer, it symbolized how broad-based the antislavery movement was and how multifaceted its appeal might be. Grounded in Christian faith and pitched as a political manifesto, the poem rises to moments of slashing rhetoric ("And thou, white savage! whether lust of gold / Or lust of conquest ruled thee uncontrolled!"). The names of literary predecessors such as Southerne and Thomson dot her writings, but More in her own right may have done as much as any writer to spread antislavery ideas among certain classes of the British reading public.

from "The Slave Trade"

... Was it decreed, fair Freedom! At thy birth,
That thou shouldst ne'er irradiate all the earth?
While Britain basks in thy full blaze of light,
Why lies sad Afric quenched in total night?

Thee only, sober goddess! I attest,
In smiles chastised, and decent graces dressed,
To thee, alone, pure daughter of the skies,
The hallowed license of the bard should rise! . . .

O plaintive Southerne!* whose impassioned page
Can melt the soul to grief, or rouse to rage!
Now, when congenial themes engage the muse,
She burns to emulate thy generous views;
Her failing efforts mock her fond desires,
She shares thy feelings, not partakes thy fires.
Strange power of song! the strain that warms the heart
Seems the same inspiration to impart . . .
No individual griefs my bosom melt,
For millions feel what Oroonoko felt:
Fired by no single wrongs, the countless host
I mourn, by rapine dragged from Afric's coast.

Perish th' illiberal thought which would debase
The native genius of the sable race!
Perish the proud philosophy, which sought
To rob them of the powers of equal thought!
Does then the immortal principle within
Change with the casual colour of a skin?
Does matter govern spirit? or is mind
Degraded by the form to which 'tis joined?

No; they have heads to think, and hearts to feel,
And souls to act, with firm though erring zeal;
For they have keen affections, kind desires,
Love strong as death, and active patriot fires;
All the rude energy, the fervid flame,
Of high-souled passion and ingenuous shame:
Strong but luxuriant virtues boldly shoot
From the wild vigor of a savage root.

Nor weak with sense of honor's proud control,
For pride is virtue in a pagan soul;
A sense of worth, a conscience of desert,
A high, unbroken haughtiness of heart;
That self-same stuff which erst proud empires swayed,
Of which the conquerors of the world were made;
Capricious fate of men! that very pride,
In Afric scourged, in Rome was deified.

* [More's note:] Author of the tragedy of Oroonoko.

No muse, O Quashy!* shall thy deeds relate,
No statue snatch thee from oblivious fate!
For thou wast born where never gentle muse
On valor's grave the flowers of genius strews;
And thou wast born where no recording page
Plucks the fair deed from time's devouring page
Had fortune placed thee on some happier coast,
Where polished pagans souls heroic boast,
To thee, who sought'st a voluntary grave,
Th' uninjured honors of thy name to save,
Whose generous arm thy barbarous master spared,
Altars had smoked, and temples had been reared.

    Whene'er to Afric's shores I turn my eyes,
Horrors of deepest, deadliest guilt arise;
I see, by more than fancy's mirror shown,
The burning village and the blazing town;
See the dire victim torn from social life,
The shrieking babe, the agonizing wife;
She, wretch forlorn! is dragged by hostile hands
To distant tyrants sold, in distant lands!
Transmitted miseries, and successive chains,
The sole sad heritage her child obtains!
E'en this last wretched boon their foes deny,
To weep together, or together die.
By felon hands, by one relentless stroke,
See the fond links of feeling nature broke;
The fibres twisting round a parent's heart,
Torn from their grasp, and bleeding as they part. . . .

---

* [More's note:] It is a point of honor among negroes of a high spirit, to die, rather than to suf-
fer their glossy skin to bear the mark of the whip. Quashi had somehow offended his master,
a young planter, with whom he had been bred up in the endearing intimacy of a playfellow.
His services had been faithful, his attachment affectionate. The master resolved to punish
him, and pursued him with that purpose. In trying to escape, Quashi stumbled and fell; the
master fell upon him: they wrestled long and with doubtful victory: at length Quashi got up-
permost, and being firmly seated on his master's breast, he secured his legs with one hand,
and with the other drew a sharp knife; then said, "Master, I have been bred up with you from
a child; I have loved you as myself: in return, you have condemned me to a punishment, of
which I must ever have borne the marks — thus only can I avoid them." So saying, he drew
the knife with all his strength across his own throat, and fell down dead, without a groan, on
his master's body.

                   RAMSAY'S *Essay on the Treatment of African Slaves.*

What wrongs, what injuries does oppression plead,
To smooth the crime and sanctify the deed?
What strange offence, what aggravated sin?
They stand convicted—of a darker skin!
Barbarians, hold! th' opprobrious commerce spare;
Respect His sacred image which they bear.
Though dark and savage, ignorant and blind,
They claim the common privilege of kind;
Let malice strip them of each other plea,
They still are men, and men should still be free.
Insulted reason loathes th' inverted trade—
Loathes, as she views the human purchase made;
The outraged goddess, with abhorrent eyes,
Sees man the traffic, souls the merchandise!
Man, whom fair commerce taught with judging eye,
And liberal hand, to barter or to buy,
Indignant Nature blushes to behold
Degraded man himself trucked, bartered, sold;
Of every native privilege bereft,
Yet cursed with every wounded feeling left.
Hard lot! each brutal suffering to sustain,
Yet keep the sense acute of human pain.
Plead not, in reason's palpable abuse,
Their sense of feeling* callous and obtuse:
From heads to hearts lies nature's plain appeal;
Though few can reason, all mankind can feel. . . .
    When the fierce sun darts vertical his beams,
And thirst and hunger mix their wild extremes;
When the sharp iron† wounds his inmost soul,
And his strained eyes in burning anguish roll;
Will the parched negro own, before he expire,
No pain in hunger, and no heat in fire? . . .
    O thou sad spirit, whose preposterous yoke
The great deliverer death, at length, has broke!
Released from misery, and escaped from care,

---

* [More's note:] Nothing is more frequent than this cruel and stupid argument, that they do not
  feel the miseries inflicted on them as Europeans would do.
† [More's note:] This is not said figuratively. The writer of these lines has seen a complete set
  of chains, fitted to every separate limb of these unhappy, innocent men; together with instru-
  ments for wrenching open the jaws, contrived with such ingenious cruelty as would gratify
  the tender mercies of an inquisitor.

Go, meet that mercy man hath denied thee here.
In thy dark home, sure refuge of th' oppressed,
The wicked vex not, and the weary rest.
And if some notions, vague and undefined,
Of future terrors have assailed thy mind;
If such thy masters have presumed to teach,
As terrors only they are prone to preach;
(For should they paint eternal mercy's reign,
Where were th' oppressor's rod, the captive's chain?)
If, then, thy troubled soul has learned to dread
The dark unknown thy trembling footsteps tread;
On Him, who made thee what thou art, depend,
He, who withholds the means, accepts the end.
Thy mental night thy Savior will not blame,
He died for those who never heard his name.
Not *thine* the reckoning dire of light abused,
Knowledge disgraced, and liberty misused;
On *thee* no awful Judge incensed shall sit
For parts perverted, and dishonored wit.
Where ignorance will be found the safest plea,
How many learned and wise shall envy *thee!*

    And thou, white savage! whether lust of gold
Or lust of conquest ruled thee uncontrolled!
Hero or robber!—by whatever name
Thou plead thy impious claim to wealth or fame;
Whether inferior mischiefs be thy boast,
A tyrant trader rifling Congo's coast;
Or bolder carnage track thy crimson way,
Kings dispossessed, and provinces their prey:
Whether thou pant to tame earth's distant bound;
All Cortez murdered, all Columbus found;
O'er plundered realms to reign detested lord,
Make millions wretched, and thyself abhorred . . .
Who makes the sum of human blessings less,
Or sinks the stock of general happiness,
Though erring fame may grace, though false renown
His life may blazon, or his memory crown;
Yet the last audit shall reverse the cause,
And God shall vindicate his broken laws. . . .

    The purest wreaths which hang on glory's shrine,
For empires founded, peacefull Penn! are thine;
No blood-stained laurels crowned thy virtuous toil,

No slaughtered natives drenched thy fair-earned soil.
Still thy meek spirit in thy flock* survives,
Consistent still, *their* doctrines rule their lives:
Thy followers only have effaced the shame
Inscribed by slavery on the Christian name.

    Shall Britain, where the soul of freedom reigns,
Forge chains for others she herself disdains?
Forbid it, Heaven! O let the nations know
The liberty she loves she will bestow;
Not to herself the glorious gift confined,
She spreads the blessing wide as human kind;
And, scorning narrow views of time and place,
Bids all be free in earth's extended space.

    What page of human annals can record
A deed so bright as human rights restored?
O may that godlike deed, that shining page,
Redeem our fame, and consecrate our age! . . .

    And see, the cherub Mercy, from above
Descending softly, quits the sphere of love!
On Britain's isle she sheds her heavenly dew,
And breathes her spirit o'er th' enlightened few;
From soul to soul the spreading influence steals,
Till every breast the soft contagion feels.
She speeds, exulting, to the burning shore,
With the best message angel ever bore:
Hark! 'tis the note which spoke a Savior's birth!
Glory to God on high, and peace on earth!
She vindicates the power in heaven adored;
She stills the clank of chains, and sheathes the sword;
She cheers the mourner, and with soothing hands
From bursting hearts unbinds th' oppressor's bands;
Restores the lustre of the Christian name,
And clears the foulest blot that dimmed its fame. . . .

    And now, her high commission from above
Stamped with the holy characters of love,
The meek-eyed spirit waving in her hand,
Breathes manumission o'er the rescued land:
She tears the banner stained with blood and tears,
And, Liberty! thy shining standard rears!
As the bright ensign's glory she displays,

* [More's note:] The Quakers have emancipated all their slaves throughout America.

See pale Oppression faints beneath the blaze!
The giant dies! No more his frown appals:
The chain, untouched, drops off; the fetter falls.
Astonished Echo tells the vocal shore
Oppression's fallen, and slavery is no more!
The dusky myriads crowd the sultry plain,
And hail that mercy long invoked in vain.
Victorious power! she bursts their two-fold bands,
And faith and freedom sprung from Britain's hands.
    And Thou! great Source of nature and of grace,
Who of one blood didst form the human race,
Look down in mercy, in thy chosen time,
With equal eye on Afric's suffering clime;
Disperse her shades of intellectual night,
Repeat thy high behest—Let there be light!
Bring each benighted soul, great God, to Thee,
And with thy wide salvation make them free!

(1787)[200]

EDWARD RUSHTON (1756–1814)

Rushton's life was heroic: childhood hardships, seafaring adventures, abolitionist activism, a difficult literary career, and great works of charity, all despite being blind for most of his adult life. Apprenticed early to a West Indies company (and for a time stationed in Jamaica), Rushton later, on his first slave-trading voyage, was nearly thrown in the brig for "mutinously" intervening on behalf of the African captives. It was during this voyage that he went blind from an ophthalmic disease he caught from the slaves to whom he was ministering.

He spent the rest of his life in Liverpool struggling with blindness, poverty, and local hostility, while working as a writer, social reformer, and abolitionist. Perhaps his moral idealism and courage were best displayed when in 1797 he wrote *An Expostulatory Letter to George Washington on his continuing to be a Proprietor of Slaves* and sent Washington himself a copy. Rushton was one of a circle of Liverpool abolitionist poets that included Hugh Mulligan, William Sheperd, and William Roscoe, all represented elsewhere in this anthology.

Thus it was as a blind poet that Rushton brought to the staid eclogue form the exoticism of his remembered Caribbean experience and the energy of his moral indignation at slavery. At the same time, his text is embedded with extensive footnotes from eyewitness accounts and historical sources, as if to fortify his imaginative presentation with authenticating fact. In the first eclogue two slaves, enraged at a typical atrocity (the whipping of a mother and infant), contemplate rebellion.

EDWARD RUSHTON

from West-Indian Eclogues
Eclogue the First*

Scene: Jamaica. Time: Morning.

ADOMA:

      . . . Yesterday,
As in the field we toil'd our strength away,
My gentle YARO with her hoe was nigh,
And on her back she bore my infant Boy.
The sultry heats had parch'd his little throat,
His head reclin'd I heard his wailing note.
The Mother, at his piteous cries distress'd,
Now paus'd from toil and gave the cheering breast.
But soon alas! the savage Driver† came,
And with his cow-skin cut her tender frame;
Loudly he tax'd her laziness,—and then
He curs'd my boy, and plied the lash again!
—JUMBA, I saw the deed,—I heard her grief!
Could I do less?—I flew to her relief;
I fell before him—sued, embraced his knee,
And bade his anger vent itself on me,
Spurn'd from his feet I dar'd to catch his hand,
Nor loos'd it, JUMBA, at his dread command:
For, blind with rage, at one indignant blow
I thought to lay the pale-fac'd villain low!
But sudden stopp'd;—for now the whites came round,
They seiz'd my arms,—my YARO saw me bound! . . .

JUMBA:

Enough:—Our glorious aims shall soon succeed,
And thou in turn shall see th' oppressors bleed.
Soon shall they fall, cut down like lofty Canes,
And (oh! the bliss) from us receive their pains.

---

* [from the publisher's preface:] The author of the following Eclogues has resided several
years in the West-Indies. They, who have spent only a small portion of time there, must have
been frequent witnesses (it is to be hoped, unwilling ones also) of barbarities similar to those,
which are here related.

† [from Rushton's note:] THOUGH the Negro-drivers . . . are in general black-men, yet
sometimes a subordinate European is stationed on the field, in order to superintend the
whole. Wishing to ingratiate himself with his superiors, and to gain the reputation of being
active and vigilant, he daily, under the mask of what is termed *necessary discipline*, inflicts the
severest punishments, for the most trifling offences.

Oh! 'twill be pleasant when we see them mourn,
See the fell cup to their own lip return,
View *their* pale faces prostrate on the ground,
Their meagre bodies gape with many a wound . . .

In the second eclogue, Rushton delves deeper into the psychology of planta-
tion slaves by demonstrating the seeming impossibility of revenge or escape, no
matter how intolerable their circumstances.

Eclogue the Second

ADOMA:
Oh! think on PEDRO, gibbetted alive!*
Think on his fate—six long days to survive!—
His frantic looks,—his agonizing pain,—
His tongue outstretch'd to catch the dropping rain;
His vain attempts to turn his head aside,
And gnaw the flesh which his own limbs supplied;
Think on his suff'rings, when th' inhuman crew,
T' increase his pangs, plac'd Plantains in his view,
And bade him eat—

JUMBA:
              . . . He possess'd a soul,
Which nobly burst the shackles of controul.
He fell betray'd, but boldly met his death;
And curs'd his tyrants with his latest breath.
—But go, ADOMA, since to live is sweet,
Go, like a dog, and lick the white men's feet;
Tell them that hunger, slav'ry, toil, and pain
Thou wilt endure, nor ever once complain:
Tell them, though JUMBA dares to plot their fall,
That thou art tame, and wilt submit to all,
Go poor submissive slave.—Go, meanly bend,
Court the pale butchers, and betray thy friend. . . .

ADOMA:
              But, friend, there still remain
Two ways to free us from this galling chain.
Sure we can bid our various sorrows cease
By quitting life, or how, or when we please:

* [Rushton's note:] A PUNISHMENT not uncommon in the *West-Indies*. Some of the miserable
sufferers have been known to exist a week in this most dreadful situation. (See a most affect-
ing account of one instance of this kind, in the Rev. Mr. RAMSAY's Treatise.)

Or we can quickly fly these cruel whites
By seeking shelter on the mountains' heights,
Where wild hogs dwell, where lofty Cocoas grow,
And boiling streams of purest waters flow.
There we might live; for thou with skillful hand
Canst form the bow, and jav'lin, of our land.
There we might freely roam, in search of food,
Up the steep crag, or through the friendly wood . . .

JUMBA:

　　　　Alas! thou dost not know
The King of all those mountains is our foe;*
His subjects num'rous, and their chief employ
To hunt our race, when fled from slavery.
Lur'd by the hope of gain such arts are tried,
No rocks can cover us, no forests hide.

　　The third eclogue presents a new story, told by Quamina, exemplifying yet
another kind of slavemaster cruelty. The weak and aged Angola, after a life of
hard labor, was whipped to death for accidentally breaking a water jug he was
struggling to carry.

Eclogue the Third

QUAMINA:

Didst thou e'er see, when hither first we came,
An ancient Slave, ANGOLA was his name?
Whose vig'rous years upon these hills were spent,
In galling servitude, and discontent:
He late, too weak to bear the weighty toil,
Which all endure who till this hated soil,
Was sent, as one grown useless on th' estate,
Far to the town to watch his Master's gate,
Or to the house each morn the fuel bring,
Or bear cool water from the distant spring:
With many a toil, with many a labour more,
Although his aged head was silver'd o'er,
Although his body like a bow was bent,
And old, and weak, he totter'd as he went. . . .

* [from Rushton's note:] The chief service expected from [the maroons], was, and still is,—to
bring back to the planters those wretches, whom hunger, or cruelty, forces to the mountains
for shelter. They are allowed a premium for every fugitive they restore, and are remarkably
vigilant in their employment.

Often, each labour sped,
Has he with aching limbs attain'd his shed.
Attain'd the spot, dejected and forlorn,
Where he might rest his aged head 'till morn:
Where, wearied out, he op'd the friendly door,
And, entering, prostrate sunk upon the floor.
Feeble and faint some moons he toil'd away;
(For trifles toil become as men decay)
When late beneath the driver's lash he fell,
And scourg'd, and tortur'd, bade the world farewell.

CONGO:
But why the scourge? Wherefore such needless rage?
Is there no pity, then, for weak old age?

QUAMINA:
'Twas part of his employ, with empty pail,
To crawl for water to a neighb'ring vale:
And as he homeward bore the liquid load,
With trembling steps along the rugged road,
His wither'd limbs denied their wonted aid:
—The broken vessel his mishap betray'd.
This his offence:—for this, thrown on the ground,
His feeble limbs outstretch'd, and strongly bound,
His body bare, each nerve convuls'd with pain,
I saw and pitied him—but ah! in vain.
Quick fell the lash: his hoary head laid low,
His eyes confess'd unutterable woe.
He sued for mercy: the big tear apace,
Stole down the furrows of his aged face.
His direful groans (for such they were indeed!)
Mix'd with his words when e'er he strove to plead,
And form'd such moving eloquence, that none,
But flinty-hearted Christians could go on.
At length releas'd, they bore him to his shed:
Much he complain'd, and the next morn was dead.

CONGO:
May ev'ry curse attend this pallid race,
Of earth the bane, of manhood the disgrace.

For Rushton the gravest atrocity was rape, which is explored in horrifying detail in the fourth eclogue. The savagery of white men raping black women is set against the heroic courage of black men, which Rushton is at pains to document in the examples he cites—one from his own experience—in the final footnote.

from "Eclogue the Fourth"

The sad LOANGO mourn'd his absent love.
    "Three nights in this appointed gloom I've past,
No QUAMVA comes,—and this shall be my last,
Hoarse thunder, cease thy roar:—perchance she stays,
Appall'd by thee, thou light'ning's fiery blaze . . .
Let QUAMVA come, my wife, my sole delight,
Torn from my arms by that accursed white;*
That pale-fac'd villain,—he, who through the day
O'erlooks our toils, and rules with bloody sway;
By him, who proud of lordship o'er the field,
By daily tortures made my QUAMVA yield;
Him, who has stolen my treasure from my arms,
And now perhaps, now riots on her charms!
Oh! 'tis too much:—Come dark revenge and death;
He bravely falls, who stops a tyrant's breath.

---

* [from Rushton's note:] THIS cruel practice of the white master, or driver, in forcing the wives of the Negroes to a compliance, cannot be too severely reprobated. . . . In the first skirmishes which happened with the *Spaniards,* after the *English* obtained possession of [Jamaica], those *Spanish* slaves . . . who had deserted from their former masters, fought under the *English* banners with great courage. One slave, in particular, was observed, by Colonel D'OYLEY, the then *English* governor, to have exerted himself with uncommon intrepidity, and to have killed several Spaniards in close engagement. On inquiry it was found that this Negro had loved a young female slave to distraction; that he had been married to her for some years before the *English* invaded the Island; and that a short time before that invasion the tyrant, his master, had barbarously torn her from him, and compelled her to submit to his rapacious will. The injured husband implored, and remonstrated: and he was answered—by the whip. . . . The *English* invasion afforded him an opportunity of an interview with his beloved wife. He told her, in a few words, that he still loved her with too sincere a passion, not to be sensible of what he had lost; but as their former days of love, and purity, could never return, he would not live to see her another's, when she could not be his own; for that, however innocent she might be in intention, he never could take an adulteress into his arms. "*Thus, therefore*" (says he) "*I now exert the rights of a husband:*"—and plunged his poniard into her heart! He immediately fled to the *English.* And, in his first engagement with his former masters, having observed his cruel tyrant in the *Spanish* line, he flew to the place where he fought, and soon laid him, with several other *Spaniards,* at his feet. Colonel D'OYLEY declared him free, on the field of battle; and accompanied . . . his freedom with the gift of a small plantation, upon which he lived ever afterwards in quiet, but with a . . . melancholy, which he could never overcome. He survived to a very advanced term of life, dying in the year 1708.

Roar on, fierce tempests:—Spirits of the air . . .
And hurl destruction on each cruel White:—
Sweep canes, and Mills, and houses to the ground,
And scatter ruin, pain, and death around:—
Rouse all you blasting fires, that lurk on high,
And, 'midst his pleasures, let the plund'rer die!
But spare my QUAMVA, who, with smother'd sighs,
The odious rape endures, but not enjoys,
Wishing the Tyrant's senses drown'd in sleep,
That she enraptur'd may her promise keep.
Oh! 'tis too much:—Come dark revenge, and death;
He bravely falls, who stops a tyrant's breath.

Yet let me pause. 'Tis said that woman's mind,
Still changes like the Hurricane's fierce wind,
Ranging from man to man, as shifts the Bee,
Or long-bill'd Humming-bird, from tree to tree.
How if she like the White, his gaudy cloaths,
His downy bed for pleasure and repose;
His shrivel'd frame, his sickly pallid face;
And finds a transport in his weak embrace.
It may be so.—Oh! vengeance on her head,
It is, it is:—She likes the Driver's bed.
For this she stays. . . .

'Tis too plain:—Come dark revenge, and death,
And steel my soul to stop a wanton's breath. . . .
            —Come, pointed blade,
And poor LOANGO's vengeance justly aid.*
Three, three must fall! for Oh! I'll not survive;
I dread the white men's gibbeting alive,
Their wiry tortures, and their ling'ring fires:—
These he escapes, who by the knife expires.
Come, then, revenge!—The deed will soon be o'er,
And then LOANGO views his native shore;

* [from Rushton's note:] The desire of revenge is an impetuous, a ruling passion, in the minds of these *African* slaves. . . . *"Being heathens . . . they give themselves up freely to the grossest immoralities, without being even conscious they are doing wrong."* (Bishop of *Chester's* Sermon, before quoted.) But . . . many instances might be adduced to shew, that some Negroes are capable of kind, nay even of heroic, actions. The story of QUASHI, related by Mr. RAMSAY, is one signal proof of this assertion. Another can be given by the Author of these Eclogues; who was preserved from destruction by the humanity of a Negro slave. His deliverance, however, was purchased at a price which he must ever deplore. For, in saving his life, the brave, the generous, *African* lost his own!

Rides on the fleeting clouds through airy roads,
Nor stops 'till plac'd in *Afric's* bless'd abodes.
Come pointed blade;—the Tyrant's house is nigh:—
And now for vengeance, death, and liberty!—"
    Then to the place, with frenzy fir'd, he fled,
    And the next morn beheld the mangled dead!—

                    (1787)[201]

The following poem, which circulated transatlantically in 1808, seems almost certainly to be by Edward Rushton, who alone fits the editor's description of its author as a blind poet, resident in Liverpool, active in the antislavery movement. Rushton's blindness is the key to understanding the poem's ironic thrust: it takes a blind poet to put before the American public a fundamental contradiction which the new nation is reluctant to see. In a further twist, the poem was published in a Philadelphia periodical called *The Eye*.

from "Song for America"*

By those fields that were ravaged, those towns that were fired,
    By those wrongs which your females endured,
By those blood-sprinkled groves where your warriors expired,
    O, preserve what your prowess procured:
And reflect that your rights are the rights of mankind,
    To all they were bounteously giv'n,
That he who in chains would his fellow man bind,
    Uplifts his proud arm against heav'n.

How can you who have felt th' oppressor's proud hand,
    Who for freedom all perils would brave,
How can you have peace while one foot of your land
    Is disgraced by the toil of A SLAVE!
O rouse then in spite of a *merciless few*,
    And pronounce this immortal decree—
Whate'er be man's tenets, his fortune, his *hue*,
    He is man—and shall therefore be free.

                    (1808)[202]

---

* [Editor's note:] The following song was composed by a *blind man* in *Liverpool;* and, as far as I know, has never been printed, at any rate not in *America*. A copy of it was recently sent in a letter from *Ireland* to a gentleman in *Philadelphia*.

ELIZABETH SOPHIA TOMLINS
(1763–1828)

Born into a family of prominent lawyers and writers, Tomlins became a widely published novelist and occasional poet. Inspired, she said, by a "fact related in Mr. [James] Ramsay's *Treatise on the Treatment of Negroes* [1784]," she published this darkly romantic verse tale in a book of poems, *Tributes of Affection* (1797), in which she also included poems about slavery by her brother Sir Thomas Edlyne Tomlins (see his poems, below). In something over 360 lines, "The Slave" tells the tragic story of a favorite, Quashi, who long remains steadfastly loyal to his cruel master Alvaro, once even turning against his fellow Africans to protect Alvaro's sister from a slave insurrection. At last breaking under the slave owner's hot-tempered brutality, Quashi flees into the forest. Alvaro pursues him, they struggle, and the slave gains the upper hand. With a knife at his master's chest, Quashi confesses his long-concealed love for Alvaro's sister and then, rather than killing the master, commits suicide. (To measure how far Tomlins modified the original story to stress the interracial love affair, compare Hannah More's sparer rendering of the Quashi tale in "The Slave Trade," also 1787.)

from "The Slave"

    The young Alvaro of Castilian race,
In wealth and honors held the foremost place:
Whene'er he turns his eye, or waves his hand,
A thousand Slaves all move at his command . . .
Yet 'twas remark'd, one Slave above the rest
He long had smil'd on, and had lov'd the best;
In youth, in childhood, he the boy had known,
And from his infant hours had call'd his own. . . .
Obedient still, and true to ev'ry trust,
For ever faithful, and for ever just.
And once when, anger'd by repeated woes,

Hostile in arms, unnumber'd Negroes rose,
Firm and unwav'ring in that trying hour,
He snatch'd Alvaro's Sister from their pow'r . . .

Thus lov'd, and trusted, and for faith renown'd,
Year after year the favour'd youth was found:
He liv'd unconscious of immediate woe,
In such sad peace as Slavery can know. . . .

One sumptuous vase . . .
[L]ong had glitter'd near Alvaro's side,
And oft been mark'd the object of his pride . . .
[F]rom [Quashi's] grasp the polish'd surface flies,
And on the floor in broken fragments lies.
His Master's vengeful soul full well he knew,
Which trifles could enflame; but nought subdue.
Trembling he stood, and mark'd his future doom,
In each bright fragment scatter'd o'er the room. . . .

When [Quashi] heard the ignominious sound
Of whips and lashes rudely echo round;
He view'd Alvaro with a scornful look,
And in his hand a pointed weapon shook:
Then, wildly firm, and bursting through them all,
Scarce in a moment's space, he left the hall.

Alvaro gaz'd on all, and all he blam'd:
Then with a fierce and sudden rage inflam'd,
With hasty paces follow'd like the wind,
Those foot-steps, swifter than the mountain hind.

Long he pursued; and long pursued in vain,
His limbs grew weary, and he breath'd with pain;
Then faint and sinking with deep dread he found
Thick shades and solitude inclose him round . . .

The Slave, quick turning with a single bound,
Threw his pursuer prostrate on the ground.
Yet though he fell, Fear brac'd Alvaro's arm,
Whom love of life, and dread of death, alarm;
In his fierce Soul a thousand passions burn—
The victor Slave he vanquish'd in his turn . . .
But soon . . . the momentary joy was o'er;
Again the Slave beheld Alvaro low,
The shades of Terror dark'ning on his brow:

With one strong hand, his trembling throat he press'd,
And fix'd one nervous knee upon his breast. . . .

"O! Master!"—twice he said, and turn'd aside,
The struggling passions of his soul to hide . . .
"For thee the hopes of Freedom I withstood,
The bonds of Friendship, and the ties of blood:
And quell'd for thee the passions of my soul,
Which once in madd'ning torrents seem'd to roll,
When with this arm I struck Matilda's foes,
Chas'd all her terrours, and reliev'd her woes:
Matilda! Brighter than the beam of Day,
And milder than the Ev'ning's parting ray!
For whom this heart long heav'd with many a groan,
Which now, Alvaro, now I dare to own. . . ."

"But why my Soul this vain recital make?
Think on thy wrongs, and to Revenge awake!
Think on the guilt of that degen'rate race,
On Europe's sons, mean, mercenary, base:
Think in this prostrate Spaniard you behold
Each grov'ling wretch, whose curst desire of gold
Has banish'd Freedom, and has murder'd Peace,
And bade the sounds of Truth and Mercy cease!
Think on the guiltless Millions, now no more,
Whose ghosts yet hov'ring on the dreary shore,
In sad procession strike these aching eyes,
And bid, with all her daggers, Vengeance rise.
Yes, injur'd Countrymen! this heart can glow,
This hand, yet undishonour'd, deals the blow:
This arm shall strike, this heart shall cease to groan,
And EUROPE's dastard Sons the great revenge shall own!"

So spoke the Slave—and, Weep ye few who feel!
In *his own gen'rous breast* he plung'd the steel:
His Soul exulting burst its narrow cell,
To seek the home where happy Spirits dwell! . . .

Blush, Europe, blush! And, prostrate at his grave,
Go learn that Conquest which adorns the brave.
To Quashi's mem'ry tears of Pity shed,
A Slave when living, but a Hero dead!

(wr. 1787/pub. 1797)[203]

JOHN WILLIAMS (1761–1818)

A satirist and gadfly who wrote under the pseudonym of "Anthony Pasquin," Williams focused on theater, art, and politics in London before emigrating to America in 1796, where he became a noted Federalist. In this piece, criticizing a London actor named Pope for the excessive sentimentality of his technique, Williams incidentally reveals much more: how contemporary audiences reacted to depictions of slaves on stage, how frequently plays about slavery—such as *Oroonoko* and *The African Captive*—appeared in the theatrical repertoire of the late eighteenth century, and how such plays shaped the sensibility of the time.

from "The Children of Thespis"

In the African Captive, see Pope wake surprize,
And call Pity's tears into feminine eyes;
When poor Oroonoko is goaded by foes,
The player outrageously pictures his woes:
Tho' his person is fashion'd, and prun'd by Perfection,
His weakness incessantly meets our detection;
With a fine rounded voice, full of Melody's tones,
He wastes half its compass in sighs and in groans;
And thinks 'cause the busking he's ta'en into keeping,
His duty directs he should always be weeping.
—When the tear of a man, from his eye-lids will start,
It should seem as a tribute that's wrung from the heart;
As an offering that's paid to the cause of a crime,
To woe that's unmeasur'd, and grief that's sublime:
But if they're call'd forth on each trivial occasion,
Their worth is no more, and they lose their persuasion;
Then Ridicule laughs at the tears as they roll,
To tell us the man has—a half-finish'd soul.

(1787)[204]

ANONYMOUS

Apparently composed by an early American abolitionist, this poignant ballad focuses—first in the voice of a distraught mother, then of her daughter desperate to save a little brother—on the destruction of families and the emotional pain that slavery inflicted. Originally published in *The New-Haven Gazette, and Connecticut Magazine* (February 21, 1788), the poem remained popular into the nineteenth century, appearing in anthologies and children's readers at least as late as 1815.

[Untitled]*

"HELP! oh, help! thou GOD of Christians!
  Save a mother from despair!
Cruel white-men steal my children!
  GOD of Christians, hear my prayer!

From my arms by force they're rended,
  Sailors drag them to the sea;
Yonder ship, at anchor riding,
  Swift will carry them away.

There my son lies, stripp'd, and bleeding;
  Fast, with thongs, his hands are bound.
See, the tyrants, how they scourge him!
  See his sides a reeking wound!

---

* [Author's note:] The distress which the inhabitants of Guinea experience at the loss of their children, which are stolen from them by the persons employed in the barbarous traffic of human flesh, is, perhaps, more thoroughly felt than described. But, as it is a subject to which every person has not attended, the Author of the following lines hopes that, possibly, he may excite some attention . . . to an attempt to represent the anguish of a mother, whose son and daughter were taken from her by a Ship's Crew, belonging to a Country where the GOD of Justice and Mercy is owned and worshipped.

See his little sister by him;
    Quaking, trembling, how she lies!
Drops of blood her face besprinkle;
    Tears of anguish fill her eyes.

Now they tear her brother from her;
    Down, below the deck, he's thrown;
Stiff with beating, thro' fear silent,
    Save a single, death-like groan.

Hear the little creature begging!—
    'Take me, white-men, for your own!
Spare! oh, spare my darling brother!
    He's my mother's only son.

See, upon the shore she's raving:
    Down she falls upon the sands:
Now, she tears her flesh with madness;
    Now, she prays with lifted hands.

I am young, and strong, and hardy;
    He's a sick, and feeble boy;
Take me, whip me, chain me, starve me,
    All my life I'll toil with joy.

Christians! who's the GOD you worship?
    Is he cruel, fierce, or good?
Does he take delight in mercy?
    Or in spilling human blood?

Ah! my poor distracted mother!
    Hear her scream upon the shore.'"—
Down the savage Captain struck her,
    Lifeless on the vessel's floor.

Up his sails he quickly hoisted,
    To the ocean bent his way;
Headlong plunged the raving mother,
    From a high rock, in the sea.

              (pub. 1788/rev. 1793)[205]

ANONYMOUS

As the newly founded Abolition Society pushed for legislation in the late 1780s, political argument often took poetic form. The unidentified author of this poem was obviously involved in the cause, whose principals (Pitt, Burke, Wilberforce, and Clarkson) he praises heartily. He was also, according to his preface, collaborating with the painter George Morland (1764–1804) to produce a painting of "the execrable Traffic carried on by Europeans on the Slave Coast" that might further sway public opinion. In the course of three hundred lines the poem touches conventional themes, but is remarkable nonetheless for its indictment of European "savagery" and the dramatic vignette it uses to condemn the sexual predations of slave traders.

from The Slave Trade

"Can this be so?" the human soul replies,
    "No monster sure in manly form thus rules!
Can free-born Britons hear poor Negro cries,
    Yet whip them on, like vicious restive mules?

It ne'er can be—this savages may do,
    Who know not aught of sacred freedom's laws!"
Yet they are worse who dare defend it too,
    And undertake the sordid Planter's cause. . . .

Hence vain distinctions, prejudice of sight!
    The social union knows no diff'rent hue,
And Nature's pencil paints him purest white,
    Who feels for others, and most good will do.

Ah! could the men of fellow-feeling view
    The inward struggles of parental woe!
How Nature's eloquence in gestures true,
    Declares with sad reluctance Blacks must go.

ANONYMOUS

Lo! the poor captive with distraction wild,
    Views his dear partner torn from his embrace!
A diff'rent Captain buys his wife and child;
    What time can from his soul such ills erase?

A sight, like this, our feelings sure would move;
    What fiend denies that Blacks like feelings have?
They give us proofs of chaste, exalted love,
    And, to our ships, prefer a wat'ry grave. . . .

Two British captains with their barges came,
    And quickly made a purchase of the young;
But one was struck with Ulkna, void of shame,
    And tore her from her husband where she clung.

Her faithful Chief, tho' stern in rugged war,
    Seeing his Ulkna by a White caress'd,
To part with her, and little son Tengarr!
    His gentler feelings could not be supprest. . . .

With hands uplifted, he with sighs besought
    The wretch that held a bludgeon o'er his head,
And those who dragg'd him, would have pity taught
    By his dumb signs, to strike him instant dead.

While his dear Ulkna's sad entreating mien,
    Did but increase the brute's unchaste desire;
He vaunting bears her off, her sobs are vain,
    They part the man and wife whom all admire.

Their constancy, their grief, and wild despair
    At parting, mov'd those harden'd in the trade;
Their cries, their groans far pierc'd the noxious air,
    And some strange Converts to soft Pity made. . . .

For Pitt's support to injur'd Negro's claim,
    Against the cry of giant-Int'rest's voice,
The woodland Muse shall cheerful sing his fame,
    And for each friend to mercy still rejoice.

Rejoice, while eloquence and wisdom join!
    Hear Burke's melodious accents charm the cause,
Bold Fox, for manly candor fam'd, is thine,
    And Wilberforce no less demands the laws. . . .

Nor Clarkson's rev'rend worth that all revere,
    Shall be forgotten in the Muse's theme!

May that great Phalanx* ev'ry blessing share,
    And ev'ry friend to virtue join his name. . . .

First, Britons, then, the bright example show,
    Which breaks the chain for millions, yet unborn!
Whilst other *states* with emulation glow,
    Which *next* the wreath of Mercy shall adorn.

                (1788)[206]

---

* [Author's note:] The Society for the Abolition of the Slave Trade.

HARRIET FALCONAR (1774–?)

With her older sister Maria (see following entry), the fourteen-year-old Harriet Falconar published a pair of antislavery poems in 1788, dedicated with gratitude to the Duchess of Devonshire. The young prodigies produced two other books of poetry, one also in 1788, the other in 1791, and then—despite attracting the support of major writers such as Hugh Blair, William Roscoe, and Helen Maria Williams—disappeared from history. Nothing else is known of them. In these excerpts from a poem of more than two hundred lines, Harriet warns complacent Britons that pleasures derived from slave labor will carry a price one day, and argues that sympathy for African slaves is a point of national honor.

from "Slavery. A Poem"

Think not, ye slaves in pleasure's venal train,
The weeping orphan's tears are pour'd in vain . . .
   Heav'n, indignant, views the impious deed
That bids the injur'd sons of Afric bleed;
Soon shall the voice of angry Justice call,
And bid the pointed sword of vengeance fall . . .
   The slave: oppress'd with secret care,
He sinks the hapless victim of despair;
Or, doom'd to torments that might even move
The steely heart, and melt it into love;
Till worn with anguish, with'ring in his bloom,
He falls an early tenant of the tomb!
Shall Britain view, unmov'd, sad Afric's shore
Delug'd so oft in streams of purple gore!
Britain, where science, peace, and plenty, smile,
Virtue's bright seat, and freedom's favour'd isle!

                  (1788)[207]

MARIA FALCONAR (1771–?)

The elder of a pair of teenage prodigies, Maria Falconar was seventeen when she published the poem below in one of three books of verse she jointly authored with her sister Harriet (included elsewhere) between 1788 and 1791. Whether because of early death or the pressures of married life or some other factor, neither of them ever published again—despite having gained positive notice in the *Monthly* and *Critical* reviews, and the support of prominent literary figures. In this passage from her poem of 250 lines, Maria uses a moral argument derived from the idea of racial equality to attack sophisticated defenses of the slave trade based on economic self-interest and global competition.

from "Slavery. A Poem"

Ye foes of heav'n, and Britain's dire disgrace,
Unjust oppressors of an injur'd race,
Tell us, who form'd the slave you thus deride,
The sport of insult, indolence, and pride?
With mis'ry should he sink so meanly down,
Adore your smile, and tremble when you frown;
At your command with servile swiftness fly,
And mark with dread the language of your eye?
Tell, why such baleful tyranny should reign,
Caprice empow'ring to distribute pain?
Yet, you will say, surrounding foes combine
To catch th'advantages that we decline;
But, sure, that impious land must deeply bleed,
And dark dishonour all its fame succeed;
Then let them hence the guilty commerce bear,
And what heav'n sanctions be Britannia's care.

(1788)[208]

JOHN FERRIAR (1761–1815)

Born and educated in Scotland, Ferriar was a physician who also pursued literary, philosophical, and scientific interests, publishing a stream of miscellaneous writings from the 1780s until shortly before his death in 1815. Based most of his working life in Manchester, Ferriar also devoted energy to charitable causes, including public hospitals, child labor laws, and disease prevention among the poor. His altruism also generated the work from which the following poems were taken, an adaptation of Southerne's *Oroonoko* that was staged as a benefit in support of the "Manchester Society for procuring the final Abolition of the Slave Trade" in 1788. As Ferriar explains in his lengthy preface (itself a considerable critical essay about *Oroonoko*), he intended to reshape Southerne's tragedy to serve more forcefully the abolitionist mission.

The result is a text in which, as the following pieces show, Southerne's lines are sometimes modified, sometimes replaced altogether. The "Prologue" is an example of the latter. This bold manifesto on behalf of abolition is also significant for the way it focuses on women activists in the audience, emphasizing the centrality of female sensibilities and female energy in the movement.

from The Prince of Angola, A Tragedy, Altered from the Play of Oroonoko and Adapted to the Circumstances of the Present Times *

from the Prologue

> To-night, reviv'd, sad Oroonoko pleads,
> For each poor African that toils and bleeds.
> No stale poetic Tricks delude the Ear,

---

* [from Ferriar's preface:] When the attempt to abolish the African Slave Trade commenced in Manchester, some active friends of the cause imagined, that by assembling a few of the principal topics, in a dramatic form, an impression might be made, on persons negligent of simple reasoning. The magnitude of the crime, by dispersing our perceptions, sometimes leaves nothing in the mind but a cold sense of disapprobation. We talk of the destruction of mil-

Nor fancy'd Woes beguile you of a Tear.
Alas! too just the faithful Records prove,
Of ruin'd Majesty, and injured Love.

But, lost in Southern's Dress, with clouded Ray,
Deform'd and rude, the Royal Image lay . . .
Now runs the Features in a chaster Mould;
And copying Nature, offers to your View,
A son of Afric, generous, brave, and true. . . .
Let *Honour* that dogmatic Scorn efface,
Which sinks to Brutes the persecuted Race:
O! spurn th' unworthy Thought with gen'rous Zeal—
Mind has no *Colour*—ev'ry Heart can feel.

Hear Misery cry from yon blood-watered Lands;
Lo, suff'ring Crouds to you extend their Hands;
Those ghastly Seams unmeasur'd Lashes tore,
Those wasted Limbs the cleaving Fetters wore—
See mangled Victims fill th' Oppressor's Den,
And hear Compassion tell you—THESE ARE MEN. . . .

Our better Hopes within this Circle* rest;
Here Pity lives in ev'ry gentle Breast.
Folly may scoff, or Avarice may hate,
Since Beauty comes the Negroe's Advocate.
Let others boast in Fashion's Pride to glow,
To lure the Lover, or attract the Beau;
You check Oppression's Lash, protect the Slave,
And, first to charm, are still the first to save.

In the following lines, which he has adapted from Southerne's act III, scene iv, Ferriar shifts the emphasis from male heroism to female suffering, interjecting several lines that focus on the ordeal that women slaves endure. In the closing lines, where Southerne had dwelt on death as a noble alternative to slav-

---

lions, with as little emotion, and as little accuracy of comprehension, as of the distances of the Planets. But . . . when they are told of the pangs of an innocent creature, forced to a foreign country, in want of everything, and in subjection to an imperious stranger; of the anguish caused by violated ties, and unchecked brutality; of the mother fainting under her task, and unable to supply her neglected infant; of the aged abandon'd to want; and the sick compelled to exertion, by the lash; nature will rise up within them, and own her relation to the sufferers.

* [Ferriar's note:] The Ladies of Manchester have distinguished themselves very honourably in this Cause.

ery, Ferriar images the self-liberated Africans resuming normal life in their native land.

from Act III, Scene iii

> *Oroonoko:* We will not wrong
> The virtue of our women, to believe
> There is a wife among them would refuse
> To share her husband's fortune. They have born
> More dreadful ills than any now before them.
> Have they not seen the partners of their breast
> With scourges torn? Beheld them bite the ground
> In speechless agony? Has pity spar'd their sex?
> Or have a mother's cares and burden gain'd
> Compassion for their weakness? Answer me,
> Ye who so oft have felt that direct pang,
> When, in the tort'rers hands, a wretched wife,
> Has scream'd for mercy, has implor'd your aid,
> While your distraction made the Christian sport. . . .
>
> To-night our tyrant plung'd in careless sleep,
> We rendezvous behind the citron grove.
> That ship secur'd we may transport ourselves
> To our respective homes: My father's kingdom
> Shall open her wide arms to take you in,
> And nurse you for her own, adopt you all,
> All, who will follow me.
> > *Omnes:* All, all follow you.
> > *Oroonoko:* There ease and honour shall reward your suff'rings,
> And never more shall Christian plund'rers fix
> Their impious feet on fair Angola's sands. . . .
> Should fate the sceptre to this hand restore,
> The injur'd African shall mourn no more—
> Safe in his plantain grove shall tend his bounds,
> And war receding die in distant sounds.

In the following soliloquy, Oroonoko is made to display not only the heroic passion that Southerne emphasized, but also an awareness of and sympathy for the mass of ordinary slaves who were the focus of the abolition campaign—and so little visible in Southerne's seventeenth-century original.

from Act V, Scene ii

> *Oroonoko:* Forget! forgive! I must indeed forget,
> When I forgive: But while I am a man,

In flesh, that bears the living marks of shame,
The print of my dishonourable chains,
I never can forgive! My anger's honest. . . .
Friendship and love may sooth my troubled mind;
Freedom may come, and, dearer now than freedom,
Th' expected hour may offer me revenge.
But the poor slave, who vents the hourly groan
From his o'er-burden'd breast, can never know
The least of my faint hopes: his meanest ill
Is want of nature's comforts, and his best
His only kind relieving friend, is death.

In Ferriar's rendering, Blandford, the white colonial who in Southerne's version acted solely out of honor and admiration for Oroonoko's heroic stature, seems motivated instead by antislavery idealism, linked to a patriotic sense of British (rather than personal) honor. This speech is entirely original in Ferriar's version.

from Act V, Scene iii

Blandford: This talk dispatch'd, I go with joyful steps
To raise the sick'ning hearts, and right the fortunes
Of this most faithful, injur'd, royal pair.
With this same breath, would I had power to offer
Relief to ev'ry drooping African
That now must envy their deliverance!
England! my country! shall no ray of freedom
Part from thy shining cliffs to cheer these wretches?
In what blest age, shall thy exalted sons
Impart to all, the liberty they love?

The following speech, also Ferriar's addition, replaces one in Southerne's version that focused on whether Oroonoko's murder-suicide was sinful or virtuous. Ferriar dwells instead on the guilt of slaveholders whose punishment, he hints, may come in violent retribution from the oppressed slaves themselves.

from Act V, Scene iv

Blandford: The guilt is ours;
For deeds like these are slav'ry's fruit; the chain
And bloody whip bring punishment upon us.
For these the suff'rer in his tyrant's heart
Fixes his steel—The elements conspire
To our undoing, Ocean overwhelms,

Or hurricanes despoil the guilty lands.
Let mercy find us safety: Still aware
That 'tis the tyrant's lot to arm despair.

In these provocative lines from his rhyming afterword, Ferriar tries to explode complacency. Satirizing both the selfish consumer who wants cheap sugar and rum, and the merchant grown rich on slave labor, Ferriar appeals to the audience to overcome both self-interest and (unconscious) racism. They must learn to see "a Brother's Features in the Negro's Face."

from the "Epilogue"

While gen'rous Britain, touch'd with foreign Woe,
Prepare[s] for Slav'ry the last fatal Blow;
What Hosts of Foes prophetic Fancy sees
Advance their chequer'd Flags of Nickanoes!
Sir Greedy, known a Connoisseur select,
When to import the Turtle, when reject,
Fears, should our Rulers to your Wish agree,
He'd lose his Callipash and Callipee.
Grave Sugar plum foresees, with waving Head,
The Royal race extinct—in Gingerbread;
While Bibo stares, by higher fears o'ercome,
And tells, with fiery breath, the Rise of Rum. . . .
You, whose kind Breasts at Tales of Sorrow melt,
You, who can pity griefs you never felt,
With Wealth, unharden'd, who can stoop to trace
A Brother's Features in the Negro's Face;
Commerce for you shall ope' her richest Stores,
The hidden Wealth of yet-neglected Shores;
And, proud to fill the heaven-directed Sail,
Shall grateful Afric breathe a spicy Gale.

(1788)[209]

ROBERT MERRY ["DELLA CRUSCA"] (1755–1798)

Merry is best known as the flamboyant Italianate poet whose pseudonym was taken to describe the ornate "Della Cruscan School" of the 1780s. A Cambridge-educated writer, dissolute army officer, bon vivant, and supporter of the French Revolution, he was a rival to the more staid and forgettable Henry James Pye, who was then poet laureate. Merry wrote "The Slaves" shortly after his return from Italy in 1787. Florid style apart, it is remarkable for its attack on rationalized defenses of slavery, chief among them the notion that Africans were the accursed descendants of Ham and bore the mark of Cain in their coloring.

from "The Slaves. An Elegy"

Lo! where to yon *plantation* drooping goes
    A *sable herd* of human kind; while near
Stalks a *pale despot,* and around him throws
    The scourge, that wakes—that punishes the tear. . . .

O cease to think, my soul! what thousands die
    By suicide, and toil's extreme despair;
Thousands, who never rais'd to heav'n the eye,
    Thousands, who fear'd no punishment, but here.

Are drops of blood the *horrible manure,*
    That fills with luscious juice, the *teeming cane?*
And must our fellow-creatures thus endure,
    For traffic vile, th'indignity of pain?

Yes, their keen sorrows are the sweets we blend
    With the green bev'rage of our morning meal,
The while to love *meek mercy* we pretend,
    Or for *fictitious ills* affect to feel. . . .

And there are *men,* who, leaning on the *laws,*
    What they have purchas'd, claim a right to hold,

Curs'd be the tenure, curs'd its cruel cause—
    Freedom's a dearer property than *gold!*

And there are *men*, with shameless front have said,
    "That Nature form'd the negroes for disgrace;
That on their limbs subjection is display'd—
    The doom of slav'ry stampt upon their face."

Send your stern gaze from Lapland to the line,
    And ev'ry region's natives fairly scan,
Their forms, their force, their faculties combine,
    And own the *vast variety of man!*

Then why suppose *yourselves* the chosen few,
    To deal Oppression's poison'd arrows round,
To gall, with iron bonds, the weaker crew,
    Enforce the labour, and inflict the wound?

'Tis *sordid int'rest* guides you. Bent on gain,
    In profit only can ye reason find;
And pleasure too:—but urge no more in vain,
    The selfish subject, to the social mind. . . .

Say, that in future, *negroes shall be blest,*
    Ranked e'en as men, and men's just rights enjoy;
Be neither sold, nor purchas'd, nor oppress'd,
    No griefs shall wither and no stripes destroy! . . .

Then shall proud Albion's crown, where laurels twine,
    Torn from the bosom of the raging sea,
Boast, 'midst the glorious leaves, a gem divine,
    The radiant gem of *pure humanity!*

                        (1788)[210]

SAMUEL JACKSON PRATT
["COURTNEY MELMOTH"]
(1749–1814)

Son of a brewer, Pratt abandoned an early career as an Anglican preacher to go on the stage, and later became a writer. Prolific but relentlessly mediocre, Pratt produced dozens of plays, poems, critical essays, and other writings over a period of forty years, right up until his death. He had a penchant for humane causes, writing at various times about prison reform, the treatment of animals, and human rights. The excerpts below are from his ambitious verse essay *Humanity, or the Rights of Nature*, which ran to more than 1,700 lines (110 pages) in the original. Despite the conventional poetic language, Pratt's Christian piety and moral indignation give the antislavery pieces of the poem a feverish urgency.

Here in Book I, he laments the slave trade in general terms as a national disgrace.

from Humanity, or the Rights of Nature
from Book I

> Why to home confin'd
> Are the soft mercies of thy Albion's mind?
> Why, at her bidding, rolls the crimson flood,
> To deluge Afric in her children's blood?
> Why torn from sire, from children, and from wife,
> Dragg'd at her wheels, are captives chain'd for life . . .
>
> Blush, Britain blush, for thou, 'tis thou hast sold
> A richer gem than India's mines can hold;
> Traffic'd thy soft HUMANITY away,
> And turn'd her strongest objects into prey!
> Thy generous sons upon that fatal shore,
> Their nature lose, and harden into ore:
> There greedy avarice, rears his venal throne,
> 'Midst seas of blood that float the sultry zone;

With wiry lash and iron rod he sways,
The tyrant orders, and the slave obeys;
Havoc and horror rage at his command,
And dissolution covers all the land! . . .

Ah! luscious mischief, slave-creating Cane,
Of ev'ry soft HUMANITY the bane . . .
To taste thy charm are groaning nations bound,
And half mankind in kindred blood are drown'd! . . .

Soon as the vessel bore the tribes away,
What horrors seized upon the trembling prey!
Ah! hear the shrieks of kindred left behind,
Roll to the wave and gather in the wind!
Matrons with orphans, sons with sires appear,
But vain affection's shriek and nature's tear:
The Spanish pirate ploughs the wat'ry plains,
And plants his cannon at the thin remains;
The flaming balls the wailing natives reach,
And added slaughter stains the crimson beach;
All, all is lost; but with a generous pride,
E'en slaves spurn life, when freedom is deny'd.

In an unusually concrete set of images, Pratt here conjures up the bloody ordeal that African captives endure at the hands of whites, as if to justify the slaves' self-destructive despair and visceral desire for vengeance. The frenzy of the passage culminates in black-on-white infanticide.

from Book II

Yet, who the Negro's suffering can relate,
Or mark the varied horrors of their fate;
Where, blushing Truth! shall we their griefs begin,
Or how commence the catalogue of Sin? . . .
Behold that axe the quivering limb assails,
Behold that body weltering in its wails!
Ah! hear that Bludgeon fall, that lash resound,
Ah! see those wretches writhing on the ground! . . .
Behold that Christian's hands the flames apply,
At the bare feet is laid the sulfurous train,
Climbs to the heart and burns into the brain. . . .
Torn from their native land at first they come,
And then are thrown into a sailing tomb,
In Wat'ry dens like coupled beasts they lie,

And beg the mournful priviledge to die;
But Death, more kind than Man, oft brings relief,
Releases one, while one survives to grief;
The living wretch his dead associate sees,
The body clasps and drinks the putrid breeze,
Chain'd to the noxious corpse till rudely thrown,
In the vex'd sea, then left a slave alone.
Ah! wretch forlorn! thy lot the most severe,
Assassination would be mercy here!

But Heav'n is just, each tyrant in his turn
Is taught the rashness of his pride to mourn,
Oft spreads his tortur'd Slave the secret snare . . .
At length he makes the Tyrant's self his prey,
And rushes on him in the face of day,
Or desperate, seizes on the child and wife,
Mad with his wrongs, and takes their forfeit life,
That thus the White man's progeny may groan,
The Tyrant's lot to balance with his own;
Oft from the cradle and the breast will tear,
Ev'n his babes on phrenzy of despair,
With mingled rage and fondness stop their breath,
And give them freedom in the arms of death.

(1788)[211]

HELEN MARIA WILLIAMS
(1762–1827)

An ardent liberal and accomplished writer who influenced Wordsworth and others, Williams was publishing poetry by the age of twenty. She became notorious after 1789 for her unrelenting support of the French Revolution and, once she moved abroad, for various scandalous liaisons, real and rumored.

In this poem, Williams harnesses human sympathy to a plea for legislative reform. The recent passage of the Dolben bill, regulating conditions aboard slave ships, raised hopes that Wilberforce's abolition bill would soon succeed. Events proved otherwise, and though she would later translate Bernardin St. Pierre's antislavery novella *Paul and Virginia* (1795), this poem was the last major work Williams published before moving to France in 1788.

from "On the Bill Which Was Passed in England for Regulating the Slave-Trade; A Short Time Before Its Abolition"

The hollow winds of night no more
In wild, unequal cadence pour,
On musing fancy's wakeful ear,
The groan of agony severe
From yon dark vessel, which contains
The wretch new bound in hopeless chains!
Whose soul with keener anguish bleeds,
As Afric's less'ning shore recedes—
No more where Ocean's unseen bound
Leaves a drear world of waters round,
Between the howling gust, shall rise
The stifled captive's latest sighs!—
No more shall suffocating death
Seize the pent victim's sinking breath;
The pang of that convulsive hour,

Reproaching man's insatiate power;
Man! who to Afric's shore has past,
Relentless, as the annual blast
That sweeps the Western Isles, and flings
Destruction from its furious wings!—
And woman, she, too weak to bear
The galling chain, the tainted air,—
Of mind too feeble to sustain
The vast, accumulated pain,—
No more, in desperation wild,
Shall madly strain her gasping child;
With all the mother at her soul,
With eyes where tears have ceas'd to roll,
Shall catch the livid infant's breath,
Then sink in agonizing death!
Britain! the noble, blest decree
That soothes despair, is fram'd by thee!
Thy powerful arm has interpos'd,
And one dire scene for ever clos'd;
Its horror shall no more belong
To that foul drama, deep with wrong.
O, first of Europe's polish'd lands
To ease the captive's iron bands;
Long, as thy glorious annals shine,
This proud distinction shall be thine! . . .

O, Eloquence! prevailing art!
Whose force can chain the list'ning heart;
The throb of sympathy inspire,
And kindle every great desire . . .
Fill with thy noblest rage the breast,
Bid on those lips thy spirit rest,
That shall, in Britain's Senate, trace
The wrongs of Afric's captive race!

(1788)[212]

ANN YEARSLEY (1756–1806)

Sometimes called "Lactilla" or the "Milkmaid poet," Yearsley was a dairy worker who became a self-taught and fiercely independent poetic prodigy of the 1780s. The established writer Hannah More patronized her, helped her publish, and recruited buyers for her books. Yearsley shared More's hatred of slavery and, like More, wrote against it, but the two fell out over how to manage the revenue from Yearsley's writings.

Running in the original to some thirty pages, Yearsley's poem seethes with anger, to the point of rage. Her images punch home. In one, perhaps drawing on her own feelings as a mother of six, she assaults "Christian" slave-traders with imaginary scenes of their own children being sold into bondage. Another dwells on the slow death of a rebel slave ("Luco"), burned at the stake. Other lines hint at Yearsley's broader critique of society, of which the slave trade is the most egregious evil.

from A Poem on the Inhumanity of the Slave-Trade

> Behold that Christian! See what horrid joy
> Lights up his moody features, while he grasps
> The wish'd-for gold, purchase of human blood!
> Away, thou seller of mankind! Bring on
> Thy daughter to this market! Bring thy wife!
> Thine aged mother, though of little worth,
> With all thy ruddy boys! Sell them, thou wretch,
> And swell the price of Luco! Why that start?
> Why gaze as thou wouldst fright me from my challenge
> With look of anguish? Is it Nature strains
> Thine heart-strings at the image? . . .
>   Oh, throw thine arm
> Around thy little ones, and loudly plead
> Thou canst not sell thy children.——Yet, beware

Lest Luco's groan be heard; should that prevail,
Justice will scorn thee in her turn, and hold
Thine act against thy pray'r. Why clasp, she cries,
That blooming youth? Is it because thou lov'st him?
Why Luco was belov'd: then wilt thou feel,
Thou selfish Christian, for thy private woe,
Yet cause such pangs to him that is a father?
Whence comes thy right to barter for thy fellows?
Where are thy statutes? Whose the iron pen
That gave thee precedent? Give me the seal
Of virtue, or religion, for thy trade,
And I will ne'er upbraid thee; but if force
Superior, hard brutality alone
Become thy boast, hence to some savage haunt,
Nor claim protection from my social laws. . . .

          Many slaves there were,
But none who could supress the sigh, and bend,
So quietly as Luco: long he bore
The stripes, that from his manly bosom drew
The sanguine stream (too little priz'd); at length
Hope fled his soul, giving her struggles o'er,
And he resolv'd to die. The sun had reach'd
His zenith—pausing faintly, Luco stood,
Leaning upon his hoe, while mem'ry brought,
In piteous imag'ry, his aged father,
His poor fond mother, and his faithful maid:
The mental group in wildest motion set
Fruitless imagination; fury, grief,
Alternate shame, the sense of insult, all
Conspire to aid the inward storm; yet words
Were no relief, he stood in silent woe.

   Gorgon, remorseless Christian, saw the slave
Stand musing, 'mid the ranks, and, stealing soft
Behind the studious Luco, struck his cheek
With a too-heavy whip, that reach'd his eye,
Making it dark for ever. Luco turn'd,
In strongest agony, and with his hoe
Struck the rude Christian on the forehead. Pride,
With hateful malice, seize on Gorgon's soul,
By nature fierce; while Luco sought the beach,

And plung'd beneath the wave; but near him lay
A planter's barge, whose seamen grasp'd his hair,
Dragging to life a wretch who wish'd to die.

Rumour now spreads the tale, while Gorgon's breath
Envenom'd, aids her blast: imputed crimes
Oppose the plea of Luco, till he scorns
Even a just defence, and stands prepared.
The planters, conscious that to fear alone
They owe their cruel pow'r, resolve to blend
New torment with the pangs of death, and hold
Their victims high in dreadful view, to fright
The wretched number left. Luco is chain'd
To a huge tree, his fellow-slaves are ranged
To share the horrid sight; fuel is plac'd
In an increasing train, some paces back,
To kindle slowly, and approach the youth,
With more than native terror. See, it burns!
He gazes on the growing flame, and calls
For "water, water!" The small boon's deny'd.
E'en Christians throng each other, to behold
The different alterations of his face,
As the hot death approaches. (Oh, shame, shame
Upon the followers of Jesus! Shame
On him that dares avow a God!) He writhes,
While down his breast glide the unpity'd tears,
And in their sockets strain their scorched balls.
"Burn, burn me quick! I cannot die!" he cries:
"Bring fire more close!" The planters heed him not . . .

Now speak, ye Christians (who for gain enslave
A soul like Luco's, tearing her from joy
In life's short vale; and if there be a hell,
As ye believe, to that ye thrust her down,
A blind, involuntary victim), here
Is your true essence of religion? Where
Your proofs of righteousness, when ye conceal
The knowledge of the Deity from those
Who would adore him fervently? Your God
Ye rob of worshippers, his altars keep
Unhail'd, while driving from the sacred font
The eager slave, lest he should hope in Jesus.

Is this your piety? Are these your laws,
Whereby the glory of the Godhead spreads
O'er barb'rous climes? Ye hypocrites, disown
The Christian name, nor shame its cause: yet where
Shall souls like yours find welcome? Would the Turk,
Pagan, or wildest Arab, ope their arms
To gain such proselytes? No; he that owns
The name of Mussulman would start, and shun
Your worse than serpent touch; he frees his slave
Who turns to Mahomet. The Spaniard stands
Your brighter contrast; he condems the youth
For ever to the mine; but ere the wretch
Sinks to the deep domain, the hand of Faith
Bathes his faint temples in the sacred stream,
Bidding his spirit hope. Briton, dost thou
Act up to this? If so, bring on thy slaves
To Calv'ry's mount, raise high their kindred souls
To him who died to save them: this alone
Will teach them calmly to obey thy rage,
And deem a life of misery but a day,
To long eternity. . . .

              Hath our public good
Fell rapine for its basis? Must our wants
Find their supply in murder? Shall the sons
Of Commerce shiv'ring stand, if not employ'd
Worse than the midnight robber? Curses fall
On the destructive system that shall need
Such base supports! Doth England need them? No;
Her laws, with prudence, hang the meagre thief
That from his neighbor steals a slender sum,
Tho' famine drove him on. O'er him the priest,
Beneath the fatal tree, laments the crime,
Approves the law, and bids him calmly die.
Say, doth this law, that dooms the thief, protect
The wretch who makes another's life his prey,
By hellish force to take it at his will?
Is this an English law, whose guidance fails
When crimes are swell'd to magnitude so vast,
That Justice dare not scan them? Or does Law
Bid Justice an eternal distance keep
From England's great tribunal, when the slave

Calls loud on Justice only? Speak, ye few
Who fill Britannia's senate, and are deem'd
The fathers of your country! Boast your laws,
Defend the honour of a land so fall'n,
That Fame from ev'ry battlement is flown,
And Heathens start, e'en at a Christian's name.

(1788)[213]

ANONYMOUS

An unidentified friend wrote this prologue for Thomas Bellamy's play *The Benevolent Planters* (1789), to be delivered by the famous tragic actor John Philip Kemble. Kemble had the leading black role in the play, as Oran, the African captive long separated from his beloved Selima. The prologue, spoken by "an African sailor," wavers between an apology for a benevolent, paternalistic model of slaveholding and a prayer (in the closing lines) for the abolition of slavery altogether.

"Prologue" to The Benevolent Planters

AN AFRICAN SAILOR:
To Afric's torrid clime, where every day
The sun oppresses with his scorching ray,
My birth I owe; and here for many a year,
I tasted pleasure free from every care.
There 'twas my happy fortune long to prove
The fond endearments of parental love.
'Twas there my lov'd Adela, my favourite maid,
Return'd my passion, love with love repaid.
Oft on the banks where golden rivers flow,
And aromatic woods enchanting grow,
With my lov'd Adela I pass'd the day,
While suns on suns roll'd unperceiv'd away.
But ah! this happiness was not to last,
Clouds now the brightness of my fate o'ercast;
For the white savage fierce upon me sprung,
Wrath in his eye, and fury on his tongue,
And dragg'd me to a loathsome vessel near,
Dragg'd me from everything I held most dear,
And plung'd me in the horrors of despair.

Insensible to all that pass'd around,
Till, in a foreign clime, myself I found,
And sold to slavery!—There with constant toil,
Condemn'd in burning suns to turn the soil.
Oh! If I told you what I suffer'd there,
From cruel masters, and the lash severe,
Eyes most unus'd to melt, would drop the tear.
But fortune soon a kinder master gave,
Who made me soon forget I was a slave,
And brought me to this land, this generous land,
Where, they inform me, that an hallow'd band,
Impelled by soft humanity's kind laws,
Take up with fervent zeal the Negroe's cause,
And at this very moment, anxious try,
To stop the widespread woes of slavery.
But of this hallow'd band a part appears,
Exult my heart, and flow my grateful tears.
Oh sons of mercy! whose extensive mind
Takes in at once the whole of human kind,
Who know the various nations of the earth,
To whatsoever clime they owe their birth,
Or of whatever colour they appear,
All children of one gracious Parent are.
And thus united by paternal love,
To all mankind, of all the friend you prove.
With fervent zeal pursue your godlike plan,
And man deliver from the tyrant man!
What tho' at first you miss the wish'd-for end,
Success at last your labours will attend.
Then shall your worth, extoll'd in grateful strains,
Resound through Gambia's and Angola's plains.
Nations unborn your righteous zeal shall bless.

(1789)[214]

THOMAS BELLAMY (1745–1800)

After working twenty years in the hosiery business, Bellamy turned to book-selling, magazine editing, and miscellaneous writing for the last fifteen years of his life. From 1787 to 1792 he edited his own periodical, *The General Magazine and Impartial Review*, which, amid its broad coverage of books and culture, produced a steady stream of antislavery pieces, including original poems by his friend William Cowper (included elsewhere).

Although the theater was his first love, Bellamy had little success as a play-wright. His *Benevolent Planters* was staged at the Haymarket in London in July 1789, as a benefit for the actress Mrs. Kemble, wife of the tragedian John Philip Kemble. The couple played the leading black roles, as the African Oran and his lover Selima, long separated by the slave trade. Given his unflagging opposition to slavery in his other writings and editorial work, Bellamy's promotion of a benign, paternalistic slave society in this play seems to reflect a desire to achieve incremental change, rather than see the abolition cause crushed altogether by the powerful pro-slavery lobby.

In the first song Selima explains why, despite the kindness of her enlight-ened master Goodwin, she is still unhappy—wrongly believing her beloved Oran dead.

"Song" [by Selima, a slave] from The Benevolent Planters

> How vain to me the hours of ease,
> When every daily toil is o'er;
> In my sad heart no hope I find,
> For Oran is, alas! no more.
>
> Not sunny Africa could please,
> Nor friends upon my native shore,
> To me the dreary world's a cave,
> For Oran is, alas! no more.

In bowers of bliss beyond the moon,
The white man says, his sorrow's o'er,
And comforts me with soothing hope,
Tho' Oran is, alas, no more.

O come then, messenger of death,
Convey me to yon starry shore,
Where I may meet with my true love,
And never part with Oran more.

(1789)[215]

In the second song, Oran, having gained freedom, property, and marriage to his beloved Selima through the magnanimity of his master, Heartfree, closes the play with a hearty celebration—to the tune of "Rule Britannia." Bellamy may have intended to make antislavery ideas seem patriotic to his eighteenth-century audience, but his tactic can strike modern ears as incredible.

"Song. To the Tune of Rule Britannia" [by Oran, a slave] from The Benevolent Planters

In honour of this happy day,
Let Afric's sable sons rejoice;
To mercy we devote the lay,
To heaven-born mercy raise the voice.
Long may she reign, and call each heart her own,
And nations guard her sacred throne.

Fair child of heaven, our rites approve,
With smiles attend the votive song,
Inspire with universal love,
For joy and peace to thee belong.
Long may'st thou reign, and call each heart thy own,
While nations guard thy sacred throne.

(1789)[216]

WILLIAM BLAKE (1757–1827)

The famous visionary poet and artist included powerful images of slavery in several of his greatest works. An autodidact who trained as an engraver and embraced radical politics and alternative philosophies, Blake developed perhaps the most idiosyncratic poetic voice of his era.

The following ballad, first printed in his *Songs of Innocence*, builds on and refines the contemporary vogue for sentimental depictions of child victims of slavery. Using the child's voice to invoke subtle moral insights, Blake plays on black-white symbolism, both physical and metaphysical, to expose the empty ideology of racism.

The Little Black Boy

My mother bore me in the southern wild,
And I am black, but O! my soul is white;
White as an angel is the English child:
But I am black as if bereav'd of light.

My mother taught me underneath a tree
And sitting down before the heat of day,
She took me on her lap and kissed me,
And pointing to the east began to say.

"Look on the rising sun: there God does live
And gives his light, and gives his heat away.
And flowers and trees and beasts and men receive
Comfort in morning joy in the noon day.

And we are put on earth a little space,
That we may learn to bear the beams of love,
And these black bodies and this sun-burnt face
Is but a cloud, and like a shady grove.

For when our souls have learn'd the heat to bear
The cloud will vanish we shall hear his voice.

Saying: come out from the grove my love & care,
And round my golden tent like lambs rejoice."

Thus did my mother say and kissed me,
And thus I say to little English boy.
When I from black and he from white cloud free,
And round the tent of God like lambs we joy:

I'll shade him from the heat till he can bear,
To lean in joy upon our fathers knee.
And then I'll stand and stroke his silver hair,
And be like him and he will then love me.

$(1789)^{217}$

However fleetingly, images of chattel slavery surface in several of Blake's apocalyptic works, including this passage in *Daughters of Albion*.

from Visions of the Daughters of Albion

At entrance Theotormon sits wearing the threshold hard
With secret tears; beneath him sound like waves on a desart shore
The voice of slaves beneath the sun, and children bought with money.
That shiver in religious caves beneath the burning fires
Of lust, that belch incessant from the summits of the earth.

$(1793)^{218}$

In this striking passage from one of his most ambitious works, Blake integrates the emancipation of slaves into the apocalypse and the resurrection of the dead prophesied in the Bible—all under the rubric of a distinctively American vision, as if the depravity of New World slavery is symptomatic of the global degeneration that was expected to usher in the millennium.

from America: A Prophecy

The morning comes, the night decays, the watchmen leave their stations;
The grave is burst, the spices shed, the linen wrapped up;
The bones of death, the cov'ring clay, the sinews shrunk & dry'd.
Reviving shake, inspiring move, breathing! awakening!
Spring like redeemed captives when their bonds & bars are burst;
Let the slave grinding at the mill, run out into the field:
Let him look up into the heavens & laugh in the bright air;
Let the inchained soul shut up in darkness and in sighing,
Whose face has never seen a smile in thirty weary years;
Rise and look out, his chains are loose, his dungeon doors are open.

And let his wife and children return from the opressors scourge;
They look behind at every step & believe it is a dream.
Singing. The Sun has left his blackness, & has found a fresher morning
And the fair Moon rejoices in the clear & cloudless night;
For Empire is no more, and now the Lion & Wolf shall cease.

$(1793)^{219}$

Slavery even manages to press into Blake's visualization of the cosmos, in these lines from *Milton*. The evident yearning for a redemptive or transformative effect that would somehow follow from artistic depictions of the slaves' misery could describe the purpose of all the poetry written against slavery.

from Milton

When Luvahs bulls each morning drag the sulphur Sun out of the Deep
Harnessd with starry harness black & shining kept by black slaves
That work all night at the starry harness, Strong and vigorous
They drag the unwilling Orb

Thousands & thousands labour. thousands play on instruments
Stringed or fluted to ameliorate the sorrows of slavery.

$(1804)^{220}$

ERASMUS DARWIN (1731–1803)

Grandfather to the famous evolutionist Charles Darwin, Erasmus was also a scientist, as well as a physician, inventor, and man of letters. Educated at Cambridge and trained as a doctor at Edinburgh, Darwin had a prosperous medical practice based in Lichfield, where he also was the center of an intellectual circle that included antislavery figures Josiah Wedgewood, Thomas Day, and the Sewards. Like his friends, Darwin opposed slavery and managed to write against it even in the context of his old-fashioned Popean verses about plant life.

This first excerpt is from a work he published in 1789 and later revised as the basis for Part 2 of *The Botanic Garden* (1791–92). Darwin fervently hoped Parliament would pass the abolition bill immediately.

from Canto III of "The Loves of the Plants"

Hark! heard ye not that piercing cry,
Which shook the waves, and rent the sky!—
E'en now, e'en now, on yonder Western shores
Weeps pale Despair, and writhing Anguish roars:
E'en now in Afric's groves with hideous yell
Fierce SLAVERY stalks, and slips the dogs of hell;
From vale to vale the gathering cries rebound,
And sable nations tremble at the sound!—
—YE BANDS OF SENATORS! whose suffrage sways
Britannia's realms, whom either Ind obeys;
Who right the injured, and reward the brave,
Stretch your strong arm, for ye have power to save!
The close recesses of the heart within,
Stern CONSCIENCE sits, the arbiter of Sin;
With still small voice the plotts of Guilt alarms,
Lights his dark mind, his lifted hand disarms;
But, wrap'd in night with terrors all his own,

He speaks in thunder, when the deed is done.
Hear him, ye Senates! hear this truth sublime,
"HE, WHO ALLOWS OPPRESSION, SHARES THE CRIME."
(1789)[221]

Here the quatrain about "the Slave" ("ARE WE NOT BRETHREN?") alludes to his friend Wedgewood's famous medallion, depicting a slave in chains on bended knee under the motto "Am I Not A Man and A Brother?" Like many in his time, Darwin was sensitive to Britain's place in the larger cycles of history and to the moral taint the slave trade inflicted on the nation's heritage.

from Canto II, "The Economy of Vegetation," Part I, The Botanic Garden

Heavens! on my sight what sanguine colours blaze!
Spain's deathless shame! the crimes of modern days!
When Avarice, shrouded in Religion's robe,
Sail'd to the West, and slaughter'd half the globe;
While Superstition, stalking by his side,
Mock'd the loud groans, and lap'd the bloody tide;
For sacred truths announced her frenzied dreams,
And turn'd to night the sun's meridian beams.—
Hear, oh, BRITANNIA! potent Queen of isles,
On whom fair Art, and meek Religion smiles,
Now AFRIC's coasts thy craftier sons invade
With murder, rapine, theft,—and call it Trade!
—The SLAVE, in chains, on supplicating knee,
Spreads his wide arms, and lifts his eyes to Thee;
With hunger pale, with wounds and toil oppress'd,
"ARE WE NOT BRETHREN?" sorrow choaks the rest;—
—AIR! bear to heaven upon thy azure flood
Their innocent cries!—EARTH! cover not their blood!
(1791)[222]

OLAUDAH EQUIANO, OR "GUSTAVUS VASSA" (c. 1745–1797)

Although the facts of his biography have recently been questioned, Equiano is generally thought to have been born in what is now Nigeria, captured and sold into slavery at age twelve, and to have led one of the most extraordinary lives of the eighteenth century. Beginning as the slave of a British sea captain, Equiano educated himself, acquired the skills of a mariner (including navigation), became a shipboard entrepreneur, and eventually purchased his own freedom. Before settling in England in the late 1770s, Equiano spent twenty turbulent years crisscrossing the seas, enduring shipwreck, attempted murder, robbery, wrongful imprisonment, and suicidal depression. These adventures, his conversion to evangelical Christianity in 1774, and his fight against the slave trade are recorded in his autobiography, *The Interesting Narrative of the Life of Olaudah Equiano* (1789), a book whose importance is hard to overestimate. A stimulus to the fledgling abolition movement, it went through nine editions in five years and was translated into Dutch, German, and Russian. It originated the genre of the slave narrative, influenced Frederick Douglass in the nineteenth century, and inspired generations of activists from Wilberforce and Clarkson to Garrison and Sumner.

This poem, written to celebrate his spiritual awakening and apparently never separately published, appears in *The Life* after Chapter 10 (c. 1774–75). The emotional intensity and the density of biblical allusion are comparable to the religious poetry of his fellow Africans Jupiter Hammon and Phillis Wheatley.

Miscellaneous Verses; Or, Reflections on the State of my Mind during my first Convictions of the Necessity of believing the Truth, and of experiencing the inestimable Benefits of Christianity

Well may I say my life has been
One scene of sorrow and of pain;
From early days I griefs have known,
And as I grew my griefs have grown:

Dangers were always in my path;
And fear of wrath, and sometimes death;
While pale dejection in me reign'd
I often wept, by grief constrain'd.

When taken from my native land,
By an unjust and cruel band,
How did uncommon dread prevail!
My sighs no more I could conceal.

To ease my mind I often strove,
And tried my trouble to remove:
I sung, and utter'd sighs between—
Assay'd to stifle guilt with sin.

But O! Not all that I could do
Would stop the current of my woe;
Conviction still my vileness shew'd;
How great my guilt—how lost from God!

Prevented, that I could not die,
Nor might to one kind refuge fly;
An orphan state I had to mourn—
Forsook by all, and left forlorn.

Those who beheld my downcast mien
Could not guess at my woes unseen:
They by appearance could not know
The troubles that I waded through.

Lust, anger, blasphemy, and pride,
With legions of such ills beside,
Troubled my thoughts while doubts and fears
Clouded and darken'd most my years.

Sighs now no more would be confin'd—
They breath'd the trouble of my mind:
I wish'd for death, but check'd the word,
And often pray'd unto the Lord.

Unhappy, more than some on earth,
I thought the place that gave me birth—
Strange thoughts oppress'd—while I replied
"Why not in Ethiopia died?"

And why thus spared nigh to hell?—
God only knew—I could not tell!
A tott'ring fence, a bowing wall,
I thought myself e'er since the fall.

OLAUDAH EQUIANO

Oft times I mused, nigh despair,
While birds melodious fill'd the air:
Thrice happy songsters, ever free,
How bless'd were they compar'd to me!

Thus all things added to my pain,
While grief compell'd me to complain;
When sable clouds began to rise
My mind grew darker than the skies.

The English nation call'd to leave,
How did my breast with sorrows heave!
I long'd for rest—cried "Help me, Lord!
Some mitigation, Lord afford!"

Yet on, dejected, still I went—
Heart-throbbing woes within were pent;
Nor land, nor sea, could comfort give,
Nothing my anxious soul relieve.

Weary with travail, yet unknown
To all but God and self alone,
Numerous months for peace I strove
And numerous foes I had to prove.

Inur'd to dangers, griefs, and woes,
Train'd up 'midst perils, deaths, and foes,
I said "Must it thus ever be?—
No quiet is permitted me."

Hard hap, and more than heavy lot!
I pray'd to God "Forget me not—
What thou ordain'st willing I'll bear
But O! deliver from despair!"

Strivings and wrestlings seem'd in vain;
Nothing I did could ease my pain:
Then gave I up my works and will,
Confess'd and own'd my doom was hell!

Like some poor pris'ner at the bar,
Conscious of guilt, of sin and fear,
Arraign'd, and self-condemn'd I stood—
Lost in the world, and in my blood!

Yet here, 'midst blackest clouds confin'd,
A beam from Christ, the day-star, shin'd;
Surely, thought I, if Jesus please,
He can at once sign my release.

I, ignorant of his righteousness,
Set up my labours in its place,
Forgot why his blood was shed,
And pray'd and fasted in its stead.

He dy'd for sinners—I am one!
Might not his blood for me atone?
Tho' I am nothing else but sin,
Yet surely he can make me clean!

Thus light came in and I believ'd;
Myself forgot, and help receiv'd!
My Saviour then I know I found,
For, eas'd from guilt, no more I groan'd.

O happy hour, in which I ceas'd
To mourn, for then I found a rest!
My soul and Christ were now as one—
Thy light, O Jesus, in me shone!

Bless'd by thy name, for now I know
I and my works can nothing do;
The Lord alone can ransom man—
For this the spotless Lamb was slain!

When sacrifices, works, and pray'r,
Prov'd vain, and ineffectual were,
"Lo, then I come!" the Saviour cry'd,
And, bleeding, bow'd his head and dy'd!

He dy'd for all who ever saw
No help in them, nor by the law:—
I this have seen; and gladly own
"Salvation is by Christ alone!"

(1789)[223]

FRANCIS HOPKINSON
(1737–1791)

A distinguished Philadelphia jurist, writer, and signer of the Declaration of Independence, Hopkinson wrote the following ghoulish satire to settle a feud between two medical schools over access to cadavers for their research. African American corpses, like those of other poor people, were frequently purchased or stolen to supply dissection labs. In this excerpt, Hopkinson envisions the resentment of the black population and then, to mock the rival medics, unfolds a bizarre fantasy of a dissectionist obsessed with the cadaver of a black woman.

from An Oration, which might have been delivered to the Students in Anatomy, on the late rupture between the two schools in this city

Methinks I see a mob of sailors rise—
Revenge!—revenge! they cry—and damn their eyes—
Revenge for comrade Jack, whose flesh, they say,
You minc'd to morsels and then threw away.
Methinks I see a black infernal train—
The genuine offspring of accursed *Cain*—
Fiercely on you their angry looks are bent,
They grin and gibber dangerous discontent,
And seem to say,—"Is there not meat enough?
Ah! massa cannibal, why eat poor CUFF?" . . .

Think how, like brethren, we have shar'd the toil
When in the Potter's Field* we fought for spoil,
Did midnight ghosts and death and horror brave
To delve for science in the dreary grave . . .

Yet I have lov'd—and Cupid's subtle dart
Hath thro' my *pericardium* pierc'd my heart.

---

* [Hopkinson's note:] The Negro burial ground.

Brown CADAVERA did my soul ensnare,
Was all my thought by night and daily care—
I long'd to clasp, in her transcendent charms,
A living skeleton within my arms. . . .
Long were her fingers and her knuckles bare,
Much like the claw-foot of a walnut chair.
So plain was complex *matacarpus* shewn
It might be fairly counted bone by bone.

(1789)[224]

WILLIAM HUTCHINSON
(1732–1814)

A lawyer in Durham, England, Hutchinson was an antiquarian, local historian, novelist, and miscellaneous writer who published steadily from the 1770s through the 1790s. He was also an ardent abolitionist and in 1789, despite having failed to get any of his earlier plays staged, he devoted a full-length tragedy to the plight of enslaved Africans in America. The result, *The Princess of Zanfara*, was in its published form dedicated to the British Abolition Society and, although rejected by the London theaters, staged frequently in provincial playhouses.

In this first excerpt, the slave "Laura," reasserting her African identity as Jaqueena, declaims to her sympathetic mistress Amelia about the culpability of Christians holding slaves, even while acknowledging that some owners like Amelia treat their slaves with kindness.

from Act I of The Princess of Zanfara; A Dramatic Poem

> Laura: Were they not Christians that on Niger's flood,
> On board their dreadful bark, receiv'd the lost
> Jaqueena? (for the name of Laura bears
> The badge of slavery, and my reproach.)
> Are they not Christians, who, in all this land,
> Make the poor Africans perform the task
> Of beasts; not barely to sustain the toil,
> But to endure the torture; and with stripes,
> With nakedness and hunger, to lie down,
> Stall'd worse than beasts, to rankle in their sores? . . .
>
>   —Can a slave then hope
> For your humanity?—for tho' the blood
> Is of one dye, without congenial suns
> It ripens not, nor meliorates to love.

Yet will I not forget your bounteous gifts,
For Africans know not ingratitude!
I am a slave, not knowing bondage here,
But in detention from my native land;
For my kind mistress, as Amelia kind,
Nor gives me chains nor stripes, nor wears a frown.
There are some Christians of a milder soul,
And such poor Laura happily protect.

Later in Act I, the kindly Amelia refutes the view of her slaveholding beau Antonio that Africans are better off in slavery than subject to the chaos of their homelands. Very shortly, Amelia succeeds in converting Antonio to abolitionism.

Amelia: She must return to Africa again,
Her country, and her friends.—

Antonio: —Romantic thought!
The wand'ring tribe she left, perhaps dispers'd,
The government dissolv'd, new tyrants reign;
And warfare, the rough habit of their lives,
With chequer'd fortunes marks each petty Prince,
Now reigning, now in chains,—on Afric's coast,
To greater perils, greater woes expos'd;
There's not a slave that in this province toils,
But, if return'd, would worship the dire name
Of slavery, that makes them tremble now.

Amelia: Your arguments enlarge the dreadful bounds
Of that vast sin which on your traffic rests;
If restitution is impossible,
The base captivity, (that thus cuts off
All human hope, and no kind limit yields
To the sad injury, but in the tomb,)
Of all the crimes on earth, becomes the worst.

In this excerpt from Act II, the plantation owner Horatio discusses with a slave trader, the aptly named Calaban, the respective merits of different nationalities of Africans as slaves. The white men's racist language, which Hutchinson obviously intended to be shocking and revolting, treats the Africans as animals and illustrates another of the means the abolitionist playwright was using to move his audience.

Horatio: What province are they of?—For much depends
Upon the breed; some of the upland slaves,

WILLIAM HUTCHINSON

That border on the desert, are of mind
So dark and so indocile, that they seem
Of one gradation only above brutes;
Those of more eastern clime are indolent,
(As bears are sluggish, and not mov'd by stripes,)
They'll neither serve the mill nor till the ground.

Calaban: Well, master, mine are of the fav'rite breed;
Twice ten degrees remov'd from the baboon;
Their form is human, and they're almost men:
Boney and strong, of countenance acute,
And as hyaenas savage?—they're the slaves
For labour; as the mind is fierce and quick,
Their bodies in proportion active are;
On mountains skirts and wilds of Zara bred,
The topsmen drove the herd to Niger's banks,
The mart of Africa.—

In this speech from Act V, Jaqueena's lover, the newly freed African Manzara, grieves over her body and vows to transport her back to Africa to sanctify a monument he will erect in denunciation of the slave trade. In closing the play this way, Hutchinson seems to be recognizing the power not of white liberals but of Africans themselves to resist and overthrow the whole institution of slavery.

Manzara: I know not what to do!—Oh sweet remains,
Adieu!—a long adieu!—If you retain
Compassion for my woes, embalm the corpse,
That Africa may yet receive its own
We must depart,—must tear ourselves from hence,
The scene of so much terror and distress! . . .
Tho' adverse winds
May hang upon the dilatory sail;
Perhaps relenting fates will yet retain
Some pity for the Moor,—that he may land
On native shores,—and there erect on high
A monument, that shall command the hearts
Of our posterity (whilst man exists)
To an abhorrence of the Trade in Slaves.

(1789)[225]

REVEREND JOHN JAMIESON
(1759–1838)

A child prodigy who entered Glasgow University at age nine, Jamieson was a Scottish clergyman who pursued a literary and scholarly career. His publications included essays, sermons, poems, and his most important work, the *Etymological Dictionary of the Scottish Language* (1808). In a long and productive life there was also pain: he eventually outlived his wife and all fourteen of their sons and daughters.

In this long poem, Jamieson builds a three-part narrative of the typical African captive's experience: first "the methods used to procure slaves on the Guinea Coast," second "the Middle Passage," and third "their situation in the West Indies." To serve his moral and political purpose, Jamieson becomes almost anti-romantic: he stresses the factual accuracy of the details in the poem, prefacing his text with a list of authoritative sources and insisting that he "hath carefully avoided exaggeration." The opening lines of Part I are particularly striking for his assumption of a (primarily) female readership.

from The Sorrows of Slavery, A Poem. Containing a Faithful Statement of Facts Respecting the African Slave Trade *
from Part I

> Ye British fair, whose gentle bosoms heave
> The sigh of pity at the tale of woe;
> Whose lovely eyes, like sun-beams darting thro'

---

* [from Jamieson's preface:] "The principal design of the Author hath been to represent simple historical facts in the language of poetry; as this might attract the attention of some who would not otherwise give themselves the trouble of looking into the subject. Through the whole of the poem he hath carefully avoided exaggeration. Circumstances are faithfully stated from different publications, particularly those of the Rev. Messrs. [John] Ramsay, [Thomas] Clarkson, [John] Newton, and [Robert Boucher] Nicholls; and of Mr. [Alexander] Falconbridge, Surgeon."

REVEREND JOHN JAMIESON

A watery cloud, the roses underneath
In sweet profusion scatter'd oft bedew,
And lend new grace to ev'ry varying tinge;
Why purchase sorrow in the tragic scene,
Or court it in the fancy-labour'd tale . . .
While Afric forces on your sight averse;
A real tragedy, unmatch'd in song,
Where every village opes a dismal scene,
Where acts of death unnumber'd chill the soul,
And freeborn Britons act the bloodiest parts? . . .
    They are not fair like you. But can the hues
Of Nature various tinge the secret soul? . . .
Does Grief ne'er wring their heart-strings? Or can Pain
Make no nerve thrill? . . .
To him his dusky mistress is as fair
As thou art to thy lover . . .
Let the superior brightness of thy soul,
Let Nature's first-born, gentle Pity, show. . . .
    O Thou, Almighty Father! who hast made
Of one blood all the nations, and assign'd
To each on this thy earth his several spot,
Who from thy height transcendant deign'st to look
On all the various sons of men, and own
All as thy offspring, blacken'd by thy sun,
Or by thy snows made white, to Thee alike:
Inspire me, while I sing the general rights
Of human kind, and mourn the inroads fell
Man, thy poor vassal, dares to make on man.
        . . . See! where Dahomy's king,
In midst of night and darkness ominous,
His gloomy spoilers crouding after him
In dreadful silence, like some demon fell
From outer darkness loos'd for man's destruction,
Flies to a village of his own domain,
His fatal torch blue-gleaming in his hand . . .
The wavering flames, now towering high, on heav'n
A horrid lustre throw; anon they sink,
As conscious of its more than midnight-frown . . .
Bound by their countrymen, their kinsmen, friends,
In hated chains, at their own King's command;
Their souls indignant burn to meet the flames

They basely fled, not half so keen as those
That now consume them inly.

In Part II, covering the middle passage, Jamieson's imaginative gaze is un-
flinching, as he shows scenes of the squalor below decks, the forced feedings,
and the frantic suicides.

from Part II

Like undistinguish'd lumber in their hold,
Between the decks the living cargo's stow'd;
Forming, like some ant-hill, a moving heap;
Tho' not, like its laborious tenants, free.
The galling fetters each to each confine,
Their legs and arms enclosing in rude grasp. . . .
They every motion by consent must make;
Frequent in quarrels, when their Babel-tongues
The biting of distorted chains provoke.
For so inventive is the cruelty
Of their harsh jailors; as if simple bonds,
To guiltless negroes were a boon too great;
Transversely they are bound, in studied forms
Most adverse to the suffering captive's ease . . .
There, rang'd in mournful ranks, they faintly spy
Their much-lov'd country flying from their view . . .
What shrieks of grief unbridled, of despair
Deep groans and hideous yells . . .
     See! where one, watchful of the moment kind,
When from the ring-bolts loos'd to leave the deck,
Leaps overboard, the partner of his chains,
Of life less lavish, dragging after him;
And fills a monstrous shark's deep-forked jaws,
Expanding to receive its shrinking prey.
     All sustinence some obstinately scorn.
If dreadful threats avail not to subdue,
On their weak limbs, while pinion'd to the mast,
In merciless repetition, the keen scourge
Draws its deep furrows. If they still refuse,
Wrench'd open are their parched mouths, and down
Their throats reluctant are the liquid means
Of life pour'd violently. Their lips at times
Th' embrace consuming of live coals endure.
But ineffectual oft these cruelties;

The wretches find that death they long have sought
With unabated ardor, and acquir'd
At such expence of suffering exquisite;
Firmly resolv'd, by vengeance on themselves,
At last on their oppressors to be veng'd.

Here, amidst his survey of New World slavery, Jamieson indicts the particular hypocrisy of slavery persisting in America (on "Columbia's plains"), despite its founding principle of liberty for all. In the final lines, the devout Jamieson conflates the prospect of bloody insurrection with that of the divine retribution that will come to those who persist in the sinfulness of slaveholding.

from Part III

But ah! the shriek of African distress
Is not to Caribbean Isles confin'd.
I hear it echoed thro' Columbia's plains
And wilds immeasureable. Can it be?
Sure, 'tis some strange illusion on the ear!
Can those, who in the cause of Liberty
Life's noblest channels emptied, claim a right
To drain the cistern of a Negro's heart
In Slavery's constant waste? . . .

. . . Can the righteous Lord
Delight in aught but justice? This alone
Exalts a nation; sin a foul reproach
To any people, to whatever height
Of glory rais'd. Far greater now your guilt
This trade in tolerating, than before,
Its wickedness unthought of, unexplor'd,
And its extent unknown. The piteous cry
Of wretched Africans is Nature's voice
To you as parents; nay, the voice of God
To you as children of one common sire.
　　Oh! for one moment of compassion, deem
These as your sons, from your embraces torn,
Dragg'd to a distant land, in fetters bound,
With toil and hunger wasted, beaten, lash'd,
And often murder'd with impunity!
What poignancy of anguish would ye feel!
What would ye not for their deliverance dare?
Your sons they are, while of this empire wide
Ye are the common parents, bound to reach

To every suffering child your equal arm.
The time may be, when ev'n your natural sons,
Your hope, joy, pride, perpetual, dearer selves
May under merciless oppressors groan.
Ah! could ye see it, what then would ye wish
To Negroes ye had done; for ever lost
The glorious opportunity? At once
The cry of African and Indian blood
Your walls re-echo; nay, it Heav'n hath reach'd,
And if your ears ye stop, shall vengeance dread
And sudden on your guilty heads bring down
From its impartial bar.

(1789)[226]

FRANK SAYERS (1763–1817)

Described by his biographer as "a zealous friend" to the abolition movement, Sayers abandoned his medical career to pursue philosophy and poetry. He published works of literary criticism and metaphysics (influenced by Hartley), as well as plays and poems. Among his earliest efforts was the following song, first published in a Norwich newspaper and later revised and reprinted, under the title "The Dying African," in several collected editions of his writings down through the 1820s. The adoption of a slave's voice and the welcoming of death as relief from suffering are typical of what had almost become its own genre of sentimental poetry.

The Dying African

On my toil-wither'd limbs sickly languors are shed,
And the dark mists of death o'er my eye-lids are spread;
Before my last sufferings how gladly I bend,
For the strong arm of death is the arm of a friend.

Against the hot breezes hard struggles my breast,
Slow, slow, beats my heart, and I hasten to rest;
No longer shall anguish my faint bosom rend,
For the strong arm of death is the arm of a friend.

No more shall I sink in the deep-scorching air,
No more shall sharp hunger my weak body tear,
No more on my limbs shall keen lashes descend,
For the strong arm of death is the arm of a friend.

Ye ruffians, who tore me from all I held dear,
Who mock'd at my wailings, and smil'd at my tear,
Now, now shall I 'scape—every torture shall end,
For the strong arm of death is the arm of a friend.

(c. 1789–90)[227]

JAMES FIELD STANFIELD
(d. 1824)

An Irishman educated in Roman Catholic seminaries in France, Stanfield went to sea rather than enter the priesthood. Having shipped aboard a slave-trading vessel, he endured a series of terrifying, life-threatening experiences at sea and ashore in Africa. By the time he returned to England, he was one of only three survivors from the original crew. Stanfield went on to pursue a career as an actor and writer in England, while also joining the abolitionist cause and becoming friends with such figures as Thomas Clarkson (after whom he named his son).

The following passages are taken from Stanfield's epic of several hundred lines, *The Guinea Voyage*, complete with an opening invocation of the muse and all the heroic apparatus. Into the familiar saga of misery on the middle passage, Stanfield introduces a heart-wrenching dramatic climax: the birth of a baby amid the squalor and degradation of the slave decks. The closing refrain of "How long . . . How long . . . ?" has resonances both with biblical language and with the Negro spirituals that would emerge in the nineteenth century.

from The Guinea Voyage. A Poem. In Three Books
from "Book the First"

> Come then, O heav'nly Muse! with Sybil-bough,
> Lead thro' the horrors of these scenes of woe:
> Support the fainting weakness that recoils
> At well-known griefs, and long-supported toils . . .
> Help me to paint the melancholy view,
> The dismal track of ocean to pursue,
> And with the Eagle-eye of Truth pervade
> All the dark mazes of th' *inhuman Trade*.

from "Book the Third"

> Pack'd in close misery, the reeking crowd,
> Sweltering in chains, pollute the hot abode.

In painful rows with studious art comprest,
Smoking they lie, and breathe the humid pest:
Moisten'd with gore, on the hard platform ground,
The bare-rubb'd joint soon bursts the painful bound . . .
Nor can they turn to an exchange of pains,
Prest in their narrow cribs, and girt with chains,
Th' afflictive posture all relief denies,
Recruiting sleep the squalid mansion flies,
In one long groan the feeble throng unite;
One strain of anguish wastes the lengthen'd night. . . .

Hark! from yon lodge in many a wounding groan
A lab'ring fair one raise the feeble moan!
Swift to the darksome cell the females fly,
To still the tumult of th' expected cry:
Join the deep woe with one combin'd exclaim;
As pangs maternal shake her drooping frame.
Heav'ns! what a mansion for the tender woes,
The painful travail partial nature throws
Upon the gentler sex—When lenient art
And soothing care should cheer the fainting heart,
Here, with dejected wretchedness enclos'd
To brutal hands and impious eyes expos'd,
Her sacred sorrows the sad crisis press,
Occurrent horrors, premature distress,
Spread with foul clouds the inauspicious ray,
That opes the new-born victim's doleful day! . . .

    Immortal King! in whose impartial eye,
Nor clime, nor realm superior state enjoy.
No worm-rais'd station warps thy just decree,
No tinctur'd skin's a prejudice to thee;
But to thy sov'reign care the various frame
Of men and nations finds an equal claim!
How long with thou th' ascending cries withstand!
How long retain the thunder in thine hand?

                (1789)[228]

JOANNA BAILLIE (1762–1851)

A prolific dramatist and poet, from an accomplished Scottish family, Baillie didn't begin publishing until she moved to London in the 1780s. Later famous for her "plays on the passions" and involved with charitable projects over much of her career, she included these two poems "for Negro children" in her first book, *Fugitive Verses* (c. 1790). They seem to have been written for use in colonial missionary schools, perhaps commissioned by the same organization that in the 1820s enlisted her to compose works for British schools in Ceylon.

School Rhymes for Negro Children

How happy are we in that hour we love,
When shadows grow longer and branches move;
Blithe urchins then we be!
From the school's low porch, with a joyous shout,
We rush and we run and we gambol about,
So careless, light, and free!
And the good child merrily plays his part,
For all is well in his guileless heart,
The glance of his eye is bright.
We hop and we leap and we toss the ball;
Some dance to their shadows upon the wall,
And spread out their hands with delight.
The parrot that sits on her bough a-swinging,
The bird and the butterfly, light air winging,
Are scarcely more happy, I trow.
Then hey for the meadow, the glade, and the grove,
For evening is coming and branches move,
We'll have merry pastime now!

(wr. c. 1790/pub. 1851)[229]

Devotional Song for a Negro Child

When at rising morn we lave
Our dark limbs in the shiny wave,
When beneath the palm-tree shade
We rest awhile in freshness laid,
And, when our early task is done,
Whom should we love to think upon?
When we noonday slumber take,
In grassy glade or bowery brake,
Where humming birds come glancing by,
And stingless snakes untwisted lie,
And quietly sounds the beetle's drone,
Whom should we love to think upon?
When, all awake, we shout and sing,
And dance and gambol in a ring,
Or, healthful hunger to relieve,
Our stated wholesome meals receive,—
When this is past and day is done,
Whom should we love to think upon?
On God, the giver of all good,
Who gives us life, and rest, and food,
And cheerful pastime, late and early,
And parents kind who love us dearly;—
God hath our hearts with goodness won,
Him will we love to think upon!

(wr. c. 1790/pub. 1851)[230]

Baillie contrived to introduce an African character—Ohio, apparently a former slave who aids prisoners—into one of her verse dramas, although the play is set in Germany, near the Polish border. The following is from one of Ohio's blank verse speeches.

from Act V, scene 2, Rayner

Ohio ["A negro attached to the prison"]:
Thou hast loved negroes' blood, I warrant thee.
Dost sleep? ay, they will waken thee ere long,
And cut thy head off. They'll put thee to rest;
They'll close thine eyes for thee without thy leave;
They'll bloat thy white skin for thee, lily-face.
Come, less harm will I do thee than thy fellows:
My sides are cold: a dead man needs no cloak.

(1804)[231]

THOMAS DERMODY (1775–1802)

Born in County Clare, Ireland, the son of a drunken schoolmaster, Dermody was a precocious scholar and poet who in his teens ran away to Dublin. He struggled as a writer, enjoyed a period of carousing and dissipation, became a soldier, and died at twenty-seven, worn out in body and mind. Among the poems he managed to publish is this lyric tribute to African slaves. Heavily indebted to Gray's "Elegy," the poem explores the unrealized potential of slaves in life and their ultimate vindication, after death, as moral superiors to whites.

from "On a Dead Negro"

At length the tyrant stays his iron rod,
At length the iron rod can hurt no more;
The slave soft slumbers 'neath this verdant sod,
And all his years of misery are o'er.
Perchance, his soul was framed of finest mould,
His heart to goodness feelingly aspir'd;
Perchance, strong sense his every word controul'd,
And glow'd his breast with heat seraphic fir'd.
Perchance his deeds bely'd his sable hue,
And every sentiment deserv'd a throne:
But labour hid him from the general view,
And fell oppression mark'd him for her own.
O'er his low grave no tender parents weep,
Nor widow wails his loss, by all forgot;
No friends sincere their holy vigils keep,
Nor infant fingers deck the mournful spot.
Yet, far more honour'd his unsculptur'd tomb,
More sacred far than all the vaulted great;
Unwonted brightness clears his parting gloom,
And Heav'n approving smiles upon his state.
Nor thou with supercilious look deride

This votive strain, or his rough state despise;
How vain thy vaunting, impotent thy pride!
Behold him, thy superior in the skies.
Though learning fled his rude untutor'd mind,
And all the superfluities of art;
Though to his form the graces ne'er inclined,
His were the beauties of the head and heart.

(c. 1790)[232]

The following excerpt is from an elegy Dermody wrote in honor of John Howard (1726–1790), the famous prison reformer. Dermody lauds the dead man's special sympathy for slaves, born of Howard's own ordeal as a prisoner of war in 1756, as he indicts Britain for participating in the slave trade and enjoying luxuries produced by slave labor.

from "The Death of Howard"

The poor black that toils
From morn to eve, and with a heavy heart
Perceives the bondage of that day undone,
Ah! doom'd to linger out the night in chains,
And starting frantic from his moody dreams,
Feel the rough iron fester in his soul!
He felt thy bounty too; thy gen'rous heart
Repaid his sorrows, and thy plaintive groan
Bemoan'd that he was born to be a slave!
Ah, sad refinement! can a fairer skin
Bear less tormenting than the negro-train?
Have not their bosoms felt some kindred pang
For wives, and dearest children left behind,
To the rude mercy of the planter's soul!
Then why not Britain heave the gen'rous sigh,
At Indian slav'ry! ah! that she would weep
At their long woes, and make the ruffian train
That pamper lux'ry with the negro's toil,
In dire atonement pay with tears of blood!
Then would th' oppress'd uprear their drooping head,
And India's Genius, on his crystal car,
Proclaim his long, long suff'ring sons were free.
Such meed, by mild-repenting Britain paid,
Would fill the land with long-lost ecstacy,
And soothe the sorrows of her Howard's ghost!

(c. 1790)[233]

CHARLES DUNSTER (1750–1816)

An Oxford-educated cleric and man of letters, Dunster wrote an early satire on the artificiality and foppery of fashionable London life. In this excerpt, Dunster depicts a laughably ostentatious "lady" accompanied by her black servant, the latter as much a material display of her wealth as her dress and carriage.

from St. James's Street

         Before them onward march
In Garb of State, with each his lofty Cane,
His fierce-cock'd Hat, and Bouquet blooming bright,
Their powder'd Footmen.——Sometimes at their head,
Index of Rank or Opulence supreme,
A sable Youth from Ethiopia's climes,
In milk-white Turban dight, precedes the Train.——
The Fair herself, in narrow compass press'd,
(While much of outward ornament her Chair
Boasts, not unconscious of its Tassels gay,
Its jetty Varnish, and gilt Coronets
Which shine o' th' top), in posture comfortless
Rides pinion'd, while her Hoop's reverted sides
With whalebone strong her elbows cramp'd confine.
                     (1790)[234]

JOHN MARRIOTT (1762–1797)

A Lancashire native raised in a Quaker home (his mother was a well-known Quaker preacher) and educated in Greek and Latin, Marriott was a religious man who reportedly wrote verse only for his private use and reflection. Contemporaries report that as he lay dying, he burned much of his manuscript poetry. He left behind a young widow and an infant child, and a clutch of poems published posthumously by his friends in 1803.

In these excerpts from a long sentimental poem, Marriott imagines an idealized young woman, "Mialma," raised in the wild, her parents having fled the slave-catching territory to live in the desert. One day the innocent Mialma discovers a fugitive African man who is desperately fleeing the "man-stealers" and, after initial hesitation, offers him shelter. Although the poem and the incipient love story were left unfinished, Marriott managed to convey his deep sense of equality between the races.

from "Mialma; or, A Description of Some of the Miseries Resulting to the Inhabitants of Africa, from the Traffick in Men Carried on by the Europeans"

Mialma was born in a glen,
    Adjoining a desert of sand,
For fear of the stealers of men,
    Her parents had left their own land;
They had left a sweet country behind,
    And made their abode in a den,
But lions they do not much mind,
    Who fly from the stealers of men.

Mialma was fond, from a child,
    In speed with the swiftest to vie,
And somewhat untutored and wild
    Was visible oft in her eye,

Yet had she a bosom replete
   With feminine tenderness true,
And innocence made it her feat,
   Regardless of climate and hue . . .

The blackest of fruits are preferred
   To the fairest of profitless blooms;—
The blackbird's a favourite bird,
   But his merit is not in his plumes.—
And has not the spirit that sighs
   In a bosom of duskiest hue,
A judge as discerning and wise,
   Ye tyrants of Europe, as you? . . .

A moment he questioned her eyes,
   But quickly his doubting was o'er,
Subdued by a melting surprise,
   He never had witnessed before:
"O! Suffer the wretch thou surveyest
   Thy tenderest pity to claim,
I am seeking some desolate waste
   Where fetters and flames never came.

The steps of the beast in the shade
   I noted, and smiled at the sign,
But trust me, thou beautiful maid,
   I shrunk, when I happened on thine;
The lioness does not enslave,
   She kills, but it is not for gain;
I am not afraid of the grave,
   My terrour is merciless men!

I have baffled them—yes, in thy face
   Such beamings of goodness appear,
I see there is truth in this place;
   The christians have never been here. . . .

I am not afraid of the grave,
   But I cannot endure to be chained."
            (wr. c. 1790/pub. 1803)[235]

JOSEPH MATHER (1737–1804)

A working-class radical whose political poems circulated orally and in broadsheets, Mather achieved considerable fame (or notoriety) in Sheffield in the 1790s and early 1800s. In the following excerpt from a typical song of protest, Mather dramatizes the hardships of industrial workers by comparing them to those of African slaves. The poem thus marks the degree to which the conditions of New World slavery had entered the consciousness and political vocabulary of European workers, although they themselves had never observed it firsthand.

Song I. The File Hewer's Lamentation

I'm debtor to a many,
But cannot pay one penny;
Sure I've worse luck than any;
My traps are marked for sale.
My creditors may sue me,
The bailiffs may pursue me,
And lock me up in jail.
As negroes in Virginia,
In Maryland or Guinea,
Like them I must continue—
To be both bought and sold.
While negro ships are filling
I ne'er can save one shilling,
And must, which is more killing,
A pauper die when old.

(c. 1790)[236]

SUSANNA PEARSON (fl. 1780s)

A little-known provincial poet and convert to the Baptist faith, Pearson was a domestic servant in Sheffield. Her poems reflect her admiration for Anna Seward and the actress Sarah Siddons, as well as a strong taste for the conventional poetic idiom of the day. In her "African Tale," from which these stanzas are excerpted, Pearson presents a long, convoluted love story about the Africans Zarad and Zilea, and the suffering that the slave trade inflicts on them and their people. Despite the clichéd language, her poem is remarkable as an expression of sympathy by a working-class woman for African slaves.

from "An African Tale"

Sad near the creek the fetter'd wretches stand,
Who shrink from transient death to lingering woe,
And weep a final farewel to their land—
Dear scene of joys they ne'er again must know.

Onward the ruffians press to gain the bower,
And strive on Zarad's arm to lock the chain,
But vain the efforts of united power,
Till mortal wounds his manly bosom stain!

Fast streams the living crimson o'er the ground,
As his cold eye seeks an eternal shade,
While Zilea in still anguish bathes each wound,
And vainly lifts her swimming eyes for aid.

"No more my love," the gasping monarch cry'd,
"New lustre on my fluttering soul is shed—

We soon shall meet beyond the misty tide,*
In meads of bliss which tyrants never tread.

For them who cruel urge these horrid deeds,
Yet boast of finer souls, and gods more pure,
If, as their scene of youth and hope recedes,
When even riches shall no more allure;

If with their thoughts the dreadful past shall blend,
Afric will rise in tenfold terrors drest,
And with a wilder pang their bosoms rend,
Than that I feel"—he said and sunk to rest.

Save one faint shriek that pierc'd the sultry air,
Horror a momentary silence shed,
While Zilea breathless sunk beside his bier,
And her fair soul to milder regions fled.

"Dear native shades!" the parting wretches cry,
As the wide sails to rising breezes swell;
"Shades! where we lov'd to live, and hop'd to die,
Fair haunts of innocence and peace—farewel!"

Ah! sure for all that spot a charm can spread,
In which the soul's first faculties expand;
Dear to the negro is his leafy shed,
As to the Briton Albion's attic land.

Perhaps some hearts in that forlorn retreat,
Throbb'd with each virtue that refinement knows;
Some with the patriot's energies might beat,
Some melt with sympathy at friendship's woes.

For there are minds with innate beauty fraught,
On whom the arts ne'er shed their lovely light;
There are whom heavenly wisdom never taught,
That tread the paths of purity in night. . . .

Unhappy Africa! for whom in vain
Majestic nature spreads her various blooms,
Whose hunted sons from many a hostile train
Vainly seek shelter in thy thickest glooms;

---

* [Pearson's note:] The Negroes' ideas of futurity are various; some believe that their spirits
  will be conveyed to the banks of a famous inland river, where a god enquires into their past
  conduct, and if it be found unexceptionable he wafts them to the opposite shores of happiness
  and immortality.

For thee, the Muse, who loves to range thy clime,
Hear thy dread thunders down the desart hurl'd,
Stray 'mongst thy rocks where horror reigns sublime,
And shades immense! coeval with the world!

Fondly for thee, her rising hopes presage
The days are near, when all thy wrongs shall cease;
Thy sorrows, Charity's soft eye engage,
And anxious Mercy plans thy future peace.

(1790)[237]

JOSEPH SANSOM (1767–1826)

A Philadelphia Quaker from an affluent merchant family, Sansom was a painter, designer, patriot, and occasional writer. Interested in the new field of physiognomy, Sansom did artistic studies of Washington, Franklin, Madison, and other eminent Americans, published in his *Occasional Collection of Physiognomical Sketches, Chiefly North Americans*. He also designed a series of medals in 1806–1807 to commemorate major events in American history, now known as "the Sansom medals."

Sansom is equally innovative in the antislavery poem excerpted below. Essentially a dramatic monologue by a pious Christian slave, the poem addresses the fundamental objection—expressed by an animist Maroon ("Ottowah") in lines 5–17—that Christianity is the religion of the oppressor. In his systematic defense of Christianity, Sansom distinguishes between the sinfulness of nominal Christians who participate in the slave trade and the ideals of true Christianity. He reinforces his argument by invoking a long list of white Christian opponents of slavery, past and present, including George Fox, Richard Baxter, Morgan Godwyn, William Burling, Samuel Sewall, John Woolman, Anthony Benezet, the Bishop of Gloucester, Granville Sharp, William Wilberforce, Thomas Clarkson, James Madison, Benjamin Franklin, the Marquis de Lafayette, and many others.

from A Poetical Epistle to the Enslaved Africans, in the Character of an Ancient Negro

Whose Oppressors slay them, and hold themselves not guilty.

Brethren by birth, and Partners in distress,
You may the CHRISTIAN'S GOD with patience bless.
May resignation calm your Souls to peace
While your wrongs lessen, and your rights increase.

415

Hark! an indignant MARO(O)N* thus replies:
"Is not ORIFA† pow'rful, good, and wise?
Must wretched OTTOWAH *that God* adore
Whose Followers dragg'd him from his native shore,
And still (inhuman, tyger-hearted Brood)
Prowl over Africa for Human Blood?
Is't not by his command, proud Christians say,
They Negroes kidnap, whip, torment, and slay,
As Executioners of wrath DIVINE
Commission'd to destroy our fated Line?
Say, do their boasted Testaments contain
Exclusive rights to wrong their Fellow-Men?"

Not so—Who good reject, and cherish evil,
Are of their father and their lord the Devil.
GOD, for the Father, chargeth not the Son:
Each shall account for what himself hath done.
And the New-Testament commandeth, "Do
   To others as ye would 'twere done to you." . . .

If colour (the imagin'd mark of CAIN)
Condemn our Race to glut the thirst of Gain . . .
A sun-burnt skin was sure a slender plea
To rob our Sires of life or liberty,
Though *still* deny'd to breathe their native air
Their wretched Offspring languish in despair.

Yet *early* in the awful name of GOD,
Fox testified against the unnat'ral fraud.
In forms divided, but in substance one,
BAXTER and GODWYN wrote in unison.
Bondage must not be endless, neither cruel,
Said they, and pious BURLING, and learn'd SEWALL,
And MANY more of grateful memory,
Whose gentle use prepared us to be free. . . .

COLUMBIA *use* had sear'd to Negro-groans,
And distant EUROPE heard not AFRIC's moans,

---

* [Sansom's note:] In several of the West India Islands large bodies of the abused Negroes
  have occasionally fled from their Oppressors, and taken refuge in the woods and mountains.
  They are called Maroons, and defend themselves from the Usurpers of their rights, with the
  considerable fierceness of desperation.
† [Sansom's note:] In the kingdom of Benin, on the coast of Guinea, the Negroes believe in an
  infinitely great and good Being, whom they call Orifa, affirming him to be the Creator of
  Heaven and Earth.

Until thy meeker spirit, WOOLMAN, rose,
Aiming to soften rather than oppose;
And thou, lov'd BENEZET, of kindred mind,
The World thy country, and thy Friends MANKIND.
Heav'n-born (now Heav'n return'd) awhile they strove,
Subduing enmity by faith and love.
Then mitred GLOUCESTER declar'd our Race,
Equals by Nature, and co-heirs of GRACE . . .

    But my glad Soul anticipates the day,
When Men no more on Fellow-Men shall prey,
Or dare—pretending *policy* and *fate*,
Divine and human laws to violate.
Three centuries our groans have pierc'd the Skies—
But bright'ning visions light my clouded eyes:
Religion and Philosophy unite
Our Minds t'enlighten, and our wrongs to right. . . .

    Meanwhile—in silence let us wait the hour
That shall to civil-life our Race restore—
And Oh! When Liberty's enchanting smile
Height'neth enjoyment and endeareth toil,
If we remember whence the blessing flows,
To GOD 'twill lead us, as from GOD it rose—
Who solemn inquisition makes for Blood,
And turns the rod o'th' Wicked from the Good.
To him let AFRIC's dusky Sons sing praise,
His works are marvellous and just his ways.
May Time's swift course the pleasing theme prolong,
And Children's Children still repeat the Song.
Nor be their names forgot (in free estate)
Whom Love first urg'd our cause to advocate;
Or theirs who now the generous plea inforce,
SHARP, RAYNAL, DE WARVILLE, and WILBERFORCE,
CLARKSON, who lives and labours but for us,
Sage NECKAR, PINKNEY, MIFFLIN, PORTEUS,
MADISON, PARRY, aged FRANKLIN, SCOT,
LA FAYETTE, MARSILLAC, and BOUDINOT–
Illustrious groupe—yet these are but a part
Of those engraven on my grateful heart,
In distant Climes, whom wond'ring Nations see
Bound in thy seraph-band, Philanthropy.
May philosophic Minds no more embrace

Those endless feuds which martyr half the Race,
But rather Concord and her train restore—
Echo the Rights of Men from shore to shore,
Strengthen the Weak—illuminate the Blind,
Reform—convert—and humanize Mankind;
Till CHRIST proclaim the CHRISTIAN JUBILEE,
Break every yoke, and set the Oppressed free—
Sheathe up, or to a ploughshare turn the sword,
Take to himself the pow'r, and reign king, priest, and LORD.

(1790)[238]

BENJAMIN BANNEKER
(1731–1806)

The foremost African American intellectual of the eighteenth century, Banneker was born in Maryland to parents who were both free blacks, though themselves the children of African slaves. Remarkably, Banneker's paternal grandparents were a self-made white woman, formerly an indentured convict, and an African prince whom she had bought from a Guinea ship, later manumitted, and then married. A brilliant and precocious student, Banneker became an accomplished astronomer, mathematician, compiler of almanacs, and self-conscious exemplar of racial equality. A generation of abolitionists held Banneker up as the living refutation of racism, although some observers, such as Thomas Jefferson, while publicly polite, remained inwardly unmoved.

This first poem, composed in 1791, circulated only in manuscript in the 1790s. Banneker sent it, along with a copy of his famous antislavery letter to Jefferson, to abolitionist friends in the hope that both texts would be printed. The letter and Jefferson's ambivalent reply were published in 1793, but for unknown reasons the poem was not included and did not appear in print until 1989.

[Untitled]

Behold ye Christians! and in pity see
Those Afric sons which Nature formed free;
Behold them in a fruitful country blest,
Of Nature's bounties see them rich possest,
Behold them here from town by cruel force,
And doomed to slavery without remorse,
This act, America, thy sons have known;
This cruel act, relentless have they done.
                    (wr. 1791/pub. 1989)[239]

The following mathematical verses evince Banneker's playful side, but were significant to contemporaries as further evidence of the intellectual abilities of blacks.

A Mathematical Problem in Verse

A Cooper and Vintner sat down for a talk,
Both being so groggy, that neither could walk,
Says Cooper to Vintner, "I'm the first of my trade,
There's no kind of vessel, but what I have made,
And of any shape, Sir,—just what you will,—
And of any size, Sir,—from a ton to a gill!"
"Then," says the Vintner, "you're the man for me,—
Make me a vessel, if we can agree.
The top and the bottom diameter define,
To bear that proportion as fifteen to nine,
Thirty-five inches are just what I crave,
No more and no less, in the depth, will I have;
Just thirty-nine gallons this vessel must hold,—
Then I will reward you with silver or gold,—
Give me your promise, my honest old friend?"
"I'll make it tomorrow, that you may depend!"
So the next day the Cooper his work to discharge,
Soon made the new vessel, but made it too large;—
He took out some staves, which made it too small,
And then cursed the Vessel, the Vintner and all.
He beat on his breast, "By the Powers !"—he swore,
He never could work at his trade any more.
Now my worthy friend, find out, if you can,
The vessel's dimensions and comfort the man!

(c. 1793–96)[240]

ANNA LETITIA BARBAULD
(1743–1825)

Daughter of the educator John Aikin, Barbauld became an accomplished teacher, critic, and poet in her own right. Among her literary friends and acquaintances were many who also wrote against slavery, including Samuel Johnson, Joanna Baillie, Hannah More, Frank Sayers, William Roscoe, James Montgomery, and William Wordsworth. A passionate antislavery activist, Barbauld wrote this poem in response to the defeat of Wilberforce's Abolition Bill in 1791. Framed in the rhyming couplets she preferred, hers was one of the first voices to encourage the abolition movement to regroup and renew its campaign.

from Epistle to William Wilberforce, Esq., on the Rejection of the Bill for Abolishing the Slave Trade

Cease, Wilberforce, to urge thy generous aim!
Thy Country knows the sin, and stands the shame!
The Preacher, Poet, Senator in vain
Has rattled in her sight the Negro's chain;
With his deep groans assail'd her startled ear,
And rent the veil that hid his constant tear;
Forc'd her averted eyes his stripes to scan,
Beneath the bloody scourge laid bare the man,
Claim's Pity's tear, urg'd Conscience' strong controul,
And flash'd conviction on her shrinking soul. . . .
She knows and she persists—Still Afric bleeds,
Uncheck'd, the human traffic still proceeds;
She stamps her infamy to future time,
And on her harden'd forehead seals the crime.
    In vain, to thy white standard gathering round,
Wit, Worth, and Parts and Eloquence are found . . .
Where seasoned tools of Avarice prevail,
A Nation's eloquence, combined, must fail:

Each flimsy sophistry by turns they try;
The plausive argument, the daring lye,
The artful gloss, that moral sense confounds,
Th'acknowledged thirst of gain that honour wounds:
Bane of ingenuous mind th'unfeeling sneer,
Which, sudden, turns to stone the falling tear:
They search assiduous, with inverted skill,
For forms of wrong, and precedents of ill;
With impious mockery wrest the sacred page,
And glean up crimes from each remoter age:
Wrung Nature's tortures, shuddering, while you tell,
From scoffing fiends bursts forth the laugh of hell;
In Britain's senate, Misery's pangs give birth
To jests unseemly, and to horrid mirth—
Forbear!—thy virtues but provoke our doom,
And swell th'account of vengeance yet to come;
For, not ummark'd in Heaven's impartial plan,
Shall man, proud worm, contemn his fellow-man?
And injur'd Afric, by herself redrest,
Darts her own serpents at her Tyrant's breast. . . .

Friends of the friendless—Hail, ye generous band!
Whose efforts yet arrest Heav'n's lifted hand,
Around whose steady brows, in union bright,
The civic wreath, and Christian's palm unite:
Your merit stands, no greater and no less,
Without, or with the varnish of success;
For ye have sav'd yourselves—and that is all.
Succeeding times your struggles, and their fate,
With mingled shame and triumph shall relate,
While faithful History, in her various page,
Marking the features of this motley age,
To shed a glory, and to fix a stain,
Tells how you strove, and that you strove in vain.

                                        (1791)[241]

WILLIAM LISLE BOWLES
(1762–1850)

An important forerunner of Romanticism who influenced Coleridge and Words-
worth, Bowles was educated at Oxford before starting a long career as a clergy-
man, social reformer, and writer. He published works on theology, literature,
social issues, and antiquarianism, as well as volumes of poetry. He addressed the
issue of slavery repeatedly over his career, as in the poems excerpted below.

The first uses a deathbed scene to explore the African belief that after death,
slaves would be restored to their homelands. The theme recurs so frequently in
eighteenth-century poetry about slavery that it could almost be read as a reflec-
tion on the Christian belief in a celestial afterlife—the latter accepted unques-
tioningly, the former usually viewed as superstitious.

from "The African"

Afric's injur'd son expiring lay,
His forehead cold, his labouring bosom bare,
His dewy temples, and his sable hair,
His poor companions kiss'd, and cried aloud,
Rejoicing, whilst in peace his head he bow'd:—
"Now thy long, long task is done,
Swiftly, brother, wilt thou run,
Ere to-morrow's golden beam
Glitters on thy parent-stream,
Swiftly the delights to share,
The feast of joy which waits thee there:
Swiftly, brother, wilt thou ride
O'er the long and stormy tide,
Fleeter than the hurricane,
Till thou view those scenes again,
Where thy father's hut was rear'd,

Where thy mother's voice was heard;
Where thy infant brothers play'd
Beneath the fragrant citron's shade . . .
Where the dance, the festive song,
Of many a friend divided long,
Doom'd through stranger lands to roam,
Shall bid thy spirit welcome home! . . .
   Fear not now the tyrant's power—
Past is his insulting hour—
Mark no more the sullen trait
On slavery's brow of scorn and hate;
Hear no more the long sigh borne
Murmuring on the gales of morn! . . .
   Tell our brethren, when ye meet,
Thus we toil with weary feet;
Yet tell them that love's gen'rous flame,
In joy, in wretchedness, the same,
In distant worlds was ne'er forgot—
And tell them that we murmur not—
Tell them, though the pang will start,
And drain the life-blood from the heart—
Tell them, generous shame forbids
The tear to stain our burning lids!
Tell them, in weariness and want
For our native hills we pant,
Where soon, from shame and sorrow free,
We hope in death to follow thee."
               (wr. 1791/pub. 1794)[242]

Here Bowles includes the abolition of slavery in his broader vision of en-lightened reforms necessary for Britain's future.

from "The Sylph of Summer"

        But temperate airs are thine,
England; and as thy climate, so thy sons
Partake the temper of thine isle, not rude,
Nor soft, voluptuous, or effeminate;
Sincere, indeed, and hardy, as becomes
Those who can lift their look elate, and say,
"We strike for injur'd Freedom;" and yet mild,
And gentle, when the voice of Charity

Pleads like a voice from Heav'n: and, thanks to God,
The chain, that fetter'd Afric's groaning race,
The murd'rous chain, that, link by link, dropp'd blood,
Is sever'd; we have lost that foul reproach
To all our virtuous boast!

(wr. c.1801/pub. 1809)[243]

Like his admirer Coleridge, Bowles did not abandon the abolition cause even during the years when hope was low. Thirteen years after Wilberforce's first abolition bill was defeated (in 1791), Bowles continued to remind the public of slavery's moral ugliness, in these lines.

from The Spirit of Discovery

Such are thy views, Discovery! the great world
Rolls to thine eye reveal'd; to Thee the Deep
Submits its awful empire; Industry
Awakes, and Commerce to the echoing marts
From East to West unweary'd pours her wealth.
Man walks sublimer; and Humanity,
Matur'd by social intercourse, more high,
More animated, lifts her sov'reign mien,
And waves her golden sceptre. Yet the heart
Asks trembling, is no evil found? O turn,
Meek Charity, and drop a human tear
For the sad fate of Afric's injur'd sons,
And hide, for ever hide, the sight of chains,
Anguish, and bondage! Yes, the heart of man
Is sick, and Charity turns pale, to think
How soon, for pure religion's holy beam,
Dark crimes, that sully'd the sweet day, pursu'd,
Like vultures, the Discov'rer's ocean tract.

(1804)[244]

FRANCIS GARDEN, LORD GARDENSTONE (1721–1793)

A distinguished jurist, landowner, philanthropist, and man of letters, Gardenstone was a leading figure of the Scottish Enlightenment. Known for his wit, benevolence, and eccentricity (he had "an extreme fondness for pigs"), Gardenstone spent many years and much money developing a model village for his tenants, including a library, a museum, and a scheme to diversify the local economy. In 1778, Lord Justice Gardenstone voted with the majority in the Joseph Knight decision of the Court of Session, by which Scotland became the first nation in Europe to abolish slavery by judicial decree. His views on slavery, and on European colonialism in general, emerge with considerable force in this poem he published near the end of his life.

from "Horace [Book] I, Ode iii. Imitated"

Columbus first, and Gama led the way,
And wasted empires all their toil repay;
Who has not heard what more than wonted crimes
Have damn'd our conquests in the western climes.
Let blushing history with tears attest,
That Cuba's sons were once completely blest;
Unknown to care, they danc'd their time away,
And every wish was innocent and gay.
But when our pirates on their coast appear'd,
And Murther's cry the helpless victims heard,
Then welcome death allow'd a quick release,
The new made wilderness was hush'd to peace,
The proud oppressor sheath'd his reeking blade,
And Rapine mourn'd the waste herself had made.
   Nor let old England with absurd disdain,
For deeds like these insult atrocious Spain;
Since, in the task of scourging human kind,
Calm Truth can hardly rank us far behind. . . .

FRANCIS GARDEN

And sure since heaven is just, the western skies
Shall see, ere long, some Spartacus arise,
To bid our slaves the Christian yoke disown,
And seize the land they labour as their own;
Behold the hero burst Oppression's bands,
The blood of ruffians reeking on his hands;
Hark how he echoes Freedoms honour'd name,
And boasts how vict'ry vindicates his claim.
See round their chief the jetty nation throngs;
What horrid vengeance answers all their wrongs.
Extermination steeps the trembling shore;
Europa's robbers lift the lash no more.
Vindictive Justice sweeps the race away;
Our toil of ages perish'd in a day.

(1791)[245]

ROBERT SOUTHEY (1774–1843)

Though now eclipsed by his friends Wordsworth and Coleridge, Southey was in his day a leading literary figure, publishing to great acclaim (and controversy), and becoming Poet Laureate in 1813. Bristol-born, educated at Westminster and Oxford, Southey pursued a career of radical politics and prolific professional writing. Although later in life he reverted to more traditional views on religion and politics, he never lost his antislavery fervor. The several poems below, spanning two decades, are a tiny subset of his literary output, but they mark him as one of the most imaginative and unrelenting foes of slavery in his time.

First is an excerpt from an extraordinary gothic poem, written when Southey was seventeen, that foreshadows elements of Coleridge's "Ancient Mariner." Without warning, the poem suddenly concludes with a curse on slavery and a call for insurrection.

from "To Horror"

Horror! I call thee yet once more!
Bear me to that accursed shore,
Where on the stake the Negro writhes.
Assume thy sacred terrors then! dispense
The gales of Pestilence!
Arouse the opprest; teach them to know their power;
Lead them to vengeance! and in that dread hour
When ruin rages wide,
I will behold and smile by Mercy's side.

(1791)[246]

Southey wrote these sonnets in the early 1790s to assess "past and present prospects" for the abolition of the slave trade. Lamenting the defeat of Wilberforce's first efforts by the "Slave Merchants," Southey predicts that slavery would only be ended by "the introduction of East-Indian or Maple Sugar, or by the just and general rebellion of the Negroes." Miltonic both in choice of poetic form and in the supernatural grandeur of the language, Southey's sonnets are powerful both politically and aesthetically.

[Sonnet sequence] "On the Slave Trade"
Sonnet I

Hold your mad hands! for ever on your plain
Must the gorged vulture clog his beak with blood?
For ever must your Niger's tainted flood
Roll to the ravenous shark his banquet slain?
Hold your mad hands! what daemon prompts to rear
The arm of Slaughter? on your savage shore
Can hell-sprung Glory claim the feast of gore,
With laurels water'd by the widow's tear
Wreathing his helmet crown? lift high the spear!
And like the desolating whirlwinds sweep,
Plunge ye yon bark of anguish in the deep;
For the pale fiend, cold-hearted Commerce there
Breathes his gold-gender'd pestilence afar,
And calls to share the prey his kindred Daemon War.

(wr. 1791/pub. 1794)

Sonnet II

Why dost thou beat thy breast and rend thine hair,
And to the deaf sea pour thy frantic cries?
Before the gale the leaden vessel flies;
The Heavens all-favoring smile, the breeze is fair;
Hark to the clamors of the exulting crew!
Hark how their thunders mock the patient skies!
Why dost thou shriek and strain thy red-swoln eyes
As the white sail dim lessens from thy view?
Go pine in want and anguish and despair,
There is no mercy found in human-kind—
Go Widow to thy grave and rest thee there!
But may the God of Justice bid the wind
Whelm that curst bark beneath the mountain wave,
And bless with Liberty and Death the Slave!

(wr. 1791/pub. 1794)

Sonnet III

Oh he is worn with toil! the big drops run
Down his dark cheek; hold—hold thy merciless hand,

429

Pale tyrant! for beneath thy hard command
O'erwearied Nature sinks. The scorching Sun,
As pityless as proud Prosperity,
Darts on him his full beams; gasping he lies
Arraigning with his looks the patient skies,
While that inhuman trader lifts on high
The mangling scourge. Oh ye who at your ease
Sip the blood-sweeten'd beverage! thoughts like these
Haply ye scorn: I thank thee Gracious God!
That I do feel upon my cheek the glow
Of indignation, when beneath the rod
A sable brother writhes in silent woe.

(wr. 1791/pub. 1794)

Sonnet IV

'Tis night; the mercenary tyrants sleep
As undisturb'd as Justice! but no more
The wretched Slave, as on his native shore,
Rests on his reedy couch: he wakes to weep!
Tho' thro' the toil and anguish of the day
No tear escap'd him, not one suffering groan
Beneath the twisted thong, he weeps alone
In bitterness; thinking that far away
Tho' the gay negroes join the midnight song,
Tho' merriment resounds on Niger's shore,
She whom he loves far from the chearful throng
Stands sad, and gazes from her lowly door
With dim grown eye, silent and woe-begone,
And weeps for him who will return no more.

(wr. 1791/pub. 1794)

Sonnet V

Did then the bold Slave rear at last the Sword
Of Vengeance? drench'd he deep its thirsty blade
In the cold bosom of his tyrant lord?
Oh! who shall blame him? thro' the midnight shade
Still o'er his tortur'd memory rush'd the thought
Of every past delight; his native grove,
Friendship's best joys, and Liberty and Love,
All lost for ever! then Remembrance wrought
His soul to madness; round his restless bed
Freedom's pale spectre stalk'd, with a stern smile

Pointing the wounds of slavery, the while
She shook her chains and hung her sullen head:
No more on Heaven he calls with fruitless breath,
But sweetens with revenge, the draught of death.

(wr. 1791/pub. 1794)

Sonnet VI

High in the air expos'd the Slave is hung
To all the birds of Heaven, their living food!
He groans not, tho' awaked by that fierce Sun
New torturers live to drink their parent blood!
He groans not, tho' the gorging Vulture tear
The quivering fibre! hither gaze O ye
Who tore this Man from Peace and Liberty!
Gaze hither ye who weigh with scrupulous care
The right and prudent; for beyond the grave
There is another world! and call to mind,
Ere your decrees proclaim to all mankind
Murder is legalized, that there the Slave
Before the Eternal, "thunder-tongued shall plead
Against the deep damnation of your deed."

(wr. 1791/pub. 1794)[247]

In this anti-imperialist ode, Southey exerts almost incantatory force in calling on the "genius" or animating spirit of Africa to rise up and "avenge thy children's wrong."

from "To the Genius of Africa"

Ah linger not to hear the song!
Genius avenge thy children's wrong!
The Daemon COMMERCE on your shore
   Pours all the horrors of his train,
And hark! where from the field of gore
   Howls the hyena o'er the slain!
Lo! where the flaming village fires the skies!
Avenging Power awake—arise!

Arise thy children's wrong redress!
Ah heed the mother's wretchedness
When in the hot infectious air
   O'er her sick babe she bows opprest-
Ah hear her when the Christians tear

431

The drooping infant from her breast!
Whelm'd in the waters he shall rest!
Hear thou the wretched mother's cries,
Avenging Power awake! arise!

By the rank infected air
That taints those dungeons of despair
By those who there imprison'd die
Where the black herd promiscuous lie,
By the scourges blacken'd o'er
And stiff and hard with human gore,
By every groan of deep distress
By every curse of wretchedness,
By all the train of Crimes that flow
From the hopelessness of Woe,
By every drop of blood bespilt,
By Afric's wrongs and Europe's guilt,
Awake! arise! avenge!

(1797)[248]

According to Southey's own note, this ballad is based on a true story. In addition to its own amazing and eery quality, the poem also invites us (as critics have noted) to read Coleridge's "Ancient Mariner" for its comparable, if submerged, antislavery psychology. Harkening back to the real experience of penitent slave traders like John Newton and others, the poem subtly, and presciently, probes the burden of white guilt.

from "The Sailor, Who Had Served in the Slave-Trade"*

"I have done a cursed thing!" he cried:
"It haunts me night and day;
And I have sought this lonely place
Here undisturb'd to pray.

Aboard I have no place for prayer,
So I came here alone,
That I might freely kneel and pray,
And call on Christ, and groan.

* [Southey's note:] In September, 1798, a Dissenting Minister of Bristol discovered a sailor in the neighbourhood of that City, groaning and praying in a cow-house. The circumstance which occasioned his agony of mind is detailed in the annexed ballad, without the slightest addition or alteration. By presenting it as a Poem the story is made more public, and such stories ought to be made as public as possible.

If to the main-mast head I go,
The Wicked One is there;
From place to place, from rope to rope,
He follows every where. . . .

O cursed, cursed is the deed!"
The wretched man replies,
"And night and day and every where
'Tis still before my eyes.

I sail'd on board a Guinea-man,
And to the slave-coast went; . . .
Would that the sea had swallow'd me
When I was innocent!

And we took in our cargo there,
Three hundred negro slaves,
And we sail'd homeward merrily
Over the ocean-waves.

But some were sulky of the slaves,
And would not touch their meat,
So therefore we were forced by threats
And blows to make them eat.

One woman, sulkier than the rest,
Would still refuse her food, . . .
O Jesus God! I hear her cries!
I see her in her blood!

The captain made me tie her up,
And flog while he stood by;
And then he cursed me if I staid
My hand to hear her cry.

She shriek'd, she groan'd, . . I could not spare,
For the Captain he stood by; . . .
Dear God! that I might rest one night
From that poor creature's cry!

What woman's child a sight like that
Could bear to look upon!
And still the Captain would not spare,
But made me still flog on.

She could not be more glad than I
When she was taken down:
A blessed minute! 'twas the last
That I have ever known!

I did not close my eyes all night,
Thinking what I had done;
I heard her groans, and they grew faint
Towards the rising sun.

She groan'd and moan'd, but her voice grew
Fainter at morning tide;
Fainter and fainter still it came
Until at noon she died.

They flung her overboard; poor wretch
She rested from her pain,
But when, O Christ! O blessed God!
Shall I have rest again?

I saw the sea close over her:
Yet she is still in sight;
I see her twisting every where;
I hear her day and night.

Go where I will, do what I can,
The Wicked One I see:
Dear Christ, have mercy on my soul!
O God, deliver me!

Oh, give me comfort, if you can!
Oh, tell me where to fly!
Oh, tell me if there can be hope
For one so lost as I!"

What said the Minister of Christ?
He bade him trust in Heaven,
And call on Him for whose dear sake
All sins shall be forgiven.

He told him of that precious blood
Which should his guilt efface;
Told him that none are lost but they
Who turn from proffered grace.

He bade him pray, and knelt with him,
And joined him in his prayers:
And some who read the dreadful tale
Perhaps will aid with theirs.

(wr. 1798/pub. 1799)[249]

These lines mark an historic moment: at the installation of Grenville as Chancellor of Oxford, Southey chooses—from all of his accomplishments—

Grenville's role in securing the abolition of the slave trade as his greatest achievement. In context and tone, Southey's poem thus differs dramatically from the personal and despairing utterances of so many antislavery writers before him.

from "Verses Spoken in the Theatre at Oxford, upon the Installation of Lord Grenville"

They
Who fear the Eternal's justice bless thy name,
Grenville, because the wrongs of Africa
Cry out no more to draw a curse from Heaven
On England; for if still the trooping sharks
Track by the scent of death the accursed ship
Freighted with human anguish, in her wake
Pursue the chase, crowd round her keel, and dart
Toward the sound contending, when they hear
The frequent carcass from her guilty deck
Dash in the opening deep, no longer now
The guilt shall rest on England . . .
                    The red-cross flag,
Redeemed from stain so foul, no longer now
Covereth the abomination.
                    This thy praise,
O Grenville! and, while nations roll away,
This shall be thy remembrance. . . .

Afric with all her tongues will speak of thee,
With Wilberforce and Clarkson, he whom Heaven
To be the apostle of this holy work
Raised up and strengthened, and upheld through all
His arduous toil. To end the glorious task,
That blessed, that redeeming deed was thine:
Be it thy pride in life, thy thought in death,
Thy praise beyond the tomb. . . .
                    Long ages hence,
Nations unborn, in cities that shall rise
Along the palmy coast, will bless thy name;
And Senegal and secret Niger's shore,
And Calabar, no longer startled then
With sounds of murder, will, like Isis now,
Ring with the songs that tell of Grenville's praise.
                    (1810)[250]

JOHN WALSH (?1725–1795)

From an early career in the East India Company, Walsh went on to become a member of Parliament and an award-winning scientist elected to the Royal Society. He was opposed to the slave trade and the lines below express his frustration at Parliament's defeat of Wilberforce's Abolition Bill in 1791. His verse is noteworthy not only for his passionate insistence that defenders of slavery should be ashamed, but for his refusal to present graphic details of the slave trade because they would be, he says, "too horrid for Poetical Language."

from An Elegy Occasioned by the Rejection of Mr. Wilberforce's Motion for the Abolition of the African Slave Trade

O *Wilberforce*! Thou Friend of human kind!
    My Heart with fervor would thy Goodness bless,
But that th'Emotions of my swelling Mind
    Are all too warm for Language to express.

Curse on the hateful Pow'r whose noxious breath
    Its taint infectious thro' the Senate blew;
Turning thy Words of Life to Threats of Death,
    While Avarice round its jaundic'd Terrors threw. . . .

Ye say they lead a Life of Joy and Peace;
    Your country's Children often feel a worse;
Oh that yourselves might taste their vaunted *Ease*,
    And feel awhile Oppression's Iron Curse:

Then should you blush your rude Barbarian Souls,
    Enshrin'd in vain Refinement's semblant Form,
Should learn to blush that they whom Fate controuls
    Are yet by Nature more humanely warm.

Then should ye blush, to call their Slavery Bliss;
　　Then should ye blush to call them rude and base;
Then should ye know what Nature's Feeling is,
　　And learn Compassion from the injured Race. . . .

When torn from Parents, Friends, and kindred Ties,
　　Must they not feel the agonizing Smart?
Must not the Drops which swell their streaming Eyes
　　Betray the Anguish of the bleeding Heart.

When they look back on all the Friends they leave;
　　When they behold them weeping on the Shore;
Do ye, as human Beings, then believe
　　They Friends nor Country agonized deplore?* . . .

The while not distant is, the joyful Time,
　　To Virtue sacred, and to Freedom dear,
Your manly Eloquence shall raise sublime
　　The pious Train who Nature's Voice revere.

Taught by your forceful Arguments to know;
　　Taught by your generous Ardency to feel,
The Nation's Bosom shall determin'd glow,
　　And one bold Effort our disgrace repeal. . . .

(1791)[251]

* [from Walsh's note:] It appeared in Evidence, that upon a Husband, Wife, and Child being kidnapped, they were all put in different Ships, merely to increase the pungency of their Sufferings. The Author had intended, in this Place, to have introduced a Description of the Method of stowing the slaves on board the Ships, in the passage to the West Indies; but the Description would be too horrid for Poetical Language. Suffice it to say, that 609 Slaves have been conveyed in one small Vessel, and that the Mortality during the Passage, is frequently one-fifth, or 20 per Cent.

ANONYMOUS

This ode in support of the Haitian revolution circulated in British periodicals for at least a decade after its first publication in 1792. Though it was easier to applaud an insurrection against the enemy French, the subject was still dangerous for a British writer to take on. Most remarkable is the fervor with which the African speakers embrace rebellion, incited by their god Whidah to "Bathe thy sword[s] in Christian blood!" Paradoxically, such radical utterances set back the Abolitionist cause in the 1790s by fanning fears of black violence and playing into the hands of racist defenders of slavery.

from "Ode. The Insurrection of the Slaves at St. Domingo"

Lowly sinks the ruddy sun,
Sheathe the blade, the war is done;
Cried Orrah, to his murderous band,
Who wearied stood on Cuba's strand.
But hark! what sound invades the ear?
Hark!—Sheathe the blade, no danger's near:
'Tis the gasp of parting breath,
'Tis the hollow voice of death,
'Tis the sigh, the groan of those,
Once our tyrants, once our foes. . . .
'Twas night, when bound in servile chains,
We sail'd from Afric's golden plains:
The moon had reach'd its utmost height,
Its orb disclos'd but half its light;
Darkling clouds hung o'er the deep,
And the hush'd murmurs seem'd to sleep.
Sudden floating in the skies
A shadowy cloud appear'd to rise;
Sudden gliding o'er the flood

ANONYMOUS

The dim-seen shade before me stood;
Through its form the moon's pale beam
Shed a faint, a sickly gleam;
Thrice its arm I saw it rear,
Thrice my mighty soul did fear.
The stillness dread a hollow murmur broke;—
It was the Genius groan'd; and lo!—it spoke!
"O, my troubled spirit sighs
When I hear my people's cries!
Now, the blood which swells their veins
Flows debas'd by servile chains:
Desert now my country lies;
Moss grown now my altars rise:
O, my troubled spirit sighs
When I hear my people's cries!
Hurry, Orrah, o'er the flood,
Bathe thy sword in Christian blood!
Whidah* will thy side protect;
Whidah will thy arm direct."
Low'ring frown'd the burden'd cloud,
Shrilly roar'd the whirlwind loud,
Livid lightnings gleam'd on high,
And big waves billow'd to the sky.
Astonish'd I, in wild affright,
Knew not 'twas vanish'd from my sight;
Whether on the storm it rode,
Or sunk beneath the troubled flood.
Again! along the beam-gilt tide,
Ah! see again the spirit glide!
It joins our triumph! on the sight
It bursts in majesty of light.
Mark! how it bows its wondrous head,
And hails our deed! Ah! see—'tis fled!
Now, now, ye cliffs, that frown around,
The echoes of our shouts resound,
While around the votive fire
We've sooth'd the spirit of our sire.

(wr. 1792/pub. 1797)[252]

* [Author's note:] The God whom the Africans on the Coast of Guinea worship.

ANONYMOUS

Appearing as it did in London's most popular magazine, this anonymous poem tells us something of the public's mood in 1792 despite the defeat of the Abolition Bill the year before. In six lyric stanzas, the poet conjures a planter's nightmare in which, Scrooge-like, he is visited by the ghosts of the slaves he has mistreated. Inspired by the true story of a slave suicide, the poem is also striking for its concluding threat of insurrection.

[Untitled]*

On his downy pillow lying,
    A rich Planter slumbering lay,
Yells, like tortur'd Negroes dying,
    Fill'd his heart with cold dismay.
On a sudden, all around him
    Troops of sable ghosts appear'd;
While his conscious fears confound him,
    These upbraiding sounds he heard:

"Cruel Christian! barbarous Briton!
    Who in thine own land wast free,
All the blessings which you pride on,
    Worse than fiend! you tore from me.

---

* [Author's note:] The following verses are founded on a real circumstance, of which the Author was informed by a respectable clergyman in Woodbridge, who had it of the Planter himself, whose slave the Negro was.—This gentleman, who was esteemed a humane good man by all his acquaintance went one day into the house where they were boiling sugar, and was informed by his Overseer that there was a slave who would not work. He ordered him to be whipped. Still he would not work. He was again punished. On which he said, "Massa, you flog me anymore, I die to-day." The Planter ordered his punishment to be renewed; when, to his horror, the slave immediately jumped into the boiling sugar, and perished.—Had this slave no feeling?

ANONYMOUS

In my country I was happy,
   Happy as thyself can be,
For my valour could defy
   Every savage beast but thee.

You stir up our thoughtless neighbours,
   With your liquors mad their brain;
They forsake their sports and labours,
   Cruel pillage to obtain:
Then, in darkness on us stealing,
   Set our wicker-walls on fire;
And you, Christian, more unfeeling,
   See those flames with joy aspire!

Think what tortures we endur'd,
   Wedg'd into a cursed hold,
Whipp'd, chain'd, thumb-screw'd—fast secur'd,
   Till to slavery we were sold!
Then, from each relation parted,
   Heat, and cold, and toil we bore;
Oft my back with scourging smarted,
   And my limbs were stain'd with gore.

Thus tormented, wild, despairing,
   Every hour my bosom wrung,
T'escape worse torture, blindly daring,
   O'er the cauldron's verge I sprung.
In the boiling sugar sinking,
   Cruel man! thou dids't me see;
But the cup thy slaves are drinking
   After death awaits for thee.

While the Planters are pursuing,
   From their cursed lust of gain,
A traffick, soon shall prove their ruin,
   And I vengeance shall obtain;
By fresh numbers dragg'd to slavery,
   They ere long will surely find
Negroes want not strength and bravery
   When for freedom they've a mind."

(1792)[253]

441

MARY BIRKETT (1774–1817)

This seventeen-year-old antislavery poet came from humble origins. Daughter of a candlemaker, she was brought to Dublin from England at the age of ten. A devout Quaker with radical views, Birkett emerges in this, her first major poem, as a critic of fashionable consumer society and as an early advocate of feminist involvement in political causes such as abolition. In the closing lines she urges consumer resistance to slave-produced goods and thus anticipates the boycott tactics of later activists in the antislavery and civil rights movements.

from A Poem on the African Slave Trade. Addressed to Her Own Sex

How little think the giddy and the gay
While sipping o'er the sweets of charming tea,
How oft with grief they pierce the manly breast,
How oft their lux'ry robs the wretch of rest,
And that to gain the plant we idly waste
Th'*extreme of human mis'ry* they must taste! . . .

There are, oh! scandal to the Christian name,
Who fierce of blood, and lost to sense of shame,
Dare lave their impious hands in human gore,
And barter living souls for lust of ore;
More rav'nous than the foulest beasts of prey,
They but from Nature's powerful craving slay;
More cruel than the thief, whose murd'rous knife
At once deprives the trembling wretch of life:
Him poverty, perchance, taught first to stray,
And strongly urg'd her too prevailing plea;
Yet him the justice of our laws condemn:
Beasts we destroy, but seldom think of them.
Strange paradox! we view with shrinking eye,

The murd'rer's crime, and bid him justly die;
But when our traders snatch a thousand lives,
No pain, no punishment on them derives;
The guilt's diminish'd, as increas'd its size,
And they are clear—at least in mortal eyes. . . .

There are, I know, who think and *more* who say,
That not so injur'd—so opprest are they;
That under masters *just* they earn their bread,
And plenty crowns the board at which they're fed.
Ah, sophist, vain thy subtle reas'ning's aim!
Look at the Negro's sun-burnt, grief-worn frame!
Examine well each limb, each nerve, each bone,
Each artery—and then observe *thy own;*
The beating pulse, the heart that throbs within,
All, (save the sable tincture of his skin,)
Say, Christians, do they not resemble you?
If so, their feelings and sensations too:
One moment now with you his burthen rest,
Then tell me, is he happy—is he blest? . . .

Oh, tyrants, what will then your anguish be,
When God and men shall your injustice see!
And trust me that important day will come,
Which fixes your irrevocable doom,
When all your basely murder'd slaves shall rise,
And publish all your crimes throughout the skies.
Here cease, oh Muse! nor dare the secret tell,
The dread event, which but with God must dwell. . . .

Now dead to hope they see resistance vain,
They in their manly breasts conceal their pain;
A silent grief to furious rage succeeds,
And by resentment stung—their whole soul bleeds.
Firm in despair their hands refuse the yoke,
We call them stubborn—and apply the stroke;
Their reeking backs the dire correction shew,
Yet they unmov'd, nor fear nor tremor know;
Their strength heroic claims a nobler name,
And shews not their's—but their oppressor's shame.
Say not, that if not humbled they rebel;
Tyrant! the cause, the guilt with thee must dwell;
For when they view the authors of their woe,
No wonder if fierce passion aims the blow!

They all their blasted hopes and comforts see,
Condemn'd to linger life in misery. . . .

Plant there our colonies, and to their soul,
Declare the God who form'd this boundless whole;
Improve their manners—teach them how to live,
To them the useful lore of science give;
So shall with us their praise and glory rest,
And we in blessing be supremely blest;
For 'tis a duty which we surely owe,
We to the Romans were what to us Afric now. . . .

Yes, sisters, yes, to us the task belongs,
'Tis we increase or mitigate their wrongs.
If we the produce of their toils refuse,
If we no more the blood-stain'd lux'ry choose;
If from our lips we push the plant away
For which the liberties of thousands pay,
Of thousands once as blest, and born as free,
And nurs'd with care, (tho' not so soft,) as we.
If in benev'lence *firm*, we this can dare,
And in our brethrens sufferings hold no share,
In no small part their long-borne pangs will cease,
And we to souls unborn may whisper peace.

$$(1792)^{254}$$

ROBERT BURNS (1759–1796)

The famous Scottish poet's response to slavery was muted and contradictory. Celebrated for his lowly origins, his years as a farmer, and his lyrical depictions of rural and working-class life, Burns was not consistent or extensive in his expression of sympathy for African slaves. Only the success of his landmark volume *Poems, Chiefly in the Scottish Dialect*, which earned him money and established him as the Scottish national poet, moved him to abandon his plans, in 1786, to emigrate to Jamaica and work as overseer on a plantation. This poem, based not on African sources (as was long rumored) but on an old English ballad, is apparently the only verse Burns ever wrote on the subject of African slavery.

The Slave's Lament

It was in sweet Senegal that my foes did me enthral
    For the lands of Virginia, —ginia, O!
Torn from that lovely shore, and must never see it more,
    And alas! I am weary, weary, O!

All on that charming coast is no bitter snow and frost
    Like the lands of Virginia,—ginia, O!
There streams for ever flow, and flowers for ever blow,
    And alas! I am weary, weary, O!

The burden I must bear, while the cruel scourge I fear,
    In the lands of Virginia,—ginia, O!
And I think on friends most dear with the bitter, bitter tear,
    And alas! I am weary, weary, O!

                       (1792)[255]

SAMUEL TAYLOR COLERIDGE
(1772–1834)

The great Romantic poet's interest in slavery was kindled while he was still a student at Cambridge, which was a seedbed for abolitionists in the late eighteenth century (Clarkson, Wilberforce, and Wordsworth were all Cambridge graduates). Through all the vicissitudes of his career as philosopher, lecturer, critic, and creative writer, Coleridge never lost his antislavery fervor. In addition to the poems printed here, Coleridge wrote magazine articles and gave public lectures against slavery. In the last year of his life (as scholars have recently discovered), he was still writing private letters in support of the abolitionist cause. Some critics have argued that abhorrence of slavery so informed Coleridge's imagination that even his "Rime of the Ancient Mariner" is inspired, at one level, by guilt over the slave trade. (See also Robert Southey, included elsewhere.)

Coleridge's first antislavery writing was an ode composed in classical Greek for a university competition. The poem won Coleridge the Browne Gold Medal and simultaneous publication. But apart from Coleridge's English rendering of a few lines in 1796, no translation was to appear until the late twentieth century, and that in a scholarly article. The following is an original translation provided by the classicist Dr. Stephen Marsh.

The Wretched Lot of the Slaves in the Islands of West India*

O DEATH, now leave the gates of dark,
And haste thee to a doom-bound folk.
No nail-rent face will greet thee there,
Nor cries of woe.

---

* For the original Greek text, see *The Poetical Works of Samuel Taylor Coleridge*, ed. J[ames] D[ykes] Campbell (London, 1893), 476–77.

But circles of the merry dance,
And joyful leapings: feared art thou,
But dwell'st withal with freedom fair,
Harsh tyrant thou.

I would take wing with thee to fly
Through rugged Ocean's massy swell,
To seats beloved of pleasures rare,
Where I was born.

There lovers tell their mistress sooth
'Neath fountains by the citron groves
What mortal man to man can do,
Such frightful things.*

Ah, isles which brim with bloody pride
That bloom amid such awful ill!
HUNGER dwells here as does the whip
Which drips with gore.

Ah, woe is us! How oft hath come
The tearful mist unto our eyes?
How oft again our heart hath groaned?
With suff'ring dire

I mourn as one with those who slave,
As they lament with voiceless pain,
Who, whirled upon the tides of toil,
Rule not their fate.

Their days are girt by scorching HEAT,
PLAGUE, and TOIL Man cannot bear
Are e'er their foes, and bitter thoughts
Of MEM'RY dire.

---

* [Coleridge's 1796 note:] The Slaves in the West-Indies consider death as a passport to their native country. This sentiment is thus expressed in the introduction [stanzas 1–4] to a Greek Prize-Ode on the Slave-Trade, of which the ideas are better than the language in which they are conveyed. . . . [Coleridge then translates the stanzas into prose, as follows:] Leaving the Gates of Darkness, O Death! hasten thou to a Race yoked with Misery! Thou wilt not be received with lacerations of cheeks, nor with funereal ululation—but with circling dances, and the joy of songs. Thou art terrible indeed, yet thou dwelleth with LIBERTY, stern GENIUS! Borne on thy dark pinions over the swelling of Ocean, they return to their native country. There, by the side of Fountains beneath Citron-groves, the lovers tell to their beloved what horrors, being Men, they had endured from Men.

Alas, the sleepless LASH doth urge them on
Before the dawn can wake the sun,
And when the Daystar sinks so sweet
Their woes do bloom:

For midnight fears affright their souls
And fill their hearts with rancour dire
Their eye is dimmed with suff'rings sad
And FEAR sleeps not.

And should they chase sweet lies of hope
Amid the darkling realm of dreams,
Waking, their hope is brought to naught
By tyrants' goad.

Woe unto you whom BONDAGE gluts
Fed by the chase of wretches frail,
Proud sons of GREED, full well ye reap
Your kinsmen's blood.

Does not the EYE that naught escapes
Behold, as JUDGEMENT shakes her fiery doom?
Hear ye, or hear ye not? The winds
Do shake the roots

And ev'ry corner rings of Earth
And vasty deeps do murmur woes
And pledge the gods below to rage against
The murd'rers vile.

But what soft sound approaches now
Like strains divine of Dorian lyre?
What soft sweet voice drips murmur low
Unto my ears?

Ah me, I see the herald clad
In boughs of olive, MERCY's friend
Oh joy! WILBERFORCE, I hear
Thy golden voice.

"Sacred fount of tears, hast dript enough!
The stranger-saving light'ning-bolt
Of JUSTICE now hath brought pain low
And it will die.

No longer will, on Libyan shore,
The foul and graceless love of gold
Charge like the dire and crackling blasts
Of PESTILENCE.

No longer will bereft OLD AGE
Far from the love of kin and home
Strive with unlawful chores and gasp
As life decays.

No more will mother's grimy babe
Be clutched to breast, in fear of doom,
No more: for bondage has gone on
For far too long.

For you, who slaved for masters cruel
Who never saw the tear run down
The cheek of MERCY, and who bore
What no ear heard,

Your daughters fair taste JUSTICE now
And pluck the rose of heav'nly CALM
With FREEDOM's holy bloom, the one
Mother of wretches."

Hail, well thou pliest MERCY's helm,
LOVE that changeth woe for mirth
On wings of deeds that work for good
Shall crown thee fair.

The Muse, of VIRTUE handmaid e'er
Shall take delight to hymn thee long
And victims' praise shall take thy name
To Heav'n on high.

(wr. 1792/trans. 1999)[256]

In this excerpt from a poetic meditation on what he calls the search for "religious meanings in the forms of nature," Coleridge offers a kind of national confession for the sin of the slave trade. While political in implication, the poem is noteworthy for its intensely personal psychological charge.

from Fears in Solitude, Written in 1798, During the Alarm of an Invasion

We have offended, O my countrymen!
We have offended very grievously,
And have been tyrannous. From east to west
A groan of accusation pierces heaven!
The wretched plead against us, multitudes
Countless and vehement, the sons of God,
Our brethren! like a cloud that travels on,

Steam'd up from Cairo's swamps of pestilence,
Ev'n so, my countrymen! have we gone forth
And borne to distant tribes slavery and pangs,
And, deadlier far, our vices, whose deep taint
With slow perdition murders the whole man,
His body and his soul! Meanwhile, at home,
We have been drinking with a riotous thirst
Pollutions from the brimming cup of wealth,
A selfish, lewd, effeminated race,
Contemptuous of all honourable rule,
Yet bartering freedom, and the poor man's life,
For gold, as at a market! The sweet words
Of christian promise, words that even yet
Might stem destruction, were they wisely preach'd,
Are mutter'd o'er by men, whose tones proclaim,
How flat and wearisome they feel their trade.
Rank scoffers some, but most too indolent,
To deem them falsehoods, or to *know* their truth.
O blasphemous! The book of life is made
A superstitious instrument, on which
We gabble o'er the oaths we mean to break,
For all must swear—all, and in every place,
College and wharf, council and justice-court,
All, all must swear, the briber and the brib'd,
Merchant and lawyer, senator and priest,
The rich, the poor, the old man, and the young,
All, all make up one scheme of perjury. . . .
                        Evil days
Are coming on us, O my countrymen!
And what if all-avenging Providence,
Strong and retributive, should make us know
The meaning of our words, force us to feel
The desolation and the agony
Of our fierce doings?—
                        Spare us yet a while,
Father and god! O spare us yet a while!

                                    (1798)[257]

In this excerpt from what were meant as light verses of social criticism (pub-
lished in a newspaper), Coleridge nonetheless finds the frustrations and set-
backs of the abolition campaign haunting his imagination.

SAMUEL TAYLOR COLERIDGE

from "The Devil's Thoughts"

IX

As he went through Cold-Bath fields he saw
    A solitary cell;
And the Devil was pleased, for it gave him a hint
    For improving his prisons in Hell.

X

He saw a Turnkey in a trice
    Fetter a troublesome blade;
"Nimbly," quoth he, "do the fingers move
    If a man be but used to his trade."

XI

He saw the same Turnkey unfetter a man,
    With but little expedition,
Which put him in mind of the long debate
    On the Slave-trade abolition.

(1799)[258]

JOHN COLLINS (1742–1808)

Born the son of a tailor, Collins was an actor, lecturer on elocution, playwright, and, in his later years, editor of *The Birmingham Chronicle*. The following two poems, each of uncertain date (but published in 1804), show how antislavery sympathies and racist jocularity could coexist in one man's work.

The first had a significant record of public performance. Originally set to music for orchestral accompaniment (perhaps in a musical drama), by 1792 it had been reset for solo recitals and its musical score published in London. In a song full of pathos, a blind African beggar recounts his enslavement, mutilation, and near death. Whether in a London theater or the drawing room of a country house, Collins's song encourages his listeners to imagine, behind the abstract idea of poor blacks, real human beings whose lives had been destroyed by the slave trade.

The Desponding Negro *

On Afric's wide Plains, where the Lion now roaring,
With Freedom stalks forth, the vast Desert exploring,
I was dragg'd from my Hut, and enchain'd as a Slave,
In a dark floating Dungeon, upon the salt Wave.
    Spare a Halfpenny—spare a Halfpenny—
    Spare a Halfpenny to a poor Negro.

Toss'd onto the wild Main, I all wildly despairing,
Burst my Chains, rush'd on Deck, with mine Eye-balls wide glaring,
When the Lightning's dread Blast struck the Inlets of Day,
And its glorious bright Beams shut for ever away.
    Spare a Halfpenny, &c.

---

* The title page of the 1792 printing of the musical score by William Reeve (1751–1815) describes it as "a favourite new song" and mentions a "version for German flute" also appended.

The Despoiler of Man, then, his Prospect thus losing,
Of Gain by my Sale, not a blind Bargain choosing,
As my Value, compar'd with my Keeping, was light,
Had me dash'd overboard, in the Dead of the Night.
    Spare a Halfpenny, &c.

And but for a Bark, to Britannia's Coast bound then,
All my Cares by that Plunge in the Deep had been drown'd then;
But by Moonlight descry'd, I was snatch'd from the wave,
And reluctantly robb'd of a watery Grave.
    Spare a Halfpenny, &c.

How disastrous my Fate, Freedom's Ground though I tread now,
Torn from Home, Wife, and Children, and wand'ring for Bread now;
While Seas roll between us, which ne'er can be cross'd,
And Hope's distant Glimm'rings in Darkness are lost.
    Spare a Halfpenny, &c.

But of Deeds fair and foul, when the Judge and the Ponderer,
Shall restore Light and Rest to the Blind and the Wanderer,
May the poor Sable Flock, here by Christians outcast,
Find a peaceful long Home their sweet Refuge at last.
    Spare a Halfpenny, spare a Halfpenny;
    O, spare a Halfpenny to a poor Negro.

(c. 1792)[259]

In a kind of ribald comedy as old as Chaucer, Collins spins a tale of cuckoldry, superstition, and domestic deceit. As wife and midwife conspire to fob an illegitimate black baby on the white husband, the racist edge of the story is muted not only by the fact that the slow-witted plantation owner is the butt of the joke, but also that the white lady and her black lover emerge the comic victors.

Conjugal Credulity (Founded on Fact)

Blind Wittols will wink at their Spouses' defects,
When as plain as the sun at noon day;
And suppose Madam's honour their temples protects,
From the weapons of Bucks when at bay.

Thus a Planter, who liv'd in Antigua's warm isle,
Whose Wife took a Black to her bed;
With Raleigh's fam'd plant all his cares would beguile,
While She planted Horns on his head.

For he smok'd it by night and he smok'd it by day,
From his pipe never wishing to stir;
And though He, for her jigging, the piper must pay,
'Tis certain he never smok'd Her.

When at length pregnant symptoms of danger appear'd,
Which, in less than nine months must make known,
Whether young Pickaninny, with Sable besmear'd,
The good man would embrace as his own.

Such a plight to be in, she perceiv'd with alarm,
When on taking the Midwife aside,
She thought the best way to prevent future harm,
Was in her secret faith to confide.

So the whole truth came out, who the brat had begot,
And what colour of course he must be;
When the matron heard all, and surpris'd not a jot,
Reply'd—"Leave the matter to me:

I'll make old Cornuto leap out of his skin,
Or near it, for joy of an heir,
And all fears to remove, a fine tale will I spin,
Which to swallow, I'm sure he won't spare.

For you're Longing for Charcoal's the thing I'll avow,
And in secret you've told it to me;
That you've got a strange whim, and 'tis strange I'll allow,
To devour it where no one can see."

The scheme thus concerted, Old Goody repair'd
To the husband, to wish him much joy;
"For," says she, "my good Sir, all your pray'rs have been heard,
And you'll soon have a fine chopping Boy:

Or suppose it a Girl, 'tis your own flesh and blood,
And you'll not want an heir for your wealth;
But I've found out a thing that must not be withstood,
And the thing must be done, too, by stealth.

Madam's longing for Charcoal, and, wond'rous to tell,
Though miscarriage and death should ensue,
If not plac'd in the dark at her bedside,—full well
I'm assur'd, not a grain will she chew.

But I'll undertake, if you'll say but the word,
That when you fast asleep seem to lie,
She'll crunch it and munch it, so sharply she's spurr'd,
Her capricious odd gust to supply."

"Eat Charcoal! Lord, Lord, (says the husband) how strange!
The thought fills me full of dejection."
"Phoo, phoo, (replies Goody) at worst 'twill but change
The young Hans in Kelder's complexion.

And what if it does, be the Bairn fair or brown,
'Tis better than no Bairn at all;
For if still-born the Babe, 'twill be murder you'll own,
If as white as a Greenland snow ball."

With reluctance the Husband his doubts did dismiss,
And the Charcoal was plac'd as directed,
For Madam to munch in the dark,—but mark this,—
Sugar Candy the business effected.

So forth from her pocket the sweetmeat she drew,
And she crunch'd it with glee in the dark,
While in pocket the Charcoal was hid from all view,
When at morn rose the old doting spark.

Yet so stinted the medicine was every night,
That the Midwife betrayed many fears;
If the poor little thing should at last see the light,
That 'twould live but a very few years.

"May be so," says the Husband, "but this I'll be sworn,
Long or short let its life be ordain'd,
I'd rather 'twould kick up as soon as 'twas born,
Than my wife should with slander be stain'd.

For the neighbours will say, if I give her too much,
Being ignorant all of the cause,
When they see a black dye the young bantling besmutch,
That the mother has made some Fore Paws.

And crouds after crouds, then to scandal's foul school,
Will, to make game of me, every one go;
Saying, she's a young strumpet, and I an old fool,
That have got for an heir a young Mungo."

When, the sequel to wind up, on one Monday morn,
And a black Monday 'twas to be sure,
Young Snowball as black as an Ethiop was born,
And his colour no washing could cure.

"Look you there," says the Midwife, "I knew how 'twould be,
Had you given her Charcoal enough,
Instead of this sable complexion you see,
You had saved the young gentleman's buff."

"Hold your tongue, you damn'd jade," says the Husband, quite mad,
   "'Tis the Charcoal has caus'd all this evil,
And I'm sure if a single grain more she had had,
My poor boy had been black as the devil."

$(1804)^{260}$

JAMES GRAHAME (1765–1811)

A Scottish lawyer, clergyman, and poet, Grahame distinguished himself at Glasgow University before coming to Edinburgh to train as an advocate in the late 1780s. Although he became a writer for the *Signet* and practiced law in the 1790s, in 1802 he changed careers to pursue his true aspirations as an Anglican clergyman and poet. He achieved considerable acclaim for his writings, especially *The Sabbath* (1804), *The Birds of Scotland* (1806), and *British Georgics* (1809), before dying, after chronic illness, at the age of forty-six.

Long an opponent of slavery, Grahame seems to have written the first poem below in the early 1790s, as an angry response to the British Parliament's rejection of Wilberforce's Abolition Bill. Undoubtedly influenced by the atmosphere in Edinburgh, where established figures such as James Beattie, Francis Garden, and John Maclaurin (all represented elsewhere in this volume) had made antislavery attitudes a mainstay of the Scottish Enlightenment, Grahame notably focuses his indictment on specifically English ("*your* Commons") governmental policy.

To England, on the Slave Trade

Of all thy foreign crimes, from pole to pole,
None moves such indignation in my soul,
Such hate, such deep abhorrence, as thy *trade*
In human beings!
Thy ignorance thou dar'st to plead no more;
The proofs have thundered from the Afric shore.
Behold, behold, yon rows ranged over rows,
Of dead with dying linked in death's last throes.
Behold a single victim of despair,
Dragged upon deck to gasp the ocean air;
Devoid of fear, he hears the tempest rise,—
The ship descending 'tween the waves, he eyes

With eager hope; he thinks his woes shall end:
Sunk in despair he sees her still ascend.

  What barbarous race are authors of his woe?
With freights of fetters, who the vessel stow?
Who forge the torture-irons, who plait the scourge?
Whose navies shield the pirates o'er the surge?
Who, from the mother's arms, the clinging child
Tears? It is England,—merciful and mild!
Most impious race, who brave the watery realm
In blood-fraught barks, with Murder at the helm!
Who trade in tortures, profit draw from pain,
And even whose mercy is but love of gain!
Whose human cargoes carefully are packt,
By rule and square, *according to the Act!*—
And is that gore-drenched flag by you unfurled,
Champions of right, knights-errant of the world?
"Yes, yes," your Commons said, "*Let such things be,
If* OTHERS *rob and murder, why not* WE?"
In the smoothed speech, and in the upraised hand,
I hear the lash, I hear the fierce command;
Each guilty *nay* ten thousand crimes decreed,
And English *mercy* said, Let millions bleed!
     (wr. c. 1792–95/pub. 1807)[261]

Grahame was invited, along with James Montgomery and Elizabeth Ogilvy
Benger, by the London publisher Robert Bowyer to contribute an original poem
to a special volume celebrating the abolition of the slave trade in 1807. The re-
sult was Grahame's fifty-page blank verse saga in four parts, "Africa Deliv-
ered," from which the following excerpts are taken. In the first of these, Gra-
hame paints the picture of slave ships cruelly gathering their cargo on the
African coast.

from Part I of "Africa Delivered; Or, The Slave Trade Abolished. A Poem"

    Now the sails appear
Hung in the dim horizon: freedom's flag,
Britannia's glowing ensign, is descried;
Then full in view the floating prison-house,
The Pandorean ark of every curse
Imagination can combine to blast
Poor human life, comes rolling o'er the surge.

The mother strains her infant to her breast,
And weeps to think her eldest-born has reached
Those years, which, tender though they be, provoke
The white man's thirst of gain: more dreadful far
The white man's scowl, than the couched lion's glare! . . .

        The murderous league,
The bribe for blood, is struck, the doom pronounced,
By which a peaceful unoffending race
Are sentenced to the sword, to exile, chains . . .
The pale-faced, ruthless author of the war,
Surveys the human harvest reaped and bound.
Fire, sword, and rapine, sweep away at once
The cottage with its inmates, and transform
The happy vale into a wilderness;
No human being, save the bowed down,
And children that scarce lisp a father's name,
Is left: as when a forest is laid low,
Haply some single and far sundered trees
Are spared, while every lowly shrub and flower,
That sheltered smiled, droops shivering in the breeze.
    And now the wretched captives, linked in rows,
In sad community of chains, drag on
Their iron-cumbered limbs, while oft the scourge
Or unclosed wound leaves in the thirsty sand
The traces of their miserable way.
At last the fainting victims reach the shore,
Where low they lie, dispersed in mournful bands;
Then are unbound, to bear the butcher gripe
Of brutal traffickers, or join the dance,
Mockery of mirth! to harmony of whips.
    The bargains finished, piteous is the sight,
Most lamentable are the peals of cries,
The groans of parents from their children torn,
Of brother, sister severed; every tie
Of kindred by one rude revulsion riven.
    Yet such is not the cruel lot of all:
Some kindred groups remain entire, and feel
The solace of society in woe.
Behold a father driven with his sons,
The mother with her nursling in her arms.—
To meet yon ship, now newly hove in sight

And unsupplied, the trader with his flock
Hastes to the water edge, where waits his boat
Its human cargo: first the sire is bound
And thrown beneath a bench; the rest unbound
Implicit follow where affection leads:
His darling boy hastes in and lays him down,
A gentle pillow to his father's head,
And with his little hand would dry the tears
That fill the upward-turned, despairing eye.
Quick plunge the oars; fleetly to eyes unused
The land retreating seems, while the huge ship
Comes towering on with all her bulging sails;
And now she nighs, and now her shadow spreads
Dark o'er the little barge's captive freight,
Like vulture's wings above the trembling lamb.
　　Alas, another captive-loaded keel
Plies from the shore to meet the floating mart.
Ah, who is he that in the dimpling track
Elbows the brine? He is a boy, bereft
Of sight, and worthless in the trader's eye;
The only remnant to a father left
Of all his children; he the best beloved,
Because most helpless; yet no prayer will move
The felon merchant to admit the child
To share the fetters which his father bind:
And now he gains upon the sounding oars
That guide his following course, and now the side
Eager he grasps, and, though still pushed away,
Still he returns, till frequent on his hands
He feels the bruising blow; then down he sinks,
Nor makes one faint endeavor for his life.

In the next excerpt, Grahame mixes realistic detail, such as the cacophony of
languages among the captives, with stories of appalling brutality to convey life
aboard ship.

from Part II of "Africa Delivered"

　　　　　　　The sails are reefed;
All hatches closed; the coffined captives pant
For air; and in their various languages
Implore, unheard, that but a single board

Be raised: vain prayer, for now the beetling surge
Breaks o'er the bow, and boils along the deck.
Oh then the horrors of the den below!
Disease bursts forth, and, like th' electric shock
Sudden strikes through at once the prostrate ranks.
Fierce fever pours his lava from the heart
And burns through every vein; convulsion writhes
Foaming, and gnaws and champs his twisted arm;
Dire trismus bends his victim on the wheel
Of torment, rivets close the firm-screwed jaw
In fearful grin, and makes death lovely seem.
Dreadful the imprecations, dire the shrieks,
That mingle with the maniac laugh; the gnash
Of teeth, delirium's fitful song, now gay,
Plaintive at times, then deeply sorrowful.
In such a scene Death deals the final blow,
In pity, not in wrath: 'tis he alone
That here can quench the fever's fire, unloose
The knotted tendon; he alone restores
The frantic mind, that soon as freed ascends
To Him who gave it being . . .

    There was (almost incredible the tale!)
A wretch whose lips condemned a mother's hands
To drop her murdered infant in the deep.
Murdered! yes foully murdered, is each one
Who dies a captive in the horrid trade.
And yet there have been men, and still there are,
Who vindicate such murder; men who preach
That gain and custom sanction every crime.

Part III covers slave life on colonial plantations. Here especially one senses Grahame's desire to make visible to the British reading public the reality of slave experience. He is at pains to establish credibility, including long and dreadful passages from parliamentary testimony and eyewitness accounts in his footnotes.

from Part III of "Africa Delivered"

O 'tis most piteous to behold the child,—
A daughter to a widowed mother left,—
Kneel to the hardened purchaser, and clasp
His knees in agony, praying by signs

Not to be parted: stern the ruffian spurns
The grasp of filial love: her hands unloosed
Clasp in a last embrace her mother's neck,
And scarcely yield to force of many arms.

    Dispersed, with eyes unlifted from the ground,
They take their various ways, to various tasks condemned.
Most part, with hoe in hand, fill up the ranks
That in the cane-field toiled, by suffering thinned.
Beneath the scorching ray, the aged man,
The tender maid, the boy, the nursing mother
Sinking beneath the double load, her work
And infant, all must ply an equal task,
Without regard to age, or strength, or sex;*
Must ply and must perform; the flagging step
That breaks the line, or arm that slurs its work,
Is prompted by the driver's biting lash,
And tears and blood bedew the rising plants.

    Nor is it only in the field of toil
The whip resounds; no, every petty fault
Is duly journalled, till the wretch, whose trade
Is torture, comes in stated round, with cry
Of *slaves to flog*! then stretched upon the ground,
The trembling victim, to the ringbolts fixed,
Receives at once the sentence and the stroke.
In agony the soil he gnaws; his shrieks,
Heard in the festive hall,† are drowned in peals

---

* [from Grahame's note:] But a nearer and more particular view of the manner of working
may be necessary to those who have never seen a gang of Negroes at their work: "The Slaves
of both sexes, from twenty, perhaps, to four score in number, are drawn out in a line, like
troops on a parade, each with a hoe in his hand; and close to them in the rear is stationed a
driver, or several drivers, in numbers duly proportioned to that of the gang." [from] *Wilber-
force's Letter on the Abolition of the Slave Trade, 3d Edit.* p. 66.

† [from Grahame's note:] "The corporal punishment of slaves is so frequent, that instead of
exciting the repugnant sensations, felt by Europeans on first witnessing it, scarcely does it
produce, in the breasts of those long accustomed to the West Indies, even the slightest feeling
of compassion. The lady I have above alluded to appears of good natural disposition, and in
no degree disposed to general cruelty; but the frequency of the sight has rendered her callous
to its common influence upon the feelings. Being one morning at her house, while sitting in
conversation, we suddenly heard the loud cries of a negro suffering under the whip. Mrs. ___
expressed surprise on observing me shudder at his shrieks, and you will believe that I was in
utter astonishment to find her treat his sufferings as matter of amusement. It proved that the
punishment proceeded from the arm of the lady's husband, and fell upon one of her own

Of mirth; and, should a stranger's voice presume
To plead for mercy, even the female hand
With taunt demoniac fills the cup brim-full,
And sends it to give spirit to the arm
That brings out music from a pipe so rude.
  And what the crime that merits such a doom?
Perhaps some word less servile than beseems
The lips of slave addressed to tyrant's ear:
Perhaps a look of conscious worth and pride,
Interpreted contempt by him who feels
How well he merits that contempt he dreads.

In Part IV Grahame praises the abolition of the slave trade and looks forward to the era of continuing progress it seemed to augur. After a poignant image of Scottish sailors weeping on the coast of Africa (from homesickness or guilt), Grahame goes on to predict that antislavery poems, such as those by his Scottish friend Thomas Campbell (included elsewhere), will one day be translated into African tongues and passed down to future generations of the "slave-descended race."

from Part IV of "Africa Delivered"

Ye generous band, united in the cause
Of liberty to Africa restored,
O may your hands be strong, and hearts be firm
In that great cause! so may you reap the meed
Most grateful to your hearts, the glorious view
Of peace reviving, ignorance dispelled,
The arts improved, and, O most blessed thought!
That faith which trampled Slavery under foot,
And led captivity in captive chains,
Embraced by men in superstition sunk . . .

  On the banks
Of Gambia's tide the Scottish seaman starts
To hear Lochaber's strain or Flodden field,
Then mounts the mast to hide the bursting tear.
  The rugged accents, gradually refined,
Come forth a language, musical and full,

---

slaves; and, can you believe that on learning this, she exclaimed with a broad smile, 'Aha! it will do him good! a little wholesome flagellation will refresh him.—It will sober him.—It will open his skin, and make him alert. If Y___ was to give it them all, it would be of service to them!'" [from] *Pinckard's Notes on the West Indies, Vol. II.* p. 192.

Sonorous, gentle, forceful, rapid, bold,
As suits the changes of the poet's lay,—
Not yet unpliant to a foreign strain:—
Yes, Campbell, thy imperishable strains
Shall live in languages but now half formed,
And tell the slave-descended race the tale
Of Africa restored to human rights.

(1809)[262]

HENRY EVANS HOLDER
(fl. 1780–1792)

A native of Barbadoes, educated and trained as a clergyman in England, Holder
was an Anglican minister who divided his career between Barbadoes and Bris-
tol, while writing on scholarly and theological topics. He also published works
in defense of slavery and the slave trade, including *A Short Essay on the Subject
of Negro Slavery* (London, 1788) and the poem below. Here, responding partic-
ularly to J. Marjoribanks's fiercely abolitionist *Slavery: An Essay in Verse* (1786;
included elsewhere), Holder offers three rationales against abolition: the
Africans are materially better off enslaved than free, the masters' self-interest in
preserving their property prevents them from harming slaves, and the abolition-
ists themselves are vain, deluded, and self-interested. Some contemporaries
found Holder's poem atrocious: the *Monthly Review* for April 1792 accused him
of "prostituting the powers of versification . . . [to produce] a poem written in
defence of slavery."

from Fragments of a Poem, Intended to have been Written in Consequence of Reading Major Majoribanks's [sic] Slavery

    And are you sure, Reformer, fiery red!
That what you give is worth acceptance?
Can you suppose that freedom is a boon
Where competence is wanting? Can the Black
Hail you his benefactor, when you give
A name, and strip him of realities?
When you curse him with a *fancied* liberty,
And leave him to endure the many cares
Which people each domestic head and heart,
To rear a tender offspring, and provide
For tott'ring age and fell infirmity? . . .

But who, you'll say, shall guard the wretched slave
From tyrant-cruelty and bloody scourge?
Believe me he requires no hand to guard,
No interference from your mad'ning zeal. . . .
The voice of interest will be heard aloud;
Nor yet in any state of life more loud,
Than when she teaches ev'ry master's heart,
That all his wealth is center'd in his slave. . . .

But after all, when this great work is done,
When you have fill'd this hemisphere with rage,
Against the children of the Western world,
Can you look up to GOD, and boldly say,
My motive was to serve his creatures,
And further his designs of genial love? . . .
Hang your heads, and smite your guilty breasts,
As you confess, because you can't deny,
That pride, or vanity, or envy mean,
Or malice fell, or private views, first arm'd
Your zeal; and shame has since impell'd you on,
Your cruel work of darkness to complete.

(1792)[263]

SARAH WENTWORTH APTHORP MORTON (1759–1846)

Daughter of the wealthy and cultured Apthorp family of Boston, Sarah Morton combined intellect, personal beauty, social position, and literary talent. Even as she moved in the highest circles of New England society, her poetic writings earned her the reputation of America's leading female poet, "the American Sappho." Over the decades, her verse appeared in the *Massachusetts Magazine, The New York Magazine,* and *The Tablet,* earning the praise of Thomas Paine, Joseph Dennie, and others.

The first of her poems below remained popular throughout the nineteenth-century. The great antislavery poet John Greenleaf Whittier proclaimed "The African Chief" one of his favorite poems. Blending a ballad stanza with historic argument, Morton links the righteousness of the antislavery fight to a series of heroic struggles for freedom, from the Messenians in antiquity to Paoli's Corsicans and Washington's Americans in the eighteenth century.

The African Chief

See how the black ship cleaves the main,
    High bounding o'er the dark blue wave,
Remurmuring with the groans of pain,
    Deep freighted with the princely slave!

Did all the Gods of Afric sleep,
    Forgetful of their guardian love,
When the white tyrants of the deep,
    Betrayed him in the palmy grove.

A Chief of *Gambia's* golden shore,
    Whose arm the band of warriors led,
Or more—the lord of generous power,
    By whom the foodless poor were fed.

Does not the voice of reason cry,
"Claim the first right that nature gave,
From the red scourge of bondage fly,
  Nor deign to live a burdened slave."

Has not his suffering offspring clung,
  Desponding round his fettered knee;
On his worn shoulder, weeping hung,
  And urged one effort to be free!

His wife by nameless wrongs subdued,
  His bosom's friend to death resigned;
The flinty path-way drenched in blood;
  He saw with cold and phrenzied mind.

Strong in despair, then sought the plain,
  To heaven was raised his steadfast eye,
Resolved to burst the crushing chain,
  Or mid the battle's blast to die.

First of his race, he led the band,
  Guardless of danger, hurling round,
Till by his red avenging hand,
  Full many a despot stained the ground.

When erst *Messenia's* sons oppressed,
  Flew desperate to the sanguine field,
With iron cloathed each injured breast,
  And saw the cruel Spartan yield.

Did not the soul to heaven allied,
  With the proud heart as greatly swell,
As when the *Roman Decius* died,
  Or when the *Grecian victim* fell.

Do later deeds quick rapture raise,
  The boon *Batavia's William* won,
Paoli's time-enduring praise,
  Or the yet greater *Washington*!

If these exalt thy sacred zeal,
  To hate oppression's mad controul,
For bleeding *Afric* learn to feel,
  Whose Chieftan claimed a kindred soul.

Ah, mourn the last disastrous hour,
  Lift the full eye of bootless grief,
While victory treads the sultry shore,
  And tears from hope the captive Chief.

While the hard race of *pallid hue*,
    Unpracticed in the power to feel,
Resign him to the murderous crew,
    The horrors of the quivering wheel.

Let sorrow bathe each blushing cheek,
    Bend piteous o'er the tortured slave,
Whose wrongs compassion cannot speak,
    Whose only refuge was the grave.

                (1792)[264]

The following excerpts are from Morton's unfinished epic about the American Revolution, published in part in 1797. In heaping praise one by one on the colonies that fought the War, Morton does not flinch from condemning the moral inconsistency of freedom-loving societies that practice slavery.

from Book I of Beacon Hill. A Local Poem, Historic And Descriptive.

Virginia! blest beyond each bordering clime,
The noblest plume, that lifts the wing of time!—
Not that luxuriance decks her festive bowers,
While the rich weed its curling fragrance pours;
That fatal weed, with many a blossom fair,
Was nursed by tears, and ripen'd in despair!—
Not that her ample skirts redundant spread,
And towering mountains crown her princely head;
The wasteful wilderness unheeded lies,
And round those heights the fiend of Slavery hies!—
Yet thou, *Virginia*, fairest of the fair,
More bright than all thy radiant sisters are,
Shalt rise supreme, and every wreath of fame
Twine its rich foliage round thy *elder* name . . .

—Child of the sun, proud *Carolina*, rise!
And say what chief thy haughty hand supplies!
Canst thou contend for freedom, while yon vale
Pours its deep sorrows on the sultry gale!
Thus rise with patriot heart supremely brave,
Nor heed the scourge, that breaks thy shackled slave! . . .

Bright *Georgia*, hail!—Though fiery Summer pours
His fierce electric round thy blasted bowers,
While in black streams the turbid clouds descend,

469

And peals on peals the flashing concave rend,—
Though many a reptile rear its slimy brood
On the moist bosom of thy breezeless wood,—
Though *Afric* feel thee on her ravaged plain,*
And stay thy step, and stop thy hand in vain.

(1797)[265]

---

* [Morton's note:] GEORGIA for a long time after its first settlement opposed the importation of
African slaves; but finally, influenced by the bad example of the neighboring colonies, she fell
into the pernicious traffic, and the lands are now generally cultivated by that unhappy people.

SAMUEL ROGERS (1763–1855)

A man of affluence, Rogers was a prolific but second-rate poet who wielded major critical and social influence throughout the Romantic era and beyond. Acquainted with all the leading figures of the day, both literary and political, he had a reputation for being charitable in person and acerbic in print. Influenced by the poetics of an earlier generation, especially Johnson and Gray, Rogers also embraced the vogue for a poetry of feeling. This excerpt is from an early poetic meditation that, in its emphasis on memory, anticipates Wordsworth. Here, stirred by the indignities that slavery inflicts on the "heroic spirit" of Africans, Rogers imagines slaves consoling themselves with memories of their homeland.

from The Pleasures of Memory

From Guinea's coast pursue the lessening sail,
And catch the sounds that sadden every gale.
Tell, if thou canst, the sum of sorrows there;
Mark the fixt gaze, the wild and frenzied glare,
The racks of thought, and freezings of despair!
But pause not then—beyond the western wave,
Go, view the captive barter'd as a slave!
Crush'd till his high heroic spirit bleeds,
And from his nerveless frame indignantly recedes.

Yet here, ev'n here, with pleasures long resign'd,
Lo! MEMORY bursts the twilight of the mind:
Her dear delusions sooth his sinking soul,
When the rude scourge presumes its base controul;
And o'er Futurity's blank page diffuse
The full reflection of their vivid hues.
'Tis but to die, and then, to weep no more,
Then will he wake on Congo's distant shore;

Beneath his plantain's ancient shade, renew
The simple transports that with freedom flew;
Catch the cool breeze that musky Evening blows,
And quaff the palm's rich nectar as it glows;
The oral tale of elder time rehearse,
And chant the rude traditionary verse;
With those, the lov'd companions of his youth,
When life was luxury, and friendship truth.

(1792)[266]

SIR THOMAS EDLYNE TOMLINS
(1762–1841)

Oxford-educated lawyer and writer, for a time editor of the London newspaper the *St. James's Chronicle* and later a government official knighted for his services, Tomlins as a young man wrote poems on slavery that were published in his sister Elizabeth's volume called *Tributes of Affection* (1797). Though his abolitionist sentiments are similar to hers (see "The Slave" by Elizabeth Tomlins, included elsewhere), he expresses them in terser, more political language than she in her narrative mode.

Tomlins's poem voices a well-intentioned but mistaken response to news of the vote on Wilberforce's first abolition bill. Though the bill passed, it had been so amended as to be without any real effect, calling vaguely for "gradual" abolition. It thus represented a setback for abolitionists—something Tomlins had not yet realized.

To the House of Commons, on Their Vote for the Abolition of the Slave-Trade. April 2, 1792

> Ye bold Assertors of the public voice,
> Whose virtues justify your Country's choice,
> On you the Sons of Africk shall bestow
> Their pray'rs, their thanks, their tears from joy which flow.
> Th' historick page, to worth and honour true,
> Shall to your Sons transmit your praises due:
> And as of old were former Senates known
> For acts of vice or virtue most their own,
> Recorded in the genuine rolls of Fame,
> *The* Parliament *of* Mercy be *your* Name.

(c. 1792)[267]

In this sonnet, the poet links the suffering of African slaves to that of European (i.e., continental) soldiers compelled to fight wars for their covetous and corrupt rulers.

XII. To Mr. Wilberforce

Friend to the Human Race! whose heart benign,
    Still listens to the calls of sad Distress;
    And bids thy hand relieve, thy bounty bless,
The African who toils beneath the line;
    And those of Europe's Sons, who, Slaves no less,
Reluctant drag Ambition's vengeful car
O'er plains once smiling, now laid waste by War;
    Vain hope! to check fair Freedom's rising sway:
    Thine, Wilberforce, the Muse's purest lay;
Thine the glad homage of the gentle soul.
Thy precepts would the storm of War controul,
    Bid Tyranny its wasteful ravage cease,
    And spread the reign of Liberty and Peace,
Far as the Sun can light, or boundless Oceans roll.

                    (1795)[268]

T. WOOLSTON (fl. 1792)

Nothing is known of Mr. "T. Woolston" of Adderbury (near Banbury), except that he was a regular reader of the *Northampton Mercury*, an admirer of William Cowper, and an opponent of slavery. His poem offers a glimpse of how amateur writers might respond to the lead taken by major literary figures and how even provincial newspapers could be forums for antislavery activism.

Sonnet. To William Cowper, Esq. of Weston-Underwood, Bucks *

COWPER, I much revere thy honest muse,
    Which oft has cheer'd my solitary hours;
For, well I know, thou never wilt abuse,
    Those heav'n-inspir'd sweet soul-commanding pow'rs.

Humane and virtuous, scorning sordid views,
    Glad to promote the welfare of mankind;
In all the charms of verse thou would'st infuse
    The noblest morals which adorn the mind.

What tho' I ne'er must hope to match thy strains;—
    While Britons Afric's native rights invade,
And forge for simple freedom horrid chains,
My heart in sympathy with thine complains;
And while the tide of life flows through my veins
    Shall reprobate the black infernal trade.

(April 23, 1792)[269]

* [Woolston's note:] I am quite surfeited with the mean tricks, paltry shifts, pitiful evasions, gross misrepresentations, and partial extracts, which the friends of the *blessed* Slave Trade have exhibited in support of their *benevolent* opinions; and to express their *humane* wishes and *fine feelings*, upon the one step made good towards its abolition, and I could not but rejoice, to find the amiable Mr. Cowper's sentiments upon that subject, still remain unchanged:— Upon reading his Sonnet to Mr. Wilberforce, I could not help scribbling the following one.

ANONYMOUS

One of several antislavery works published in the *Gentleman's Magazine* in the 1790s, this poem, like so many, was contributed anonymously by an amateur poet. (The magazine did not pay for poetical submissions.) In its sympathetic attempt at Negro dialect and its rendering of the not-uncommon belief among Africans (e.g., Olaudah Equiano) that the whites were cannibals come to eat them, the poem goes beyond the sentimental conventions of so many abolitionist works of the day.

The African's Complaint On-Board a Slave Ship

Trembling, naked, wounded, sighing,
    On dis winged house I stand,
Dat with poor black-man is flying
    Far away from their own land!

Fearful water all around me!
    Strange de sight on every hand,
Hurry, noise, and shouts, confound me
    When I look for Negro land.

Every thing I see affright me,
    Nothing I can understand,
With de scourges white man fight me,
    None of dis in Negro land.

Here de white man beat de black man,
    'Till he's sick and cannot stand,
Sure de black be eat by white man!
    Will not go to white man land!

Here in chains poor black man lying
    Put so tick dey on us stand,
Ah! with heat and smells we're dying!
    'Twas not dus in Negro land.

ANONYMOUS

Dere we've room and air, and freedom,
    Dere our little dwellings stand;
Families, and rice to feed 'em!
    Oh I weep for Negro land!

Joyful dere before de doors
    Play our children hand in hand;
Fresh de fields, and sweet de flow'rs,
    Green de hills, in Negro land.

Dere I often go when sleeping,
    See my kindred round me stand;
Hear 'em toke—den wak in weeping,
    Dat I've lost my Negro land.

Dere my black love arms were round me,
    De whole night! not like dis band,
Close dey held, but did not wound me;
    Oh! I die for Negro land!

De bad traders stole and sold me,
    Den was put in iron band—
When I'm dead dey cannot hold me
    Soon I'll be in black man land.

(1793)[270]

477

ANONYMOUS

The following is from an anonymous lampoon about the events of 1792, first published January 1, 1793, in Hartford, and then circulated throughout New England. Here the unidentified satirist mocks the "Equality Ball" thrown by Massachusetts Governor John Hancock for the blacks of Boston in December 1792. Hancock, who was also known for supporting the suppression of the theater on moral grounds, comes under fire for his liberal treatment of blacks, in terms that, for all their jollity, are openly racist.

from Addressed by the Boy Who Carries the *American Mercury*, to the Subscribers

Now HANCOCK . . .
    Prompt to assert the *rights of man*
On Nature's most extensive plan,
Behold him, to his splendid Hall,
The noble Sons of Afric call;
While, as the sable bands advance,
With frolic mien, in sportive dance,
Refreshing clouds of rich perfume
Are wafted o'er the spacious room.
There he, with keen delight, surveys
Their graceful tricks, and winning ways;
Their tones enchanting, raptur'd hears,
Surpass the music of the spheres;
And, as he breathes the fragrant air,
He deems that FREEDOM's self dwells there;
While CUFFEY near him takes his stand,

Hale-fellow met, and grasps his hand;
With pleasure glistening in his eyes,
"Ah! Massa Gubbenur!" he cries—
"Me glad to see you, for de peple say,
You lub de Neeger better dan de play."
(1793)[271]

ANONYMOUS

This poet may well have been a free black, but nothing else is known of him except that he admired the two African American heroes in the title. The lives of Absalom Jones (1746–1818) and Richard Allen (1760–1831), both born slaves who later purchased their own freedom, converged in Philadelphia in the 1780s. After years of struggle, both had emerged as prominent Christian ministers and community leaders. Together they founded the Free African Society in 1787, which Charles Wesley called the first organization of its kind "among Negroes of the western world." This poem pays tribute to their heroism in personally leading the volunteer corps of African Americans that nursed the sick and buried the dead during the yellow fever epidemic of 1793.

Eulogiam in Honour of ABSALOM JONES and RICHARD ALLEN, Two of the Elders of the African Church, Who Furnished Nurses to the Sick, During the Late Pestilential Fever in Philadelphia

Brethren of Man, and friends to human kind,
　　Made of that blood which flow'd in Adam's veins!
　　A muse, who ever spurn'd at adulation's strains;
Who rates not colour, but th' immortal mind,
With transport guides the death redeeming plume;
Nor leaves your names a victim to the tomb.

'Twas your's, amid that life destructive hour,
When terror's monarch rode in pomp of pow'r,
And swept a nation to the silent grave;
His two edged sword with fortitude so brave;
Nor did ye heed the pallid courset's rage,
Who trampled youth in dust, and and trod on age.

ANONYMOUS

Brethren of Man, and friends of fairer clay!
Your godlike zeal in Death's triumphant day
    Benignant Angels saw—they lent a smile,
'Twas temper'd with the dew of sympathy divine;
      And whilst they kenn'd your more than mortal toil,
      To both, they cried, "the praise of *doing well* be thine."
                         (1793)[272]

JOHN THELWALL (1764–1834)

A self-educated teacher of elocution and a social reformer, Thelwall was jailed for his radical utterances in the 1790s but eventually enjoyed considerable success as a writer, lecturer, and speech therapist. Although Voltaire and others had publicized the connection between slavery and cheap sugar decades earlier (e.g., *Candide*, 1759), Thelwall was among the first to elaborate it—as he does here—into a political position. Explicitly addressed to women readers, the poem marks an important increment in the feminization and domestication of the abolition movement.

from *Untitled Poem in* THE PERIPATETIC

Daughters of Albion's gay enlighten'd day!
To *man* alike your sympathy display!
Heedless of groans, of anguish, and of chains,
Of stripes inflicted, and tormenting pains,
At morn, at eve, your sweeten'd beverage sup,
Nor see the blood of thousands in the cup.

   What though each sweet effluvium, ere it rise,
Have clogg'd the western gale with Afric's sighs,
Each sweeten'd drop yon porc'lain cell contains,
Was drawn, O, horror! from some brother's veins;
Or, wrought by chemic art, on terms too dear,
Is but transmuted from some negro's tear,
Which dropt, 'midst galling bonds, on foreign strand,
His bride still answers from his native land!—
Still turn indiff'rent from these *foreign* woes,
Nor suffer griefs so distant to oppose
The sickly taste, whose languid pulse to cheer
Two rifled worlds must drop the bitter tear!—

JOHN THELWALL

For what is Afric, what the Eastern Ind
To Europe's race, by polish'd arts refin'd?
Or why should pamper'd Luxury enquire
Who by the sword, or by the lash expire?

(1793)[273]

RICHARD BINGHAM DAVIS
(1771–1799)

Educated at Columbia College, Davis was a writer, editor, and reluctant businessman. Part of the New York literary world of the 1790s, he was known for his unprepossessing physique, his shyness around women, and his melancholic world view. He died young (age twenty-eight), from yellow fever. In this poem, Davis depicts the experience of a white refugee from the bloody and prolonged racial wars in Santo Domingo (modern Haiti). Accounts of the violence, which began as massive slave insurrections and led to ten years of civil war, prompted reactionary fears in American and other slaveholding societies.

from "Le Malheureux de St. Dominique"

Impell'd by sanguine rage, by vengeance fir'd,
  With deadly haste the sable myriads rush'd;
  Beneath their steps *humanity* was crush'd,
Reluctant from their presence *hope* retired.

Far off the sufferer saw his harvest blaze;
  But 'twas no time such distant fears to heed;
  Approaching fast he heard their bloody tread—
He heard such yells as fiends alone could raise.

The shrieks of death proclaim'd their furious course;
  O'er each devoted dome the flames roll'd fast:—
  Not the dread earthquake or tornado's blast,
Could hurl more rapidly destruction's force.

Wing'd by despair he fled the mingled roar;
  Through hostile bands, o'er mangled friends he flew;
  Panting he reach'd, among a wretched few,
The ships just parting from th' ensanguine shore. . . .

From the sad retrospect he fain would shrink:
  Where are his friends? their hearts' blood dyes the shore;

His dearest relatives?—Alas! No more;
His wife and children, where?—he dares not think.

From these dread scenes of frantic horror borne,
    Can ev'n Columbia's regions *him* delight?
    Though liberty and plenty greet his sight,
Can others' blessings bid *him* cease to mourn?
               (wr. 1794/pub. 1807)[274]

TIMOTHY DWIGHT (1752–1817)

Among the most accomplished Americans of his era, Dwight was a scholar, theologian, teacher, pastor, writer, academic leader, and public servant. He served as a military chaplain during the Revolutionary War, held the presidency of Yale for twenty-one years (1795–1816), rose to prominence as a founding member of the Hartford or Connecticut Wits, and produced some of the most important poetry of the first decades of the American republic.

The following lines are from a long work he composed when he was minister at Greenfield Hill, Connecticut, the second of two epic-length poems he wrote to demonstrate the worthiness of America as a source and subject of literature. The excerpts below fall into three thematic sections, all to do with slavery. The first examines, with unforgiving acuity, the pernicious effects on human beings of even the most "benign" forms of slavery, such as those Dwight's fellow northerners might congratulate themselves for practicing. The second presents a horrific vision of plantation slavery, replete with shockingly graphic images. The third builds on his earlier idea of slavery as the overarching sin of the modern world ("Satan's triumph over lost mankind"), to prophesy cataclysmic fates for those nations that sustain it.

from Greenfield Hill: *Part II, "The Flourishing Village"*

He never, dragg'd, with groans, the galling chain;
Nor hung, suspended, on th'infernal crane;
No dim, white spots deform his face, or hand,
Memorials hellish of the marking brand!
No seams of pincers, fears of scalding oil;
No waste of famine, and no wear of toil.
But kindly fed, and clad, and treated, he
Slides on, thro' life, with more than common glee. . . .

    He toils, 'tis true; but shares his master's toil;
With him, he feeds the herd, and trims the soil;

Helps to sustain the house, with clothes, and food,
And takes his portion of the common good:
Lost liberty his sole, peculiar ill,
And fix'd submission to another's will. . . .

    See fresh to life the Afric infant spring,
And plume its powers, and spread its little wing!
Firm is its frame, and vigorous is its mind,
Too young to think, and yet to misery blind.
But soon he sees himself to slavery born;
Soon meets the voice of power, the eye of scorn;
Sighs for the blessings of his peers, in vain;
Condition'd as a brute, tho' form'd a man.
Around he casts his fond, instinctive eyes,
And sees no good, to fill his wishes, rise:
(No motive warms, with animating beam,
Nor praise, nor property, nor kind esteem,
Bless'd independence, on his native ground,
Nor sweet equality with those around;) . . .
Thus, shut from honour's paths, he turns to shame,
And filches the small good, he cannot claim.
To sour, and stupid, sinks his active mind,
Finds joys in drink, he cannot elsewhere find;
Rule disobeys; of half his labour cheats;
In some safe cot, the pilfer'd turkey eats;
Rides hard, by night, the steed, his art purloins . . .
And makes revenge the balsam of his woe. . . .

    O thou chief curse, since curses here began;
First guilt, first woe, first infamy of man;
Thou spot of hell, deep smirch'd on human kind,
The uncur'd gangrene of the reasoning mind;
Alike in church, in state, and houshold all,
Supreme memorial of the world's dread fall,
O slavery! laurel of the Infernal mind,
Proud Satan's triumph over lost mankind! . . .

Ceaseless I hear the smacking whip resound;
Hark! that shrill scream! that groan of death-bed found!
See those throng'd wretches pant along the plain,
Tug the hard hoe, and sigh in hopeless pain!
Yon mother, loaded with her sucking child,
Her rags with frequent spots of blood defil'd,
Drags slowly fainting on . . .

487

Why glows yon oven with a sevenfold fire?
Crisp'd in the flames, behold a man expire!
Lo! by that vampyre's hand, yon infant dies,
Its brains dash'd out, beneath its father's eyes.
Why shrinks yon slave, with horror, from his meat?
Heavens! 'tis his flesh, the wretch is whipp'd to eat.
Why streams the life-blood from that female's throat?
She sprinkled gravy on a guest's new coat! . . .

Hark, hark, from morn to night, the realm around,
The cracking whip, keen taunt, and shriek, resound! . . .
The damned, sure, here clank th'eternal chain,
And waste with grief, or agonize with pain.
A Tartarus new! inversion strange of hell! . . .

Why surge not, o'er yon isles its spouting fires,
'Till all their living world in dust expires.
Crimes found their ruin's moral cause aloud,
And all heaven, sighing, rings with cries of brother's blood.

(1794)[275]

In the wake of the 1800 Virginia slave insurrection known as Gabriel's Re-
bellion and of Thomas Jefferson's election to the presidency, the Federalist
Dwight saw slavery as the gravest danger for America's future. In this excerpt
from a mocking tribute (and warning) to Jefferson's home state, Dwight might
also be seen to distantly foretell the outcome of the Civil War.

from "Triumph of Democracy"

Proceed great state—thy arts renew,
With double zeal thy course pursue,
Call on thy sister states t' obey,
And boldly grasp at sovereign sway—
Then pause—remember ere too late,
The tale of St. Domingo's fate,
Though Gabriel dies, a host remain
Oppress'd with slavery's galling chain,
And soon or late the hour will come,
Mark'd with Virginia's dreadful doom.

(January 1, 1801)[276]

ANONYMOUS

Its origins lost in the local humor of eighteenth-century London lawyers, this squib is simply a witty piece of graffiti recorded earlier in the century and passed down in various collections. The anti-lawyer wit depends, of course, on recognition of the African slave ("the Moor") as a symbol of victimhood.

Found Stuck on the Statue of the Moor Which Supports the Sun-Dial in Clements-Inn

In vain, poor sable son of woe,
    Thou seek'st the tender tear;
From thee, in vain, with pangs they flow,
    For mercy dwells not here.
From cannibals thou fled'st in vain;
    Lawyers less quarter give;
The first won't eat you till you're slain,
    the last will do't alive.

$$(1794)^{277}$$

EAGLESFIELD SMITH (c. 1770–1838) and HANNAH MORE (1745–1833)

A complex collaboration between Smith and More, recently discovered by Professor Alan Richardson, gave rise to this poem, which had long been attributed to More only. First published in More's "Cheap Repository Tracts" in 1795, the text combines Smith's poem about a female slave with More's additions that emphasize Christian themes. Smith, a minor Scottish romantic poet, seems to have submitted his poem to More, who augmented it and edited the final version. In these excerpts from a hymn of forty stanzas, all in the voice of a West Indian slave, the first nine (by Smith) focus on the slave's personal ordeal and suicidal despair. The remaining stanzas bespeak More's priorities and didactic aims: not only the salvation of individual slaves, but the conversion of the whole of Africa.

from "The Sorrows of Yamba, or the Negro Woman's Lamentation"

[stanzas 1–9:]
"In St. Lucie's distant isle,
    Still with Afric's love I burn;
Parted many a thousand mile,
    Never, never to return.

Come kind death and give me rest,
    Yamba has no friend but thee;
Thou can'st ease my throbbing breast,
    Thou canst set the prisoner free.

Down my cheeks the tears are dripping,
    Broken is my heart with grief;
Mangled my poor flesh with whipping,
    Come kind death! And bring relief.

Born on Afric's golden coast,
    Once I was as blest as you;

Parents tender I could boast,
    Husband dear, and children too.

Whity man he came from far,
    Sailing o'er the briny flood,
Who, with help of British tar,
    Buys up human flesh and blood.

With the baby at my breast,
    (Other two were sleeping by)
In my hut I sat at rest,
    With no thought of danger nigh.

From the bush at even tide
    Rush'd the fierce man-stealing crew;
Seiz'd the children by my side,
    Seiz'd the wretched Yamba too.

Then for love of filthy gold,
    Strait they bore me to the sea;
Cramm'd me down a slave-ship's hold,
    Where were hundreds stow'd like me.

Naked on the platform lying,
    Now we cross the tumbling wave;
Shrieking, sickening, fainting, dying,
    Deed of shame for Britons brave. . . .

[stanzas 26–28:]
And with grief when sinking low,
    Mark the road that Yamba trod;
Think how all her pain and woe
    Brought the captive home to God.

Now let Yamba too adore
    Gracious heaven's mysterious plan;
Now I'll count thy mercies o'er,
    Flowing thro' the guilt of man.

Now I'll bless my cruel capture,
    (Hence I've known a Saviour's name)
'Tis my grief is turn'd to rapture,
    And I half forget the blame. . . .

[stanzas 37–40:]
Where ye once have carried slaughter,
    Vice, and slavery, and sin;
Seiz'd on husband, wife, and daughter,
    Let the gospel enter in.

Thus where Yamba's native home,
  Humble hut of rushes stood,
Oh if there should chance to roam
  Some dear Missionary good;

Thou, in Afric's distant land,
  Still shalt see the man I love;
Join him to the Christian band,
  Guide his soul to realms above.

There no fiend again shall sever
  Those whom GOD hath join'd and blest;
There they dwell with him for ever,
  There 'the weary are at rest.'"

(1795)[278]

ANONYMOUS

The following lines, apparently written by a white supporter of Benjamin Banneker, were published in the preface to the 1796 edition of Banneker's *Almanac*. Banneker, born to free blacks descended from Maryland slaves, was an ingenious mathematician and scientist whose abilities antislavery activists cited to refute racialist theories of black inferiority. As this poet says elsewhere in his preface, "the colour of the skin is no ways connected with strength of mind or intellectual powers."

[Untitled] from Bannaker's Maryland, Pennsylvania, Delaware, Virginia, Kentucky, and North Carolina Almanack and Ephemeris, for the Year of Our Lord 1796

Nor you ye proud, impute to these the blame
If Afric's sons to genius are unknown,
For Banneker has prov'd they may acquire a name
As bright, as lasting as your own.

(1796)[279]

ANONYMOUS ["MATILDA"]

The author of the following poem, apparently a white female amateur writer and admirer of Phillis Wheatley, sent it in for publication in the *New York Magazine* of 1796. Despite her opposition to slavery, the poet's ideas about racial difference seem to vacillate between "missing-link" speculations and assertions of full equality.

On Reading the Poems of Phillis Wheatley, the African Poetess

His servile lot the beast of burden bears,
Unstung by memory, and unvext with cares,
With glad release returning evening smiles,
And food and slumber closes all his toils.
   If Afric's sable sons be doom'd to know
Nought but long bondage and successive woe,
Why did just Heav'n their sun-born souls refine
With passions, virtues, as our own, divine?
What tho' the sanguine flushes that adorn
Our limbs with tinges like the roseate morn,
Ah, partial Nature! on the race be lost;
Yet leave them peace and freedom still to boast:
For, as a just gradation still we find,
Up from the grov'ling to the enlighten'd mind,
And all the graces of the human form
Allied, in system, to the meanest worm;
The unfavor'd race in shade are meant to be
The link between the brutal world and we.
   In flowers we see that beauteous order rise
From earth to purest substance of the skies;
Rough and unformed in its first degree,

ANONYMOUS

More polish'd verdure in the next we see;
The third claims perfect beauty to its share,
And breathes its fragrant soul in kindred air.
    Free and impartial still, the gifts of Heaven
In just degrees to all mankind are given:
This boasts of mental, that corporeal grace,
Or the vain merits of a beauteous face;
And these no grace, no scientific art,
But all the nobler virtues of the heart;
As our's their souls with great ambition glow,
Or melt in softer sympathy of woe.
    Long did the hapless race in bondage groan,
In grief unheeded, and in worth unknown,
And long in vain their weeping genius bore
The sighs of sorrow to the eternal shore.
Oft when the Lover in some fav'rite grove,
Told the soft raptures of successful love,
Rude ruffian force the guiltless youth would tear
From all that love and nature render'd dear,
To unrelenting rigour's cruel sway,
To drudge his fond unhappy soul away.
    'Tis done! at length the long-withheld decree
Goes forth, that Afric shall be blest and free;
A PHILLIS rises, and the world no more
Denies the sacred right to mental pow'r;
While, Heav'n-inspir'd, she proves her Country's claim
To Freedom, and her own to deathless Fame.

$(1796)^{280}$

ANONYMOUS ["L.B.C." OF ARLINGTON, BENNINGTON COUNTY, VT.]

Though this poet remains unknown, the citizens of Vermont had a strong record of antislavery sentiment. In 1777 they passed the first state constitution to prohibit slavery. In L.B.C.'s powerfully eloquent poem, the author mounts a methodical, reasoned argument for abolition based on the contradiction between America's founding principles and its tolerance of slavery. Most remarkable are his defense of slave insurrections then raging in the Caribbean and his vivid Thomsonian invocation (see Thomson's "Summer," elsewhere included) of an Atlantic Ocean "crimsoned" by the "gore" of millions of slaves transported over it.

from "Reflections on the Slavery of the Negroes, Addressed to the Conscience of Every American Citizen"

We broke our fetters, yet enchain our kind.
We boast and glory in our liberty,
And in our sweet equality rejoice,
And joy that we be so supremely blest,
In wealth, peace, safety, wise, and virtuous laws;
Yet, fifty myriads of our kindred kind,
The hapless children of rich Afric's shores,
Groan round our land, in base captivity,
And weep, and sigh, bound in Columbia's chains.
Alas! our boasted justice how absurd!
We exercise our reason but by halves:
We make a mockery of sacred truth,
To which we feign our hearts so much adhere.
The shafts we aim at tyrants and their crews,
Again rebound, and sorely wound ourselves.
The murd'rous sons of savage, curst Algiers,
Who seize, distress, enslave, and plunge in woes,

ANONYMOUS

Bound in vile chains, our hapless brothers dear,
We execrate, enrag'd and fraught with ire:
But we reflect not, that for ONE of ours,
In Afric groaning, HOSTS of Afric's sons,
Than beasts worse us'd, Columbians hold enslav'd.
Why thus so partial? why so blindly judge?
Why suffer passion reason to controul?
Why suffer lust of wealth, and venal pride,
To suffocate, triumphant, thus our virtue?
Why hope we justice, whilst unjust ourselves?
Sweet liberty, enamour'd of our souls,
From one of us if snatch'd, our bosoms blaze,
We're anger, pity, wrath, and feeling all.
But, for those thousands of poor purchas'd slaves,
Debas'd, insulted, victims to our power,
Who, toiling, bleed and sweat t'enlarge our store,
We feel no pity, and we breathe no sigh.
Let us be just, beneficent, and fair,
And deal with all, as we would be dealt by;
Nor from *our* colour dare to deem ourselves
The *only* men who're worthy to be free.
Was liberty the right of whites alone,
How *few* were free compar'd to mankind all;
And if *own'd* only by the *major* part,
Then whites should toil the slaves of sable men. . . .
The fierce revolt of Afric's tortur'd tribes.
Which now wide range around Carribean isles,
Our half reflecting minds too quick condemn.
Were we in dire captivity and chains,
Opprest, degraded, as they've been for ages,
We would revolt, had we the means and pow'r,
And deal destruction to our tyrant foes,
Strowing our way with carcasses and blood,
And deem it justice, reason, noblest virtue.
Whips, chains, swords, so long in tyrants' hands,
Are now destroying—Is this more than just?
If blacks are cruel, vengeful, and unfeeling,
And deal to Christians terrors, sword, and fire,
As they now strive to break their galling yokes—
Do they not act from Christian precedent:—
Wrote, round the globe ten thousand times, in blood?
Were sable men to pour on Christian lands

Each bitter woe, that human rage could cause,
Such as fam'd Titius' death to Judah's tribes,
What human soul could prove them aught unjust,
Or, that Europeans did not merit all?
"O shocking! horrid!" Some, perhaps, exclaim:
But pause, good reader—and reflective muse—
What myriads, annual, of each age and sex,
For twelve score years, have been from Afric torn,
Torn from each joy that men could taste or lose,
And doom'd to every anguish men could feel—:
What equal numbers, prematurely fell,
Destroy'd and butcher'd by innumerous means,
Yet unoffending, in their own defence:—
What ruin, havoc, and devouring flames,
Hath rag'd for cent'ries thro' that hapless land;—
What miseries keen, astonishing, and vast,
Complex and countless, and yet undeserv'd—
Hath mourning Afric's suff'ring tribes endur'd—
Yea—such endur'd as mortal can't depict,
The task requires a far superior pow'r.
Now—by whom caus'd, and wrought these horrors all,
These pungent, stern, and unutterable woes,—
This havoc of humanity and man,—
Which reign'd o'er Afric's various tongues & climes,
Thro' such a vast revolving lapse of years?
But, why demand we? Do we not well know
The savage authors of these direful deeds?—
And, are they not—O! truth disgraceful! Christians?
They Christians? Yea—so call'd, but truly fiends! . . .
Could we appeal to thee, O, thou Atlantic!
Thou could'st support our charge; for, thou didst bear
Our captive millions o'er thy boist'rous waves,
In gloomy, floating prisons, bound in chains,
And round invested by ferocious crews,
The vicious dregs of tyrant Europe's slaves:
And oft our gore hath crimson'd thy green serge,
Pour'd copious from our purple tort'ring wounds:
And thousands, while transporting o'er thy tide,
Did in thy liquid bosom find their tombs;
By hunger, sickness, thirst, and pains destroy'd,
By sorrows, griefs, ill usage, and despair.
Bear witness to our woes, ye virtuous men . . .

ANONYMOUS

Who, in a venal, hostile, vicious world,
Have spoke and wrote the friends of Afric's tribes.
In spite of tyrants, wits, and learned fools,
And hosts of haughty, selfish impious foes,
You've nobly dar'd t'assert the rights of men,
And spread humanity and reason round.

$(1796)^{281}$

ANONYMOUS AFRICAN WOMAN (fl. 1796) and GEORGIANA CAVENDISH, DUCHESS OF DEVONSHIRE (1757–1806)

The two poems below arise from an extraordinary episode in Mungo Park's *Travels in the Interior Districts of Africa* (1799). In July 1796, while waiting for the King of Bambarra's slaves to ferry him across the Niger to the capital city of Sego (in modern-day Mali), Park was suddenly turned away and forced to seek shelter in an outlying village. Anxious about his safety, he was welcomed by a group of women who fed him, gave him a place to sleep, and sang him the following improvised song as they worked.

Untitled

The winds roared, and the rains fell.
The poor white man, faint and weary, came and sat under our tree.
He has no mother to bring him milk; no wife to grind his corn.
Chorus. Let us pity the white man; no mother has he, &c. &c.

(composed 1796/pub. 1799)

Sometime between Park's departure from Africa in 1797 (aboard an American slave ship) and the publication of his book in 1799, Georgiana Cavendish, the Duchess of Devonshire, saw this little lyric and was moved to rewrite it in her own version and commission a composer to set it to music. A longtime friend of Charles James Fox, one of the leaders of the abolitionist movement, the Duchess was obviously sympathetic to the plight of Africans and eager to commemorate this instance of kindness by these African women to a European stranger. The resulting song can be read as a striking example of cross-cultural connection, with possible overtones of feminist identification, the vogue for primitivism, and the politics of abolitionism.

A Negro Song, From Mr. Park's Travels

I.

The loud wind roar'd, the rain fell fast;
The White Man yielded to the blast:

He sat him down, beneath our tree;
For weary, sad, and faint was he;
And ah, no wife, or mother's care,
For him, the milk or corn prepare:

CHORUS.

The White Man, shall our pity share;
Alas, no wife or mother's care,
For him, the milk or corn prepare.

II.

The storm is o'er; the tempest past;
And Mercy's voice has hush'd the blast.
The wind is heard in whispers low;
The White Man, far away must go;—
But ever in his heart will bear
Remembrance of the Negro's care.

CHORUS.

Go, White Man, go;—but with thee bear
The Negro's wish, the Negro's prayer;
Remembrance of the Negro's care.

(1799)[282]

CHARLES CRAWFORD
(1752–post 1825)

Born in Antigua to a landowning family and educated at Cambridge University, Crawford spent much of his later life in England, where he wrote poetry and tracts on various subjects, including his 1790 abolitionist pamphlet *Observations Upon Negro-Slavery*. Controversy touched his life: a rumored expulsion from Queens' College, Cambridge, in 1773 and, in the early 1800s, his opportunistic assumption—without official recognition—of the title "Earl of Crawford and Lindsay."

In this excerpt from a much longer poem, Crawford argues against slavery on the basis of both Christian doctrine and classical precedent (the "awful doom" of "ancient Rome"). But he also—perhaps because of his firsthand knowledge of island life—argues for gradual rather than immediate emancipation, to avoid harm to blacks as well as whites.

from The Progress of Liberty; A Pindaric Ode

> To form on equal* rules the plan
> He taught, which fastens man to man;
> That all who feel th'ethereal fire,
> Are sons alike of one great sire.
> O could the doctrines which he deign'd impart,
> Not on the tongue be planted but the heart;
> No more the sons of Afric opprest,
> In servitude and ignorance should pine;
> But when by freedom, animated, blest,
> Of genius also know the flame divine;
> Then should the chearless desart raise her voice†

---

* [from Crawford's note:] According to the principles of christianity we should consider the Africans as our equals and our brethren.

† [Crawford's note:] Those who planned the settlement of Sierra Leone, are worthy of the highest praise. It may be the means of extirpating the slave-trade, and of gradually introduc-

And like the fragrant rose should blossom and rejoice. . .

O Britain, form'd by nature's partial hand,
The seat of arts, renown'd, delightful land;
Think oft upon the fame of ancient Rome,
Whose eagle to remotest regions flew;
And learn this lesson from her awful doom,
That the same judgments the same crimes pursue;
The God who her chastis'd may not spare thee,
Revere his laws, give others freedom,* and be free.

(1796)[283]

---

ing science, religion, freedom, and happiness into every part of Africa. In the company's schools at Sierra Leone, 300 children are educated, among whom are some young African princes.

* [from Crawford's note:] The slave-trade is the opprobrium of England and several nations, as well as the scourge of Africa. It would tend to the interest, as well as the honor, of England, to abolish it *immediately*. The emancipation of the negroes, however, in the West Indies should be *gradual*, for their own advantage, as well as the advantage of others. An abrupt emancipation of the negroes, according to the mad schemes of that seditious and profane scribbler Thomas Paine, would make every island in the West Indies, and some of the states of America, like St. Domingo, the scenes of anarchy, vice, cruelty, and misery.

CHARLES ISAAC MUNGO DIBDIN (1768–1833)

The eldest of three illegitimate children born to Charles Dibdin and the dancer Harriet Pitt (whom Dibdin later abandoned), Charles Isaac Mungo may have the distinction of being the first white person named after a black character. His father had starred as Mungo, the African slave in Bickerstaffe's *The Padlock*, a few months before he was born. Despite his disadvantages, "Dibdin the younger" became a successful playwright, songwriter, and, at Sadler's Wells, theater manager. Unlike his father's verse, young Dibdin's sentimental poem is free of slave dialect and unmixed with any comic or stereotypical effects. Indeed, the opening couplet could be read as a reproach to his father and others who treat slavery lightly, and the poem as a whole makes a claim for the wretchedness of slavery eclipsing the triviality of European life.

Negro Slave. A Pathetic Ballad

Ye children of Pleasure! come hither and see,
A sight that shall check your irreverent glee;
Ye children of Woe! hear a tale which awhile
A sense of your own various griefs shall beguile:
Thy tear, at the tale, divine Sympathy! shed;
Rejoice, sweet Compassion! at viewing this grave;
Here Wretchedness hides, unmolested, its head—
For under this turf lies a poor Negro Slave!

Depriv'd of whatever endears us to life,
His country, his freedom, his children, and wife;
Grown mad with reflection, his spirit he freed—
With pity, ye rigid, contemplate the deed!
His corpse, unregarded, disgrac'd the highway,
Till, blushing, Humanity's credit to save,
With tenderness Charity hasten'd to pay
Mortality's due to the poor Negro Slave!

CHARLES ISAAC MUNGO DIBDIN

Ye kind passers by, who this spot turn to view,
The tribute bequeath to his memory due—
May Peace watch his pillow, whose breast can bestow
A generous tear o'er the annals of woe!
The sigh that you heave, and the tear that you shed,
Remembrance on Heaven's blest records shall 'grave;
But vengeance shall heavily fall on each head,
That spurn'd and oppress'd him, a poor Negro Slave!

(1796)[284]

SUSANNA MASON (1749–1805)

A Philadelphia Quaker and associate of Benezet and other abolitionists, Mason met the extraordinary Benjamin Banneker on a visit to Maryland. Deeply impressed by his accomplishments, she sent him this poem in his honor. Banneker responded warmly, apparently unbothered by the double standard implied by her closing admonition.

from "An Address to Benjamin Banneker, an African Astronomer, Who Presented the Author with a Manuscript Almanack"

Genius smil'd upon thy birth,
And application call'd it forth;
That times and tides thou couldst presage,
And traverse the celestial stage,
Where shining globes their circles run
In swift rotation round the sun:
Could'st tell how planets in their way,
From order ne'er were known to stray;
Sun, moon, and stars, when they will rise,
When sink below the upper skies;
When an eclipse shall veil their light,
And hide their splendor from our sight.
Now we'll apply thy wond'rous skill,
The wise may oft be wiser still. . . .
Now, as I've said, though thou art wise,
Permit me here to moralize. . . .
Thou, a man exalted high,
Conspicuous in the world's keen eye,
On record now thy name's enrolled,
And future ages will be told,

SUSANNA MASON

There lived a man called Banneker,
An African astronomer.
Thou need'st to have a special care
Thy conduct with thy talent square,
That no contaminating vice,
Obscure thy lustre in our eyes,
Or cast a shade upon thy merit
Or blast the praise thou might'st inherit:
For folly in an orb so bright,
Will strike on each beholder's sight:
Nay, stand exposed from age to age,
Extant on some historian's page. . . .
Let fair examples mark thy round
Unto thine orbit's utmost bound.
"The good man's path," the scriptures say,
"Shines more and more to perfect day."

(1796)[285]

THOMAS JAMES MATHIAS
(1754–1835)

The continuing debate over abolition in the 1790s inevitably meant that African slavery and race would surface in the political satire of the day. Here the Cambridge-educated Tory satirist Mathias mocks the practice of printing Parliamentary speeches in the newspapers. Among his targets are the abolitionist MPs William Wilberforce and Sir Francis Burdett (the latter known for his swarthy complexion).

from Dialogue III of The Pursuits of Literature. A Satirical Poem

Mere talkers now, not writers, are preferr'd.
Look at that paper: if you print the speeches,
Pitt seems George Rose, or like Sir Richard, preaches,
Nor tone, nor majesty, nor patriot fires;
Methinks the wit of Sheridan expires;
Lost in Dundas the Caledonian twang,
Though Pitt, and port, and property he sang;
Print negro speeches, and in reason's spite,
Lo, Wilberforce is black, and Francis white.

(1796)[286]

CAPTAIN THOMAS MORRIS
(1732–post 1806)

A scholar at Winchester who then spent twenty years in the British army, Morris served in various campaigns in the West Indies and North America, before marrying and turning to a literary life in England in 1767. He became well known as a songwriter, published a variety of literary works, and was still writing occasional verse to amuse Bath society as late as 1806.

The story of Quashy (and her doomed lover Quaco) is set against the chaos of factional fighting in the French colony of Martinique in 1794, which erupted with the Republic's edict ending slavery and the arrival of the British fleet. Morris's poem exhibits remarkable attitudes: criticism of British policies, sympathy for the French Revolution, proto-feminist ideas about the abilities of women, and fierce antipathy to slavery. Much of the power of the poem emerges from Morris's firsthand knowledge of Caribbean slavery: the abomination of white men raping their own mulatto daughters to produce fairer and fairer offspring, and the widespread suicides that were not just a literary convention but a gruesome fact of slave life.

from "Quashy; or the Coal-Black Maid"

There Quashy dwelt; a slave of lowliest kind;*
A state ill suited to her noble mind.
Her eyes like gems beneath her brows were set;
Her teeth were iv'ry, and her face was jet;
Tall was her stature, as her shape was neat;
Her fingers small, and delicate her feet;
Then from her lips such melting accents broke,†
That drivers almost felt when Quashy spoke:

---

* [Morris's note:] She was a field-negro, not a domestic one: slaves of the latter sort are seldom ill treated.

† [Morris's note:] The negro women have often voices of wonderful sweetness.

509

Such was her person; her superior part,
An honest principle and tender heart. . . .

O Quashy, could thy foes thy beauty see,
Yet mock that color which gives grace to thee?
Could they behold thy manners and thy face,
And not compassionate thy hapless race?
Yes; there are men with brutal passion curst,
To women prone, but ever to the worst:
Unprincipled, unfeeling, unrefin'd,
Who scarce admit that woman has a mind.
Dull, sensual beings, quite absorb'd in self;
The dupes of harlots, and the slaves of pelf;
In filthy revels roll the human swine,
Made sick with gluttony, or mad with wine . . .
Of this licentious crew was Quashy's lord;
A noble once, by simple clowns ador'd:
Faln from his state, and frantic at the loss,
His little title gone, and little cross,
He rush'd to war; exposing, in despair,
That life his pride conceiv'd below his care.
His partner was a high, imperious dame,
Still proudly glorying in a fancied name;
The style of *citizen* too great to brook,
She yet was *madam with the haughty look*;
And when her nation made their negroes free,
Like her mad consort, spurned the just decree. . . .
Quashy, resolv'd her legal rights to claim,
Approach'd the mansion of her stately dame:
She crept with timid step and falt'ring tongue,
Where madam in her hammock gently swung;
And, softly warning her that slaves were freed,
Begg'd for that liberty the law decreed.
Long did the sable beauty plead her cause;
But what care dames of birth for rights and laws!
Her, stript of privilege, no truth could reach;
As well might lambs the hungry wolves beseech . . .
She next address'd her lewd, inhuman lord;
For freedom argued, and his grace implor'd:
Mark'd for his prey,* he durst her claim deride;

---

* [Morris's note:] The amorous intercourse of masters with black slaves is too well known to
need explanation; the poor creatures dare not resist: and the horrid practice of "washing the

Of his black haram, Quashy was the pride:
Tho' brutes love brutes, by tender flames inspir'd,
He, worse than brute, could scorn what he desir'd.
She fear'd the ruffian might her spoiler prove;
And Quashy's heart had felt the force of love:
The maid had charmed a youth from Afric's plains,
Sold, like herself, to wear this tyrant's chains:
From the same region both the lovers came;
The same their beauty, and their worth the same:
[Quaco], tall and strong, and full of manly grace,
She, blest with softness and the charms of face. . . .

O Liverpool, O Bristol, brave not fame;
Bid your youth feel, and hide their fathers' shame;
Extend their commerce; trade where 'er they can;
But never more presume to deal in man:
And thou, sage Glasgow, for thy learning fam'd,
With Oxford and with Cambridge often nam'd,
Art thou engag'd in this ungodly work;
Thou, boastful of thy faith in holy kirk?
Reflect what ills from self-delusion spring;
Faith void of morals is a dang'rous thing;
Mistaken mortals pray but to their cost,
If, while they pray, humanity is lost. . . .

[After Quaco's death]
Despair now whisper'd, and her heart approv'd,
Not to survive the constant man she lov'd;
Mild, but resolv'd, and hiding her intent,
Forth to the woods the beauteous Ethiop went:
She fell'd the tree . . .
Whose vapor oft the wretched negro tries,
Till, by its strange effects, he swells and dies.
Her hut was clos'd, the pile funereal laid;
A cloud of smoke involv'd the coal-black maid;
One tear she dropt . . .
But home and Quaco open'd to her view:
She yielded to the fate her soul desir'd,
Call'd on her lover, and in peace expir'd.

                                    (1796)[287]

---

blackmoor white" has by some old wretches been gloried in; that is, intriguing with the
mother, daughter, granddaughter, &c. till the black color disappear.

ANONYMOUS ["A VERY INGENIOUS LADY, AND A DEVOUT CHRISTIAN"]

Nothing is known of this anonymous Englishwoman except that she was a friend of Sir Philip Gibbes (1731–1815), who was a prominent Barbadian planter, a humane if unrepentant owner of slaves, and author of *Instructions for the Treatment of Negroes* (London, 1786). It was to Gibbes that she sent the following five poems, all of which were first published in the enlarged third edition of his tract, printed in London in 1797. The absence of any local detail or insider knowledge of West Indian life, together with the platitudinous tone of the poems, suggests that the "ingenious Lady" (as Gibbes called her) had no firsthand experience of slavery in the Caribbean.

The following is the first of three little poems apparently imagined (however implausibly) as songs the slaves could sing in the fields to console themselves with the idea of religious salvation as reward for earthly labor.

[Untitled]*

See! The Great God sends forth his Sun
To ripen all the fields of canes:
'Tis just as if he said, "Well done
Good negroes! I'll reward your pains."

And so he will:—a little while
We have to labour here below,
And for our honest faithful toil
God will his heaven bestow.

(1797)[288]

---

* [from Gibbes's introduction:] I desire that [the slaves] . . . may be taught to sing psalms.—I wish they could be engaged to use the following stanzas, which were sent me by a very ingenious Lady, and a devout Christian; who imagines that the singing such little pieces in rhyme would cheer and enliven their spirits.

The second hymn is also paternalistic: it would have the slaves voice their gratitude for being kept from "mischief," "folly," and "sloth" by their forced labor, as well as their acceptance that "the master we serve, knows for us what is best."

[Untitled]

How useful is labour, how healthful and good!
It keeps us from mischief, procures wholesome food;
It saves from much sickness and loathsome disease
That fall on the idle and pamper'd with ease:
Then let us work chearful, nor think it is hard,
That from folly and sloth we thus are debarr'd.
God, the master we serve, knows for us what is best:
And when life's toils are ended we sweetly shall rest;
For ev'ry good deed in God's book is recorded.
So faithful good negroes will be surely rewarded.
                                        (1797)[289]

The third in the set offers a variation on the same themes, but is designed for slaves to sing not at work but during the "free" time of their holidays.

A Grace to be sung on festive days

Come dear companions, let us sing
To God our gracious, glorious king:
To him our chearful songs we raise:
Glory to God on high, and praise—
            Hallelujah!
Bless the fields we dig and plant!
Lord! supply our ev'ry want:
Give our souls and bodies food,
And grateful hearts for ev'ry good.
            Hallelujah!
                                        (1797)[290]

The next two poems, probably by the same lady, also appeared in Gibbes's 1797 pamphlet. The first of them is a significant, if to modern ears repulsive, apology for slavery that recites familiar (and flawed) arguments: that Africans were the cursed descendants of Ham, that they would have been killed in African wars had not the slave trade made captives saleable, and that the slaves' access to Christian salvation is worth any amount of worldly suffering. The ef-

513

fort to exculpate whites in this poem extends even to the claim that European slave traders would never have bought African slaves "if *Black Men* had not sold them."

The Negro's Address to His Fellows

We're children of Cham!* He his father offended,
Who gave him the curse, which to us is descended.
"A servant of servants" alas! is our curse;
And bad as it is, it has sav'd us from worse.
For, *Master of Masters,* say friends are we fitted?
Our passions unbridled.—Our self-will unbitted.
In our own country free, we Savages ran;
And negro made war on his brother *Black Man.*
To those ta'en in battle no mercy we gave:
Each pris'ner was murther'd or sold for a slave.
So that if to White Men now slaves you behold them,
White Men had not bought, if *Black Men* had not sold them.
Nay, were we more happy, or felt we less evil,
When snakes were our Gods, and we worship'd the devil?
A servant of servants much more were we then:
We labour'd for devils.—We now work for men.
A blessed exchange we may make, if we chuse,
The knowledge of God for the freedom we lose:
A far better freedom than knowledge shall give,
And children of God we, Cham's children, shall live.
Belov'd by our masters, kindly treated, esteemed,
And, in God's own due time, from Cham's curse quite redeem'd.
Mean time ev'ry slave, who his duty doth here,
Shall receive his reward when God shall appear
To take away evil, and sickness and pain:
And find that his labour hath not been in vain.
If we suffer with Christ, with him we shall reign;
For he came a servant, to death was obedient
To crucify pride THUS he found it expedient.

(1797)[291]

The irony of the final poem, which was probably written in the comfort of an English household, lies in its titular assumption that plantation slaves regularly had meat for their meals. Again here the effort to conjure up an image of

* [Author's note:] Ham, the son of Noah, from whom the negroes are descended, is written Cham in the Hebrew.

"happy Negroes" thankful for their masters' beneficence is as unsubtle as it is unpersuasive.

A Grace after Meat

> God loves a thankful heart:——and we
>   Have nothing more to give.
> First, Lord, we sing our thanks to thee
>   For all that we receive.
> Our master too for this day's feast
>   We thank with chearful voice:
> Give us to see him, Lord, thy guest,
>   And in his good rejoice.
>
>   (1797)[292]

ANONYMOUS (fl. 1775–1796)

The "sable bard" who wrote this long poem poses a mystery: identifying himself as a black American, the speaker tells a story of capture and sale into slavery as a child, eight years in the American army fighting the Revolutionary War, and then manumission, followed by marriage and family, financial struggles, enlistment as a commercial sailor, and the wretched luck of being captured by Algerian pirates and sold as a Christian slave in Islamic North Africa.

To whatever degree the biographical details are true, in Canto II the speaker uses the clamor then raging in America (for military action against these North African slavetakers), as the ironic backdrop for his indictment of American slavery. The speaker's patriotism deepens his anger at America for not rejecting a slave system inherited from European imperialists.

from Canto II of The American in Algiers, or the Patriot of Seventy-Six in Captivity

Now gentle reader, think thy task not hard
Awhile to listen to a sable bard,
Whose pen undaunted thus shall dare address
A world of critics, and her thoughts express,
Th' envenom'd source of every ill to trace,
That preys incessant on his hapless race;
And trump the inconsistency of those
Feign'd friends to liberty, feign'd slavery's foes;
From that piratic coast where slavery reigns,
And freedom's champions wear despotic chains;
Turn to Columbia—cross the western waves,
And view her wide spread empire throng'd with slaves;
Whose wrongs unmerited, shall blast with shame
Her boasted rights, and prove them but a name.

ANONYMOUS

... To make mankind in vicious habits bold,
By bart'ring virtue for the love of gold.
For these, old Europe's fleets first cross'd the flood,
And bath'd the coast of Africa in blood;
For these, her sons have rob'd the world of peace,
And sluic'd the veins of half the human race;*
For these, Hispania's pious children hurl'd
Death and destruction round the western world;
For these, Britannia loos'd the dogs of war ...
For these, French, Dutch, and Portuguese, and Danes,
Have slaughter'd millions on Columbia's plains;
And with our sable sons the place supply'd
Of tribes less suited to sustain their pride. . . .†

Ye rev'rend Sages! who first fram'd the plan,
And rear'd the fabric of the rights of man,‡
To you I speak, in truth's undaunted tone,
And plead the cause of Afric's injur'd sons.
Say then, ye Sires! who, by a just decree,
O'erturn'd a *throne,* and made a nation *free;*
Does not that Sacred Instrument contain
The Laws of Nature, and the Rights of Man?
If so—from whence did you the right obtain
To bind our Africans in slav'ry's chain?
To scourge the back, or wound the bleeding heart,
By all the base tyrannic rules of art?
Nature ne'er gave it.—Read that first of laws,
The Manifesto of Columbia's cause;
'Tis your own act, on which you found your claim
Thro' endless ages to unrival'd fame;

---

* [Author's note:] Witness millions of the natives of both Indies, wantonly sacrificed by the Spaniards, French, Dutch, Portuguese, and British. To say nothing of the unhappy Africans, whose seacoasts have for more than two hundred years been the theatre of wars, massacres, &c. instigated by speculators in flesh and blood for the sole purpose of procuring slaves, by purchasing prisoners from all parties; yet the perpetrators of those enormities, their heirs and assigns, appeal to the mandates of heaven for justification.

† [Author's note:] The natives of America are of so turbulent a disposition as to render abortive every effort to enslave them and it is this together with their inability of body to withstand the fatigues of constant manual labour, that accounts why the Europeans chose to extirpate them, and fill up their places with slaves brought 5000 miles.

‡ [Author's note:] The Declaration of Independence.

Whose well form'd sentences thus spread abroad
The Rights of Nature, and the Gift of God:
"We hold these Truths self-evident to be,
All men are Equal and created Free;
Endow'd with Rights, no Law can e'er suppress,
Life, Liberty, Pursuit of Happiness."
Recall the feelings of each Patriot mind,
When first this mighty Instrument was sign'd,
Hear the loud echoes rend the distant sky,
And *death*, or *freedom*, was the general cry.

What then, and are all men created free,
And Afric's sons continue slaves to be,
And shall that hue our native climates gave,
Our birthright forfeit, and ourselves enslave?
Are we not made like you of flesh and blood,
Like you some wise, some fools, some bad, some good?
In short, are we not men? and if we be,
By your own declaration we are free. . . .

Great son of Mars, with deathless honour crown'd,
Mount Vernon's pride o'er earth and seas renown'd,
Freedom's first born, who stem'd the hostile flood;
And march'd to liberty through fields of blood;
Oh how my bowels yearn to see the brave,
The worthy WASHINGTON possess a slave;
If you whose sword still reeks with despots blood,
Have drench'd your fields with Afric's purple flood;
Sure some malicious fiend to blot your fame,
Has sanction'd usurpation with your name:
Look o'er your fields, and see them black with slaves,
Where freedom's flag in boasted triumph waves,
Nor let your soul despotic laws despise,
Since as despotic ones yourself devise,
And now convert to slavery's galling chain,
That sword you drew to aid the rights of man:
Such, mighty chieftain, is thy portrait drawn,
By one who knows not basely how to fawn.

And you brave patriots who in private ranks,
Laid claims well founded to your country's thanks;
Who now the last, o'er trembling slaves extend,
And insult daily with oppression blend. . . .
You say all men were first created free,

Whence then the right t' usurp their liberty?
Hath not the African as good a right,
Deriv'd from nature to enslave the white?
As whites to say the hue our climate gave,
Our rights shall forfeit and ourselves enslave? . . .

   Near where the Gambia's mighty current rolls,
My ancestors from immemorial time
Had liv'd contented in old Afric's clime;
Here on the summit of a verdant hill . . .
My father liv'd—of all mankind the friend,
Whose constant care was virtue to defend.
And sweet relief to ev'ry want extend. . . .
Beneath this tender parent's fost'ring care,
My father's joy, my mother's only dear,
In youth's gay hours, I spent a joyous life,
Free from contention, care, or feudal strife;
Nurs'd in the lap of luxury and ease . . .
Life was one continued scene of bliss. . . .

   But oh! what mis'ries tread on heels of joy!
How soon dark clouds oft' veil the beautious sky! . . .
Swift to the shore a band of ruffians came
And wrap'd our peaceful mansion in a flame,
While unarm'd warriors met the desp'rate clan,
And fought impetuous for the rights of man,
But skill or bravery here could nought avail
'Gainst foes well arm'd, who ev'ry side assail;
Friends, children, lovers, age nor sex they spare,
But wife from husband, child from parent tear. . . .
In haste the monsters now their pris'ners strip,
And with a lash more keen than phaeton's whip,
Drive them unfeelingly toward the ship. . . .

   A faint description of which floating hell,
Aid me, ye heav'nly muses, to reveal.
Here groans of anguish, screams, and dismal cries,
Forth from the deep and noxious hole arise;
Lashes, and oaths, and threats, and clanking chains,
From the hoarse music of those curs'd domains;
Hundreds of human beings here confin'd,
In liquid torrents melt away their mind;
While savage seamen with ferocious pride,
Damn, huff, and beat, the slaves on ev'ry side;

For eight long weeks amidst this doleful scene,
I liv'd confin'd upon the boist'rous main;
Parching with thirst, and threat'ned with starvation;
Nor in that time beheld the fair I prize,
Though oft' I heard her agonizing cries.

At length in sight Columbia's shores appear,
Where Baltimore her lofty turrets rear,
And Albion's flag in haughty triumph wav'd,
The proud insignia of a world enslav'd.
Now money'd crouds advance with eager pace
To cull this cargo of the human race;
With caution great, and scrutinizing eyes,
Each jockey views the slaves before he buys . . .
My father, mother, sister, self, and wife,
To diff'rent ones were sold, and sold for life.

One short embrace we crave, this they refuse—
The drivers lash precludes all interviews;
By vi'lence parted, each reluctant mov'd
With tardy steps from objects so belov'd.
Since which, the earth has round yon central sun
Full five and twenty times her orbit run . . .

I'm now worn out with servitude and woe,
And patient wait for death to strike the blow
That ends each care, each suffering and dread . . .
And sends me headlong to the silent dead. . . .

And now base tyrants, who no mercy shew,
I crave no sympathetic tears from you;
Callous to every feeling of the heart,
Language must fail, your baseness to impart.
But you, whose breasts with warm affections glow . . .
Whose softer bosoms feel paternal care,
Fraternal love or filial duty share;
And you whose hearts, a tender passion warms,
Who know the pow'r of love's ten thousand charms,
To hearts like yours, which soft impressions feel,
Of Afric's race, I make the just appeal;
And leave the portrait which my pen has drawn,
A short, concise, and comprehensive one.

(1797)[293]

These lines, appended to "The American in Algiers," seem to be by a supportive white writer, who may have assisted the "sable bard" in producing the poem to which this coda is attached.

Conclusion. A Word of Comfort to the Author

Hapless descendant of old Afric's race,
Check the big tear that damps thy aged face;
See o'er the south, the Gaulic flag unfurl'd,*
Proclaiming peace and freedom to the world:
That splendid sun that gilds the Indian isles,
On tyrants frown, but on your brethren smiles;
Anon Columbia'll rouse, from prej'dice freed,
To share the glories of that godlike deed;
E'er long (to set no more) shall Freedom rise,
Emancipate the world, and glad the skies.

(1797)

* [Author's note:] The French have declared all their negroes in the West-Indies free.

ANONYMOUS

Poetic tributes to slaves and their descendants turn up in unexpected corners of the English landscape. These simple rhyming couplets from St. Andrew's church-yard in Chesterton, Cambridge, commemorate the child of Olaudah Equiano ("Gustavus Vassa"), the former slave whose life and work are treated elsewhere in this book. The poem offers a touching instance of interracial kindness, in describing the burial rites performed by the children of the village for the poor girl whose parents had died earlier.

[Gravestone inscription]

ANNA MARIA VASSA
Daughter of GUSTAVUS VASSA, the African
She died July 21, 1797
Aged 4 years
Should simple village rhymes attract thine eye,
Stranger, as thoughtfully thou passest by,
Know that there lies beside this humble stone
A child of colour haply not thine own.
Her father born of Afric's sun-burnt race,
Torn from his native field, ah foul disgrace:
Through various toils, at length to Britain came
Espoused, so Heaven ordain'd, an English dame,
And follow'd Christ; their hope two infants dear.
But one, a hapless orphan, slumbers here.
To bury her the village children came.
And dropp'd choice flowers, and lisp'd her early fame;
And some that lov'd her most, as if unblest,
Bedew'd with tears the white wreath on their breast;
But she is gone and dwells in that abode,
Where some of every clime shall joy in God.

(c. 1797)[294]

FRANCES HOLCROFT
(c. 1780–1844)

Daughter of the English writer and radical Thomas Holcroft, as a girl Frances (or "Fanny") suffered the death of her mother and the suicide of her older brother within a year of each other in 1789–90. She nonetheless went on to pursue a career as a novelist and translator, while also producing occasional poetry. The poem below, composed while she was still a teenager, appeared in *The Monthly Magazine*, a new literary journal. An editorial note disclosed that the eighth and ninth stanzas were contributed by someone else, opening some very interesting possibilities, as the magazine regularly published the young Coleridge, Southey, Lamb, and others destined for later fame. The overtones of Christ's crucifixion in the opening line ("transpierc'd," "streaming wound") lend particular force to the critique of Christian hypocrites that informs this emotional attack on the inhumanity of slavery.

The Negro

Transpierc'd with many a streaming wound,
    The Negro lay, invoking death:
His blood o'erflow'd the reeking ground—
    He, gasping, drew his languid breath.

His sable cheek was ghastly, cold;
    Convulsive groans their prison broke:
His eyes in fearful horror roll'd,
    While thus the wretch his anguish spoke:

"Accursed be the Christian race;
    Insatiate is their iron soul:
To hung our sons—their fav'rite chace—
    They goad and lash without control.

Torn from our frantic mother's breast,
    We bear our tyrant's galling chains;

Deny'd e'en death, that lulls to rest,
   The keenest woe, and fiercest pains.

From sun to sun the Negro toils;
   No smiles approve his trusty care;
And, when th'indignant mind recoils,
   His doom is whips, and black despair.

Yet, Christians teach faith, hope, and love:
   Their God of mercy oft implore;
But can barbarians mercy prove,
   Or a benignant God adore?

Hear then my groans, oh, Christian God!
   Thy curses hurl—but, no! Forbear.
Let Christians wield Oppression's rod,
   Spread hatred, woe, and wild despair.

While I a nobler course pursue,
   Yes, let me die as I would live!
Yes, let me teach this Christian crew,
   The dying Negro can forgive.

And if, indeed, that pow'r be thine,
   O Christian God! In mercy move
Thy people's hearts, by pow'r divine,
   To justice, gentleness, and love."

The suff'rer ceas'd, death chill'd his veins;
   His mangl'd limbs grew stiff and cold;
Yet whips nor racks inflict the pains
   Men feel who barter Man for Gold.

            (1797)[295]

WILLIAM SHEPHERD (1768–1847)

A shoemaker's son, educated in dissenting academies, Shepherd was a Unitarian minister, schoolmaster, and member of the Liverpool abolitionist circle that included Edward Rushton and William Roscoe. An enthusiast for religious and civil liberty, he was active in local and national politics, gained notice as an orator, and published many works on reform issues.

In this poem, Shepherd's radicalism is evident. Implicitly countenancing violent insurrection, he foregoes any discussion of the wrongs of slavery and instead plunges directly into the underworld of Obi ritual and slave resistance. Focusing on the role of Obi in the Jamaican insurrection of 1760 (drawn from Edwards's *History of the West Indies*), Shepherd may also have been stirred by news of the Haitian and other uprisings of the 1790s.

The Negro Incantation*

I.

Hail! ye sacred horrors hail!
Which brooding o'er this lonely vale,
Swell the heart, impearl the eye,
And raise the rapt soul to the sky.
Hail! spirits of the swarthy dead,
Who, flitting thro' the dreary shade,
To rouse your sons to vengeance fell,

---

* [from Shepherd's note:] In the year 1760, a very formidable insurrection of the Jamaica negroes took place.—This was instigated by the professors of a species of incantation, known among the blacks by the name of OBI. The OBI, says Mr. EDWARDS, is usually composed of a farrago of materials, viz. *blood, feathers, parrots' beaks, dogs' teeth, alligator's teeth, broken bottles, grave dirt, rum,* and *egg-shells.* By the proper mixture and application of these materials, the Negroes imagine they can effectuate the destruction of their enemies. The account . . . in EDWARDS's History of the West-Indies, gave birth to the following Ode.

Nightly raise the troublous yell!
Hail! Minister of Ill, whose iron pow'r
    Pervades resistless earth, and sea, and air,
Shed all thy influence on this solemn hour,
    When we with magic rites the white man's doom prepare.

II.

    Thus Congo spake, "what time the moon,
    Riding in her highest noon!"
    Now beam'd upon the sable crowd,
    Now vanish'd in the thickening cloud.
    'Twas silence all—with frantic look,
    His spells the hoary wizard took:
    Bending o'er the quiv'ring flame,
    Convulsion shook his giant frame.
Close and more close the shuddering captives throng,
    With breath repress'd, and straining eye, they wait—
When midst the plantains bursts the awful song,
    The words of mystic might, that seal their tyrants' fate.

III.

    Haste! the magic shreds prepare—
    Thus the white man's corpse we tear.
    Lo! the feathers from the raven's plume,
    That croaks our proud oppressor's doom.
    Now to aid the potent spell,
    Crush we next the brittle shell—
    Fearful omen to the foe,
    Look! the blanched bones we throw.
From mouldering graves we stole this hallow'd earth,
    Which, mix'd with blood, winds up the mystic charm;
Wide yawns the grave for all of northern birth,
    And soon shall smoke with blood each sable warrior's arm.

IV.

    Hark! the pealing thunders roll,
    Grateful to the troubled soul.
    See! the gleamy lightnings play,
    To point you to your destin'd prey.
    Hence! with silent foot and slow,
    And sudden strike the deadly blow:
    Your foes, the palmy shade beneath,
    Lie lock'd in sleep—their sleep is death!

Go! let the memory of the smarting thong
    Outplead the pity that would prompt to save:
Go! let the oppressor's contumelious wrong,
    Twice nerve the hero's arm, and make the coward brave.

                         (1797)[296]

ROBERT ANDERSON (1770–1833)

Born poor, educated in charity schools, Anderson was by age ten an apprentice working in the textile industry of his native Carlisle. He emerged as a leading regional poet, writing in the Cumbrian dialect (as Burns had in Scottish) and influencing Wordsworth, among others. Given his local focus, and a career pursued far from cities such as London or Liverpool where awareness of the slave trade was more prevalent, Anderson's antislavery attitudes indicate the degree to which the subject was part of the consciousness of Britons everywhere.

In the first poem, Anderson uses chattel slavery as the framing metaphor for his radical critique of ambition.

from "The Slave"

Torn from every dear connection,
Forc'd across the yielding wave,
The Negro, stung by keen reflection,
May exclaim, Man's but a Slave!

In youth, gay Hope delusive fools him,
Proud her vot'ry to deprave;
In age, self-interest over-rules him—
Still he bends a willing Slave.

The haughty monarch, fearing Reason
May her sons from ruin save,
Of traitors dreaming, plots and treason,
Reigns at best a sceptr'd Slave.

His minion, Honesty would barter,
And become Corruption's knave;
Won by ribband, star, or garter,
Proves himself Ambition's Slave. . . .

The soldier, lur'd by sounds of glory,
Longs to shine a hero brave;

And, proud to live in future story,
Yields his life—to Fame a Slave. . . .

Thus dup'd by Fancy, Pride, or Folly,
Ne'er content with what we have;
Toss'd 'twixt Hope and Melancholy,
Death at last sets free the Slave.

(1798)[297]

In this poem, Anderson pursues his interest in dialect, inventing an idiomatic voice for a distraught African woman lamenting the capture of her lover by slave traders.

Negro Affection

Poor Zeila on wide water gaze,
Where white man tear her love away;
In vain she to poor Oran prays;
In vain she call the ship to stay.
Back to her hut can Zeila go?
From Oran dear how can she sleep?
When Zeila breast swell big wid woe,
When Zeila eye do nought but weep.
Rise, Sun of Morn! but give no light
To cruel man who him enslave!
Poor Oran pine, far, far from sight,
Or now lie dead below cold wave.
But if him live, him see no more
The big tear drop from Zeila' eye;
Then where white man poor Oran tore,
I'll sit me down, and soon will die.

(1798)[298]

THOMAS GISBORNE (1758–1846)

Educated at St. John's College, Cambridge, Gisborne was a clergyman, poet, and religious writer whose friends included Hannah More, William Wilberforce, and other abolitionists. Gisborne's most important writing against slavery took the form of a prose work, *Remarks on the Decision of the House of Commons on 2 April 1792, respecting the Abolition of the Slave Trade* (London, 1792).

In this elegy for William Mason (1724–1797), Gisborne devotes several stanzas to Mason's antislavery sentiment as the mainstay of his moral excellence. Interestingly, Gisborne identifies William Cowper, the great antislavery poet and Mason's friend, as the next in line to succeed to the English poetic pantheon.

from "Elegy to the Memory of the Rev. William Mason"

His breast, of lawless anarchy the foe,
    For Britain swell'd with Freedom's patriot zeal;
Nor thus confin'd, for every clime could glow,
    And in a Slave's a Brother's wrongs could feel:

Could feel, o'er Afric's race when avarice spread
    Her bloody wing, and shook in scorn the chain;
While Justice, hand in hand by Mercy led,
    To Christian senates cried, and cried in vain!

Now their new guest the sacred hosts include,
    They who on earth with kindred lustre shone;
Whom love of God to love of Man subdu'd,
    Nor Pride nor Avarice fear'd the heart to stone.

There shall he join the Bards whose hallow'd aim
    Sought from the dross of earth the soul to raise;

THOMAS GISBORNE

Disdain'd the meed of perishable fame,
    And sunk the Poet's in the Christian's praise.

There 'mid empyreal light shall hail his GRAY;
    There MILTON thron'd in peerless glory see;
The wreath that flames on THOMSON's brow survey;
    The vacant crown that, COWPER, waits for thee.

                (1798)[299]

JAMES ORR (1770–1816)

An Irish weaver without any formal education, Orr lived in the northern Irish county of Antrim, where he was known as the "Bard of Ballycarry." Written both in English and in Ulster-Scots dialect, Orr's poems show that an awareness of racial slavery had penetrated even remote Irish villages where the population might never have seen a black person.

Orr was a political radical and in this sonnet he develops an idealistic vision, through the persona of "Humanity," of a postmillennial world informed by peace, love, and liberty. All the evils of the world are to be overcome, including the bloody persecution of Africans for their "faulty hue."

Humanity

How fine her form! her face was sweetly sad,
   Like May's mild skies, half smiling while they rain,
When thus she spoke: "View mortal!—view unaw'd,
   The mild Millenian Queen about to reign.

Then man shall live for man. Soft pity's tear
   Shall wash the crimson from the sword of strife:
The friend of lore the orphan babe shall rear;
   The friend of worth shall shield the widow'd wife.

Then savage churls who tortur'd beasts before,
   Shall spare the nest from which a *parent* flew:
No conscience shall be cross'd; no Negroes gore
   Gush, as if glad to change his faulty hue.

I am HUMANITY. My precepts mark,
Happy my friends must be." She said; and all was dark.
               (c. 1798)[300]

Having fought for the United Irishmen in the failed Irish Rebellion of 1798, Orr briefly went to America, though whether as a political refugee or an immigrant is unclear. This stanza from his dialect poem about the voyage to America suggests how African slavery could instill a sense of racial identity in immigrants even at the first moment of contact. Not only are the new arrivals struck by the sight of black slaves, but—despite their own foreignness—the Irish immediately began to see themselves as part of the white ascendancy ("We mixt amang the Yankies").

from "The Passengers"

Whan glidin' up the *Delaware,*
    We cam' forenent *Newcastle,*
Gypes* co'ert the wharf to gove,[†] an' stare,
    While out, in boats, we bustle:
Creatures wha ne'er had seen a black,
    Fu' scar't took to their shankies;[‡]
Sae, wi' our best rags on our back,
We mixt amang the Yankies,
        An' skail't,[§] that day.
            (c. 1798)[301]

Taking as his motto Pope's antislavery passage from *The Essay on Man* (anthologized above), Orr invents a monologue by a dying slave. Orr's African rejoices in the prospect of rejoining his family in the afterlife and then, remarkably, devotes the closing stanzas to an encomium on Charles Fox, a longtime parliamentary supporter of abolition.

The Dying African

    "Simple Nature to his hope has given,
      Behind the cloud-capt hill, an humbler Heaven,
      Where slaves once more their native land behold,
      No fiends torment, no Christians thirst for gold."
                      POPE

Farewell life! before to-morrow's
    Orient beam shall gild the plain,
Freed from all my pains and sorrows,
    I'll defy fell slavery's chain:

---

* Foolish people.
[†] To stare.
[‡] Legs; i.e., they ran.
[§] Scattered.

Yes, ere then, this longing spirit,
  That misfortune's pressure bends,
Shall once more my home inherit,
  In the village of my friends.

Father fond, and faithful brothers,
  Soon I'll join you—free and blest;
Soon I'll soothe you, best of mothers!
  Who with war-tales fir'd my breast:
Soon the maid who priz'd my brav'ry
  I'll attend, and share her smiles!—
Hence, fond Hope! perhaps proud slav'ry
  Tasks them now in other isles.

If their wrongs, like mine, are over,
  Freed by death from earthly ills,
With their shadowy band I'll hover
  In the clouds that top our hills:
Hence I'll mark the hunter, bringing
  Home the spoil he joyed to chase,
And hereafter hear him singing
  Of the friends who freed his race.

Afric's friends are Albion's glory,
  Fox, their chief, in death I bless
He'll proclaim the negro's story,
  He'll the negro's wrongs redress:
How he'll paint his toils and dangers,
  Gory wounds, and gushing eye!
Fiends who flogg'd th' offenceless strangers,
  Blushing deep—even they will sigh!

"Favour'd Britons, free from troubles,
  Mourn the wretched"—thus he'll plead—
"Should rude pirates task your nobles,
  And condemn your dames to bleed;
Should they sell your babes, and sunder
  Plighted lovers, how you'd sigh!"—
"Keep the thieves from human plunder!"
  Every village will reply.

Sire of white men and of sable!
  Friend of all on every plain!
Though our foes be formidable,
  May our friends the victory gain!

JAMES ORR

Avarice grim! my heart forgives you,
    Justice comes to end your sway!—
Farewell life! the slave who leaves you,
    Homeward gladly wings his way!

(c. 1804)[302]

MARY STOCKDALE
(c. 1769–post 1818)

Daughter of a London publishing family (founded by father John, continued by brother John Joseph), Mary Stockdale was a poet and translator who produced at least two collections of original verse and an English version of Berquin's *The Family Book, or Children's Journal* (1798). In this poem, Stockdale dramatizes, in the voice of a child, the emotional pain caused by the slave trade. Parent-child separations were a cruel fact and a literary commonplace, but Stockdale deepens the pathos of her depiction by having the child dwell not on her own suffering but on the grief of her father back in Africa.

Fidelle; or, the Negro Child

An outcast from my native home,
    A helpless maid forlorn,
O'er dangerous seas I'm doom'd to roam,
    From friends and country torn.
No mother's smile now sooths my grief;
    A Christian me beguil'd;
But, ah! he scorns to give relief,
    Or ease a poor black child.

My father now, unhappy man!
    Weeps for his lov'd Fidelle,
And wonders much that Christians can
    Poor negroes buy and sell:
O had you heard him beg and pray,
    And seen his looks so wild!
He cried, "O let me bless this day;
    O spare my darling child!"

But, O! their hearts were hearts of stone;
    They tore me from his arms;

A Christian savage scoffs the groan
   Caus'd by a black's alarms.
They chain'd me in this dungeon deep,
   And on my sorrows smil'd,
Then left, alas! to sigh and weep,
   The slave! the negro child!

(1798)[303]

THOMAS CAMPBELL (1777–1844)

Born and educated in Glasgow, Campbell was a major poet, critic, and editor whose fame rivaled that of Walter Scott and whose accomplishments ranged from best-selling works (including "Gertrude of Wyoming" and "Specimens of the British Poets") to a role in founding the University of London. The excerpts below are from his first great poetic success, a work published when he was only twenty-one. Written in the tradition of Mark Akenside and Samuel Rogers, *The Pleasures of Hope* is a meditation on human nature and the mood of hopefulness generated by the many reforms and revolutions that dominated world events at the turn of the eighteenth century. Thus Campbell's indictment of the slave trade is one part of a larger vision of progress. His lines here are remarkable not so much for their depiction of the suffering slave as heroic outcast (which had become a type) as for Campbell's vision of enlightenment as a Christian rather than merely a secular development.

from Part I of The Pleasures of Hope

Truth, Mercy, Freedom, yet shall find a home;
Where'er degraded Nature bleeds and pines,
From Guinea's coast to Sibir's dreary mines,
Truth shall pervade the unfathom'd darkness there,
And light the dreadful features of despair —
Hark! the stern captive spurns his heavy load,
And asks the image back that Heaven bestow'd!
Fierce in his eye the fire of valor burns,
And as the slave departs, the man returns! . . .

Lo! once in triumph on his boundless plain,
The quiver'd chief of Congo lov'd to reign;
With fires proportion'd to his native sky,
Strength in his arm, and lightning in his eye;
Scour'd with wild feet his sun-illumin'd zone,

The spear, the lion, and the woods his own;
Or led the combat, bold without a plan,
An artless savage, but a fearless man!

    The plunderer came:—alas! no glory smiles
For Congo's chief on yonder Indian isles;
For ever fallen! no son of Nature now,
With Freedom charter'd on his manly brow!
Faint, bleeding, bound, he weeps the night away,
And, when the sea-wind wafts the dewless day,
Starts, with a bursting heart, for ever more
To curse the sun that lights their guilty shore! . . .

    Poor fetter'd man! I hear thee whispering low
Unhallow'd vows to Guilt, the child of Woe!
Friendless thy heart; and, canst thou harbor there
A wish but death—a passion but despair? . . .

Come, Heav'nly Powers! primeval peace restore!
Love!—Mercy!—Wisdom!—rule for ever more!

                    (1799)[304]

ARCHIBALD M'LAREN
(1755–post 1814)

A Scottish soldier, strolling player, and miscellaneous writer, M'laren fought for the British army in the American Revolutionary War before returning to pursue a hand-to-mouth career writing farces, musical dramas, and other popular entertainments throughout Britain. The songs below are taken from a one-act musical drama first performed in Edinburgh in the late 1790s as *The Negro Slaves*. It was later brought to London, where it was staged in 1799 at the popular Amphitheatre (near Westminster Bridge) under a new title, *The Blackman and Blackbird*.

M'laren's antislavery sympathies are evident throughout, despite the motleyness of the cast and the unevenness of the piece. In the first song below, set on a plantation, the whole chorus of African slaves voices a strange desire: they pray to their gods to be made insensate, like beasts, rather than have to endure slavery as human beings.

four untitled songs from The Negro Slaves, A Dramatic Piece, of One Act
Air [sung by Quako, Sela, and other slaves]

> Ye tedious sun, oh, do make haste,
> And hide your head in yonder west;
> Come friendly sleep and seal my eyes,
> Dry up my tears and heal my sighs.
> Ye airy dreams recall no more
> Sad thoughts of what I was before;
> For now ye sons of India's soil,
> Here we are bound to slave and toil.
>
> Ye pow'rs, who made us what we are,
> Since we no more are worth your care,
> Recall from us each human thought,
> To make us fitting for our lot.

That henceforth we may never know,
One beam of hope or pang of woe;
But like the beasts, unus'd to smile,
Drag on a life to slave and toil.

(1799)

In this song, the African romantic lead tells a familiar story of capture and enslavement, including his painful reunion with his beloved Sela, now also a slave in the New World. At times M'laren breaks the plane between fiction and reality, trying to awaken a new consciousness in his British audience: "White man and white woman from sorrow secure, / They never consider what negroes endure."

Song [by Quako, a slave]

When the ship came to Guinea, the white man we 'spy,
Like the great Nankaponie come down from the sky;
He shew'd the fine trinket, the glass, and the bead,
The lace and the ribbon, and the cap for the head.
One day I was happy, with friends by my side,
To give me my Sela, my sloe-colour'd bride,
To buy her fine trinket, I go to the shore,
But white man he seize me, I get back no more,
When bound in the vessel, I saw in my mind,
The grief of my Sela, and friends left behind.

I thought all my sorrows to drown in the wave,
But white man refus'd me the peace of the grave;
When here I first landed, like beast I was sold,
With many more blackmen companions of old;
Sometimes I seem merry, to keep up poor heart,
Yet here I still carry sad grief's poison'd dart.
When I past in my slavery a twelvemonth or more,
One day to plantation some slaves came ashore;
I haste with my labour, and run to the place,
To try if remembrance cou'd point out some face.

Oh, great Nankaponie, how much was I blest,
To see my dear Sela along with the rest;
I laugh and I jump, and I dance and I rave,
But my happiness died when I found her a slave.
White man and white woman from sorrow secure,
They never consider what negroes endure;
They laugh when they're merry, they drink and they eat,

And to find them fine dainties, poor Negroes must sweat.
Sometimes when I'm weary, they make me to strip,
And the wage of my labour, is lash of the whip:
Oh, great Nankaponie, look down on my woe,
For nobody pities poor negro below.

(1799)

In the next song the enslaved lovers console themselves with their belief that after death they will be reunited and restored to their homeland in Africa.

Duet

Quako.	Come wipe the tear from your bright eye,
	Keeping up your sinking heart.
Sela.	How can you bid my cheek be dry,
	Yet say that we must part.
Quako.	No beams of hope my bosom chear,
	Through life I'm doom'd a slave;
Sela.	No prospect ever to get clear,
	Till laid down in the grave.
Quako.	When this sad weary life-time ends,
Sela.	Then all our troubles o'er,
Quako.	We'll meet again with former friends
	Upon sweet Guinea's shore—
Sela.	When by the roaring river streams,
	On flowery banks we stray:
Quako.	Our present griefs we'll mind, like dreams
	That long since fled away.

(1799)

In a typical reversal at the end of the comedy, the master shows charity, Quako and Sela are given their freedom, and the lovers look forward to a happy married life. This excerpt captures M'laren's effort to close with an upbeat message, where noble slaves are free, rascals are punished, and even prisoners find a silver lining.

from "Finale"

Rac[oon].	My sable pair, I'm very glad,
	That you're reliev'd from slav'ry:
M[ac].	And sae wou'd I, my honest blade,
	That you were cur'd of knav'ry.

Just[ice].	Come drown your care, and hang despair,
	And banish grief and sorrow;
Prison[er].	Why shou'd we grieve, who may not live
	Perhaps to see to-morrow.
Quako.	May peace and love with liberty,
	Extend to all the creation.

(1799)[305]

ANONYMOUS

Even in slave states, some voices were raised against slavery. Here an anonymous Maryland versifier of 1800 uses a phonetic, but not unsympathetic, rendering of slave dialect to indict the profane and racist mindset of the slave driver. The poem appeared in the widely circulated *Baltimore Weekly Magazine*.

The Planter's Reason for His Cruelty to His Brethren

OH! Massa what make you so cruel to me?
Why slave me? Me fadder and mudder was free!
Why 'tarve me? Why cuttee de kin off me back?
Why cuss me? Because, you d——n'd rascal, you're black.

(1800)[306]

JAMES COBB (1756–1818)

A London dramatist who produced some twenty-four plays between 1779 and 1810, Cobb was one of several English writers to take up Bernardin de Saint-Pierre's best-selling romance *Paul et Virginie* (Paris, 1789). Translated into English by Helen Maria Williams in 1795, the novella is a story of Rousseauvian innocence set on a Caribbean island. Paul and Virginia, white youths raised apart from the corruptions of Europe and of the plantation society on the other side of the island, pursue a tragic romance, meanwhile showing their virtue by aiding the slaves and free blacks who come to them for help. Cobb's adaptation was first staged at Covent Garden May 1, 1800, and afterward published in London, Dublin, and America in several editions.

In the first of six songs excerpted from Cobb's musical drama, the antislavery theme is set up in the opening scene, as a chorus of slaves heckles the slave catcher Diego when he threatens to disrupt Virginia's birthday celebrations.

from Paul and Virginia, A Musical Entertainment
Trio and Chorus [sung by slaves and Diego the slave-catcher]

Women	Bold intruder, hence, away!
& boys.	Let no rude act profane this day!
	Tis Virginia's natal day.
Diego.	Hence, ye idle pack, away!
	Instead of hard and healthy labor,
	Jigging to the pipe and tabor,
	Serenading, masquerading—
	Go home, go home, and work, I say.
Women.	Against decorum—tis a sin.
Diego.	Let me pass—I will go in.
Women.	With these flowery wreaths to-day,

> Our debts of gratitude we pay:
> Your flinty heart can nothing feel.

Diego.   You pay your debts with what you steal.

(1800)

In the next song, the free black Dominique romanticizes the midnight revels and courtship rites of the African slaves. His presentation owes more to the pastoral traditions of literature than to the realities of slave life.

Song [by Dominique, the free mulatto]

I.

When the moon shines o'er the deep,
Ackee-O,
And whisker'd dons are fast asleep,
Snoring fast asleep,
From their huts the negroes run,
Full of frolic—full of fun,
Holiday to keep.
Till morn they dance the merry round,
To the fife and cymbal.
Few so brisk,
Now they frisk,
Airy, gay and nimble;
With gestures antic,
Joyous, frantic,
They dance the merry round,
Ackee-O,
To the cymbal's sound.

II.

Black lad whispers to black lass,
Ackee-O,
Glances sly between them pass,
Of beating hearts to tell;
Though no blush can paint her cheek,
Still her eyes the language speak,
Of passion quite as well.
Till morn, &c.

(1800)

In the next song, the slave girl Mary extols the wonders of being in love. Her remarkable song defies convention two ways: in her acceptance of her dark-skinned lover's complexion and in the way her love relationship is set up as a model that the young whites might hope to emulate.

Song [by Mary, a slave]

Mary.   There they go! innocent and happy pair! love reigns in their hearts, and prepares them to enjoy every blessing around them. I wish they may be as happy as Dominique and I. Though ten years older than I am and ten shades darker, I find his want of youth made up by good-nature, and the darkness of his skin by the fairness of his dealings; and I love him better and better the older we grow together.

I.

Glorious the ray glancing over the ocean,
  That bids hill and valley display each gay hue,
Graceful the orange grove waves in commotion,
  With joy as it hails the fresh morning in view.
Yet vainly her beauties shall nature impart,
But for love's cheering sunshine, that reigns in the heart.
All is delight, if kind love lend his aid,
And all is despair if fond hopes are betray'd.

Virginia here intercedes on behalf of the runaway slave Alambra, begging Diego not to pursue him.

Air [sung by Virginia]

Oh! could my faultering tongue impart
The tale of woe that pains my heart,
Then in vain I should not crave
Your pity for a wretched slave!
The injur'd ne'er in vain addrest,
In plaints of woe a noble breast:
Compassion ever marks the brave,
Oh, pity, then, your wretched slave!

(1800)

Sung by whites and blacks together, the final song in Act I celebrates Paul and Virginia's resolution to confront Diego over his cruelty to Alambra. As the song begins, Dominique predicts that "Paul's hatred of slavery is such that he may be provoked to insult the owner of the plantation."

Finale [to Act I, sung by whites and blacks]

Chorus.   Oh! blest for ever be this day!
When charity asserts her sway;

547

> When beauty, generous as fair,
> Deems not the slave beneath her care;
> And bids the beams of mercy smile
> Upon the suffering sons of toil.
>
> (1800)

Where the novella had ended tragically, Cobb's version provides a joyful conclusion. The ship on which Virginia is being forced to leave the island sinks offshore and the distracted Paul plunges into the waves to save her. Moved by his gratitude to both of them, the heroic Alambra risks life and liberty to go to their rescue, bringing all to shore safe and singing.

Song [by Alambra, the runaway slave]

> Of winds and waves I'll brave the strife—
>   Tis honor's call, fearless I go:
> What tho' I risk my ransom'd life,
>   The debt I to Virginia owe.
>
> (1800)[307]

DAVID HUMPHREYS (1752–1818)

A Revolutionary War officer who served as aide-de-camp to Washington, Humphreys afterwards pursued a career as diplomat, farmer, innovator, and writer. A member of the Hartford Wits in the 1780s, Humphreys also produced a series of poems consciously written as national literature on behalf of America. As with Dwight, Trumbull, and the others, Humphreys's patriotic pride motivated, rather than compromised, his antislavery sentiments.

In this elegy for his beloved Washington, Humphreys makes sure to include among the great man's virtues his benevolence toward his slaves and his careful plans for their manumission.

from "A Poem on the Death of General Washington"

> Where that foul stain of manhood, slavery, flow'd
> Through Afric's sons transmitted in the blood;
> Hereditary slaves his kindness shar'd,
> For manumission by degrees prepar'd:
> Return'd from war, I saw them round him press,*
> And all their speechless glee by artless signs express.
>
> (1800)[308]

Coming from an ex-army officer and a man of public affairs, the emotional tones of this poem are remarkable. In language evocative of the New Testament ("Their bleeding bosoms bathe with oil and wine / Bind up their wounds"), Humphreys suggestively conflates the suffering of slaves and that of Christ. The abolition of slavery thus becomes not just a national necessity, but a sacred duty.

---

* [Humphreys's note:] General Washington, by his will, liberated all his negroes, making an ample provision for the support of the old, and the education of the young. The interesting scene of his return home, at which the author was present, is described exactly as it existed.

from "A Poem on the Industry of the United States of America"

Thy sap, more sweet than Hybla's honey, flows,
Health for the heart-sick—cure of slavery's woes—
Then, as th' unfailing source, balsamic, runs,
Dispense that cordial, hope, for Afric's sons!

    Oh, could my song impressive horror bring,
Of conscious guilt th'insufferable sting;
From eyes untaught to weep the tear should start,
And mercy melt the long obdur'd of heart.
See naked negroes rear the sugar'd reeds!
Behold! their flesh beneath their driver bleeds!
And hear their heart-heav'd groans! then say, how good,
How sweet, the dainties drugg'd with human blood!

    Though night's dark shades o'ercast th' ill-favour'd race,
Nor transient flushes change the vacant face;
Though nature ne'er transforms their wooly hair
To golden ringlets, elegantly fair!
Yet has not God infus'd immortal powers,
The same their organs and their souls as ours?
Are they not made to ruminate the sky?
Or must they perish like the beasts that die?
Perish the thought that men's high worth impairs,
SONS OF OMNIPOTENCE, AND GLORY'S HEIRS!

    Come, ye who love the human race divine,
Their bleeding bosoms bathe with oil and wine,
Bind up their wounds—then bless the dulcet tree,
Whose substituted sweets one slave may free. . . .

    Thou, slavery, (maledictions blast thy name!)
Fell scourge of mortals, reason's foulest shame!
Fly, fiend infernal! To thy Stygean shore,
And let thy deeds defile my song no more.

    Heav'ns! Still must men, like beasts, be bought and sold,
The charities of life exchang'd for gold!
Husbands from wives, from parents children torn,
In quivering fear, with grief exquisite, mourn!
No, soon shall commerce, better understood,
With happier freight promote the mutual good.

(c. 1802)[309]

ANONYMOUS

Although commonplace in many ways, this antislavery poem is still remarkable for being published in Maryland, a slave state. Lapsing briefly into an imaginary slave's voice, the poet posits the slave's craving for freedom as proof of his essential equality as a human being. The appeal to reason gives way, in the closing, to the emotional force of the slave's dramatic suicide.

from "The Slave"

The moon in silent majesty arose,
And weary negroes fought for calm repose.
Scorch'd by the burning sun's meridian ray,
All wish'd refreshment from the blaze of day—
But one unhappy slave oppress'd with care,
O'erwhelmed with grief, and mad with fell despair,
Forsook the grove. On Afric's burning shore
He'd left his friends, his absence deplore;
His wife, his children, in their native land,
(Subjected to a tyrant's curs'd command)
In poverty and wretchedness retire;
Nor know the friend, the husband, or the sire.
Such sad reflection never left his breast,
His eyes forgot the balmy sweets of rest;
His tongue forgot to sing the songs of joy,
No more did mirth or love his hours employ;
Far from his country, from his native race,
Far from his little children's much lov'd face,
And doom'd to bear forever slav'ry's chain,
To grieve, to sigh, alas! To live in vain.

O, christian! Friends to our unhappy race,
Why do we wear those ensigns of disgrace?

Did nature's God create us to be slaves,
Or is it pride, which God's decree outbraves?
Had he design'd that we should not be free,
Why do we know the sweets of liberty?

He could no more; but mounting on a rock,
Whose shaggy sides o'erhung the silver brook—
Thence tumbling headlong down the steepest side,
He plung'd determin'd, in the foaming tide.
His mangled carcasse floated on the flood,
And stained the silver winding stream with blood.

(1801)[310]

ANONYMOUS

The following is the third in a succession of antislavery poems, clearly by different authors, to appear within a few months in the *Baltimore Weekly Magazine* in 1800–1801. If this poem's prefatory stanza is true, it may have been written or adapted by the editor of the magazine, John B. Colvin. Cast in an African slave's voice, and filled with detail about the miseries slaves endure, the poem explicitly calls for an end to slavery. Such a series of poems, published in a popular forum, makes impossible any easy generalization about the consensus of opinion in a slave state.

The Negro's Prayer

The Poet's corner in Gazette,
Is often fill'd by some Coquette;
Or cap in Hand to do his duty,
Will satirize his female beauty;
But as I now have room to spare,
I'll insert a Negro's Prayer.

LORD if thou dost with equal eye,
See all the sons of Adam die;
Why dost thou hide thy face from slaves,
Consign'd by fate to serve the knaves?
Stolen or sold in Africa,
Imported to America,
Like hogs or sheep, at market sold,
To stem the heat or brook the cold,
To work all day and half the night,
And rise before the morning light,
Sustain the lash, endure the cane,
Expos'd to storms of snow and rain,
Pinch'd with hunger and with cold,

And if we beg we meet a scold,
And after all the tedious round,
At night to stretch upon the ground.
Has Heaven decreed that negroes must,
By cruel men be ever curst!
For ever drag the galling chain,
And ne'er enjoy themselves as men!
When will *Jehova* hear our cries!
When will the sun of freedom rise,
When will a Moses for us stand,
And free us from Pharaoh's hand?
What tho' our skin be black as jet,
Our hair be curl'd, our noses flat,
Must we, for this no freedom have,
Until we find it in the grave?

(1801)[311]

LEIGH HUNT (1784-1859)

Descended from a family with roots in Barbados and in Quaker Pennsylvania, Hunt was an influential London writer, critic, and editor whose career spanned half a century, from the 1790s well into the Victorian period. He published the following poem at age sixteen. In subject and voice, it resembles other child-focused poems by Jerningham, Blake, and Mary Stockdale. Here the young Hunt romanticizes the suffering of "Ozmyn," a black boy living in the streets, shivering in his rags, weeping with distress, and looking forward to death as a relief.

The Negro Boy

Cold blows the wind, and while the tear
    Bursts trembling from my swollen eyes,
The rain's big drops quick meet it there,
    And on my naked bosom flies!
        O pity, all ye sons of Joy,
        The little wand'ring Negro-boy.

These tatter'd clothes, this ice-cold breast
    By Winter harden'd into steel,
These eyes, that know not soothing rest,
    But speak the half of what I feel!
        Long, long, I never knew one joy,
        The little wand'ring Negro-boy!

Cannot the sigh of early grief
    Move but one charitable mind?
Cannot one hand afford relief?
    One Christian pity, and be kind?
        Weep, weep, for thine was never joy,
        O little wand'ring Negro-boy!

Is there a good which men call Pleasure?
    O Ozmyn, would that it were thine!

Give me this only precious treasure;
   How it would soften grief like mine!
         Then Ozmyn might be call'd, with joy,
         The little wand'ring Negro-boy!

My limbs these twelve long years have borne
   The rage of ev'ry angry wind:
   Yet still does Ozmyn weep and mourn,
Yet still no ease, nor rest can find!
         Then Death, alas, must soon destroy
         The little wand'ring Negro-boy!

No sorrow e'er disturbs the rest,
   That dwells within the lonely grave;
Thou best resource the woe-wrung breast
   E'er ask'd of Heav'n, or Heav'n e'er gave!
         Ah then, farewell, vain world, with joy
         I die the happy Negro-boy!

                  (1801)[312]

JOHN LEYDEN (1775–1811)

A Scottish physician, poet, philosopher, and preacher, Leyden published several works in Edinburgh (including a book on European settlements in Africa) before going to India in 1803. Regarded by many as the most accomplished scholar of Asian languages in his era, Leyden spent the last eight years of his life in India and Malaysia researching, translating, and writing about such languages as Sanskrit, Persian, Hindustani, Malay, Maldivian, and others. He died of fever, still immersed in his work, in Malaysia, aged thirty-six.

In the first of the poems below, written while still in Edinburgh, Leyden yokes pastoral images ("sweet bird," "citron-flowers," "plaintive song") with scenes of violence and gore. Given readers' preconceptions about the bloodiness of slave insurrections, the poet seems intent to shock them with his explicit call for black vengeance.

The Wail of Alzira. A Negro Song

Sweet bird of twilight, sad thy notes,
That swell the citron-flowers among!
But sadder on the night-breeze floats
Forlorn Alzira's plaintive song.
While, bending o'er the western flood,
She soothes the infant on her knee,—
Sweet babe! her breast is streak'd with blood,
And all to ward the scourge from thee.
Green are the groves on Benin's strand;
And fair the fields beyond the sea:
Where, lingering on the surf-beat sand,
My youthful warrior pines for me.
And, each revolving morn, he wears
The sandals his Alzira wore,
Ere whites, regardless of her tears,

557

Had borne her far from Benin's shore.
And, each revolving morn, he bears
The sabre which his father bore:
And, by the negro's God, he swears
To bathe its glimmering edge in gore.

(c. 1801)[313]

In this poem about his Scottish homeland, Leyden contrives to interject an antislavery passage. After imagining the anguish of capture and the suffering aboard a slave ship, culminating in suicide, Leyden unexpectedly veers back and contrasts the condition of African slaves with that of Scottish peasants, who enjoy relative freedom and prosperity.

from "Scenes of Infancy: Descriptive of Teviotdale"

Hope not, tyrants! in the grave to rest,
(The blood, the tears of nations unredress'd,) . . .
For still, to heaven when fainting nature calls,
On deeds accurs'd the darker vengeance falls.

Nor deem the negro's sighs and anguish vain,
Who hopeless grinds the harden'd trader's chain . . .
In dreams he sees Angola's plains appear;
In dreams he seems Angola's strains to hear;
And when the clanking fetter bursts his sleep,
Silent and sad he plunges in the deep.

Stout was the ship, from Benin's palmy shore
That first the freight of barter'd captives bore:
Bedimm'd with blood, the sun with shrinking beams
Beheld her bounding o'er the ocean-streams;
But, ere the moon her silver horns had rear'd,
Amid the crew the speckled plague appear'd.
Faint and despairing on their watery bier,
To every friendly shore the sailors steer;
Repell'd from port to port they sue in vain,
And track with slow unsteady sail the main. . . .

Untainted yet, thy stream, fair Teviot! runs,
With unatoned blood of Gambia's sons:
No drooping slave, with spirit bow'd to toil,
Grows, like the weed, self-rooted to the soil,
Nor cringing vassal on these pansied meads
Is bought and barter'd, as the flock he feeds.

Free as the lark that carols o'er his head,
At dawn the healthy ploughman leaves his bed,
Binds to the yoke his sturdy steers with care,
And, whistling loud, directs the mining share;
Free, as his lord, the peasant treads the plain,
And heaps his harvest on the groaning wain;
Proud of his laws, tenacious of his right,
And vain of Scotia's old unconquered might.

(1803)[314]

ANONYMOUS ("A PERSON CONFINED IN THE STATE-PRISON")

The author of this ballad presents himself in a remarkable way: as "Itaniko," an African slave, now a convict in New Jersey. First written to be sung to the tune of "Ellen O'Moore," the poem was published in a volume entitled *The Prisoner: or, A Collection of Poetical Pieces, Written by a Person Confined in the State-Prison.* Whether imprisoned for rebellion or some other crime, Itaniko never discloses. But he does tell his life's story, from capture in Africa to field labor in America, including a dramatic suicide attempt aboard the slave ship.

The African Slave

YE SONS OF COLUMBIA, who taste every blessing
    That Liberty, Plenty, and Peace can bestow,
Give ear to my story, and think how distressing!
    Ah! hear the sad tale of an African's woe:
Tho' guiltless my life was, without provocation
I was torn from my country, companions, and nation,
And doom'd to the toils of a life's Mancipation;
    Ah! such the hard fate is of *Itaniko.*

One morn, I my juvenile gambols was playing,
    No ill did I bode, for no fear did I know,
As thro' the palm-forest, thus carelessly straying,
    A prey I was seiz'd by the steel-hearted foe:
Who dragg'd me on board, where in fetters they bound me,
While pale-visag'd hell-hounds in horror surround me
I plung'd in the deep hoping death would have found me,
    They snatch'd from the billows poor *Itaniko.*

My father! I utter'd in wild exclamation,
    When life's crimson current a while ceas'd to flow:
Awake, O my Country! in just indignation,
    The swift-feather'd vengeance elance from the bow!

ANONYMOUS

In vain were all efforts their power to vanquish,
What language can picture my heart-rending anguish!
In cold galling chains for my freedom to languish!
   Oh! such the hard fate is of *Itaniko.*

On board of our ship there arose a dire faction,
   I let my curs'd fiends the conspiracy know;
But mark the reward of this life-saving action,
   Altho' I befriend them no pity they show;
For when on the shores of Columbia we landed,
The caitiffs I sav'd with what infamy branded!
The christian's base gold was the boon they demanded,
   And sold as a slave was poor *Itaniko.*

You boast of your Freedom—your mild Constitution
   See tears undissembled for Liberty flow!
Unmov'd can you witness such cruel delusion,
   Who feel in your bosoms Philanthropy glow?
Were we not by the same common Parent created?
Why then for the hue of my race am I hated?
Why, faultless, to mis'ry and chains am I fated?
   Ah! why is thus wretched poor *Itaniko?*

Each morn to fresh toils I awake broken-hearted
   The blood-streaming lash & the sweat-reeking hoe;
By Country, by Hope, by all Pleasure deserted,
   A victim, alas! to unspeakable woe:
O, GOD Of Columbia! behold with compassion,
The Cruelties, Insults, and Wrongs of my nation,
And blast, by thy justice, that Tyrant-Oppression,
   That holds from his country poor *Itaniko!*

                 (1802)[315]

ANONYMOUS

This and the next two poems appeared in one of the earliest books published in Washington, D.C., an anthology edited by Richard Dinmore called *Select and Fugitive Poetry* (1802). Dinmore was born in Britain but emigrated to America, where he became fiercely anti-British and sympathetic to the abolitionist cause.

This anonymous poem, apparently written by a new resident of Jamaica who found the island desperately disappointing, offers a kind of anti-pastoral catalog: terrible climate, grim landscape, rampant disease, and a dearth of social amenities. The poet's revulsion at slavery, perhaps sharpened by his perspective as an outsider, becomes a key element of his private hell.

from "Letter to a Friend. Written from Jamaica"

Despair here lifts her baleful hand,
While fell Disease pervades the land;
And meagre Death near couching lies,
To snatch the wretched, destin'd prize:
These, and a thousand evils more,
Alas! are here reserv'd in store,
To blast our joys, and render life,
One tragic scene of pain and strife. . . .

Here Afric's sable race deplore,
Their bondage on this hostile shore;
Where, crush'd beneath the galling chain,
The voice of pity pleads in vain:
Relentless despots hold the sway,
And rigid laws devote their prey
Each agonizing pang to find,
Each racking torture of the mind.

(1802)[316]

ANONYMOUS

Like the preceding and following poems, this antislavery lyric comes from Dinmore's *Select and Fugitive Poetry* (1802). Even those inured to tragic tales about despairing slaves could hardly fail to be moved by the final lines of Monimba's story. There is also a modern self-reflexive quality in Monimba, who—as the poem's readers themselves are doing—had herself "wept at mis'ry's tale." Her sympathetic response to suffering seems to mirror, or perhaps determine, that of the reader.

Monimba

MONIMBA, pride of Afric's plain,
    The beauty of the burning zone,
Was led to Hymens holy fane,
    By Zanga, prince of Ebo's throne.

Six moons revolving, saw them blest;
    The seventh, a base, enslaving band
Lodg'd the cragg'd ball in Zanga's breast,
    And sever'd love's united hand.

In vain the widow's piteous wail:
    Nor heard her soul-distressing cries:
Borne passive on the pinion'd gale,
    To distant climes the mourner hies.

There, doom'd to rounds of endless toil,
    Her life was soon to waste away,
On curst Port Royal's torrid soil
    Amid the fires of blazing day.

Her child—the tender babe unborn,
    Must share its mother's iron fate:

Doom'd ere it saw the rising morn,
   To horrid slav'ry's death-like weight.

Monimba own'd a feeling mind;
   Oft had she wept at mis'ry's tale;
The tender heart, by love refin'd,
   With firmness bids misfortune, hail.

Confin'd below, in bolted chains,
   Deep musing o'er a world of woes,
The sudden gush of spouting veins,
   At once announce parturient throes.

Rais'd to the deck—she ey'd the wave,
   Plung'd with her babe beneath the flood,
And, buried in a watery grave
   Escap'd the madd'ning sons of blood.

               (1802)[317]

ANONYMOUS

The following is the third antislavery poem Dinmore included in his *Select and Fugitive Poetry* (1802). This simple song, reportedly based on a real episode, explores an unexpected moral dimension: the guilt of an African leader for having engaged in the slave trade. The poem is thus unusually subtle for its time. Most writers who discussed Africans selling other Africans into slavery did so to mitigate white guilt or to defend the slave trade. Here the African's repentance proves his moral equality and models the kind of conversion that abolitionists hoped to effect in white slave traders.

The Negro Boy

> *The African Prince who lately arrived in England,*
> *being asked, What he had given for his watch? replied,*
> *"What I'll never give again.—I give a fine Boy for it."*

When avarice enslaves the mind,
    And selfish views alone bear sway:
Man turns a savage to his kind,
    And blood and rapine mark his way
        Alas: for this poor simple toy,
        I sold a blooming Negro Boy.

His father's hope, his mother's pride:
    Tho' black yet comely to their view:
I tore him helpless from their side,
    And gave him to a ruffian crew:
        To fiends that Afric's coast annoy,
        I sold the blooming Negro Boy.

From country, friends, and parents torn,
    His tender limbs in chains confin'd,
I saw him o'er the billows borne,

And mark'd his agony of mind:
    But still to gain this simple toy,
    I gave away the Negro Boy.

In isles that deck the western wave,
  I doom'd the hopeless youth to dwell:
A poor forlorn insulted slave,
  A beast that Christians buy and sell:
    And in their cruel task employ,
    The much enduring Negro Boy.

His wretched parents long shall mourn;
  Shall long explore the distant main,
In hopes to see the youth return;
  But all their hopes and sighs are vain:
    They never shall the sight enjoy,
    Of their lamented Negro Boy.

Beneath a tyrant's harsh command,
  He wears away his youthful prime
Far distant from his native land
  A stranger in a foreign clime:
    No pleasing thoughts his mind employ,
    A poor dejected Negro Boy.

But he who walks upon the wind,
  Whose voice in thunders heard on high,
Who doth the raging tempest bind,
  Or wing the light'ning thro' the sky,
    In his own time will soon destroy
    Th'oppressors of the Negro Boy.
            (1802)[318]

ANONYMOUS

In this short political poem, written by a Connecticut Federalist against the Jef-
fersonians newly arrived in power, the rift between north and south over slavery
is already evident. The poet's remarks, though incidental and self-serving, fore-
shadow the whole trajectory of nineteenth-century American politics.

from The Political Nursery for the Year Eighteen Hundred Two

But firm New-England feels repose,
Nor fears a host of Southern foes:
These despots boast of Liberty
Of Freedom and Equality,
And yet O! dire disgraceful clan,
They tread in dust their fellow man.
From galling chains, and slavery,
We thank the Lord, that we are free!

(1802)[319]

[?JOSEPH DENNIE], (1768–1812)

As author or editor, Joseph Dennie was responsible for all eight of the following poems about Thomas Jefferson and slavery. Scholars have determined that one of them ("Song by the Sage of Monticello") is definitely by Dennie. Others may be, as they all appeared anonymously in his anti-Jeffersonian periodical *The Port Folio* (published in Philadelphia) within a few months in 1802–3. A Harvard-educated lawyer and writer who served briefly in the Adams administration, Dennie was still smarting from Jefferson's election in 1800 and the ascendancy of the Republicans. When allegations of Jefferson's affair with his slave Sally Hemings erupted in 1802, Dennie, like many Federalist propagandists, leapt into action. The result, even if based in fact, was some of the most scurrilous, obscene, and racist political satire in American history.

In the first, the poet affects a slave dialect to mock Jefferson for espousing universal freedom while owning slaves. In his ironic depiction of a slave embracing "Jeffersonian democracy," his loathing for Jefferson is eclipsed by the unrelieved racism of his own assumptions about black people.

*[Untitled]**

> Our massa Jeffeson he say,
>   Dat all mans free alike are born;

---

* [from the editor's note:] I was yesterday sympathizing with a friend, at the fate of poor captain Jack, alias Quashee, who was unfortunately hung at Winston, North-Carolina, only for an "intention to rise, and commence a general massacre of the white inhabitants." My friend told me, that, among the accomplishments he was universally known to possess, his poetical talents had not been much noticed; that many of his fugitive pieces possessed considerable merit, and he hoped they would be collected and published by the democratic society, of which he (poor fellow!) had been a member; in proof of this, he produced from his pocket the following copy of admirable verses, which I requested, and obtained permission to send you. . . . The orthography I have not dared to alter, as . . . it would have lost much of its inimitable wildness and simplicity.

Den tell me, why should Quashee stay,
    To tend de cow and hoe de corn?
    Huzza for massa Jeffeson!

And if all mans alike be free,
    Why should de one, more dan his broder,
Hab house and corn? for poor Quashee
    No hab de one, no hab de oder.
    Huzza, &c.

And why should one hab de white wife,
    And me hab only Quangeroo?
Me no see reason for me life!
    No! Quashee hab de white wife too.
    Huzza, &c.

For make all like, let blackee nab
    De white womans. . . . dat be de track!
Den Quashee de white wife will hab,
    And massa Jef. shall hab de black.
    Huzza, &c.

Why should a judge (him alway white)
    'Pon pickaninny put him paw,
Cause he steal little? dat no rite!
    No! Quashee say he'll hab no law.
    Huzza, &c.

Who care, me wonder, for de judge?
    Quashee no care. . . . no not a feder;
Our party soon we make him trudge,
    We all be democrat togeder.
    Huzza, &c.

For where de harm to cut de troat
    Of him no like? or rob a little?
To take him hat, or shoe, or coat,
    Or wife, or horse, or drink, or vittle?
    Huzza, &c.

Huzza for us den! we de boys
    To rob and steal, and burn and kill;
Huzza! me say, and make de noise!
    Huzza for Quashee! Quashee will
    Huzza for massa Jeffeson!
            (July 10, 1802)[320]

The following is the earliest poem in Dennie's magazine to attack Jefferson over the Sally Hemings scandal. A ribald song originally set to the tune of "Yankee Doodle," the poem shows how raucous and vicious early American political life could be. Although Jefferson highmindedly declined to answer the Hemings allegations and was elected to a second term as president, modern scholarship has determined that his affair with Hemings was real and that she bore children by him. The poet's main accusation, therefore, was devastatingly true.

from "A Song Supposed to Have Been Written by the Sage of Monticello"

> Et etiam *fusco grata* colore Venus. OVID.
> *And Venus pleases though as black as jet.*

Of all the damsels on the green,
　　On mountain, or in valley,
A lass so luscious ne'er was seen
　　As Monticellian Sally.

　　Yankee doodle, who's the noodle?
　　　　What wife were half so handy?
　　To breed a flock, of slaves for stock,
　　　　A blackamoor's the dandy. . . .

When press'd by loads of state affairs,
　　I seek to sport and dally,
The sweetest solace of my cares
　　Is in the lap of Sally.
　　　　　　Yankee doodle, &c. . . .

You call her slave—and pray were slaves
　　Made only for the galley?
Try for yourselves, ye witless knaves—
Take each to bed your Sally.

　　Yankee doodle, whose the noodle?
　　　　Wine's vapid, tope me brandy—
　　For still I find to breed my kind,
　　　　A negro-wench the dandy!
　　　　　　(October 2, 1802)[321]

Written in a colloquial, bantering idiom, this satiric ode offers mock consolation even as it lacerates Jefferson for his alleged indiscretions with Sally Hemings. Its jocular tone can be contrasted with the more elaborate and elevated style of John Quincy Adams's version of the same Horatian ode, also published in 1802 and included elsewhere in this anthology.

Another Imitation of Horace, Book II. Ode 4 . . . Addressed to a Certain Great Man

Nay hang not Tom, your nether lip;
Tho' you with Quashee made a slip,
    Your fame it will not blight;
Ajax a captive maid admir'd;
Achilles by a slave was fir'd;
    Both damsels tho' were *white*.

Who knows but Quasheba may spring
From some illustrious sable King;
    And mourns her chang'd degree:
Odsbodikins, if this were true,
And son-in-law t'a monarch, you,
    How devilish proud you'd be.

Certes, a wench, though strait and tall,
With lips so large and teeth so small,
    Though lively plump and mellow,
Descended of ignoble race,
Would ne'er be suffered to solace
    The *sage of Monticello*.

But banish, Tom, all vain alarm,
Altho' I paint each 'witching charm
    That grac'd your sooty bride;
The heyday of my blood is o'er;
For I am verging to three score,
    And have a wife beside.
              (October 30, 1802)[322]

Framed, like so many of these attacks, in "Jefferson's" voice, the following mock love song is similarly indecent, but much more cruel. Heartlessly invoking Jefferson's loss of his wife, Martha (who had died in 1782), the satirist presents a lonely widower turning for consolation to his attractive black servant Sally Hemings.

from "A Philosophic Love-Song. To Sally"

In glaring red, and chalky white,
    Let others beauty see;

Me no such tawdry tints delight—
   No! *black's* the hue for me!* . . .

Thou, Sally, thou, my house shalt keep,
   My widow'd tears shall dry!
My virgin daughters—see! they weep—
   Their mother's place supply.

Oh! Sally! hearken to my vows!
   Yield up thy swarthy charms—
My best belov'd! my more than spouse,
   Oh! take me to thy arms!
              (November 6, 1802)[323]

In these mock-heroic lines, "Phyllis" (Sally Hemings) addresses "Demo-phoon" (Jefferson), pleading with him to return to Monticello from Washington. The poem bespeaks sexuality run rampant: Phyllis is surrounded by her mulatto children (fathered by Jefferson), while faithful Cudjoe complains about the overseer neglecting the plantation in order to dally with one of the slaves, "aunt Dinah."

from "Phyllis *to* Demo-*Phoon*"†

For thee I sigh, and thy long absence mourn,
O haste then to my arms; return, return.
Oft do the beauteous pledges of our love
Disconsolate around their mother move,
With whining sob demand their father dear,
Till bread and butter dry the glist'ning tear.
Thy faithful servants frequent ask me when
From the *great town* thou will come back again;
Old Cudjoe cries, to duty's bidding true,
"Do make the paper peak, do missy, do;
Tell massa quick come home; now he no here,
De corn field neber see de overseer;
Him all day sleepin in de fodder-house

---

* [Author's note:] In Addison's *Cato*, we find a warm advocate for African beauty. Syphax, when observing Juba to be enamoured with the Roman maids, thus speaks to his Prince of the beautiful damsels of Numidia: "The glowing dames of Zama's royal court, have faces flush'd with more exalted charms. Were you with these my Prince, you'd soon forget the pale unripen'd beauties of the North."

† [from author's note:] The following ludicrous letter, supposed to be addressed to a *philosophic* personage, by a *jetty* mistress, has made us laugh and sneer at *republican* morality.

While neger workin; him no wort a louse.
Him often wid aunt Dinah in de barn;
I peep one day; dey no go dere for corn;
I no been bab um, but I bet a guinea,
'Fore Christmas next, she hab a pickaninny."
                    (December 4, 1802)[324]

This little ditty draws on an instance of slavery shaping history from be-
neath. The song bids defiance to an army that Napoleon had sent to refortify
Louisiana: en route, the French forces stopped in Haiti to quell the slave insur-
rection, and were decimated by disease. This compounded the difficulty of de-
fending Louisiana, and the French were soon willing to let Jefferson purchase it.
As the poem suggests, the question of how to apportion the Louisiana Territory
into slave and free states would soon sharpen the ongoing American debate be-
tween pro- and antislavery advocates.

Patriotic Song *

At last the French have come my boys!
    What then? we do not fear 'em!
We scorn their sansculottish noise;
    Besides—we're not yet near 'em.

Chorus.   Columbia has no cause for dread,
                While freedom smiles upon her,
            Bold JEFFERSON her troops shall head,
                And lead them on to honour. . . .

On southern states the tempest raves;
    And, lo!—not Gallic cattle—
The demos, mustering up their slaves,
    March, ardent, to the battle.

Chorus.   Columbia, &c.
                    (March 5, 1803)[325]

Composed as a medley, this polyphonic ode plays upon every anti-Jeffersonian
theme: the lover of freedom who thrives in a slave-based society, the patriot
who somehow fails to serve in the military, the virtuous republican who in-

---

* [from author's note:] A patriotic song, intended to be published, should we be obliged to de-
clare war against the French, for attempting, (as some think they will, soon after their arrival
in Louisiana,) to deprive our southern democratic citizens of their property, by exciting their
negroes to run away from them.

dulges his lust with slave women. The poet seems little concerned about slavery itself, except as a weapon with which to attack Jefferson.

from "A Piece of an Ode to Jefferson"
The God of this new world [Milton, Par. Lost]

Muse, bid the song commence from that blest morn,
When to a wondering world a patriot chief was born,
   When first his durance ended,
      While gossips round grew witty,
   The boy, by slaves attended,
      Heard Dinah sing this ditty.

   Peaceful slumber in de cradle,
      Lilly Tommy, Dinah nigh,
   Stirring hominy wid de ladle;
      Den sing, Tommy, lullaby:
   Lullaby, lullaby, lullaby, lullaby;
      Den sing, Tommy, lullaby. . . .

Haste from the schools, from science' simple lore,
   To where, enlarg'd, on nature's boundless plan,
His ardent mind would freedom's wilds explore,
   As Mungo taught the sacred *rights of man.*

   Ah! massa Tom, you litty tink
      When Mungo work all de day,
   Midout one drop of rum to drink,
      Dat Mungo wish to run away.

   Though you born here, and white as snow,
      Poor Mungo black, from Guinea shore;
   Yet both alike—for Mungo know,
      All white mans are all blackamoor. . . .

In the cornfield I stand, with my negroes around,
Their glances from all sides my passion confound;
For Sal, Peg, and Quash, my inconstancy burns;
Though I'll take Sal the first, they shall all have their turns.

   War, is but a peck of troubles;
   Honour, virtue—empty bubbles;
   Ne'er will I, for either sighing,
      Slight my Sal—though love is cloying,
   If the wench is worth the buying,
      Surely she is worth enjoying:

Lovely Sally stands beside me,
She's the girl my purse provides me.
(March 19, 1803)[326]

In response to rumors of Jefferson's displeasure over earlier poetic attacks, the poet here mocks Jefferson's resolute silence, especially on the subject of Sally Hemings.

Ego et Rex Meus. Myself and the President

So, Tom, you do not like my ode!
Now, 'pon my word, that's very odd,
    For 'tis a mighty good one;
And, when 'tis finish'd, I'll declare,
'Twill fit your honour to a hair;
    Or call my muse a rude one.

Tell me where you can find a fault?
Is the verse lame? does the rhyme halt?
    In what is it amiss?
May I no speeches get to print,
If 'tis not good!—the devil's in't,
    If you're not pleas'd with this!

Why then, I'll say where 'tis not right:
You make me "scamper"—for his flight,
    The feds your friend will rally;
You speak of "Gossips"—that I blame;
And then about the blacks—for shame!
    Say not a word of *"Sally."*
(March 19, 1803)[327]

JOHN QUINCY ADAMS
["THOMAS PAINE"] (1767–1848)

Son of President John Adams, and himself sixth President of the United States, John Quincy Adams pursued a career in public service spanning more than fifty years. A Federalist from early in life, Adams joined in the mockery of Jefferson when the Hemings scandal erupted. As this satire suggests, the young Adams was not concerned about the moral aspects of slavery so much as its political implications. But later, during the eighteen years he served in Congress after his presidency, Adams would become the champion of antislavery petitioners to Congress—so indefatigable in his efforts that the notorious "gag-rule" (1838–44) was passed to silence him. Perhaps the highest moment of his antislavery activity came in 1841, when, as an old man, he argued the case of the *Amistad* captives before the Supreme Court and won their freedom. In this early poem, as his prefatory material wryly suggests, Adams takes as his premise the absurd postures into which human beings are cast by the institution of slavery.

Horace, Book II, Ode 4. To Xanthia Phoceus
Imitated by Thomas Paine (Not the Boston Poet, but the Sophist of Thetford,) and Addressed to Thomas Jefferson

"Young as we are, and with such a country before us to fill with people and with happiness, we should point in that direction the *whole generative force of nature,* wasting none of its efforts in mutual destruction."

—Jefferson's notes on Virginia, page 257.

See also the same sentiment repeated in the President's first message to Congress.

Ancillam amare, heroum exemplo turpe non esse.

That he had no occasion to be ashamed of being in love with his maid; for that had been the case with many great men.

Dear Thomas, deem it no disgrace
    With slaves to mend thy breed,

Nor let the wench's smutty face
   Deter thee from the deed.
At Troy's fam'd seige the bullying blade
Who swore no laws for *him* were made,
   Robs, kills, sets all in flame—
A SLAVE in petticoats appears,
And souse! in love! head over ears
   The Lion's heart is tame!

Lord of the world, when *Nero* reign'd,
   When fires were his delight
A SLAVE the Tyger's bosom chain'd,
   That slave indeed was white.
Lo! at his feet the fawning train,
His Smith, Blake, Cheetham and Duane,
   Howling his praise are seen!
Vice turns to virtue at his nod;
Imperial Nero, grows a GOD
   And ACTE* grows a Queen.

Speak but the word! alike for thee
   Thy venal tribe shall swear
PUREST OF MORTALS thou shalt be
   And SALLY shall be fair.
No blasted brood of Afric's earth
Shall boast the glory of her birth
   And shame thy daughter's brother,
To prove thy panders shall conspire
Some king of Congo was her sire—
   Some Ethiop Queen her mother.

Yet, from a princess and a king
   Whatever be their hue,
Since none but drivelling idiots spring,
   And GODS must spring from you.
We'll make thy Tommy's lineage lend;
Black and white genius both shall blend
   In him their rays divine.
From Phillis Wheatley we'll contrive

* [Adams's note:] For the history of *Acte*, the Emperor Nero's Sally, and the methods taken by
  him to correct the procedure of her genealogy, consult his life in Suetonius.

Or brighter Sancho to derive*
    Thy son's maternal line.

Though nature o'er thy Sally's frame
    Has spread her sable veil,
Yet shall the loudest trump of fame
    Resound your tender tale.
Her charms of person, charms of mind
To you and motley scores confin'd
    Shall scent each future age;
And still her jetty fleece and eyes
Pug nose, thick lips and ebon [?thighs]†
    Shall blacken Clio's page.

Nay, Thomas, fumble not thy head,
    Though Sally's worth I sing,
In me, no rival canst thou dread,
    I cause no horns to spring.
Besides my three score years and ten
I was not form'd like other men
    To burn for beauteous faces—
One pint of brandy from the still
My soul with fiercer joys can fill
    Than Venus and her graces.
           (October 30, 1802)[328]

---

* [Editor Joseph Dennie's note:] It appears that Paine before he wrote this incomparable Ode or Epithalamium, had attentively studied his friend's *Notes on Virginia*. Phyllis Wheatley and Ignatius Sancho are there mentioned as the two prodigies of African intellect. *There* is to be found a learned and ingenious comparison between the blacks and the whites, both in a moral and physical point of view. The *immoveable* veil of black, the *scented bodies,* and sundry other properties of the negroes delicately alluded to here, are all noticed in that immortal work. It contains moreover the important discovery that "the difference between the black and the white complexion is *as real* as if its seat and cause were better known to us."

    With respect to the amatory propensities of the blacks, the *Notes on Virginia* remark, that "love seems with them to be more an eager desire, than a tender delicate mixture of sentiment and sensation." And again, "Their love is ARDENT, but it kindles the senses only, not the imagination." Upon this point the Author's testimony is beyond all exception. *Crede experti.*

† Bracketed word omitted in original.

AMELIA OPIE (1769–1853)

A successful novelist and poet, Opie counted among her literary friends Wordsworth, Godwin, Byron, and Scott. A lifelong reformer and philanthropist, she became a Quaker in 1814 and helped lead the antislavery movement in later years. She published an influential poem, *The Black Man's Lament, or How to Make Sugar*, in 1826, and in 1840 she represented her town of Norwich at the British Anti-Slavery convention in London.

In this poem written at the beginning of her career, Opie dramatizes the story of a slave child in Jamaica begging a departing English woman to take him with her. Perhaps inevitably, the story ends in tragedy. But Opie's poem has unusual twists, including resentment at the impotence of women in British society and rueful acceptance that the slave boy may be better off dead.

from "The Negro Boy's Tale"

"Haste! hoist the sails! fair blows the wind!
Jamaica, sultry land, adieu!—
Away! and loitering Anna find!
I long dear England's shores to view!" . . .

　　An earnest suit to press,
To Anna flew the Negro boy.

"Missa," poor Zambo cried, "sweet land
Dey tell me dat you go to see,
Vere, soon as on de shore he stand,
De helpless Negro slave be free.

Ah! dearest missa, you so kind!
Do take me to dat blessed shore,
Dat I mine own dear land may find,
And dose who love me see once more. . . .

And ven I'm in my moder's arms,

And tell de vonders I have know,
I'll say, Most best of all de charms
Vas she who feel for negro's woe. . . .

Dat heart love you, and dat good land
Vere every negro slave be free,—
Oh! if dat England understand
De negro wrongs, how wrath she be! . . .

O missa's God! dat country bless!"
(Here Anna's colour went and came,
But saints might share the pure distress,
For Anna blushed at others' shame.)

"But, missa, say; shall I vid you
To dat sweet England now depart,
Once more mine own good country view,
And press my moder on my heart?"

Then on his knees poor Zambo fell,
While Anna tried to speak in vain:
The expecting boy she could not tell*
He'd ne'er his mother see again. . . .

But woe betides an ill-timed suit:
His temper soured by her delay,
Trevannion bade his child be mute,
Nor dare such fruitless hopes betray.

"I know," she cried, "I cannot free
The numerous slaves that round me pine;
But one poor negro's friend to be,
Might (blessed chance!) might now be mine."

But vainly Anna wept and prayed,
And Zambo knelt upon the shore;
Without reply, the pitying maid
Trevannion to the vessel bore.

Mean while, poor Zambo's cries to still,
And his indignant grief to tame,
Eager to act his brutal will,
The negro's scourge-armed ruler came.

The whip is raised—the lash descends—
And Anna hears the sufferer's groan;

---

* [Opie's note:] "I could not tell the imp he had no mother." Vide *Series of Plays on the Passions*, by Miss [Joanna] Baillie, *Count Basil*, p. 111.

But while the air with shrieks she rends,
The signal's given—the ship sails on.

That instant, by despair made bold,
Zambo one last great effort tried;
He burst from his tormentor's hold,—
He plunged within the foaming tide. . . .

Anna, I mourn thy virtuous woe;
I mourn thy father's keen remorse;
But from my eyes no tears would flow
At sight of Zambo's silent corse:—

The orphan from his mother torn,
And pining for his native shore,—
Poor tortured slave—poor wretch forlorn—
Can I his early death deplore?—

I pity those who live, and groan:
Columbia countless Zambos sees;—
For swelled with many a wretch's moan
Is Western India's sultry breeze.

Come, Justice, come! in glory drest,
O come! the woe-worn negro's friend,—
The fiend-delighting trade arrest,
The negro's chains asunder rend!

(1802)[329]

SUSANNA WATTS (fl. 1802)

Ostensibly framed in the voice of a female slave, Watts's poem assumes a natural link between feminine sensibility and the antislavery movement. Appealing especially to maternal feelings about the pain of losing one's children, the poem becomes something of an anthem, calling British women to action in support of the abolition movement.

The Slave's Address

Natives of a Land of Glory,
    Daughters of the good and brave!
Hear the injured Negro's story;—
    Hear and help the kneeling Slave.

Think how nought but death can sever
    Your lov'd children from your hold;—
Still alive—but lost for ever—
    Ours are parted, bought, and sold!

Seize, oh! Seize the favouring season—
    Scorning censure or applause;
JUSTICE, TRUTH, RELIGION, REASON,
    Are your LEADERS in the cause!

Follow!—faithful, firm, confiding;—
    Spread our wrongs from shore to shore;
Mercy's God your efforts guiding,
    Slavery shall be known no more.

                (1802)[330]

WILLIAM WORDSWORTH
(1770–1850)

One of the most important poets in all of English literature, Wordsworth (like his friend Coleridge) was awakened to the evils of slavery while still a student at Cambridge. The subject surfaces in his early poems and like his literary friends (including Southey, Hunt, Helen Maria Williams, Amelia Opie, and others), Wordsworth loathed the institution. But he was less active in the movement than many people. He seemed to regard slavery as one of many interconnected evils, all likely to be eliminated as the revolution that had begun in France in 1789 spread its influence across western civilization. In later years, even after his disillusionment with France, he supported abolition, but in the quiet manner of one who saw it less as a political cause than as a topic in his endlessly evolving autobiographical poetry.

In this first sonnet, Wordsworth pays tribute to the great leader of the Haitian Revolution, Toussaint L'Ouverture. Born of slave parents, Toussaint was a free black who took a leading role in the slave insurrection of 1791, and from 1793 to 1801 led black Haitian forces that defeated other factions, repulsed a British invasion, and gained control of Haiti. Wordsworth's poem takes as its moment Toussaint's defeat and capture by French forces in 1802. Despite such protests, Toussaint was never released and died a prisoner in France.

To Toussaint L'Ouverture

Toussaint, the most unhappy man of men!
Whether the whistling Rustic tend his plough
Within thy hearing, or thy head be now
Pillowed in some deep dungeon's earless den;—
O miserable Chieftain! where and when
Wilt thou find patience! Yet die not; do thou
Wear rather in thy bonds a cheerful brow:
Though fallen thyself, never to rise again,
Live, and take comfort. Thou hast left behind

Powers that will work for thee; air, earth, and skies;
There's not a breathing of the common wind
That will forget thee; thou has great allies;
Thy friends are exultations, agonies,
And love, and man's unconquerable mind.

(1802)[331]

Returning from a visit to the continent, Wordsworth was moved by the sight of a black refugee fleeing a recent edict reinstating slavery in France. A brilliant example of his ability to capture a "spot of time," the sonnet dramatizes the up-welling of powerful feelings in response to a keenly observed moment of human suffering.

September 1, 1802 *

We had a female Passenger who came
From Calais with us, spotless in array,—
A white-robed Negro, like a lady gay,
Yet downcast as a woman fearing blame;
Meek, destitute, as seemed, of hope or aim
She sate, from notice turning not away,
But on all proffered intercourse did lay
A weight of languid speech, or to the same
No sign of answer made by word or face:
Yet still her eyes retained their tropic fire,
That, burning independent of the mind,
Joined with the lustre of her rich attire
To mock the Outcast—O ye Heavens, be kind!
And feel, thou Earth, for this afflicted Race!

(1802)[332]

In this excerpt from his famous autobiographical poem, Wordsworth recalls his return to England after a year abroad in France (1791–92). Wilberforce's bill had been defeated, but the abolition movement had shaped public opinion greatly; in Wordsworth's view, "a whole Nation crying with one voice . . . had been cross'd." As he candidly admits here, for him the slavery question was subsumed in the need for larger reforms. (Wordsworth returned to this passage

---

* [Wordsworth's headnote:] Among the capricious acts of tyranny that disgraced those times, was the chasing of all Negroes from France by decree of the government: we had a Fellow-passenger who was one of the expelled.

in later years, shifting its emphases in subtle but significant ways for the 1850 edition.)

from The Prelude

When to my native land,
After a whole year's absence, I returned,
I found the air yet busy with the stir
Of a contention which had been raised up
Against the traffickers in Negro blood,
An effort which, though baffled, nevertheless
Had called back old forgotten principles
Dismissed from service, had diffused some truths,
And more of virtuous feeling, through the heart
Of the English people. And no few of those,
So numerous—little less in verity
Than a whole nation crying with one voice—
Who had been crossed in this their just intent
And righteous hope, thereby were well prepared
To let that journey sleep awhile, and join
Whatever other caravan appeared
To travel forward towards Liberty
With more success. For me that strife had ne'er
Fastened on my affections, nor did now
Its unsuccessful issue much excite
My sorrow, having laid this faith to heart,
That if France prospered good men would not long
Pay fruitless worship to humanity,
And this most rotten branch of human shame
(Object, as it seemed, of a superfluous pain)
Would fall together with its parent tree.

Such was my then belief—that there was one,
And only one, solicitude for all.

(1805)[333]

Less spontaneous than his best poetry, Wordsworth's sonnet in honor of his fellow Cantabrigian Thomas Clarkson (1760–1846) has more of the formality of a ceremonial poem, which it is. Characterizing the abolition movement that Clarkson founded as "this pilgrimage sublime," Wordsworth celebrates the recent passage of the abolition bill of 1807 with an optimism that subsequent events were to dispel.

Sonnet, to Thomas Clarkson, on the Final Passing of the Bill for the Abolition of the Slave Trade, March, 1807

Clarkson! it was an obstinate Hill to climb;
How toilsome, nay how dire it was, by Thee
Is known,—by none, perhaps, so feelingly;
But Thou, who, starting in thy fervent prime,
Didst first lead forth this pilgrimage sublime,
Hast heard the constant Voice its charge repeat,
Which, out of thy young heart's oracular seat,
First roused thee.—O true yoke-fellow of Time
With unabating effort, see, the palm
Is won, and by all Nations shall be worn!
The bloody Writing is for ever torn,
And Thou henceforth shalt have a good Man's calm,
A great Man's happiness; thy zeal shall find
Repose at length, firm Friend of human kind!

(wr. 1807/pub. 1815)[334]

JOSEPH WARREN BRACKETT
(1775–1826)

Defenders of slavery turn up in surprising contexts. Brackett was a New York lawyer and alderman who delivered this poem at the Dartmouth College Phi Beta Kappa commencement ceremonies on August 23, 1803. As he surveys the progress of civilization, Brackett reveals, in this excerpt, his racist and anthropologically misinformed views of Africans, including the unenlightened idea, so agreeable to apologists for slavery, that these "sons of Ham" were predestined "to toil and bleed, and shackles wear." Few can regret that no other poems by Brackett are known to have survived.

from The Ghost of Law, or Anarchy and Despotism

Thence turn to Afric, where the god of day,
With force solstitial, pours his fervid ray;
There savage still, wild man his waste explores,
And still the tyger yells, and lion roars.
Through dewy vales, and aromatic groves,
And wild'ring wilds, where satyrs scream their loves,
But aping human kind, the vagrants roam,
In soul high fever'd, and neglecting home,
Poor sons of Ham, as sons of av'rice swear,
Born but to toil and bleed, and shackles wear,
At once rapacious, indolent, severe,
In drowsy ignorance their offspring rear:
While o'er their woes the war-torn suff'rers brood,
And Koromantyns drink their brother's blood.
Thus time has roll'd, and still unalter'd rolls;
Still, still the same,—no brighter scene unfolds:
Then drop, ah then, the kindly curtain drop,
O'er these rude tribes; and turn to climes of hope!

(1803)[335]

WILLIAM C. FOSTER
(fl. 1798–1805)

A self-described workingman of little formal education, but a passionate auto-didact, Foster disseminated liberal ideas and occasional publications from his base in upstate New York. True to his pseudonym "Timothy Spectacles," Foster focused his gaze on the dynamics of liberty and oppression in Europe and America.

In this poem Foster uses the Haitian slave rebellions to call for an end to slavery everywhere, including the United States. His closing lines refer to James Callender's allegations about President Jefferson's affair with Sally Hemings, to show the extent to which American life is permeated with the moral taint of slavery. Modern revelations about the Jefferson-Hemings relationship confute Foster's opinion that the matter had "dy'd without much joy or grief."

from "An Address, Presented to the Readers of the 'Waterford [N.Y.] Gazette,' January 1, 1803"

In St. Domingo, as they say,
Equality has forc'd her way;
Where *Toussaint* and *Christophe*,
(Resolv'd on death or liberty)
The Lodian victors have withstood,
And drench'd their native hills with blood!
Can those who breathe fair freedom's air
Wish not *all* men the boon to share
Whose sacred altars long have stood
Seal'd with ten thousand patriots' blood?
Can they wish those of deeper dye
Within the tyrant's chain to lie?
No!—let it sound from shore to shore
That "*Man is Man,* and who is more?"
From Afric's shore (to man's disgrace)

They've hither brought this hapless race;
For ages doom'd the lash to bear,
And slavery's galling yoke to wear;
Forc'd cruel lordlings to obey—
Branded and shot, like beasts of prey;
Till, sick of life, they all conspire,
And vengeance moves the kindled ire!

    And thou, O *Guadaloupe!* must share
The sad disasters of the war!
Thy flaming towns but faintly show
A picture of thy future woe!
Each tortur'd black, whose bosom bleeds,
To nature's God for vengeance pleads—
Whose slumb'ring wrath but waits the call
On thy devoted isle to fall! . . .

    Jim Callender . . .
With crimson'd face he sounds the horn,
To tell a negro child is born—
Says the Presiding democrat
Was father of the yellow brat!
This furnish'd up a luscious mess,
A handsome story for the press:
'Twas told, and told, without belief,
And dy'd without much joy or grief.
                (1803)[336]

ANONYMOUS ["A. A."]

The following ballad was written by an anonymous English woman on a visit to Virginia in 1804. Although nothing is known of the author, her poem was later anthologized by the American abolitionist Abigail Mott, whose collection was republished from the 1820s into the 1850s. Unlike so many British critics of American slavery, the poet not only condemns American slaveholders, but also implicates her fellow Britons for their part in the transatlantic slave trade.

Pity the Slave *

1. PENSIVE, lonely, while I wandered
   Dark Virginia's woods among,
       Soon I heard the thrilling locust,
   Stood and listened to its song,

2. When the sound of human footsteps,
       Soft approaching, caught my ear;
   Quick I started, looked around me,
       Lo! a black boy stood so near.

3. He from cold could ne'er be sheltered,
       By his garments ragged and bare,
   Yet his looks bespoke good nature
       With a smile as wild as air.

4. And is this the land of Freedom,
       Soon my throbbing heart rejoined,
   While the poor afflicted negroes
       Still in fetters hard they bind?

* [Abigail Mott's note:] In 1804, A. A., when travelling in Virginia, stopped in the woods with her companions to refresh themselves and horses. After taking refreshment, she took a solitary walk, when a circumstance occurred which gave rise to the following reflections.

5. Sad disgrace to human nature—
   And must England bear a part?
   Cast away the shameful traffic,
   Prove thou hast a feeling heart,

6. That, aroused by thy example,
   Columbia too may break the chain,
   Nor the mournful sons of Afric,
   Longer curse your lust of gain.

   (c. 1804)[337]

THOMAS MOORE (1779–1852)

An Irish poet whose popularity (for such works as *Lalla Rookh* [1817]) rivaled that of Scott and Byron, Moore was one of the first Roman Catholics educated at Trinity College, Dublin. Although he pursued his literary career in England, the following poems were inspired by an eight-month sojourn in America in 1804. As with many foreign visitors, especially liberals like himself who admired the American republic, Moore was struck by the incongruity of slavery in the land of freedom. In both of the poems below, slavery emerges as a focal point of his criticism.

In the first, addressed to Sir William Forbes, the Scottish banker and member of Samuel Johnson's literary circle, Moore becomes one of the first to attack the grotesqueness of slave markets operating in the new American capital. Moore's revulsion at the continuance of slavery in America anticipates the response of other foreign observers over the next several decades.

from "Epistle VI. To Lord Viscount Forbes. From Washington"

Oh! freedom, freedom, how I hate thy cant!
Not Eastern bombast, not the savage rant
Of purpled madmen, were they number'd all
From Roman Nero down to Russian Paul,
Could grate upon my ear so mean, so base,
As the rank jargon of that factious race,
Who, poor of heart, and prodigal of words,
Born to be slaves, and struggling to be lords,
But pant for licence, while they spurn controul.
And shout for rights, with rapine in their soul!
Who can, with patience, for a moment see
The medley mass of pride and misery,
Of whips and charters, manacles and rights.

Of slaving blacks and democratic whites,*
And all the pye-bald polity that reigns
In free confusion o'er Columbia's plains?
To think that man, thou just and gentle God!
Should stand before thee, with a tyrant's rod
O'er creatures like himself, with souls from thee,
Yet dare to boast of perfect liberty!
Away, away—I'd rather hold my neck
By doubtful tenure from a sultan's beck,
In climes, where liberty has scarce been nam'd,
Nor any right but that of ruling claim'd,
Than thus to live, where bastard freedom waves
Her fustian flag in mockery over slaves;
Where (motley laws admitting no degree
Betwixt the vilely slav'd and madly free)
Alike the bondage and the licence suit
The brute made ruler, and the man made brute!
                    (wr. 1804/pub. 1806)[338]

In another poem addressed to a friend back in Britain, Moore satirizes the grandiose pretensions of Americans who, even as their new capital was just emerging from the wilderness, imagined it a second Rome. Although he was introduced to President Jefferson and elsewhere reported being favorably impressed by "this remarkable person," here Moore slyly ridicules Jefferson for his indiscretions with Sally Hemings ("Aspasia") and the pall they cast over his reputation as a champion of freedom.

from "Epistle VII. To Thomas Hume, Esq. M.D. From the City of Washington"

'Tis evening now; the heats and cares of day
In twilight dews are calmly wept away.
The lover now, beneath the western star,
Sighs through the medium of his sweet segar,

---

* [Moore's note:] In Virginia the effects of this system begin to be felt rather seriously. While the master raves of liberty, the slave cannot but catch the contagion, and accordingly there seldom elapses a month without some alarm of insurrection amongst the negroes. The accession of Louisiana, it is feared, will increase this embarrassment; as the numerous emigrations, which are expected to take place, from the southern states to this newly acquired territory, will considerably diminish the white population, and thus strengthen the proportion of negroes, to a degree which must ultimately be ruinous.

And fills the ears of some consenting she
With puffs and vows, with smoke and constancy!
The weary statesman for repose hath fled
From halls of council to his negro's shed,
Where blest he woos some black Aspasia's grace,
And dreams of freedom in his slave's embrace!

In fancy now, beneath the twilight gloom,
Come, let me lead thee o'er this modern Rome,
Where tribunes rule, where dusky Davi bow,
And what was Goose-Creek once is Tiber now!—
This fam'd metropolis, where fancy sees
Squares in morasses, obelisks in trees;
Which travelling fools and gazetteers adorn
With shrines unbuilt and heroes yet unborn,
Though nought but wood and [Jefferson]* they see,
Where streets should run and sages *ought* to be!
                        (wr. 1804/pub. 1806)[339]

* Jefferson's name left blank in the original.

CHARLOTTE SMITH (1749–1806)

An accomplished woman of letters whose private life was sad and difficult, Charlotte Smith endured an arranged marriage to the son of a West India merchant, to whom she bore twelve children. In the late 1770s, with her husband in debtors' prison, she turned to writing. Her "Elegiac Sonnets" (1784) attracted the admiration of Cowper, Walpole, the Wartons, young Wordsworth, and many other poets. She continued to produce popular poetry, novels, and criticism to the end of her life.

The following passage, inspired by the sight of a firefly displayed as an entomological specimen, moves from a piece of scientific evidence to a series of imaginative associations. The dead firefly evokes images of captive Africans struggling to escape, with distant hints (perhaps foreshadowing Eliot's Prufrockian insect "pinned and wriggling on the wall") of Smith's own sense of entrapment.

from "To the Fire-Fly of Jamaica, Seen in a Collection"

The recent captive, who in vain,
Attempts to break his heavy chain,
And find his liberty in flight;
Shall no more in terror hide,
From thy strange and doubtful light,
In the mountain's cavern'd side,
Or gully deep, where gibbering monkies cling,
And broods the giant bat, on dark funereal wing.

Nor thee his darkling steps to aid,
Thro' the forest's pathless shade,
Shall the sighing Slave invoke;
Who, his daily task perform'd,
Would forget his heavy yoke;
And by fond affections warm'd,
Glide to some dear sequester'd spot, to prove,
Friendship's consoling voice, or sympathising love.

(1804)[340]

ANONYMOUS

By 1805 the notion was spreading that New World slavery was an evil whose apocalyptic end was at hand. In the following excerpt from an American newspaper's review of the year's events, the poet invokes Haiti's insurrections and civil wars as a warning to his fellow Americans of the divinely sanctioned violence to come, if slavery is not abolished.

from "New Year's Address of the Carrier of the Mercantile Advertiser to His Customers"

How much—ah! pr'ythee think awhile,
We've said of sad Domingo's isle!
Ill fated Isle! what crime unknown
Has drawn from Heav'n its vengeance down,
To whelm your fields with Ruin's flood,
And float your streets with murder'd blood?
Is it that Afric's ceaseless groan
At length has reach'd mild Mercy's throne,
Who calling Justice (not in vain)
Justice has stept on earth again?
Columbia! let Domingo's fate
Give warning ere it prove too late;
Rouse! and pronounce the bold decree,
"Death to the Monster, Slavery."

(1805)[341]

THOMAS BRANAGAN (1774–1843)

Born to a middle-class Catholic family in Ireland, Branagan (a self-described "dunce") left school early to pursue life at sea. Already a widely traveled sailor, at age sixteen Branagan began serving aboard a Liverpool slave ship and entered a world of cruelty that he described later as "truly inconceivable." In one pivotal episode, Branagan deserted his ship in Africa and found himself a fugitive in the interior, where various African families sheltered him before he was captured and returned to his ship—a remarkable inversion of the experience of so many fugitive slaves, and one that left a lasting impression on him. A series of jobs on West Indies ships led to a stint as a plantation overseer in Antigua. During these years he also underwent a religious conversion and began an idealistic but doomed effort to develop a Christian ministry among the slaves he oversaw.

After a brief return to Ireland in 1798, Branagan emigrated to Philadelphia and began his American career as a pious and indefatigable abolitionist. In addition to the poetry presented below, Branagan wrote several prose works against slavery, joined abolitionist societies, and entreated public figures for support, including President Jefferson. Jefferson was flattered by Branagan's compliments, but his writings made him uneasy. Jefferson declined to endorse them publicly, though he kept both of Branagan's antislavery epics in his library.

The first poem below is Branagan's massive, overwrought epic ("written in imitation of Homer's Iliad"), set in Africa and meant to dramatize in heroic battle scenes the running war between slavers and Africans. In Book I, the bereaved Avenia laments the capture of her beloved Angola, while the African chiefs Louverture and Mondingo take the field against packs of European invaders with names like Hodge, Dundas, and O'Brien.

from Avenia, or A Tragical Poem
from Book I

> Awake my Muse, the inharmonious strain!
> I sing of arms on Afric's crimson'd plain:

Of war, 'gainst Afric's sons by Christians wag'd,
With all the accursed love of Gold enrag'd.
What pen can half their villanies record!
What tongue can count the slaughters of their sword! . . .

With sacred transport glows *Avenia*'s breast,
While with the swains her lov'd *Angola* sings,
And wakes to love, the banjoe's well-taught strings;
Behind irreg'lar move the chaunting train,
And time the voice, and answer to the strain.
Twice twenty warriors as their guardians stand,
Six shepherd's dogs complete the rural band,
And fleecy flocks that crop the tender green,
Skip, o'er the lawns and heighten all the scene—
When lo! the *Christians* suddenly arise
In arms, and furious rush upon their prize;
The sable nymphs they seize to sate their lust,
While heaps of slaughter'd swains bestrew the dust.
One youth escap'd of all the warrior train,
Swift speeds his flight across the ensanguin'd plain.
While brave *Angola* by the Fiends oppress'd
Undaunted wields his weapon—bares his breast—
That breast which heaves with sorrow not his own,
But for his lov'd *Avenia*—her alone.
To rescue her he strives, but strives in vain.
O'erpower'd by numbers, to the galling chain
He yields reluctant, and from her he loves,
Toward the floating dungeon, pensive moves;
While from his numerous wounds the noble blood,
Slow streaming, marks his footsteps thro' the wood,
The widow'd bride, in misery complete
Now swoons a victim at the tyrant's feet.
Impatient he beholds the royal prize,
While lust and rapine swell his brutish eyes,
Grudging he views her short reprieve from woe—
And waits, till life's returning current flow.
Avenia now to hated life restor'd,
In plaintive sounds bewails her absent Lord:
"Where have ye borne my soul's far better part!
She said, while anguish fill'd her widow'd heart,
Ah, tell me, *Christians:* whither have ye borne,
My *Angola*, from his lov'd partner torn" . . .

Louverture leads; all fix on him their eye,
Resolv'd with him to conquer or to die.
And now, my Muse assist me to proclaim,
Who fac'd him first, and press'd the purple plain.
Imperious *Hodge,* advancing, void of fear,
First met the vengeance of his thirsty spear;
Prone in the dust the panting tyrant lay,
While brave *Louverture* lopp'd his head away.
The fight begun, promiscuous shouts arise,
And dreadful clangors echo through the skies;
Next the fam'd *Dundas* felt the fatal wound;
Sudden he fell, and falling bit the ground.
Louverture left him in the shades of night,
Then press'd amidst the thickest ranks of fight . . .
The brave *Louverture* with resistless hand,
Pursues, o'erturns, confounds the Christian band;
On strong *O'Brien* next inflicts a wound,
And lays proud *Thompson* gasping on the ground.
While he lay foaming on the purple plain,
The far fam'd villain, *Barrington* by name,
Wing'd with wild fears, in vain did strive to fly,
The ships too distant and the foe too nigh:
The eager dart transfixt him as he fled,
And soon enroll'd him with th' ignoble dead. . . .
Mondingo now, a chief well skill'd in arms,
Leads forth to combat his infuriate swarms;
He fights, he conquers, prodigal of breath,
And seeks the certain, glorious path to death:
See, while he fires the brave victorious throng,
Prince urge on prince, and chief drive chief along;
Heaps upon heaps, the slaughter'd *Christians* lie,
And hideous shouts of conquest rend the sky.

In Book II, the Africans' early victories are overshadowed by the arrival of large fleets of British ships on the African Coast. A mood of despair begins to infect the warriors.

from Book II of *Avenia*

The Christians flee in terror from the plain,
The fierce *Louverture* rushing stern before,
His chieftains follow, thundring to the shore . . .

599

But now, the prince beholds far on the sea,
Full twenty ships direct their watery way;
Straight for the shore the tilting vessels stand,
Then furl their sails and anchor near the land.
Each held full forty troops, a cruel train,
And each prepar'd to scour the ill fated plain.
And while the sight the sable host appals,
The vanquish'd robbers gain their wooden walls . . .

Now o'er the fields dejected he surveys,
From fifty ships as many fires blaze;
And looking forward to the fleet and coast,
Anxious he sorrows for his father's host:
Inward he groans, while duty and despair,
Divide his heart, and wage a doubtful war.
And while a thousand cares his breast revolves,
To seek sage *Quaco* now the chief resolves;
With him in wholesome council to debate,
What yet remain'd to save th' afflicted state.

After more battles in Book III, in Book IV the white slavers finally triumph
and, true to Branagan's larger vision, take brutal vengeance on the vanquished
Africans. Here an unnamed slaver commits genocide by hanging unwanted
women and children, while taking men to sell into slavery.

from Book IV of *Avenia*

"Die, wretches die, your suppliant arts give o'er
To me no negro need for grace implore.
The hour t'avenge our soldiers now is come,
Impending fate is yours, and instant doom;
Not all the gold in your detested town
With all in Africa join'd with your own,
If offer'd for you should for mercy call,
'Tis negroes offer, and I scorn them all."
   Thus speaking, from a lofty tree he strung,
A ship's tough rope that to another hung;
Near the high boughs he strain'd it strongly round,
Whence no contending foot could touch the ground:
Their necks tied up, connected in a row,
Both babes and mothers, spectacles of woe,
All beat the air with quiv'ring feet below.
Soon fled their harmless souls, and left behind
The lifeless bodies wav'ring with the wind.

In a symbolic dramatization of the middle passage, Book V presents an epic-scale transportation of the defeated Africans into slavery in the West Indies. For all the parallels with the *Aeneid,* there is no hint of later regeneration, only scene after scene of dehumanization and degradation, culminating in the brutal rape of Avenia by her white master, and then her suicide.

from Book V of *Avenia*

> Behold, and blush, ye first born of the skies,
> Behold the complicated villanies,
> Practis'd by Christian hypocrites, unjust,
> Full of rage, rapine, cruelty and lust,
> Who, smooth of tongue, in purpose insincere,
> Hide fraud in smiles, while death is harbor'd there. . . .
>
> The unfeeling tyrant, bent on wickedness,
> Eager beheld her, in her keen distress . . .
> He bids her follow where he leads the way.
> And as they to the place prepar'd, proceed,
> The lustful ruffian meditates the deed,
> Which stamps for ever poor Avenia's fate . . .
> In vain the sable captive lifts her hand,
> In vain she strives his pity to command;
> Invokes her lov'd Angola, tears her hair,
> And lifts to heav'n her unavailing prayer:
> And oh, what various passions struggling, rise
> Swell her vex'd bosom, and inflame her eyes;
> What sobs of anguish, what hysteric screams,
> What shrieks of frenzy, in their fierce extremes!
> The monster braves them all, by wild lust driv'n,
> And violates the dame, in face of heav'n!
> Cease my indignant muse, by shame suppress'd,
> Let tears and burning blushes speak the rest . . .
>
> The foaming billows, mounting to the shore,
> High on the rock the mangled body bore;
> There in the craggy bason, long it lay,*
> To ev'ry wind, and rav'nous bird, a prey.
> Hapless Avenia! whither art thou gone;
> Launch'd in a moment to a world unknown.
> No more, alas, for thee the chaunting train,

* [Branagan's note:] One morning as I was walking round our estate I saw [the body of] a slave who had previously committed suicide by plunging in, and continuing under water till drowned.

Shall join harmonious on the verdant plain;
No more, with grace superior to the rest,
Shalt thou inflame the wond'ring hero's breast;
For thee no more awake the tuneful strings;
No more to charm thee thy Angola sings.

(1805)[342]

In his next major poem, Branagan built a first-person epic out of remorse over his own involvement in the slave trade. More than two thousand lines in length, *The Penitential Tyrant* is both an agonizing personal confession and a bold assertion of discomfiting truth. Although Branagan's verbal artistry is of a different quality, the power of his personal experience—of both damnation and redemption—gives his vision an intensity like that of another slaver turned evangelical poet, John Newton. His poem extends to four cantos of psychological and theological rumination, of which the most vivid, Cantos I and II, are excerpted below. Canto I, in its graphic lists of the sufferings of the slaves, becomes also something of an exercise in self-denunciation and self-flagellation.

from The Penitential Tyrant; or, Slave Trader Reformed: a Pathetic Poem, in Four Cantos
from Canto I

Oh! may I never stand where once I stood—
View hills and dales all red with crimson blood,
See verdant fields all clotted stiff with gore,
Which ne'er were stain'd with human blood before;
Where mortals wounded pil'd on mortals dead,
Made verdant green be ting'd with crimson red,
No more I see that thrice unhappy ground,
Where heaps of human bones are spread around;
Hear screams—hear groans—hear agonizing sounds
Pierce hell—pierce heav'n—pierce earth's remotest bounds!
Alas! my soul the shocking din sustains,
Which makes the blood hang shiv'ring in my veins!
Their wrongs I saw and heard, their mighty woes
I now relate, and more than I'll disclose.
I've seen behaviour in this cruel race,
Which naming would the very brute disgrace . . .
Have I not seen the wounds their sabres gave,
To each dejected, weeping, dying slave;
Have I not seen the blood of hundreds shed!
The injur'd maid forc'd to her tyrant's bed!

THOMAS BRANAGAN

The frantic father stain'd with filial blood,
Who with his children ting'd the crimson wood
His violated consort dragg'd away
Thro' woods, o'er seas, to wicked man a prey,
And doom'd to misery, though once possess'd
Of love, peace, joy, with ev'ry blessing bless'd . . .

    Remembrance sad exhibits to my view,
Sights which must open all their wounds anew;
I view their wrongs, while on the roaring waves,
I saw them languish, and I saw them slaves,
Been basely seiz'd while in the dire alarms
Of war, rage, slaughter, and the clash of arms;
What first, what last, what here I now relate,
Brings to my wounded mind their wretched fate;
Nay, as I write, methinks I hear them moan,
Tear following tear, and groan succeeding groan;
Struck at the sight, I melt at human woe,
While down my cheeks the tears unbidden flow . . .

    Th' Impartial Judge, and Sov'reign of the skies,
Has heard, and hears the mourning captives cries;
And, with benignant love, he now declares,
Their cares are his, his boundless mercy their's:
Their potent friend in their behalf will rise,
Their numerous foes the injur'd God defies . . .

With penitential tears, I this affirm,
For, to my grief, I've borne the baneful term;
For I myself have oft stood by unmov'd,
Dead to entreaty I have often prov'd;
Dead to remorse, I often have stood by,
And still as often did the lash apply!
But, lo! I saw the vengeful hand of God,
His fury, judgments, and tremendous rod,
His flaming sword, just lifted for the blow,
T' avenge th' opprest, and slay the murd'rous foe;
From thence I haste, my trembling steps I bend
Far hence, before consuming deaths descend,
Smit with a conscious sense of guilt in mind,
I shun the fate I well deserv'd to find . . .

Thus from the paths of wickedness I run,
Lest the Almighty's vengeance once begun,
I share the doom which tyrants will not shun!

In Canto II, in a guilt-ridden dream vision worthy of Macbeth or the Ancient Mariner, a succession of maimed and bloody specters reproaches Branagan for all the evils perpetrated under slavery. Later, as he feels himself redeemed by God's mercy, Branagan rejoices in language reminiscent ("wondrous grace, amazing love") of Newton's hymn of thanks, "Amazing Grace."

from Canto II of *The Penitential Tyrant*

One night, methought about the midnight hour,
A double darkness o'er me seem'd to lower;
Pensive I lay, to know what God design'd,
Sensations awful fill'd my boding mind!
The poor unhappy slaves rose to my view,
My former guilt, their wounds now bled anew;
I heard their sighs, and saw their big round tears,
Wept as they wept, and fear'd with all their fears;
Methought I saw once more their natal shore,
All stain'd with carnage, red with human gore;
Shrouded in blood they now appear'd to stand,
And pointed to their agonizing land;
I saw the thousands, thousands, thousands slain,
On their primeval, their parental plain;
Their lacerated limbs, with chains opprest,
Their minds, alas! with mighty woes distrest!
Each body mangled, scourged in every part,
While sighs and groans burst from each swelling heart!
I saw in tides of tears their sorrows flow,
And still new anguish added to their woe. . . .

As the bold sailor, when his daring soul,
Has drawn, too vent'rous, near the freezing pole,
Who having slighted caution's tame advice,
Seems wedg'd within impervious isles of ice;
If from each chilling form of peril free,
At length he makes th' unincumber'd sea;
With joy superior to his transient pain,
Rushes exulting o'er the expansive main:
Thus sav'd, by wondrous grace, amazing love,
I long to shout my Saviour's praise above.
Impell'd by gratitude, I now declare,
His tender mercy, and his guardian care.

(1805)[343]

In this lyric poem, buried as a footnote to *The Pentitential Tyrant,* Branagan converts Robert Burns's skepticism into an ingenious rationale for faith. Taking up Burns's tactic of questioning conventional rationalizations for human suffering, Branagan goes on to argue that the abject misery of slaves is itself a paradoxical evidence of God's larger plan. Otherwise, an existence so bleak would have no purpose.

Untitled ["Written in imitation of Burns"]

If he's designed that lordling's slave,
    By nature's law design'd;
Why was an independent wish
    E'er planted in his mind?

If not, why is he subject to
    His cruelty or scorn?
And why has man the power and will
    To make his fellow mourn?

But this, even this should not disturb
    The honest negro's breast;
This partial view of human kind
    Is surely not the last.

The poor oppressed virtuous slave
    Had never sure been born,
Had there not been some recompence
    To comfort those that mourn.

               (1805)[344]

Here, in the first of two untitled lyric poems embedded in a tract against the abuse of women, Branagan digresses on the abject condition of African slaves, for whom—as for Avenia—death comes as a relief.

Untitled, *from* The Excellency of the Female Character Vindicated *

O death! the negro's welcome friend,
    "The dearest and the best;"

---

* [from Branagan's introduction:] In attempting to investigate the cause of female degradation, my mind is led imperceptibly to contemplate the miserable state of millions of poor unhappy females, who, at this very moment, are the victims of the avarice, and consequently the promiscuous lust of the traitors and tyrants of mankind; I mean the exiled daughters of the African race, from whose chains death alone is expected to relieve them.

How joyful is the hour you bring,
    The weary slave to rest.

When from the cruel tyrants grasp,
    By friendly death he's torn;
To taste the bless'd relief of those,
    Who cease on earth to mourn.

His tyrant, though he seems thus vain,
    In fortune's lap carest;
Yet think not while he seems thus great,
    That he is truly blest.

The thought, he'll soon be food for worms,
    From all his pleasures torn;
Blasts ev'ry op'ning bud of joy,
    And makes the tyrant mourn.

(1807)[345]

In the second lyric, Branagan focuses on the sexual vulnerability of female slaves and the anguished helplessness of their loved ones. While elsewhere Branagan connected New World slavery with old world serfdom, here he isolates it as a national disgrace for America in particular.

Untitled, from The Excellency of the Female Character Vindicated

"Ah! how can he whose daily lot is grief,
Whose mind is vilify'd beneath the rod;
Suppose his Maker has for him relief?
Can he believe the tongues that speak of God?

For when he sees the female of his heart,
And his lov'd daughters torn by lust away;
His sons the poor inheritors of smart,
Had he religion, think ye he could pray.

E'en at this moment on the burning gale,
Floats the weak wailing of the female tongue;
And can that sex's softness nought avail?
Must feeble women shriek amid the throng?

Haste, haste, ye winds on swiftest pinions fly,
Ere from this world of misery they go;
Tell them their wrongs bedew a nation's eye,
Tell them Columbia blushes for their wo."

(1807)[346]

THOMAS GREEN FESSENDEN ["CHRISTOPHER CAUSTIC"], (1771–1837)

A New England poet, journalist, and inventor, Fessenden, like his friend Joseph Dennie, was a rabidly anti-Jeffersonian Federalist. Among the many satires he wrote was the elaborate mock epic *Democracy Unveiled*, excerpted here. Like other anti-Jeffersonians, he jumped at the Sally Hemings scandal, cleverly using it to mock the three-fifths provision of the Constitution. Fessenden crudely suggests that, in siring children by their slave mistresses, southerners like Jefferson not only expand the population base for their states' representation but also provide an alternative to importation, thus enabling them to support the abolition of the overseas slave trade.

from "Canto IV. The Jeffersoniad," in Democracy Unveiled; or, Tyranny Stripped of the Garb of Patriotism

A Chief who stands not shilly shally,
But is notorious for—a *Sally*,*
Might Mars defy in "war's dire tug,"
Or Satan to an Indian hug.

Therefore, ye Feds, if you should now hard
Things mutter of a nerveless coward,
'Twill prove your characters, ye quizzes,
Black as an Empress's black phiz is.†

'Tis true, some wicked wags there are,
Who laugh about this dark affair,

---

* [from Fessenden's note:] [We] leave it to our commentators to decide, whether, by the term *Sally*, we mean an attack upon an *enemy*, or dalliance with a *friend*.

† [from Fessenden's note:] [We] cannot determine, whether we mean to allude to the jetty visage of the Empress of Morocco, or any particular paramour of the Emperor of America.

607

But I can tell the shameless faction,
They ought t'admire the same transaction . . .

For I will prove, sans disputation,
Our Chief has wondrous calculation;
And is in Politics, as able,
As Mazarine or Machiàvel.

For where's a readier resource
For that sweet, "social intercourse,"
Which, at a grand inauguration,
Was promis'd this our happy nation.

And, if by his example he goes,
To recommend the raising negroes,
The chance is surely in his favour,
Of being President for ever.

A southern negro is, you see, man,
Already three fifths of a freeman,
And when Virginia gets the staff,
He'll be a freeman and an half!*

Great men can never lack supporters,
Who manufacture their own voters;
Besides, 'tis plain as yonder steeple,
They will be *fathers to the people.*

And 'tis a decent, clever, comical,
New mode of being economical,
For when a black is rais'd, it follows,
It saves a duty of ten dollars.†

And he's a wayward blockhead who says
That making negroes, or pappooses,
Is not consistent with the plan,
Of Tom Pain's precious "Rights of Man."

---

* [Fessenden's note:] The preponderance which Virginia has already obtained in the scale of
representation, will enable her to proceed to increase the privileges and immunities of her
black population. In this she will be governed by the strict rules of Republican propriety;
which always consults the *greatest good* of the *greatest number.*

† [Fessenden's note:] This is a duty which has been proposed, and probably will, at some future
period, be adopted in the Southern States, to prevent the importation of slaves. It is surpris-
ing, that, among all the calculations for political economy, which have distinguished our
penny-saving administration, this pleasant scheme has not been adopted more generally. But
a word to the wise will not be thrown away. Our southern Nabobs will improve on this hint,
and sable *Nabobbesses* will be fashionable articles.

THOMAS GREEN FESSENDEN

Then Mister Opposition-prater,
Since that reproach to human nature,
The most nefarious Guinea trade
May fall by *Presidential* aid.

(1805)[347]

JAMES HAMMOND (fl. 1805)

The anxieties of a free black man opening a restaurant in a slave-holding community—here Alexandria, Virginia—are evident in this versified ad in a local newspaper.

[Untitled]

He hopes the color of his face
Will his calling never disgrace,
But that his conduct and attention
Will be a means to gain him custom.

(1805)[348]

JAMES MONTGOMERY
(1771–1854)

Born in Scotland to devout Moravians, Montgomery was sent to a Moravian school near Leeds while his parents pursued their radical Protestant ministry, first in Ireland and then in the West Indies, where both died within a few years. In England young Montgomery struggled, running away from an apprenticeship in a bakery, taking a job in a shop, and clerking for a Sheffield newspaper, all the while trying to publish his poetry. At the newspaper he flourished, rising to become editor and then proprietor by the age of twenty-four, and beginning what would become a significant literary career. As an active reformer and working journalist, Montgomery produced, from 1798 through the 1830s, a stream of poetry, criticism, and literary biography.

The first excerpt below is from a stanzaic meditation on the sea, written in the tradition of James Thomson and John Dyer, inflected by the site-specific subjectivity of Wordsworth. In these lines Montgomery harnesses the forces of nature to his moral imagination: "the gloomy Ocean," the site of so much carnage in the slave trade, gives rise to tempests and hurricanes that serve as portents of the coming apocalypse. Montgomery later lifted and revised these four stanzas as a separate poem, published as "The Slave Trade," which circulated in many anthologies and antislavery collections of the early nineteenth century.

from "The Ocean. Written at Scarborough, in the Summer of 1805" [or "The Slave Trade"]

There are, gloomy OCEAN! A brotherless clan
Who traverse thy banishing waves,
The poor disinherited outcasts of man,
Whom Avarice coins into slaves:
From the homes of their kindred, their forefathers' graves,
Love, friendship, and conjugal bliss,
They are dragg'd on the hoary abyss;

The shark hears their shrieks, and, ascending today
Demands of the spoiler his share of the prey.

Then joy to the tempest that whelms them beneath,
And makes their destruction its sport!
But woe to the winds that propitiously breathe,
And waft them in safety to port,
Where the vultures and vampires of Mammon resort;
Where Europe exultingly drains
The life-blood from Africa's veins;
Where man rules o'er man with a merciless rod,
And spurns at his footstool the image of GOD!

The hour is approaching,—a terrible hour!
And Vengeance is bending her bow;
Already the clouds of the hurricane lour,
And the rock-rending whirlwinds blow;
Back rolls the huge OCEAN, Hell opens below:
The floods return headlong,—they sweep
The slave-cultured lands to the deep;
In a moment entomb'd in the horrible void,
By their Maker Himself in his anger destroy'd!

Shall this be the fate of the cane-planted isles,
More lovely than clouds in the west,
When the sun o'er the ocean descending in smiles
Sinks softly and sweetly to rest?
—NO!—Father of mercy! befriend the opprest;
At the voice of thy Gospel of peace
May the sorrows of Africa cease;
And the slave and his master devoutly unite
To walk in thy freedom, and dwell in thy light!*

(1805)[349]

The poem below was commissioned by the London publisher Robert Bowyer, for inclusion in a lavish volume of antislavery poetry (with works by Grahame and Benger) timed to celebrate the abolition of the slave trade on January 1, 1808. Montgomery's "West Indies" is an epic about the peopling of the Caribbean with African slaves, ranging from their first importation to replace the extinguished Caribs, through decades of the slave trade, to the present moment of imminent insurrection.

* [Montgomery's note:] Alluding to the glorious success of the Moravian Missionaries among the Negroes in the West Indies.

JAMES MONTGOMERY

from "The West Indies, A Poem in Four Parts"
from Part I

　　Let nobler bards in loftier numbers tell
How Cortez conquer'd, Montezuma fell;
How grim Pizarro's ruffian arm o'erthrew
The sun's resplendent empire in Peru. . . .
　　Give me to sing in melancholy strains,
Of Charib martyrdoms, and negro-chains;
One race by tyrants rooted from the earth,
One doom'd to slavery by the taint of birth!

In Part II, for all his romanticization of Africans, Montgomery hammers out
his insistence on their shared humanity and equality by repeating the phrase "Is
he not man?"

from Part II

　　In these romantic regions Man grows wild;
Here dwells the negro, nature's outcast child,
Scorn'd by his brethren; but his mother's eye,
That gazes on him from her warmest sky,
Sees in his flexible limbs untutor'd grace,
Power on his forehead, beauty in his face;
Sees in his breast, where lawless passions rove,
The heart of friendship, and the home of love;
Sees in his mind, where desolation reigns,
Fierce as his clime, uncultur'd as his plains,
A soil where virtue's fairest flowers might shoot,
And trees of science bend with glorious fruit;
Sees in his soul, involv'd in thickest night,
An emanation of eternal light . . .
Is he not *Man*, though knowledge never shed
Her quickening beams on his neglected head?
Is he not *Man*, though sweet religion's voice
Ne'er bade the mourner in his God rejoice?
Is *he* not man, by sin and suffering tried?
Is *he* not man, for whom the Saviour died?
Belie the Negro's powers:——in headlong will,
Christian! *thy* brother, thou shalt prove him still;
Belie his virtues; since his wrongs began,
His follies and his crimes have stampt him Man.

In Part III, Montgomery links a series of images: the African slave styled as Romantic exile or outcast, the African homeland as pastoral ideal, and an epic rendering of the second coming when the African dead shall rise in triumph over their tormentors. In such phrases as "the shark's appointed prey" and "the unremember'd millions" Montgomery shows his imaginative kinship with poets such as Thomson and Gray.

from Part III

[I]s the Negro outlaw'd from his birth?
Is he alone a stranger on the earth?
Is there . . .
No land, whose name, in exile heard, will dart
Ice through his veins and lightning through his heart?
Ah! yes; beneath the beam of brighter skies,
His home amidst his father's country lies;
There with the partner of his soul he shares
Love-mingled pleasures, love-divided cares;
There, as with nature's warmest filial fire,
He soothes his blind, and feeds his helpless sire;
His children sporting round his hut behold
How they shall cherish him when he is old,
Train'd by example from their tenderest youth
To deeds of charity and words of truth . . .

When the loud trumpet of eternal doom
Shall break the mortal bondage of the tomb . . .
Then shall the sea's mysterious caverns, spread
With human relics, render up their dead . . .

Myriads of slaves, that perish'd on the way,
From age to age the shark's appointed prey,
By livid plagues, by lingering tortures slain,
Or headlong plung'd alive into the main,
Shall rise in judgment from their gloomy beds,
And call down vengeance on their murderers' heads.

Yet small the number, and the fortune blest,
Of those who on the stormy deep found rest,
Weigh'd with the unremember'd millions more,
That scaped the sea, to perish on the shore,
By the slow pangs of solitary care,
The earth-devouring anguish of despair,
The broken heart which kindness never heals,
The home-sick passion which the Negro feels,

When toiling, fainting in the land of canes,
His spirit wanders to his native plains . . .
                Then before his eyes,
The terrors of captivity arise.
—'Twas night: his babes around him lay at rest,
Their mother slumber'd on their father's breast:
A yell of murder rang around their bed;
They woke, their cottage blazed, the victims fled;
Forth sprang the ambush'd ruffians on their prey,
They caught, they bound, they drove them far away;
The white man bought them at the mart of blood;
In pestilential barks they cross'd the flood;
Then were the wretched ones asunder torn,
To distant isles, to separate bondage borne,
Deny'd, though sought with tears, the sad relief
That misery loves,—the fellowship of grief.

In Part IV, invoking Cowper as his inspiration, Montgomery balances lamentations over the wrongs of slavery against his sense that, with the abolition of the slave trade, a new age of Christian enlightenment is dawning.

from Part IV

    And thou, poor Negro! scorn'd of all mankind;
Thou dumb and impotent, and deaf and blind;
Thou dead in spirit! toil-degraded slave,
Crush'd by the curse on Adam to the grave!
The messengers of peace, o'er land and sea,
That sought the sons of sorrow stoop'd to thee.
—The captive rais'd his slow and sullen eye;
He knew no friend, nor deem'd a friend was nigh,
Till the sweet tones of Pity touch'd his ears,
And Mercy bathed his bosom with her tears . . .

    Meanwhile among the great, the brave, the free,
The matchless race of Albion and the sea,
Champions arose to plead the Negro's cause;
In the wide breach of violated laws,
Through which the torrent of injustice roll'd,
They stood:—with zeal unconquerably bold,
They raised their voices, stretch'd their arms to save
From chains the freeman, from despair the slave;
The exile's heart-sick anguish to assuage,
And rescue Afric from the spoiler's rage . . .

615

Lamented Cowper! in thy path I tread;
O that on me were thy meek spirit shed!
The woes that wring my bosom once were thine;
Be all thy virtues, all thy genius mine! . . .

    Quick at the call of Virtue, Freedom, Truth,
Weak withering age, and strong aspiring youth,
Alike th' expanding power of pity felt;
The coldest, hardest hearts began to melt . . .

    Dim through the night of these tempestuous years
A sabbath dawn o'er Africa appears;
Then shall her neck from Europe's yoke be freed,
And healing arts to hideous arms succeed;
At home the bonds of peace her tribes shall bind,
Commerce abroad espouse them with mankind,
While pure Religion's hands shall build and bless
The church of God amidst the wilderness . . .
Unchanging seasons have their march begun;
Millennial years are hastening to the sun;
Seen through thick clouds by Faith's transpiercing eyes,
The New Creation shines in purer skies.
—All hail!—the age of crime and suffering ends;
The reign of righteousness from heaven descends.

                    (wr. 1808/pub. 1809)[350]

ISABELLA OLIVER [SHARP]
(1777–1848)

Daughter of James Oliver, a mathematician and prominent citizen of Cumberland County, Pennsylvania, Isabella Oliver (later Sharp) was a devout Christian of modest education who had great poetic gifts. She was known to compose all her poetry from memory, while working at household tasks or walking in the woods, and then dictate it to others to transcribe. She had considerable local support, as evident in the fifteen-page list of subscribers who signed for copies of her first book of poetry, edited by her friend Robert Davidson and published when she was twenty-eight.

In these excerpts from a poem of over two hundred lines, Isabella Oliver attacks slavery on religious, historical, and patriotic grounds. Perhaps most impressive are her studied refutations of the specious biblical precedents cited by slavery's defenders and her careful proof, in the final lines, that racism itself is contrary to Christ's teachings.

from "On Slavery"

AMONG the evil morals which disgrace
The page historic of the human race,
Slavery seems most to blacken the records;
It militates against our blessed Lord's
Divine instructions. Is it not a shame
For any that assume the christian name,
Who say the influence of his blood extends
From sea to sea, to earth's remotest ends,
To trade in human flesh, to forge a chain
For those who may with them in glory reign?
But, independent of the christian light,
Humanity is outrag'd, every right
Of human nature trampled to the ground;
By men who deify an empty sound,

And call it liberty, or what they please;
But God will visit for such crimes as these.
Behold the fruitful islands of the main . . .
The cords of slav'ry were so tighten'd there,
Its hapless victims could no longer bear;
But desperation work'd in every brain,
And gave them strength to break the iron chain. . . .
Slavery's a very monster on the earth,
Which strangles every virtue in its birth:
From the first dawning of the human mind,
Children should be instructed to be kind;
To treat no human being with disdain,
Nor give the meanest insect useless pain:
Yet mark how babes and sucklings learn to rack,
And trample down, the poor defenceless black . . .
God's image in his creature they deride,
And daily grow in indolence and pride,
With ignorance and cruelty combin'd;
A Slavery of the most ignoble kind!

O ye, who make and execute the laws,
Exert your influence in so good a cause;
Pursue with zeal some well-arranged plan,
To stop this most unnat'ral trade in man . . .

Each southern state unnumber'd slaves commands,
Who steel their hearts, and enervate their hands.
There knotted whips in dreadful peals resound,
While blood and sweat flow mingled to the ground,
So fame reports, and rising in her ire
She adds, that some beneath the lash expire.
Ah stop! inhuman! why provoke the rod,
The dreadful vengeance of an angry God! . . .

Oh, slavery! thou hell-engender'd crime!
Why spoil this beauteous country in her prime,
Corrupt her manners, enervate her youth!
Blast the fair buds of justice, mercy, truth!
But, Europe! know, to thy eternal shame,
From thee at first this foul contagion came;
Before we to a nation's stature grew,
We learn'd this trade, this barb'rous trade, from you:
Should not we now exert a noble pride,
And lay your follies, and your crimes, aside? . . .

ISABELLA OLIVER [SHARP]

How many futile reasons have been given
For mixing God and mammon, sin and heaven!
Some say, they are of Canaan's cursed race,
By God ordain'd to fill this servile place:
Was then their lineage fully ascertain'd,
Before they in the cruel hold were chain'd?
Before the tenderest ties of human life
Were torn asunder; the beloved wife
Dragg'd without mercy from her husband's breast,
And the sweet babes they mutually caress'd,
Carried like cattle;—(Let it not be told!)
By christians too, to be to christians sold? . . .
In Joseph's case we may a parallel see;
Sent into Egypt by divine decree,
His brethren's evil, God intends for good,
Yet they, as guilty, in his presence stood.
Some plead the precedent of former times,
And bring example in, to sanction crimes:
Greece had her Helots, Gibeonites the Jew;
Must then Columbia have her Negroes too! . . .
Our blessed Lord descended to unbind
Those chains of darkness which enslave the mind;
He draws the veil of prejudice aside,
To cure us of our selfishness and pride:
These once remov'd, then Afric's sable race
No more among the brutal herd we place:
Are they not blest with intellectual powers,
Which prove their souls are excellent as ours?
The same immortal hopes to all are given,
One common Saviour and one common heaven.

(1805)[351]

619

ELIZABETH OGILVY BENGER
(1778–1827)

Daughter of an enlightened tradesman, Benger was sent to a boys' school and encouraged to pursue a formal education. At age thirteen she wrote "The Female Geniad," an epic celebration of women writers from classical times to the 1790s. The death of her father left her in financial straits and she never married, but Benger achieved modest success as a professional writer in London. With all the dignity that genteel poverty afforded, she moved in circles that included Anna Letitia Barbauld, the Lambs, Dr. George Gregory, and the artist Robert Smirke.

This excerpt is from a long poem (850 lines) she started in 1806 and published in 1809, in an ornate volume of antislavery verse commissioned by William Bowyer, edited by James Montgomery, and illustrated by Smirke. Her lines about Granville Sharp are from her account of the history of the abolition movement. The final section encourages Britain (with overtones of paternalism) to heal Africa's past wrongs through a concerted missionary effort.

from "A Poem, Occasioned by the Abolition of the Slave Trade, in 1806"

Time was, that Britain to no distant land
Her mandate breath'd, or stretch'd her sceptral wand . . .

Yet to this isle, beneficent as blest,
Truth's sacred haunt, and freedom's shelter'd rest,
By fraudful wiles, the demon Av'rice bore,
A monster-form, distain'd with human gore;
Whose tainted breath a cloud of darkness cast,
Whilst grim oppression swell'd the boding blast.
The patriot sigh'd, indignant, and dismay'd,
For martyr'd piety—and faith betray'd;
For man, in slavery's abject form disgrac'd,
For man, yet most by brutal might debas'd,

For captive Africa, who wept in dust!
For Britain, treach'rous to her plighted trust!
Yes, there was one, unmeasur'd in his woe,
Poorer than penury, supremely low . . .
A wretch to hope estrang'd, but ne'er redeem'd from fear.
That blasted man was Afric's exil'd son,
Wreck'd on each coast, in ev'ry realm undone.
For him no boons had charity assign'd . . .
Till thou, oh! Sharp, didst launch the gallant oar,
And bear him to the hospitable shore—
Friend to the wretched! once his only guide,
Now raise thine eyes with patriarchal pride;
Thy gen'rous children in his champions trace,
Bless, fondly bless, the wide encircling race;
See future sons, in ages far from thine,
Champions of truth, the guard of Honour's shrine.
To distant climes see Britain's bounty run,
Whilst Virtue's triumph and her own are one. . . .

    Afric's outcast meets no kindred hand,
He mourns unsolac'd in a foreign land;
To him the heavens a fearful aspect wear,
Strange are the accents murmur'd in his ear.
He steals no balm from pity's lenient breath,
Hope sheds no gleam but thro' the vale of death:
An alien, far from nature's bosom cast,
He broods on wrongs, the present and the past;
And asks what vengeance shall the wretches wait,
Who bade him mourn within the stranger's gate.
Devoted victim of the crimes accurst,
By hatred cherish'd, and by av'rice nurs'd;
Crimes that with Europe's sordid sons began,
The rude barbarian's gift from polish'd man. . . .

    Is there a spell the Negro's soul to wean
From childhood's lov'd traditionary scene?
No—long estrang'd, through slow revolving years,
The exile pours his unexhausted tears . . .

    Thou, who loath'st thy fellow-man to trace
In the dark aspect of the Negro's race,—
Go seek his home, his native worth behold,
Unspoil'd by lucre, and uncurst with gold—
True to his brother, to the stranger kind,

Nor fraud, nor treachery pollutes his mind;
Falsehood he spurns, and sacred holds his trust;
Till scorn'd beneficent, till injur'd just.
And shall not peace his thirst for vengeance tame,
When freedom fires him with a nobler aim?
Has heaven no gracious ministry design'd
To ripen reason in his simple mind?
To lead him on where science sheds her ray,
And glad his soul with truth's eternal day?
Let Britain's sons the fruitful coast explore,
And kindly bless the race they wrong'd before;
With gentle promises invite to toil,
With precious gifts endow the docile soil;
Till Afric's race in grateful rev'rence bend,
And hail the teacher where they find the friend.

(c. 1806/pub. 1809)[352]

CHARLOTTE SMITH
RICHARDSON (1775–c. 1850)

Educated in a York charity school and trained as a domestic servant, Richardson overcame poverty, illness, early widowhood, and the burden of raising a blind child to become a successful poet. Through the kindness of locals and an appeal in the *Gentleman's Magazine* in 1805, her first book of poetry had six hundred subscribers, including Anna Barbauld and other London literary figures. In this poem, she consciously frames 1806 as a pivotal year, the year in which Wilberforce succeeded in getting the bill passed in the House of Commons that would abolish the slave trade as of January 1, 1808. That her images and style seem somewhat clichéd is itself a measure of how widely, by this date, such anti-slavery sentiments were held.

The Negro, Sept. 1806

Whence that agonizing groan?
   Whence those shrieks that rend the air?
'Tis the sable negro's moan,
   'Tis the language of despair.
See the hapless mourner stand,
   Hear him all his woes deplore,
Stolen from his native land,
   Never to behold it more!

Yet, though dear his native lot,
   Higher griefs his bosom swell,
For in yon far distant spot,
   His love'd wife and children dwell.
Far from wife and children torn,
   All his bosom held most dear,
Can he cease his loss to moan?
   Can he dry the flowing tear?

Fancy oft before his eyes
    Brings the objects of his love;
Bids his native valleys rise,
    Tow'ring hill and orange grove.
Soon the whip's heart-rending sound
    Wakes him from his pleasing dream;
Hark! the echoing strokes rebound—
    Stop, monsters! see that crimson stream!

Blush, ye Britons! blush for shame,
    Let compunction seize your mind;
Dare ye boast the Christian name,
    While ye prey on human kind?
Is it thus the Faith ye spread?
    Thus advance your Saviour's cause?
While you on his precepts tread,
    Will you disobey his laws?

Rise ye noble friendly band,
    In whose hearts compassion glows;
Rise, ye patriots of our land,
    Ye who feel for Afric's woes.
Wilberforce shall lead the way,
    His exertions ne'er shall cease,
Till Oppression yields her sway,
    And the oppressed, taste of peace.
             (wr. 1806/pub. 1809)[353]

HENRY KIRKE WHITE
(1785–1806)

Another prodigy poet who, like William Pattison and Thomas Chatterton, died young, White was a butcher's son who started his adolescence working in a textile factory before moving on to a law clerkship and then a brilliant academic career at Cambridge. Said to have been exhausted by his prize-winning academic performances, White died in his college rooms at St. John's on October 19, 1806, aged twenty-one. His work attracted the support of many, including the Duchess of Devonshire, William Wilberforce, Robert Southey, and Josiah Conder, and he had a wave of popularity (much of it posthumous) in the early nineteenth century.

In this, the first stanza of a survey of oppression around the world, White paints a gothic, impressionistic vision of slavery. The reader senses the preternatural evil of slavery, but may feel torn between sympathy and horror at the Blakean image of the "lash'd Angolan" roaring in his cage.

from *"Ode to Liberty"*

Hence to thy darkest shades, dire Slavery, hence!
    Thine icy touch can freeze,
    Swift as the Polar breeze,
The proud defying part of human sense.
    Hence to thine Indian cave,
To where the tall canes whisper o'er thy rest,
    Like the murmuring wave
Swept by the dank wing of the rapid west:
    And at the night's still noon,
The lash'd Angolan, in his grated cell,
    Mix'd with the tyger's yell,
Howls to the dull ear of the silent moon.

(c. 1806)[354]

GEORGE DYER (1755–1841)

A charity-school boy who went on to Emmanuel College, Cambridge, Dyer was a second-rate London writer noted for his eccentric ways. Praised for his idealism by Lamb, Barbauld, and others, he nonetheless was the object of gentle mockery for his unworldliness, evident in his slovenly appearance and propensity for accidents. He wrote this irregular ode to celebrate the passage of the 1807 bill abolishing the slave trade. In this and parallel legislation in America, Dyer senses a turning point in Anglo-American civilization, and forsees a wave of further progress under Charles Fox's parliamentary leadership.

from "Ode IX: On Considering the Unsettled State of Europe, and the Opposition Which Had Been Made to Attempts for the Abolition of the Slave-Trade"

See! I view a distant land;
And, hark! I hear a minstrel band.
The negro-slaves, now slaves no more,
Have struck a chord untouch'd before.
Of Afric's wrongs, and Afric's pains,
Oft had they sigh'd in lonely strains;
    A tale it was of woe,
    Discordant, sad and slow!
But, now 'tis Freedom's song.—And, see!
    How the rapt soul fills the eye!
And, hark! was ever minstrelsy
So wing'd with fire, and strain'd to notes so high? . . .

For see o'er fair Columbia's plains
    Peace extend her halcyon wings;
And tho' no Washington now reigns,
    Still Freedom laughs and sings.

GEORGE DYER

This civic wreath with song I blend to thee,
For thou, oh! Fox, wast first to hail Columbia free.

And lives there still a generous band
Studious to raise our sinking land?
Foremost amidst the group I trace
Thy form superior rise with manly grace;
And many a tear I see thee shed
O'er slaves oppress'd, and heroes dead:
On thee thy country's blessing still attend;
Oh! live thy country's hope, the people's generous friend.

(c. 1807)[355]

RICHARD MANT (1776–1848)

An Oxford-educated Anglican clergyman and writer, Mant rose to become a Bishop in Ireland, meanwhile producing more than forty publications over his career. As a poet, he was formed and influenced by the Wartons (Joseph at Winchester, Thomas at Oxford). His politics are less easy to characterize, given his support for abolition on the one hand, and his opposition to toleration for Catholics on the other. Still, it is significant that someone who would later be a high official in the Church of England should be so outspoken in his criticism of slavery. The following excerpts from his long poem *The Slave* capture in vivid terms the predations of slave traders, the mentally and spiritually debilitating effects of slavery on its victims, and the tide of vengeance predicted to overwhelm colonial societies that fail to renounce slavery.

from "The Slave"

On Congo's or Angola's spicy shore,
Or Koromantyn's sands of golden ore,
Or northward, where to swell th' Atlantic deep
Majestic floods thro' Senegambia sweep,
Before them horrour, and despair behind,
Speed to their task the stealers of mankind.
Their's is the honied tongue, and specious smile;
The open outrage; and the covert wile:
'Tis their's to quench the intellectual light,
And whelm the negro's mind in grosser night:
'Tis their's to rend with impious force apart
The ties, which nature winds around his heart:
But most 'tis their's to spread the woes afar,
The crimes and horrours of intestine war! . . .

Thine Av'rice, Europe, preys on lands unknown;
Thy bribes prevail; and Afric's millions groan.

Kings, lur'd by thee, forget their people's claim,
And yield a father's, for a traitor's, name:
While rous'd by mutual wrongs to mutual rage,
In open war contiguous tribes engage . . .

    From country, home, and kindred torn;
Of hope, the wretch's privilege, forlorn;
Denied in woe to clasp his infant race;
Denied the comfort of a last embrace;
And doom'd to tremble at a tyrant's nod,
Writhe at the lash, and kiss the vengeful rod . . .

    Thou, degraded Afric's abject son,
Drear is the course of sorrow, thou must run. . . .
The ceaseless weight of the reproachful chain
Shall quell each nobler purpose of thy mind;
Benumb thy feelings, and thy reason blind;
Down to the earth thy tow'ring spirit draw;
Defeat thy Maker's will, reverse his law:
Till thy immortal nature it imbrute,
Thy earthly frame's celestial attribute;
Forbid thy soul superiour worlds to scan;
Displace, degrade thee in creation's plan;
And leave a worthless form, the semblance of a man.

So shall at length thy nobler part be broke,
Cleave to the ground, and hug the slavish yoke:
Or proudly spurning at the name of slave,
Too fierce to yield, yet impotent to save,
A willing victim to the tomb go down:
Or, leagu'd with high-born spirits, like thine own,
Rise in wild vengeance o'er the trembling foe,
Repay the wrong, and lay th' oppressor low.

Thus o'er Jamaica's pallid isle of late
Hung the black cloud, with ruin charg'd and fate:
Thus rolling on with gather'd fury, shed
Its night of tempest on Domingo's head.

Thron'd on the storm, and all his soul on flame,
A thirst for vengeance, Afric's Genius came.
His sons beheld him, tow'ring in his might;
And clank'd their chains with horrible delight;
Wav'd the red banner o'er the murmuring flood;
And yell'd to war; and bath'd the land in blood.

Nor rest; nor respite: death to death succeeds:
The negro triumphs, and the white man bleeds.
E'en Europe trembled, as she heard from far
The sounding march of injur'd Afric's war . . .
Britannia, watch! the spreading tempest stay,
Ere o'er thy trembling isles it burst its way;
With timely pity hear the Negro's pray'r,
Or, if unmov'd by pity, dread despair! . . .
O, spread thy blessings: be the glory thine,
The first in mercy, as in pow'r, to shine . . .
Till Freedom's voice the song of gladness pour
From Niger's flood to western India's shore;
And Afric, starting from her Pagan dream,
Behold the day-spring break, and bless the heav'nly beam.

(1807)[356]

RICHARD ALFRED MILLIKIN [OR MILLIKEN] (1767–1815)

A lawyer by training but not inclination, Millikin was an Irish poet, amateur painter, and patron of the arts who worked all his life in his native Cork. This poem harkens back to a tradition of riverbank or riparian meditations, ranging from Pope's *Windsor-Forest* to Wordsworth's "Tintern Abbey." The passage shows that antislavery sentiment flourished among the Anglo-Irish, although they had little involvement in the trade and very limited experience of African slaves living in their midst. Millikin's sympathies did not extend to all oppressed peoples: as a loyalist militia volunteer, he had eagerly participated in putting down the Irish rebellion of 1798.

from Book III of The River-Side

[The sun] downward pours
His rays intense upon the woolly crowns
Of her black sons, who down the Gambia's stream
Or Senegal, float yearly to augment
The cries of slavery in foreign lands,
And bleed, that Europe's pamper'd sons may glut
On delicacies which their climes refuse.
O! violated nature, every tie,
Each fond endearment, every anxious wish,
And every tender ligament that binds
Man to his home, his country and his friends;
Torn, cruel torn, while nature pours in vain
The burning tear and heaves the heavy sigh.
But Britain hears the hapless negro's groans,
And bids him hope; throughout the western isles
The tidings fly, and at the joyful sound
The slave already drags a lighter chain.
Yes, from thy senate, Britain, comes a voice

That bids aloud the dreadful traffick cease,
Bids human blood no more your commerce stain,
Nor human flesh deform. Happy thine Isle,
And happy he, who with unwearied zeal
And truth in bright robed eloquence arrayed
Pleaded the Captive's cause, and dauntless stood
Th'unconquer'd champion of Humanity.

(1807)[357]

ANNE RITSON (fl. 1799–1810)

Nothing is known of Ritson except that she was an Englishwoman who lived eight years in Virginia and then, after her return to London, published a colossal poem about America (177 pages long). Her poem is remarkable as an early instance of what would become common over the course of the nineteenth century: foreign observers, predominantly British but also from other nations (e.g., Tocqueville), commenting about the institution of slavery in their writings on American life. Ritson seems to maintain a carefully balanced neutrality: she avoids discussing the recent debate over the abolition of the slave trade, she says of the African slaves "some are good and some are bad," and, although she takes pride in never having "bought or sold a slave," she does not scruple at renting slaves to work as her personal servants.

from A Poetical Picture of America . . . 1799 to 1807

As much of negroes, and their fate,
Have been discuss'd so very late,
I shall not dwell upon their case,
Tho' there are thousands in the place;
No other servants can be had,
They some are good and some are bad;
I think myself that much depends
With those on whom the slave attends;
Nature most certainly has given,
A cunning that with sense is even;
For in their looks you oft descry
Knavery lurking in their eye.
While I their service did require,
I always chose their time* to hire;
And this great satisfaction have,
I never bought or sold a slave.

(c. 1807/pub. 1809)[358]

* [Ritson's note:] Negroes can always be hired for the year on the first of January, for which you pay forty or fifty dollars a year, and clothe them.

ANONYMOUS ("A YOUNG MAN [WHO SERVED UNDER] COMMODORE DECATUR")

This poem dramatizes how the fear of insurrections reverberated within and among slave societies, across geographic and linguistic boundaries. It was apparently composed by an American in honor of Duncan Mc'Intosh, a Scottish expatriate who, at great personal risk, rescued French plantation owners during the Haitian revolution. For those who regarded Mc'Intosh as a hero and welcomed him to Baltimore in 1808, this poem marked a fusion of American and French plantocratic interests, and perhaps allayed some of their underlying anxieties.

*[Untitled]**

When ruthless slaughter, piercing ev'ry wood,
Wasting each plain, and staining ev'ry flood,
Fair St. Domingo, in thy peaceful shade,
"Bared his red arm, and grasp'd his bloody blade;"
And breathing flames of dread intestine war,
In breathless fury drove his blood-stain'd car;
Hope to thy children bade a sad farewell,
And vengeful havoc toll'd the white man's Knell.

Oh! shall the muse, here summon in review,
The saddening scenes which this assembly knew;

* [Author's note:] During the slaughter of the white inhabitants of the island of St. Domingo, by their own slaves, who had revolted in the years 1803–4 and 5, Mr. DUNCAN MC'INTOSH, a merchant of Aux-Cayes, most humanely and heroically interposed to save the lives of the unhappy and devoted planters—He succeeded in saving the lives of 2,400 prisoners, at the risk of his own, and at the expence of $100,000, which sum has never been repaid to him by the French government.

   On the arrival of Mr. Mc'Intosh at Baltimore, in the year 1808, the gratitude of the French refugees, prepared for him a splendid *fete*—The following lines were written for the occasion, and read to a grateful and numerous audience, by the president of the day.

ANONYMOUS

While melting gratitude now fills each mind
To him, the benefactor of mankind;
Shall I, to cloud, the present scene relate,
The deeds of death that sealed the planters fate?
Ah! no—the woes of that devoted race,
The sad historian pensively may trace,
A grateful and applausive task is mine,
To shew the care of providence divine. . . .

          Heav'n at once surveyed;
The various works its providence had made,
And to a son of Scotia's summits gave
The task to rescue thousands from the grave:
A man whose dauntless soul and valiant arm,
Should shield each victim from impending harm,
And 'midst dread scenes of peril and of strife
To save each captive, risk his valued life.

How he performed the dangerous task thus given,
For his reward;—is register'd in Heav'n;
That he fulfill'd it, and fulfill'd it well,
Those grateful tears that stream in torrents tell.

But who is he, fame cries, who thus could charm,
The heart of steel and stay the murderous arm:
Who was it dared, in that dread hour oppose
His breast between the victims, and their foes?
Tell to the world—and let his sainted name
Fill the loud clarion of exulting fame;
A nations gratitude shall stamp the rest;
Then let the name of MC'INTOSH be bless'd.

                    (1808)[359]

ANONYMOUS

These two hymns are both a mystery and a marvel. The mystery is the identity of the author, who may have been a white abolitionist, but could equally have been one of the "people of colour" who "prepared and performed" the music on this occasion. The marvel is the occasion itself: an interracial celebration of the abolition of the slave trade, held on July 14, 1808, in the African Meeting-House in Boston, conducted by Dr. Jedidiah Morse and other leading Boston clergy.

The hymns formed a deliberate sequence. The first gives thanks to God the father and to Jesus for the abolition of the slave trade, all in the voice of African captives ("We lose the terrors of the slave, And *Abba,* Father, cry"). The second, in the same voice, prays for blessings on the nations—especially Britain and America—that have finally restored to slaves "the rights that God bestow'd on all." Both hymns bespeak the elation and widespread optimism that had broken out and briefly created a mood of epochal change. Within a few years, however, events were to overtake and dissipate that spirit.

[Untitled Hymn]*

Hark! for 'tis God's own Son that calls
    To life and liberty;
Transported fall before his feet,
    Who makes the prisoners free.

The cruel bonds of sin he breaks,
    And breaks old Satan's chain;
Smiling he deals those pardons round,
    Which free from endless pain.

* [from Editor's note:] Delivered at the African Meeting-House, in Boston, July 14, 1808, in Grateful Celebration of the Abolition of the African Slave-Trade, by the governments of the United States, Great Britain and Denmark. . . . The religious services, beside the sermon, were performed by the Rev. M[r]. Blood, Rev. Mr. Channing, and Mr. Codman. The music, prepared and performed principally by the people of colour, was appropriate and excellent.

Into the captive heart he pours
    His Spirit from on high;
We lose the terrors of the slave,
    And *Abba,* Father, cry.

Shake off your bonds, and sing his grace;
    The sinner's Friend proclaim;
And call on all around to seek
    True freedom by his name.

Walk on at large, till you attain
    Your Father's house above:
There shall you wear immortal crowns,
    And sing immortal love.

                    (1808)

[Untitled Hymn]

To thee, Almighty, gracious power,
    Who sit'st, enthron'd, in radiant heaven,
On this bless'd morn, this hallow'd hour,
    The homage of the heart be given!

Lift up your souls to God on high,
    The fountain of eternal grace,
Who with a tender father's eye
    Look'd down on Afric's helpless race!

The nations heard his stern commands!
    Brittania kindly sets us free;
Columbia tears the galling bands,
    And gives the sweets of Liberty.

Then strike the lyre:—your voices raise!
    Let gratitude inspire your song;
Pursue religion's holy ways,
    Shun sinful pleasure's giddy throng.

From Mercy's Seat may grace descend,
    To wake contrition's heart-felt sighs;
O! may our pious strains ascend
    Where ne'er the sainted spirit dies.

Then, we our freedom shall retain,
    In peace, and love, and cheerful toil,
Plenty shall flow from the wide main,
    And golden harvests from the soil.

Ye nations that to us restore
   The rights that God bestow'd on all
For you his blessing we implore;
   O! listen further to his call.

From one parental stem ye spring,
   A kindred blood your bosoms own.
Your kindred tongues God's praises sing,
   And beg forgiveness at his throne.

O! then your mutual wrongs forgive,
   Unlock your hearts to social love,
So shall ye safe and happy live,
   By grace and blessings from above.

                (1808)[360]

ANONYMOUS ["ALIQUIS"]

These elegiac stanzas exemplify the transatlantic nature of the antislavery movement. Reprinted here from an American magazine that had devoted an entire issue to John Newton's legacy, the poem had originally appeared a few months earlier in an English periodical, *The Evangelical Magazine*. Newton and his works were revered by abolitionists everywhere. Here the poet focuses on Newton's personal history, as a slave trader reawakened through Christian faith and converted to the abolitionist cause. The final stanza printed below pays tribute to Newton's powers as a poet, deliberately echoing the opening phrase of his most famous hymn, "Amazing Grace."

from "An Elegiac Tribute to the Memory of the Rev. John Newton"

Like Jonah, on the mighty deep,
    He strove to fly from God;
But fled, alas! to sin, and weep
    Beneath his chast'ning rod.
A wretch upon a wretched shore,
    A slave by slaves confin'd,
A doubly galling yoke he bore,
    Of body and of mind.

In deep distress, and bitter woe,
    Corruption's rankling smart,
Mysterious Wisdom made him know
    His own rebellious heart!
Unconscious of the future sphere
    That he was form'd to fill,
With application most severe
    He sought for knowledge still!

Cut off from ev'ry human aid,
    On Afric's burning sand
The depths of science he essay'd,
And mystic Euclid scann'd;
While o'er the liquid way he mov'd,
    He studied many a tome;
With Tacitus and Livy rov'd,
    To scenes of ancient Rome.

Almighty grace the rebel tam'd;
    And deep contrition drew
The wand'ring prodigal, reclaim'd,
    And form'd his heart anew!
No more on grov'ling themes confin'd,
    His ardent spirit soar'd,
With ready gifts and soul refin'd,
    To glorify his Lord!

            (1808)[361]

ANONYMOUS ["A"]

By 1808 the conventions of sentimental antislavery poetry were well established and this poem repeats most of them: the misery of separated families, the indignities of slavery, and the captives' downward spiral into despair and suicide. Although the mood of the poem (first published in a Philadelphia magazine) runs counter to the optimism generated by the recent abolition of the slave *trade*, it provides a useful reminder that the institution of slavery itself had yet to be ended.

The Slave

How oft when tempests dire, obscure the sky,
    While by fierce winds and waves o'er ocean borne;
Regret's warm torrent fills my sadden'd eye;
    I mourn for peace, now never to return.

Once on me smiled a wife and blooming boy,
    Once I with pleasure till'd my native soil;
Then work was pastime, labour was my joy,
    But pleasure, now alas! is turned to toil.

How sweet! How sweet! when in the shade of eve,
    My wife would meet me at our cottage door;
When her lov'd lips affection's kiss would give,
    And joy to think my labour was no more.

And are these joys from me, forever gone,
    Must I forever plough th' Atlantic wave!
Shall I no more, with rapture, hail the dawn,
    But ever wand'ring seek a distant grave!

Was it for this I rose to active life,
    Are these the endless joys I had in view?

Was it for this, I woo'd a tender wife,
    Are these the happy scenes my fancy drew?

ORAM a slave! Alas, and can it be?
    Can he endure the scoffs of wanton pride?
Can slav'ry's bands bind him who once was free?
    No—give me freedom—then take all beside.

But ah! the white man will not heed my pray'r;
    He hears—but pity moves him not, to save:
Then in the sleep of death I'll drown each care,
    Come thou dark heaving billow be my grave!
                                    (1808)[362]

JAMES FENN (1745–1824)

Born in Kent, England, Fenn was a religious writer, farmer, and landlord who settled in Schenectady, New York. By the end of his life he had become quite wealthy, owning several buildings and businesses in Schenectady, in addition to his two-hundred-acre farm. Starting in his fifties, Fenn produced a series of religious and poetic writings, including *Hymns and Poems on Various Subjects* (1808), *A Poem on Friendship and Society* (1815), and *A Humble Plea for the Benevolence of God* (1816). Remarkable as the utterance of a wealthy property owner, the following piece from Fenn's first book combines the themes of universal rights, abolitionism, and national pride. Implicit in this poem is the emerging rift between the northern and southern states.

Civil Liberty the Right of All Men

True liberty, the glory of our land,
The natural right of ev'ry son of man.
This, well to use and manly to maintain,
Will be our wisdom and the nation's gain.
Sweet liberty, some will for thee contend,
But 'tis for self and not for other men.
Do they deserve the sacred right to wear,
Who do not wish all men with them to share?
Too selfish they of such a turn of mind,
When others right, is not in their design.
Should freedom's cause on such men e'er depend,
Our rights and liberty is at an end.
True freedom stands on better ground than this,
Tho' some will dare assume to act amiss.
Should I presume, the simple truth to tell,
Some boast of freedom tho' they act not well.
Have we not many in this favorite land,

In slav'ry kept and feel oppressive bands?
Is this the liberty that is our pride,
And yet to others shamefully deni'd?
Let none, pretend, to own her sacred cause,
Who openly oppose her noble laws.
Dare fools contend, that Guinea's sons can't be
Of human race, as well as you and me?
Some have been found to plead in freedom's cause,
And yet by acts destroy her very laws.
If Liberty, you truly would maintain,
Release your slaves, knock off their heavy chains:
Then whites and blacks, in freedom shall unite,
God will approve, and men shall own it's right.
Then, may America of freedom tell,
And boast of liberty we love so well.

(1808)[363]

MICHAEL FORTUNE (fl. 1808)

Although no biographical information survives, it seems clear that Michael Fortune was an African American hymn-writer and member of St. Thomas, the African Episcopal Church in Philadelphia where Absalom Jones was Rector. Apart from a glimpse at the poetic talent of an obscure African American at the turn of the nineteenth century, Fortune's hymn also adds to our knowledge of the ceremonies that were held on the anniversary of the abolition of the slave trade in African American churches in various American cities. Similar hymns appear elsewhere in this volume by Henry Johnson, Robert Y. Sidney, Peter Williams Jr., William Hamilton, and an anonymous Boston poet of 1808.

"New Year's Anthem" from A Thanksgiving Sermon

Sung in St. Thomas's, or the African Episcopal, Church,
in Philadelphia. Jan. 1, 1808.

I. TO Thee, Almighty, gracious power,
    Who sit'st, enthron'd, in radiant heaven,
    On this bless'd morn, this hallow'd hour,
    The homage of the heart be given!

II. Lift up your souls to God on high,
     The fountain of eternal grace,
     Who, with a tender father's eye,
     Look'd down on Afric's helpless race!

III. The nations heard His stern commands!
      Britannia kindly sets us free;
      Columbia tears the galling bands,
      And gives the sweets of Liberty.

IV. Then strike the lyre! your voices raise!
     Let gratitude inspire your song!
     Pursue religion's holy ways,
     Shun sinful Pleasure's giddy throng!

V.   From Mercy's seat may grace descend,
To wake contrition's heartfelt sighs!
O! may our pious strains ascend,
Where ne'er the sainted spirit dies!

VI.   Then, we our freedom shall retain,
In peace and love, and cheerful toil:
Plenty shall flow from the wide main,
And golden harvests from the soil.

VII.   Ye nations that to us restore
The rights which God bestow'd on all;
For you His blessing we implore:
O! listen further to His call!

VIII.   From one parental stem ye spring,
A kindred blood your bosoms own;
Your kindred tongues God's praises sing,
And beg forgiveness at his throne:

IX.   O, then, your mutual wrongs forgive,
Unlock your hearts to social love!
So shall ye safe and happy live,
By grace and blessings from above.

(1808)[364]

JOSHUA MARSDEN (1777–1837)

Born near Liverpool and raised in poverty, Marsden went to sea as a youth, led a dissolute life, and survived two shipwrecks before undergoing a religious conversion at about age twenty. Immersing himself in Methodism, he became a missionary to America, with postings in Nova Scotia (eight years) and then, more dangerously, in Bermuda and nearby islands (four years). It was in Bermuda in about 1807–8 that, confronted with the evils of slavery, Marsden began writing the antislavery poems he did not (perhaps *could* not) publish until after he left the Caribbean. By early 1812 he was in New York City, where all of the poems below were first published in his volume *Leisure Hours*.

Marsden's poems occupy a pivotal position in the history of slavery and abolition. Unmoved by the fleeting euphoria of the recent abolition of the slave trade (though he welcomed it), Marsden already in 1808 looked ahead to the larger imperative, the abolition of slavery itself. He rejected false optimism and consciously positioned himself in the historical moment: "Some will perhaps say, 'you are kicking a dead wolf; slavery is now abolished.' Where is it abolished? . . . in the British Colonies? . . . the United States? . . . Oh, when will this curse of nature and humanity be removed from the earth?"

In the first of the poems below, Marsden takes an actual event—the theft of a Bible by a black man—to reflect on the laughable irrelevance of legal systems in slaveholding societies. In such societies, built on evil premises, *all* ethical codes become relative and discreditable.

from "The Spiritual Theft, or Stolen Bible: Written on Having My Gilt Pocket Bible Stolen by a Black Man in St. George, Sommer Islands. In the Year 1808"

> *Jove fix'd it certain that whatever day,*
> *Man makes a slave, takes half his worth away.* (HOMER)

An African, void of uprightness within,
Who, like many others, thought stealing no sin;

Intent on converting whatever he saw
To private account, without license or law;
Saw my gilt pocket Bible, laid by on a shelf,
And stole it to barter for liquor or pelf.
It was my instructor; I lov'd it more dear
Than misers their lucre, or tiplers their beer . . .
Men rifle the young, and purloin from the old,
Rob maidens of virtue, and misers of gold:
While bigots deprive you of conscience's right;
And tyrants may rob you of liberty bright:
But a Bible to steal is uncommonly odd:
Was there ever a thief who delighted in God? . . .
Mayhap the poor black had some latent intent,
And thought by this conduct to give it a vent.
He might feel a fancy to favour his plan,
'Twas no greater crime than to pilfer a man!
The argument's just, and I feel its sharp edge;
It cuts like a razor, and cleaves like a wedge;
Strikes home on my reason, I blush in a minute,
And feel all the truth and the reason that's in it:
A Bible to steal is a theft it is true, man,
But stealing and slaving the blacks is inhuman!

(1808)[365]

Moral indignation also sparked this poem, which again (per Marsden's foot-note) draws on an actual event. Although Marsden mentions other whites who protested the removal of Molly's ("Negro Mary's") corpse from the parish bur-ial ground, his poem seems to provide a private outlet for opinions that would have been dangerous to voice in public.

from "The Negro Mary, or Inhumanity to the Dead"*

Respectfully Inscribed to the Manumission Society of the City of
New-York

Under ground
Precedency's a jest; vassal and lord,
Grossly familiar, side by side consume.
Surely there's not a dungeon slave that's buried
But lies as soft and sleeps as sound as he. (BLAIR)

---

* [Marsden's note:] Black Mary was married to one of the band belonging to the seventh Regi-
ment; she was a pious, sensible, diligent creature; beloved and esteemed by both the officers

Molly was of Guinea race,
Deeply sable was her hue;
But her placid eyes and face
Spoke a feeling heart and true.

Sympathy is not confin'd,
To the noble, rich and high;
Molly had a gentle mind,
And a bosom form'd to sigh.

Colours may be white or dark,
For the body is a clod;
'Tis the intellectual spark,
Shows the lineaments of God. . . .

Molly knew the Saviour's love,
She had felt the blood applied;
Tasted of the powers above,
Pardon thro' the crucified.

But she sick'ned and she died;
Princes must resign their breath!
And her end exemplified,
How the saint is blest in death. . . .

What, deny her dust a place
On its genuine mother's breast!
O ye slave-oppressing race!
She is now the Saviour's guest.

Yes, the consecrated spot,
Africans shall ne'er invade;
Where the whites corrupt and rot,
Not a negro shall be laid.

Is the wide distinction nought,
'Twixt a white man and a slave?

---

and men, and noted for her faithfulness, cleanliness, and honesty. While in St. George, Bermuda, she lost several children; at last she sickened and died herself, and was buried by her infants in the church-yard; but in defiance of nature, decency, and humanity, the worthy parish of St. George had her taken up again, thinking the hallowed spot would be desecrated by such a deposit. The conduct excited a sentiment of indignation in the officers of the corps, and the whole Regiment was ordered to honour and attend her reinterment near the St. George Ferry; and the Paymaster of the Regiment dying soon after, requested to be laid along side black Mary, which was complied with.

Who can bear the horrid thought,
To have blacks beside his grave?

O ye hypocritic drones!
Curst with hearts that cannot feel,
Callous to the negro's groans;
As a rock or bar of steel!

If the judge of all mankind
As ye measure mete to you;
What comparison will ye find?
Only rigour is your due!

Bright the golden precept shines,
But ye spurn the rights of men!
Nature's claims, and scripture lines,
Plead with you, but plead in vain.

Tho' ye now a grave deny,
Can ye shut the gates of light?
Lo, her spirit mounts on high;
Wonders at your impious spite.

Let the slave oppressor dread!
Lest a just and angry God
Pour upon his impious head
Woe for woe! and rod for rod!

Yes, the final hour appears,
Vengeance will not always spare,
Negroes' sighs, and groans, and tears,
Are not lost in empty air.

They are bottled up on high,
By and by the bolt shall fall;
Sevenfold vengeance from the sky,
Shall o'erwhelm and crush you all.

(c. 1810)

Combining the eye of a painter with the conscience of a moralist, Marsden depicts in the following poem a gorgeous natural world undermined by the evil in its midst. More troubling still, however, is his quiet observation that some slaves are lulled into complacency by the idyllic setting.

from "The Slaves of the Beautiful Isle"

Bermuda, thy rocks are the mariner's dread,
But calm and pellucid thy seas;

Thy skies in a vest of pure azure array'd,
  Waft sweetly the health-giving breeze.

Fair blooms thy gilt orange and beautiful lime,
  Whose acid refreshes the taste;
The sun never viewed a more temperate clime,
  For the plains never felt a cold blast. . . .

From the clamour of battle removed afar,
  Thy vales are the harbours of peace;
But slavery all the mild blessings can mar,
  Sweet Island, it is thy disgrace.

Thy vessels are rapid that skim the blue deep,
  Thy cedars glide over the flood;
But the mariner slave is predestin'd to weep,
  And mingle his tears with his food.

But still they are fond of the health-giving spot,
  And prefer it to liberty's smile;
In love with their chains, and content with their lot,
  They delight in the beautiful Isle.

(c. 1810)

Starting from a Cowper quotation about the common humanity of whites and blacks, the following poem is the only one in which Marsden affects a slave dialect. Like so many before him, the weary slave, in his innocence, reveals the cruelty and hypocrisy of his masters with devastating clarity.

from "The Weary Negro. A Dialogue"

> *Still in thought as free as ever,*
> *What are England's rights, I ask,*
> *Me from my delight to sever,*
> *Me to torture, me to task;*
> *Fleecy locks and black complexion*
> *Cannot forfeit nature's claim;*
> *Skins may differ, but affection*
> *Dwells in white and black the same.* (COWPER)

Negro, is thy treatment cruel?
  Is thy master kind or not?
Hast thou food enough, or do ill
  Overseers oppress thy lot?

Art thou easy and contented?
  Satisfied to be a slave?

651

Hast thou ever yet repented
   Crossing the Atlantic wave?

"Easy! dat be great ting, massa,
   Negro easy, cannot be,
While de white-man make us passa
   Life of pain and misery.

Back is whipp'd, and food is scanted,
   One poor quart of corn a day;
Tho' we labour'd, sweat, and panted,
   In de sun's consuming ray."

Can poor negro cease to sorrow,
   When his wife and children rise?
Snatch'd perhaps before to morrow
   From his arms and longing eyes?

Black man, do thy hardships never
   Make thee think of God above?
In thy sorrows dost thou ever
   Dread his vengeance, ask his love?

"Yes, good massa, dat be truly
   In my thoughts, both night and day;
Yet poor Cato has but newly
   Known de narrow blessed way.

Tho' de white man whip and strike us,
   When we faint beneath our toil;
Still de gracious Saviour like us,
   Make de negro bosom smile."

Tell me, Cato, who has taught thee,
   Jesus died a world to save?
Surely not the wretch who bought thee,
   Or convey'd thee o'er the wave.

"No, no, massa, dey were bad men,
   And would fight, and curse, and swear;
Sing, and drink, and shout like madmen,
   But dey never made a prayer.

De poor negro wrapt in blindness,
   Hardly knew a God above:
Till de missionary kindness
   Point us to a Saviour's love."

                     (c. 1810)

JOSHUA MARSDEN

In the following excerpts, Marsden uses the preferred rhyming couplet form of such earlier neoclassical moralists as Pope and Johnson. Taking as his motto a famous passage of Cowper's *The Task* (1785), Marsden proceeds to refute one by one the racist apologies for slavery that were the orthodoxy of the white Bermuda society in which he lived.

from "West-India Logic, or Negroes Have No Souls"

I would not have a slave to till my ground,
To carry me, to fan me while I sleep,
And tremble when I wake, for all the wealth
That sinews bought and sold have ever earned.
No: dear as freedom is, and in my heart's
Just estimation priz'd above all price,
I had much rather be myself the slave,
And wear the bonds, than fasten them on him. (COWPER)

Because their skin is black as ink or coals,
Have injured negroes no immortal souls!
If they are bought and sold at every mart
As drudging beasts, have they no better part?
'Tis thy detested avarice has made
The selling human flesh a legal trade;
And if a qualm should twinge thee from within,
And something whispers 'tis a cruel sin;
'Tis answered with a blasphemy as ever fell,
As ever issued from the pit of hell;
"They are but cattle, born to drudge and toil,
To boil the sugar, or to hoe the soil!"
Proud white-man, cease to blame their sable skin,
Has the dark casket no pure pearl within?
Are they not made in God's own image, say?
And form'd and fashion'd with the self-same clay
As thee and other men? Then why contest
The spark divine that glows within their breast? . . .
A skin of purest ivory or jet,
Is no true test of heaven's love or hate.
A black man's heart may be as white and fair
As polar snows or cherubs' garments are;
While thine as black as hell, and stain'd within,
Belies the lily-whiteness of thy skin:

Jehovah looks within, he only knows
Whose black as ink, or white as polar snows. . . .
Perhaps, vain mortal, 'tis thy shocking pride,
That sets his immortality aside;
Or else thy fears deny his future state,
Lest thou shouldst meet thy slave at heaven's gate
At heaven's gate! thou canst not bear the thought,
That one so basely sold, so cheaply bought,
Should be a tenant of immortal bliss,
Which possibly his haughty lord may miss.
Mayhap thy doubts suggest a judgment seat,
Where thou thy lacerated slave shalt meet;
Before a judge inexorably just,
To answer for thy cruelty and lust.
Some of thy injured slaves may then appear,
Whiter than snow-drops on the early year;
Not whipp'd, and tied, not brutalized, and sold,
A starry diadem their heads infold;
And purest robes of dazzling light invest,
The pious African by thee opprest.
O bright reverse of all their former woe! . . .
But, monster! not to thee their thanks are due,
Nor thy inhuman negro-driving crew;
Thou hast oppos'd this bliss with hellish spite,
Thou hast refus'd the negro sacred light;
Thou hast, to prove intelligence a clod,
Denied thy negroes all access to God;
Repress'd each anxious wish their hearts might feel,
For present bliss, and everlasting weal;
And made as lust or av'rice might suggest,
Thy slave a mindless sod, machine, or beast.

                                                   (c. 1810)

    At the heart of the following poem is the poet's indictment of European con-
sumers grown used to cheap sugar, coffee, and other colonial products, and in-
different to their massive cost in human suffering. Again Cowper is Marsden's
touchstone: the motto is spliced together from two stanzas of "The Negro's
Complaint" (1788). Here, in stanzas that hammer home his point, the speaker
attacks the displacement of moral values by economic interests.

JOSHUA MARSDEN

from "The Sale of Slaves, or a Good Bargain"*

Men from England bought and sold me,
Paid my price in paltry gold;
But though theirs they have enroll'd me,
Minds are never to be sold:
Is there as ye sometimes tell us?
Is there one who reigns on high?
Has he bid you buy and sell us;
Speaking from his throne, the sky? (COWPER)

Monster, check thy scurril clack,
    She thy mother's sister is;
Though her polish'd skin is black,
    She's an heir of endless bliss.

If she be a child of Ham,
    She's a child of Adam's race;
Marble man, O blush for shame!
    If a blush can stain thy face.

Did I say she was thy kin?
    Will she thank me for the tie?
Though thou boast a whiter skin,
    Blacker is thy moral die!

Is a soul design'd for bliss,
    On the shambles to be sold?
At a crime so black as this,
    God of love, my blood runs cold!

In thy lovely image made,
    Ransom'd by the cross divine;
Shall we, Oh forbid the trade,
    Buy and sell a child of thine!

O base avarice of gold!
    Sorest curse beneath the sun;
Pen of man can ne'er unfold
    Half the evils thou hast done.

Look upon her woolly hair,
    Look upon her sable skin;

* [Marsden's note:] On being at a sale of furniture in Bermuda, several blacks were put up at auction, when the unfeeling auctioneer told his auditors to bid away, as the slave he was selling, (a pensive looking dejected young woman) was not so dear as butcher's meat.

Reason, honour, truth declare,
    Slavery a dismal sin.

Hast thou reason? so has she;
    Warm affections she can glow;
Dost thou weep at misery?
    See her tears already flow. . . .

We have slav'd the human race,
    Sunk the mortal to a brute;
Tumbled manhood from its place,
    To get sugar, rum, and fruit.

Sweet our coffee, sweet our tea,
    But in bitterness of soul,
Many a wretch has pin'd away,
    To ameliorate the bowl.

Still we love the sparkling glass,
    Though it cost a negro's groans;
But to negro's woes, alas!
    We are obdurate as stones!

O Omnipotence of love!
    Rise and crush the hellish trade;
Look in mercy from above,
    Send the injur'd negro aid.

           (c. 1810)

The sexual exploitation of black women, widespread in slaveholding societies, here comes in for stinging attack. Framed in the unwittingly self-parodic voices of two "pillars of the community" (a judge and a colonel), the poem exposes the lechery, hypocrisy, and racism of such men. The "damn'd parson" who so enrages these leading citizens seems to have been a colleague of Marsden's, according to his note.

The Converted Mulattoes, or Enraged Junto*

Says the Judge to the Colonel, dear Colonel, I say,
The Methodist dogs get our lasses away;

---

* [Marsden's note:] The following dialogue was written extempore from an authentic circumstance; a lively Methodist missionary in the island of T[rinida]d, had awakened some mulatto girls, in the keeping of several official characters, which so exasperated the gentlemen, that they contrived to send God's minister to prison for the terrible crime. Some have said Paul was beheaded for converting one of Nero's favourite women.

Our lovely mulattoes and sweet jolly lasses
Will all be undone by their canting grimaces.

Yesterday my dear Molly sigh'd sadly and said,
It griev'd her to think what an ill life she led;
She blubber'd, and whin'd about stuff and salvation,
Till I swore she was mad, and got into a passion.

So I met the damn'd parson, and told him right roundly,
If he preach'd any more so I'd drub him most soundly;
But he like a canting knave told me he'd do it,
I shook my cane at him, rascal, sirrah, you'll rue it.

And now, my dear Colonel, some method let's fall on,
Or this devil will stamp, threaten, wheedle, and bawl on,
Will rob us of all our mulattoes, I swear it,
But confound the vile babbler, there's no one can bear it.

I'll go to old H—p,* and tell him forsooth,
For they say he has still a most lickerish tooth;
To watch his mulattoes, it has been asserted,
They'll slip through his fingers, and all get converted.

But stay, a good notion has enter'd my head,
I may but have dream'd it, or it has been said;
These rascally parsons will kindle sedition,
And therefore to stop them I'll quickly petition.

Yes, dam'em, petition, says the Colonel with speed,
Or else they'll sedition or something worse feed;
Their cant, and their clamour, there is no enduring,
For the villains launch out against drinking and wh[orin]g.

Had I my own way, I would tip them a bullet,
'Tis the best recipe for a noisy man's gullet;
For were they allow'd to go on with their ranting,
The Island would echo with whining and canting.

So betwixt the gay Colonel and head of the bench,
Who lov'd his full bottle, his cards, and his wench;
The parson was sent to the jail in a trice, sir:
To repent of converting mulattoes from vice, sir.

(c. 1810)

It is no surprise that Marsden should dedicate the following poem to Free-born Garrettson, as Garrettson was a much beloved and indefatigable itinerant

---

* [Marsden's note:] The Governor [of Trinidad, Sir Thomas Hislop, 1764–1843].

preacher and Methodist elder who had freed his own slaves in 1775 at the moment of his conversion and aggressively opposed slaveholding throughout his fifty-year ministry.

from "The Spread of the Gospel"

Affectionately Inscribed to the Rev. Freeborn Garrettson

Brighter glows the day of grace,
    Wider spreads the happy sound,
Ev'ry land and ev'ry place,
    Shall with the gospel bliss abound.

Africa, so long forlorn,
    Jesus now will richly bless,
With salvation's joyful morn,
    Tidings of delightful grace.

Every toil-degraded slave,
    Bow'd beneath oppression's rod,
Bleeding clemency shall save;
    Lead the African to God.

(c. 1810)

Drawing on the motto made famous by Josiah Wedgewood's antislavery medallion ("Am I not a brother, and a Man?"), Marsden here explores, like Wheatley, Blake, and others before him, an image of heaven that is color blind. As with so many abolitionists, Marsden trusted finally that what he saw as the rational, irrefutable truth of Christianity would prevail.

from "A Black Man's Plea, 'Am Not I a Brother'"

Ah, why should a white man despise
A brother of African race?
Ah, why should his enmity rise,
If a black man but enter the place?
Sure there will be negroes above,
As white as the purest of lime;
In the regions of heavenly love,
Will be natives of every clime. . . .

If wash'd in the blood of the Son,
If robes of salvation they wear,
The nations of every zone
Shall have their blest delegates there:
For Europe its millions shall send,

JOSHUA MARSDEN

While favour'd America vies
With Asia and Afric to bend,
And people the dazzling skies.

If sable and dusky our skin,
We are not to blame for the deed;
If deeply defiled by sin,
The more a salvation we need;
We need, and the Saviour hath died
To save the poor African race,
Nor will he reject us through pride,
Or blame for our colour or face. . . .

Though we are benighted and blind,
A captive illiterate race,
The Saviour is loving and kind,
And free and extensive his grace.
No riches or honour have we,
No learning, no wisdom to bring,
Yet mercy for us is as free
As 'tis for a prince or a king.

And mercy is all that we want,
To make us both happy and wise;
Thy fulness of mercy, O grant,
Thou King of the star-paved skies.
Are we not the work of thy hands,
The purchase of Jesus's blood?
O save the poor African bands,
Thou Son of Jehovah, our God.

(c. 1810)

659

ANONYMOUS

A remnant of a source that is now lost, the following poem was included in a collection entitled *Poems, Chiefly Amatory; by a Lady,* compiled by a woman called Mary De Krafft and published in Washington, D.C., in 1809. Although nothing is known of the editor, the entire collection focuses on what were thought at the time to be the "natural" sensibilities of women. Notable among these is a particular sympathy for the plight of slaves, which informs this plaintive and consciously feminine ("Shall not pity, gentle maiden, / Wet the eye . . . ?") ballad.

The African Slave

Occasioned by the recent insurrections of the oppressed Blacks in the West Indies.

Shall the muse that's wont to wander
    Where the wretched sigh and cry,
Forbear upon the slave to ponder,
    Dying beneath the burning sky.

Shall not pity, gentle maiden,
    Wet the eye of freedom's son
When he beholds the slave o'erladen,
    See him lash'd, and hear him groan.

O'er Atlantic's sky hu'd billows
    Fancy guides my weeping way,
To mourn the toiling wretches' sorrows,
    Doom'd to servitude a prey!

O hark! I hear their plaintive anguish
    Murmur on the foaming shore;
Yes, I see the females languish,
    Spent with loss of purple gore!

Say, thy rich and lordly tyrant,
   Speak what reason bids thee say,
Were these made for thee to torment,
   Scourge and make to death a prey?

O no, blest freedom's sacred fire
   Shall in the sable bosom glow;
With fortitude the slave inspire
   To break the chain of galling woe!
               (c. 1809)[366]

ANONYMOUS

The authorship of the following poem remains uncertain, but it can be narrowed down to one of a group who collaborated on the landmark book in which it was published: the publisher Robert Bowyer; the poets James Montgomery, James Grahame, and Elizabeth Benger; and the artist Robert Smirke, F.R.A. Inspired to commemorate the passage of the abolition bill in 1807, Bowyer commissioned these artists to produce an illustrated volume of *Poems on the Abolition of the Slave Trade*. The following unsigned lines were presented as a gloss on Smirke's title-page illustration of Prometheus chained to the rock, an image of Africa's persecution at the hands of Europe.

Prometheus Delivered

"Come, Outcast of the human race,
Prometheus, hail thy destined place!
This rock protects the dark retreat,
Unvisited by earthly feet;
We only shall thy mansion share,
Who haunt the chamber of despair!
The vulture, here, thy loathed mate—
Rapacious minister of fate!
Compels life's ruddy stream to part
With keenest torture from thy heart.
Yet not to perish art thou doomed,
Victim unspared, but unconsumed;
Death shall not sap thy wall of clay,
That penal being mocks decay;
Live, conscious inmate of the grave,
Live, outcast, captive, victim, slave!"
    The Furies ceased; the wrathful strain
Prometheus hears, and, pierced with pain,

Rolls far around his hopeless gaze,
His realm of wretchedness surveys;
Then maddening with convulsive breath,
He moans or raves, imploring death.
Thus hours on hours unnumbered past,
And each more lingering than the last;
When lo! Before his glazed sight,
Appears a form, in dauntless might.
'Tis he! Alcides, lord of fame!
The friend of man, his noblest name!
Swift from his bow the arrow flies,
And prone the bleeding vulture lies.
He smites the rock, he rends the chain,
Prometheus rises man again!

   Such, Africa, thy suffering state!
Outcast of nations, such thy fate!
The ruthless rock, the den of pain,
Were thine—oh long deplored in vain,
Whilst Britain's virtue slept! At length
She rose in majesty and strength;
And when thy martyr'd limbs she viewed,
Thy wounds unhealed, and still renewed,
She wept; but soon with graceful pride,
The vulture, Avarice, she defied,
And wrenched him from thy reeking side;
In Britain's name then called thee forth,
Sad exile, to the social hearth,
From baleful Error's realm of night,
To Freedom's breath and Reason's light.

              (1809)[367]

[?HENRY JOHNSON]
(fl. 1809–1810)

Little is known about Henry Johnson, the apparent author of this poem and other religious writings, except that he was a member of the African Church of New York and that he lived in lower Manhattan in Ward 2, an area bounded by the East River, Pine, Nassau, and Ferry Streets. These two stanzas, perhaps adapted from another source, were part of an introductory address delivered by Johnson at a ceremony on January 2, 1809, to commemorate the first anniversary of the abolition of the slave trade. Rising to introduce the program's orator, the African American Henry Sipkins, Johnson expressly framed his remarks as being on behalf of "us Africans and descendants of Africans."

[Untitled] from An Oration on the Abolition of the Slave Trade; Delivered in the African Church, in the City of New York, January 2, 1809

I long to lay this painful head,
    And aching heart, beneath the soil;
To slumber in that dreamless bed,
    From all my toil.

For misery stole me at my birth,
    And cast me naked on the wild,
I perish, O my mother earth;
    Take home thy child.

(1809)[368]

BERNARD BARTON (1784–1849)

An English Quaker whose verse is little remembered today, Barton published more than twenty books of poetry (mostly on social issues) before his death in 1849. Formerly a merchant, the pious poet became friends with Lamb, Southey, and other literary figures of the day. Both of the following poems were written early in his career.

The first is an example of the false optimism inspired by the abolition of the slave trade January 1, 1808. Writers like Barton thought the tide of reform had turned and would soon sweep before it not only the slave trade, but the whole institution of slavery and other inequities. Instead, history brought decades of disappointment.

from "Stanzas on the Anniversary of the Abolition of the Slave Trade"

Respectfully Inscrib'd to the Members of the African Institution

My muse! commemorate, with joyful sound,
An hour which unborn ages shall revere.
E'en that glad hour which wip'd the bitter tear
From Afric's cheek, and cast her chains away . . .

All hail, ye heavenly band! your holy fire
Inflam'd with virtuous ardour Clarkson's breast;
Awoke that zeal which labour ne'er could tire,
Danger affright, nor av'rice lull to rest.
He saw poor Afric's sable sons opprest;
Saw them, transported from their native shore,
Meet stern-eyed death in all his horrors drest,
Or life more horrible than death deplore.
Such were the scenes he saw—scenes we behold no more.

Clarkson! and Wilberforce! thrice honour'd names!

Ye shine conspicuous 'mid that chosen band,
Whose steady zeal a nation's reverence claims,
Whose generous labours have redeem'd the land. . . .

Among the hosts who hail with just applause
This joyful hour, my partial eyes survey
A sect, whose ardent zeal in virtue's cause,
Prompts me the tribute of respect to pay.
Ye Friends of Peace! to you this glorious day
Is doubly sanctified, is doubly dear;
On Afric's shores no more shall martial fray
Infringe that sacred law your souls revere;
But strife and war shall cease, and happier days appear.

On Guinea's coast, where once the shriek of woe
Proclaim'd the reign of anguish and despair;
Where avarice sunk the man the brute below,
And christian monsters mock'd the captive's prayer;
A different aspect shall that region wear:
There scenes of bliss shall once more greet the eye;
The festive song the evening gale shall bear
In broken accents to the distant sky—
Blest sounds of peaceful mirth, and village revelry.

O Thou! whose sceptre sways this earthly ball,
This trivial atom in creation's round;
"Who seest with equal eyes as God of all,"
A Negro fetter'd, or a Monarch crown'd:
O Thou! whose power and goodness none can bound,
Heal Afric's wrongs, and pardon Europe's crime;
Proclaim through torrid wastes that joyful sound,
Which Jordan's vallies heard in earlier time:
Salvation's gladdening voice, and Gospel truths sublime!

(1809)[369]

Like many antislavery poets, Barton was conscious of his generation's debt
to earlier writers and activists. In this excerpt from his tribute to the philanthro-
pist and poet William Roscoe, Barton singles out Roscoe's "Wrongs of Africa"
(1788) as an example of imaginative literature that helped shape history.

from "To William Roscoe, Esq."

Beneath the burning equinoctial line
The negro tribes shall grateful sing thy praise;

Their children's children shall in concert join
To hail the Bard who pour'd his generous lays,
And turn'd on "Afric's Wrongs" a nation's pitying gaze.
With Poesy shall History unite,
To crown with civic wreath her favour'd son,
Whose classic pen again recals from night
Statesmen and Bards who once in splendour shone.

(c. 1809)[370]

MARY AND CHARLES LAMB
(1764–1847 and 1775–1834)

Behind this co-authorship lies a tale of sibling devotion and a shared life of suffering. Charles, who became one of the most prolific and well-known writers of the Romantic period, served as guardian for his older sister Mary from the time of her first breakdown in 1796 (when in a mad rage she murdered their mother) until his death thirty-eight years later. During her lucid intervals, she joined with him in writing works for children, including the volume from which the two poems below are taken.

In the first, the ambiguities of racial identity play out beneath the deceptively simple story of a West Indian boy's acculturation in England. The "dark Indian" identifies ultimately, and tragicomically, with the "boys of colour" he sees in the streets of London—the chimney sweeps who are in fact poor white orphans blackened with soot.

Choosing a Profession

A Creole boy from the West Indies brought,
To be in European learning taught,
Some years before to Westminster he went,
To a Preparatory School was sent.
When from his artless tale the mistress found,
The child had not one friend on English ground,
She, ev'n as if she his own mother were,
Made the dark Indian her peculiar care.
Oft on her fav'rite's future lot she thought;
To know the bent of his young mind she sought,
For much the kind preceptress wish'd to find
To what profession he was most inclin'd,
That where his genius led they might him train;
For nature's kindly bent she held not vain.
But vain her efforts to explore his will;
The frequent question he evaded still:

Till on a day at length he to her came,
Joy sparkling in his eyes; and said, the same
Trade he would be those boys of colour were,
Who danc'd so happy in the open air.
It was a troop of chimney-sweeping boys,
With wooden music and obstrep'rous noise,
In tarnish'd finery and grotesque array,
Were dancing in the street the first of May.

(1809)[371]

A remarkable feature of this poem, which could as easily have applied to twentieth-century as to eighteenth-century school integration, is that it is addressed to children. Beneath its optimistic moral, the poem offers insights into the psychology of prejudice, peer pressure, and human affection.

Conquest of Prejudice

Unto a Yorkshire school was sent
A negro youth to learn to write,
And the first day young Juba went
All gazed on him as a rare sight.

But soon with altered looks askance
They view his sable face and form,
When they perceive the scornful glance
Of the head boy, young Henry Orme.

He in the school was first in fame:
Said he, "It does to me appear
To be a great disgrace and shame
A black should be admitted here."

His words were quickly whispered round,
And every boy now looks offended;
The master saw the change, and found
That Orme a mutiny intended.

Said he to Orme, "This African
It seems is not by you approved;
I'll find a way, young Englishman,
To have this prejudice removed.

Nearer acquaintance possibly
May make you tolerate his hue;
At least 'tis my intent to try
What a short month may chance to do."

Young Orme and Juba then he led
Into a room, in which there were
For each of the two boys a bed,
A table, and a wicker chair.

He locked them in, secured the key,
That all access to them was stopt;
They from without can nothing see;
Their food is through a skylight dropt.

A month in this lone chamber Orme
Is sentenced during all that time
To view no other face or form
Than Juba's parched by Afric clime.

One word they neither of them spoke
The first three days of the first week;
On the fourth day the ice was broke;
Orme was the first that deigned to speak.

The dreary silence o'er, both glad
To hear of human voice the sound,
The negro and the English lad
Comfort in mutual converse found.

Of ships and seas and foreign coast
Juba can speak, for he has been
A voyager: and Orme can boast
He London's famous town has seen.

In eager talk they pass the day,
And borrow hours even from the night;
So pleasantly time passed away,
That they have lost their reckoning quite.

And when their master set them free,
They thought a week was sure remitted,
And thanked him that their liberty
Had been before the time permitted.

Now Orme and Juba are good friends;
The school, by Orme's example won,
Contend who most shall make amends
For former slights to Afric's son.

(1809)[372]

ROBERT Y. SIDNEY (fl. 1809)

Probably a relation of Joseph Sidney, the African American preacher and abolitionist, Robert Sidney produced the following anthems for the "National Jubilee of the Abolition of the Slave Trade" celebrated in New York on January 2, 1809. Joseph Sidney delivered the "Oration" that day, before the Wilberforce Philanthropic Association. Anthems and hymns were a standard feature of these ceremonies and offer a window into African American life at the beginning of the nineteenth century. The abolition anniversary poems from 1808–10 mark the high point in the morale of the African American and abolitionist communities, which languished for decades thereafter, until the Emancipation Proclamation and the Thirteenth Amendment in the 1860s.

Anthem I

1. Dry your tears, ye sons of Afric,
   God has shown his gracious power,
   He has stopt the horrid traffic,
   That your country's bosom tore.
   See through clouds he smiles benignant,
   See your nation's glory rise;
   Though your foes may frown indignant,
   All their wrath you may despise.

   CHORUS.
   Dry your tears ye hapless nation,
   Banish all your cares away;
   God has given great salvation,
   On this ever glorious day.

   SOLO.
   O raise to heaven a grateful voice,
   Through every age rejoice, rejoice.

RECITATIVE.

What objects meet the piteous eye,
　　What passions fill the soul of man,
To see a hapless nation rise,
　　And all its various actions scan,
In deep disgrace, depriv'd of peace,
　　And every blessing dear,
Now blest with peace, rais'd up in fame,
　　And free from every fear.

2. Thus the clouds the light obscuring,
　　Vainly try to veil the day:
　　Thus shall you all toils enduring,
　　See your troubles pass away.
　　Though the clouds of night have hover'd,
　　On your nation's hapless head;
　　See the blushing morn discover'd,
　　See the dawn of glory shed.

　　　CHORUS.——Dry your tears, &c.

3. See each science round you blooming,
　　Like the flowers at dawn of day,
　　　With their sweets the air perfuming,
　　With their beauties cheer the way.
　　See with eagle wings expanded,
　　　See each hidden talent rise;
　　See each slavish fear disbanded,
　　　See your genius mount the skies.

　　　CHORUS.——Dry your tears, &c.

　　　　　　　　　(1809)[373]

Anthem II

1. Ye sons of Afric, loud rejoice,
　　In songs of triumph raise your voice;
　　The night of slavery now is past,
　　The dawn of freedom shines at last.

　　　CHORUS.

　　Rejoice that you were born to see,
　　This glorious day, your jubilee.

2. O praise the Lord enthron'd on high,
　　The Lord that heard your piercing cry;

That made his wond'rous light to spread,
And shed his blessings on your heads.

CHORUS.——Rejoice, &c.

FINALE.

3. Ye worthy friends our thanks receive,
'Tis all that Afric's sons can give;
And for the kindness you have shown,
May GOD receive you as his own.

CHORUS.——Rejoice, &c.

(1809)[374]

NANCY DENNIS SPROAT
(1766–1826)

Born into an old Rhode Island Quaker family, Nancy Dennis married the Revolutionary War veteran James Sproat in 1788 and settled in Taunton, Massachusetts. She published poetry and children's books in Boston, New York, and other cities. The poem below is one of her earliest. At one level "Mount Pleasant" is an homage to domesticity, celebrating the pleasures of her own comfortable family life. But it is also a consciously nationalist poem, albeit from an appropriately modest female perspective. For a woman of Sproat's beliefs, the national sin of slavery loomed large and shaped her message to the nation: "Oh! may I never hear beneath thy shades / The moan of slavery!"

from "Mount Pleasant. Written in 1809"

> "All various Nature pressing on the heart."
>
> THOMSON.

When groaning millions own a tyrant's sway,
And war's hoarse clangor turns the nations pale;
When man, more savage than the forest wolf,
Uplifts the blade, still wet with human blood,
Again to plunge it in a brother's breast.
From scenes so dire the sicken'd heart recoils,
And pants to find on earth some favour'd spot,
Where slavery's chains were never heard to clank,
But freedom's plant, by every virtue nurs'd,
Spreads its wide branches o'er the happy land.
America! this precious grant is thine!
Thy spiry cities, fraught with honest gains . . .
    Thy territory vast,
Crowded with hosts of gallant, sturdy sons,
Beneath no tyrant's nod, to no decrees
Subjected, save the *golden* rule of *right*. . . .

All proclaim . . .
The joyous reign of *Liberty* and *Law*.
These are our nation's sinews and her shield.
Rob man of *Freedom,* and his nerveless arm
Drops from its destin'd task; his spirits droop,
His genius withers, and his sickly soul,
Desponding, shrinks from every great pursuit.
Restore him *lawless* liberty, and strait
His passions seize the empire of his mind,
And tyrannize with wild, demonic rage.
Unaw'd by discipline, and *just* restraint,
Society were like an instrument
Of jarring sounds, which grate the tortur'd ear.
But tun'd by *Law* and *Liberty,* it moves
In concord sweet, and perfect harmony.
Oh, blest Columbia! this has been thy state:
Let not the demon *Discord* mar thy peace . . .
Oh! may I never hear beneath thy shades
The moan of slavery! In thy sweet retreat,
Mount Pleasant, safe secluded, I will breathe
A wish for this dear land's prosperity.
But what avails a feeble woman's wish?
I leave the cares of empire to the minds
Which ought to wield them, and solace my thoughts
With the lov'd scenes of this delightful spot.
(wr. 1809/pub. 1813)[375]

PETER WILLIAMS, JR.
(? 1780–1840)

Son of a slave who fought in the American Revolution, Peter Williams, Jr., became the first black Episcopalian priest and a leader in the American abolitionist movement. Based in New York City, he established St. Philip's African Church in 1819, helped found the first African American newspaper (*Freedom's Journal*) in 1827 and the Phoenix Society to support black education in 1833, preached, wrote, and occasionally stirred controversy. In 1834, amid white backlash at abolitionists and rumors that Williams had performed interracial marriages, rioters burned his church and he was forced to resign from the board of the New York Antislavery Society. Although he supported African colonization projects and refuge communities in Canada, Williams continued to hope that eventually America would include blacks as equals.

These two hymns were published with William Hamilton's *Address to the New York African Society, for Mutual Relief, delivered in the Universalist Church, January 2, 1809,* and were sung during the service held to celebrate the second anniversary of the abolition of the slave trade. In the first, for all his gratitude, Williams focuses his listeners on the larger political message: "*All men are free by right / Of Nature's laws.*"

Hymn I

To the Eternal Lord,
By saints on earth ador'd
   And saints above.
Let us glad honors rear,
In strains of praise and pray'r
His glorious name declare,
   The God of Love.

When the oppressor's hands
Bound us in iron bands
   Thou didst appear.
Thou saw our weeping eyes,

And list'ning to our cries,
In mercy didst arise,
    Our hearts to cheer.

Thou did'st the trade o'erthrow,
The source of boundless woe,
    The world's disgrace,
Which ravag'd Afric's coast,
Enslaved its greatest boast,
A happy num'rous host,
    A harmless race.

In diff'rent parts of earth
Thou called the Humane forth,
    Our rights to plead,
Our griefs to mitigate,
And to improve our state,
An object truly great,
    Noble indeed.

Thou didst their labours bless,
And gave them great success,
    In Freedom's cause.
They prov'd to every sight
By truth's unerring light,
All men are free by right
    Of Nature's laws.

They to insure our bliss,
Taught us that happiness
    Is from above.
That it is only found
On this terrestrial ground,
Where virtuous acts abound,
    And Mutu'l Love.

                    (1809)[376]

In the second hymn, in terms that distantly foreshadow the self-sufficiency ethos of later African American nationalist movements, Williams focuses on the closeness and mutual support within the black community.

Hymn II

The Sov'reign ruler of the skies
    To bless the human kind,

Implanted in the breast of man,
   A sympathetic mind.
Hence we, participating woe
   Each other's griefs alloy,
And by reciprocating bliss
   We swell the tide of joy.

Instructed thus by Nature's God,
   The good and great first cause;
We find that Fellowship and Love
   Stand high in Nature's Laws.
As brethren are to brethren near,
   So let us be combin'd:
Knit by the bonds of Mutu'l Love
   In social compact joined.

With unremitting tender care,
   Let us the sick attend;
Defend from want the fatherless,
   And prove the Widow's friend.
So shall we cheer affliction's night,
   And soothe the fiercest grief;
So shall we ease the aching heart,
   By MUTUAL RELIEF.

          (1809)[377]

ROBERT TANNAHILL (1774–1810)

A Scottish poet and songwriter, Tannahill began life as an apprentice weaver. Influenced by Burns, he produced scores of sentimental songs, many in Scots dialect, and became moderately famous before committing suicide in 1810. This poem combines the standard elements of a ballad about a lovelorn woman, so characteristic of Tannahill, with the particular sadness of an African captive in Britain pining for her native land.

The Negro Girl

Yon poor Negro girl, an exotic plant,
    Was torn from her dear native soil,
Reluctantly borne o'er the raging Atlant,
    Then brought to Britannia's isle.
Though Fatima's mistress be loving and kind,
    Poor Fatima still must deplore;
She thinks on her parents, left weeping behind,
    And sighs for her dear native shore.

She thinks on her Zadi, the youth of her heart,
    Who from childhood was loving and true,
How he cried on the beach, when the ship did depart!
    'Twas a sad everlasting adieu.
The shell-woven gift which he bound round her arm,
    The rude seaman unfeelingly tore,
Nor left one sad relic her sorrows to charm,
    When far from her dear native shore.

And now, all dejected, she wanders apart,
    No friend, save retirement, she seeks,
The sigh of despondency bursts from her heart,
    And tears dew her thin sable cheeks.

Poor hard-fated girl, long, long she may mourn!
 Life's pleasures to her are all o'er,
Far fled ev'ry hope that she e'er shall return
 To revisit her dear native shore.
(wr. c. 1810/pub. 1815)[378]

WILLIAM HAMILTON
(fl. 1808–1815)

Once rumored to be a descendant of Alexander Hamilton, William Hamilton left few biographical traces. An African American writer, actor, composer, and activist based in New York City, he produced hymns and orations, and, with Peter Williams, Sr., founded the New York African Society for Mutual Relief in 1808. These hymns were composed and set to music by Hamilton, and sung during services at the African Church in New York.

Hymns Sung on the Second Anniversary of the Abolition of the Slave Trade
Hymn I

Great God, what wonders have been wrought,
    For us by thy almighty hand,
In cutting off the trade which brought
    Direful confusion in our land.

Its cruel power with dreadful sway,
    On Afric's peaceful, happy shore,
Spread war, confusion and dismay,
    And drench'd its fields with human gore.

Those dwellings where true happiness,
    Did long and constantly reside,
Were robb'd of peace, content, and bliss,
    And every pleasing hope beside.

Those knit by soft conjugal love,
    Were sever'd by a barb'rous stroke;
And doom'd in distant climes to prove
    A tyrant's cruel galling yoke.

Parents from children oft were torn,
    Relations from relations near;
And doom'd forever thence to mourn
    The loss of friends by nature dear.

But in supreme, unbounded love,
    Thou did'st behold their suff'ring plight,
And from thy splendid courts above
    Asserted injur'd Afric's right.

Thy powerful arm the host restrain
    Which ravag'd wide its golden shore;
And crowns its spicy, fertile plains,
    With peace and happiness once more.

Let ev'ry heart then join to bless
    And glorify thy holy name,
Let every tongue thy love confess,
    And shout aloud thy matchless name.

                 (1810)[379]

Hamilton's tone of untempered celebration differs sharply from the mixed emotions of Peter Williams's hymns on this occasion the previous year. Hamilton's private feelings remain unknown, but the circumstances suggest that perhaps some had objected to Williams including complaints about slavery in lines ostensibly giving thanks for the abolition of the trade itelf.

Hymn II

Now let a burst of sacred joy,
    And unmingled delight,
Ascend the hill of God our king,
    Who doeth all things right.

Now let the sons of Africa,
    In loudest strains rejoice;
God is our king, his loudest praise
    Sing forth with cheerful voice.

No more can avarice, that foul fiend,
    To human peace a foe;
Thy sons, O Africa, beguile,
    And liberty o'erthrow.

No more shall foul oppression's arm,
    From your once peaceful shore,

Drag your defenceless, harmless sons
    To slavery no more.

God is our king, let all rejoice,
    The SLAVE TRADE is no more;
God is our king, let Afric's sons
    His matchless name adore.

              (1810)[380]

ANONYMOUS ["J. LOWBARD"]

These lines come from a long poem submitted anonymously by a Harvard student to the college literary magazine, *The Harvard Lyceum*, which published it in serial installments beginning in August 1810. Here the poet digresses on the popular view that blacks had a better sense of humor than whites. In spite of the racial stereotyping and initial tone of satiric irreverence, the poet soon falls into sympathy with the African slaves whose self-protective wit he admires.

from Book VIII of "The Ad: A Poem in Ten Books"

Whence comes it then that blacks in wit excel,
And, if they serve completely, joke as well.
For still we find the readiest wit has place
Behind the vizor of a smutty face.
Whether, when nature formed the race at first,
She baked and browned them like a Sunday crust;
So that their brains at easiest impulse snap,
Like sailors' biscuit, at the gentlest rap.
Whether, to show their ivory teeth the while,
'Twas given them aye to joke and aye to smile:
Whether, since wit and musick, hand in hand,
Are knit and joined by sympathetick band,
The black must be the master of the jest,
And joke the better as he fiddles best:
Are knotty questions in dame nature's book,
On which, though none can read, the world will look.
Perhaps (for let the laughing muse bestow
Her tribute too, to mourn unpitied woe,)
Perhaps the giddy head and thoughtless heart
To the poor *slave* a soothing charm impart.
When lawless power locks on her heaviest chains,

And savage tyrants mock defenceless pains,
When the poor wretch to some dark nook would creep,
To sigh with pine trees and with torrents weep,
Blest is he, if his spirits bear the weight,
The dull dead burden of his hopeless fate;
Blest, if a playful fancy cheer him on
To toils for others borne, and work for others done.

(wr. 1810/pub. 1811)[381]

MARY RUSSELL MITFORD
(1787–1855)

Despite having to support a profligate and delusional father, Mary Mitford became one of the most admired writers of the early nineteenth century. This passage is from an early poem, published when she was twenty-three. Here she recalls her days at a London girls' school. "Zosia" is apparently based on a beloved classmate or junior teacher who, having been raised on a colonial plantation, regaled the girls with tales of life in a slave-holding society. The poem, with the heroine's sympathy for slaves, forms a female counterpoint to Thomas Day's famous novel *Sandford and Merton* (1783), in which a colonial boy brings his racist attitudes to an English boarding school and is converted to more enlightened ways by his right-minded classmates.

from "On Revisiting the School Where I Was Educated. Addressed to Mrs. Rowden, of Hans Place"

> With lofty tales of feudal power
> Would Zosia charm the ling'ring hour,
> Describe her father's princely dome,
> The splendors of her native home;
> The slaves, that follow'd where she trod,
> And swift obey'd her slightest nod;
> Yet, had she learnt on this blest shore
> To wish that slav'ry liv'd no more,
> For many a tale of negro woe
> Had bid her gen'rous bosom glow,
> Pitying, she sigh'd at their distress,
> And languish'd for the pow'r to bless.
>
> (1810)[382]

GEORGE WHITE (1764–1836)

A former slave, White was born in Virginia, separated from his mother by the age of one, and, after a succession of masters in Virginia and Maryland, was manumitted in the early 1780s. He made his way north, spending three years in New Jersey and then finally settling in New York, where he became a Methodist preacher. From 1795 he was involved in founding a separate African Methodist church and in the factional wrangles that ensued. Although he did not become literate until the age of forty-two, he published a narrative of his life in 1810 that includes this elegy for a young African American, Mary Heanery. White explained that "God had made me instrumental in the awakening and conversion of this young sister, and being present at her death, her parents requested me to preach her funeral sermon [which] I shall here insert; with an Elegy." Free of any political or sociological self-consciousness, the poem offers a direct insight into the emotional and spiritual life of an African American family and their minister in the early 1800s.

[Untitled]

How wond'rous are thy ways, Almighty God!
Deep are thy councils; and severe thy rod!
Thy chast'ning hand, what mortal man can stay?
Or who can turn thy tenderness away?

Our friend is gone, but let us not repine:
The gem was ravish'd by the hand divine.
Call'd to adorn the dear Redeemer's crown,
And add new honours to Immanuel's throne.

Her virtue lives; and ever live it must;
Although her flesh lies slumb'ring in the dust.
Wipe off the tear, suppress the swelling sigh;
For she that lives in Christ can never die.

Grieve not, ye parents, give your sighing o'er:
The deep felt cause will soon be felt no more.
Your daughter lives in pleasures ever new,
On Zion's hill, where she looks out for you.

(1810)[383]

Notes

1. *Gentleman's Magazine* 12 (July 1742): 384.

2. E[dmund] H[ickeringill], *Jamaica Viewed* (London, 1661).

3. *The Works of John Dryden*, ed. Sir Walter Scott, rev. George Saintsbury (Edinburgh, 1882–92), vol. 9. Dryden later incorporated the poem almost verbatim into the text of the prologue to his tragedy *Amboyna* (1672).

4. *The Works of John Dryden*, ed. H. T. Swedenberg, John Harrington Smith, et al. (Berkeley: University of California Press, 1962), vol. 8.

5. "Prologue Written by Mr. Dryden *Spoken by a Woman*" to Aphra Behn's *The Widow Ranter or The History of Bacon in Virginia, A Tragicomedy* (performed 1689; pub. 1690), reprinted in *Aphra Behn: Oroonoko, The Rover and Other Works*, ed. Janet Todd (London: Penguin Books, 1992), 251–52.

6. *The Poems of John Dryden*, ed. James Kinsley (Oxford: Clarendon Press, 1958).

7. Ibid.

8. John Dryden, *The Satires of Juvenal and Persius* (London, 1693; repr. in *John Dryden*, ed. Keith Walker, [Oxford: Oxford University Press, 1987]).

9. Samuel Butler, *Hudibras Parts I and II and Selected Other Writings*, ed. John Wilders and Hugh de Quehen (Oxford: Clarendon Press, 1973), 115.

10. *The Golden Coast, or a Description of Guinney* (London, 1665).

11. *The Poems of Michael Wigglesworth*, ed. Ronald A. Bosco (New York: University Press of America, 1989).

12. Thomas Jordan, *London Triumphant: or, The City in Jollity and Splendour* (London, [1672]).

13. Thomas Jordan, *The Triumphs of London: Performed on Tuesday, October XXIX. 1678* (London, 1678).

14. Thomas Flatman, *Poems and Songs* (London, 1674).

15. A[phra] Behn, *Abdelazer, or the Moor's Revenge. A Tragedy* (London, 1677), as printed in *The Works of Aphra Behn*, ed. Janet Todd (London: William Pickering, 1996), vol. 5, p. 252.

16. A[phra] Behn, *To the Most Illustrious Prince Christopher Duke of Albemarle, on His Voyage to His Government of Jamaica. A Pindarick.* (London, 1687).

17. *Female Poems On Several Occasions. Written by Ephelia* (London, 1679).

18. James Revel, *The Poor Unhappy Transported Felon's Sorrowful Account of His Fourteen Years Transportation, at Virginia, in America*, ed. John Melville Jennings, in *The Virginia Magazine of History and Biography* 56 (April 1948): 187–94.

19. [Thomas Tryon], *Friendly Advice to the Gentlemen-Planters of the East and West Indies* ([London], 1684; repr. in *Caribbeana: An Anthology of English Literature of the West Indies, 1657–1777*, ed. Thomas W. Krise, Chicago: University of Chicago Press, 1999).

20. [Anonymous], "To Their Graces, the Duke and Dutchess of Albemarle, Upon Their Voyage for Jamaica," printed in "Miscellanea: or, the Second Part" of Jane Barker, *Poetical Recreations: Consisting of Original Poems, Songs, Odes, &c.* (London, 1688), p. 280–81.

21. *The Triumphs of London, Performed on Thursday, Octob[er] 29, 1691* (London, 1691).

22. Thomas Southerne, *Oroonoko* (London, 1695).

23. [Anonymous], "Prologue to *Oroonoko*. Sent by an Unknown Hand. And Spoken by Mr. Powell," printed in Thomas Southerne, *Oroonoko* (London, 1695).

24. [William Congreve], "Epilogue, Written by Mr. Congreve, and Spoken by Mrs. Verbruggen," printed in Thomas Southerne, *Oroonoko* (London, 1695).

25. William Congreve, *The Mourning Bride, A Tragedy* (London 1697), as printed in *The Complete Plays of William Congreve*, ed. Herbert Davis (Chicago: University of Chicago Press, 1967), p. 347.

26. *A Poem Upon the Undertaking of the Royal Company of Scotland Trading to Africa and the Indies* (Edinburgh, 1697).

27. John Saffin, *A Brief and Candid Answer to . . . The Selling of Joseph* (Boston, 1701), repr. in George H. Moore, *Notes on the History of Slavery* (1866; rev. ed. New York: Negro Universities Press, 1968).

28. [Daniel Defoe], *Reformation of Manners: A Satyr* (London, 1702).

29. Samuel Sewall, *The Selling of Joseph, A Memorial*, ed. Sidney Kaplan (Northampton: University of Massachusetts Press, 1969), 44.

30. [Anonymous], *The Tryal of Skill: or, A New Session of the Poets. Calculated for the Meridian of Parnassus, in the Year, MDCCIV* (London, 1704), repr. in *Poems on Affairs of State: Augustan Satirical Verse, 1660–1714*, ed. Frank H. Ellis (New Haven: Yale University Press, 1970), vol. 6, 708.

31. [?Bernard Mandeville], *The Planter's Charity* (London, 1704).

32. Edmund Arwaker, *Truth in Fiction: or, Morality in Masquerade. A Collection of Two Hundred Twenty-Five Select Fables of Aesop, and other Authors. Done into English Verse* (London, 1708).

33. Thomas Walduck, letter to James Petiver, 12 November 1710, printed in "T. Walduck's Letters from Barbados, 1710," *The Journal of the Barbados Museum and Historical Society* 15.1 (November 1947): 50.

34. *The Poems of Alexander Pope*, ed. John Butt (London: Methuen & Co., 1963).

35. Ibid.

36. Ibid.

37. Anonymous broadsheet, "The Cavalcade" (Dublin, [1717]), repr. in Andrew Carpenter, ed., *Verse in English from Eighteenth-Century Ireland* (Cork: Cork University Press, 1998).

38. [Frances Seymour], *The Story of Inkle and Yarico* (London, 1738), as reprinted in *Eighteenth Century Women Poets*, ed. Roger Lonsdale (Oxford: Oxford University Press, 1989).

39. *The Poetical Works of Mr. William Pattison, Late of Sidney College Cambridge* (London, 1728).

40. John Gay, *The Beggar's Opera* (London, 1728).

41. [John] Gay, *Polly: An Opera. Being the Second Part of the Beggar's Opera* (London, 1729).

42. *American Weekly Mercury* (5–12 June 1729).

43. Stephen Duck, *Poems on Several Subjects* (London, 1730).

44. Duck, *Avaro and Amanda*, as printed in *The Lady's Poetical Magazine, or Beauties of British Poetry*, vol. 4 (London: Harrison and Co., 1782), 216–230.

45. *The South-Carolina Gazette* (11 March 1732).

46. *The South-Carolina Gazette* (18 March 1732).

47. John Whaley, *A Collection of Poems* (London, 1732).

48. Ibid.

49. *London Magazine* 3 (May 1734): 257–58.

50. [Anonymous], "An Essay on Humanity. Inscrib'd to the Bristol Captains," printed in *The Bath, Bristol, Tunbridge and Epsom Miscellany* (London, 1735).

51. *Yarico to Inkle: An Epistle* (London, 1736).

52. *The Poetical Works of Richard Savage*, ed. Clarence Tracy (Cambridge: Cambridge University Press, 1962).

53. *Gentleman's Magazine* 8 (March 1738): 158.

54. Samuel Richardson, *Pamela; or, Virtue Rewarded* (London, 1740; reprinted Harmondsworth, England: Penguin, 1980, ed. Peter Sabor), 295.

55. *Some Excellent Verses on Admiral Vernon's Taking the Forts and Castles of Carthagena, in the Month of March Last [1741]*, facsimile repr. in *American Broadside Verse: From Imprints of the 17th & 18th Centuries*, ed. Ola Elizabeth Winslow (New Haven: Yale University Press, 1930).

56. *Is Slavery Contrary to Christian Liberty? A Politico-Theological Dissertation, by James Elisha John Captain* [sic], *an African . . . 1742*, trans. from the original Latin [by anon.] (Leyden, 1742; repr. Louisville, Ky.: Morton and Griswold, 1860).

57. Ibid.

58. [Robert Blair], *The Grave* (London, 1743).

59. [Kimber], "Fidenia," printed in *London Magazine* 13 (March 1744): 147–48.

60. *The Works in Verse and Prose of William Shenstone, Esq.* (London, 1744).

61. James Thomson, "Summer," *The Seasons* [rev. ed.] (London, 1744).

62. Thomas Bacon, *Sermons Addressed to Masters and Servants, and Published in the Year 1743* (repr. Winchester, Va.: John Heiskell, [c. 1813]).

63. Terry, Untitled ["August 'twas the twenty-fifth"], as printed in Josiah Gilbert Holland, *History of Western Massachusetts* (1855).

64. *Gentleman's Magazine* 19 (July 1749): 323–25.

65. *Gentleman's Magazine* 19 (August 1749): 372–73.

66. "The Vanity of Human Wishes," in *Samuel Johnson: Poems*, ed. E. L. McAdam, Jr. (New Haven: Yale University Press, 1964), 107 and note to l. 330.

67. *Translations from Boethius, "De Consolatione Philosophiae,"* in *Samuel Johnson: Poems*, ed. E. L. McAdam, Jr. (New Haven: Yale University Press, 1964), 259.

68. John Winstanley, "Yarico's Epistle to Inkle," from *Poems Written Occasionally*, vol. 2, reprinted in *Inkle and Yarico Album*, ed. Lawrence Marsden Price (Berkeley: University of California Press, 1937), 19.

69. Cornelius Arnold, *Commerce: A Poem*. (London, 1751).

70. *A Poem, on the Joyful News of the Rev. Mr.* Whitefield's *Visit to* Boston (Boston, 1754).

71. Samuel Bowden, M.D., *Poems on Various Subjects* (Bath, 1754).

72. John Dyer, *The Fleece: A Poem in Four Books* (London, 1757).

73. "Extract of a Poem, intitled INDICO," *The South-Carolina Gazette*, 25 August 1757.

74. Francis Williams, "To . . . George Haldane . . . An Ode," printed in [Edward Long], *The History of Jamaica* (London, 1774), vol. 2, 481–83.

75. John Hawkesworth, *Oroonoko, A Tragedy, as it is Now Acted at the Theatre Royale in Drury-Lane* (London, 1759).

76. [Anonymous], *Oroonoko, A Tragedy, Altered from the Original Play of That Name by the Late Thomas Southern* (London, 1760).

77. James Beattie, *Original Poems and Translations* (London, 1760).

78. *The Works of the Late John Maclaurin, Esq. of Dreghorn* (Edinburgh, 1798).

79. Ibid.

80. Ibid.

81. Ibid.

82. [Bryan Edwards], *Poems Written Chiefly in the West Indies* (Kingston, 1792).

83. Ibid.

84. Ibid.

85. Ibid.

86. Ibid.

87. Jupiter Hammon, *An Evening Thought. Salvation by Christ, with Penetential Cries* ([New York, 1761]).

88. Jupiter Hammon, *An Address to Miss Phillis Wheatly, Ethiopian Poetess, in Boston, who came from Africa at eight years of age, and soon became acquainted with the Gospel of Jesus Christ* ([Hartford], 1778).

89. Jupiter Hammon, *An Evening's Improvement. Shewing, The Necessity of Beholding the Lamb of God* (Hartford, [1783]).

90. [Isaac Teale], *The Sable Venus: An Ode. Inscribed to Bryan Edwards, Esq.* (Kingston, 1765).

91. [Charles Churchill], *Gotham, Book I* (London, 1764).

92. James Grainger, *The Sugar-Cane: A Poem. In Four Books* (London, 1764).

93. Michael Wodhull, *The Equality of Mankind: A Poem* (Oxford, 1765).

94. Edward Jerningham, "The African Boy," as printed in *The African Repository* (April 1826).

95. *Poems by Mr. Jerningham* (London, 1779).

96. *Poems and Plays, by Mr. Jerningham* (London, 1806).

97. John Singleton, *A Description of the West-Indies. A Poem, in Four Books*, 2d ed. (London, 1777).

98. *Phillis Wheatley and Her Writings*, ed. William H. Robinson (New York: Garland, 1984).

99. Phillis Wheatley, "On Messrs. Hussey and Coffin," *Newport Mercury*, December 21, 1767.

100. Robert C. Kuncio, "Some Unpublished Poems of Phillis Wheatley," *New England Quarterly* 43 (June 1970): 287–97.

101. Phillis [Wheatley], *An Elegiac Poem, on the Death of that Celebrated Divine, and Eminent Servant of Jesus Christ, the Reverend and Learned George Whitefield* (Boston, [1770]).

102. Phillis Wheatley, *Poems on Various Subjects, Religious and Moral* (London, 1773).

103. Ibid.

104. Ibid.

105. Ibid.

106. Ibid.

107. Phillis Wheatley, "To His Excellency General Washington," *Virginia Gazette*, no. 1286 (March 30, 1776).

108. Isaac Bickerstaffe, *The Padlock* (London, 1768).

109. Anonymous, [Epilogue], Isaac Bickerstaffe, *The Padlock* (London, [?1768]).

110. [Thomas Chatterton], "Heccar and Gaira. An African Eclogue," *Court and City Magazine* 1 (February 1770).

111. [Thomas Chatterton], "An African Song," *Court and City Magazine* 1 (February 1770).

112. [Thomas Boulton], *The Voyage, a Poem in Seven Parts,* 2d ed. (Boston, 1773).

113. [Jane Dunlap], *Poems, upon several sermons, preached by the Rev'd, and renowned, George Whitefield, while in Boston. A new-years gift, from a daughter of liberty and lover of truth* (Boston, 1771).

114. Ibid.

115. S. E. [Thomas Thistlethwaite], "Bambo and Giffar; an African Eclogue," *Every Man's Magazine* (Sept. 1771).

116. *The Poetical Works of William Roscoe* (London, 1857).

117. [William Roscoe], *The Wrongs of Africa, A Poem. Part the First.* (London, 1787).

118. [William Roscoe], *The Wrongs of Africa, A Poem. Part the Second* (London, 1788).

119. Reprinted in George Chandler, *William Roscoe of Liverpool* (London: B. T. Batsford, 1953), 272–73.

120. Bliss, Untitled Epitaph for John Jack, printed in Angelika Krüger-Kahloula, "Tributes in Stone and Lapidary Lapses: Commemorating Black People in Eighteenth- and Nineteenth-Century America," *Markers VI: Journal of the Association for Gravestone Studies* 6 (1989): 75.

121. [Thomas Day], *The Dying Negro, a Poetical Epistle, Supposed to be Written by a Black, (Who lately shot himself on board a vessel in the river Thames;) to his intended Wife* (London, 1773).

122. *The Poetical Works of Percival Stockdale* (London, 1810).

123. Ibid.

124. *The Association, &c. of the Delegates of the Colonies, at the Grand Congress, Held at Philadelphia, Sept. 1, 1774* (Philadelphia, [1774]).

125. [Untitled], in [Edward Long], *The History of Jamaica. Or, General Survey of the Antient and Modern State of that Island,* (London, 1774), vol. 2.

126. Rev. W[illiam] H[ayward] Roberts, A Poetical Essay on the Existence of God. Part I. (1771); repr. in *Poems* (London, 1774).

127. [Mary] Scott, *The Female Advocate; A Poem. Occasioned By Reading Mr. Duncombe's Feminead* (London, 1774).

128. John Wesley, *Thoughts Upon Slavery* (London, 1774).

129. "Remarks on the Slavery of the Negroes," *London Magazine* 44 (May 1775): 262, and (June 1775): 317–18.

130. "On Seeing a Beautiful Young Lady Kiss a Black Boy," *London Magazine* 44 (July 1775).

131. "Adam's Fall: The Trip to Cambridge. 1775," *Songs and Ballads of the American Revolution,* ed. Frank Moore (New York: D. Appleton & Company, 1866).

132. "To the Dealers of Slaves," *Pennsylvania Ledger: or the Virginia, Maryland, Pennsylvania, & New-Jersey Weekly Advertiser* 28 January 1775.

133. "A Fragment," *A Family Tablet: Containing a Selection of Original Poetry* [ed. Abiel Holmes] (Boston, 1796).

134. [Myles Cooper], *The Patriots of North-America: A Sketch* (New York, 1775).

135. *Black Preacher to White America: The Collected Writings of Lemuel Haynes, 1774–1833,* ed. Richard Newman (New York: Carlson, 1990).

693

136. Letter XXIV, To Mr. B[rowne], 12 August 1775, *Letters of the late Ignatius Sancho, an African, to which are prefixed memoirs of his life* (London, 1782); repr. in *Letters of the Late Ignatius Sancho, An African*, ed. Vincent Carretta (New York: Penguin, 1998).

137. Letter XXVI, To Miss L[each], 27 August 1775, *Letters of Ignatius Sancho, an African, to which are prefixed memoirs of his life* (London, 1782); repr. in *Letters of the Late Ignatius Sancho, An African*, ed. Vincent Carretta (New York: Penguin, 1998).

138. [John Trumbull], *M'Fingal: A Modern Epic Poem. Canto First, or The Town-Meeting* (Philadelphia, 1775). In later revised editions, these lines appear in Canto II of *M'Fingal*.

139. [John Trumbull], *M'Fingal. A Modern Epic Poem, in Four Cantos* (Hartford, 1782).

140. *New York Journal* ([?May] 1776); repr. in *The Virginia Gazette*, 25 May 1776.

141. [James Boswell], "Prologue," William Whitehead, *Variety: A Tale for Married People* (London, 1777).

142. [James Boswell], *No Abolition of Slavery; or the Universal Empire of Love: A Poem* (London, 1791).

143. *The Poems of Philip Freneau* ([Philadelphia], 1786); repr. *The Poems of Philip Freneau: Poet of the American Revolution*, 2 vols., ed. Fred Lewis Pattee, Princeton: Princeton University Library, 1902–3, 1:262–64.

144. *Poems of Philip Freneau*, ed. Fred Lewis Pattee, 2:115.

145. *Poems of Philip Freneau*, ed. Harry Hayden Clark (New York: Harcourt, Brace and Company, 1929).

146. *Poems of Philip Freneau*, ed. Fred Lewis Pattee, 2:255–56.

147. *The National Gazette*, 21 July 1792; repr. *Poems of Philip Freneau*, ed. Fred Lewis Pattee, 2:258–60.

148. First published under the title "Stanzas Written at the foot of Monte Souffriere, near the Town of Basseterre, Guadaloupe;" text here from *The Miscellaneous Works of Mr. Philip Freneau* (Philadelphia, 1788), 155–57.

149. [Philip Freneau], "On the Migration to America, and Peopling the Western Country," *The Columbian Muse: A Selection of American Poetry* (Philadelphia, 1794).

150. *Poems Written Between the Years 1768 & 1794 by Philip Freneau, of New Jersey* (Monmouth, 1795).

151. [Anonymous], *Jamaica, A Poem, in Three Parts. Written in that Island, in the Year 1776* (London, 1777).

152. [Anonymous], "A Poetical Epistle, from the Island of Jamaica, to a Gentleman of the Middle-Temple," appended to *Jamaica, A Poem, in Three Parts. Written in that Island, in the Year 1776* (London, 1777).

153. William Julius Mickle, *The Lusiad . . . Translated from the Original Portuguese of Luis de Camoëns* (Oxford, 1776).

154. [Anonymous], "Palinode to Phillis Wheatley," from *The Public Advertiser*, No. 13350 (July 23, 1777).

155. [Mary] Robinson, *Captivity, A Poem. And Celadon and Lydia, A Tale* (London, 1777).

156. M[ary] Robinson, *Poems* (London, 1791).

157. [Mary Robinson], "The Progress of Liberty," *Morning Post*, April 14, 1798, reprinted in *Mary Robinson: Selected Poems*, ed. Judith Pascoe (Toronto: Broadview Press, 2000), pp. 300–302.

158. [Mary Robinson], "The African," *Morning Post*, August 2, 1798, reprinted in *Mary Robinson: Selected Poems*, pp. 313–14.

159. Mary Robinson, *Lyrical Tales* (London, 1800).

160. *The Poems of John Bampfylde,* ed. Roger Lonsdale (Oxford: Perpetua, 1988), 50.

161. Joel Barlow, *The Prospect of Peace. A Poetical Composition, Delivered in Yale-College* (New Haven, 1778).

162. Joel Barlow, *The Columbiad. A Poem. With the Last Corrections of the Author* (Paris, 1813).

163. *Poems by the Revd. James De-La-Cour A.M.* (Cork, 1778); repr. in Andrew Carpenter, *Verse in English from Eighteenth-Century Ireland* (Cork: Cork University Press, 1998).

164. *Poems, on Subjects Arising in England, and The West Indies . . . by a Native of the West Indies* (London, 1783).

165. Ibid.

166. Ibid.

167. Ibid.

168. [John Newton and William Cowper], *Olney Hymns, in Three Books* (London, 1779).

169. Edward Thompson, *Nauticks; or, Sailor's Verses,* 2 vols. (London, 1783).

170. Ibid.

171. Ibid.

172. Ibid.

173. [Charles Dibdin], *Songs, Duetts, Trios, &c. in the Islanders, A Comic Opera* (London, 1780).

174. Ibid.

175. *A Collection of Songs, Selected from the Works of Mr. [Charles] Dibdin* (London, [1790]), vol. 2.

176. Epitaph "In memory of CAESAR," repr. in Angelika Krüger-Kahloula, "Tributes in Stone and Lapidary Lapses: Commemorating Black People in Eighteenth- and Nineteenth-Century America," *Markers VI: Journal of the Association for Gravestone Studies,* ed. Theodore Chase, 6 (1989): 67.

177. M[ary] Deverell, *Miscellanies in Prose And Verse, Mostly Written in the Epistolary Style: Chiefly upon Moral Subjects, and particularly calculated for the Improvement of Younger Minds,* vol. 2 (London, 1781).

178. William Cowper, *Poems* (London, 1782).

179. William Cowper, *The Task, A Poem, in Six Books* (London, 1785).

180. [William Cowper], "Pity for the Poor Africans," *Northampton Mercury,* vol. 69, no. 23 (9 August 1788).

181. W[illiam] Cowper, "The Morning Dream, A Song," *General Magazine and Impartial Review* 2 (May 1788): 261–62, reprinted in *Gentleman's Magazine* 58 (November 1788): 1008–9.

182. *The Works of William Cowper,* ed. Robert Southey (London, 1836), vol. 1.

183. "The Negro's Complaint," *A Subject for Conversation and Reflection at the Tea Table* (London, 1788), reprinted in *Gentleman's Magazine,* vol. 63, pt. 2 (December 1793).

184. William Cowper, "Sonnet, Addressed to William Wilberforce, Esq.," *Northampton Mercury,* vol. 73, no. 7 (21 April 1792).

185. "An Epigram," *Northampton Mercury,* vol. 73, no. 10 (12 May 1792).

186. [George Gregory], "American Eclogues, Eclogue I: Morning; or the Complaint," *Gentleman's Magazine* 53 (December 1783): 1043–44.

187. [George Gregory], "American Eclogues, Eclogue II: Evening; or, the Fugitive," *Gentleman's Magazine* 54 (January 1784): 45–46.

188. George Crabbe, *The Village: A Poem. In Two Books* (London, 1783).

189. Henry James Pye, *The Progress of Refinement. A Poem in Three Parts* (Oxford, 1783).

190. H[ugh] M[ulligan], "The Lovers, An African Eclogue," *Gentleman's Magazine* 54 (March 1784): 199–200.

191. William Hayley, Canto XXXIII, "A Sketch of the Araucana," in "Notes to the Third, Fourth, and Fifth Epistles, of an Essay on Epic Poetry," *Poems and Plays*, vol. 4 (London, 1785).

192. Captain J. Marjoribanks, *Slavery: An Essay in Verse* (Edinburgh, 1792).

193. [John Wolcot], *Bozzy and Piozzi, or the British Biographers, a Town Eclogue. By Peter Pindar*, 4th edition (London, 1786).

194. [John Wolcot], *A Poetical, Serious, and Possibly Impertinent, Epistle to the Pope . . . by Peter Pindar* (London, 1793).

195. [John Wolcot], "Yarico to Incle," *Scots Magazine*, vol. 55 (May 1793): 242.

196. [John Wolcot], *Pindariana; or Peter's Portfolio* (London, 1794).

197. "Tempora Mutantur. An Ode," *The Works of Peter Pindar* (London, 1812), vol. 4.

198. George Colman, *Inkle and Yarico: An Opera, in Three Acts* (London, 1787).

199. Eliza Knipe, *Six Narrative Poems* (London, 1787).

200. *The Works of Hannah More*, 7 vols. (New York, 1843), 5:383–93.

201. Edward Rushton, *West-Indian Eclogues* (London, 1787).

202. "Song for America," *The Eye: by "Obadiah Optic"* [Philadelphia], vol. 2, no. 13 (29 September 1808): 155–56.

203. [Elizabeth Sophia Tomlins], "The Slave," *Tributes of Affection: With The Slave; And Other Poems. By A Lady; And Her Brother* (London, 1797).

204. John Williams, *The Childen of Thespis. A Poem* (Dublin, 1787).

205. [Anonymous], *American Poems, Selected and Original*, vol. 1 (Litchfield, [Conn.], [1793]), 217–19.

206. [Anonymous], *The Slave Trade; A Poem. Written in the Year 1788* (London, 1793).

207. *Poems on Slavery: By Maria Falconar, aged 17, and Harriet Falconar, aged 14* (London, 1788).

208. Ibid.

209. [John Ferriar], *The Prince of Angola, A Tragedy, Altered from the Play of Oroonoko and Adapted to the Circumstances of the Present Times* (Manchester, 1788).

210. Robert Merry, "The Slaves. An Elegy," in *The Poetry of the World*, ed. E. Topham, vol. 1 (London, 1788).

211. [Samuel Jackson Pratt], *Humanity, or the Rights of Nature: A Poem* (London, 1788).

212. Helen Maria Williams, *Poems on Various Subjects* (London, 1823).

213. Ann Yearsley, *A Poem on the Inhumanity of the Slave-Trade* (London, 1788).

214. [Anonymous], Prologue, printed in Thomas Bellamy, *The Benevolent Planters* (London, 1789).

215. Thomas Bellamy, *The Benevolent Planters* (London, 1789).

216. Ibid.

217. W[illiam] Blake, *Songs of Innocence* (London, 1789).

218. William Blake, *Visions of the Daughters of Albion* (London, 1793).

219. William Blake, *America: A Prophecy* (London, 1793).

220. W[illiam] Blake, *Milton: A Poem in Two Books* (London, 1804).

221. [Erasmus Darwin], *The Botanic Garden, Part II. Containing the Loves of the Plants, A Poem. With Philosophical Notes. Volume the Second* (Lichfield, 1789).

222. [Erasmus Darwin], *The Botanic Garden; A Poem, in Two Parts* (London, 1791).

223. Olaudah Equiano, "Miscellaneous Verses; Or, Reflections on the State of my Mind during my first Convictions of the Necessity of believing the Truth, and of experiencing the inestimable Benefits of Christianity," *The Interesting Narrative of the Life of Olaudah Equiano, or Gustavus Vassa, the African. Written by Himself* (London, 1789), repr. in *The Interesting Narrative and Other Writings,* ed. Vincent Carretta (New York: Penguin, 1995).

224. [Francis Hopkinson, L.L.D.], *An Oration, which might have been delivered to the Students in Anatomy, on the late rupture between the two schools in this city* (Philadelphia, 1789).

225. [William Hutchinson], *The Princess of Zanfara; A Dramatic Poem* (London, 1789).

226. J[ohn] Jamieson, *The Sorrows of Slavery, A Poem. Containing a Faithful Statement of Facts Respecting the African Slave Trade* (London, 1789).

227. *Collective Works of the Late Dr. Sayers,* ed. W[illiam] Taylor (Norwich, 1823).

228. James Field Stanfield, *The Guinea Voyage. A Poem. In Three Books* (London, 1789).

229. *The Dramatic and Poetical Works of Joanna Baillie* (London, 1851).

230. Ibid.

231. Joanna Baillie, "Rayner," *Miscellaneous Plays* (London, 1804).

232. *The Harp of Erin, Containing the Poetical Works of the Late Thomas Dermody* (London, 1807).

233. Ibid.

234. [Charles Dunster], *St. James's Street, A Poem, in Blank Verse. By Marmaduke Milton, Esq.* (London, 1790).

235. John Marriott, *Poems* (London, 1803).

236. *The Songs of Joseph Mather; to which are added a Memoir of Mather, and miscellaneous songs relating to Sheffield* (Sheffield, 1862).

237. S[usanna] Pearson, *Poems, Dedicated, by Permission, to the Right Honourable the Countess Fitzwilliam* (Sheffield, 1790).

238. [Joseph Sansom], *A Poetical Epistle to the Enslaved Africans, in the Character of an Ancient Negro, Born a Slave in Pennsylvania, but liberated some Years since, and instructed in useful Learning, and the great Truths of Christianity* (Philadelphia, 1790).

239. Benjamin Banneker, Untitled ["Behold ye Christians . . ."], *The Black Presence in the Era of the American Revolution,* ed. Sidney and Emma Nogrady Kaplan (Amherst: University of Massachusetts Press, 1989).

240. Banneker, "A Mathematical Problem in Verse," *Black Writers of America: A Comprehensive Anthology,* ed. Richard Barksdale and Keneth Kinnamon (Upper Saddle River, N.J.: Prentice Hall, 1997).

241. Anna Letitia Barbauld, *Epistle to William Wilberforce, Esq., on the Rejection of the Bill for Abolishing the Slave Trade* (London, 1791).

242. W[illiam] L[isle] Bowles, "The African," *Sonnets (Third Edition) with Other Poems* (Bath, 1794).

243. W[illia]m Lisle Bowles, "The Sylph of Summer," *Poems, (Never Before Published,) Written Chiefly at Bremhill, in Wiltshire* (London, 1809).

244. W[illia]m Lisle Bowles, *The Spirit of Discovery; or, the Conquest of Ocean. A Poem, in Five Books* (Bath, 1804).

245. [Francis Garden], Lord Gardenstone, *Miscellanies in Prose and Verse,* 2d ed. (Edinburgh, 1792).

246. "To Horror," *The Poetical Works of Robert Southey, Collected by Himself* (London, 1838).

247. Robert Southey, *Poems* (Bristol and London, 1797).

248. Ibid.

249. Robert Southey, "The Sailor, Who Had Served in the Slave-Trade," *Poems* (Bristol and London, 1799).

250. "Verses Spoken in the Theatre at Oxford, upon the Installation of Lord Grenville," *Poems of Robert Southey*, ed. Maurice H. Fitzgerald (London: Henry Frowde and Oxford University Press, 1909).

251. [John] Walsh, *An Elegy Occasioned by the Rejection of Mr. Wilberforce's Motion for the Abolition of the African Slave Trade* (London, 1791).

252. Anonymous, "Ode. The Insurrection of the Slaves at St. Domingo. (Written in the Year 1792)," *Spirit of the Public Journals for 1797* (London, 1799).

253. Untitled ["On his downy pillow lying"], *Gentleman's Magazine* 62 (March 1792): 260.

254. M[ary] Birket[t], *A Poem on the African Slave Trade. Addressed to Her Own Sex* (Dublin, 1792).

255. *The Complete Works of Robert Burns*, ed. James A. Mackay (Ayr: Alloway, 1986).

256. "The Wretched Lot of the Slaves in the Islands of West India" is an original translation provided by classics scholar Stephen Marsh (D.Phil, Oxon).

257. S[amuel] T[aylor] Coleridge, *Fears in Solitude, Written in 1798, During the Alarm of an Invasion* (London, 1798).

258. [Samuel Taylor Coleridge], "The Devil's Thoughts," *Morning Post*, 6 September 1799.

259. John Collins, *Scripscrapologia: or, Collins's Doggerel Dish of All Sorts* (Birmingham, 1804).

260. Ibid.

261. James Grahame, *Poems*, (London, 1807), vol. 1, 130–31.

262. "Africa Delivered," *Poems on the Abolition of the Slave Trade; Written by James Montgomery, James Grahame, and E[lizabeth] Benger* (London, 1809).

263. H[enry] E[vans] Holder, *Fragments of a Poem, Intended to have been Written in Consequence of Reading Major Majoribanks's [sic] Slavery* (Bath, 1792).

264. [Sarah Wentworth Apthorp Morton] "The African Chief," *The Columbian Centinel*, 9 June 1792; reprinted in Sarah Wentworth Morton, *My Mind and Its Thoughts, in Sketches, Fragments, and Essays* (Boston, 1823).

265. [Sarah Wentworth Apthorp Morton], *Beacon Hill. A Local Poem, Historic and Descriptive. Book I.* (Boston, 1797).

266. [Samuel Rogers], *The Pleasures of Memory* (London, 1792).

267. [Sir Thomas Edlyne Tomlins], "To the House of Commons, on Their Vote for the Abolition of the Slave-Trade. April 2, 1792," *Tributes of Affection: with The Slave; and Other Poems. By a Lady; and her Brother* (London, 1797).

268. [Sir Thomas Edlyne Tomlins], "XII. To Mr. Wilberforce," *Tributes of Affection: with The Slave; and Other Poems. By a Lady; and her Brother* (London, 1797).

269. T. Woolston, "Sonnet. To William Cowper, Esq. of Weston-Underwood, Bucks," *Northampton Mercury*, vol. 73, no. 10 (12 May 1792).

270. Anonymous, "The African's Complaint On-Board a Slave Ship," *Gentleman's Magazine* 63 (August 1793): 749.

271. [Anonymous broadside], *Addressed by the Boy Who Carries the* American Mercury, *to the Subscribers* (Hartford, 1 January 1793).

272. Anonymous, "Eulogiam in Honour of ABSALOM JONES and RICHARD ALLEN," *The Massachusetts Magazine, or Monthly Museum* 5 (December 1793): 756.

273. [John Thelwall], *The Peripatetic; or, Sketches of the Heart, of Nature and Society; in a Series of Politico-Sentimental Journals, in Verse and Prose. of the Eccentric Excursions of Sylvanus Theophrastus* (London, 1793).

274. Richard B. Davis, *Poems . . . with A Sketch of His Life* (New York, 1807).

275. Timothy Dwight, *Greenfield Hill: A Poem, in Seven Parts* (New York, 1794).

276. "Triumph of Democracy," *New-England Palladium*, 6 January 1801.

277. "Found Stuck on the Statue of the Moor Which Supports the Sun-Dial in Clements-Inn," *The Poetical Farrago . . . of Epigrams and Jeux d'Esprit* (London, 1794), vol. 2.

278. [Eaglesfield Smith and Hannah More], *The Shepherd of Salisbury Plain. Part II. To Which Is Added The Sorrows of Yamba, A Poem* (Philadelphia, 1800).

279. Untitled ["Nor you ye proud . . ."], *Bannaker's Maryland, Pennsylvania, Delaware, Virginia, Kentucky, and North Carolina Almanack and Ephemeris, for . . . 1796* (Baltimore, [1796]).

280. Anonymous, "On Reading the Poems of Phillis Wheatley, the African Poetess," in "The American Muse" [poetry section], *New York Magazine* (October 1796).

281. "L.B.C.," "Reflections on the Slavery of the Negroes, Addressed to the Conscience of Every American Citizen," *The Rural Magazine: or, Vermont Repository* 2 (July 1796).

282. Anonymous African Woman, Untitled ["The winds roared, and the rains fell . . ."], and Georgiana Cavendish, Duchess of Devonshire, "A Negro Song, From Mr. Park's Travels," printed in Mungo Park, *Travels in the Interior Districts of Africa: Performed Under the Direction and Patronage of the African Association, in the Years 1795, 1796, and 1797* (London, 1799).

283. Charles Crawford, *The Progress of Liberty; A Pindaric Ode* (Philadelphia, 1796).

284. "C. I. Pitt," [Charles Isaac Mungo Dibdin], *The Pedlar. A Miscellany, in Prose and Verse* (London, 1796).

285. *Selections from the Letters and Manuscripts of the late Susanna Mason*, ed. R. Mason (Philadelphia, 1836).

286. [Thomas James Mathias], *The Pursuits of Literature. A Satirical Poem in Four Dialogues* (London, 1798).

287. Captain Thomas Morris, *Quashy; or the Coal-Black Maid. A Tale* (London, 1796).

288. [Anonymous], untitled poem, in [Sir Philip Gibbes], *Instructions for the Treatment of Negroes*, 3d ed. (London, 1797).

289. Ibid.

290. [Anonymous], "A Grace to be sung on festive days," in [Sir Philip Gibbes], *Instructions for the Treatment of Negroes*, 3d ed. (London, 1797).

291. [Anonymous], "The Negro's Address to his Fellows," in [Sir Philip Gibbes], *Instructions for the Treatment of Negroes*, 3d ed. (London, 1797).

292. [Anonymous], "A Grace after Meat," in [Sir Philip Gibbes], *Instructions for the Treatment of Negroes*, 3d ed. (London, 1797).

293. [Anonymous], *The American in Algiers, or the Patriot of Seventy-Six in Captivity. A Poem, in Two Cantos* (New York, 1797).

294. [Gravestone inscription], "Anna Maria Vassa," Web site: *www.ely.anglican.org/parishes/chesandr/plaque* (as of 2 September 1999).

295. Frances Holcroft, "The Negro," *The Monthly Magazine; and British Register*, vol. 4 (October 1797): 286.

296. W[illiam] Shepherd, "The Negro Incantation," *The Monthly Magazine, and British Register* 4 (July 1797): 51.

699

297. R[obert] Anderson, *Poems on Various Subjects* (Carlisle [England], 1798).

298. Ibid.

299. Thomas Gisborne, *Poems, Sacred and Moral* (London, 1798).

300. James Orr, "Humanity," *Poems on Various Subjects* (Belfast, 1804), repr. in *Poems on Various Subjects by James Orr of Ballycarry With a Sketch of His Life* (Belfast: Wm. Mullan & Son, 1935).

301. James Orr, "The Passengers," *Poems on Various Subjects.*

302. James Orr, "The Dying African," *Poems on Various Subjects.*

303. [Mary] Stockdale, *The Effusions of the Heart: Poems* (London, 1798).

304. Thomas Campbell, *The Pleasures of Hope: in two parts* (Edinburgh, 1799).

305. Archibald M'Laren, *The Negro Slaves, A Dramatic Piece, of One Act . . . Being the Original of the Blackman and Blackbird, Performed at the Amphitheatre, Westminster Bridge* (London, 1799).

306. "The Planter's Reason for His Cruelty to His Brethren," *Baltimore Weekly Magazine,* 7 June 1800, 51.

307. James Cobb, *Paul and Virginia, A Musical Entertainment, in Two Acts* (New York, 1806).

308. David Humphreys, "A Poem on the Death of General Washington," in *The Miscellaneous Works of David Humphreys* (New York, 1804).

309. David Humphreys, "A Poem on the Industry of the United States of America," in *The Miscellaneous Works of David Humphreys.*

310. "The Slave," *Baltimore Weekly Magazine,* 28 January 1801, 197–98.

311. "The Negro's Prayer," *Baltimore Weekly Magazine,* 16 February 1801, 216.

312. J. H. L. Hunt, *Juvenilia; or, A Collection of Poems. Written between the Ages of Twelve and Sixteen* (London, 1802).

313. *The Poetical Remains of the Late John Leyden, with Memoirs of His Life, by the Rev. James Morton* (London, 1819).

314. John Leyden, *Scenes of Infancy: Descriptive of Teviotdale* (Edinburgh, 1803).

315. "The African Slave," *The Prisoner: or, A Collection of Poetical Pieces, Written by a Person Confined in the State-Prison* (Trenton, [N.J.], 1802).

316. "Letter to a Friend. Written from Jamaica," *Select and Fugitive Poetry. A Compilation,* ed. Richard Dinmore (Washington City, [D.C.], 1802).

317. "Monimba," *Select and Fugitive Poetry. A Compilation,* ed. Richard Dinmore (Washington City, [D.C.], 1802).

318. "The Negro Boy," *Select and Fugitive Poetry. A Compilation,* ed. Richard Dinmore (Washington City, [D.C.], 1802).

319. *The Political Nursery, for the Year Eighteen Hundred Two* (Norwich, [Conn.], 1802).

320. *The Port Folio* [ed. Joseph Dennie], vol. 2 (10 July 1802).

321. *The Port Folio* [ed. Joseph Dennie], vol. 2 (2 October 1802).

322. *The Port Folio* [ed. Joseph Dennie], vol. 2 (30 October 1802).

323. *The Port Folio* [ed. Joseph Dennie], vol. 2 (6 November 1802).

324. *The Port Folio* [ed. Joseph Dennie], vol. 2 (4 December 1802).

325. *The Port Folio* [ed. Joseph Dennie], vol. 3 (5 March 1803).

326. *The Port Folio* [ed. Joseph Dennie], vol. 3 (19 March 1803).

327. *The Port Folio* [ed. Joseph Dennie], vol. 3 (19 March 1803).

328. [John Quincy Adams], "Horace, Book II, Ode 4. To Xanthia Phoceus," *The Port Folio,* [ed. Joseph Dennie], vol. 2 (30 October 1802).

329. [Amelia] Opie, *Poems* (London, 1802).

330. Susanna Watts, *Original Poems and Translations* (London, 1802); repr. in Moira Ferguson, *Subject to Others: British Women Writers and Colonial Slavery, 1670–1834* (New York: Routledge, 1992), p. vii.

331. William Wordsworth, *Poems, in Two Volumes, and Other Poems, 1800–1807*, ed. Jared Curtis (Ithaca: Cornell University Press, 1983), 160–61.

332. Ibid., pp. 161–62.

333. William Wordsworth, *The Prelude: 1799, 1805, 1850*, ed. Jonathan Wordsworth (New York: W. W. Norton & Company, 1979), 368 and 370.

334. William Wordsworth, *Poems, in Two Volumes, and Other Poems*, 246–47.

335. J. Warren Brackett, *The Ghost of Law, or Anarchy and Despotism. A Poem* (Hanover, N.H., 1803).

336. William C. Foster, *Poetry on Different Subjects, Written Under the Signature of Timothy Spectacles* (Salem, N.Y., 1805).

337. "Pity the Slave," *Biographical Sketches and Interesting Anecdotes of Persons of Color*, ed. A[bigail] Mott (New York, 1839).

338. Thomas Moore, *Epistles, Odes, and Other Poems* (Philadelphia, 1806).

339. Ibid.

340. Charlotte Smith, *Conversations Introducing Poetry: Chiefly on Subjects of Natural History. For the Use of Children and Young Persons*, 2 vols. (London, 1804).

341. Anonymous, "New-Year's Address of the Carrier of the *Mercantile Advertiser* to His Customers," reprinted in *The Port Folio*, vol. 5 (2 February 1805).

342. Thomas Branagan, *Avenia, or A Tragical Poem, on the Oppression of the Human Species; and Infringement of the Rights of Man. In Five Books.* (Philadelphia, 1810).

343. Thomas Branagan, *The Penitential Tyrant; or, Slave Trader Reformed: A Pathetic Poem, in Four Cantos* (New York, 1807).

344. Ibid.

345. Thomas Branagan, *The Excellency of the Female Character Vindicated; Being an Investigation Relative to the Cause and Effects of the Encroachments of Men Upon the Rights of Women, and the Too Frequent Degradation and Consequent Misfortunes of the Fair Sex* (New York, 1807).

346. Ibid.

347. [Thomas Green Fessenden], Canto IV, "The Jeffersoniad," *Democracy Unveiled; or, Tyranny Stripped of the Garb of Patriotism* (Boston, 1805).

348. [James Hammond], advertisement, unidentified Alexandria, Va., newspaper, in Charles William Janson, *The Stranger in America, 1793–1806* (London, 1807); repr. with intro. by Carl S. Driver (New York: Press of the Pioneers, 1935).

349. James Montgomery, *The Poetical Works. . .Collected by Himself* (New York, 1850).

350. James Montgomery, "The West Indies, A Poem," *Poems on the Abolition of the Slave Trade; Written by James Montgomery, James Grahame, and E[lizabeth] Benger* (London, 1809).

351. Isabella Oliver [Sharp], *Poems, on Various Subjects* (Carlisle, Penn., 1805).

352. *Poems on the Abolition of the Slave Trade; Written by James Montgomery, James Grahame, and E[lizabeth] Benger* (London, 1809).

353. Charlotte Richardson, *Poems, Chiefly Composed During the Pressure of Severe Illness* (London, 1809).

354. Henry Kirke White, "Ode to Liberty," *The Remains of Henry Kirke White*, ed. Robert Southey, 2 vols. (London, 1823).

355. George Dyer, *Poetics: Or, a Series of Poems, and Disquisitions on Poetry* (London, 1812).

356. Richard Mant, "The Slave, and Other Poetical Pieces," appendix to *Poems by Rev. Richard Mant* (London, 1807).

357. R[ichard] A[lfred] Millikin, *The River-Side, A Poem, in Three Books* (Cork, 1807).

358. [Anne Ritson], *A Poetical Picture of America, Being Observations . . . in Virginia . . . 1799 to 1807* (London, 1809).

359. *Poems on Several Occasions by a Young Man, Formerly Attached to the Squadron under the Command of Commodore S. Decatur* (Winchester, Va., [n.d.]).

360. Untitled hymns, in Jedidiah Morse, *A discourse delivered at the African Meeting-House, in Boston, July 14, 1808, in Grateful Celebration of the Abolition of the African Slave-Trade* (Boston, 1808).

361. "An Elegiac Tribute to the Memory of the Rev. John Newton," *The Panoplist, and Missionary Magazine United* [Published by "An Association of Friends to Evangelical Truth," Boston], n.s. 1 (July 1808): 95–96.

362. [Anonymous], "The Slave," in *The Eye: by "Obadiah Optic"* [Philadelphia], vol. 1, no. 19 (12 May 1808): 227.

363. J[ames] Fenn, *Hymns and Poems on Various Subjects* (Schenectady, N.Y., 1808).

364. Michael Fortune, "New-Year's Anthem," in *A Thanksgiving Sermon, Preached January 1, 1808 . . . By Absalom Jones* (Philadelphia, 1808).

365. This and all the following poems by Joshua Marsden taken from *Leisure Hours; or Poems, Moral, Religious, & Descriptive. By Joshua Marsden, Missionary* (New York, 1812).

366. Anonymous, "The African Slave," *Poems, Chiefly Amatory; by a Lady*, ed. [Mary De Krafft] (Washington City, [D.C.], 1809).

367. "Prometheus Delivered," *Poems on the Abolition of the Slave Trade; Written by James Montgomery, James Grahame, and E[lizabeth] Benger* (London, 1809).

368. [?Henry Johnson], untitled poem, in Henry Sipkins, *An Oration on the Abolition of the Slave Trade; Delivered in the African Church, in the City of New York, January 2, 1809* (New York, 1809).

369. [Bernard Barton], *Metrical Effusions, or Verses on Various Occasions* (Woodbridge [England], 1812).

370. Ibid.

371. [Mary and Charles Lamb], *Poetry for Children, Entirely Original. By the Author of "Mrs. Leicester's School,"* 2 vols. (London, 1809).

372. Ibid.

373. Robert Y. Sidney, Anthem I, in Joseph Sidney, *An Oration Commemorative of the Abolition of the Slave Trade in the United States; Delivered before the Wilberforce Philanthropic Association. In the City of New-York, on the Second of January, 1809* (New York, 1809).

374. Robert Y. Sidney, Anthem II, in Joseph Sidney, *An Oration Commemorative of the Abolition of the Slave Trade in the United States.*

375. [Nancy Dennis Sproat], *Poems, on Different Subjects. By A Lady* (Boston, 1813).

376. Peter Williams Jr., Hymn I, in William Hamilton, *An Address to the New York African Society, for Mutual Relief, Delivered in the Universalist Church, January 2, 1809* (New York, 1809).

377. Peter Williams Jr., Hymn II, in William Hamilton, *An Address to the New York African Society*.

378. Robert Tannahill, *Poems and Songs, Chiefly in the Scottish Dialect* (London, 1815).

379. William Hamilton, Hymn I, appended to Henry Johnson, *An Oration on the Abolition of the Slave Trade. . . . Delivered in the African Church in New-York, January 1, 1810.* (New York, 1810).

380. William Hamilton, Hymn II, appended to Henry Johnson, *An Oration on the Abolition of the Slave Trade*.

381. "The Ad: A Poem," *The Harvard Lyceum*, vol. 1, no. 17 (23 February 1811): 389–90.

382. Mary Russell Mitford, *Poems* (London, 1810).

383. George White, *A Brief Account of the Life, Experience, Travels, and Gospel Labours of George White, an African; written by himself and revised by a friend.* (New York, 1810).

Index

INDEX

INDEX

INDEX